DATE			

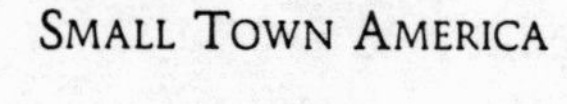

SMALL TOWN AMERICA

Also by Richard Lingeman

Don't You Know There's a War On?
Drugs from A to Z

SMALL TOWN AMERICA

A Narrative History 1620-The Present

Richard Lingeman

G. P. Putnam's Sons
New York

 Published simultaneously in Canada by Academic Press Canada Limited, Toronto.

Library of Congress Cataloging in Publication Data

Lingeman, Richard R
Small town America.

1. Cities and towns—United States—History.
I. Title.
HT123.L47 1979 301.36'3'0973 79-14760
ISBN 0-399-11988-4

Printed in the United States of America

To Jenifer

"The country town is one of the great American institutions; perhaps the greatest, in the sense that it has had . . . a greater part than any other in shaping public sentiment and giving character to American culture."

—Thorstein Veblen, "The Country Town" (1923)

"The Jonesvilles, Smithtowns, Greenfields and all the other -villes, -towns and -fields of America are essentially alike. . . . No two American habitations are identical, but all of them, big or little, bear the strong family resemblance of the same parentage. . . . The lives of the ten thousand citizens of Jonesville express the basic values of 180,000,000 Americans."

—W. Lloyd Warner, *Democracy in Jonesville* (1949)

"The phrase 'small town' has come itself to carry a double layer of meaning, at once sentimental and condescending. There is still a belief that democracy is more idyllic at the 'grass roots,' that the business spirit is purer, that the middle class is more intensely middling. There is also a feeling that by the fact of being small the small town somehow escapes the corruptions of life in the city and the dominant contagions that infest the more glittering places. History, geography, and economics gave each American town some distinctive traits of style that are imbedded in the mind, and the memory of this style is all the more marked because of the nostalgia felt, in a largely urban America, for what seems the lost serenity of small-town childhoods."

—Max Lerner, *America as a Civilization,* Vol. I (1957)

"While residing in a small town I had often heard people say what a friendly place it was, how kind and neighborly the people were, and what a fine place it was in which to live. From my own experience I had to agree. And yet, evidently not everyone in the town shared the same favorable image. On the highway sign at the town entrance one night somebody crossed out the town name and painted over it the word HELL."

—Father Bernard Quinn (1970)

"This Midwest. A dissonance of parts and people, we are a consonance of Towns. Like a man grown fat in everything but heart, we overlabor; our outlook never really urban, never rural either, we enlarge and linger at the same time, as Alice both changed and remained in her story."

—William Gass, *In the Heart of the Heart of the Country* (1968)

TYPICAL U.S. TOWN
KEEPS 1920's VALUES
A New Look at Muncie, 50 Years
After Famous Study, Finds
"Surprising" Similarities

—Headline in *The New York Times,* March 15, 1979.

My deep gratitude for assistance, patience, understanding, professionalism, advice, faith, friendship, love, loyalty, efficiency, sustenance, and much else in appropriate degrees, from various quarters as needed, and always at the right time to:

Editors: Harvey Ginsberg, Phyllis Grann

Agent: Lynn Nesbit

Typing: Michelle Friedman, Yolande Andrews

Copyediting: Kathleen Howard

Wife: Anthea Lingeman

(Note: The Epilogue originally appeared, in considerably different form, in *The New York Times* Travel Section.)

Contents

SMALL TOWN AMERICA

1
"A World Within Itself"

The New England town with its town meeting hall, saltbox houses, green common, and white churches with jutting spires is stored like a faded postcard in the attic of American memory. Stout yeomen, stern elders, repentant sinners in the stocks, all dressed in somber Puritan gray, people its streets. These towns were the cradles of democracy, the mythos has it, the incubators of our prematurely born liberties, home of the men who fired the first shots in the War for Independence.

It is curious that nowhere else among the colonies along the East Coast did the town form implant itself as firmly as it did in the glacial soil of New England. In the South, settlement followed a markedly different course, one in which towns played a minor role, save for a few seats of government and important ports such as Baltimore and Charleston. This variant southern pattern stemmed from different geographical conditions, religious ideals, and agricultural practices. To be sure, the settlers of both regions were English and, at least initially, under charters of the London Virginia Company. But differing social, cultural, and geographical mixes produced contrasting societies in the New World—two unique pools of social genes that produced two variant American cultural strains. These strains would eventually intermingle in the democracy of the western frontier to produce a new hybrid America, even as the two societies were on the collision course that produced the Civil War.

But the lack of towns in the Virginia Tidewater region was not for want of directives from London: that the settlers should form towns was practically an article of faith with authorities in the mother country who attempted to instruct the parties they sent across the Atlantic. England had become relatively urbanized by the end of the seventeenth century. Three out of every ten urban dwellers lived in cities of more than one hundred thousand—and one third of these lived in London. At the other end of the urban spectrum was the traditional English agricultural village, the basic social unit of country life where dwelled clusters of farmer-laborers who went forth each day to farm their adjacent strips in common fields. A third type of urban unit lay somewhere between the folk village and the city—the towns, hubs of commercial activity, markets, ports, seats of cathedrals or universities. In short, the more or less deliberately formed sites of some important economic or social activity, centralized rather than dispersed, drawing in the energies, labors, and products of the surrounding countryside. It was these commercial centers that the London "adventurers" (capitalists) had in mind when they adjured their "planters" (settlers) to form towns. Towns were considered the mode of organizing the settlers' labors in order to exploit whatever riches the new land contained, of providing protection in the wilderness, and—an important consideration—of preventing the settlers from reverting to some dimly imagined but strongly deplored state of barbarism. America might be the "new Eden" or Arcadia of the myths, but London businessmen feared nonproductive indolence or worse.

Of the three types of settlement the planners in London had as loose models, the commercial town exercised the strongest attraction, while the rural village and the city were more passive influences. The city—London—served as a kind of object lesson in perils to be avoided. London's pullulating social ills—specifically fire, plague, and poverty—were a stimulus to city planning in the New World. For all its wealth, culture, and far-flung trade, London had become a catch basin for the landless rural poor, serving as a convenient warehouse of food distributed under relief programs and, of course, providing some of them with jobs as laborers. The New World would provide a partial solution to the surplus agricultural population, although this was not uppermost in the minds of the adventurers and planters of the Virginia company, who put up capital in exchange for a share in whatever profits the venture yielded. They gradually came to see that labor was needed in the New World, and that obviously this could be drawn from the poor, who would be sent as indentured servants. But where some saw London's problems purely as a source of cheap labor, others were moved to envision a better city and, by extension, other better cities in America. A school of city planners arose, who gained practical experience, and considerable sophistication in their plans for rebuilding London after the Great Fire of 1666. And so enlightened town-founders such as William Penn were prodded into experimenting with new ideas. Penn, of course, laid out Philadelphia with well-spaced houses and with its streets and squares serving as firebreaks and attractive prospects; there was also provision for trees, gardens, and fields. Penn had in mind, he said, "a green country town, which will never be burnt, and always be wholesome."[1] He thus "solved" London's plague, fire, and poverty problems in a single plan. Penn was not alone; other similar town plans emerged, few of them actually tried, for reasons that will be described, but often involving such innovations as regular streets laid out in a grid pattern.

The English agrarian village had a more diffuse, subtle influence—the influence of custom, tradition, and memory. It was not an example that galvanized a scientific planner's vision, yet it exercised a strong hold over the minds of the common folk who came to the New World; and in New England it became the preeminent town form. Even though social forces that had been in motion since at least the thirteenth century were eroding its traditional identity, the nucleated village endured. The timeworn stability of this ancient human social unit* remained a fixed star in the changing social firmament—defined, in the ideal, as an autonomous, nearly classless, democratic association of households of freeholders, tenants, and laborers, who lived and worked in the same place, handing down their customs and land to succeeding generations, intermarrying, sharing traditional festivals, farming land in common, having little contact with the larger world. But such villages were becoming a rarity. Although the notorious enclosure laws, by which Parliament transferred land from smallholders to the gentry, enabling them to amass large estates, did not begin until the eighteenth century, the practice of engrossing—taking land by force, fraud, chicanery, or purchase—was already eating up the landed heritage of many of these small villages, leaving their inhabitants with a single small plot and working for the squire. Sometimes the village was simply destroyed, its inhabitants scattered. Thomas More in his *Utopia* wrote of "noblemen and gentlemen, yea and certain abbots, holy men no doubt" who "leave no ground for tillage, they enclose all into pastures; they throw down houses; they pluck down towns, and leave nothing standing, but only the church to be made a sheephouse."[2] And 250 years later Oliver Goldsmith wrote his elegy to a village destroyed by enclosure, *The Deserted Village.*

The human waste of these decimated villages was tossed into the growing sea of transient paupers, who in the seventeenth century were required to wear a scarlet *P* and were hounded through the countryside by overseers of

*"The small community has been the very predominant form of human living throughout the history of mankind. The city is a few thousand years old, and while isolated homesteads appeared in early times, it was probably not until the settlement of the New World that they made their 'first appearance on a large scale.' To Tocqueville, the village or township was the 'only association so perfectly natural that wherever a number of men are collected it seems to constitute itself.' One estimate is that today [1942] three-quarters of the human race still live in villages; and to these villages are to be added the relatively very few who still live in nomadic bands or other unstable small settlements." Robert Redfield, *The Little Community*,p. 3.

the poor in each village—for only their home villages had an obligation to care for them. If that village had been destroyed, they had to starve or seek charity in the cities. Many of the poor men who eventually came to the New World as indentured servants had been thus expelled, or else they could not make an adequate living in their home place. In their minds there must have been a deep ambivalence—a longing for the traditional homeplace, and yet a disillusionment with village ways, a freedom from the primary ties that had once rooted them to the soil. In America they could either cut the ties entirely and aim to become independent farmers, or they could seek to reconstitute an ideal village—the village they had lost in England—amidst the wilderness. The settlers in the South did the former and those in New England, the latter. As the British social historian Peter Laslett observed in *The World We Have Lost*, the models for the villages that flourished in the New World were the villages of Stuart England, "where no gentlemanly household was to be found and where the yeoman and the husbandman ran things themselves"[3]—in other words, the dwindling ranks of autonomous, unenclosed villages left in England, perhaps one fifth of the total number.

The settlers in New England were imbued with Puritan Congregationalist ideals; in the colony of Virginia, however, this traditional English village inspirited by Puritanism did not take hold. They brought with them the established Church of England, with its parish and vestry, but they did not make town and congregation one, as did the Puritans. Instead, they permitted scattered settlement within the boundaries of the parish; they held to the moral strictures of the church—at least at first—but the need for the kind of close-knit community of neighbors who were enjoined to look after each other's souls was not a guiding precept for them, as it was for the Puritans.

Still, although it was only implicit at first, because it was simply assumed, the early settlers of Virginia were expected to plant towns, but the kind of town that was envisaged was a modern town, inhabited by tradesmen and craftsmen and shopkeepers and professionals—not an agricultural village. This is shown by a recruitment handbill issued by the Virginia Company in 1610, which called for "only such sufficient honest and good artificers as smiths, shipwrights, sturgeon-dressers, joiners, carpenters, gardeners, turners, coopers, saltmakers, ironmen for furnace & hammer, brickmakers, bricklayers" and so on, down to "surgeons and physicians for the body, and learned divines to instruct the colonies, and to teach the infidels to worship the true God."[4] A notable omission from the list was farmers, and the idea was, apparently, that the colony would exploit the mineral wealth and trade with the native inhabitants for food and objects of value, while being supplied from home. There were instructions to plant corn, but this was treated as a matter of detaching a dozen or so men to scatter seed in a convenient spot. Whatever the plan, the failure of the early Virginia colonies to grow their own food contributed to their high mortality rate. Later, the assumption was modified, and the vision of "handsome towns" was scaled down to include at least "compact and orderly villages."[5]

The instructions to the first party attempting to settle at Jamestown in 1607 were perhaps typical of the early thinking. The planters were ordered to "fortify and build of which your first work must be your Storehouse for Victual."[6] Although a fortified place was obviously in mind, it was also to be a town, and later instructions often distinguished between forts and towns. Jamestown was referred to as a "Seat for habitation" and was to be laid out in an orderly way: "Set your houses Even and by a line that you[r] streets have a good breadth and be carried square about your market place and every street's end opening into it that from thence with a few field pieces you may command every street throughout which marketplace you may also fortify if you think it needful."[7] The Jamestown that was actually built—fatally located in marshy, unhealthful environs, despite the company's instructions—was probably a triangular palisade with the houses inside along each wall.

Jamestown was wiped out several times by famine, sickness, fire, and Indian attack. It was eventually established with some permanence but was never highly regarded as a site. After it was burned down in 1676, during Bacon's Rebellion, it was abandoned. Other towns were planted farther up the James River during the next decade—Bermuda Hundred or City and Henrico Hundred (a "hundred," derived from the Anglo-Saxon term for a political unit, was employed to describe large grants of land to a group of Virginia Company colonist-stockholders). But these towns never amounted to much.

As time went on, and the initial tacit assumption that settlers would plant towns was belied, instructions became more explicit and admonitory—especially after the Virginia Company went bankrupt in 1624, and the colony was taken over and administered directly by the Crown. By then, the Virginia colonists were developing a unique society in the wilderness, one in which towns had at best a peripheral role. A major reason for this was the nature of the country. Tidewater Virginia and the neighboring colony of Maryland around the Chesapeake Bay were in a region of creeks, inlets, bays, estuaries, and other outlets which emptied into the ocean, providing a direct, if arduous highway of commerce to London. These waterways provided no access to the interior, and thus tied the colony to England, a four-week journey away. Thomas Jefferson recognized the significance of this coastal bond in his *Notes on the State of Virginia,* written in 1781, when Virginia was still a state of plantations and farms: "We have no townships. Our country being much intersected with navigable waters, and trade brought generally to our doors, instead of our being obliged to go in quest of it, has probably been one of the causes why we have no towns of any consequence."[8]

Not only did this network of waterways fail to provide access to the interior, it also blocked the construction of roads. Thus it was difficult to establish agricultural trading centers, had the colonists been of a mind to, and several towns that were established withered away in their isolation. To travel from Williamsburg to Annapolis entailed taking over a dozen ferries. Towns such as London Town in Maryland were perfectly positioned for access to the sea (and London Town did indeed become a tobacco-exporting center), but they could draw no sustenance from the interior, unlike Baltimore to the north, and Charleston to the south. London Town was limited to handling the produce and serving the population within its immediate environs; in London Town's case that produce was, of course, tobacco. The town lived—and eventually died—by the tobacco trade.

For it was Virginia's tobacco economy itself that held back the formation of towns, even though it saved the colony from economic ruin. After John Rolfe brought in a strain of West Indian tobacco that provided a smoother smoke than the indigenous variety, the colonists abandoned other forms of agriculture and concentrated on growing *Nicotiana tabacum*. By the nature of the trade, each planter became his own merchant, and he often dealt directly with London, carting his hogsheads of tobacco to ships anchored in the creeks and estuaries. The ships provided him with necessities and luxuries imported from the homeland and carried back the tobacco to a London merchant who sold it on consignment. In such a trade there was little need for a town—for local merchants, for warehouses to store the produce, or for local brokers, since the planter dealt directly with the ship's captain. In the case of London Town, there were several London agents on the scene who had credit and ties with London dealers and who provided the town with an economic base. Their presence encouraged the rise of a permanent town with a few houses, stores, taverns for the sailors and visiting planters, and warehouses. But the town offered few services for the plantations round about beyond those allied with the tobacco trade. As Carville Earle and Ronald Hoffman point out in their study of London Town, the Virginia tobacco economy had engendered a decentralized, agrarian way of life, consisting of scattered planters, large and small. On the large plantations, there were indentured servants who could provide the necessary skills and crafts needed, while in the countryside the smaller farmers doubled as tradesmen, even doctors; and the entire society—or "neighborhood" as it was sometimes called—lived sufficiently close for anyone who needed some particular specialty to go to the man who practiced it and hire him. There were also a few stores scattered about, all within a day's travel. And so London Town survived only as long as it shipped tobacco; when a system of inspection stations was established by the colonies and these were located at other places, London Town had no more purpose for its existence and went into abrupt decline.

The large landholdings—plantations in the contemporary sense—of certain planters also no doubt enhanced this pattern of scattered settlement and prevented formation of towns. Also, even in that early day, land speculators were buying up large tracts and holding them until the time when the country was populated and prices went up. They and the plantation owners often amassed these holdings by manipulating headrights—the grant of fifty acres of land to each man who paid his own way or that of another man to Virginia. There were many ways of taking out headrights fraudulently, then selling them to speculators (who kept the land idle). Furthermore, indentured servants who had served their three-year term became eligible for a headright, and many of them, being possessed of no other marketable skills, took up tobacco farming on their land. They gravitated inland, however, while the great landowners clustered on the best land in the tidewater area.

Thus, two societies grew up, centered around two different economic classes. The plantation owners were often court favorites, who had received their large holdings in outright grants, or younger sons of good families, who had no patrimony since under the English system of primogeniture the entire estate went to the eldest son. These ambitious, young landless aristocrats were seeking their fortune, and they brought with them money to buy up land. Over time they formed a local gentry; they dominated the parish and county governments and monopolized their district's seats in the legislature. Their considerable ambitions were directed toward economic, political, and social power, in emulation of the English gentry.

The poorer sort who settled inland were probably of a rural-laborer background and possessed of at least rudimentary handyman skills. In other words they were superb fledgling pioneers, and they formed a kind of early frontier society in the back country, living isolated and independent lives. A contemporary observer, John Aubery, who was contemptuous of their rude way of life, described them as "mean people who live lawless, nobody to govern them, they care for nobody, having no dependence on anybody."[9] Such men did not need the services of a town, for they were relatively self-reliant, just as the plantation owners, with their large establishments, did not need towns because they presided over large, self-contained economic establishments, serviced at first by indentured servants and later by black slaves.

And so Robert Beverely could write in 1704 that the people of Virginia "have not any place of cohabitation among them that may reasonably bear the name of town."[10] In contrast, Massachusetts alone boasted one hundred towns by 1717. The government in London sought to remedy this failing (for it was still regarded as a failing) by passing town acts. A typical statute called for "a town to be built [which] shall consist of thirty-two houses, each house to be built with brick, forty foot long, twenty foot wide, within the walls, to be eighteen foot high above the ground, the walls to be two brick thick to the water table. . . . The houses shall be all regularly placed one by another in a square or such other form as the honorable Sir William Berkeley [the governor] shall appoint most convenient."[11] Such laws had little effect in Virginia and Maryland, but they became a precedent that was invoked in the other regions of the South with somewhat more success. Notable about these acts, even though they were sometimes framed with only a remote idea of the conditions under which the settlers actually lived, was their vision of planned towns, laid out in grid pattern, and embodying all the best thinking of the urbanologists of the day. But planners could not change habits, nor could laws for that matter. For, as Governor Francis Nicholson observed about the inhabitants of Virginia and Maryland: "People in these parts have been used to live separately. . . . It is very difficult to bring them at once to cohabit, especially by restraint."[12]

Yet, for all the fears of the London authorities, the Virginia system worked well, and indigenous institutions took root—institutions whose growing independence of action was also not to the liking of the London authorities. Rural life in Virginia centered around church and courthouse. Unlike New England, the churches were infrequently located in a town; nor were town and congregation coterminous. Rather, the churches stood alone in the countryside, and the farmers and planters traveled to them each Sunday. Each church served a parish, as in England; and for a time, the parish was a geographical unit of local government, although it came to be replaced by the county. The church retained its traditional moral authority to try to punish sinners in ecclesiastical courts for a time, but this authority too gave way to that of the county courts.

These courts became the central unit of local government. They were presided over by justices of the peace, who had the power to try smaller offenses separately, but who joined together as a court to try felony cases. New England had this system too, of course, and in both places the justices were appointed by the governor. But in New England, these officials—and other county functionaries, such as the sheriff and collector—came to be seen as puppets of the governor and, through him, the Crown. The towns held themselves above the county officials as the true representatives of local interests; they also sent their own representatives to the legislature. In Virginia, however, the governor's appointment power became a formality, and the justices of the county court were chosen locally (generally, the large plantation owners usurped the offices for themselves). And so, in New England townships—the town and its surrounding area, as described in an original grant—became the significant unit of local government, while in Virginia, the county court assumed that role, and townships were almost nonexistent.

Like the churches, the county courthouses were often sited in the countryside; a few were in towns, and sometimes towns grew up around a courthouse. Generally, though, the courthouse remained a decentralized complex, coming to life when court was in session. The typical courthouse was a compound, surrounded by a brick wall, inside which was the courthouse proper, a brick structure with a cupola, the jail, the caretaker's house, and a row of attached houses where the lawyers had their offices. A tavern was often located nearby, serving to house those who had business with the court and who came from a distance. When the courthouse was open, it was a busy place, with planters in their colorful coats and high boots riding up, paying their taxes, checking deeds for land sales (Virginia's system of land tenure was poorly contrived and necessitated close attention to matters of record, and the courthouse served as a repository for these all-important documents upon which family fortunes were founded). Trials drew people from far and near to hear the lawyers plead; and militia musters were held at the courthouse, which served as a central assembly point of the county.

Thus did the society of the Tidewater region constitute itself in the first century of American life. It formed under the long shadow the motherland cast across the sea, yet it developed independent representative bodies that, although dominated by the plantation gentry, were representative from the parish and county level up to the colony level. These institutions, in turn, cast their own shadow over the America that was forming as the stream of southern culture eventually joined with that originating in New England, like two rivers that flow into one, yet retain a separate alluvial coloration of particles from the lands of their source.

The New England tradition also had its origin in geographical and economic factors, as well as the spiritual considerations that preoccupied the religious dissenters who settled there. The land itself was considerably different in topography and soil. The Appalachian barrier to the west, turned back any who had thoughts of migration, while the Atlantic, brimming with schools of cod, herring, and haddock and serving as a natural highway for trade, held the settlers close to the coastline with its fine natural harbors such as the one at Plymouth, where the Pilgrims chose to found the first New England town. The soil was mostly glacial, not overly fertile yet not quickly exhausted. Unlike the rich alluvial soil of the South, it was not suited for large plantations devoted to raising a staple crop such as cotton or tobacco. Nor could it grow a surplus adequate to feed hosts of inefficiently laboring slaves. New England was a country for small farms, and in early times these were best worked by men living clustered together for mutual aid and protection in villages and towns. There were no rivers or valleys forming natural gateways to the west and thus encouraging further migration into the hinterlands (as was the case with the French in Canada), and this kept the population as it grew and spread out over the colony in a relatively compact state.

The settlers themselves brought with them memories of the English village and town, and their habits from their earlier way of life no doubt biased them in favor of a similiar pattern in the New World. Add to this the dominant influence of the Puritan groups whowere imbued with utopian ideals of community which they promptly sought to implant in New England. These people—a disproportionately influential minority—were intent on founding their churches and busying themselves with improving the spiritual as well as the material well-being of the congregation. In addition to the groups of settlers who had been members of the same congregation in England, there were also parties of colonists from the same village or parish or shire; they had come as groups and intended to remain together as groups. These non-

Puritans, who made up perhaps four fifths of the total number of colonists, were primarily motivated by a desire to better themselves economically, and for practical reasons—primarily for protection against the Indians, but also for economic cooperation and companionship in the hostile-seeming wilderness—they banded together into towns. Having little religious feeling of their own, they were content to delegate the care of their souls and morals to the Puritans, whose strongly held beliefs made them well qualified for this task, and who gained early political control.

The high motives of the Puritan colonizers made them envision a new utopian society which would bond men together in Christian love. John Winthrop, who was the first governor of the Massachusetts Bay Colony, expressed this ideal in a sermon he delivered to his fellow settlers aboard the *Arbella* in 1630. "We must uphold a familiar commerce together in all meekness, gentleness, patience and liberality," he said. "We must delight in each other, make others' conditions our own, rejoice together, always having before our eyes our commission and community in the work, our community as members of the same bond. . . . For we must consider that we shall be as a city upon a hill."[13] That Winthrop's vision, given tongue by fanatical preachers such as John Cotton, actually took the form of a rigid, intolerant theocracy was another matter, but the gentle, honorable, and righteous Winthrop—a superior, cultivated man who willingly assumed the heavy burden of other men's salvation—set his sights far above mere survival or economic betterment (although the decay of his own personal fortunes in England, where he had been a wealthy man, may have been among his reasons for emigrating).

Winthrop's vision of "a city upon a hill"—of a religious utopia—was carried by weaker reeds into the New England wilderness, but vestiges of his pellucid idealism survived in the covenants that preceded the founding of some of the new towns. The town covenant was indigenous to New England. It derived from the Congregational church covenants, by which men bound themselves together in one body and promised to obey God and the church's ordinances. It was only natural for the Pilgrims (who lived the congregational ideal even more intensely than did Winthrop and his company), to sign such a compact, only seven lines in length, crammed together in their tossing ship off Cape Cod before they landed in 1620. They knew that they made up only one third of the *Mayflower*'s passengers; the rest were a motley group, some of excellent character, some not. If this whole company was to live together, the Pilgrims had better make a contract among all of them to legitimize a single authority whom all would obey. There was no king in Massachusetts to give legitimacy to the law, no lord or squire or mayor or burgess, as there had been in England; indeed, unlike the green villages of England whence many of them came, where their ancestors had lived since time immemorial, there was no body of familiar neighbors, no kinship bonds. They were starting anew and they instinctively recognized the need for a basis for civil, as well as religious society.

In the Puritan theology man had a covenant with God—a covenant between a fallen sinner and the source of his redemption—which called for obedience from below in return for grace flowing from above (although it fell only on the elect, according to the Calvinist doctrine the Puritans adhered to). And the civil covenants framed by the Puritans required every man to obey the laws and the men who had been placed in authority. A covenant was neither a constitution nor a bill of rights; it was rather an undertaking of obedience without dissent or opposition, taken as a condition precedent to living communally. He who disobeyed the law broke the covenant and was thus outside the pale of organized society: he was cast out into the literal and symbolic wilderness, the dominion of the Devil. Within the bosom of the town there was to be love and charity, but the price was unquestioning obedience to the community's rules. A failure to adhere to the covenant was more than a betrayal of the community; it was a defiance of God.

Thus, in a typical covenant, the settlers of Dedham, Massachusetts, subscribed "in the fear and reverence of our Almighty God" to live according to "that most perfect rule, the foundation whereof is everlasting love." They made a corollary promise to exclude the "contrary minded" and to accept only those who walked in "a peaceable conversation with all meekness of spirit . . . seeking the good of each other out of which may be derived true peace."[14] They anticipated and provided for disputes (man was contentious by nature, was he not?) by advising that these be referred to arbitrators chosen from among themselves. Neighbors, rather than courts, would judge neighbors in love and fellowship and would seek to settle disputes in a spirit of reconciliation and compromise. More practically, every man was guaranteeed a plot of land—that is, a livelihood—and enjoined to pay his share of taxes and "become freely subject unto all such orders and constitutions as shall be . . . made now or at any time hereafter."[15]

The church—and specifically the Congregational church—formed the nucleus of the early New England town. Its covenant provided an analogy in the civil realm. Many of these early towns were settled by a minister and his flock. Every town was required by law to have a minister and the people in it were obliged to pay his salary and attend his church whether they were members or not. The church was made up of visible saints—those who had undergone some vigorous requirements and had thus demonstrated that they were "visible saints" in a state of grace. An embryonic democratic ideal informed the conduct of the church's business, and the entire congregation participated in the decisions on church affairs.

The seventeenth-century theocrats in Boston also followed a rigid Calvinism, believing in the rule of the elect and regarding democracy as an immoral form of government. John Winthrop called it "the meanest and worst of all forms of government,"[16] and John Cotton asked, "If the people shall be governors, who shall be governed?"[17] Nonetheless, the ideals of Congregationalism implied some democratic rule. As the Cambridge Platform—the definitive statement of Puritan doctrine—had it: "A church being free cannot become subject to any but a free election."[18]

The New England Congregationalist church diverged from the Church of England not only in its "purification" of the services by banning music and ritual and enforcing the Sabbath by strict observance of Old Testament laws, but also and most crucially in according all power to the congregation, a fundamental tenet with the Pilgrims. Each congregation was a *self-gathered* body, governed by a covenant written by its own communicants—such as the compact composed aboard the *Mayflower* or the covenant drawn up by the settlers of Salem in 1629. The Pilgrims held that "any competent number of such persons [those only who appear to believe in Christ and obey him] have a right to embody themselves in a church" and that "this ought to be done by express covenant."[19] Each church was in effect "a city, compact within itself, without subordination under or dependence upon any other but Jesus Christ."[20]

Undoubtedly this attitude lead naturally to the establishment of the town meeting for the conduct of the town's affairs. The town meeting was simply the congregation reconstituted for civil affairs. The town meeting was the greatest and most justly famous innovation of the New England town, and as time went on, it ripened into the democratic ideals that had their expression in the Revolution. As Tocqueville observed, "the doctrine of sovereignty of the people came out of the townships and took possession of the states."[21] Once this idea of a forum for the expression of popular sentiment was unleashed there was no reining it in; each town was an extension of its congregation—"a city, compact within itself, without subordination under or dependence upon any other . . ."

Perhaps the closest thing to the town meeting in the old country was the parish council with its vestrymen, which supervised the affairs of the local church and thus acquired some influence over the townspeople's daily lives. But most of the little villages in England were firmly under the thumb of the local lord or squire. Further, men held their land at the sufferance of local nobility. But the settlers who migrated to New England became freeholders—indentured servants excluded—and they were beholden, in theory, to no class of gentry.

The founding of the typical seventeenth-century New England town was accompanied by a rudimentary form of planning, which centered around the allocation of land. The model was the English agricultural village. The preferred locations were near a stream; a meadow or salt marsh nearby was considered highly desirable, to provide pasturage for animals. And if the land was already cleared, all the better, which was why the colonists frequently planted towns on the sites of abandoned Indian villages. But the most characteristic aspect was the system of land allocation, under which each townsman received a plot of land as a freehold—usually without having to pay quitrent or any of the other encumbrances common in the mother country. Legally, the town was a corporation, the model being the Plymouth and Massachusetts Bay colonies. Thus, the first settlers—the proprietors—in each town were regarded as stockholders with varying shares in the town's assets—its land. Such a system implied that the "stockholders" share in the profits and so all the crops must be pooled in common, with each family taking a share—a kind of capitalistic communism. But the experience of the Pilgrims at Plymouth pointed up the inadequacies of this system. The Pilgrims allowed each household a share of the year's harvest, with a surplus earmarked for paying off the colony's debts to the adventurers back in London who had financed them. But dissension soon arose: The idle and incompetent were receiving the same as the industrious and able. And so the policy was quickly abandoned, and each family was alloted a plot of land and allowed the subsistence, plus any surplus, that this land produced.

In subsequent towns, a pattern of common farming might be followed in the initial years, to prevent anyone from going hungry, but ultimately each man could feel that the land he farmed was his. His neighbors regarded it as such; the town government recognized his claim; and the colonial legislature gave each town considerable autonomy, so that they became in fact independent governmental units. A town was, after all, a group of settlers who had been granted permission to settle a plot of land that had been inspected and surveyed by the legislature. They had collectively been granted a patent (deed) to this land and the power to divide it up among themselves according to certain general principles of law. From this power, present at the town's founding, flowed its subsequent power to govern itself.

The land allocation in Andover, Massachusetts, was perhaps typical of the way the early towns went about it. A meeting of the proprietors—the group of men who had expressed their intent to settle and who had been granted a patent for land by the General Court (the colonial legislature)—met prior to settlement and covenanted at the "first planting" of the town to give "every inhabitant whom they received as a townsman a house lot proportionable to his estate, or otherwise as he should reasonably desire."[22] Each "inhabitant"—that is, each person who had been accepted by the rest of the town—was given a "house lot"—land he would build on and farm.

In the early days, house lots averaged from one to ten acres, thus giving the settler room for a house, an orchard, and a garden. The grant also included a piece of common land—that is, the open field suitable for cultivation of corn, wheat, barley, or oats—and shares in pasture, woods, and meadowland. Usually, the shares in these lands were laid out in strips that were scattered about rather than contiguous. This strip pattern followed the English open-field system, which allowed communal planting and harvesting by men working next to one another; in time, however, New England farmers came to operate more individualistically, planting when they thought best. And, as will be seen, they also would consolidate their dispersed holdings into a single farm plot large enough to support a family and to produce a surplus for sale. (By the midseventeenth century at least twenty-five acres of land were needed to support the average family with six children). The original and all subsequent assignments of specific tracts of land were made by drawing lots—hence the term "house lot." Some men drew more lots than others.

In parceling out land, the men of Andover reverted at least partially to their old-country habits and varied the amount of land according to rank, status, and "estate"—and size of family. Thus, Simon Bradstreet, a gentleman, received the largest lot (twenty acres). But old-world status was only partially controlling. John Osgood, a yeoman whose rank would be considered lower than Bradstreet's in the mother country, was also granted twenty acres. And Edmund Faulkner, the only man besides Bradstreet to be called "mister," received only six acres. There was an aristocracy of sorts, but it was a rough-hewn aristocracy of the New World: Both Bradstreet and Osgood were regarded by their fellows as the leading settlers, they also had more capital (or labor, in the case of large families) to invest in farming. The same standards prevailed in Springfield, whose founding regulations stated, "Every inhabitant shall have a convenient portion for a house lot, as we shall see meet for everyone's quality and estate."[23]

A man's house lot constituted his share in the town's total land. Land was also set aside for the meetinghouse. All of the land was not distributed, and in accordance with English practice, this undistributed remainder was designated common land. It was to be used for haying, timbering, grazing, hunting, and fishing by the townspeople; some was often set aside in the center of the town for public use as a green or as a "cow common." Eventually parts of it would be parceled out in amounts proportionate to each man's initial house lot, thus insuring the continuance of the hierarchy established by the original land division. These land divisions were voted by the proprietors and benefited the proprietors—a source of future conflict with the newer settlers.

At the same time there was a rough egalitarianism at work. Every townsman was given ample land to support himself, and the extremes of wealth and poverty were deliberately avoided. Although there was vestigial deference to rank, there was also an abundance of land and a policy that each man would have enough to survive and even prosper. To have their own land, free and clear of the rents and duties paid to the local gentry back in England, must have been an exhilarating experience to these settlers—if they had time to raise their thoughts above the harsh necessities of scrabbling for a living. It instilled in them an independence of spirit and an ingrained suspicion of centralized government.

Another striking fact about the initial distribution of land was the relatively small size of the plots given to each man. Andover had, after all, sixty square miles of land under its original patent. (Thirty-six square miles was the customary township grant, but some went as high as two hundred square miles). Wouldn't it have been understandable for these men to accord themselves large estates of perhaps a thousand acres each (the settlers in Watertown had done just that)? Or even to create a local squiredom? The answer is that, even if there were such an itch to ape the aristocracy, the hard realities of New England life made it impracticable of expression. Most of these men were without families, which meant that they lacked labor to clear and work the land. Then too, they were used to small holdings in England and perhaps could not conceive of any need for farming large plots—and if they could not farm them, why own them? Lastly, the small plots, clustered tightly about a town center, contributed to the cohesiveness of the town and made certain that men were kept under the watchful eye of the church.

The early town plan most typically emulated the layout used since time immemorial in England. The houses abutted in two parallel rows along the main street with their house garden plots jutting out behind. The fields beyond the town were in adjacent strips. In the center of the town, within easy reach of each house, was the meetinghouse (in Massachusetts it was forbidden by law to locate houses more than a half hour's journey from the meetinghouse.) The meetinghouse stood on its own plot of ground, typically the town green—a cleared green space in the center which provided a kind of physical axis of the community and served other community functions—militia muster, farmers market, even in some places, common pasture for animals. Rising ground—a hill—was the favored site for the meetinghouse itself, which was supposed to be placed in the exact center of the township bounds (if the rising ground and the geographical center did not coincide, the rising ground was chosen, and christened Watch Hill, Town Hill, or Meetinghouse Hill). The building itself was of no preordained style, but simplicity and modesty were its hallmarks, in keeping with Puritan austerity and pioneer exigencies. Thus, no great cathedrals or traditional spired stone churches rose upon New England soil. Instead, rough, square wooden structures—ranging from only seventeen feet by ten feet up to fifty feet by fifty feet, in New Haven—were common. These buildings usually had four-planed pyramidal roofs capped by modest bell cupolas. The meetinghouse was never referred to as a church. It served as house of worship, community center, and seat of town government.

And beyond the fields were the common lands, which as time went on would be subdivided among the proprietors, and which in the meantime served as common pasturage and wood lots. Other matters of town planning, such as highways and fences, were also determined by the proprietors. The proprietors laid out the town and retained for themselves the sole right to vote in future land distributions, until sufficient newcomers had moved in, captured the town meeting, and wrested this right from them. Then too, as land became scarcer because of the rising tide of immigration, the colony governments took to selling plots of land at auction, and the scheme of land dividends for the proprietors broke down in favor of private property system. But in the early days exclusivity was the rule and the number of proprietors was deliberately limited—a kind of planning in itself. Exclusivity was written into the covenant. Sudbury barred "such whose dispositions do not suit us, whose society will not be helpful to us."[24] Dedham proposed "to keep off from us all such as are contrary-minded. And receive only unto us as be such as may be probably of one heart."[25] Some towns set the precise number of families they wished to live there in their founding covenant. The Articles of Agreement of Springfield, Massachusetts, for example, carried this codicil: "We intend that our town shall be composed of forty families, or, if we think after to alter our purpose, yet not to exceed the number of fifty families, rich and poor."[26] The limit of forty to fifty families was a common one and was evidently considered the ideal size of a town. This was derived from a principle laid down by the Pilgrims on church size: "No particular church ought to consist of more members than can conveniently watch over one another and usually meet and worship in one congregation."[27]

The desired end of these early planners, then, was a tight, homogenous community—"rich and poor" but with no great differences of holdings. The town turned inward and fields were close at hand. Obviously, the settlers could have divided the land into relatively isolated farms with large plots; but for reasons of self-protection, mutual assistance, the salvation of their souls, and good morals and order, they preferred to bunch tightly together around the meetinghouse under the minister's wing. Each man checked the conduct of the others, for under Puritan belief each man *was* his brother's keeper, obliged to watch his conduct as carefully as he presumably watched his own. Further, the original townsmen as "stockholders" in the further divisions of the land bank had an economic interest tying them to the town. So they worked close to one another in their adjacent fields, in the early years gathering the harvest cooperatively as they had done in England.

But the utopian Puritan town—Winthrop's "city upon a hill"—began to decline almost as soon as it was covenanted. Internal strains on the covenant were being felt in Dedham as early as 1686. The practice of having disputes mediated by one's neighbors, for example, fell into desuetude. The minister's salary could no longer be met by voluntary contributions and had to be raised by taxation. Of course other towns, less idealistic perhaps, raised their minister's salaries by taxation, but in Dedham voluntarism grew out of the covenant; when support of the covenant declined, so did voluntarism. Then too, the original elders—the elect or visible saints—had all died, to be replaced by ordinary townsmen who were much less awesome figures.

The sheer refractoriness of human nature ate away at the utopian ideal. John Demos in his imaginative study of Plymouth noted the high number of legal actions between neighbors—suits involving property, debt, trespass, and slander. Demos lays the blame for this litigiousness on the hearth of the Puritan family. Such families were tightly knit and large in size—ten to twelve members on the average—living and working in close proximity in single-roomed frame houses. In such a family the members would be perpetually tripping over one other. Add to this an authoritarian father who ruled with iron discipline. The obvious result is an environment productive of much suppressed hostility. This hostility, Demos theorizes, would threaten to wrench the family asunder unless it could be directed outward, toward one's neighbors. But this contentiousness rarely erupted into violence. Rather, it vented itself in petty hostilities, bickering, property-line disputes, and verbal violence. In many towns ministers were disturbed by the malicious gossip that accompanied each new application for membership in the church and by the constant unneighborly—and un-Christian—quarrels that they were called upon to mediate.

Another cause of the breakup of the small, tightly knit, utopian village was, paradoxically, increasing economic prosperity which in turn led to a faster rate of population growth, a higher fertility rate, and larger families. In the last decades of the seventeenth century and the first of the eighteenth, most of the established towns experienced sharp increases in the birthrate. Each family had an average of eight children, with six or seven of these surviving to the age of twenty-one. Hand in hand with the higher birth rate went a declining death rate. Life in the towns proved healthy (until the eighteenth century when epidemics spread to the countryside from the cities). In Andover half the men who reached the age of twenty-one would live on to past seventy. The average life span was forty-five years—nearly ten years higher than it was back in the old country. Towns doubled in population in the space of a generation. In Connecticut, the overall population increased 280 percent between 1700 and 1730. Strict immigration laws in Massachusetts, giving the colony government the power to turn away "undesirables," stifled the growth of population in that colony for a time.

The population explosion put pressure on the once-abundant land resources of a single town. By custom a father had an obligation to provide his sons with a means of livelihood so that they might marry; this meant land, primarily, or a trade. A son's "portion" was spoken of as a claim to a share of his father's land—almost a right—so long as he did not incur his father's disapproval. The sons were thus dangling at their father's dispensation and obedient to his will; theoretically they would have to wait until his death to come into their own. In practice, a father often settled his sons' portions on them before his death, with title passing to them on his demise. By the third or fourth generation, however, there was, in many of the settled places, not enough desirable land; an alternative was emigration and often fathers would buy their sons land at auction in the new towns that were forming. Many sons were reluctant to leave the tight bonds of family and community and venture into a hostile wilderness where hardship was the rule and Indian raids a likely possibility until well into the eighteenth century. Nonetheless, while barely one percent of the population migrated in the early days of most covenanted towns, after the third or fourth generation the rate rose to 50 percent.

Another centrifugal factor was, paradoxically, the open-field system. Its pattern was predicated upon and enhanced the closed community, but it was ill-adapted to the growing desire among the colonists for a large, self-contained plot of land for farming, rather than several small ones scattered about the town's environs. The open-field system belonged to the ancient villages in land-scarce England, not the New World. Its function was primarily social, but the inhabitants began to look beyond survival and subsistance and think in terms of producing a surplus and selling it. Men began to desire to consolidate their holdings in one large parcel, which was more sensible for farming, rather than have them scattered about as each division of the common land added to their holdings. So men traded land and often they moved away from the town center, clustering into new communities that in turn demanded their own church, minister, and town services.

The itch for more was asserting itself even in early Plymouth, William Bradford noted disapprovingly: "No man thought he could live, except he had cattle and a great deal of ground to keep them; all striving to increase their stock."[28] The communal ideals of the Puritans were at war with the economic energies they unleashed in their exaltation of work, in their sense of a man's work as his "calling," and their honoring of those who prospered as deserving their prosperity. Yet the man who sought to better himself by moving out of the town onto a larger holding was accused of disruption, of seeking to escape communal supervision, and of defying the elect's tenderness for his soul. Indeed, the articles of the church specifically forbade moving away from the town without the church's permission.

As the new towns were settled, individual plots of land were sold at auction, because the single-plot farm was more attractive to buyers. Meanwhile, within the villages, men traded among themselves with the end in mind of consolidating their plots. The wealthiest men usually organized their plots around improved land close to the meetinghouse, while the less wealthy gravitated toward cheaper land in the outlying districts. These "outlivers" soon clamored for the right to set up their own independent communities, and they were opposed in this by the "old town."

From the earliest times, those who moved out of the town were regarded with suspicion; they were seen as a threat to the cohesion of the community and were sternly admonished. In the early days, when many divisions of common land left men with large plots at a distance from the meetinghouse, these men began to think about erecting outbuildings or even moving their houses to the land. Towns passed laws forbidding such buildings or imposing a heavy tax on them. But that did not stop the emigration. Inevitably, the outlivers began demanding their own minister, schools, and roads to market. (Since the roads were laid out with the meetinghouse as their hub, the center became the natural market; the outlivers found themselves too far removed from the hub—a journey of hours by foot or oxcart, over rutted, muddy roads, which in winter were impassable.)

Attempts to found new towns were resisted fiercely by the old towners. They feared, they said, for their scattered brethrens' souls in their wilderness diaspora; there a man would degenerate into "heathenish ignorance and barbarism."[29] But this tender concern was more practical than spiritual; the real worry was lost tax revenues: Individual assessments for the minister's salary—the main municipal expense—would go up. Naturally the outlivers did not want to pay for services they were no longer receiving. The colonial legislatures often had to intervene in these squabbles when they threatened to tear a town asunder. Or the outlivers might seek to gain their ends through the town meeting. A fight for control of the meeting ensued, with the "old-towners" mustering their supporters and quelling the schismatics by force of numbers. Yet despite their taint as secessionists and renegades, the outlivers were impelled by the simple urge to found a town of their own, which would be little different from the one they had left. They usually won in the end, for the old-towners simply could not allow the dispute to drag on for too long and upset the harmony they prized; for the sake of peace and stability they let the new town go its own way. By this process of hiving off, the New England towns spread.

As land became scarcer and men were no longer satisfied with a subsistence, many—especially the young men and women of the second and third generations—found their economic and marital opportunities under the parental wing in their hometowns so constricted that life was no longer endurable. Many of them moved on to the frontier, to the new speculative towns where they bought land with money advanced by their fathers. Others turned to trade, again with a stake from their fathers, as a way of supplementing the income from a small farm. As the number of tradesmen and shopkeepers increased, so did the undercurrent of incipient rivalry among them. As farmers, they were not in competition, unless one man wanted another man's land; but as tradesmen they were—one man's increase could mean a decline in another man's business. Still, the overriding impulsion in these early towns was noncompetitive. There were laws fixing wages and prices, which were medieval in origin, and each tradesman enjoyed a monopoly in his specialty. But rising competition among merchants and a chronic labor shortage made fixed prices and wages an anachronism.

For all these reasons, then, the covenanted utopian town founded by a homogeneous group of men and women or a minister and his congregation on land given them by the colonial legislature gradually became obsolete. In its place came a new kind of town—the town founded as a real-estate speculation. Colonial legislatures came to realize that land was too valuable a commodity to be given away and eyed it as a source of revenue—or graft if they were so inclined. Land auctions began to be held on the frontier in western Massachusetts, northern Connecticut and Vermont and New Hampshire, giving birth to a new generation of speculative towns. It is true that not all of the earliest towns were covenanted towns; some of them were planted by a man who had surveyed a plot of wilderness, purchased or stole title to it from the Indians, and then sold off plots to others. Its articles of incorporation were correspondingly bare of the references to God and adjurations to brotherly love and community harmony that the usual covenants contained; instead they dealt solely with property matters. In the speculative towns the old religious idealism was secondary to the cash nexus, the real-estate transaction; shares in common land were replaced by deeds to single plots of land; community was replaced by individualism. Although the tradition of the covenanted town never died—and was even mingled with the newer style of town, for the Yankee was nothing if not pragmatic—the speculative town, consisting of a collection of parcels of real estate to be sold to the highest bidder, became the norm as the frontier moved westward.*

One of the immediate byproducts of the speculative town was fraud. Wealthy speculators along the coast bought land in the interior and sold it without giving clear title. When the buyers became aware of how they had been duped, they vainly petitioned an indifferent legislature (the same legislature whose complicity had given the swindle its original momentum). Such disputes could drag on for as long as twenty years. The speculative system created a class of absentee proprietors in some towns. These owners conducted business from afar in their own towns, where of course they lived at a comfortable remove from the hardships the settlers were undergoing. These speculators had no intention of becoming farmers, and they had no stake in the town other than watching the value of their land rise.

Some scholars believe the notion of an absentee proprietor–settler conflict has been overstated. A close study of Kent, Connecticut, for example, showed that sixteen of the twenty-five original purchasers at auction actually settled there. Colony laws were passed in Massachusetts and Connecticut requiring purchasers to improve their land and build a house upon it within two years, as well as pay taxes on unimproved land. As a result, the absentees often sent agents to do this for them; sometimes these agents were sons or relatives, sometimes they were simply tenants who would hold the land until it was ripe for resale. Certainly it was in the interest of the proprietors that a town prosper upon the original grant, for otherwise their land would be worthless. In Kent, at any rate, most of the speculation was done by residents, and the turnover in land there was brisk indeed; many of the great white houses, still standing, were built by landed wealth.

In the older towns there were also conflicts, but these were between the proprietors and the new settlers. The newcomers wanted a share in the undivided common lands while the original proprietors were defending their

*See in this connection, Page Smith, *As a City Upon a Hill.* (New York: Alfred A. Knopf, 1966).

vested rights in further subdivisions of these lands. In Haverhill, Massachusetts, in 1720, the newcomers sought to participate in future divisions and the proprietors opposed them, often offering land bribes to their leaders. The nonproprietors were more numerous, however, and although they employed the town meeting to confiscate the land, they sometimes resorted to theft and violence and destruction of records. Finally, the legislature intervened in favor of the proprietors, and the poorer newcomers had to buy what additional land they wanted, thus lining the pockets of the old families.

Such disputes flared up in many towns; eventually they would be settled in some manner and the town would go on. In a few towns the disputes were so rending that the town was abandoned. In some of the speculative towns, settlers who had been gulled by absentee proprietors also quit the town en masse. But in other such towns, the settlers learned to stand on their hind legs and fight. Their fierce determination to survive and build up their town ultimately defeated the speculators who had no interest in founding a community.

Having cited the various causes of dissension, we must stress the *stability* of the New England town. Its collective drive was fueled by ideals of peace and order, homogeneity and harmony, conformity and orthodoxy. It may well be said that the New England town government was the seedbed of the American form of democracy, but it was also the locus of the local tyranny of the majority—or rather the ruling minority.

This nascent conformity had much encouragement in the Puritan religion, but there may also have been deeper roots in the psychological needs of the colonizers. They brought with them an atavistic, almost superstitious fear of chaos and an English penchant for order. Set down in the "hideous, howling wilderness"[30] (as one traveler described it), they projected their own fears upon their environment in the form of lurking, unspeakable menaces. Yes, there were Indians—and perhaps primeval evil itself lay in wait in the deep forest. They had come to the New World to escape England's unrest and upheaval, disorder and arbitrary tyranny by those in power, but they now found a menace in nature—the sins of the old Adam were set loose from the constraints of law and tradition.

Buttressing these dark fears was the Puritan credo, with its Calvinistic superstructure of obedience to authority and its inveighing against factionalism, contention, dissent, nonconformity, heresy, and any other "different" behavior. As Gurdon Saltonstall, the minister who became governor of Connecticut, wrote, "Divine Wisdom [provided civil government] to give check to those wretched Principles of Pride and Contradiction, Disorder and Confusion, which the first Rebellion hath unhappily brought into the hearts of men."[31] Such statements could be multiplied many times over. To the Puritans, man was a fallen sinner, basically evil; rigid laws were needed to curb his unruly nature; true, the church held out a hope of divine grace—darkly hedged by the doctrine of predestination—but he must confess his sins and gain control over himself. Only the hierarchial authority of the state and the church could curb the base nature of man in society. Authority must be eternally vigilant and seek out and smite error wherever it raised its seductive head.

"Factions" and "parties" were feared; authority was firmly grounded in the admonition to obey those whom God had set over one—primarily the "visible saints," the elect, those who had partaken of divine grace. William Perkins, an English theologian, highly regarded by the Puritans, wrote: "God hath appointed that in every society one person should be above or under another, not making all equal, as though the body should be all head and nothing else."[32] This promise to obey was embodied in the covenant—such as that of the church in Kent under which the covenantors promised to "submit to our betters." Or as the Cambridge Platform had it: "Yet when such a people do choose any to be over them in the Lord, then do they become subject and most willingly submit to their ministry in the Lord."[33]

Authority percolated down through the society; there was a natural hierarchy in church, school, family, and government, based upon each man's "calling"—the work he did—and estate. Richard Bushman has speculated that in the Puritan temperament the desire to submit was yolked to the desire to dominate. The father or schoolmaster whose word was law feared disobedience; the son or student who submitted feared arbitrary rule and deprival of his chances in life—an economic castration, if you will. This gave rise to psychological tensions, especially an acute defensiveness about what was seen to be authority overstepping its bounds at one pole, and "fractiousness," "unruliness," mob action at the other. As the threshold of grievance, real or fancied, was crossed, the wronged one lashed out against usurping authority. As Bushman wrote, "Among men so hypersensitive to encroachments on their rights, the innate fear of oppression magnified the controversies brought by social change and added to the pressure on established institutions."[34] So warring with Puritanical conformity was an unruly touchiness, which might flare up at any time. The Puritanical character in New England contained within itself the Yankee temperament, which was independent, cantankerous, shrewd, acquisitive, and individualistic, and had "Don't Tread on Me" stitched prominently on its ensign. In the late eighteenth century this resentment of unjust authority would be directed against the mother country and the tyrannical acts of her agents, and explode into revolution.

But within the town, each institution was conjoined with the others in a tacit conspiracy to produce a docile, obedient, law-abiding citizenry. These institutions governed the individual from cradle to grave. Family, church, school, and town government all interwove to wrap the individual in a shroud of regularity and "steady habits."

The Puritan family was an outpost of order on the edge of the wilderness, as well as an economic unit of production. At its head was the father; the wife and children were not independent persons but rather subsumed into his authority. In conditions of acute labor shortage, everyone in the family was needed to work the land or run the house. Children in the Puritan family were thus designated young adults, fit to work from the age of six or seven; there was no childhood, no adolescence. A boy could expect to put in twenty years laboring for his father before he could strike out on his own. Marriage came late—at an average age of twenty-six for men, and three to five years younger for women. The son's main hope of bettering himself lay in receiving from his father either land or a sum of money adequate to allow him to set up in a trade or migrate; the daughter's lay in making a good marriage—often an economic contract to which the bride's father contributed money or property as part of the bargain. The economic dependence of both thus lasted a long time, and the father had an economic whip hand, as well as the authority custom and law conferred on him. This is not to say the Puritan father was necessarily harsh and unloving, but he had the power, if a son or daughter displeased him, to cut them off economically and thus blight their chances for marriage, home, and children.

The legal aspects of paternal authority were numerous. By law the father led family prayers. Parents were held responsible and punished for the infractions of their offspring. The family also performed certain social welfare functions, acting as an agency of the town government to care for the poor, for example. It also was a hospital; sick people who needed extended care were boarded in families at town expense. Orphaned children were placed with families. The family could be a trade school with young people bound over as apprentices to learn a skill. Some strict Puritan families, not trusting themselves to discipline their own children properly, boarded them out with other families so that their unruliness would be chastised without inhibition. Old people without relatives to care for them could be placed with a family. Fathers provided for their own old-age assistance, and for that of their widows, in their wills. These testaments typically stated that in consideration for the land a father was bequeathing, a designated son was to provide care for his parents so long as they should live; if the care was not given, the will became null and void. The kind of care and its monetary value were often set down in fine detail; one man, for example, providing for his wife who would live with his son, bequeathed her a cow, "which my said wife shall have liberty to choose [from] among all my cattle. Also I allow unto my said wife five pounds a year as long as she lives, for which my wife had a bond of me before marriage. The said five pounds [is] to be paid in wheat and peas and rye and Indian [corn]. . . . Also my will is that my said wife shall, if she please, continue in my house. She shall have the new bed chamber for her use, with all my furniture in it, for a space of seven months, as also, a sufficiency of firewood for her own particular burning."[35] The family was even a correctional institution: Delinquents were bound over to private households to work off their sentences.

When there were no schools, the family served as one, but only the earliest towns lacked a school. Schools were required by colony law; the Puritans lived by the literal word of the Bible and demanded the literacy of all, so that all could learn the Commandments. The newer towns always set aside a plot of land for the school. This "school right" land was sold; the money gained from the sale was lent out at interest and the interest was used to support the school. The parents also paid tuition fees, and there was money from the colony government as well. Teaching in school was authoritarian, learning by rote. In the Kent, Connecticut, school the curriculum consisted of memorizing the three R's, the catechism, and the laws on capital punishment. State law required that town wardens and the minister inspect the schools to see that the required subject matter was being taught. Such schools turned out (or were intended to turn out) docile citizens with a healthy respect for authority. Their minds were imprinted with the catechism; their primers warned them of the fires awaiting the sinner in the afterworld—the "easiest room in Hell" was reserved for children; and they learned of the numerous transgressions in this life for which the penalty was death.

The long list of capital crimes in Massachusetts would be sufficient to plunge a child into a permanent state of gloom. They included worshiping "any other God but the Lord God," witchcraft, certain blasphemies, premeditated murder, murder out of anger or "cruelty of passion," murder "through guile, either by poisoning or other such devilish practice," bestiality, homosexuality, adultery "with a married or espoused wife," kidnapping, false testimony that resulted in the death of another, subversion, and treason. A child above sixteen could be put to death if he cursed or struck his mother or father, except in self-defense. The law stated that a "stubborn or rebellious son" of sixteen years who refused to obey his parents should be brought before the magistrates by the parents. Upon their testimony "that their son is stubborn and rebellious and will not obey their voice and chastisement, but lives in sundry notorious crimes; such a son shall be put to death."[36]

Caring for the townspeople's spiritual welfare—indeed the most crucial matter of their salvation—as well as their morals was the church—the Congregational church. The church also taught obedience to one's betters, and ministers hurled anathemas at noncomformist behavior; they condemned antisocial acts such as slander, feuding, family discord, and assault, and vigorously denounced "unwarrantable anger," "contentious or quarrelsome disposition" and "ill temperedness." Jonathan Edwards denounced "contention and party spirit" as "iniquity" which left men's souls "destitute."

In accord with Calvinist doctrine the Puritan church admitted only those into full communion who had experienced divine grace—the "visible saints." Salvation involved a direct, mystical experience of God, but in practice a mere mystical experience was far from sufficient proof of sanctity (as it was among the scorned Quakers). Rather, the candidate for admission into the elect had to undergo an obstacle course of rigid tests of faith, including the obligatory confession of sins before the congregation. The suppliant had to offer sufficient evidence that he or she had truly experienced divine grace, submit to the congregation's questions, then be voted upon. If he had any enemies, he could expect his affront to that person to be fully ventilated before the congregation; no right of a hearing was accorded.

Despite their insistence upon exclusivity, the local congregations found that the large numbers who did not formally join the church, either through indifference or because they despaired of ever passing the tests of membership, posed a dilemma to the church; it meant that a majority of the town would be outside its purview. A significant faction of unchurched citizens in a town could lead to divisiveness. Several formal and informal compromises were worked out to patch over this difficulty. Most important was enforced sabbatarian communion (that is, everybody was required to attend church on Sunday). Another approach was to forget sterile purity and loosen up admission requirements. Many townspeople were allowed to "own the covenant"—that is, profess their belief in Puritan doctrine—and become partial members. Under the Halfway Covenant the grandchildren of such partial members were made eligible for baptism. The reason for this was that the children of the original members, who could be baptized and were subject to church discipline, were showing reluctance to run the admissions gauntlet and become full members. Thus it appeared unlikely that their children would become members and so to retain them in the fold they were conscripted in infancy by baptism.

In the political arena, the church was also faced with a dilemma. Under law, only church members were politically enfranchised as "freemen" (the term originally meant a member of the company, that is, stockholder who was entitled to vote). In Boston this tight little oligarchy thrived, but out in the towns, men instinctively realized that exclusivity would divide the town and place the few over the many, whose cooperation was after all needed. So in practice the religious test was dropped. The local churches retained almost complete autonomy in choosing their composition, even though Puritan theory, with its emphasis on the "elect," tended toward exclusivity. Small-town reality pushed the church toward a greater openness. The church, after all, was God's earthly "thought police," spying out men's hidden transgressions and smiting sinful behavior, but its ultimate sanction—"churching" or expulsion—and the lesser penalties of shaming or flogging, had little influence upon nonmembers.

The church's job—perhaps its chief job—was moral surveillance. As Cotton Mather put it, ministers were "*Watchmen,* because they should watch the action of all men, and with an aim of religious curiosity spy out, how every one liveth, with his household in his house."[37] In fact, every member of the church was supposed to act as a watchman. Many took to this task with holy zeal, and undoubtedly spite and petty quarrels colored the judgment of some of them. Town officials, church elders, especially the tithingman, were also empowered to inquire into private family affairs. Was Jedediah Smart drinking too much? Was Goodwife Browne gossiping? Was Edward Small a dilatory farmer? All these matters were of legitimate concern to church and community, and the boundaries between sacred and secular were elastic.

The pastor could admonish his flock from the pulpit and speak to errant individuals privately and prayerfully ("labor with them," as it was called); however, in cases of persistent and willful misbehavior, the church would constitute itself as a court, hear the case, and render judgment if necesssary. The penalties ranged from admonishment to the ultimate sanctions of censure and excommunication. But the object of these exercises was not punishment, rather it was to mobilize the power of public opinion against the sinner, making him aware of his transgression so that he might sincerely repent. Ideally, the sinner, seeing the error of his ways, would confess to his sins before the whole church and ask for its forgiveness, which was readily forthcoming. The objective was not banishment beyond the pale, but rather reaffirmation of the community's organic unity, its common values; the sinner was taken back to the church's breast—but at the price of admitting he had wronged his fellows. And this capacity for forgiveness was bottomless; records might show Ephraim Starbuck confessing to, and being duly forgiven for, the sin of drunkenness again and again over the years.

Still, there remained the ultimate sanction of excommunication. This was indeed a matter of utmost gravity, for it meant delivering up the sinner to the embrace of the Devil, while simultaneously leaving the gate open for his return into the fold. The record of one such case in Boston reveals with what deliberation the congregation went about its business—and with what anathemas it meted out its punishment. The year was 1640; the case involved Mistress Ann Hibbens, who had quarreled with a carpenter over the price of some work he had done for her. Two church-appointed arbitrators had ruled that the price charged had been a fair one, but Mrs. Hibbens, who apparently had a sharp tongue, continued to slander the carpenter. When the case came before the assembled church, she remained unrepentant—to the anguish of her husband, who urged her to relent. Two hearings were held within the year, but Mrs. Hibbens remained obdurate. Even in the face of her impenitence, some church members continued to urge charity, citing scripture to show that God Himself was sometimes slow to punish. Others, however, compared her to a leper and urged the "great censure of excommunication." This punishment, it was argued, "is not to destruction but for salvation, that the sin may be destroyed and mortified and that the soul may be saved in the day of the Lord."[38]

Ultimately the minister, the Reverend John Cotton, handed down the sentence of excommunication in these terrible words:

> For these and many more foul and sinful transgressions, I do here in the name of the whole church and in the name of the Lord Jesus Christ and by virtue of that power and authority which He hath given to His church, pronounce you to be a leprous and unclean person; and I do cast

> you out and cut you off from the enjoyment of all those blessed privileges and ordinances which God hath entrusted his church withal, which you have so long abused. And because you have scorned council and refused instruction and have like a filthy swine trampled those pearls under your feet, I do now in the name of Jesus Christ deprive you of them and take them from you in order that you may learn better to prize them by the want of them. And I do exclude you not only from the fellowship of the church in all the public ordinances of the same, but also from all private fellowship and communion with any of the servants of God in this church, except only in those relations in your own family—to your husband, children and servants. And for the greater terror and amazing of you, I do here in the name of Christ Jesus and His Church, deliver you up to Satan and to his power and working, that you who would not be guided by the council of God may be terrified and hampered by the snares and power of Satan—for the destruction of your proud flesh and for the humbling of your soul, that your spirit may be saved in the day of the Lord Jesus, if it be His blessed will. And so as an unclean beast and unfit for the society of God's people, I do from this time forward pronounce you an excommunicated person from God and His people.[39]

Mrs. Hibbens's chief sin, more serious than her slander, was her defiance of the judgment of her fellows and her lack of contrition. She may have been a stubborn, spiteful woman, but recall that her offense really involved a simple quarrel over price. The whole thing escalated—as quarrels often do, feeding on the stubbornness on both sides—until she was placed in a position of defying her entire church. This was not the last mention of Mrs. Hibbens in the records of the day. In 1656 she appears again—on trial as a witch. She was sentenced to death, stubborn to the end, it appears, still living outside the church, ostracized by her fellow townspeople, and thus probably more vulnerable to a charge of witchcraft during the hysteria of those times.

Excommunication, however, was a religious sanction; it did not theoretically impose civil disabilities. Massachusetts law provided that censure of a church could not "degrade or depose any man from any civil dignity, office, or authority he shall have in the commonwealth."[40] Members were forbidden to eat and drink with excommunicants or to have anything to do with them "farther than the necessity of natural or domestical or civil relations require." Although expellees were barred from spiritual communion, they could still attend church. But no doubt, some stubborn sinners found the church's relentless solicitude for their souls oppressive and rejected its dominion. In Suffield, Connecticut, Brother Apollos Hastings simply told the congregation "that he could not belong to the church because he would not fit, he considered it oppression, monarchy, tyranny, and aristocracy to be confined to its regulations."[41] In the same town, Stephen Steadman had left his wife to live with another woman and the church "labored" with him to bring him around but gave up when Steadman said that his wife was not really his wife "because [while] she had married *him,* he had not married *her.*"[42]

In its role as guardian of community morals, the church was not then, as it is now, isolated from the power structure. The town magistrates enforced the laws against idolatry, blasphemy, heresy, "open contempt for the word preached," breaking the sabbath, and similar misdemeanors. Each Sunday the church reflected the social hierarchy of the town. Seating in church was set by a committee whose members had the exquisite sense of rank now seen in a State Department protocol officer. As the church covenant in Kent had it, "We shall seat each person according to age, dignity and list [that is, ranking on the tax list]."[43] The town's wealthiest and most powerful citizens were seated closest to the pulpit, there presumably to bask in the divine flame at its warmest. Perhaps too much can be made of this, for the church seating was changed every year, indicating that rank was fluid, rather than rigidly oligarchical. At least the rankings had a democratic aspect; they were actively and heatedly debated, rather than being a preordained hierarchy. Still, the church honored wordly substance, which was evident in tangibles such as profession, income, and property and in intangibles such as "dignity," "calling," and estate in the Puritan lexicon.

The minister had a powerful role to play in the town. This presence was required by law, and if a minister had not actually been a leader in the town's founding, the town made it its first order of business to bring in a suitable person. The first article in the founding document of Springfield, Massachusetts, read: "We intend by God's grace as soon as we can with all covenient speed, to procure some godly and faithful minister with whom we purpose to join in church covenant to walk in all the ways of Christ."[44] Land was set aside for the minister and a house was built. He was paid a good salary, and townsmen were required to contribute labor as well as money to his well-being. For their part, the divines sometimes showed a considerable worldliness in negotiating favorable contracts for themselves with the town's representative, the church agent; and they protested strongly if their salary was in arrears. Many ministers owned slaves—a sign of wealth.

For five or six hours every Sunday the minister had the town as his captive audience. The early Puritan churches banned music and other trappings of popishness; the congregation sat rigidly upright, many of them taking notes, as waves of scholarly rhetoric about divine love and eternal damnation rolled out over them from the pulpit. It cannot be said, however, that the minister's words fell upon an entirely docile and sedate people. Hostility toward a too stern or otherwise unpopular minister often welled up, and one Hartford divine wrote that he could not quiet the minds of his "fierce and wrathful people."[45] Quarrels over salary between a punctilious clergyman and his congregation were not infrequent. A minister in the Congregational church was after all chosen by his flock, and they could remove him or make life so miserable for him that many ministers favored a peaceable parish over a better-paying one. Then too, the conscientious minister was often in the unpopular post of umpire between feuding parties, who blew up petty quarrels and personal animosity into religious zealotry. Censure proceedings often opened long-festering sores of animosity within the community.

The Reverend Ebenezer Parkman, who lived from 1703 to 1782, was in many ways an emblematic New England divine, a country preacher who served the village of Westborough, Massachusetts, for nearly half a century. He kept a detailed diary which recorded the quotidian events of his life—raising chickens, building a house, appointments, his pastoral duties, and his private, unrelenting scrutiny of his spiritual health (about which he was a bit of a hypochondriac). Parkman emerges from the minutely handwritten pages of his diary as a stereotypical Puritan, a lesser version of Nathaniel Hawthorne's Reverend Dimmesdale in *The Scarlet Letter.* He was a professional policeman of souls, a rather dry, legalistic man whose sermons were lengthy, scholarly, and often provoked by an incident of backsliding in the town. In the dark nights of his soul, he scourged himself as an unregenerate sinner, but he never wavered in his belief in God—only in his belief in his belief. He felt acutely his own unworthiness of God's grace, and held his faith frequently to the whetstone of introspection; it was both his strength and a tool, like a woodsman's ax, for clearing the wilderness of sin and error around him. Yet, he was also a concerned father who loved his wife and children, a man who forgave his enemies and cultivated a patient resignation against the blows of the world. He was a country man, yet he did not allow his mind to go to seed; he read widely, kept up with the topics of the day, attended to the new currents in theology which his innately conservative nature instinctively opposed, and maintained his ties with the intellectual life of Boston, which was, in any case, only thirty-five miles away.

Parkman's moral inventories and inner debates are sprinkled through his pages, but there is also much about the weather, the crops, the country life. In his very first entry, written while he was still a student at Harvard, he accuses himself of "many great and heinous sins,"[46] and such moral flagellations recur through the years, gathering the deeper resonance of age, failing health, and weariness. In his twenty-sixth year he draws up an elaborate moral ledger itemizing his sins like a storekeeper inventorying his goods. But as the years settle upon him, he becomes less facile, sinking into "great concern respecting . . . my own spiritual state"[47] or crying out, "Alas! My great darkness and perplexity!"[48] He shared the inclination of Puritan preachers to melancholia. Their lives were an intense lonely war within the self, whose sinful nature and pride—the cardinal Puritan sin—they sought to scourge and abnegate, to subsume in total obedience to a loving, angry, inscrutable God the Father. They saw God's hand in everything; He was instinct in nature, and in society. Indian wars provided moral lessons. Miracles—"remarkable Providences"—occurred daily; there were signs in the sky and the weather was to be taken as a judgment of God, as were deaths from illness and epidemics, fire, and accident. To Parkman, an earthquake represented "that great and terrible operation of the Divine Hand,"[49] sent to remind him to put his moral house in order.

Yet Parkman was a prosaic, industrious man, much involved in the affairs of his parishioners, of course, and he describes dispassionately his attempts to reform a drunkard, settle peaceably a quarrel, persuade an impenitent sinner to seek the forgiveness of the congregation. He does not punish, although at times he deals with disputes that in another day—or even in his—were primarily legal matters, wrestling with them before they reach the civil authorities. Like a doctor prescribing placebos to hypochondriacal patients, he administers a bit of routine prayer to an old man who fancies himself a great sinner. His forbearance when evil is done to him seems almost saintly. After his indentured servant attempts to rape his fourteen-year-old daughter, he merely sells the man's contract to another person. He keeps one slave, but when the man dies, he records his passing as "The First Death in My Family."

He also worries a good deal about money, and his parishioners complain about his salary being too high or about the cost of his new parsonage. He nearly weeps on his pages over his inability to "do for" his children. He is very strict about demanding that the town perform its obligation to supply him with firewood, but he is a working farmer himself, deeply involved in practical problems. He performs numerous services for his parishioners—doctoring them, drawing up wills, teaching school from time to time—in addition to preparing two lengthy sermons for each Sunday (and if he should try to fob off an old sermon on his audience, they will immediately complain). He must stand for hours in his pulpit in the unheated meetinghouse, glaring at those who fall asleep (who are awakened by a beadle with a stick tipped by a squirrel's tail); once his daughter is spattered by a misaimed gob of tobacco juice. He lectures the younger generation on their frivolous amusements, yet enjoys the social life of the country village—the huskings and barn raisings—and also his wine, beer, and rum, which, judging from one entry, he orders by the eleven-gallon barrel.

Parkman was a protean mix of confessor, censor, marriage counselor, psychologist, judge, lawyer, intellectual, and moral philosopher. No doubt, his parishioners found him a spiritual busybody at times; certainly they argued with him, and he with them; but his influence was often directed to bringing peace and harmony to village life, to damping down the spites and quarrels. Nor did he particularly enjoy admonishing sinners; he was no spiritual sadist. His attitude toward this not always pleasant task is revealed in an entry he set down shortly after telling some roistering men in an adjacent room to stop the party and go to bed: "This exerting my authority gave me great uneasiness, but I was resolute to show impartiality and not be partaker of other men's sins, as likewise to discharge my own duty as watchman in this place and as having the care of their souls."[50] Parkman was a good and faithful watchman, but he belonged to an era that was gradually passing, as the dark, primeval wilderness was cleared and as ideas of civil government replaced the Puritan theocracy.

For the church's power was declining by the end of the seventeenth century. The Puritan monopoly had been broken and other sects allowed to propagate. A certain sterility had set in, a religious formalism, and when the New Light movement swept over New England with its emphasis on grace through direct experience of God, its revivalism and emotionalism, many a Puritan soul embraced it. Those weak, vulnerable egos, brought up in families where their individuality was suppressed, were empty vessels crying out to be filled by the holy spirit.

There were other symptoms of decline in the Puritan church. Ministers' salaries were often in arrears, and the parsons complained that inflation was eating away their livelihood. Church self-government was threatened by a move toward presbyterianism, fostered by the antidemocratic theocrats in Boston who sought to have committees of ministers rather than the congregations choose new pastors. "Certification"—a device for avoiding the church tax by declaring oneself a member of the Anglicans, Baptists, or some other sect—was on the rise. In 1802 a Connecticut minister named Daniel Parker observed that "preachers of every description had passed through and many of the inhabitants were certified in other denominations, mostly to avoid the expense."[51] Many of these were undoubtedly outlivers—or even schismatics who had fled the old-town church but not its taxes and who as yet had no church they felt was their own. Eventually, after sometimes epic battles in the town meeting, the new communities were allowed to found their own churches, often of another denomination. A few of these people may have been rebels against the local church's all-seeing eye—perhaps the first village atheists.

The dissenter had a choice of either fighting or moving away. Fighting from within was all the more difficult because he was treated like a pariah. The troubles Abel Wright of Kent, Connecticuut, brought down on himself are illustrative. Wright was a wealthy man, Kent's largest property owner, and had served as selectman, moderator of the town meeting, and captain of the militia. Evidently he fell under the sway of the religious fervor stirred up by the New Light movement in the early 1740s. (The New Light movement was regarded as disruptive and, worse, democratic by many conservatives and was thus a fertile source of town divisions. The spectacle of common people rising up and crying that they were saved, of young ministers preaching a new, looser doctrine of salvation, and of unlearned mechanics and poor farmers arguing theology was repugnant to the orthodox, and they boycotted the young New Light ministers Harvard was graduating. Of course, others embraced them, and the young parsons did revive moribund congregations in more than the spiritual sense. The saved then became intolerant of those who clung to the old religion.) Abel Wright held meetings at which New Light evangelists preached, and this caused him to fall out with the church, whose minister brought him to trial. Wright's gospel privileges were suspended, but he refused to truckle. Instead he stuck to his nonconformist path, taking up with some Moravians and attempting to spread their doctrine, which taught, among other things, that man was not always in a state of grace. The townspeople were outraged, and thirty-eight "yeomen" petitioned the General Assembly to remove him from the captaincy of the militia. Wright was forced to move away, although he eventually returned and lived out his days quietly in Kent as a general storekeeper. Even the town's leading citizen was vulnerable when he defied the ruling religious orthodoxy.

In Concord, Massachusetts, the demand of a prominent but unpopular citizen to be admitted to membership in the church set off an internecine feud that shook the town to its foundations. Joseph Lee, a doctor and the town's largest landowner, had long nursed a grudge against the town leadership because he had never been chosen as selectman or elected to serve on the General Court. Moreover, he was an Old Light and joined a separatist church in town when a New Light minister was installed. The dissenting West Church eventually withered away, and Lee decided to make formal application for membership in the main church, which had a liberal young minister in the pulpit. Lee applied and awaited the requisite period of probation, during which objections to his candidacy were to be raised. They were immediately forthcoming; several widows accused him of mishandling, for his own profit, their husbands' estates, of which he had served as executor. The church elders called upon Lee to refute the charges—or make peace with his accusers. He refused, demanding a public hearing and castigating both the elders and his accusers in violent language. He even "threatened and bull raged"[52] one deacon he happened to run into.

The case became the kind of polarizing *cause célèbre* that was the antithesis of the New England ideal of harmony—of every town a "peaceable kingdom" free of "contention" and "party" or "faction." Lee felt, with considerable justification, that he had not been given a proper hearing or a chance to confront his accusers. Since the local minister was identified with the anti-Lee faction, he called upon a committee of ministers from nearby towns to mediate. The church elders agreed, and the peacemakers were summoned. They promptly prescribed soothing words for the inflamed situation, absolving all parties; yet after this pastoral balm had been applied, Lee was still outside the church—and the political establishment. He and his sympathizers—about one third of the town's voters—remained a divisive force in Concord politics. Lee could take care of himself, but he was still, as Robert A. Gross points out, a victim of the tyranny of the majority. Lee's course of confrontation politics aroused "intense anxiety" in Concord, and the majority had formed a solid front of opposition against him, instead of laboring with this contentious man, as was their Christian duty. Eventually, on the eve of the Revolution, the church's hand of forgiveness was extended to Lee and his group in an attempt to bury the old quarrel and unite against the common threat. But by then Lee's cause was hopeless—he had declared his support for the Crown in this nest of angry rebels.

At the center of the storm of doctrinal controversy and political faction that periodically raged through the towns was the meetinghouse on the hill—site of the town meeting. It was here that the myriad individual interests of townspeople were raised and debated; and here that these common concerns were translated into policy and governance. The town meeting spoke for the townspeople as a whole and dealt much more intimately with the urgent concerns of their daily lives—straying animals, fences, roads, bridges, the town militia, and so on—than did the remote colonial legislatures.

The story of the evolution of the town meeting is the story of an evolution from oligarchy to democracy. At the earliest meetings voting was confined to freemen, a status determined by property and church membership, or proprietors. But this practice—a clear derivation from the church's concept of "visible saints"—soon deteriorated; it was simply not feasible to govern with a minority. Eventually only minors, women, tenants, and persons who had not been accepted as inhabitants were excluded.

The meetings were presided over by a moderator. Although the post of moderator was perhaps the most important the town could bestow, the moderator's power was informally circumscribed. He did not represent a party or faction—at least in an organized sense—and his main responsibility was the reconciliation of conflicting viewpoints. His function was not to force a consensus where none was present, but rather to seek out compromises among dissident factions. Not that he always succeeded in this and not that the meetings were always sweet and reasonable. Unruly elements sometimes seized the floor forcibly. But generally the goal of debate or discussion was unanimity; mere majority rule was not sufficient, for this suggested the existence of factions or parties and thus threatened the ideal of unity.

The town's executive arm was made up of the selectmen—usually seven in number. They were at first the secular equivalent of the church's elders. Each new congregation at its formation was supposed to select seven men as a kind of executive committee. These were supposed to be "visible saints"—men purified in the flame of confession. They were chosen by election and were indeed the worldly equivalent of the heavenly elect of Calvinist theology—whose real identity was, of course, revealed only on judgment day by an inscrutable God. The elders were the pillars of the church, and each congregation was to select seven of them. This was as prescribed in Proverbs 9:1—"Wisdom hath builded her house, she hath hewn out her seven pillars."[53]

Like the church elders, the selectmen made up an executive committee that gave overall direction to town affairs. They called the town meetings and drew up the agenda; they assumed the town meeting's powers when it was not in session, and executed its decisions. Thus they carried on the town's day-to-day business in conjunction with such elected town officials as the constable, tithingmen, grand jury men, justice of the peace (an appointee of the colony government), hogsreave (who watched over the common herds of animals in the pasture land), fence warden (who saw that neighbors kept up strong fences), and the other minor specialized functionaries.

Originally, it appears, the selectmen possessed the primary governing power, and the town meeting acted as a rubber stamp. In Dedham, Massachusetts, for example, the meeting decided that since "it has been found by long experience that the general meeting of so many men in one [assembly to consider] of the common affairs thereof has wasted much time to no small damage, and business is nothing furthered thereby, it is therefore now agreed by general consent that these seven men hereunder named [the selectmen] we do make choice of and give them full power to contrive, execute, and perform all the business and affairs of our whole town—unto the first of the tenth month next."[54]

But while the selectmen continued to function as a sort of executive council between town meetings, the meetings themselves gradually gained the upper hand in policy matters. The idea of the selectmen as a Platonic committee of wise rulers, to whom all decision making was delegated, clashed with the townspeople's diverse, conflicting economic interests. Then too, the first selectmen had been a natural aristocracy—proprietors, visible saints, and wealthy men; when these patriarchs died off, there was inevitably a diminishment of awe for their successors. In most towns the body of selectmen, which was elected every year, began to show a brisk turnover. Before, the same men had served for decades, but now new—often newly wealthy—candidates emerged from a wider popular base. The old cohesiveness broke down, as did the utopian ideals of the covenant; this change was especially evident in the newer speculative towns, where men were busy improving their fortunes. Sectionalism also arose as the outlivers formed their own communities and demanded greater independence. Increasingly, the selectmen were bypassed as men turned to the town meeting as a forum for influencing policy. Matters affecting the whole community were too important to be left, out of deference, to the selectmen to decide. Typical of this process was the Dedham town meeting's recovery of control over the agenda by the device of ritually appending the phrase "and all other business" to the order of business presented by the selectmen.

For many reasons, the town meeting became the decision-making body. It laid taxes, determined how much each man would pay, spent town money, authorized land divisions, settled title disputes, approved new immigrants as inhabitants, arranged for fencing of common land and settled the endless disputes over common-land use, located highways, arranged for animal pounds, granted economic concessions to exploit various local resources, and gave permission to engage in various kinds of businesses. The town meeting was, in sum, the town's economic planning board, and the issues before it were overwhelmingly local, economic, nonideological, and secular.

As the selectmen's power diminished, the participation in the town meeting's deliberations broadened. This reflected a broadening of the franchise; the towns had assumed greater power over determination of who should vote. As they established themselves economically, the towns became more autonomous, and their geographic isolation from the seat of the colonial government contributed to their independence. As a result, although the colonial legislatures passed laws defining who could participate in town meetings as well the procedures for holding them, in practice these decisions were pretty much left up to local custom.

There evolved two kinds of franchise: that of freemen, who were legally eligible to vote in all elections, and that of "townsmen," who were eligible to participate in the town meeting (the two overlapped, of course, and were sometimes synonymous). In Connecticut, to qualify as a freeman, a man had to own a freehold with an income of 50 shillings annually—the "fifty-shilling freehold" of England—or a personal estate valued at £40 (in Massachusetts, where the same law obtained, this amount was ultimately lowered to £20). The freeman also had to be of age—twenty-one in Connecticut, twenty-four in Massachusetts—and of quiet, peaceable behavior and "honest conversation." Massachusetts also required church membership.

Theoretically, only freemen were eligible to participate in the town meetings, but in practice the franchise was widened to include all male adult inhabitants who had some property or regular income. The property requirement was easily fulfilled. Usually a man took an oath that he had the requisite amount and that was that; so long as a man earned a subsistence from his land it was enough. The religious qualification was a dead letter. In effect, the town meeting was open to all men who were accepted as inhabitants of the town and who were relatively free. That is, it was open to all townspeople, except those who were tenants or adult but propertyless sons (and thus subject to the control of landlords or fathers); those who were "strangers" with no fixed address (strangers were not likely to remain; they would be "warned out" after a certain time—usually thirty days—or even whipped out); and those who were minors or women. Women, like children, had few rights (in Massachusetts they were considered to be "civilly dead" upon marriage, and completely subject to husbandly authority). The town meeting's aim, then, was to involve all its independent citizens, consult with them, and, most important, solicit their participation in and agreement to any decisions made affecting the whole town. A unified, cohesive, harmonious, peaceable town was the objective.

As a result of this loosely defined franchise, anywhere from 40 to 90 percent of the town's adult males were eligible to participate in its politics. The only links connecting the town with the larger world in the colonial capital were the deputy it sent to the legislature, and the county officials—the sheriff and the circuit judges—who were appointed by the governor. The legislators were dispatched solely as agents of the town and were given explicit instructions which had been debated upon and drawn up by the town meeting. The towns paid their own legislators, and they received journals of the debates and actions of the legislature by which they could check their performance. There were no higher statewide offices to vote upon in Massachusetts and Connecticut, and it would be fair to say that the towns were not interested in colonywide issues (until the pre-Revolutionary fervor spread across the land); nor were there political parties. Town politics were local and autonomous, and there were no splits among townsmen down party lines.

There were, of course, elections for the town offices, but campaigning seems to have been minimal and informal. The taverns, usually located close to the meetinghouse, were the center of town politics. There, in face-to-face contacts, men argued, lobbied, and persuaded. Candidates did not formally announce for office, but let their intention be known casually. It was unnecessary for a man to campaign, since he was familiar to his neighbors. Voting was also conducted informally; it was common practice, for example, for a man to vote two or three times.

Colony law required that an elaborate notice be prepared by the selectmen and distributed by the constable before a town meeting was held, but in practice town meetings were held as frequently as the town deemed necessary. By all evidence debate was lively at a town meeting, but when there was strong dissent to a proposed action by a significant group, the moderator would defer a decision until all could be won over. When conflict got out of hand, it was a sign that the basic cohesion of the town had broken down. Fractiousness could result from a splinter group demanding its own town services or from different sections of the town opposing one another—perhaps the waterfront area of the town with its merchants and storekeepers would clash with a section consisting entirely of farmers. In one bitter dispute in Dedham, a group from a splinter community was so intent upon having its way that it forced through a voting plan that created new voters. The dissidents took over the town meeting by force, bringing in three men with muskets to force the moderator to step down. But such tactics were extreme and highly unusual.

When conflicts became unbridgeable, the town meeting system broke down. To preserve at least one segment of the community, the dissidents might be given a certain measure of autonomy. Since they were usually located in a distinct neighborhood or cluster of houses, they could be given a geographical designation such as "ward" or "north ward" or "precinct" or "parish" and allowed their own church or even representation in the town meeting (a concession that eroded the idealized monolithic harmony of the meeting, creating within it a "fraction" or "party").

Or they might be allowed to secede and form a new town, but this ultimately required the permission of the colonial legislature, as well as the local town meeting. In practice, a precinct represented a stage halfway between being subsumed into one town and becoming a separate town. A separatist incident in Concord's history, peripherally related to the Lee affair, illustrates the process. Another faction in the town, which was also unhappy with the New Light minister and which lived farther out from the center, decided that the meetinghouse was too distant for convenient Sunday journeys (this was a common precipitator of such split-offs, although it might actually be a pretext masking another complaint such as unhappiness with the minister or simply a desire to evade the town taxes). They won designation as a precinct in 1746, after several petitions, and in time duly prayed the Concord meeting to grant them township status. The Concord meeting, with another rebellious faction on its hands at the time and fearing for its revenue base, rejected the request, pointing out that the town had built a road to make travel to the meetinghouse easier for the dissidents—a road they stood to inherit without cost if they were allowed to break away. At that time, the governor of Massachusetts, William Shirley, was inundated with similar petitions and sought to discourage them. With each new town sending its two representatives to the General Court, that body would become more unmanageable and populist in hue. A citizen of the embryo town had a father on the Governor's Council, however; strings were pulled and the new town, which was named Lincoln, was allowed to be born.

Concord's experience reveals the inner dynamics of the New England town when it was torn by fractiousness. It had two alternatives, other than resolving the dispute through compromise—either confrontation, as in the Lee case, or allowing the dissidents to go their own way. There was no party machinery, no political tradition of putting such disputes to the test in the electoral arena.

Many town meetings threw up their hands and asked the colonial legislature to arbitrate. This was done in Dedham, and the General Court had to send a special investigating committee to settle the sectional conflicts that were dividing the town. In Kent, a newer speculative town, the townsmen resorted to the General Assembly with a monotonous regularity on questions as mundane as where a bridge should be built or a highway laid (a sign, incidentally, of the weakness of community spirit in such towns).

Despite loose eligibility requirements, however, participation in the town meeting was not always universal. In the town of Kent, three quarters of the population in the early days was eligible for freemanship. And of the thirty-four who couldn't meet the standards, twenty-eight eventually made it. Yet by 1745, 30 percent of the eligible men did not take the required freeman's oath; this rose to 53 percent in 1796. Furthermore, during the same period the number of eligible adult men gradually declined from 71 percent to 63 percent of the male population. The reason for this decline seems to have been an economic downturn. A sort of "voteless proletariat" grew up in Kent; those who were chronically unable to meet the economic qualifications for the vote rose from 3 percent to 11 percent of the male population.

Analyses of voter eligibility by economic class have also revealed a decrease in enfranchisement as economic differences increased among men. George D. Langdon Jr. observed that in seventeenth-century Plymouth a society was formed "in which the opportunity to share in the political life of the colony was initially great but became more exclusive."[55] A statistical breakdown of qualified voters in Newburyport, Rhode Island, shows that the highest income levels had the highest proportion of qualified voters and the bottom levels the lowest. Merchants and professionals, for example, who made up 24.8 percent of the town's 699 males, had 79.1 percent of their number eligible to vote whereas only 36.7 percent of the laborers were qualified to vote. Thus the New England town in reality was hardly the font of pure democracy portrayed by sentimental myth. The voter qualifications were applied liberally, and men who started with little or nothing could work themselves up to qualification in a few years. But there was a hard core of apathy among a growing class of permanent poor who could not make the grade.

Then too, the impression persists that there was a small group of wealthy and powerful men who "really ran things"—an oligarchy in short. Although there was a good deal of equality when the towns were laid out, some men were more equal—got more land—than others. Moreover, the speculative towns that grew up on the frontier fostered an absentee class of proprietors who attempted to run things from afar. Although the real power of this class has been exaggerated, many historians have identified a kind of squirearchy of the wealthiest who ran the town and elicited conformity to their values—when they frowned, the entire town frowned. In this view, the proprietors—the original founders and the largest landowners—made up the aristocracy, while the yeomen chafed under their iron rule. In fact, the truth lies in some middle ground. Kenneth A. Lockridge described Dedham as: "an oligarchy which was not an oligarchy and a democracy which was not a democracy."[56]

The tendency toward oligarchy was rooted in the Puritan's belief that there was a natural hierarchy among men, just as there was a predetermined elect who would be saved from the pit on the Day of Judgment. As John Winthrop said in his sermon aboard the *Arbella*: "God Almighty in his most holy and wise providence hath so disposed of the condition of mankind as in all times some must be rich, some poor, some high and eminent in power and dignity, others mean and in subjection."[57] The hierarchy reflected a belief in an organic society, with each man in his place, each man following his calling, whether high or low. Those highest placed had an obligation not to overstep their authority, to eschew "convetousness," and to extend charity to the less fortunate. The lowest members of the hierarchy had the duty of deference to their betters, but they also had a right (not always enforceable in fact) to economic self-sufficiency, to raise at least a bare subsistence. And if they attained prosperity, then perhaps God had foreordained this just as he had foreordained that some men would be more able than others. Vagabonds, black slaves, bond servants, and others without a calling were excluded from the Puritan hierarchy. Reverend Perkins wrote, "It is a foul disorder in any commonwealth that there should be suffered rogues, beggars, vagabonds; for such kind of persons commonly are of no civil society or corporation, nor of any particular church, and are as rotten legs and arms that drop from the body."[58]

The initial landowners—the proprietors—obviously had a legup in the economic struggle. Each further division of land increased their estates and preserved the difference between them and the lesser folk. Naturally, the have-nots often raised a fuss, and there were seemingly endless disputes over land arising out of the proprietors' attempts to expand their holdings.

In the speculative town, the bonds of the covenant were loosened, releasing egoistic energies, validating the acquisitive itch.* Opportunities were more available—primarily in the form of virgin land. And the awareness of others' good fortune made men even less patient with subsistence farming. Although eight out of ten men in colonial America were farmers, the majority of farms returned only four percent of their total value a year. Men were drawn to the growing opportunities for wealth outside farming—in trade, in extracting minerals such as iron or copper, in hauling produce to market, in peddling, in running an alehouse or an inn, and in numerous other activities. The "happy yeoman" of Jefferson's vision was, if not a creature of the past, certainly dissatisfied with his lot and eyeing other paths to wealth. Puritan tradition may have compelled him to defer to his betters, but it did not keep him from becoming one himself. Men could rise, even if only a small minority did. Land, though, was the readiest source of wealth. The first fortunes were made from land; those who came endowed with an "estate," those with capital, as well as those who acquired it, the proprietors, were favored in the race. From farming it was a short step for those with money to land speculation—using the profits of the original acquisition to acquire more land on the frontier and sell it to new settlers. Then, as time went on, trade provided an alternate mode of rising, and it was to this, and away from the land, that other ambitious men turned.

Naturally economic differences arose among men, but these differences do not in themselves imply class distinctions. Members of a class have interests in common other than their bank accounts. A prime example is the British

*"Some were for staying together in this place, alledging men might hear live, if they would be contente with their condition; and that it was not for waste or necessitie so much that they removed, as for the enriching of themselves." William Bradford, *Of Plymouth Plantation*, p. 213.

class system which was really, as Peter Laslett has written, a one-class system—the gentry, with privileges conferred by law, versus all the rest. No doubt the British attitude toward class was carried to America—witness the colonists' awarding land by rank and estate, their use of the terms "esquire," "gentleman," "yeoman" or "goodman," "mister"—a variant pronounciation of "master"—and "goodwife." But the situation in New England was too fluid and land too readily available to allow the colonies to emulate the English system of a privileged gentry versus all the rest.

One mode of advertising class distinctions is dress. The Puritans believed in simplicity in dress, and their daily wear emphasized subdued grays and butternut. They were, however, the children of Stuart England, and in church and on festival days the men wore purple, green, or scarlet hues and the women red and blue petticoats, green or tawny brown aprons, and red stockings. William Bradford, it is said, had a turkey-red suit over which he wore a violet cloak. Lace and froufrou were eschewed, however. There were sumptuary laws forbidding those of "middling" or lower orders from dressing above their station, but these were loosely enforced. Reverend Parkman felt compelled to inveigh from his pulpit against "the growing extravagance of velvet and scarlet among people of low rank."[59]

Clothes were regarded as an investment, and hats and other more durable items were counted in with a man's fortune in his will. The size of the investment, reflected in the quality of a man's clothes, clearly established his rank. There was a similar attitude toward possessions, and such household items as quilts, bolsters, crockery, and tableware were carefully itemized in wills. Possessions were clearly correlated with economic differentiation, and although a rising prosperity was reflected in a rising number of possessions among all ranks, the social distance was maintained.

Although there was no squirearchy, there were indeed squires. In Kent, for many years there were only two men entitled to be called squire, but they ranked twenty-third and twenty-seventh in wealth. A tendency for yeomen (a yeoman was a husbandman or shopkeeper with substantial property; a gentleman was a man who did not have to work with his hands and lived very well) to style themselves gentlemen and thus take the title "mister" was also noted in some towns. "Esquire" was a title that could be assumed only by those holding high electoral and appointive offices in the colony.

So there were class distinctions in the towns, imported whole cloth from England, but not nearly so rigid or carefully defined as they were in the mother country. There was a group of men in the town who generally ran things, but the town was no tight, closed oligarchy. Theoretically any man could rise, and the highest village offices were spread among a broadly based electorate. Hereditary wealth there was, but it was generally divided among the several sons through partible inheritances, rather than passing entirely to the oldest through primogeniture, which would preserve a large estate.

Income distribution solidified into gradations with no great fortunes or plantation aristocracy at the top. Wealth in the town's early days was derived from land speculation. The proprietors and later substantial holders who shared in the divisions of the common land were able to amass larger holdings than the newcomers with little capital. There was upward mobility, at least into the middle ranks, and often the poorest people were only temporary poor—sons or new arrivals who started small and increased the worth of their holdings. There was also geographical mobility—to other towns, to the frontier, to the city. But those who fell into poverty found themselves warned off each town in which they tried to start anew (a custom that went back to England when enclosure acts put men off the land and created an itinerant poor). Eventually, these unfortunates were sent back to their home towns, where there was an obligation to care for them. Even home towns might warn off, however, starting the wandering all over again.

Land was cheap in the seventeenth century—less than ten cents an acre in today's money—and even in the eighteenth century £25 could buy a holding. In Andover, the proprietors provided land to newcomers on a quit-rent basis, payable in produce; the rent was low. The marquis de Chastellux, a French officer who served in America during the Revolution, observed how quickly a settler could become a "comfortable planter." "At the end of two years," he wrote, "the planter has the wherewithal to subsist and even send some articles to market. At the end of four or five years he completes the payment of his land and finds himself a comfortable planter."[60] In the late eighteenth century, Charles S. Grant found, two-thirds of the men of Kent owned farms valued at £30 or more and therefore had a surplus from their land.

There was inevitably a poor class, which in Kent in the 1790s reached as high as 42 percent of the total population. Furthermore, a class of permanent poor grew larger. In Andover, the tenants who rented the twenty-acre plots the town made available to newcomers never amounted to much; twenty-one out of twenty-seven of them remained poor, while most of the original proprietors grew prosperous. Nearly every town had a servant-laborer class, a propertyless proletariat who were never able to get together enough money to buy a farm large enough to produce a surplus. The indentured servants were provided for, often with land, when their seven-year bondage was completed, but Richard Hofstadter estimates that nine out of ten of them remained poor (Benjamin Franklin's father was a notable exception). Slaves could buy their freedom—at an astronomical price (a slave in Concord paid £120 for his freedom, which was several years' earnings for many a white farmer). There was a "welfare" system in that the town provided for its indigenous poor, but poor people were often bound out to work for families. Many were widows, old people, or orphans and hence unable to care for themselves. Even the transient poor were eligible for relief in some towns if they managed to remain for three months.

Generally, then, the social structure of the town was an admixture of the Old World class system and the New World opportunity. With all its institutions for keeping people "regular" and in their place—the family, the church, the schools, the class system—the New England town was a small, stable, conservative, conformist society, closer to a peasant village than a modern town. It was ethnically and religiously homogeneous. The townspeople had a distaste for anarchy and disorder, and obedience to the law was demanded. To enforce the law there was the local constable, the justices of the peace, and the county courts. Actually, popular opinion dictated the degree to which laws were enforced; the constable had little power in areas where local custom and popular sentiment did not back him up. The job itself was not a desirable one, and men avoided it when possible, at the risk of a heavy fine. Stern punishment was meted out for a variety of crimes such as desecration of the Sabbath, blasphemy, adultery, fornication, impiety, and debt default. The rate of crime as we think of it—murder, rape, theft—was surprisingly low; instead, most legal actions rose out of debts and such interpersonal matters as slander, trespass, and battery, the result of feuds, animosity, and quarrels. Men wanted law and order, but there was a fair amount of aggression, verbal and physical, directed against one's neighbors (possibly because of the reservoir of hostility engendered within the family, as we have remarked). John Demos states that "on the one hand, the records [in Plymouth] show relatively few episodes of violent crime: murder, rape or even ordinary assault. Yet, on the other hand, they report literally countless suits for debt, trespass, wrongful withholding of property, slander and the like. Moreover, in many cases where details are available, it seems clear that considerable feeling was invested in the matter at issue, from all sides. Hostility was, then, controlled beyond a certain point (where life and limb might be threatened), but was rampant in a host of lesser, everyday contexts."[61]

What sociologists refer to as social deviance or "victimless" crimes were usually confined to drunkenness, adultery, and fornication—mainly premarital intercourse. Marriage was largely a secular affair, an economic nexus, a matter of negotiations and contract worked out between the two families, though the young people might well have chosen one another and also had a right to veto at least one match they didn't like. Premarital philandering disturbed the symmetry of this system; it provided the consummation without the contract, and society frowned upon this subservience to sexuality rather than more sensible considerations of property and income (the Puritans were not antisex per se). At a time when marriage came relatively late in life, it is not surprising that premarital sex was fairly common. The town kept a stern eye on young couples who were just married and counted the months. If a birth occurred within eight months, the town immediately intervened, and the midwife was asked to testify if in her judgment the baby was premature. Their testimony was usually decisive. A typical such deposition ran as follows: "Lidiah Standish aged fifty-five years testifieth and saith I being at the house of John Merrite after his wife [had delivered] her child and I saw the child and by the behavior of the child I cannot judge but that the child was born before the mother of the child had gone her full time, I being a mother of many children myself and have nursed many but I never saw none as that . . . except it were such which the mother had not gone her full time with."[62] (Mothers who gave birth on Sundays were also punished, the Puritans believing that a child was born on the same day, nine months later, as it was conceived. Sexual relations on the Lord's day were of course sinful.)

The incidence of premarital intercourse seemed to vary from place to place in the colonies; it also increased in the mid-eighteenth century, reflecting a growing independence of youth and a weakening of the father's economic control as the size of estates diminished. Couples whose parents disapproved of their proposed marriage might force the issue by presenting the adamant parents with a fait accompli—a pregnant girl. Another escape valve was the custom of public betrothals, after which premarital sex was tolerated. Studies of marriage and birth records in Andover show that the average length of time between marriage and the birth of a first child was 15.1 months. In Bristol, Rhode Island, though, between 1720 and 1740, 10 percent of the married couples had a child within eight months of their wedding; this figure rose to 49 percent between 1740 and 1760 and remained at 44 percent between 1760 and 1780. In Concord, Robert A. Gross discovered one third of all births in the twenty years before the Revolution resulted from out-of-wedlock conceptions. This trend may have reflected the growing revolutionary sentiments in the air, but it also had deeper roots in the breakdown of parental authority. As has been already mentioned, sons expected to inherit land from their fathers and were kept on dutiful behavior by this expectation. But by the third and fourth generation, the available land was dwindling, and young men could no longer expect to be set up in this way (nor, by the same token, could daughters expect dowries). Thus, Gross concluded that the younger generation had less reason than ever for patience with parental restraints and rebelled.[63]

Whipping was the usual punishment for fornication, as it was for other crimes. The stocks were also used, and occasionally a weight was attached to the transgressor's leg. Of course there were fines, imprisonment, especially for debt, and capital punishment. The stocks were often placed near the meeting house to deter disturbers of the peace on the Sabbath.

But the sternness of Puritan punishment in the small towns has been overstated. In most places, physical punishment was used sparingly and the law was largely applied to nonconformists, vagabonds, and unpopular people. As Michael Zuckerman remarks, "The sanctions of the law were no solution to dissension."[64] In other words, the majority preferred not to be constantly punishing dissenters; it preferred that they depart or recant. The Puritan ideal of harmony necessarily presumed voluntarism rather than coercion through punishment. There is also ample evidence that the extreme sanction of imprisonment for debt was rarely used in Connecticut; it seems to have been a last-resort measure employed when a defendant withheld his property as a settlement for the debt. Most debts never reached the trial or foreclosure stage. When a creditor was determined, however, the suit would go to trial, and in Massachusetts, the debtor could be imprisoned as long as the creditor paid for his maintenance. Otherwise, he would be released in a year or so.

Above all, informal controls outweighed formal sanctions. The town actively sought to extirpate idleness since it might lead to delinquency; hard work was the cure for the dissolute. If a man was wasting his substance (or growing too old to look after himself and his family), the town stepped in and appointed an overseer to keep him on the track. Moses Rowless of Kent was found "guilty of poor husbandry" and "thereby in great danger of wasting his estate." An overseer was appointed. This was the solution in the case of Nehemiah Sturdevant, of whom it was said that "he spends his time to no good purpose and his family will likely be reduced to want."[65] Idleness bred poverty and poverty bred sin or crime; to the Puritan mind there was little difference.

In sum, given the Puritan abhorrence of anarchy and disorder, and given the threatening wilderness around the colonists, there was strong incentive to enforce conformity. Transgressors, criminal types, deviants, dissenters or simply people who were "different" had no place in the town and were punished or packed off somewhere else. What was wanted were men of peaceable disposition, steady habits, and "honest conversation." Like the Puritan congregation, the town valued its exclusivity.

A final force for cohesiveness was the economic interdependence of the town residents. They were engaged in subduing an unfriendly land and building an economy. Cooperative effort was needed if men were to survive and eventually prosper. As Richard Bushman observed, "Few considered any course but to live within the town. The economic ambitions of the people were attainable only because, living together in a town, they cooperatively mitigated the difficulties of exploiting the wilderness. Land distribution, road building, supervision of fencing, supplementation of pasturage, the recruitment and subsidy of millers, tanners, and blacksmiths, and the destruction of pests made the town's participation in the economy crucial to a farmer's success. Without aid from the community, few indeed could have produced a surplus and taken it to market."[66]

Many of the town offices had primarily economic functions related to an agricultural community. There were fence wardens to inspect the all-important fences between men's lands, which had to be maintained to keep sheep or cattle from straying and trampling crops. There were poundkeepers who corralled the stray animals. And in order to keep trade honest, there was a man in charge of weights and measures.

Before the widespread introduction of paper money, the towns depended upon a barter economy. Men pledged their crops to a merchant for his goods; debts were thus commonplace—nearly everybody was in debt, the merchants, like as not, most of all, for they bought their stock on credit from the port towns. No wonder that debt collection was a last-resort measure; the town depended upon debts to grease the wheels of commerce. Prices were based upon produce, with each bushel of wheat having a set value. Labor was another valuable commodity, and townsmen were required to work on the roads or for the minister, as part of his salary, or simply for each other in exchange for goods.

The rise of small shops and industries came when men sought more than the subsistence provided by their plot of land. Most men worked their land, but set up some other kind of business part-time. To lure needed industries, such as grain and saw mills, to a new town, there were subsidies in the form of grants of land. There were also opportunities to become tanners, weavers, fishermen, carpenters, coopers, blacksmiths, shoemakers, glaziers, wheelrights, and stonemasons; they forged iron, distilled rum or cider, built ships, and ran taverns or tippling houses.

Storekeepers imported a variety of goods from the port cities which they sold to their neighbors on credit. This was often a part-time business, and the storekeepers had often gotten their start by transporting farm produce to the market towns and bringing back in exchange necessities and luxuries. The credit system, based as it was on payment when the crops came in, effectively bound the buyer to the store; if he traded elsewhere, he could be sued for debt. The system favored local merchants who knew how much credit they could extend to each customer. When paper money became widely circulated, the old system broke down. A man could then pay his debts and shop around for the best prices, instead of being forced to deal with one merchant charging inflated prices.

If a store in Suffield, Connecticut, is any indication, the local shopkeeper offered a rich variety of goods. In the late eighteenth century this merchant advertised "wine, rum, plates, earthen plates, pewter, and all such, shoebinding, twist, thread, ashes . . . blue bowls, candlesticks, brass rails and escutcheons, shoes, hats (napped, chip, and leghorn), cups, Florentine shoes, skillets, fry pans, dish kettles, brass tea kettles, shoe buckles, ribbon, flaxseed, meat, tea pots, . . ."[67] and a hundred other items.

It is difficult to overestimate the importance of the general store. It brought amenities to a rude frontier life and provided the ease of manufactured conveniences and the pleasure of consumption to these hard-scrabbling folk. Indeed, when some ministers sensed that people were enjoying themselves, they lashed out against the evils of "trade" and excessive attachment to material things. It is doubtful that an increasingly materialistic people paid them much heed.

That general store's bounty signifies the achievement of a higher level of material prosperity, a level at which men's work was producing a sufficient surplus so that they could afford to buy some of the luxuries of life. In short, the towns had achieved material success. These collections of unpainted clapboard-sided saltbox houses with their shingled roofs sloping steeply down front and back had grown and prospered in the wilderness. No longer were they made up of determined yet fearful men living on the razor's edge of subsistence. They had arrived.

With material success came greater self-reliance. The various taxes imposed by Parliament on imported goods in the 1770s encouraged the development of local industry. With the severing of the economic umbilical to the mother country, the birth trauma of Revolution came. The towns had become semiautonomous political units; they found that they too were threatened by tyranny when the representatives of the Crown imposed laws aimed at stamping out the power of the town meetings; they resisted attempts to strengthen the colonial administration during the 1770s. Autonomy and self-government were bred into the bone and sinew of most townsmen, and when it was usurped, they rebelled. Their placid life was roiled by mob action against loyalist sympathizers, who were burned in effigy and tarred and feathered. The intolerance of nonconformity bred into the village soul was inflamed against those still loyal to the king. When war came, the towns equipped and financed soldiers for the cause; symbolically, the first shot was fired in a New England town, at Concord bridge.

The towns, which had been so insular and self-preoccupied, were suddenly seized by international events. By then they had come to regard their liberties as part of their patrimony. It was easy for them to choose which side they were on. They were not demanding new rights, but rather the preservation of rights they already had.

But, by the same token, the revolution, the first step toward the formation of strong national and state governments, presaged the end of their unique autonomy. No longer could townspeople be preoccupied with purely local issues; however remote and parochial they remained in many ways, they became a part of a larger national scene, with its parties and factions. The inbred exclusivity they cherished would gradually give way to the rising democracy of the Jacksonian era. Homogeneity would give way to pluralism.

But only to a degree. Many traditions of small-town life would persist through the ensuing years—the conformity, the suspicion of strangers and new ideas, the informal, personal politics, the avoidance of divisive issues, the reliance on accommodation, the "neighborliness" accompanied by a proclivity to pry into the private lives of those neighbors, and the sporadic outbursts of populist opposition to centralized authority, whether governmental or economic. And the covenants that imbued the founding of so many New England towns with idealism and law-abidingness would continue in the newer towns founded along the wagon trails westward. The idea that in forming themselves into a town men and women were fundamentally recreating some ideal human society of law and orderliness, with obedience to authority standing as the alternative to chaos and darkness, endured as the pioneers pushed farther into the wilderness, even though it took newer forms. In the

Old World, America was often imagined as an Edenic wilderness where men might live amidst abundance, free from the curse of work—happy savages unfettered by the constraints of civilization. Perhaps Thomas Morton's anti-Puritan revelers at Merrymount, who had their anarchic settlement not far from the sober Pilgrims' Plymouth and spent their days carousing, were parodying this dream. But most men instinctively chose the Puritan vision of the state of nature—after the fall. They believed that hard work and harsh laws were needed to curb man's innately sinful nature, so they sought to bind themselves into a society as a defense against the terrors of sinfulness within, as well as external dangers of the hostile wilderness. The covenant symbolized their need to fetter their unruly natures in a web of reciprocal obligations, an entangling network of laws. Yet, in a more liberal sense, it made society in the new land possible—a society inspirited by the biblical tales of the Israelites who fought heroically to regain their own Zion or Canaan in the desert.

Less philosophically, life in the New England towns was for the greater majority—idlers, drifters, dissenters, outlivers, and cantankerous antisocial types excepted—a life of close involvement with one's neighbors. In the ideal, everyone watched over everyone else and did not hesitate to intervene if another got off the track. Others were ever around you; you were involved in their lives from birth until death, and they were involved in yours. You saw them every day, from the time you were very young. If there was spite and meanness, gossip and nosiness, there was also helpfulness and cooperative effort. And in the church and the town meeting, there was a rough democracy and nearly every man could be heard. If the Puritan family snuffed out any traces of uniqueness in a child, when he grew up he found that he at least had an identity bound up with a homeplace, a town where he belonged. No wonder that many preferred to remain where they were known, rather than venture out into the unknown. The ties of the town became even stronger than those of the family for those who remained behind: families broke up and spread, the town remained. No wonder too, perhaps, that the more restless souls found opportunity so limited or their spirit so deadened by town life that they were moved to strike out for the territory ahead—where they founded new towns like the ones they had left behind.

The sentimental place that the town came to occupy in the hearts of many New Englanders was expressed by the Reverend Timothy Dwight in a poem:

In every village smil'd
The heav'n-inviting church, and every town
A world within itself, with order, peace,
And harmony, adjusted to all its weal. [68]

That was the ideal of the town—peace, order, and harmony, with God smiling (or frowning) down from above. William Bradford meditated on the town with less easy sentimentality, remembering the utopian ideals of brotherhood that had informed the founding of Plymouth. He had in mind, perhaps, the "declension" that so many ministers preached against—a loss of the community of love, stable and unchanging, which the Puritans had been determined to found. Bradford lived to see many sons and grandsons of Plymouth's original Pilgrim settlers move on, driven by an itch to better themselves economically, no longer satisfied with a modest share of the old town's limited bounty. He compared their leaving to that of children—"the town like an ancient mother [is] grown old and forsaken of her children."[69]

The spiritual ideals and organic unity of the covenanted town faded away into a dim but persistent memory. Men were driven by material concerns—survival and then amassing property and wealth. The bustle of trade and expansion drowned out the still, small voice of Christian utopianism. Democracy and economic opportunity overwhelmed the Calvinistic code of order and hierarchy. Founded upon John Winthrop's dream, the New England town later developed through the death of that dream. But in each of those towns were the seeds of newer towns farther west and the ideals of liberty, representation, and constitution that were the foundation of a new nation.

2
"The Garden of the Universe"

In April 1788, a small flotilla of boats drifted downstream on the broad expanse of the Ohio River, almost lost in the immensity of the eddying brown waters. They glided past green islands which loomed up before them and then receded, dreamlike, into the timeless backdrop. On either shore the somber forests and sheer bluffs bore mute witness to their incursion. As the poet-pioneer James Kirke Paulding later wrote of his own journey down the river:

> Down Ohio's ever ebbing tide,
> Oarless and sailess silently they glide,
> How still the scene, how lifeless, yet how fair,
> Was the lone land that met the strangers there!
> No smiling villages or curling smoke,
> The busy haunts of busy men bespoke. . . .
> Nothing appear'd but Nature unsubdu'd,
> One endless, noiseless, woodland solitude.[1]

The little flotilla comprised one large bargelike hulk, trailed by several small flatboats and three bateaux. The mother craft, a low fortresslike superstructure with sloping sides constructed of heavy timbers, was forty-four feet long and twelve feet wide and displaced fifty tons; the name inscribed on her prow was *Mayflower.* A name full of historical overtones for the forty-eight

Massachusetts men who made up the ships' complement; it symbolized their sense of mission, their conception of themselves as harbingers of civilization, like the first Pilgrims. They had come to plant a settlement on the soil of the Northwest Territory—the land northwest of the Ohio River and east of the Mississippi ceded to the United States by the British under the treaty ending the Revolutionary War. This land had been officially opened up for settlement by the ordinances of 1785 and 1787, passed by the Continental Congress of the Confederation of the United States.

It was one of those moments when the present loops back to make a slipknot with the past. The party was heir to the Puritan traditions of its native Massachusetts and to the ideals of the New England towns that had shaped the settlement of the Bay State. But it was also imbued with the ideals of the Revolution. Three fourths of the men were veterans of that war; as veterans, they were entitled to military land warrants, negotiable for government land—land that would enable many of the men, whose long service had left them improverished, to make a new start.

Commanding the body was an old hero of the Revolution, General Rufus Putnam, who was also a friend and comrade-at-arms of General George Washington. Washington had given his blessing to the expedition. He had explored this territory himself, and as an erstwhile land speculator, he had a keen grasp of the economic opportunities that the new territory offered. The men were shareholders in the Ohio Company, one of three land companies that purchased the first large holdings of public land in the Northwest Territory. The Ohio Company's tract comprised 964,000 acres around the Muskingum River in the surveyed part of the Northwest known as Ohio Territory—a land heretofore inhabited only by Indians, a few French colonists, itinerant fur traders, and small forces of soldiers posted at scattered forts.

The uneventful passage of the *Mayflower* and her companions ended near one of these forts, Fort Harmar, which had been erected in 1785 near where the Muskingum empties into the Ohio and the great river takes a majestic bend. There the settlers did as their Pilgrim forebears had done; they planted a town, which they patriotically called Marietta, after Marie Antoinette, who had been considered a patroness of the American cause in the Revolution (some of the party favored Adelphia, meaning "brethren," but the ill-starred Marie, about to become a victim of another revolution, received her only democratic tribute). Marietta was the first town in the Northwest Territory legally planted by Americans.

Actually, Marietta was a fortified town, in the tradition of the Kentucky stations—blockhouses and palisades set down in hostile Indian territory. And these in turn traced their lineage to the earliest Puritan towns, which followed the dictum of John Cotton, the Puritan divine, in 1630: "Neglect not walls and bulwarks and fortifications for your own defense."[2] There was a more direct link to the frontier towns in western Virginia, however. The Virginia General Assembly in 1701 had set down very detailed plans for fortified settlements, under a system called "settling in cohabitations." A minimum of twenty families was required for a colony. Each man was to be granted 200 acres of land for farming and a half acre for his house. The houses were to be built inside a 200-acre square surrounded by a palisade of heavy logs, ten feet high and set three feet deep.

Certainly these exsoldier-settlers did not expect to encounter any friendly Squantos; one hundred and fifty years of Indian-white bloodshed intervened between their incursion and the Pilgrims' encounter with curious, helpful Indians. The Native Americans who inhabited these lands knew that the first parties of whites presaged a flood of settlers, bent on claiming the land for their own; they were readying themselves to resist. Their British allies, who had second thoughts about their cession of terrritory, were stirring them up, while the American government had, largely by inept diplomacy, kept the Indians poorly informed of its intentions and their rights under the cession. Bloody fighting had already taken place in Kentucky, and the Indians of the Ohio Territory had committed hostile (or defensive) acts, although a loose confederation of tribes in the area had entered into treaties with the Americans. These treaties had settled nothing, and the Indians, encouraged by the British and their Canadian agents with vague (and, it turned out, false) promises of support, chose war.

When the Massachusetts men arrived in 1788, the situation was still murky, but it was obvious from the construction of the *Mayflower* was in effect a floating blockhouse—that they expected trouble. They further strengthened their defensive posture by constructing their fortified town, which was a hollow square of adjoining buildings and blockhouses, surrounded by a palisade fence. As a town, Marietta had a distinctly martial character, rather like an ancient Roman fort in the land of the barbarians—a comparison enhanced by the Latin names chosen by the exsoldiers (many of whom were Dartmouth and Harvard graduates), such as Campus Martius for the fort, Cecelia, Quadranaou and Capitolium for the open spaces, and Sacra Via (sic) for the wide road leading up from the river to the town. (The remaining streets were named for Washington and other revolutionary generals.)

But New England's peacetime concern for schools and religion was embodied in the person of the Reverend Daniel Story, a scholarly Congregationalist divine from Worcester, Massachusetts, who had been hired as a combination minister and schoolteacher. In surveying its land, the Ohio Company, at General Putnam's behest, had set aside school and ministerial lands, in the New England town tradition. The school-land idea came to be applied on a large scale in the Northwest, as the federal government set aside lands for the states to sell, witth the proceeds going to education—a practice in line with the exhortation in the Ordinance of 1787 that "schools and the means of education shall forever be encouraged." The idea was generally poorly administered, however, and public education was slow in coming to the region. The first land-grant college was founded within the Ohio Company's territory—

Ohio University at Athens, which for a time lived off the income produced by designated school lots within the town. The ministerial-land concept, however, contravened the First Amendment to the Constitution, which stated that "Congress shall make no law respecting an establishment of religion." In addition, the ordinance also provided for freedom of religion, and the Puritan (Congregational) church had long lost its quasi-official power. Moreover, a number of dynamic younger faiths had risen up that would actively proselytize in the Northwest. Public support for any one religion was obviously discriminatory—not to say politically impossible.

So, while the Mariettans honored New England tradition by bringing along a Congregationalist pastor and erecting a church for him among the first structures, his duties already were divided between religion and education (Reverend Story founded the first school in the Northwest Territory). Further, the civil law reigned supreme in the little town. Four months after their arrival, the colonists drew up a criminal code, which was promulgated by nailing it to a tree on August 2. There was perhaps an implicit, if not openly taken, civil convenant to submit to these laws, as there was in the other early towns of the Northwest. The early Ohio historian Jacob Burnet speaks of similar promulgations of criminal law in the next three towns to be founded in the Ohio Territory—Cincinnati, North Bend, and Columbia—adding, "To these regulations they all agreed; and each gave a solemn pledge to aid in carrying them out."[3] Further, the Ordinance of 1787, the new territory's "higher law," was also read to the assembled company on July 15 "with much solemnity in the midst of profound silence."[4] To enforce the criminal code, a court of quarter sessions for the territory was set up, and the right of trial by jury, enunciated in the Ordinance, was reaffirmed. Two weeks after the publication of the criminal code, the court was convened in a ceremony for which all the townsmen turned out in full regalia. After a parade and the blessing by the Reverend Manasseh Cutler (one of the Ohio Company's founders), Sheriff Sproat called out, "Oyez, oyez," and the court was officially in session—and promptly adjourned, there being no business before it. The ceremony honoring the court's existence evidently had an important meaning for the Mariettans, and such solemn ceremonies, minus any military cast and sometimes enlivened by rustic horseplay, would take place in many other newly organized counties in the territory. To the more civilized of the settlers, law, rather than religion, was accorded supreme importance.

But the first priority, of course, was given to the basic necessities of food, defense, and shelter. Trees were felled or girdled and structures erected, while corn was planted on the cleared land. The mood in the early days was optimistic. "The climate is exceedingly healthy," one man wrote home, "not a man sick since we have been here. We have started twenty buffalo in a drive—deer are as plenty as sheep in New England. Turkey are innumerable.

We have already planted a field of 250 acres of corn. . . . The corn has grown nine inches in twenty-four hours for two or three days past."[5]

These words, and those of the other settlers, made their way back to Massachusetts, where they were eagerly read. More immigrants began to arrive in the area, this time including women and children. In August, 8 families and 132 men; in 1789, 152 men and 57 families. Some came in wagons with black canvas covers on which were painted in white letters the words "To Marietta on the Ohio." The first virus of what would become an epidemic of "Ohio fever" had entered the New England bloodstream.

The new colony's fortunes soon changed, however, with the beginning of five years of intermittent warfare with the Indians, ending in 1794 when thirty-five hundred regulars and frontiersmen under General Anthony Wayne defeated two thousand of Chief Joseph Brant's warriors at the Battle of Fallen Timbers near the Maumee Rapids. The well-fortified settlers at Marietta came through the war without serious loss, although Reverend Story held his services in the blockhouse for the duration. Worse depredations than the Indians could devise were visited upon them in the form of famine caused by the black frost of 1790. The people of Marietta were reduced to eating boiled nettles, pigeonberry shoots, game, and spicebush tea. But Marietta was well organized and discliplined, and its settlers were sufficiently resourceful to survive in the wilderness; after the war the town became a shipbuilding center and entered its golden age.

After defeating the Indians at Fallen Timbers, General Wayne took his men into winter quarters rather than immediately ram a peace treaty down the throats of the vanquished. Sensitive to Indian ways, Wayne gave the Indians time to prepare for their formal capitulation. This came the following year when the tribes gathered at Fort Greenville to sign the first of a series of treaties with the white men that inexorably extinguished their title to the Northwest territory (the Treaty of Greenville gave the victors the Ohio Territory). Officially the policy of the Americans, like that of the British before them, was to recognize a fundamental Indian title to these lands and to forbid settlement until the rights of usage had been transferred to the United States in exchange for whiskey, blankets, trinkets, and small annuities. It was all to be done under the color of law, even though it was obvious that the Americans' legal power emanated from the barrels of their guns. In Chief Justice Marshall's words, the Indians were "domestic dependent nations in a state of pupilage."[6] In the course of 370 treaties during the settlement of the West, the United States spent $270 million paying off the Indians, plus $46 million surveying the land; total receipts by the federal government from the sale of this public domain land were $120 million less than its total expenditures. (One analysis of purchases in Illinois showed that the government had payed for the state twice over.) By those standards the Indians were rather handsomely paid off, with the government the loser. In actual fact, the wealth these rich lands produced would be hundreds of times greater than their cost.

The white settlers had their moments of terror and tragedy during the Indian wars, but the small but steady stream of newcomers did not abate. News of massacres that trickled back east interrupted the flow temporarily, while keeping those living in vulnerable parts in a state of anxious alert. Yet Jacob Burnet, a lawyer and leading citizen of early Cincinnati, could speak philosophically of the Indian menace in those days. He recalled that people did not let the Indians dominate their thoughts but rather occupied themselves with the material concerns of daily life. The stories of massacres, tortures, and abductions of whites were told and retold along the frontier grapevine, however, provoking terror and revanchism. Such notorious incidents as the atrocious torture of Colonel William Crawford, who was captured in General Harmar's retreat and subjected to a daylong roasting at the stake, became part of folklore. More poignant were the captivity stories, involving women and children who were swept up in Indian raids and taken off, never to be heard from again. A pioneer mother, captured by Indians in Kentucky who killed her children, met up by chance in Ohio with another captive, a young boy named Jonathan Adler, in 1782. Adler was later freed and set down this recollection of the encounter:

> She asked me how I had been. I told her I had been very unwell, for I had had the fever and ague for a long time. So she took me off to a log and there we sat down and she combed my head and asked me a great many questions about how I lived, and if I didn't want to see my mother and little brothers. I told her that I should be glad to see them, but never expected to again. She then pulled out some pieces of her daughter's scalp, that she said were some trimmings that she had trimmed off the night after she was killed and that she meant to keep them as long as she lived. She then talked and cried about her family, that was all destroyed and gone, except the remaining bits of her daughter's scalp. We stayed here a considerable time, and, meanwhile, took many a cry together; and then we parted again, took our last and final farewell, for I never saw her again.[7]

But the Indian Wars were only a brief, violent interlude in the settling of the Northwest Territory. There were comic episodes as well, such as the story of the effete Frenchmen who founded a town called Gallipolis on the banks of the Ohio. This "city of the French" was the abortive offspring of the Scioto Land Company, one of the three such companies that bought up vast acreage in the southern Ohio Territory in the late 1780s. The others were the Ohio Company, a company of shareholders, and Judge John Cleves Symmes's company, a speculative operation that bought land for resale to whatever settlers it could lure there. The original congressional contracts of sale transferred one and a half million acres to the Ohio Company, three and a half million to the Scioto Company, and one million to the Symmes Company. Of the three, only the Ohio Company retained any degree of rectitude and fiscal probity. Judge Symmes and his partners never raised the money to purchase clear title to the lands; however, this did not stop them from promoting them heavily. Some of the land Symmes sold lay outside his original grant, and much of the rest was sold and resold with Symmes seeing very little of the money. He did not make good his original contract with Congress, and eventually the government abrogated it. Symmes, a former chief justice of New Jersey, who became known as "the greatest land-jobber on the face of the earth,"[8] lost most of his money in the tangle of litigation that followed. For his own ends he did do much to promote the West in the early days, and he also became the father-in-law of William Henry Harrison, first governor of Indiana Territory, congressman, and hero of the West.

The Scioto Company was even more shady financially. It had been the product of an under-the-table deal between the unscrupulous William Duer, secretary of the treasury, and Manasseh Cutler and Winthrop Sargent of the Ohio Company. The three advanced $143,000 to the Ohio Company, which made a down payment on an option to purchase an additional five million acres, concealing Duer's and his backers' part in the transaction. Congress granted the option without a qualm. Duer became a silent partner in the Scioto Company, whose assets consisted of a contract transferring to it part of the Ohio Company's option to buy five million acres. The Scioto Company planned to raise the necessary capital by land sales abroad and appointed as its overseas salesman a young Hartford lawyer named Joel Barlow, who had gone abroad to make his fortune. Barlow met with Duer in London's Threadneedle Street, the English bourse of American land jobbing, and was assigned the French sales territory. Duer supplied a sheaf of authentic-looking deeds, which appeared to convey clear title but actually didn't, since there was none to convey until the Scioto Company paid for the land on which it had an option. With the prestige gained from the early sales, other buyers could be lured in, and eventually the company would accumulate enough money to exercise its option—or such was the plan.

In France, Barlow formed the Compagnie de Scioto and circulated grandiose promotional literature (Ohio was said to be "the garden of the universe, the center of wealth, a place destined to be the heart of the great empire.")[9] In a time of social upheaval and revolution, the distant arcadia conjured up in the company's brochures had a seductive allure. The comte de Volney, a French scholar, wrote, "Nothing was talked of, in every social circle, but the paradise that was opened for Frenchmen in the western wilderness, the free and happy life to be had on the blissful banks of the Scioto."[10] Eventually Parisians bought one hundred thousand acres, and an advance party of five hundred "cultivators" was assembled to prepare the land for settlement (the town, they were told, had already been begun, and the territory surrounding it tamed and settled, which was, of course, untrue). It would be difficult to find a group of people more ill-suited for the rigors of the wilderness. They were mostly small craftsmen—jewelers, wigmakers, wood-carvers, coachmakers, gilders. There were as well a small number of professional men, *petit* noblemen and courtiers and ten or twelve indentured servants brought along to perform any necessary hard labor. The terms were that the Compagnie de Scioto would pay their expenses and that they, in turn, would work for the company for three years, after which they would receive fifty acres, a house, and a cow.

The untried band set sail from Le Havre-de-Grâce in January 1790. Whatever visions they harbored of a land of milk and honey were quickly dissipated upon their arrival in Philadelphia, where officials informed them that the land they had come to settle on did not belong to them. Furthermore, the Ohio Territory was a long, arduous journey away, rather than the short distance promised in the prospectus. ("The land travel is about thirty miles but will very probably be diminished in a little while, by means of a plan which is actually in contemplation for opening a communication between the Potomac and Ohio rivers.")[11] Bilked, abandoned without prospects, the Frenchmen composed a letter to President Washington complaining of their treatment. It was arranged that the Ohio Company would temporarily take over the Scioto Company's obligations. General Putnam hired a crew of laborers in Massachusetts and transported them west to clear the land and erect habitation. The Frenchmen were put up by hospitable Philadelphians until they left in the summer for the journey across Pennsylvania to the Monongahela River and thence down the Ohio to their new town.

They arrived in the fall of 1790 and found awaiting them a village of eighty cabins in rows of twenty, along with palisades and blockhouses, located at a point four miles south of the mouth of the Kanawha River. General Putnam's men had built well by frontier standards, but the rough lodgings must have come as a still further shock to the already disillusioned Frenchmen. They were soon plunged into the rigors of winter, during which they subsisted on what food they had brought and game supplied by Ohio Company hunters. When spring at last came, they set to planting gardens, even though their agricultural experience was so slight that they consulted books for instructions. They planted grapes, berries, artichokes, beans, peas, and olive and almond trees—appropriate crops for Eden, no doubt, but in some cases dubiously suited to Ohio country. After chopping down trees, they buried the logs instead of burning them as was standard pioneer practice.

The settlement miraculously lasted another fifteen years. One third of its populace died from malaria. There were bitter winters when they subsisted almost entirely on boiled beans, and a later chronicler, the Ohio antiquarian Henry Howe, wrote, "May the happy of this day, never feel as they did, when all hope was blasted, and they were left so destitute!"[12] Still, they dabbled in their crafts, played flutes and violins, and held weekly balls on the rough-hewn puncheon floor of the blockhouse, dressed in their imported finery as though they were still in Paris. One of their leading citizens, Dr. Antoine François Saugrain, a 4′6″ naturalist, scientist, *philosophe*, friend of Ben Franklin, set up the first laboratory in the West and busied himself making ink, thermometers, barometers, and phosphorous matches. He later moved to St. Louis, where he supplied Lewis and Clark with scientific instruments for their expedition.

By the time the Scioto Company bubble burst, as it was bound to do, many of the surviving Frenchmen had drifted away, either back to civilization or deeper into the wilderness as hunters. The remaining populace dispatched a representative to Congress with a list of their grievances. Again the government acted with kindness, awarding the Frenchmen twenty-four thousand acres of public-domain land—or about 217 acres each (there were only 110 left by then). But few had the stomach for further pioneering and gradually Gallipolis, the city of the French, was abandoned, its buildings rotting away or preempted by squatters, the vanguard of a ruggeder breed of settlers who would efface all traces of Gallic culture so briefly scratched in Ohio soil.

Atypical as they were, Marietta and Gallipolis embodied in embryo some of the traits of the towns of the pioneer period in the old Northwest. Marietta was the obvious forerunner of the New England–style towns that sprouted along the northern tier of the territory; but its well-planned layout showed a conservative urging toward stability and permanence. Gallipolis played the fool and stands for all the ephemeral towns founded in fraud and energized by impossible dreams. These two—stability, by whatever cultural coloration, and speculation, form contrapuntal themes in the settlement of the West.

In contrast to the controlled, orderly settlement of New England by homogeneous groups in towns planted under the aegis of the Puritan church and the supervision of the government, the western migration was a mixture, part pell-mell anarchy, wave after wave of all manner of people, rich and poor, skilled and unskilled, churched and unchurched, foreign and native, New England and Middle Atlantic and southern. It began with the ubiquitous squatters, who moved in before the land was even surveyed, then moved on when they acquired neighbors, and embraced every social stratum from eighteenth-century outliver to nineteenth-century urban proletarian and foreign immigrant. Among the native cultural strains, two distinct types can be singled out as dominant in the migratory flood—the New Englanders and the southerners; these were the groups that most decisively put their stamp on the area that was to become the American Middle West.

The Yankees from New England—"Brother Jonathans" they were dubbed—did sometimes come in communal groups, in keeping with their tradition. Indeed the three million acres of land on the northern tier of Ohio known as the Western Reserve was dotted with replicas of New England towns. "No other 5,000 square miles of territory in the United States," wrote

B. A. Hinsdale, "lying in a body outside New England, ever had, to begin with, so pure a New England population."[13]

Connecticut men and women—and New Englanders in general—were driven by population pressures. The growing number of people living on a limited amount of good land was especially acute in the Nutmeg State, and the prospect of land selling for one fifth as much—and better land at that—was an obvious lure. After the War of 1812, conditions conspired to eject a great outflux of people. Economic depression gripped the cities as the British dumped their surplus goods in America. On the farms the strange summer of 1816, known as "1800 and froze to death" or "the year without a summer," when frost withered the crops in the fields, snow fell in June, and water froze in July and August, brought ruin and foreboding. "Thousands feared or felt that New England was destined henceforth to become a part of the frigid zone," wrote Samuel Griswold Goodrich under his pen name of Peter Parley.[14] A song of the day caught the popular escape dream:

'Tis I can delve and plough, love,
And you can spin and sew;
And we'll settle on the banks
Of the pleasant Ohio.[15]

Because it was a primarily agricultural state, Connecticut was hit especially hard; whole towns were decimated, as communal groups picked up stakes and headed west. A foretaste of this was provided in 1804 when the entire population of East Granville, Massachusetts—234 men and women in all—simply abandoned the town. These people from Massachusetts had their own song:

Adieu, my friends! come on my dears,
The journey we'll forgo
And settle Licking Creek
In yonder Ohio.[16]

Many of these Yankees were third-, fourth-, or fifth-generation sons whose patrimony had been so carved up among preceding generations that their fathers had nothing left to settle on them. The poet and essayist Edward Everett painted a sentimentalized picture of the young man, whose "portion of the old farm is too narrow to satisfy his wants and desires," leaving the "old family farm" and heading west, there to found a new town, on which "he piously bestows the name of the spot where he was born."[17]

Everett's peroration, however inaccurate it was as a description of the realities of settlement of the West, did evoke the propensity of New Englanders to recapitulate their traditions in the new towns they founded. It also reflected New England's imperial vision of perpetuating itself across the

West, in recompense for the many sons and daughters it had lost. Finally, he touched on the familiar theme of the landless youth, free to go west and make it on his own, no longer dependent upon his father for the inheritance that would give him economic independence. In the dynamics of the family and its generational relationships may be found the seeds of the intangible spirit of the frontier that Turner idealized—the antiauthoritarianism, the independence and individualism, the egalitarianism, with every man as good as the next and all starting the race at the same place. The New England men who went west were landless, uprooted; they had rejected their dependence upon an authoritarian paterfamilias.

The archetypal Yankee had the reputation of being a sharp trader and close with a dollar, but he also carried that messianical Puritan urge to reform his neighbor's conduct, to be his brother's keeper and reconstitute Winthrop's religious utopia as a "city upon a hill." The New England communal groups were often led by a minister and held their first church services among the towering trees which covered their town site. Agents of the Connecticut Association, who were sent ahead to lay out a town, were instructed to "begin your own labors . . . with morning and evening prayers and reading the Scriptures. On your first Sabbath and every following one till you have a preacher hold a prayer meeting and read a sermon. In this be neither negligent or discouraged and while you make it a steady object to promote the public good of the Connecticut Association and of the settlement as a whole, regard especially the literary, moral and religious improvement of the town.[18]

In 1805, the 234 men and women of East Granville arrived at the site of Granville, Ohio, on land purchased from the Scioto Company. Their first business upon arrival was to assemble beneath a great tree to hear a sermon by their minister. The tree was the first one cut down in the new settlement, and on this site a Presbyterian church was later erected. Their first Sabbath was celebrated among the trees, and the scene kindled poignant longings for home. As Henry Howe imagined it, "When they began to sing, the echo of their voice among the trees was so different from what it was in the beautiful meetinghouse they had left, that they could no longer restrain their tears." [19]

But the New England groups were frequently organized as land companies rather than congregations, each member purchasing shares that were converted into a proportionally sized lot. The capital raised was used to buy the land for the town site, and any further profits were divided among the stockholders. The impetus, though, was not primarily speculative, but rather communitarianism combined with good business. Indeed, the town's profits might be dedicated to idealistic ends, as was the case in Galesburg, Illinois, promoted by George Washington Gale. Gale, a Presbyterian minister in Oneida, New York, had circulated a prospectus among his flock of mostly transplanted New Englanders and had raised fifty thousand dollars from fifty families. The money was used to buy twenty square miles of Illinois prairie land. The town was carefully planned from the start; the settlers lived outside the town site in temporary shelters until houses of planed boards were built on their own town lots. The town's primary spiritual mission was to serve as the seat of Knox College, for the training of ministers. The college was supported by the profits of further land sales to outsiders.

Galesburg and many other towns settled by New Englanders were characterized by a rigid morality codified in their town ordinances which was strongly reminiscent of the Sabbatarian laws of the Puritans. The traditional exclusivity of the early New England towns was also practiced—at least in the beginning. Thus, a group of "intelligent Christian men in Connecticut" purchased a tract near Peoria, Illinois, for the purpose of planting a town. "By their laws, no undesirable characters could purchase land and were so kept away, while those who were worthy were in every way encouraged, which assured a good society from the start."[20]

New England's attitude toward the West melded missionary zeal with a kind of economic imperialism; the new land was to be cultivated for both souls and profits. Early missionaries sounded the call for more good Christian men to come out and do battle with sin in the wilderness. "We have heard the cry," one missionary wrote. "Come into Macedonia and help us."[21] "Infidelity and profaning the Sabbath are general in this place; they bid fair to grow into a hardened, corrupted society,"[22] the Reverend Joseph Badger thundered. "The Sabbath is greatly profaned, and but few good people can be found in any one place,"[23] lamented another divine, speaking of the region south of the Western Reserve after the War of 1812.

Hand in hand with New England's conversion of the West would procede economic hegemony. This economic-religious mission was obliquely expressed in a letter from Eliah Parker Mackintire, a New England merchant, to one William Salter: "The same resources that can support trade can throw a religious influence into every part of [the West], until New England institutions are established from the lakes to the shores of the Pacific, and you may travel from the Atlantic to the Pacific, and every six miles find a New England village, with its church spires pointing to the skies, and the school by its side."[24]

These New England–style towns with their greens or commons, white church spires, and neat frame houses did proliferate in the Reserve and continued on farther west; but their pristine New England quality crumbled away before the tides of migrants of diverse ethnic and cultural stocks. The towns in the Reserve that remained truest to New England traditions were usually idle backwaters, bypassed by the mainstream of progress; those towns in the main current accepted newcomers and found themselves adapting. This happened in Galesburg, which received both religious liberals (who started a college to rival Knox and protested the blue laws) and Swedes, who left their cultural stamp. One product of this admixture was the poet Carl Sandburg, the Whitmanesque bard of the common man.

The steam soon went out of New England cultural imperialism. The West was a great homogenizer, for one thing. Then too, the rising business-industrialist class in the East began to fear the loss of the sturdy, landless farmboys who seemed ideal fodder for the textile mills. As early as 1817, the year after the cold summer and the resultant exodus that threatened to decimate Connecticut, that state's General Assembly debated a bill forbidding emigration. A kind of counterpropaganda in the form of books critical of the West began to appear. Peter Parley published an anti-Ohio, Yankee-stay-home tract called *T'other Side of the Ohio,* based on his travels through the state, which played up the hardships the settlers endured. The uprooteed Yankees he encountered invariably "mourned the land they had left with its roads, schools and meetinghouses, its hope, health and happiness."[25] Other books followed, emphasizing the sickliness, ungodliness, and ruggedness of pioneer life in contrast to New England's green and peaceful fields and neat picket-fenced towns. Eventually New England made its peace with the West, its intellectuals idealizing it as a font of democracy, and its businessmen seeing it as an escape valve for the area's discontented poor (by this time there was plenty of cheap immigrant labor to man—and woman and child—the mills).

The southern migrants who came from the Carolinas, Virginia, and later Tennessee and Kentucky, were a different breed. They never came as towns of communal groups (save in the early days of fortified settlements), but as individuals. Many of them shied away from town life, preferring to work small farms on the bottom land in southern Ohio, Indiana, and Illinois. As Turner put it, "The northern stream of migrations was communal and the southern individual."[26] The southerners often came from societies dominated by large plantation owners and slaveholders—the great tidewater aristocracy who dominated the government of their states, while disenfranchising the small farmers who scratched out a living on the poorer land in the hills west of the fall line. The Quakers among these small farmers were antislavery and the rest tolerant of slaveholding while antipathetic to the slaveholding class. The only governments they had known had not represented their interests; they tended, in consequence, to be antigovernment. Most of these poor whites had had little and asked for little—just a plot of subsistence land of their own and otherwise to be left alone. They were independent, beholden to no man, suspicious of the law, indifferent to schooling, hair-triggered at fancied slights to their honor; they were also tough, hardy, crack shots, gifted at surviving in the wilderness. The southerners were generally less religious than the New Englanders, although prone to revival-meeting purgation; they were less likely to link up public morality and religion than the New Englanders and were thus more tolerant of the kinds of vice the New Englanders were always attempting to legislate out of existence with blue laws.

When these two highly divergent cultural strains met, the initial result was apt to be a mutual suspicion. The southerners feared the legendary Yankee sharp practices; the Yankees thought the southerners irreligious, immoral, lazy, and dissolute. An early traveler named Estwick Evans wrote, "The

Yankees are everywhere considered an intelligent, hardy, bold, active and enterprising people; but they are supposed to be excessively fond of money and frequently to obtain it by fraudulent means."[27] Yankees generally came west with more money, from the sale of their farms, and were better educated, while the southerners came from a society that relegated the poor to ignorance.

In an article published in 1821, the Edwardsville, Illinois, *Spectator* ruminated on the dialectics of the confrontation of these two groups:

> "The southern emigrants consider the eastern to be all cheats; the eastern man imagines the southern to be all savages. The white man [southerner] damns the Yankee and the Yankee, the white man—the one term synonymous with rascal, and the other with outlaw, with those who reproachfully use them; and when they come together, the one expects swindling, the other personal abuse. . . . The *one* associates with an eastern name, ideas of intelligence and industry; with a southern, ignorance and laziness. The *other* considers avaricious meanness for the former, and careless independence for the latter, to be more appropriate terms."[28]

In the mixing bowl of the frontier the two subcultures managed to coexist peaceably more often than not and join together against common hardships; pre-Civil War abolitionist politics was the flash point of their relationship. During the 1850s, in towns in the southern and middle part of the section, where the two regions were most equally intermingled, southern sympathizers and abolitionists clashed. When war came and the old Northwest lined up on the union side, the rift deepened. Some southerners went off to fight with their own people. Confederate raiding parties, abetted by Southern sympathizers who were known as Copperheads, carried out guerrilla incursions into southern Indiana and Illinois. But despite the war, the Middle West remained a crucible in which disparate national elements formed a new American alloy. The southerners contributed to frontier life their hospitality and generosity to strangers, as well as a love of liberty and an ingrained distrust of authority. Their speech overlaid that of the Yankees in the formation of what is generally considered to be the middle western dialect. For their part, the Yankees bequeathed their abiding respect for education, their enterprise, their puritanical morality, and their township system of settlement. As a result, the Middle West became an amalgam of these strains, with neither dominant, except in certain more or less isolated pockets.

Nor should the contributions of the Middle Atlantic states be overlooked. The institutions of local government, for example, were patterned after the county-township system of New York and Pennsylvania, rather than the New England town-meeting system, which never "took" except as an *ad hoc* convocation to approve some major town undertaking such as a new bridge or a railroad-stock subscription. The peculiar southern institution of slavery had been banned from the Northwest Territory by the Ordinance of 1787, and while southerners brought slaves to the territory, and indentured servitude was permitted for years, the region remained predominantly antislavery—yet not abolitionist. Economically, after the heyday of New Orleans as the point of export of goods from the interior, the West's ties were increasingly with the eastern seaboard. Nor were southerners a majority of the population. They were an estimated ten percent of the population of Indiana and Illinois in the 1820s, for example, and by 1850 it was calculated that one-sixth of Ohio's people were of New England birth, one-eighth southern, one-eighth foreign (with Germans leading, Irish next, followed by Scandinavians, Scotch-Irish, and Welsh), and three-fifths midwestern born. Certainly New Jerseyans, Pennsylvanians, New Yorkers, and Marylanders were among the immigrants, while the foreign born sometimes settled whole towns or formed colonies in the cities and small towns. The West, in short, was heterogeneous.

To the New Englanders, "heterogeneous" was a pejorative word, and they frequently applied it to the peoples they met in the West. Where they came from, a man's neighbors were of like origin, mind, and convictions. Yet, except where they settled as communal groups, the New Englanders, like all the other pioneers, were likely to land among diverse strangers—from "everywhere in general and nowhere in particular,"[29] as the popular phrase went. What they had in common, though, was the overriding hardship of frontier life; necessity ground down individuality to the nub of basic needs. It effaced differences, throwing people back on one another. The settlers (who tended to have rather attenuated roots to begin with) thus played down origins in favor of the here-and-now; they looked forward not back, except in homesickness. Clinging to one's back-home identity was positively frowned on by western writers. In an immigrant's guide of the 1850s, foreign immigrants were advised against importing any ancient European nationalistic animosities: "The American laughs at these steerage quarrels."[30] Communal settlement was also condemned by self-appointed frontier social arbiters as excessively insular. George Flower, Morris Birbeck's collaborator in establishing an English settlement in Illinois until they had a falling-out, wrote, "The idea of forming exclusive settlements of Germans, English, or Irish is very erroneous and highly prejudicial to the interests of the settlers themselves."[31] In Illinois, where twenty-two colonies of New Englanders planted towns in the 1830s alone, the *Illinois Advocate and State Register* was critical of this traditional Yankee practice. Wishing the new arrivals well, it went on to opine that it was better for immigrants to come as individuals and families. The *Western Monthly Magazine* said that the settler "so strongly imbued with the peculiar manners, notions, and ways of thought of that home, as to be unable to shake them off and adopt those of his adopted country"[32] would do best to stay home.

The key to getting along on the frontier was to avoid putting on airs or displaying a sense of superiority—in other words, adopting a kind of aggressive egalitarianism. This advice was proffered by the author of *View of the Valley of the Mississippi;* who signed himself "R.B.," and pointedly aimed at easterners, who were evidently the worst offenders in this regard:

> The eastern emigrant will find warm-hearted friends in every neighbourhood in this state. The people of the West have much plain and blunt, but sincere hospitality. And any emigrant who comes among them with a disposition to be pleased with the country and its inhabitants,—to partake of their hospitality cheerfully—to make no invidious comparisons,—to assume no airs of distinction,—and in a word, to feel at home in this region, where, of course, everything is very different from what he has been accustomed to, will be truly welcome. Fastidious and reserved manners, a disposition to be forever unfavourably contrasting the West with the East,—and to find fault with everything around him,—will speedily render any emigrant an object of dislike and neglect.[33]

On the frontier people ate, dressed, were housed alike; they helped each other, and individual merit and self-sufficiency were prized. But social distinctions set a man apart from his neighbors—and on the frontier a man sometimes desperately needed his neighbors. Those who held themselves apart—who were standoffish in the social or physical sense of the term, who kept to themselves, who maintained an exclusive group identity and an implied superiority—were to be regarded with suspicion and hostility. In her book *Western Clearings* (1845) Mrs. Caroline Kirkland described this tendency of frontier life:

> There seems to be in the forming stages of society, at least in this Western county, a burning, restless desire to subject all habits and manners to one Procrustean rule. Whoever ventures to differ essentially from the mass, is sure to become the object of unkind feeling, even without supposing any bitter personal animosity. . . . As was the accusation of witchcraft in olden times . . . so with us of the West is the suspicion of pride—an undefined and undefinable crime, described alike by no two accusers, yet held unpardonable by all. Once establish the impression that a man is guilty of this high offense against society and you have succeeded in ruining his reputation as a good neighbor. Nobody will ask you for proof; accusation is proof.

Mrs. Kirkland was speaking of the embryonic society of the towns and settlements that had progressed beyond the survival stage, like the towns she called "Tinkerville" and "Monacute" in her semifictional *A New Home—*

Who'll Follow? It was in this beginning-to-be-organized society that the western paradox of extreme individualism and extreme conformity resolved itself. The solution was *social* conformity but *economic* individualism. That is, one was free to pursue gain, but one must pay homage to the egalitarian values of the frontier. One could earn—amass land or money—but not spend—at least in a manner that seemed to proclaim excessive pride or to imitate effete eastern values. Pioneer virtues were simplicity and frugality, and display of an egregious sort aroused criticism. One must not take on any kind of airs of being superior to anyone else.

Later, after the passing of the pioneer period, economic differentiation, rising fortunes, and industrialization would impose a class structure on the towns, but in the early days every person who came west was new-minted, sui generis—without a past. "What part of the world you from?" was a western greeting, but this question indicated curiosity about geographical, not social origins "Kin and kin-and-law didn't count a cuss," as the saying had it. Pioneering was a great leveler, with a man's individual talents and physical prowess the only currency of social worth. As Frederick Jackson Turner put it: "The early society of the Middle West was not a complex, highly differentiated and organized society. Almost every family was a self-sufficing unit and liberty and equality flourished. . . . Both native settler and European immigrant saw in this free and competitive movement of the frontier the chance to break the bondage of social rank, and to rise to a higher plane of existence. The pioneer was passionately desirous to secure for himself and for his family a favorable place in the midst of these large and free but vanishing opportunities."[34]

Pioneer men, foreign travelers often observed, displayed an absence of servility and a kind of haughtiness of mien. They exhibited a disdain for title and rank and any other "airs" of the effete East and a distrust and irreverence for all officialdom. As for manners, they wolfed down their food like animals and chewed tobacco, spitting copiously anywhere they fancied (to the disgust of Charles Dickens and Mrs. Trollope). One traveler described the manipulation of the tobacco cud as being "like a toad in a monkey's mouth."[35]

The pioneer man was also seen as brave, honest, kind to children, helpful in time of sickness, and, to a point, respectful to women (though he referred to his wife as "the old woman" and made her walk behind him). He was single-minded in his ambition to aggrandize himself—"His spirit is eminently encroaching,"[36] as John Ludlum McConnell put it—and would take what he wanted even if it belonged to someone else, yet he was quick to punish severely trespassing and theft when he was the victim. He was selfish—yet his hospitality was legendary, and he was sociable with his neighbors. He was rather gloomy of temperament, though his rough sense of humor was evident in his tall tales and braggadocio. His dissipations had an air of desperation about them. He was pragmatic, materialistic, and scornful of philosophy and art. His religion, if such a dedicated materialist could be said to have one, was of the primitive, emotional sort, tending toward excess and fanaticism, then swinging back to passivity and indifference. Like political arguments, disputes over fine points in the Bible were a favorite time-passer of general-store idlers. He was violent and physical, quick to take up a challenge to his prowess. Above all he was calmly self-reliant, confident of his practical abilities, contemptuous of organization, protective of what he conceived to be his rights and his dignity.

The westward itch was not confined to men; many wives followed them willingly, though others hated to exchange the familiar comforts of home for the wilderness. The pioneer wife may have been subservient to her husband, eating last, carrying the bundles, and getting up first in the morning to lay the fire, milk the cows, do the gardening; but she had the respect due to one who pulls her own weight, and she had authority within her own considerable sphere. At once slavey and paragon mother, she displayed a calm, earned sense of self-reliance and a sometimes venomous tongue. A good number of spinsters and widows also came west; the former taught, characteristically, and the latter took over a claim and farmed it or lived in a town, supporting their brood "with the needle."

For all his egotism, the pioneer was neighborly. The Englishman Morris Birbank was struck by the reciprocal kindness he observed in settlements in the Wabash Valley. There was, he said, "such a genuine warmth of friendly feeling, a disposition to promote the happiness of each other, that the man who is lonely among them is not formed for society. . . . There is a great amount of social feeling, much real society in new countries, compared with the number of their inhabitants. Their importance to each other . . . creates kind sentiments."[37] One old settler reminisced that "common hardships and labors begot a fellow feeling. If there was a cabin to raise, every man for miles around turned out with alacrity to help raise it and put on the last clapboard. If there was any job too heavy for one man to do, all assisted. When a hunter or traveler was belated, be he stranger or acquaintance, he found a home and a welcome in any log cabin he might chance to find."[38]

The old settler was referring to the prevailing custom of "change [exchange] work." Underlying the kindliness and mutual assistance so many old pioneers recalled nostalgically was a hardheaded notion of reciprocity which had a compulsory aspect—a kind of forced barter of labor, as it were. The sense of compulsion comes through in the recollection of a pioneer woman from Fountain County, Indiana: "Each settler had to go and assist his neighbors ten or fifteen days, or thereabouts, in order to get help again in log rolling time. This was the only way to get assistance in return."[39] An Ohio man, turning away another's thanks for his help in raising a barn, spoke in softer terms of a generalized duty: "No, Daniel, what we've done today, we owe to everyone that makes a like call."[40] There was a chronic labor shortage on the frontier; one man could not go it alone, therefore all men had to help one another. Even if one could afford to pay wages—which most pioneers couldn't—there was little labor for hire. Hired hands were relatively well paid, but the average man looked down on doing such work and regarded it as a stopgap until he could stake himself to his own land. Every man's ideal was "working for himself." Similarly, the scarcity of inns or other public accommodations made hospitality to strangers a necessity—people never knew when they might be caught out in the woods far from home. And the isolation of the pioneer family made the arrival of a visitor a welcome event and a chance to acquire news of the great world.

The proud, "stuck-uppetty," standoffish person was thus not wanted on the frontier, for he or she would not lend a helping hand in the barn raisings, harvesting, huskings, and myriad other jobs of cooperative labor the pioneers engaged in. An eccentric loner might be tolerated, but a man who was not open, who did not proffer the bland, friendly expression of neutrality was considered potentially hostile, or at least suspicious.

Likeness in dress, the reluctance to take on airs, the avoidance of superior ways, the bland expression—these were a complex of verbal signals that one was not different, and therefore not threatening—behavioral flags of truce, as it were, earnests that one was friendly. Such body language was necessary on the frontier, for to set oneself apart from others was to sever the bond of reciprocal help that enabled people to survive. It followed that any group that insisted on maintaining its unique traits and keeping to itself was suspect—and possibly a threat.

Two groups on the frontier who gained the enmity of their neighbors did so because one *could not* conform and the other *would not*, thus committing the sin of pride. These groups were the blacks and the Mormons; the former bore the stigma of historical racial attitudes, while the latter was a classic case of a group that clung to—even flaunted—its special identity and would not assimilate.

Attitudes toward blacks in the West were essentially the same as they were in the East and the South; the white immigrants simply imported them. Except in pockets of strong abolitionist sentiment, which is to say towns settled by New Englanders, blacks were regarded as inferior and subjected to segregation. Undoubtedly there was opportunity for black people in the West, but few could take advantage of it in pre-Civil War days. Some freed slaves did come in groups and attempted to make a new life for themselves with mixed success. An experimental settlement of black people in southern Ohio founded by a Connecticut abolitionist, Augustus Wattles, for example, was eventually scattered by threats and pressures from the white people in the area. Wattles had purchased thirty thousand acres of land upon which a colony of two hundred people settled. They farmed the land, and Wattles also established a manual labor school, to teach the settlers trades. Another group of freed slaves, formerly belonging to John Randolph of Virginia, tried to take up three thousand acres of land nearby that had been purchased for them with a legacy from their former master's estate, but local whites forcibly prevented them from settling. These were highly visible groups of blacks, living in an area largely inhabited by southerners. If the settlements had been in the northern part of Ohio, where New Englanders dominated, things might have been different. It was in Ohio, after all, that a group of New England abolitionists founded Oberlin College in 1832. The college not only admitted women on equal footing with men, which was liberal enough; but it also admitted colored persons "on terms of equality and brotherhood,"[41] which was unheard of at the time.

So while blacks were relatively few in the West during the pioneer period, there was discrimination against them, and even violence where they settled in groups. There was an urban riot in the growing little city of Cincinnati in 1841. The blacks, who lived in their own neighborhood, were attacked by Irish toughs. The Irish, significantly, were probably the next poorest group to the blacks. Often coming as laborers on the canals and railroads, they joined the poorer classes in the towns and cities, rather than taking to the land. The Irish were also subjected to imported prejudice—only in this case the prejudices were those of the cities of the Northeast.

The Mormons, however, were not poor; they were well equipped to prosper, and they did. There was undoubtedly prejudice against them, but their own pride, exclusiveness, and undiplomatic ways with the Gentiles surely fomented the hostility they met in Ohio, then Missouri, and finally Illinois, before they began their great hegira to Utah under Brigham Young.

Their first stopping point in the West was the central Ohio town of Kirtland. The town had been founded by Sidney Rigdon, a Campbellite. The Campbellites, under their founder, Alexander Campbell, espoused a form of primitive Christianity. Rigdon broke with Campbell and took his followers to Kirtland. When he heard of Joseph Smith's miraculous teachings, Rigdon converted to Mormonism and became Smith's second-in-command. Kirtland became a prosperous town, and the Mormons practiced communism for a while, but this system was modified because of internal dissensions in 1834. Thenceforth church members could keep enough for their individual needs and give the rest to the church. They built a magnificent temple in Kirtland, as would become their practice.

For a spiritual leader who recommended communism to his flock, Joseph Smith retained well-developed capitalistic instincts. After the breakdown of the communal system, he opened a bank, not an unusual thing to do at the time. Everybody was opening banks on little or no capital, and these same banks were failing with such regularity that a newspaper in Cleveland had made up a linecut of a log cabin blowing sky-high to use routinely when it ran a bank-failure story. Smith's motives may have been to serve the best interests of his flock; certainly the Mormon colony was short of money at the time, as was most of the West. At any rate, Smith founded the Kirtland Safety Society Anti-BanBing (sic) Company. The bank issued notes, like all private banks were doing at the time, and these were used to pay off the colony's debts. Eventually some of the Mormons' creditors—perhaps out of anti-Mormon prejudice, perhaps not—questioned the soundness of these notes. Challenged, Smith staged a charade for the creditors. He offered to open the bank's vaults to the creditors, so that they could see for themselves that his bank's notes were backed by specie. The creditors took him up on his offer and were duly shown rows of boxes, each labeled "$1,000" and apparently full of silver coins. Actually, beneath the surface layer of coins there was a ballast of sand, gravel, lead, and scrap iron. (Non-Mormon banks engaged in less flagrant but similar deceptions to forestall a run on their funds in bad times.) This fiscal shell game stalled the creditors for a time, but eventually there was a run on the bank and it collapsed. Smith, it turned out, was guilty of operating an illegal bank, although he had attempted to avoid the intent of the statute by the device of printing the words "anti-BanBing" in small letters on the notes. A mob—the first of many—menaced Smith, and he and Rigdon fled. The rest of the Mormons followed, leaving Kirtland and their fine temple behind.

They settled in Missouri for a time but were harassed by vigilantes and moved on to Illinois. There, on land purchased by Brigham Young, near the Mississippi River, they founded the town of Nauvoo, which became even more prosperous than Kirtland and had an equally imposing temple. The town was laid out according to Mormon doctrine, drawing upon the Book of Revelation. The plot was a mile square with right-angle streets, each of which was eight rods wide, and ten-acre blocks containing twenty houses, each set on a half-acre lot. Smith was constantly in debt, despite land speculations, and his practice of refusing credit at his general store (contrary to the near-universal pioneer custom) caused ill feelings. He began stirring up the political waters, seeking greater influence in the state. He became cozy with the state Democratic party, and the upshot was that Smith delivered his people as a sizable voting bloc to the Democrats in exchange for various concessions, the most significant of which was the right to maintain a Mormon army, the Nauvoo Legion. No doubt Smith was again thinking of his people in trying to form a protective alliance with the power brokers of the Gentile world, but again his public-relations sense failed him. He was inspired to add polygamy to the Mormon canon, which was a red flag to his neighbors. They were also becoming nervous about the sizable Nauvoo Legion, which had become the second largest army in America (the largest being the U.S. Army). A newspaper in Nauvoo criticized Smith's revelations on the number of wives a man should have, and he promptly closed it down. Tension between the well-armed Mormons and their neighbors grew, and fearing insurrections, Governor Thomas Ford raised a militia and persuaded Smith to surrender himself and face criminal charges relating to his suppression of the paper. No sooner was Smith in jail than he was murdered by a mob, while the militia guarding him looked the other way. After a power struggle, Brigham Young gained the leadership of the church and imposed a virtual police state in Nauvoo. The Mormons' state charter, which had given them powers of self-government and the right to organize the Mormon Legion, was revoked in 1845. Incidents of Mormon thievery from surrounding farmers rose, and the locals retaliated by burning Mormon farms; Brigham Young took to wearing two pistols and threatened to shoot any one who tried to serve a writ on him. The upshot was that in 1846 the Mormons once again picked up and headed west, on the Great Trek that took them to the Great Salt Lake, where they founded a spacious, well-planned city in the desert they would make bloom.

The Mormons' penchant for violence did them in more than any other characteristic; it caused the hostility that their aloofness provoked among their frontier neighbors to flare up in retaliatory acts. Had they been more peaceable they might have emulated the career of another religious group that had some similarities to the Mormons and an even greater aloofness and exclusivity. This was the band of German separatists known as Rappites or Harmonists who founded Harmony, Indiana. In 1814 they had migrated from Pennsylvania, after they had aroused enmity among their neighbors; in Indiana they again aroused dark emotions—a compound of envy for their material success, resentment over their sharp business practices, and rancor against their coldness with strangers. Yet none of this animosity ever spilled over into violence, although the stirrings of hostility were at least one reason why George Rapp and his band sold their prosperous, beautiful little town on the Wabash River, with its great brick granaries, ingenious prefabricated frame homes, and thriving mills and breweries to another communalist, Robert Owen. Rapp claimed to have received a direct command from God and moved his flock back to Pennsylvania en masse in 1824. Recall, too, the milder yet distinct disapproval felt in Illinois toward the New England community groups that settled there. In time these towns abandoned the outmoded New England tradition of exclusivity. Foreign-immigrant groups also frequently stuck together, for which they won disapproval from the dominant "Americans"; but such was the living space—the social elbow room—provided by the West that they were generally not bothered.

Socially a conformist, the frontiersman was dependent primarily upon his own efforts in getting a living, supplemented by reciprocal-help arrangements with his neighbors. There was plenty of land for all, and each could seek his own prosperity without diminishing his neighbor's. Politically, too, the frontiersman was an individualist, scorning organized government and parties, often indifferent to political matters, yet capable of being swept up by crowd fervor. A robust nationalist, he responded most strongly to those national candidates who embodied frontier values and spoke for western interests. Thus, the two most popular national figures in the West were Andrew Jackson and William Henry Harrison. Both locally and nationally, issues were less important than personalities; men were either "nominal"

Jacksonians (for the man) or "whole hog" or "whole cloth" Jacksonians (for the man and his program). Harrison, as an adopted son of the West, won overwhelming support in that region, even though he was a handpicked candidate of the eastern-dominated Whigs. Later the slavery question would harden ideological party lines, but the point is that while pioneer politics could be violently partisan, political differences were not a divisive force on the frontier.

Frontier society also successfully mingled successive, overlapping "generations," each reflecting a different stage of settlement. These stages, in Frederick Jackson Turner's classic description, were first the fur trader, then the cattle-raising pioneer, then the small primitive farmer, and finally the serious husbandman who raised a surplus. The fur trader passed off the stage of history by the end of the eighteenth century, his role as pathfinder completed, but he left a legacy of skills that were employed by many early settlers who sold pelts to John Jacob Astor's men to raise dearly needed cash. The primitive farmers were next—wild, reclusive, individualistic folk who were always moving on. These were the squatters who barged in before the land was even surveyed and made their "tomahawk claims" (blazing the "witness trees" on each of the four corners of their parcel), built rude cabins, cleared a few acres on which to raise a subsistence crop, supplemented by hunting, then sold out or simply abandoned their land to the next wave of settlers and headed deeper into the wilderness. The squatter began to feel hemmed in as soon as a neighbor's chimney smoke smudged his sky, but some lingered on in the settled regions. They clung to the old ways, defiantly wearing their coonskin caps, linsey-woolsey shirts, buckskin breeches, and moccasins and carrying long knives; their women wore homespun cotton or wool frocks and went barefoot. They were haphazard farmers, raising the two crops easiest to grow—corn and hogs. Hence their appellation "hog and hominy" people. In Illinois they were also called the "butcher knife boys" because of their ever-present long knives, and politicians were careful to appeal to them, Governor Thomas Ford recalled in his history of Illinois. They were a subbreed of pioneers who refused to progress to more civilized ways when those became available. Governor Ford stated reprovingly that "they would have been better contented to live in their old log cabins, go barefooted, and eat hog and hominy."[42] These people believed in being self-sufficient and practiced the old home-crafts rather than wear "store bought."

These early arrivals had been the pathbreakers, however. The explorers and fur traders and hunter-farmers opened up by trial and error the trails the later migrants followed. For one hundred and fifty years America had been a coast-locked country, walled off from the rich West by the Appalachian Mountains. The early sojourners found cracks in this seemingly impenetrable barrier, and rivulets of settlers, which later grew into floods, poured through them to the West. By the end of the eighteenth century four routes had emerged as the main highways to the West.

The northernmost was called the Genesee Road. It ran west through the Mohawk Valley from Albany to Buffalo, then by trek along the shores of Lake Erie to the Western Reserve. This was the favored way of the Connecticut settlers of the Reserve, as well as other New Englanders who had already taken a first migratory hop that had landed them in upstate New York. Later the Erie Canal, which linked Albany to Buffalo on Lake Erie and thence to the booming port city of Cleveland, made the route popular with foreign immigrants who landed in New York and went up the Hudson River to Albany.

The second route was known as the Forbes Road or Pennsylvania State Road. This led the traveler west from Philadelphia through Lancaster, Carlisle, and Bedford to the confluence of the Monongahela and Allegheny rivers at Pittsburgh. The Forbes Road had been opened in 1758 by Colonel Henry Bouquet and George Washington. It was by this route that William Henry Harrison came west with eighty men, and so did the ill-fated John Cleves Symmes, bringing sixty colonists to settle his newly purchased land. The route was well traveled by settlers from New York, New Jersey, and eastern Pennsylvania, as well as by foreign immmigrants off the ships docking at Philadelphia.

George Rapp's German Harmonists came this way, as did, much later, Robert Owen's people on their way to occupy the Rappites town which Owen had purchased. Upon arrival at Pittsburgh, the emigrant often sold his horse, if he had one, to a traveler going in the opposite direction and bought passage on a boat going down the Ohio or had one built. Pittsburgh, Redstone on the Monongahela, and Kittanning on the Allegheny were the great jumping-off places. These towns had carpenters, axmen, and boat builders who could build all manner of river craft from a skiff up to a seventy-foot barge with sails and poling platforms. Those who had boats built often dismantled them upon arrival and used the wood to make temporary shelters. The boat traffic on the Ohio included a variety of craft—pirogues, bateaux, schooners, keelboats, flatboats, broadhorns—ranging from large canoes and dugouts to barge-type vessels (flatboats which were typically forty feet long and fifteen feet wide). Some travelers hired crews, and pilots were needed to negotiate the falls of the Ohio. The journey from Pittsburgh to the falls took ten days or more.

A third route was the Cumberland Road (sometimes called Braddock's Road). The settler jumped off at Baltimore, proceeded to Cumberland on the Potomac, thence due west for one hundred and fifty miles to the head of the Potomac and then across the Allegheny Mountains to Redstone, where he either forked north to Pittsburgh or headed west to Wheeling and Ohio. On this route the mountains took a fearsome toll, and the trail was littered with so many abandoned wagons that it looked as if a retreating army had passed over it. Most hazardous was descending the mountains; the best method was to drag a good-sized tree behind the wagon as a brake.

The last route was the Wilderness Road, which the explorer-trapper Daniel Boone had opened up. It ran through the Cumberland Gap, across the Clinch River, over Clinch Mountain, past Shelby's Fort, over Moccasin Gap and across the Powell River, past Martin's Station and up a steep pass to Louisville on the falls of the Ohio. There the migrant could cross the river and follow the Vincennes Trace through southern Indiana and Illinois. This was the most rugged, demanding route and the one most often taken by southerners by way of the Shenandoah Valley. It was also the first route to be abandoned.

These were the ways west, conduits that dropped the emigrant off at the edge of the wilderness, leaving him to make the rest of his way by water, Indian trail, or later by rugged local roads. The first of these roads was laid out by Ebenezer Zane and was completed in 1798. Called Zane's Trace, it proceeded from Wheeling, West Virginia, through Ohio and terminated at Limestone (now Maysville), Kentucky. This road was little more than an improved path, hemmed in by forest and bristling with stumps and roots, yet along it developed the Ohio towns of Zanesville, Lancaster, and Chillicothe.

Zane's Trace was inevitably followed by a more ambitious thoroughfare—the National Road. The idea of a federally built road reaching from the Atlantic seaboard to the Mississippi River was first raised in Congress in 1806; after delays, sectional squabbles, and legal problems that reached the Supreme Court, construction was begun in 1811. The National Road followed the old Cumberland Road across Pennsylvania to the Monongahela and then continued to the towns of Washington and Alexandria, Pennsylvania, and Wheeling, West Virginia. By 1818, mail coaches were in regular service between Washington and Wheeling. More legal tangles followed. President Madison vetoed a bill for improving the already deteriorating completed sections of the road and surveying the rest of it. But under growing pressure from the Middle Atlantic states, who saw the road as their trade link with the West in competition with New York's Erie Canal, which had been completed in 1825, Congress allocated more money and approved a route through the capitals of Ohio, Indiana, and Illinois (Columbus, Indianapolis, and Vandalia, respectively) to St. Louis. For the next twenty-five years the road inched westward. It reached Cambridge, Ohio, by 1825; Zanesville by 1830; Springfield by 1838; Indiana by 1840; and Vandalia by 1850.

In its eastern segments, at least, the National Road was a marvel of engineering. Eighty feet wide, it had a thirty-foot macadam center and stone culverts and bridges. Its greatest importance was for Pennsylvania and Ohio; by the time it reached farther west, the canals and railroads were furnishing competition. Only the Ohio Canal, built between 1825 and 1833 and connecting the Ohio River with Lake Erie at Cleveland, did as much for the economy of the region. The canal's role, of course, was primarily as a conduit of trade, rather than immigrants.

New York's Erie Canal did play an important role in immigration. The project was a farsighted effort by the state, under the leadership of Governor De Witt Clinton, to link the interior with New York City. After the federal government refused aid, the state carried out the venture on its own, at an ultimate cost of $13 million. The canal was a tremendous feat for the day, and it also had far-reaching, if short-lived, effects. Once New York proved it could be done, canal-building fever began in earnest in the West. And other eastern states, fearing New York's monopoly of the trade with the interior, were prodded into building their own routes west. The urgency felt in Pennsylvania was translated into an ingenious canal system which was in operation between Harrisburg and Pittsburgh by 1834. It employed a horse-car railroad with stationary steam engines to pull the cars over the western mountains by cable. There were 172 miles of canal and the passenger also traveled one leg of the journey by stagecoach. Later canal boats were built in sections so that they could be hoisted onto rail cars and transported over land. The entire journey took four days, compared with eight days by fast horse, ten days by stage, and sixteen to twenty days by Conestoga wagon.

Other improvements for the traveler followed in the 1820s and 30s—mostly local roads built by the army and the states, with the aid of federal land grants, and by private turnpike companies. Ohio's system of roads was good for its day, but farther west, the roads were poor. In Indiana, for example, even the National Road was permitted by law to contain stumps nine to fifteen inches high, "rounded and trimmed" so as to present "no serious obstacles to carriages."[43] There was no stone or gravel for surfacing, and roads twisted around hills or through the tall timber. Such were the most advanced improvements the immigrants could expect until railroad links were completed between Chicago and the East in the 1850s.

Over these routes flowed a tide of immigrants, ebbing and rising in bad times and good, yet never stopping. The Treaty of Greenville opened the flood gates of immigration; within a year over one thousand boats filled with settlers passed Fort Harmar on the Ohio and a contemporary observer wrote:

> Never since the golden age of the poets did "the syren song of peace and of farming" reach so many ears, and gladden so many hearts, as after Wayne's treaty at Greenville in 1795. "The Ohio," as it was called, seemed to be, literally, a land flowing with milk and honey. The farmer wrote home of a soil "richer to appearance than can possibly be made by art"; of "plains and meadows without the labor of hands, sufficient to support millions of cattle summer and winter"; of wheat lands that would vie with the island of Sicily; and of bogs from which might be gathered cranberries enough to make tarts for all of New England; while the lawyer said that as he rode the circuit, his horse's legs were dyed to the knee with the juice of the wild strawberry.[44]

Reports in this tenor continued to emanate from the West in the coming decades. Some of them were sheer puffery—advertisements of the land-jobbers—but a primary source was the letters the settlers themselves wrote to friends, relatives, and fellow townsmen back east. Whole new settlements might be populated on the strength of one or two letters. Another source was the young newspapers of the West, which advertised land sales and new towns, accompanied by boomish editorial fanfare touting the paper's particular area. Since much of the Western papers' income was derived from land-sale advertisements, they were hardly disinterested parties; more settlers meant economic growth in their towns and even more advertisers of a different kind.

Another source of information on the West were the immigrant's guides and gazeteers, which purported to advise the newcomer on what to expect when he arrived, but which considerably colored their "factual" editorial matter—especially the guides subsidized by land speculators. *The Western Gazeteer and Emigrant's Guide,* for example, talked glowingly of corn fourteen feet high, of soil like black gunpowder, of land as level as a barn floor, of seven-acre farms producing seven hundred bushels of corn, of hogs growing fat on the rich mast in the woods without the farmer lifting a finger, of potatoes as large as Connecticut pumpkins. Books written by travelers provided a more realistic picture but were also positive in tone; between 1815 and 1825 more than a dozen of them on "the Ohio" alone were published. Even if the hardships had been highlighted, it is doubtful that potential emigrants would have paid them much heed anyway; those who worried about such things did not emigrate in the first place. The West, after all, represented a longshot bet on a golden future; and there were plenty whose present lives were so bitterly straitened that they were more than eager to stake them on that bet paying off.

"Old America seems to be breaking up and moving westward,"[45] wrote Morris Birbeck, the Englishman who had come to America in 1817 to plant a colony of his countrymen in the Illinois Territory. An observer in Philadelphia predicted that same year in the pages of *The Philanthropist* that within twenty years the majority of Americans would live west of the Alleghenies (it actually took forty years). Birbeck, who had been astonished by the number of people he met traveling across Pennsylvania in 1817, remarked, "We are very seldom out of sight, as we travel on this grand track towards the Ohio, of family groups behind and before us. . . . Add to these the numerous stages loaded to the utmost, and the innumerable travelers on horseback, on foot, and in light wagons, and you have before you a scene of bustle and business, extending over three hundred miles, which is truly wonderful."[46]

A Danville, Kentucky, newspaper reporter watched the stream along the backbreaking Wilderness Road: "Emigrants—the number of movers passing daily through the place westward is astonishing. They are generally poor, having their plunder packed on horses, or in carts drawn by calves, cows, and horses, or in some instances by oxen and horses. Several days during the last week the road was literally filled with movers. Nine-tenths of the movers are from North Carolina, South Carolina, Virginia, and other southern and eastern slaveholding states; the remainder are all our citizens, all pressing to the free states on our western frontier."[47]

And farther north, a correspondent writing in the *Genesee Farmer* in 1832, a year of another great wave of migration: "Several steamboats and vessels daily depart for the far west, literally crammed with masses of living beings. . . . Some days, near a thousand of them depart. Hundreds and hundreds of horse wagons arrive every spring and fall with emigrants from our own state; and when at Buffalo, the whole caravan, consisting of family, horses, dog, wagon and furniture, are put on board the steamboats and landed either in Ohio and Michigan. Some even go round through the upper lakes and land in Chicago, and pursue their course to Indiana, Illinois or Missouri."[48]

They came in a variety of conveyances from stagecoaches, carrying as many as twelve persons (of which the traveler B. F. Fearon said, "the pain of riding exceeded the fatigue of walking";[49] the coaches employed leather belts in lieu of springs), to light wagons or traps that a man could lift. And some came on foot, carrying their worldly goods on their backs or in pushcarts. The most popular vehicle for large groups was the Conestoga wagon; Birbeck saw one with twenty passengers. The trip evidently cost little, with a coach ticket of 140 miles, say, costing fourteen dollars. The cost of outfitting a large wagon ranged from fourteen dollars on up to as high as seventy to ninety dollars, depending upon the degree of comfort desired. One historian has estimated that a Maryland family of ten with five slaves would pay seventy-five dollars for the 300-mile journey from Baltimore to Wheeling. Whatever the precise figures, it is clear that migration west could be done cheaply.

The people came singly, in husband-wife pairs, and in large families. Birbeck was struck by the number of large families he saw. "The wagons swarm with children. I heard today of three together, which contain forty-two of these young citizens."[50] Other travelers also described Conestogas with father, mother, and six to twelve children either riding inside or walking behind. Piled in the wagons were the worn belongings they were taking to start a new life—beds, chests, washstands, churns and crocks, dishes, gridirons, quilts, feather mattresses, and old clothes. There were a few books, too, for long, cold winter nights before the fireplace. The most popular titles were the Bible, Watts's *Psalms and Hymns*, a Webster's speller, and Foxe's *Book of Martyrs.*

There were eccentricities among the migrants that were sometimes reflective of national character. Germans, for example, typically brought heavy, carved furniture—as though they could not set up a home in the West without it. An observer on a Great Lakes steamboat noted that Yankees traveled light—a Dearborn wagon, a feather bed, some harness, and a few gadgets—while Englishmen seemed to be attempting to bring "even the fast-anchored isle itself."[51] The Swiss and Germans aboard brought their heavy museum pieces, costing in fare four or five times what they were worth. He noted a general tendency for families to bring their entire possessions. "What an indignity it is to overwhelm the triumphal chariot with the beds and ploughs, shovels, saddles and sideboards, chairs, clocks, and carpets that fill its interior, and to hang those rusty pots and kettles, bakepans, frying pans, and saucepans, iron candlesticks, old horseshoes and broken tobacco pipes, like trophies of conquest over Time, along its racked and wheezing sides."[52] Most people, if they had the means, attempted to transplant every familiar comfort from their old life to the new. Of course, from what we know of the living arrangements of many pioneer families, there were those who brought little or nothing and made do with furnishings contrived in the wilderness. But we also know from early pioneer wills that many had a surprising number of possessions, implying that the romantic ideal of the pioneer hewing a new life in the wilderness with his bare hands was partly fictional.

The high-tide years of migration were 1816–18, 1830–37, and the early 1850s. During financial panics immigration fell, only to rise again with inflation and easy money. Flush times released speculative energies, reflected in land sales, but also loosed countervailing depressive forces that affected not only the West but the entire nation. Between 1810 and 1820 the population of Ohio increased 152 percent, that of Indiana 500 percent, and that of Illinois 350 percent. In 1800 Ohio's population had been 45,365, Indiana's 5,461, and Illinois's negligible. Between 1815 and 1818 the population of Illinois increased from 15,000 to 40,000, while 42,000 immigrants entered Indiana in 1816 alone. By 1830 Ohio's population was nearly a million, and it had become a major state in the Union. By 1860 the median population line of the nation had moved from West Virginia to a point near Columbus. Meanwhile the population of Illinois was tripling in each decade between 1820 and 1840. From 1825 onward, the northern states of Michigan and Wisconsin filled up at a similar rate, mostly with New Englanders—the population of these two states grew from 30,000 to 300,000 between 1840 and 1850. By 1900 the Middle West had 26 million people, against 21 million in New England and the Middle Atlantic states combined, and the region had provided six of the seven presidents elected in their own right since 1860.

The waves of humanity beat against the Alleghenies, spilled through the passes, and flowed down the river courses through the valleys, along Indian trails in silent forests which blocked out the sky. At the end of this mass hegira was the stuff of these migrants' dreams—land! The great natural resource that "'constituted the richest free gift that was ever spread out before civilized man,"[53] in Turner's words. The availability of land had become a cardinal article of American faith in the first half of the nineteenth century. As Harriet Martineau wrote in 1837, "Land was spoken of as the great unfailing resource against over manufacture, the great wealth of the nation; the grand security of every man in it."[54] Land—the symbol of a better life—a home, a farm with ploughed black fields, serried by green ranks of corn or wheat reaching to the farthest horizon. Land that would bear fruit and perpetually rise in value. And land as an abstract commodity, a deed of title, a town plat, a piece of paper to be held and sold and resold by speculators, town jobbers, those gamblers in the evanescent future to whom the West was a great Monopoly board. Land was the stuff of the American dream, and this dream had set a whole people in motion.

Yet, Turner to the contrary, this land was not a "free gift" to the people who settled on it. It was government land, purchased, or wrested, from the Indians and theoretically belonging to "we the people." But the people who actually settled it had to buy it from their government. When Congress first began wrestling with the problem of disposing of the vast holdings ceded to the United States by the British at the end of the Revolutionary War, it was moved by a congeries of policy considerations, some of them contradictory. The most immediately pressing problem was the large debt the young country had incurred fighting the war, but there was also the grander question of what kind of country the United States was to become. In the Jeffersonian, populist vision it would be a nation of yeomen, in which small, independent farmers would be encouraged to the maximum extent. Then there was the Hamiltonian view, which saw stability in a centralized fiscal aristocracy and the development of industry and cities. Finally, there was the clash of sectional and nascent economic interests, as well as the claims of the poor.

As these pressures evolved and shifted through time, the foundations of United States land policy also altered. Originally, Congress regarded the sale of the vast public domains as a revenue-raising measure. Accordingly—and with considerable enlightenment—the land was surveyed before settlement was permitted. Surveyors set forth into the wilderness with their chains and poles, beginning at the Ohio-Pennsylvania border, and slowly worked their way West, dividing the land up into townships six miles square—the size of the New England township. A north-south line of townships was called a range, and each township was subdivided into sections of 640 square acres, which were further subdivided into quarter and half sections, with the quarter section (160 acres) becoming the basic unit purchased by the average settler. Thus each buyer's plot was registered by descriptive notations referring to range, township, and section number. The land was thus divided up into a grid of salable parcels (though the accuracy of their boundaries was considerably less precise in practice than in theory). Further, the adoption of the township system by Congress reflected a policy judgment, a leaning toward the New England system, which promoted settlement by communities. This was a more orderly mode of settlement than the southern method of indiscriminate settlement, followed by surveys.

For its first land sales, the Congress dealt with large purchasers—among them the Ohio Company, the Scioto Company, and the Symmes Company already described. The reason was the need to raise large amounts of revenue relatively quickly through large downpayments; also such sales permitted the delegating to these land companies of all the paperwork involved in smaller land sales to individuals. The land companies, on their part, hoped to take in sufficient money from their sales to pay off the remainder of the installments due, though in fact they never did.

To complicate matters, not all of Ohio was federal land. Substantial parts of the territory had been granted to Virginia and Connecticut, the states that had original title to them under royal charters which proclaimed them sovereign over all lands to the western sea. To settle these claims, the government reserved certain tracts for the two states in exchange for their relinquishment of their overall claims. Virginia's tracts was set aside for her revolutionary veterans who had been given military land warrants as a bonus for their services. This section was known as the Virginia Military District. Connecticut kept what came to be known as the Western Reserve in northern Ohio. The state sold this land to the Connecticut Land Company, with the eventual proceeds to be applied to public education in the state. (These proceeds were finally collected, but only after the incredibly complicated titles were disentangled, a process taking decades.) Connecticut was also ceded a section adjoining the Reserve, which was known as the Fire Lands because it was to be parceled out among Connecticut citizens whose towns and homes had been burned by the British during the Revolution. The rest of Ohio—still a considerable tract—and on west into the area separated off in 1800 and known as Indiana Territory was public domain land.

After its unsatisfactory dealings with the large land companies, Congress took a new tack and sought to reach a larger number of buyers. Federal land offices were set up and public domain land was offered in 640-acre sections at a minimum price of $2 per acre. Terms were stiff: The buyer had to come up with half the $1,280 within thirty days and pay off the remainder within a year. Obviously only the wealthy could afford these terms, and as a result, most of the sales were made to speculators. For the common man, the only option was to squat—and an increasing number of people did just that despite desultory government efforts to expel the squatters. ("They will settle the land in spite of everybody," Jefferson had written long before.[55]) Actually the squatters were forging their own land policy, and they had excellent precedent for it under English common law, as expressed in the familiar adage "Possession is nine tenths of the law." English law held that the possessor held title, unless there was a superior claim. Why was the claim of a speculator who happened to buy the same land later at a public auction superior to that of the man improving the land? Congress waffled on this question, but half a century later came around to de facto recognition of the squatters' rights.

The next step was the Land Act of 1800, passed under the leadership of William Henry Harrison, the territorial delegate to Congress from the Northwest. This legislation provided for the sale of half sections of 320 acres. The price was still two dollars an acre, but it could be paid in installments over four years. The act was further amended to allow the sale of quarter sections, also at $2 an acre. The settler who wanted to buy a quarter section paid "entry money" of eighty dollars and then paid off the rest in annual installments of eighty dollars over the next three years. Now the common man could afford his farm in the West, and instead of having to buy it from speculators at inflated prices, he could buy land at the government land offices in Pittsburgh, Marietta, Chillicothe, and Cincinnati. The effect of the law on land sales was striking. Under the old law, fewer than fifty thousand acres had been purchased; during the first eighteen months the Harrison Land Act was in force four hundred thousand acres were sold, and sales reached three quarters of a million acres by 1802.

Land sales continued apace as the waves of immigrants flowed into the Northwest, but at the same time the region's burden of debt also grew. The settler-farmers were handicapped by a chronic shortage of money, low prices for farm produce, and a lack of markets because of poor transportation and the high cost of shipping. Lacking money, a farmer couldn't settle his debts; the prices he got for what he raised precluded a profit, and the cost of shipping his produce to market was so high that the price he received there would not cover it. The Northwest became a debtor nation within a nation, and a major creditor was the federal government. In addition there were a large number of state-chartered banks that pursued inflationary fiscal policies.

All this came to a boil in the panic of 1819, which was caused at least in part by the West's fiscal irresponsibility. At any rate, in that year the total land debt was $22 million, which was more than three times the total amount of money in circulation in the Northwest, Jacob Burnet wrote; one half the men in the Northwest were in debt, and nine tenths of the debtors would have to forfeit. Western legislatures began to feel the pressures from their constituents and passed "stay laws" and "relief acts" which in effect required creditors to accept devalued bank notes or extend even more credit—actions that, because they abrogated contracts, were in violation of the Constitution as interpreted by Chief Justice Marshall in the *Dartmouth College* case of 1819. There was even talk of secession. In the *Kentucky Reporter*, a writer warned darkly that a government owed money by a large segment of its people could not be assured of their loyalty. The people would become disaffected and the end result would be secession.

The western legislatures might abet the debtors in evading individual creditors, but the federal government could not be denied. As men in the Northwest worried about losing their land, Congress became concerned about the loss of revenues. It was obvious that some easement plan was needed, and leading citizens of the Northwest began petitioning Congress for relief. Jacob Burnet drew up a petition calling upon Congress to allow landholders to forfeit the portion of their land that they hadn't paid for while retaining the part upon which they had made improvements. This petition was widely circulated throughout the territory and presented to Congress with thousands of signatures. Proposals were also made to end the credit system of buying land entirely and replace it with cash-only terms. The land-policy issue split the Northwest's representatives in Congress, with some feeling that stopping credit would discourage immigration. Despite their objections, Congress overwhelmingly passed the land law of 1820, which abolished the credit system, reduced the price of land to $1.25 an acre, and allowed minimal purchases of eighty acres. Land would still be sold by auction at the land offices—thus wealthy speculators could still jack up the prices at which settlers bought it—but the measure opened the door still wider to the independent smallholder. Any man with $100 in his pocket could theoretically buy land. Not the best land perhaps—that still went to speculators and wealthier immigrants—but land nonetheless and there was plenty of land for everybody.

The Relief Law passed in 1821 was intended to assuage the pains of debtors already on the land. It offered a choice of three modes of relief: (1) the Burnet plan; (2) payment of the total purchase price discounted by 37.5 percent (to reflect the new lower price per acre) for those who completed payments on their land by September 30, 1821; or (3) further extension of credit for periods in indirect proportion to the amount of the downpayment (that is, the higher the downpayment the shorter the term of credit). Within seven months the unpaid balance on all lands was reduced by half. Further refinements were added, always tilted slightly in favor of the debtor, with the result that forfeitures fell off markedly. A large measure of relief had at last been granted to the people of the West—all predicated on an implicit faith in the region's ultimate prosperity. The talk of secession, such as it was, died out.

Further legislation aided squatters, who had become an increasingly vocal interest group and had found a champion in Senator Thomas Hart Benton of Missouri. Most of the "little people" on the frontier were, after all, squatters—that is, people who had made a claim and intended to pay for it at land-office prices, rather than letting it go to speculators or paying them for it. Thus a series of preemption acts ensued. The Pre-emption Act of 1830 guaranteed that people who had settled on land prior to its sale at auction had the right to purchase up to 160 acres at $1.25 an acre; the Pre-emption Act of 1841 accorded full legal rights to squatters. The overall tendency of the land laws was thus in a Jeffersonian, populist direction; the ultimate step would be free land, but that did not come until the Homestead Act of 1862. In the meantime, Congress was reluctant to give up entirely its revenue from the public domain; instead it moved toward increasingly cheaper land at terms the poor man could afford. (Some unsold land was later marked down to a rock-bottom $0.125 an acre.)

But throughout its history federal land policy had given encouragement to the speculator by the auction system of land sale and by placing no limits on the amount of land a purchaser could buy. This is why individual speculators, banks, and land companies were able to buy up large tracts, which they either held idle waiting for the price to go up or resold to settlers at a price higher than the government price. What was more, nearly every man who went west had a bit of speculator in him; many an ordinary settler bought up all the land he could on credit, taking advantage of cheap money. He now had more land than he could farm and on a set day was required to come up with the purchase money, if he was exercising preemption rights. Short of cash and with little hope of arranging any sensible kind of mortgage financing, the squatter was confronted with the choice between relinquishing his dream or borrowing from the bank or the ubiquitous frontier loan sharks at usurious rates. Assuming he chose to borrow, he had to find out the date on which his parcel of land was being auctioned off and then, assuming he did not miss the notice in the local paper, travel what might be a considerable distance to the government land office. If he succeeded in buying his land, the farmer was now even deeper in debt. The upshot was that many settlers who could not meet their payments abandoned their farms and headed farther west. Others became tenants—more than a third of all farmers in some areas.

The squatter—the word is a bit too pejorative; he should be called merely a settler—was also in competition with the speculators who haunted every land office, seeking to buy up the best land. As a result, many settlers organized themselves into land-claims associations and pressured sympathetic local officials and juries to side with their claims. They also took to arriving on auction day armed with sticks and guns; they drove away any speculators present, leaving the field to themselves. In some cases the pioneer did not even need to display his hardware; his mere presence with his fellows could imply the force he had in reserve, should it be necessary. Such was obviously the case in an auction at the Crawfordsville, Indiana, land office in 1824, which was described by an eyewitness:

> The land sales commenced here today, and the town is full of strangers. . . . There is but little bidding against each other. The settlers, or "squatters" as they are called by speculators, have arranged matters among themselves to their general satisfaction. If, upon comparing numbers, it appears that they are after the same tract of land, one asks the other what he will take not to bid against him. If neither will consent to be bought off, they then retire and cast lots, and the lucky one enters the tract at Congress price, $1.25 per acre, and the other enters the second choice on his list. If a speculator makes a bid, or shows a disposition to take a settler's claim from him, he soon sees the whites of a score of eyes snapping at him, and at the first opportunity he crawfishes out of the crowd. The settlers tell foreign capitalists to hold off till they enter the

tracts of land they have settled on, and that they may then pitch in—and there will be land enough, more than enough, for them all.[56]

The presence of speculators, loan sharks, and land agents upset the system. The loan sharks were often acting as agents for big eastern banks, which were also among the largest landholders, buying up property both at auctions and foreclosures. These and other absentee investors often worked through land agents, who scouted out, bought, and entered land for them in exchange for a 5 percent commission. Along with the registrars and receivers at the land offices, these agents became powerful figures in local communities, doing everything from note shaving to managing the property of absentee investors. Cases of land agents cheating their eastern clients, who could not come out personally to oversee their activities, were legion. In extreme cases investors lost all, while the land agent, wheeling and dealing on the spot, parlayed his holdings into wealth. Many a pillar family of many a community made its first-generation fortune from shrewd dealings in land by a land-agent ancestor.

Land speculation in the Northwest reached its zenith in the 1830s. The peristaltic waves of immigration which had slowed in the late 1820s began to throb faster as good times returned. As more people came west, investors foresaw rising land values, so their money came too—big eastern money, as well as the smallholder's money. Once more the West was in the throes of a land rush. Land became a commodity to be traded like wheat or pork bellies, rather than a resource to be husbanded. Men dealt in futures, not permanencies. And Everyman could play. D. W. Mitchell, an Englishman who traveled through the West, later wrote: "Speculation in real estate . . . has been the ruling idea and occupation of the Western mind. Clerks, labourers, farmers, storekeepers, merely followed their callings for a living, while they were speculating for their fortunes. . . . The people of the West became dealers in land, rather than its cultivators."[57] Why improve one's land, the thinking of many farmers ran, when in a year or so one could sell it at a profit greater than the amount one would have made farming it. Besides, the process of clearing the land was a laborious one, taking years.

Loose credit policies by local banks aggravated the speculative fever. President Jackson's veto of the renewal of the charter of the Second Bank of the United States loosed all constraints on the state banks and set off an inflationary spree, fueled by sheaves of notes run off by undercapitalized local banks. As a result of easy credit policies, purchasers overextended themselves. It was the familiar story; instead of buying an eighty-acre plot with his cash on hand, the speculative-minded settler would plunge into debt in order to buy a half or whole section. The United States government's credit sales were replaced by private credit of a more pernicious sort with a killing interest load.

By this time, Ohio was no longer the frontier; people were pushing on to Indiana, Illinois, Michigan, and Wisconsin—and points west. Illinois, and Michigan to a lesser extent, were the battlefronts of the frenetic speculation of the thirties, with Chicago the financial command post. Indeed, this young city's first export to the East, it was said, was land titles. In a letter to the New York *Commercial Advertiser*, a Chicagoan wrote, "Speculators are arriving in regiments, and a heavier business is doing in lands than in any other town in the Union."[58] A rude town of a thousand inhabitants had sprung up by 1833, just two years after it was first settled—a chaos of muddy streets strewn with garbage, raw frame buildings, and people living in covered wagons because there was no permanent shelter for them. Miasmic sinkholes and frog ponds were within the town limits. (The town's name came from the Algonquian *Chicagou*, meaning "place of onions"—a reference to the plethora of wild onions growing in the area, which gave a pungent smell to the locale.) By 1835, the population was 3,300, and brick buildings were rising. Some streets were being macadamized, while others were still only dirt tracks demarcated by stakes in the ground; the Chicago Hydraulic Water Company had already been incorporated by the state legislature.

Maps were the land speculators' stock ticker; they crowded around them while a smooth-talking salesman expatiated on the glories of the particular section of country depicted, his incantatory words transforming a muddy creek into a wide river, a few cabins into a prospering town. Only Miami in the days of the Florida land boom of the 1920s equaled the Chicago of those heady days. The rutted streets were turbulent with the milling knots of buyers, surrounding one seller then surging on to the next, like carp at feeding time. Harriet Martineau described one such scene: "A negro, dressed up in scarlet, bearing a scarlet flag, and riding a white horse with housings of scarlet, announced the times of sale. At every street corner where he stopped, the crowd flocked round him; and it seemed as if some prevalent mania infected the whole people. . . . As the gentlemen of our party walked the streets, storekeepers hailed them from their doors, with offers of farms and all manner of land lots, advising them to speculate before the price of land rose higher. A young lawyer . . . had realized five hundred dollars per day the five preceding days, by merely making out titles to land."[59]

Town jobbing became so frenetic that some opined that the entire state would soon be papered over with town plats, leaving no land for farming. Land along projected internal improvements such as canals drew the highest prices, but the rich prairie land—which earlier settlers tended to avoid because they erroneously believed that it was infertile and because it lacked timber for houses and fences—also opened up. The 1837 edition of Mason Peck's gazeteer for immigrants—considered the most reliable of such publications—extolled the rich Illinois soil: "In no part of the United States can uncultivated land be made into farms with less labor than in Illinois."[60] The guide told how the average rise in property values during the last ten years had been 25 to 30 percent—and some town lots had risen 1,000 percent within a three-year span. Peck forecast a continuing rise and advised "the advantageous application of manual labor"[61] toward improving one's land. If Peck's guide was conservatively euphoric, other guides such as Samuel Augustus Mitchell's *Illinois in 1837* (parts of which were lifted from Peck's 1834 gazeteer) and Henry W. Ellsworth's *Valley of the Upper Wabash* were downright puffery subsidized by speculators seeking to lure land buyers into an area. Abner Dumnon Jones, a New Englander who wrote a reliable travel book about the West, castigated Mitchell's guide as "full of exaggerated statements, and high-wrought and false-colored descriptions."[62]

But such propaganda helped spread the galloping speculative fever, which grew more and more florid until it burned itself out in the crash of 1837. In 1831, total sales at the national land offices were about two million acres; in 1836, the peak year, twenty million acres were sold. All told, thirty-eight million acres were sold; of these an estimated twenty-nine million, or $36-million worth, went to speculators, with an inestimable but probably roughly equivalent amount paid out for town lots, also by speculators. As most serious observers had predicted, the bubble burst in 1837. The instrumentality was that old populist Andrew Jackson, who in July 1836 issued the Specie Circular, a direct assault on land speculators, moneylenders, and absentee proprietors. Jackson's remedy was simple—a requirement that only gold or silver be accepted from land purchasers at the government land offices. Squatters were excepted from this requirement and could continue to use bank notes for the remainder of the year. Jackson's motives were ostensibly, as he said in his message to Congress of December 1836, to "save the new states from a nonresident proprietorship, one of the greatest obstacles to the advancement of a new country and the prosperity of an old one."[63] The effect of his action would tend "to keep open the public lands for entry by emigrants at government prices instead of their being compelled to purchase of speculators at double or treble prices."[64] In other words, Jackson, like Jefferson before him, sought to return to a truly democratic land policy, one that favored the small freeholder. But another purpose of Jackson's action was to drive paper currency and bank notes out of existence and replace them with specie. Old Hickory was not, as many thought, an easy-money man; he just despised bank notes. Another blow at the state banks was the Distribution Act, which withdrew federal funds deposited in state banks for distribution directly to the states for internal improvements. As a result, many of the underfunded banks failed. Speculators who had been using "land office money"—bank notes backed by insufficient assets exchanged for land—were also wiped out.

Jackson's action throttled land sales—they fell to five million acres in 1837. Again the West was faced with a currency shortage, and debtors were thrown on the untender mercies of banks and moneylenders. Only the eastern banks had specie in any quantities, and they lent it out for a price—30 percent annual interest. The result was more people in debt, more foreclosures, more people abandoning land or sinking into tenancy. The land speculators and town jobbers watched their land shrink in value, while their taxes rose. Unable to liquidate their investments, they let their mortgages go into foreclosure. The way of the speculator was not always the royal road to riches—indeed more of them probably lost money in the West than made it. Corrupt land agents fleeced them; squatters moved onto their land; and the locals, who resented the absentees' low tax assessments (property taxes were mainly assessed on improvements—buildings, fences, stock, and the like, which the absentees did not have), stole timber and fences or used the land for pasturage. Taxes went unpaid on the idle land, increasing the burden on local farmers and hurting the straitened county and town governments.

The economy began recovering in the 1840s, and by the 1850s there was another even more virulent outbreak of speculation, resulting in the sale of sixty-five million acres of public-domain land farther west between 1854 and 1858. But that was to be the last of the great public-domain land sales. The Homestead Act would end them, and the western railroads, beneficiaries of huge government land subsidies after the Civil War, would take over some of the speculators' role.

Speculation was an intrinsic part of the settlement of the near West. Everybody had a little speculator in him, and it was this hope of increased wealth that inspired the migrating armies, that gave urgency to their quest, that impelled them across the mountain barriers and into the wilderness. Undoubtedly it also unleashed energies that were dissipated in airy hopes of future profits rather than serious farming or town building. Yet all the puffery and propaganda perhaps did serve to bestir men to come west and in that sense quickened the pace of settlement. And eventually the land got cleared and the crops planted; and the towns grew up, if they did not always thrive. For every Gallipolis there were many Mariettas. If speculation was a periodic fever, the West threw it off, recovered its fundamental health, and became healthily prosperous almost despite itself because of its real wealth—the rich land itself—and the hard work of the small farmers.

The brunt of the detrimental effects was borne by this same small farmer, however; undercapitalized, he often slipped into debt and tenancy, his dreams of self-sufficiency scattered to the winds. The land policy's encouragement of large holdings by absentee speculators lowered the effective tax base in many areas and retarded the growth of governmental services, as well as shifting most of the burden to the local farmers. This added tax burden raised the farmers' costs, forcing them into wasteful farming practices that depleted the soil.

Some of the absentee speculators perhaps performed a perverse service of promoting internal improvements in the West, in hopes of raising the value of their land, although the conflicts of interest these depended upon had unhealthy effects on government. Even Senator Daniel Webster of Massachusetts, the rock of the Union, was a big Illinois landowner and an ardent supporter of land-grant measures to subsidize the railroads. The town jobbers were active in pushing through county or municipal subsidies to railroads so that they would route their tracks through specific towns. They also lobbied and bribed in the state legislatures for various perquisites for their towns, ranging from state-capital designation down through county seathood, land offices, state universities, agricultural colleges, penitentiaries, and institutions for the insane and the like. Speculators entered politics directly and pushed for land grants to the railroads and easier credit terms, while opposing free land and any other progressive legislation against the interests of the banks, large property owners, railroads, and rising industrialists. A landed-money class came into being, which, if it was enterprising and kept up with the times, reformulated itself into a wealthy financial and business-owning class, with ties to the eastern financial establishment. It was against this class that the agrarian populist movements of the 1880s and 90s rose up.

Was there a better way to do it? One can see glimmers of a farsighted land policy in the early legislation. The visionary initial survey, for example, that divided up millions of acres into a great invisible grid had a kind of grand eighteenth-century lucidity and orderliness about it, however ineptly the actual squares were laid out. This grid provided a clear basis for selling off the land to the small farmers—Jefferson's yeoman, Jackson's common man. If Congress had not been so hard-pressed for money after the Revolution, such small parcels might have been sold off—or even given free to whoever would improve the land, a principle the Homestead Act later recognized. The large speculators would be barred or at least curbed more than they were.

There was also in Congress's initial vision a harking back to the New England ideal of communal settlement. Thus, the survey divided up the land into townships. If settlers had been encouraged to come in affinity groups and plant their towns, distributing their land among themselves, with the surplus held for sale to subsequent immigrants, the development of the West would have been more orderly, and the speculator would have been kept out to a degree. The town jobbers, whose activities we shall see in more detail in the next chapter, would have been prevented from advertising their paper towns to gullible settlers, and the towns would have had a better chance to "take," given the initial mutual bonds among the settlers. There would have been a more or less guaranteed base of small farmers around the town, working the land and supporting the town merchants with their surplus.

But the communal system of settlement would have been slower, and it was so uniquely New England by nature that the pioneers from the South and the Middle Atlantic states might have found it uncongenial. In New England itself, the outliver urge had vitiated communal settlement, and even in the old covenanted towns, men worked to assemble individual farms, and the original proprietors and their descendants were able to amass large holdings. Cotton Mather had put his finger on the weakness of communal settlement back in 1690 when he wondered how "at once we may Advance our Husbandry, annd yet Forbear our Dispersion."[65]

A broader trend was at work: The American farmer came to prefer the system of owning and working his own parcel of land, individually—to live alone and separate from the town, and indeed (as we shall see) develop interests hostile to it. Such a system seemed strange to Europeans, who had the ancient tradition of the peasant village, where the farmers lived, and from which they went forth each day to work the fields. The American system created a new breed of independent-entrepreneur farmers, whose economic interests were different from the cities and the towns, and who clung to this very typically American belief in improving one's fortunes by individual effort in the teeth of economic depression and exploitation originating from the distant cities. This strain of individualism had disastrous effects in times of agricultural depressions, drought, tornadoes, and the like, most particularly on the Great Plains, as will be seen. Significantly, the most successful farmers in the Far West, given the poor land they had to start with, were the Mormons, whose New England–style towns and religious discipline encouraged them to work cooperatively in the great task of irrigating the desert. Equal success came to the independent entrepreneur farmers, but the price in failure, poverty, hunger, and instability was considerable.

But such was the profligate bounty of the West that, after the wealthy had skimmed off the cream, there was still much rich land left over for the ordinary man. Despite rising debt and tenancy, a class of independent farm owners did rise up. For all the deception and corruption and the human and environmental waste it engendered, the public-land policy did encourage the creation of 867,697 farms in the West by 1860 and 2,185,492 by 1880; more than three-quarters of these were operated by their owners. Perhaps, all things considered, that represents a sizable victory for the common man who loaded his family and his plunder into a wagon and came west, seeking a plot of his own.

To Alexis de Tocqueville, there was something mystical about the great migration that had populated the West: "This gradual and continuous progress of the European race toward the Rocky Mountains has the solemnity of a providential event. It is like a deluge of men rising unabatedly, and driven daily onward by the hand of God."[66] Morris Birbeck saw something in the American character that demanded the West: "The American has always something better in his eye, further west; he therefore lives and dies on hope, a mere gypsy in this particular."[67] The more analytical Tocqueville dissected the American's restless itch to pick up and go and attributed it to his materialism, the lack of laws or customs fixing him to a place, and his sense of freedom from artificial restraints, which allowed him to strive to become whatever he dreamed of becoming. The frontier idea, as Frederick Jackson Turner saw it, was a perpetually westering grail, igniting a fire in the belly that only the waters of the Pacific could quench.

The pioneers were mystics of materialism, caught up in a contagious mass movement, a *völkerwanderung* fueled by the romantic prose that gushed forth from the pens of the western propagandizers pandering to their yearning for riches and a life of ease, or at least for a better life, a second chance, a new start, a casting off of the integuments of life in some town back east, where the land was exhausted. At the heart of this dream was the American El Dorado, the inexhaustible, ever-renewing source of prosperity—land. Land was the promise of the West—rich, black, fertile land, hundreds of thousands of acres of it, unturned by the plough. But on that land, where some envisioned farms, others saw towns.

3

"Each Town Has Its Day . . ." Pioneer Towns, 1815-1840

Among the first settlers who infiltrated the Western Reserve, the wild, Indian-haunted tract of three million acres belonging to the Connecticut Land Company, was David Hudson. Hudson had bought a six-mile-square township and, with his family and others from his hometown in Connecticut, set out to plant a town. On his first exploratory journey to the Ohio Territory, he was accompanied by a small advance party. For six days they combed the silent forest for the survey line that led to his township. The plot found, Hudson lay beneath an oak tree that night, sheltered from the rain and savoring the "grateful pleasure at owning my own land."[1] Leaving the men behind to build a log house, clear some land, and plant wheat on it, Hudson returned for the rest of his party. By autumn they were ready, and the night before they embarked on the perilous voyage across Lake Erie, Hudson lay staring into the embers of the campfire, unable to sleep:

> While my dear wife and six children, with all my men, lay sleeping around me, I could not close my eyes, for the reflection that these men and women, with almost all that I held dear in life, were now to embark in an expedition in which so many chances appeared against me; and should we survive the dangers in crossing the boisterous lake, and the distressing sickness usually attendant on new settlements, it was highly probable that we must fall before the tomahawk and scalping knife. As I knew at that time no considerable settlement had been made but what

> was established in *blood,* and as I was about to place all those who lay around me on the extreme frontier, and as they would look to me for safety and protection, I almost sunk under the immense weight of responsibility resting on me. . . . But after presenting my case before Israel's God, and committing all to his care, I cheerfully launched out the next morning upon the great deep.[2]

The dream of founding a town—how to account for it? Perhaps it was bred into the New England man who plunged into the virgin territory of the Reserve. He had an innate suspicion of outlivers—those who lived outside the pale of church and society. With the southerner it was different; he was an outliver by nature and tradition. Yet both across the northern tier of the Northwest, where the New Englanders settled, and along the rivers and streams of the southern part, into which the men and women from the South flocked, the towns sprouted up like mushrooms after a soaking spring rain. A town meant trade, a seat of rudimentary government and law enforcement, a center of sociability, a hearth fire of civilization in the forest. Above all, to the speculator, the town promised a way to make money.

The birth of the first towns was often swathed in legend and romance. There was the story of the young lieutenant marching toward Lake Erie during the Indian wars who sighted a piece of land he liked and resolved to purchase it with his military land warrants. Driving a stake into the ground, he announced to his companions, "At this spot I shall build my future home, which shall be the nucleus of a thriving town."[3] Bold words (and if he did not actually speak so dramatically at the time, the thought was probably there). Eight years were to elapse before he could return to the spot, but his dream remained intact. After much searching he found his stake still in place; he bought off with a barrel of whiskey the squatters who had occupied the area in the interim and settled down. In time his location became a crossroads; a settlement grew up, and eventually a town—Clyde, Ohio—was platted there.

Then there was Massie's Station, founded in 1790 by Nathaniel Massie, a surveyor and land locator who knew the territory like the back of his hand. Massie's Station (present day Manchester, Ohio) was located on the north bar of the Ohio across from the Kentucky town of Limestone and was the fourth settlement in the Ohio Territory, the first in the Virginia Military District. In those early days, when the Indians were widely feared, settlers were more valuable than land, so Massie peopled his town by offering anyone who came one hundred acres free (the founders of Cincinnati made the same offer, with the proviso that a house be erected and other specified improvements be made; such offers were a common way of attracting settlers, but were usually limited to the first five or ten). Indians or no, the town was a carefree place, according to one traveler's description: "The men spent most of their time in hunting and fishing, and almost every evening the boys and girls footed merrily to the tune of the fiddle."[4]

Surveying was Massie's profession and he became a prolific town-founder. In 1796 he laid out Chillicothe in the path of Zane's Trace, barely more than a widened trail through the dense woods. Again he offered free lots to settlers, and by autumn twenty cabins had been raised on the spot. Massie's towns seemed to attract an indolent lot—or perhaps such was the character of many early settlers in the Northwest. At any rate, when the town was founded, whiskey was selling for $4.50 a gallon, but the inhabitants entered the distilling trade with such force and effect that the price soon fell to fifty cents a gallon. With whiskey so cheap, everybody in Chillicothe, including children, consumed it in large amounts. Many of the settlers were veterans, or camp followers, of Wayne's army. They were a lawless breed, and Henry Howe observed that "it for a time became a town of drunkards and a sink of corruption."[5] Even so the citizenry pulled itself together and sought to establish law and order. The turning point came when a man and his wife stole a greatcoat, handkerchief, and a shirt. They fled but were caught. A judge and jury were appointed, and the couple was sentenced to a choice between ten lashes or public humiliation, which consisted of going to every house in the town and announcing, "This is Brannon, who stole the greatcoat, handkerchief and shirt."[6] They chose the latter, and Chillicothe had taken a step upward. It eventually became, for a brief while, the capital of Ohio.

If Chillicothe began as a town of drunks, Lancaster's settlers were remarkable for their sobriety. The town was laid out in 1800 by Ebenezer Zane, another active town surveyor who also surveyed Zane's Trace. He sold lots for five to fifty dollars apiece, and most of the early settlers came from Lancaster, Pennsylvania. These sober Pennsylvania Dutch passed a resolution that any person drunk in public would be required to remove one of the many stumps that covered the main street like stubble on a man's chin.

In the early days of the nineteenth century, town building progresssed slowly, especially in the Western Reserve, where Indians still roamed and communication to the East was difficult. General Moses Cleaveland, representing the Connecticut Land Company, had led the first party into the area in 1795. While surveying the territory, he laid out the town that was to bear his name (later losing the first "a" to the haphazard spelling of the time). Cleaveland selected a site at the point where the Cuyahoga River empties into Lake Erie. His first act, good New Englander that he was, was to pace off the outline of a ten-acre public square among the trees. That ritual done, he ordered his men to lay out a town around the square.

Although it was located on the beautiful blue waters of the lake, Cleveland did not have an entirely propitious site. In 1827 a visitor wrote that "the mouth of the river is choked up by a sand-bar which dams up the water and prevents it from having a free passage. It stands in a deep pool, two or three miles long; and the water being stagnant, and contaminated by decaying vegetation, affects the inhabitants on its margin with fever and ague. . . . The smell was almost insufferable."[7] In its early days the town did not thrive. Two-acre lots were first offered for fifty dollars—with no takers. The price was then lowered to twenty-five dollars, which action drew one bid of twelve dollars. By 1810 the little settlement had only fifty-seven people. It was not until the 1840s, after the Ohio and Erie Canal was completed, that Cleveland began to bustle.

The early settlers lived harrowing lives in the trackless wilderness. One of the first men in the Cleveland area left his pregnant wife alone in their cabin and trekked east to get food. When he returned in the dead of winter, after fighting his way through snowbanks carrying a barrel of flour, he found his wife lying in bed, ill, their baby dead of starvation in her arms. The settlers were scattered, enduring lonely lives in the vast forest. Children often wandered off and, despite intensive searches, disappeared forever. One woman, on her way to a spring to fetch some water, decided to pass the time of day with her husband, who was working nearby. She took a wrong turn and wandered lost all day until she luckily found an Indian trail that led her back to a familiar spot. When the Beebe family arrived in the Reserve, Mrs. Tillotson, who lived in a cabin a few miles away, went to call on her new neighbors. When the two women confronted each other, both were so overcome with emotion at seeing a new human face that they were unable to speak for many minutes. Homesickness led many to regret leaving their neat New England towns and to idealize the homes they had left. One eighteen-year-old boy whom the anti-west propagandist Peter Parley met in the woods asked Parley where he hailed from. Parley said Connecticut, and the boy asked if that was near the Bay State. He said that he had been born in Massachusetts and brought west as an infant, yet had imbibed from his parents' talk a yearning for "home." He told Parley that he longed to see a meetinghouse, a school, and "the real salt sea." "If I could see the old Bay State and ocean, I should be willing then to die," said the boy.[8]

The earliest towns in the Ohio Territory, whether they were laid out or simply grew up without planning, were sited in locations the settlers thought desirable—along rivers and streams; on trails, traces, and later roads; around crossroads taverns; near military posts; at fords and passes; or near the gristmills that ground the first settlers' corn. In this first phase, the pace of settlement was slow, and many large areas were too sparsely inhabited to support a town. Often too, these settlements, like the Kentucky stations, had as their main reason for being protection from the Indians.

During the next stage, towns were more consciously planned. They were located on what was hoped to be a place with a future and peopled by whatever drop-offs from the westward flow of immigrants could be lured there. The best natural sites had already been exploited, and the hopes for these newer towns, platted by the proprietors of the soil, were banked on the future—that is, they were modest speculations. Most of those that survived grew into small country towns, trading centers, and county seats, way stations along roads or, later, canals and railroads, which linked them with the more distant markets. They grew slowly but stubbornly, or else faded into economic decay and quiescence.

As settlement marched farther west, a third stage came into being, containing elements of the other two, but marked by a more blatantly speculative character. These were the "paper towns," founded by often absentee speculators with the profit motive uppermost, in the midst of a flat, empty nowhere near a rumored railroad, a remotely probable steamboat landing, a vaguely hinted canal. This type of town flowered in Illinois and Michigan during the late pioneer period (and continued on, farther west). As the Chicago *Democrat* laconically observed at the peak of the paper-town rush, "Each town has its day and each day its town."[9]

Whatever form it took, town jobbing was a principal occupation in the Old Northwest from the earliest days. Judge Symmes was the West's first boomer, although he was touting a tract of land rather than any specific town. His advertisements in the New Jersey papers described a land where cattle and horses could forage in the woods, where wild game and fish were there for the taking, where all varieties of grains and vegetables—as well as cotton and indigo—would flourish, where millstones lay plentifully about on hillocks, ready for any man who wished to work at the miller's trade, and from where the bountiful harvests could easily be transported by three navigable rivers to New York via the Gulf of Mexico.

Other such promotions followed. Ohio and Indiana towns-to-be were heralded in the early 1800s by western papers such as the *Liberty Hall and Cincinnati Gazette* and the *Vincennes Western Sun and General Advertiser,* and notices about them were picked up in the "exchange clippings" sections of the eastern papers. By 1816 advertisements for towns in southwestern Indiana appeared: Paoli, Washington, Terre Haute, and Evansville. Across the river in Illinois, Bloomington, Fredonia (deceased), Rockport (deceased), Portersville (deceased), Sprinklesburg (deceased), Palestine, Concord (deceased), and Clinton were some names that the boomers dangled before eager settlers.

Town jobbing in fact became a principal alternative to farming in the West. "Sparsely settled as the country was, town booming was anybody's business," a historian wrote, "and with true frontier optimism, each promoter proclaimed his townsite destined to be a metropolis of industry and culture."[10] The Englishman Morris Birbeck, himself come to found a colony dedicated to scientific farming, had his own opinion of the motives of most town founders: "Gain! Gain! Gain! Gain! Gain! is the beginning, the middle and the end, the *alpha* and *omega* of the founders of American towns."[11]

To another traveler the ubiquitous farmer-speculator-town-promoters seemed a fixture of the western landscape, like the beggars in India. "If you accost a farmer in these parts, before he returns your civilities he draws from his pocket a lithographic city, and asks you to take a few building lots at one-half their value . . . as a personal favor conferred on you."[12] Birbeck had a few choice observations on how some of these promoters went about their work: "On any spot where a few settlers cluster together . . . some enterprising proprietor finds in his section what he deems a good site for a town; he has it surveyed and laid out in lots, which he sells or offers for sale by auction. . . . The new town then assumes the name of its founder—a storekeeper builds a little frame store and sends for a few cases of goods; and then a tavern starts up . . . as the boarding house of the weary traveler; soon follows a blacksmith; a schoolmaster, who is also a minister of religion, becomes an important accession to this rising community. Thus the town proceeds if it becomes the metropolis of the neighborhood. Hundreds of these speculations may have failed but hundreds prosper."[13]

Town jobbing was particularly attractive to those settlers with more land than they could farm—a common enough situation—and, one suspects, little ambition to farm it anyhow. Compared with large-scale land speculation, little capital was required—merely the entry money and the cost of the plat (hence the frequent partnership of surveyors and proprietors)—and if the town took, the return could be one hundred to five hundred times what the land had cost—from ten to fifty dollars a house lot of, say, 25 by 125 feet, compared with the two-dollar-an-acre government price. The landowner merely had to get his plat made up after clearing title and declare himself open for business—perhaps holding an auction or simply setting up his office on the site and doing business with buyers as they came to him. Terms were usually a quarter down, and the rest in three installments over a year's time, with interest. There might also be a requirement that a house or building be erected on the lot by the purchaser within a certain time before a deed would be issued.

Of course, the new proprietor might well find it worth his while to advertise his shining city-to-be, as many did, and that raised the ante a bit. Advertisements in the local and eastern papers were a favored method. Another way was to post broadsides at travelers' way stations—taverns, stables, stores, blacksmith shops, coaching stations, or boat landings—thus catching the eye of the itinerants passing through. These broadsides were as flamboyant as the writer could devise, limited only by his wit and imagination and containing a few crumbs of necessary truth. Perhaps typical was the prospectus of the jobber named Joseph Clark, an Ohio farmer who, running true to Birbeck's law, named his town-to-be Clarksville:

> The subscriber is laying out a NEW TOWN, on the waters of Wakatomica Creek, of the town of *Clarksville*, and will offer about sixty of the lots at Public Auction, on the ground, on the 20TH OF MARCH *next*. The conditions of sale will be as follows . . . 1/4 of purchase money to be paid in hand . . . 1/4 in six months, notes with interst to be given for the last two payments. . . . If the purchaser builds a house or a stable of wood, brick, or stone within two years from the time purchase is made, sixteen feet by twenty and one story high, or larger, on each lot

purchased . . . he will be given a FULL WARRANTY DEED with a provision that the actual owner or occupant shall pay one dollar a year forever to be appropriated for the support of a school; but if the house or stable is not built, at the end of two years then the lots shall be forfeited together with all the improvements and payments made.

The site of the town possesses nearly as many advantages as the most flourishing town of the state of Ohio . . . and will, probably, before long become a county seat. . . . The local advantages of this place are particularly promising. The ground on which the town is to stand is a large hill, of a gentle ascent on every side, and on the center of the hill two important roads intersect each other in parallel lines of north, south, east and west. There is a large spring of excellent water within a few rods of the center of this hill, and an extensive bank of stone coal within 100 rods on each side of the above hill. Within one fourth of a mile runs streams of durable water, which, after running about 3/4 of a mile meet each other and form the Brushy Fork of Wakatomica Creek. This brushy fork has a rapid descent of about one mile and a half, forming several good mill seats, and then enters into the main Creek.

A grist mill and saw-mill are within two and one half miles of the place. . . . Within three miles is one of the best seats for a furnace in the state with abundance of iron ore. . . . Within six miles there are not less than 10 good mill seats—the country is generally filled with stone coal—there are immense bodies of fine clay suitable for manufacturing glass, stone and earthenware. In addition to all this the country is uncommonly fertile, producing all the comforts of life in the greatest abundance, and the country is nearly settled with industrious, enterprising farmers.

A lot each will be given for a Court-House, a Market-House and an Academy. Every reasonable encouragement will be given by the proprietor to industrious, peaceable mechanics, who will come and settle in the town; *but no countenance will be given to overgrown speculators in any shape.*

THE SUBSCRIBER IS NOW ERECTING BUILDINGS FOR A STORE, TAVERN AND OTHER PURPOSES, WHICH WILL SOON BE COMPLETED. HE WILL GENERALLY BE FOUND AT THE ABOVE PLACE, BUT IN HIS ABSENCE DANIEL ASHCROFT RESIDING NEAR THE PREMISES, WILL GIVE ALL NECESSARY INFORMATION. FEBRUARY 1, 1817. J. CLARK.[14]

Actually, Joseph Clark appears to have been a relatively restrained copywriter compared to some; perhaps all the natural advantages he cited did exist in and around the site of Clarksville. Perhaps not, for the town never got off the ground. Another unrelated Clarksville, however, was destined to grow up a hundred miles from the failed one. The flyer does reveal the vital components of a town—grist mill and saw mill, potential for industry (iron ore and "stone coal"), fertile land for farmers. The proprietor's city-planning vision also included donated land for a Court House (hoped-for), a school and a farmers' market. Lastly, he promised to allow only peaceable, industrious citizens—"mechanics"—who would provide skills needed by farmers. No "overgrown speculators" need apply; one, farmer Clark, was sufficient.

Not all promoters were fly-by-nighters. James Kilbourne was an Episcopalian clergyman who successfully planted the towns of Worthington and Bucyrus (with Samuel Norton), and, as Ohio surveyor of public lands, laid out ten more. After planting Worthington in behalf of a land company he had formed back in his home state of Connecticut, he became rector of the church for a while, and founded Worthington Academy. Next he became a colonel in the Ohio militia and was appointed Surveyor in 1805. Later, he founded the first newspaper in Ohio, was elected to Congress, and owned woolen factories in Worthington and Steubenville. In promoting Bucyrus, which he named after the founder of the Persian Empire, with a prefixial "bu" tacked on for euphony, Reverend Kilbourne resorted to poetry:

I'll tell you how Bucyrus now
Just rising, like the star of morn,
Surrounded stands by fertile lands,
On clear Sandusky's rural bourn.
Then here, my friends, your search may end,
For here's a county to your mend, [sic]
And here's a town your hopes may crown,
As those who try it soon shall find.[15]

A typical town-founding story is encapsulated in the natal history of Alamo, Indiana, founded in 1837, as related matter-of-factly by the Montgomery County historian:

> The establishment of this village was the result of an attempt at speculation made by Mr. Truax and Boyce, a surveyor, who figured in the origin of several villages in Indiana at that time. The plan was a simple one, and much the same as is now being adopted in the West: to describe a village, with streets named in honor of some revolutionary hero, blocks and lots, all regularly numbered, and a "city square," say that it "is a promising location for young men with energy," advertise it in the eastern papers and wait until the greater portion of the lots are sold to persons who think they have bought a good business location in a thriving western village and watch their discomfiture as they view their lot, the only recognizable feature of which is a small stake driven into the ground or a mark blazed upon a tree to designate its boundaries. This plan did not succeed in Alamo, however, so that after much had been

squandered in advertising, the lots were sold at auction to any who would buy, and at figures much lower than those dreamed of by the surveyor, Boyce, about a year after the imaginary city was first conceived by him.[16]

Alamo never amounted to much, though it is still on the map, a village of several hundred inhabitants. The story of its founding is remarkable only in its typicality. Hundreds of other towns were whelped in the same way.

There were cases of clear-cut fraud—including the classic real estate fraud of selling subaquatic land to nonamphibians back east. In Ohio a cluster of paper towns on empty swampland near the Maumee River was energetically promoted. Eleven towns in all were mapped, each with a different ascribed potential which was touted in the eastern papers. There was Manhattan, located near where the river emptied into Lake Erie—obviously a future port; Oregon, with unique advantages as a pork-production center; Marengo, at the head of navigation for the Maumee; and so on. The promoters' puffs attracted a flock of takers, but when they arrived at the sites they found only deserted Indian camps. The towns were not worth the paper they were platted on.

One of the gaudiest and most notorious promotions was that of Cairo, Illinois. The town did start out with a strategic location at the confluence of the Ohio and Mississippi rivers. Cairo rode the crest of the speculative bubble of the 1830s that collapsed in the panic of 1837. In that unpropititious year the state legislature chartered the Cairo City & Canal Company, under the direction of a Yankee named Darius B. Holbrook. Men were hired to build a levee and shops and houses, while Chicago real estate touts feverishly sold lots from colored maps depicting a thriving city stretching for optimistic miles up and down the river. But it was in England, where the London firm of John Wright & Company sold lots, that the Cairo speculation reached its highest pitch. Wright & Company went bankrupt in 1840, and after that Cairo went steadily downhill, its population decreasing from one thousand to one hundred in the space of two years. It was in this sorry state that Charles Dickens saw it in 1842, and he portrayed it as "Eden" in *Martin Chuzzlewit* as an example of the basest follies of town speculation. (The commonly held belief that Dickens was himself an investor in Cairo is untrue; more probably he wrote of the town as an aggrieved Englishman and as a spokesman for his countrymen who had been rooked.) His description of Cairo in *American Notes* is bathed in venom (the West, generally, seemed to have plunged Dickens into a fit of depression) but provides a jaundiced portrait of the reality of "Eden":

> We arrived at a spot so much more desolate than any we had yet beheld, that the forlornest places we had passed were, in comparison with it full of interest. At the junction of the two rivers, on ground so flat and low and marshy, that at certain seasons of the year it is inun-

> dated to the house-tops, lies a breeding-place of fever, ague, and death; vaunted in England as a mine of Golden Hope, and speculated in, on the faith of monstrous representations, to many people's ruin. A dismal swamp on which the half-built houses rot away: cleared here and there for the space of a few yards; and teeming, then, with rank unwholesome vegetation, in whose baleful shade the wretched wanderers who are tempted hither, droop, and die, and lay their bones; the hateful Mississippi circling and eddying before it, and turning off upon its southern course, a slimy monster hideous to behold; a hotbed of disease, an ugly sepulchre, a grave uncheered by any gleam of promise: a place without one single quality, in earth or air or water, to command it: such is this dismal Cairo.[17]

The taint of Cairo's birth cast a shadow over its subsequent history, and it never realized the potential of its strategic location. The vainglorious promises of its infancy set it off on a rainbow chase that always ended in failure. Illusory hopes sapped the civic spirit of its people, and encouraged the town to shoulder a killing burden of debt.

In the Northwest, where government was remote and minimal and there were no laws governing town-founding, it was almost impossible to draw a line between the efforts of the legitimate town boomer and those of the con-man. If the buyer lost his money buying town real estate, it was either because the promoter absconded with it and there was no town there, or else the promoter had promised not wisely but too well and his town flopped. In the latter case, no doubt the promoter would have been better pleased if the town had succeeded, but otherwise there was little difference between the two situations—except intent and the fact that out-and-out fraud separated the buyer from his money more quickly and cleanly. In both cases this was accomplished by identical means: the absence of a town.

Still, whatever the motives of the founders, or the hot-air quotient of their puffery, most towns succeeded after a fashion. Even Cairo prospered briefly in the 1860s, after a huge federal land grant subsidized the building of the Illinois Central Railroad, which linked Cairo to Chicago, enabling it to serve as a supply depot during the Civil War. In contrast, many religious communitarian experiments, founded out of the highest motives and selflessness, without a taint of puffery, thrived for a time, but foundered on the shoals of internal dissension or external hostility. Those that succeeded, like George Rapp's New Harmony, were marked by a strong authoritarian discipline and unquestioning obedience to the spiritual leader. Given such discipline, the utopia usually flowered.

Needless to say the average town promoter was not guided by any lofty aesthetic or religious aspiration in laying out his town—let alone any scientific principle of town planning. His main inspiration was, as Morris Birbeck said, gain; his object was to transform his land into a gridiron of salable real estate parcels. True, the town founder might throw in a town square or green, after the New England example, and he might set aside certain lots for donation to the county, in hopes of being designated as a county seat in return; he would also roughly envision a town center—either the square or the place where the "main" and "main cross" streets would intersect on his plat—which would, of course, become the town's business center. And naturally there would be streets, numbered or named after trees or patriots. But that was it; the rest was rows of numbered rectangular house lots on a plat map, to be sold as quickly as possible.

Only the towns founded by religious groups seemed to have any semblance of a unifying vision in their layouts—any sense of community purpose or aspiration over and beyond the mundane practicalities of the real estate transaction. The Mormon towns of Kirtland, Ohio, and Nauvoo, Illinois, had their imposing temples, their streets laid out according to Biblical prescription; the Rappite town of New Harmony was beautifully laid out and meticulously planned—even to the people's houses, which were prefabricated and designed in a uniform style of attractive simplicity. Somewhat more eccentric, perhaps, but certainly visionary was the layout of the Ohio town of Tallmadge, located in the Western Reserve. Many of the towns in the Reserve were replicas of the New England towns whence their inhabitants had come, and consequently they were often rather pretty in the manner of the New England town. Tallmadge, however, was a New England town run riot. The founder was David Bacon, a missionary-zealot who in 1807 built a cabin on a site he acquired in a Connecticut Land Company drawing. Other settlers, Congregationalists all, followed, and the town was run by strict Puritanical standards.

The Tallmadge plan followed the New England model of the meetinghouse and a town hall on the village green at the center and all roads leading to it. Bacon had the town surveyed into sixteen "great lots," each one thousand acres, rather than the usual small salable lots. Along the borders of these lots, running north and south and east and west, were roads sixty-six feet wide. Lastly, borrowing from the original plan of Washington, D.C., Bacon laid out roads radiating from each corner of the green to the ultimate corners of the township, and four other roads running due north, south, east and west. Double rows of elms were planted along these arterial routes. The results were aesthetically pleasing as well as theologically sound. Tallmadge's elaborate network of roads was also ahead of its time; most country road systems grew up piecemeal, laid out and maintained by entrepreneurs.

Unfortunately Bacon's road system was too costly. The inhabitants of Tallmadge were short of money, and eventually their mortgage was foreclosed by the owners of the land—who then resold it. Contributing to the demise of Bacon's Puritan town were quarrels over doctrinal differences and personality clashes between the autocratic Bacon and his flock. In any event, Tallmadge's fate was to become a suburb of nearby, booming Akron, though it still boasts the handsomest New England–style green in Ohio.

Actually the New England town was ill-adapted to the heterogeneous population of the West; not surprisingly those towns settled in this tradition by communal groups kept their New England identity only as isolated enclaves in the Reserve. The western speculative town that was simply an agglomeration of salable parcels was most suited to the laissez-faire West and best equipped to play host to the driblets of settlers trickling in from all over. There was no first-settler or proprietor class which owned valuable land and first rights on undistributed common land as in New England (there was indeed no common farmland in the New England tradition, only the land set aside for parks, schools, and the like). Thus there was no built-in schism between the first settlers and the newcomers, who in the East had often been grudgingly allowed in and denied a chance at the most desirable land. Rather, the town was simply sold off piece by piece to whoever had the money.

Because there was no proprietor class, the middle western town was not subject to the secessionist schisms of the early New England towns, the clashes between old-towners and outlivers. Always solidly planted, founded on religion rather than speculation, the New England town spread by secession, while the middle western town grew by accretion—by "additions"—or else didn't take and died. The New England town was homogeneous and centralized in spirit, and thus constantly riven by dissenting groups, whose only alternatives were to knuckle under to the town establishment or to secede and strike out on their own. There was no such homogeneity in the middle western towns, indeed there were no planned settlements at all, other than those of the New England communal groups. There was no central authority of religion and town meetings. A farmer who ploughed his clearing in the woods far from town was not regarded as ripe for the Devil; he was, after all, pursuing the Dream, though some might deplore his rude, uncivilized ways. The only inhibition placed upon the founding of a new town was potential commercial rivalry with the prior town; the founders did not need any permission from the legislature to lay out a town once they owned the land. The Ordinance of 1787 and the United States Constitution encouraged freedom of religion, so the people of a town could set up a church in any of the going religious faiths they fancied, removing another source of the schisms common in New England. True, the multiplicity of faiths reflected doctrinal disputes, which caused sputtering quarrels, but, by the same token, the ease of founding a new church provided a safety valve in contrast to the pressure-cooker effect of early Puritan theocracy. And a new part of town was not regarded with suspicion and forced to secede or, after long, acrimonious dispute, grudgingly allowed to become a separate ward. Instead, when the middle western town felt the pressure of population on land, it simply let out its belt a few notches. The Woodford County, Illinois, historian described a practice so commonplace today that it seems it was always done that way:

"When rapidly growing cities have become so compactly built that there no longer remains ground on which buildings may be placed, or when lots have become so dear that the newer owners can find no suitable location corresponding to their limited means on which to erect them a habitation, they are, necessarily, compelled to seek room at a distance from the occupied portion of the city. In this way addition after addition to the original plat of the city is made, and suburb after suburb follows, until what was at first considered a long way out into the country becomes the heart of the city."[18]

The problem with this system was that while easing pressure on residential land, it increased it on the business district in the town center as the population grew and more businesses were founded. This forced property values up, eliminating unused land that might have provided green space. Thus, the town squares were quickly eaten away by developers' rapacity. Those squares that functioned as markets to which country folk brought their produce were also vulnerable: town merchants disliked the competition. There was at least one case of town-center businessmen disguising themselves and tearing down the market stalls in the dead of night. Unlike the typical New England town with its center providing a locus of its twin concern for religion and town government, the center of the pioneer town, even in rudimentary form, was the business district. It was located at the intersection of the two main streets or around the green square, which was usually fenced to keep out the livestock that wandered freely through the town.

If the town was a county seat, it had a courthouse and a jail, also located on the square. Indeed, after the jail (a less ambitious and more immediately necessary structure, after all), the courthouse was the first major public structure erected, and the two of them symbolized the preeminence of government and law in the West. The actions of the Marietta pioneers—drawing up a criminal code and posting it on a tree and holding a parade, mobilizing all the pomp and circumstance a pioneer colony could muster, to celebrate the first, symbolic session of court—demonstrated that the civil law was to be the foundation of society in the West—the unifying core. The religious ideals of community embodied in the covenant gave way to the norms of secular law, and the power of religion always remained secondary. (True, trials and excommunications—"churchings"—for misbehavior were often employed by middle western churches as they had been in New England, but these sanctions lost much of their potency in the fluid society of the West, where people could simply pick up and move farther west if they found religious restrictions too binding. The local churches also instigated town blue laws. As will be seen, town politics often reflected the struggles between the church people and those who profited from vice.) The centrality of the courthouse was underscored by the settlers' frequent choice of the Virginia courthouse with its cupola capping a pyramidal roof (reminiscent, in its shape, of a New England meetinghouse, too) as an architectural model; the southern courthouse town seems to have been a model as often as the New England Meetinghouse Hill. These simple square, brick structures also had what may have been an architectural advantage to early town-builders—not obviously fronting in any particular direction when they were set in the square, in contrast to a building with a classical entrance façade.

Most settlers were not educated New Englanders, like the founders of Marietta, self-consciously bearing an ideal of law and order into the wilderness. Indeed, many, especially the southerners, were poor, rural folk who had lived beyond the pale of courts and government. The early farmer-hunter settlers had little contact with other human beings and little need for law, and visitors from the East—other than the missionaries, who saw only back-sliding and depravity—praised their orderliness, while admitting them to be improvident, indolent, and transitory. Thus, in 1829, an anonymous writer in the *American Quarterly Review* observed that those early settlers "are honest, and very generous. Crimes of magnitude seldom occur among them; and it is a singular fact, that at those remote points, where the *law* is almost unknown, travellers enjoy a degree of security which is scarcely known in any other part of the world." [19]

But those people could hardly covet their neighbors' property, since they were not fond of neighbors; nor did their neighbors have much to covet. If they couldn't raise a subsistence, they could move on, seeking that better land always rumored to exist in the territory ahead. It was when the country began to fill up with a more permanent population that crime began to be a problem. And the character of the people themselves no doubt contributed to this problem. These early pioneers were a rootless, rumbustious, physical people. As the Madison County, Ohio, historian wrote, "Physical prowess was the standard of merit in pioneer days." [20] In the absence of law, trial by combat was the rule, and disputes were settled by brawls—or by the knife or gun. But these private score-settlings were, after all, accepted and indeed were, in their nonlethal forms, a welcome spectator sport. More serious forms of crime arose, however, involving gangs of thieves who threatened the lives and property of a settlement. To deal with these outlaws, bands of vigilantes or regulators were frequently formed on the frontier to apprehend and punish criminals. A community still in the pioneer stage might tolerate killings in self-defense or arising out of matters of family honor; but murder by robber bands and counterfeiting and horse stealing were another matter.

Over and beyond these kinds of crime, nearly every settlement had a nucleus of citizens who identified law with a higher level of civilization and sought, with varying success, to drag the rest of the populace up to it. There were the scattering of towns like Massie's Station and Chillicothe that were taken over by the lawless, but more generally community living increased the social pressure against criminal acts. The inhabitants demanded protection from threats to life and property and exemplary punishment of wrongdoers. In towns, unlike scattered settlements, the respectable folk could be rallied, and the weight of the group brought to bear, either through vigilante action or through the work of law officers.

So wherever towns were founded, law, courts, and a constabulary were soon demanded. As soon as—or even before—the county seat (the term derives from the town's position as the seat of justice) had been designated, a circuit court, regular grand juries, and prosecuting attorneys were appointed by the territorial or state legislature, and they met in log cabins, taverns, empty sheds, churches, schoolhouses, or wherever there was a building big enough to hold them.

The presence of courts, irregular and itinerant as they were in the days of circuit-riding judges, marked the beginning of the end of the law of vengeance, of trial by combat and vigilantism. So it was in Greene County, Ohio. As was often the case, the first session of the court was held to organize the county, with the two associate judges present ordering a surveyor to lay out the townships. This was in May 1803; in August of the same year the first trial was held. A grand jury was appointed, composed of residents from all over the county who had gathered for the event. They promptly retired to a pole hut behind the log cabin that was being used as a court and jury room. Unfortunately, they had no business to discuss, and the spectators grew restive. A spontaneous decision arose to give the jurors something to do, so they began fighting among themselves. Owen Davis, a mill owner, accused a neighbor of stealing his hogs and laid into him. After Davis had vanquished the alleged pork thief, he presented himself to the judge and announced, "Well, Ben, I've whipped that damn hog thief—what's the damage—what's to pay?" He then pulled out his purse and slammed all the money it contained on the table, saying, "Yes, Ben, and if you'd steal a hog, damn you, I'd whip you too." Thomas C. Wright, Esq., the county auditor, witnessed the event and later wrote, "He had, doubtless, come to the conclusion that, as there was a court, the luxury of fighting could not be indulged in gratis and he was for paying up as he went." [21]

At first the transition from fisticuff justice to the court-ordained variety became a calculated game. As Henry Howe put it:

> In newly settled counties, there appears to be a particular fondness among people for lawsuits. After a court has been organized in a new county they will still continue to settle their quarrels by combat, until fines become troublesome. The court then becomes the arena in which their contentions and quarrels are carried and finally disposed of. If one cannot afford the fine or imprisonment which would be incurred, by taking personal satisfaction, he can bring a suit, if any cause of action can be found, and no matter how small the amount claimed or frivolous the matter, if he can only cast his adversary and throw him in the courts, he

is as much gratified as if he had made him hallow "enuf—take him off."[22]

Later, the novelty presumably wore off, and the more serious business of crime dominated the courts. Theft, armed robbery, horse thievery, murder, and dueling were on the rise from the 1820s onward—to hear the newspapers talk at any rate. It may have been that crime, then as it is now, was good for circulation, or it may have been a reflection of genuine public concern (or both), but all over the Old Northwest the papers regularly deplored serious crimes. Murders led the list: "Barbarous Murder," "'Horrible Crime," "Atrocious Outrage," "Terrible If True," "Horrid Murders," "Distressing Narrative," [23] the local weeklies headlined with monotonous regularity.

Most crime was of the rural sort; bank robbery, for example, was relatively infrequent, since banks were rare. Instead, given the shortage of money, many criminals resorted to making rather than stealing money—in other words, counterfeiting. With all the various kinds of currency in circulation, this particular crime was perhaps a natural and was popular throughout the West. The first Ohio penitentiary was built in 1815, and between that year and 1822, the leading crimes were horse stealing, larceny, and counterfeiting, in that order. By 1826, 548 miscreants had been sentenced to the penitentiary—5 of them women.

Crime in the smaller towns was undoubtedly less of a problem than it was in the cities. The gravest crime out in the rural areas was horse thievery, which directly stimulated the formation of vigilante bands. Horse thievery, highway robbery, counterfeiting, and the like were crimes of "outsiders" and were dealt with severely as a rule. Crimes of passion, vengeance, or outraged honor, as well as lesser offenses committed by locals against each other, were often treated more lightly. In his history of Illinois, Governor Thomas Ford said that the most frequent cases before the courts involved trespass, trover replevin (actions to recover personal property illegally held), slander, indictments for assault and battery, affrays, riots, selling liquor without a license, and card playing. Juries, he said, were particularly loath to convict for blue-law peccadilloes such as the last two. Furthermore, "in all cases of murder arising from heat of the blood or in fight, it was impossible to convict," he said flatly.[24] A treacherous assassin or a murderer who had taken unfair advantage, yes, but not a man who had felled his opponent in a fair fight. Such attitudes were particularly southern, reflecting the preponderant number of Kentuckians and Tennesseans in Illinois. In areas settled predominantly by New Englanders, murder was murder and regarded with a biblical finality that foreclosed any exculpatory circumstances.

Murder cases provided a real-life theater of human passion—with comedy and tragedy in equal measure. In an Indiana town a young man and a girl were in love, but her father, the squire, disapproved of the match. Finally the young man persuaded his sweetheart to elope. The squire learned about their plans and lay in wait along the road; when the couple appeared, he shot the young man and reclaimed his daughter. In the murder trial that followed, the daughter was compelled to testify against her father, an experience so wrenching that she went insane. The squire was sentenced, by a reluctant judge, to two years for manslaughter and was promptly pardoned by the governor. He succumbed to morbidity, and it was said that he never smiled again in all the remaining years of his life. Clearly public opinion sided with the father and his right to decide whom his daughter should marry; on the other hand, the murder was a deliberate, calculated, merciless act. And for the daughter to testify against her father was a dilemma so cruel that it overbore her. No one could win.

Far from reflecting the impartial dispensation of justice according to abstract principles, law in the pioneer days was mulched in the prejudices and folkways of the community. The unwritten laws, seated deep in the emotions of the people and expressed by the votes of the juries, determined the seriousness of crimes. In a subsistence economy where everyone owned little, theft could take on enlarged proportions. In Indiana the theft of a watch brought three years' imprisonment at hard labor; a first offender in a horse-thievery case was punished with thirty-one lashes, a second offender by death. Counterfeiting was seriously regarded because currency was in short supply and passing false money was stealing in another way. Counterfeiters were widely reprehended and ruthlessly hunted down (although their handiwork inevitably was circulated and sometimes tacitly accepted by local merchants). Compared to these crimes, murder was often more easily justified to frontier juries.

Even when courts sat regularly, the vigilante bands were slow to disappear. Bands of citizens, ranging from disorganized mobs acting in the heat of moment to well-organized groups of regulators, acted as an auxiliary to the regular law-enforcement agencies (which generally consisted of a county sheriff and a constable or two in the towns). The punishment they meted out ranged from whippings to banishment to hanging, and often, being untrammeled by the niceties of the law, if they couldn't catch the culprit, they grabbed a handy scapegoat, who served a cathartic purpose just as well.

In one Indiana town, the first prisoner incarcerated in the new jail escaped by setting fire to its wooden door, and the outrage over this evasion of justice—or was it the blow to their civic pride?—ran so high that the locals demanded retribution. In the absence of the escaped prisoner, they fixed upon the theory that he must surely have had a confederate, and their suspicion homed in on "a worthless chicken-thief named Jack, who had long been a lazy pensioner upon the industrious little community." A gang of regulators, "duly disguised and armed, collected to administer lynch law upon the offender."[25] How the men were disguised, the historian does not say, but it was common for mobs to disguise themselves, as though clandestineness, the anonymity of a mask, freed them from all restraint. At any rate, poor Jack was caught, thrashed with hickory sticks (known as "castigation"), and banished from the county. Another posse, this time with the sheriff along, caught up with the escaped thief and chained him to an iron staple in the courthouse until trial. Obviously, when it came to an unpopular, feebleminded ne'er-do-well, the local folk felt no obligation to accord him a trial.

Mob action against unpopular individuals or groups may not have been commonplace, but it was resorted to with some frequency. The Mormons felt the wrath of mobs in Ohio, Missouri, and Illinois. An abolitionist editor was killed by an angry mob of southerners in Alton, Illinois, while in Rockville, Illinois, a mob lynched a secessionist named Thomas J. Burke, whose views made him unpopular and who, perhaps as a result of this unpopularity, was accused of starting a wave of fires that had plagued the town. A private detective, who was hired by the town to investigate the crimes undercover, befriended Burke and claimed to have elicited a confession from him. Before Burke's trial had run its course, a mob cornered him while he was in transit under guard inside the courthouse, tied a rope around his neck, and threw him out the window to his death. The single deputy guarding him later explained that when he saw the mob coming with a rope, he assumed they were merely trying to frighten the prisoner. The leaders of the mob were later indicted for murder but exonerated by the local jury. As for Burke, he had protested his innocence all along and had been refused counsel at the trial. Later evidence proved that he was innocent of setting at least one of the fires, and perhaps all of them.

Still, such cases of mob prejudice aside, under frontier conditions there was often no alternative to taking the law in one's own hands, since there was no agent of the law. An early case in Zanesville illustrates how a good citizen sometimes had too get involved, in the absence of regular procedures. Two men accused of counterfeiting silver dollars were caught, but at that time, in the 1820s, Zanesville did not possess a jail. The nearest facility was in Marietta, sixty miles away, a prohibitive distance in winter time. A local man, however, volunteered to "prisoner-sit." Leading the men to an empty cabin, he handcuffed them and said, "Now, boys, there is your bed; with your guilt and innocence we have nothing to do—you shall have plenty to eat and drink, but *if you attempt to escape, damn you, I'll kill you.*"[26] With that, gripping an ax, he seated himself at the door.

As sheer spectacle and entertainment, legal trials had it all over vigilantism, a furtive, if invigorating, sport at best. Important trials drew big crowds of rapt spectators and functioned as local morality plays, reinactments of forbidden wishes that some fellow who had been borne over the line expressed for all, tragedies of irreconcilable alternatives or honor avenged, or, at the other extreme, comedies involving petty disputes blown all out of proportion by the sheer cussedness of the contending parties. People came hundreds of miles to watch the judges and hear the lawyers plead. And the stars of the drama played to this gallery. One lawyer delivered an eloquent three-hour harangue to the jury, in which he detailed the great provocation his client had suffered before he was moved to twist the plaintiff's nose. The judge was as appreciative as the spectators, and when the lawyer rested, he roared, "Capital; I did not think it was in him!" The jury, well swayed, quickly found the man innocent, to the "rapturous applause" of the spectators. Public hangings were even more popular, drawing large crowds; sometimes tickets were sold.

In the 1830s lawyers called themselves "squires" and wore three-inch queues, but in actuality they were only a few books more learned than the nonlawyers. They practiced by their wits and common sense, plus their volumes of Blackstone, Espinasse's *Nisi Prius*, and Peak's *Evidence* with the pages turned down at the most frequently consulted sections. Abraham Lincoln won his spurs in this rough-and-ready school, and his courtroom tactics—for example, the use of an almanac to discredit a witness who said he had seen the defendant in the light of a full moon—have become folklore; at the time they won an obscure lawyer wider renown and helped advance his political career.

Some judges too were only sketchily learned in the law. The circuit courts of the early days often had a presiding judge and two associates. The presiding judge rode the circuit, while the associates were local laymen who sometimes, in the presiding judge's absence, dispensed their own brand of folk law. Handling the lesser cases were justices of the peace, likewise untrained, who made little pretense of consulting precedents before making decisions. A well-known early J.P. in Washington County, Ohio, was John Popejoy, Esq., who kept his docket on scraps of paper stuck away in chinks in his cabin. Popejoy handed down a ruling only as a last resort; his usual technique was to urge an amicable settlement upon the disputing parties. He assessed no court costs for this service, preferring cider or beer instead, which he served up to the witnesses and spectators. The justices of the peace were often the legal authorities of first resort in a new county, and they handled the squabbles and the petty misdemeanors, as well as performing the first marriages.

The courts and the justices and constables and sheriffs were the primary source of authority in the early towns, keeping the peace, protecting property. The other units of town government, although present from the beginning, expanded more slowly, and their effect on daily life was more limited. With settlers scattered and towns small, the family assumed a preeminent role. It was the basic economic unit, self-sufficient unto itself and producing little in the way of surplus for trade. In time, however, the need for rudimentary social services grew up—roads, bridges, fences, schools—and of course a common fund to pay for them, that is to say, taxes. Gradually, scattered farms, settlements, villages, and towns were interconnected in a web of social and economic relationships, giving rise to the need for common action in very limited areas through government.

As the territorial government gave way and the states elected their own legislatures, criminal law became the responsibility of the state, replacing the *Mayflower*-style compacts of the early towns. The inferior units of government now derived their authority from the state. It was the state legislatures that created the county governments. They in turn chose the county seats and laid out the townships. The state legislatures also incorporated the towns (thus making them legal entities able to sign contracts and the like) and approved their charters.

The county-township system was essentially a territorial form of government, based on geographical rather than population units. It was best adapted to a pioneer society in which the people were scattered about on farms, and it did not anticipate the economic hegemony of the towns over the countryside. The system was woven out of a variety of historical strands. The county idea was strongest in Virginia and the Middle Atlantic states, while the township idea developed in New England, out of the pattern of town settlement. New England towns served as locus of the meetinghouse, and its bounds were set by the radius of an easy day's journey there and back, with time for a sermon. The town also had aspects of an English agricultural village; the people lived in it and worked their fields and common lands round about. In contrast, the survey townships of the Old Northwest became simply large land parcels that few could afford to buy and that were carved up into sections and half sections, with farmers living on and working individual plots. When the county governments were set up by the state, they laid out their own quasi townships, at first more or less following the government-survey townships but soon drawn up as divisions of the county; one might be coextensive with the boundaries of the largest town, and others simply geographical governmental units that embraced farms and villages alike.

At the heart of the county government were the county commissioners, usually three in number. After a county's boundaries had been surveyed by the state, the commissioners were either elected by the people in it or appointed by the legislature. The commissioners had an important role in designating the county seat and also creating the townships. Typically, their first acts included ordering surveys, establishing license fees for taverns, setting bounties on wolves and other pests, establishing ferry rates, formulating tax-assessment rates (based on house, cattle, horses, and other personal property), letting contracts to private parties to survey and build roads, specifying where court should be held (until a courthouse could be built), and designating polling places for township elections. Other county officials were either elected or appointed—usually a clerk, recorder, treasurer, assessor, collector, county agent, sheriff, coroner, surveyors (called road viewers or fence viewers), and the like. After the county had been organized, the townships held their elections; officers included a governing board, whose members were usually called trustees, and other functionaries, most important of whom were the justices of the peace, constables, and directors of the school districts which lay within the township.

Town governments assumed a variety of forms. Sometimes, where the town was conterminous with a township unit (usually this would be the county-seat town), a township government consisting of a board of trustees, president, secretary, and treasurer was established. Until the town was incorporated, it had no legal government, but in some places the townspeople went ahead and elected a council. The councilman or trustee idea—perhaps derived from the New England selectmen system—seems to have been widespread, with the chief executive officer (if any) being elected by this board. If the town grew sufficiently large, it could draw up a charter and gain municipal status, in which case it was usually divided up into wards, each of which elected an alderman or councilman. In addition a mayor and other city officials were directly elected by the people.

The right to vote in the Old Northwest evolved from the New England freeholder system into full manhood suffrage. Under the Ordinance of 1787, the vote was given to those who owned fifty acres of land; to be qualified to serve in the territorial assembly, one had to own five hundred acres. These property qualifications gradually eroded away under pressure from the large squatter population and the wave of popular-suffrage agitation of the 1830s and 40s, so that eventually a man had only to prove he was a taxpayer and had lived in the state or town for a certainn period of time (a system close to that which evolved in the New England towns). When the Ohio Constitution abolished even these qualifications in 1833, there was some grousing by the "established" citizenry. The Darke County, Ohio, historian grumbled that "for more than twenty years, the municipal government of the town, from year to year, has been created and controlled by men who, with few exceptions, pay no taxes, and care nothing how much others have to pay."[27] The act also demonstrated the preeminence of the state because it wiped from the book all city charters that had provisions contrary to it.

The Darke County historian inadvertently reveals something of the democratic nature of politics in the Old Northwest—the opportunity it offered for the nonpropertied to advance themselves. Actually, before party conventions began in the 1820s and party organizations were solidified in the 1830s, just about anybody could stand for local office; politics was informal, cliquish, entirely personality oriented. If a man wanted to run for an office, he need simply rear up at a social event such as a logrolling or county muster, or in front of a group of loafers at the general store in the county seat, and announce his candidacy. Sometimes he importuned his friends to hold a "mass meeting" to acclaim their new champion—no matter that there were only five or ten people present.

Campaigning in the pioneer days was highly personal, necessitating that the candidate stop off at little cabins in the clearings and halloo farmers in their fields. A favored technique was to post oneself at a great distance from a farmer straining his plough through the muddy soil and shout: "Halloo! I'm (name of opponent). I hope you'll vote for me." Later the candidate would come back, slog through the mud to the farmer, introduce himself by his right name, spit on his hands, and do a little ploughing. The voters liked a man who would get down in the mud with them. By the same token, they resented any candidate who was "stuckuppity" or "took on airs," so the candidate had to avoid fancy clothing or elegant speech. An Indiana politico of the 1820s purchased a fine buggy to campaign in—and was immediately advised by friends to park it for the duration of the campaign and proceed by foot or horseback. Even in the 1840s a congressman who addressed a basket supper in a silk hat caused a sensation and lost votes. And candidates had to be generous with whiskey; voters came to expect "treating" as well as—if not more than—oratory. It was said that one preacher campaigned with a Bible in one pocket and a whiskey bottle in the other. "Thus armed with the 'sword of the Lord and the spirit' he could preach to one set of men and drink with another, and thus make himself agreeable to all."[28] Another way to dispense the spirits was to place a barrel of whiskey at a local grocery a few weeks before election. These barrels were the predecessors of today's Gallup Polls, in that the pre-election popularity of a candidate could be judged by the comparative emptiness of his barrel. This polling technique was not always reliable, however, since an opponent's supporters frequently would sabotage a candidate by drinking all his whiskey.

The candidate also made sure to be present at any local assemblage, such as a sale or court day or militia muster, and to climb upon a stump and let the crowd savor his oratorical style which, in the manner of the day, was bound to be robust, flowery, and "no holts barred" when it came to vituperating his opponent. These rallies worked the voters up into a high pitch of civic-mindedness. Governor Ford recalled a typical one in Illinois: "The stump speeches being over, then commenced the drinking of liquor, and long before night a large portion of the voters would be drunk and staggering about town, cursing, swearing, halooing, yelling, huzzaing for their favorite candidates, throwing their arms up and around, threatening to fight, and fighting."[29]

The lack of party programs, the preeminence of personal politics, and the ignorance of the voters sometimes produced political apathy alternating with phases of high passion that owed as much to whiskey and demagogy as to principle. As Governor Ford observed in his disillusioned history of Illinois, "The people asked nothing and claimed nothing but to be left alone, and the politicians usually went to work to divide out the benefits and advantages of government amongst themselves."[30] Those who went to the legislature spent their time promoting special legislation for their friends and practicing the delicate art of backscratching. Governor Ford described the talents necessary for legislative success: "The man of the most tack and address who could make the most friends and the most skillful combinations of individual interests, was almost always the most successful in accomplishing his purposes. A smooth, sleek, supple, friendly manner, which by gaining favor imposed upon credulity, made a politician formidable."[31] It is not for nothing, perhaps, that the political expression "logrolling" comes from the pioneer practice of helping one another out. In Governor Ford's day the wheeler-dealers in the legislature were said to "carry a gourd of possum fat." Applying this unguent, they caused their victim to be "greased and swallowed"—that is to say, "greased" when he was won over to their purposes and "swallowed" when he acted in accord with those purposes. This process was also known by a term more familiar in our day—"soft soap."

Governor Ford's rather cynical view reflected the state-legislature politics of Illinois in the 1820s and 1830s. Visiting intellectuals from New England were appalled by the barbaric (to them) style of western politics, but some discerned beneath the crudity and gaucherie an underlying healthy vigor, a robust involvement with the political process. That was the view of Cornelius C. Felton, a professor of classics at Harvard, who, writing in 1842, contrasted his own region unfavorably with the towns of the West:

> There is more activity and stir in one of these new communities, than in the ancient towns. Public affairs more engross the minds of men, and are more discussed, within doors and without. Poetry and art,—music, sculpture and painting,—the last new novel, tomorrow evening's concert, last evening's "Lowell Lecture," are things unheard of; but political disquisitions, not always of the wisest, stump speeches, the affairs of the town, county, or State, and the pretensions of rival candidates, are vehemently argued. After a visit to the West, one cannot but be struck with the comparative apathy of the New England people. We look with wonder on communities of men who attend to their own business, and seem to care but little who is made President of the United States, or even County Commissioner."[32]

As political parties grew better organized with conventions and platforms and patronage to dispense, and party regularity became a virtue, local politics often fell under the sway of a "boss." Such a man was a Darke County, Ohio, Democrat named Andrew (Abe) Scribner. Scribner, a merchant, became leader of the local Democratic party in the 1820s and "discharged all the functions of caucuses, primary elections, and nominating conventions; those he allowed to run for office ran and were elected, and those he forbade had to keep shady and hold the peace."[33] Scribner had inherited the mantle of another power broker, Archibald Bryson, who began his career with his election to county commissioner in 1816, followed by a second two-year term. During his reign, "his influence and opinions as to men and measures served more than that of any other man to direct and control public action, and it may be said that this influence was exercised honestly and judiciously."[34] With the passing of Scribner from the scene in the 1840s, no one man dominated Darke County politics without the aid of "rings and cliques," according to the local historian.

Equality of opportunity and the absence of a moneyed oligarchy marked the politics of the pioneer West, for all its crude excesses and corruption. It was the politics of frontier democracy, reflecting a fluid, heterogeneous society that glorified the self-made man—"men who have fitted themselves for the emergencies into which they are thrown,"[35] as an article in the *New Englander* put it.

Both politics and trials provided opportunities for spectacle and entertainment, as well as government. Communal labors were another occasion for socializing, copious eating and drinking, and amusement. This was a tradition that traced back to early New England, where "raisings" provided a welcome excuse for unpuritanical license, as well as an occasion for helping one's neighbor. The festive aspects carried over in the West, with men and women gathering from all over the area—the men to work and the women to help cook a huge meal, which, accompanied by plenty of hard cider and whiskey, the host provided in symbolic payment. Among the pioneers, such occasions multiplied; they eased the curse of loneliness and satisfied the hunger for amusements. Thus there were cornhuskings for both sexes and quilting bees, fulling parties, apple parings, maple sugar boilings, rag cuttings, carpet tackings, wool pickings, chicken and goose pluckings—primarily for the women; for men only, in addition to logrollings, barnraisings, and harvests, there were pest hunts, wood choppings, stump burnings, militia musters. Husking became a competition, punctuated by raucous gaiety. After leaders were appointed, two sides chosen and the corn divided into two equal piles on the barn floor, the competition commenced: "The yells of defiance, mingled with whoops and yells in Indian style, arose in one continued medley, and reverberated far through the air. . . . Shortly after the commencement, there were some new arrivals, toward whom the tide of vociferation was directed. "Come along, Andy—go ahead—whoop, here's the major—halloo, major, graze it—well done, *Kurnel,*—look at him—see how he cuts gravel—whoop, halloo."[36] Cornhuskings also provided an occasion for the younger folk to do their courting. Whoever found a red ear won the right to kiss a member of the opposite sex of the their choice. After the corn was shucked, supper was served, followed by a barn dance. Then the boys and girls bent on courting paired off to go home.

Amusements were little different in the towns that were growing up—really clusters of log cabins scarcely distinguishable from the countryside. Social distinctions were nonexistent. People dressed as the rural folk did; the men in linsey-woolsey worked and argued, wrestled and drank, and the women in their plain homespun did chores, shopped, gossiped. Many town dwellers farmed plots of land on the edge of town. So depressed was the pioneer economy that a storekeeper or craftsmen often had to depend on his garden or out lot for food. Everybody, whether lawyer or blacksmith or storekeeper or dirt farmer, mingled in full equality. (A New England visitor, Dr. Zerah Hawley, did, however, notice a penchant for titles among the pioneers he met on his travels. Nearly every man, it seemed to him, was called judge, squire, senator, colonel, or major. Whether the honorifics were legitimate he could not say; however, it is probable that frontier inflation devalued considerably the social worth such titles had had in early New England.) A founding elder of Mount Vernon, Ohio, recalled that "the early settlers in the town all felt as one family. If one got a piece of fresh meat, he shared it with his neighbors, and when a person was sick, all sympathized. At night, they met in one anothers' cabins, to talk, dance, and take a social glass. There was no distinction of party, for it was a social democracy."[37] Effete manners and "stuckuppity" dress were regarded with bemusement or hostility. In 1824 a Crawfordsville, Indiana, man observed that "society here, at this time, seems almost entirely free from the taint of aristocracy. The only premonitory symptoms of that disease, most prevalent generally in old-settled communities, were manifested last week, when John I. Foster bought a new pair of silverplated spurs, and N. T. Catterlin was seen walking up street with a pair of curiously embroidered gloves on his hands."[38]

Actually, as these "premonitory symptoms" of the "disease" of social distinction indicated, the townspeople inevitably set themselves on a course that would put distance between them and the rural pioneer ways. As some townsmen grew more prosperous, their social life grew more citified; with increased leisure time masquerades and balls replaced huskings and raisings and dances on puncheon floors. The women doffed their homespun in favor of imported silks and satins, while the men wore broadcloth and beaver hats instead of buckskin. The pioneer amusements were still practiced—in 1837 the Piqua, Ohio, *Courier and Enquirer* observed that the townspeople still liked "to recur to the pastimes of our ancestors"[39]—but it was in the spirit of fun and nostalgia, stripped of any connection with necessary work. The old pioneers still alive no doubt observed the rise of town society with mixed emotions and turned their eyes to what now seemed the happy past. The elegiac remarks of one old fellow to Henry Howe were typical of this attitude: "What little aristocratic feeling any one might have brought with him was soon quelled, for we soon found ourselves equally dependent upon one another; and we enjoyed our winter evenings around our blazing hearths in our log huts cracking nuts full as well aye! much better than has fallen to our lots since the distinctions and animosities consequent upon the acqusition of wealth have crept in among us."[40]

Not that there wasn't leisure in the early pioneer town—not that there wasn't indolence, for that matter—but manners were rough, amusements were simple and self-generated. There was, of course, a hunger for culture among those who had had a taste for it back east, and such books as they had been able to bring along were read and reread hungrily, and lent to others. A few towns even started subscription libraries. The most famous of these was the coonskin library in Athens County, Ohio, so named because its books were purchased with the proceeds of pelts the people had trapped. There was a host of pioneer poets, whose effusions appeared in the newspapers, but their work was at best derivative and self-consciously literary. The average pioneer townsman's leisure pursuits consisted of such things as sitting around the country store gossiping or talking politics, visiting (which was popularly done by a family en masse after considerable preparation), dances, weddings, (featuring much eating and drinking, playing the customary pranks on the bride and groom—the shivaree—and dancing on puncheon floors; often guests from afar would simply sleep on their host's cabin floor), and public occasions such as trials, hangings, barbecues, rallies, and militia musters. The women had their separate social sphere, usually work sessions which were a chance for gossip, the gossip being almost as much the reason for the get-togethers as the work. The men had their own pleasures—the hunt, footraces, politics, cockfighting, wrestling, beef shoots (shooting at targets with the winner being awarded the hide and the tallow, the runner-up the choicest portion of meat, and so on down the line), gander pulling (a gander was greased, hung from a tree limb by its feet, and the contestants rode full-speed at the hapless bird, attempting to snap off its head), horse racing (both impromptu and organized), snipehunting, and practical jokes. The frontiersman's penchant for settling disputes by fighting has been remarked, but he might also wrestle for the sheer hell of it. A match might be triggered at a gathering of men by the simple challenge, "Who's the best man?" As one historian described it: "Neat clothing, correct speech and a gentlemanly bearing were often a sufficient provocation to the bully who had a distaste for these effeminacies, and lacking these he could, without departing too widely from recognized custom, 'renown it' by drawing a circle about himself with a stick and defying anyone to enter the territory thus claimed; or sometimes, after loading up with whisky, he essayed to terrorize a town, profanely swearing he could 'whup' the best man or all men in it, till some one accommodated him."[41]

Although purely for sport, wrestling matches were governed by a rough set of rules which insured a fair fight and a minimum of mayhem. Sometimes there was "bad blood," however, or the contestants lost their tempers; then the contest continued until the victor gouged out his opponent's eyes (some rougher sorts deliberately cultivated long, horny thumbnails, sharpened for added effectiveness). Generally, though, the fight would end when one man threw or pinned another and he shouted "nuff."

Another manly occasion was the militia muster, when the local defenders of women and children against the skulking Red Man turned to for periodic drills. Although the Indians had been pretty well evicted from the Old Northwest with the Black Hawk War of 1832, the militia musters continued, and judging from contemporary accounts, they were mainly an occasion for drinking, wrestling, and some desultory marching about. The pioneer was not one to cotton to military discipline anyhow, that being the very antithesis of his antiauthoritarian outlook. So what drills there were were a shambles, as a contemporary description of a muster in Sangamon County, Illinois, shows:

> Certainly there are few more ridiculous scenes than a military muster under the present (dis)order of things. Several hundred men formed in what is called a *line* (although it can hardly be called a straight, and as little a curved, or any other known mathematical line) in every variety of posture and position—some sitting, some lying, some standing on one foot, some on both, and well-spread at that; equipped, too, or non-equipped, with every variety of coat and shirt sleeves, and every variety of weapon, among the latter, however, the corn-stalk, the umbrella and riding whip predominating almost to uniformity; every man grumbling and thinking the time wholly thrown away; some impatient for the grog-shop, and some for the horse race, and some to attend to their business—certainly there is very little of the military in this display![42]

An officer became so incensed at his slovenly command that he threw his hat on the ground and shouted, "Gentlemen! form a line, and keep it, or I will thrash the whole company!"[43] The men formed the line.

When they were not occupied with ostensibly military exercises, the men whiled away the muster day with drinking and fighting. One Ohioan recalled that every muster day was marked by the spectacle of at least thirty men with their shirts off, either fighting or standing by to insure that a friend's brawl was a fair one.

The camp meeting was another popular mass assemblage, part self-improvement, part pleasure. These gatherings were convened in clearings in the woods or on the side of a hill, under the aegises of traveling evangelists. They were held out of doors because of the paucity of churches in pioneer times, one of which, in any case, would have hardly been large enough to hold the crowds of men, women, and children who streamed in from miles around to attend. Lasting for two or threee days, the camp meetings provided ample occasion for picnicking, gossip, and flirtation, as well as saving souls. Those pilgrims who were serious, however, came fully intending to flaunt publicly their fallen state and receive remission and a fresh infusion of the Spirit from the preacher. The presiding divines were, typically, unlettered, ignorant men whose only qualification was a self-ascribed "call" and a talent for religious demagogy.

The meetings reached their apotheosis each night as the great bonfires cast their light like dancing imps against trees robed in funereal black shadows. The hoarse, ranting voices of the preachers proclaimed the miseries of hell and the ecstasies of heaven to transfixed audiences, writhing in terror and guilt. Those moved by the spirit hysterically confessed their sins and were led to the penitents' pen—a fenced area spread with straw—where they received spiritual aftercare. A common testimonial to the preacher's power was the phenomenon known as "the jerks," which caused people in the throes of religious possession—or a species of hysteria—to shake and quiver violently, then fall to the ground in a dead faint. The number of such "fallings" was sometimes calculated to provide a quantitative measure of the success of a camp meeting. Women possessed would shake their long hair with such force that it made a loud snapping noise.

Whatever darker emotions—including repressed sexuality—and sincere awe it unleashed, the camp meeting served as an emotional catharsis for many, a chance for these simple, unlettered people, many of whom lived in conditions of great loneliness, to dissolve their terrors in a bath of divine love, as well as to exorcise their guilts and darker thoughts. For others of more tepid temperament, a camp meeting was a social occasion with virtuous overtones, uniting them in good fellowship under the skies; for the young, their blood warmed by the oratory, it was an opportunity to steal away beneath the trees and unite in a more directly carnal fashion. At any rate the camp meeting was a harmless, even inspirational, pastime if not indulged in to excess; there were reported cases of people who "got delirium" and went mad and of others who died while in the throes of their religious convulsions.

Death was a commonplace of frontier life, occurring with dismaying frequency; it was an event that, for all its familiarity, unlocked dark terrors. The flash of hope that religion provided, the ecstasy of conversion—washing one's thoughts clear of dark broodings, bathing oneself in an experience of divine forgiveness—were a welcome respite from frontier life. The preachers themselves were the bumpkinish epigoni of Jonathan Edwards and the other intellectual New England divines who led the New Light movement. The camp meetings were a theater at once of the aspiring and the darker sides of the pioneer temperament, both normally sublimated in a drive to conquer nature.

The pioneers' diversions were outgrowths of their main task of subsisting, of wresting a living and eventually a profit from the raw land. Like their clothes, pioneer pastimes were simple and handmade, part work and part play. Even the men's sport occupied skills that on other occasions were converted to the necessities of life—hunting, fishing, fighting. It was only after the pioneer stage had run its course that amusements became purely social and decorative, divorced from function, in the towns. But for this to occur, a town economy that provided a surplus of time and money for leisure had to be established. Until there were sufficient farmers in the area producing a surplus for export, making sufficient money to buy the town's goods and services, the town would remain a tiny hamlet, a few families clustered together. The towns were rooted in the soil, dependent upon the growth of the agrarian economy that nourished them. But that growth could only occur with access to eastern markets.

The basic economic facts of the pioneer life were: a shortage of money; a shortage of labor (on the frontier labor was in a sense capital); and a shortage of markets for produce. In the pioneer stage, the economy was a congeries of isolated, self-sufficient family farms and cottage industries. Little was bought and sold; barter was prevalent. If a man produced any surplus, he could only sell it to another person in the area—a newcomer, say, whose first corn crop hadn't come in yet, or a traveler passing through—at depressed prices. Henry Howe tells of wheat at 25 cents a bushel—when a buyer could be found at that price. One farmer offered ten bushels to a storekeeper for a pound of tea—and was refused. Another cleared fifty-five acres of land and brought in his first crop; he was able to sell only a small quantity of this to a traveler passing through for 12.5 cents a bushel as horse feed and fed the rest to his cattle. Still another farmer exchanged an entire ox wagon-load of corn, which he had transported eight miles, for three yards of satin from which his wife could make pantaloons.

And of course before the land would produce, it had to be cleared. This was a laborious, time-consuming process; the trees had to be felled or girdled, and then the corn planted in the cleared place, often amongst the stumps, which eventually would be burned out. Girdling involved stripping the tree's bark so that it would eventually die—an easier method than chopping the tree down, but since it took a tree eight to ten years to die, a long-range measure. For one man to clear a single acre of land was a job of three weeks. It was a matter of six or seven years before the settler had himself a decent-sized farm and was able to replace his rude log cabin with a more permanent house that had hewn logs, puncheon floors, a brick chimney, and perhaps glass windows to replace the paper dipped in bear's grease originally used.

Once he had his crop in, the new settler's most urgent need was for a "corn cracker," or gristmill, to grind his corn into the meal that his wife would make into corn dodgers and pone, the pioneer's bread (lacking an oven, she cooked these before the open fire). Often he had to haul his grain fifty or sixty miles to the nearest mill. Or he ground it himself on a hominy block—a mortar hollowed out of a tree stump—or with a hand mill known as a "sweat mill" because it took two hours' labor to produce a single day's supply for one person.

In their first winter on their new land, a family lived off their "capital"—whatever flour and other food they had brought with them—supplemented by game and wild fruit gathered in the woods. They had literally no bread on the table, and even if they had sufficient food otherwise, they retained a voracious craving for it. The children were told to imagine the slices of wild turkey breast on their plates were bread. The more ingenious cooks made a kind of acorn-flour bread, but nothing could really substitute for this basic item in the diet. Little wonder then that grain was the farmer's first priority; as soon as he had built his cabin, the pioneer cleared his small plot.

After the hunting and subsistence farming came the "hog and hominy" stage. Corn and hogs were best adapted to pioneer conditions. As one settler put it: "The great West would have settled slowly without *corn* and *hogs.* A bushel of wheat will produce, at the end of ten months, fifteen or twenty bushels; a bushel of corn, at the end of five months, 400 bushels. . . . Our horned cattle do not double in a year; hogs, in the same time, increase twenty fold."[44] Wheat did poorly in unprepared soil and was best planted where another crop had been raised. Otherwise the farmer got "sick wheat," which, if eaten, caused stomach upsets; even hogs, with their deserved reputation as four-legged garbage disposals, would not touch it. Corn was easier to grow, and the first crop was often put in by making a cleft in the soil with an ax and dropping the seed in. Even when ploughed, the early fields were minimally cultivated, so that there were almost as many weeds as cornstalks. A man could also take his time harvesting his corn crop—it was said to take one man a full winter to harvest, shuck, and grind ten acres of corn—while wheat had to be harvested immediately, which could be a problem in a labor-short economy. Neighbors might help, of course, but they might have wheat of their own to harvest. Wheat grew more rapidly, however; it took only twenty-four days from planting to harvest, while corn required forty days. Initially the farmer might produce from 10 to 300 bushels of corn per acre; with improved methods his yield might increase to 60, and the richest land yielded 100 to 120 bushels an acre. As for livestock, hogs could feed on acorns, wild potatoes, and other mast in the forests, while cattle required grass and grazing space (though they could, of course, forage in the woods); as a result, the latter were generally raised in quantity by a few baronial landholders rather than the average pioneer on his quarter section.

Better techniques and machinery were obvious needs of the western farms. Farm journals and articles on improved agricultural methods began appearing from the earliest days, and there were always a few enlightened farmers interested in scientific methods. But the average farmer took to such knowledge slowly and had a distrust of any information that had to be conveyed by the written word (assuming he could read, which many couldn't). As one farmer put it, "I reckon I know as much about farming as the printers do."[45] Cultivation methods often exhausted the soil, and many farmers did not practice rotation with replenishing crops such as alfalfa. Without markets the pioneer farmer had no strong incentive to overfarm, but this would come. The farmer was often heavily in debt with high interest charges and carried a heavy tax burden—disproportionately so compared with the large absentee landowners who did not improve their land, and thus did not pay their fair share. Still, interest in better farming methods and conservation existed, as shown by the increasing number of articles on scientific farming in the magazines, the burgeoning agricultural societies, and state and county fairs, descendants of the harvest home festivals in England. The first agricultural society was organized in Vincennes, Indiana, in 1809, and the first fairs began locally in the 1830s, with the first state fair being held in 1849 near Detroit. "High farming"—scientific farming for high yields—came into vogue, but the steep prices for machinery held the small farmer back.

Improved farming implements first began to appear in the 1830s. John Deere's self-scouring moldboard plough became indispensable in the Grand Prairie of Central Indiana and Illinois; the black loamy prairie soil stuck to the old-type ploughs. Prairie land presented other problems: Water collected in the sloughs, or "slashes" as they were known, and the thick, matted root systems of the prairie grass were difficult to break through (enormous breaking ploughs drawn by teams of up to eighteen oxen were used). Add to this the absence of trees for building cabins and for firewood, and it is obvious why early pioneers avoided the prairies, and why huge sections of them were later bought up by large land speculators who farmed them with tenant labor. Significantly, where these large holdings predominated, towns were few and scattered. Although we have concentrated on the idealized pioneer—the small freeholder—the tenant farmer became an increasingly significant class in the forties and fifties and remained so into the twentieth century. By the same token the landlord class waxed powerful in local politics, while objections to absentee landlords—who did not develop their land or who overfarmed it for maximum profits, while charging their tenants exorbitant rents—were recurrently raised in the West. The speculators' large holdings were land monopolies deliberately withheld from the market, thus preventing settlement by small independent farmers on the best land. These speculators also extracted from settlers prices two or more times higher than the government land price, thus foiling the purpose of the land laws, which was to provide opportunity for the average man. Local fortunes were made from farming these large holdings, but the majority of them were poorly managed and eventually fell apart. Aside from discouraging the growth of towns and viable local government, another effect of these large holdings was to stimulate emigration farther west by the tenant who could not pay exorbitant rack rents and who maintained the driving dream of working for himself.

Larger farms, whether speculator-owned or not, produced more efficiently, but required improved equipment and, eventually, mechanization. Improved ploughs had utility in the pioneer's bottomland and enabled him to farm more intensively and cover a greater area, thus producing the surplus for export necessary to support a town. Mechanical reapers and threshers increased the farmer's ambit even more and assisted the transition out of the hog-and-hominy subsistence economy. McCormick's reaper was first produced in 1831, but the early model employed eight men and ten horses and could harvest only ten acres a day—about what the same quantity of labor could accomplish by hand. It would be fifteen years before McCormick's reaper was perfected and produced on a large scale.

Threshing machines of a cumbersome stationary type started appearing in the West along the National Road in the 1830s, and eventually the traveling thresher became a familiar sight on country lanes. Drawn by six strong horses, it caused excitement in the new land, as one newspaper account of its advent shows:

> Driven by a rollicking country Jehu, and fed by an expert—the bundles being thrown upon the band-cutter's table from a wagon driven besides the thresher—[it] came rattling and rumbling along the great road on a display trip, scattering straw and chaff to the disgust of the townspeople and the great delight of the pigs, chickens, and little children, and closely followed by the inevitable fanning mill peddler with his newly painted wind-raisers, [while] the rural heart beat high and happily, and the agricultural statisticians figured out big profits for those who should thereafter cultivate cereals in the wheat belt of Ohio and Indiana.[46]

Such machinery would revolutionize farming in the West by making it practical to cultivate sufficient acreage for the farm to be profitable. If it is true that most of the independent farmers in the region had more than a little bit of the speculator in them, it followed that they would buy up as much land as they could, often going into debt to do so, and more than they could farm on their own with traditional tools. The average independent farmer, it was said, owned a spread of about two hundred acres, which, although it was large enough to make money on, was difficult to cultivate without hired hands or labor-saving devices (one answer, of course, was to have a large family). So until the farmers expanded their operation sufficiently to fill their claims, the region remained economically backward, and the growth of towns was slow.

The shortage of money also inhibited the economic growth of the West. Nearly everyone was short of capital, from big speculator to small freeholder, and nearly everybody was in debt. If the farmer could not get up the cash to pay off his debts—a chronic condition among many of them—he was subject to foreclosure. Add to this burden the depressed state of farm prices, and it is easy to understand why the West was traditionally opposed to the restrictive fiscal policies of the National Bank and was generally Jacksonian Democratic because of Old Hickory's anti-Bank views. The condition of the average pioneer farmer was expressed by the recollections of an Athens County, Ohio, man: "So scarce was money that I can hardly remember seeing a piece of coin [silver and gold coins were frequently split up into eights because of their scarcity] till I was a well-grown boy. It was with difficulty we obtained enough to pay our taxes with and buy tea for mother—as for clothes or other things we either depended on the forests for them, or bartered for them, or did without."[47]

Barter—and credit—was the expediency the pioneer merchants adopted to keep the wheels of commerce, such as they were, turning. The most prevalent such transaction was at the gristmill. The miller simply took a portion of the grain he had ground as payment. The general storekeepers followed suit, exchanging the poor and scanty stock of goods on their shelves for grain and just about any other product of field or forest. The wide variety of things accepted in trade is suggested by this advertisement for an Ohio store in the early days: "Low for cash, or in exchange for wheat, rye, corn, pork, butter, feathers, rags, calf and deer skins, fur skins, buck horns, ginseng, bees wax, etc."[48] Ginseng—or "sang" as it was popularly known—was a popular cash crop. A man-shaped root, which was dried and ground up into a powder with supposed medicinal uses, it grew wild, and many a pioneer family used it to supplement the other produce it raised. Another commodity the farmer could produce was corn whiskey, which was more easily transportable than grain (a horse could carry only four bushels of corn but it could carry the equivalent of twenty-four bushels in the form of forty-eight gallons of the clear, fiery liquid). Whiskey was also a more salable commodity, given the pioneer's legendary thirst; it was taken not only as an inebriant but also as a medicine and as a stimulant or fatigue-deadener when performing hard labor—the pioneer equivalent of the Chinese railroad worker's opium and the Bolivian peasant's coca leaves.

The hog-and-hominy economy worked well enough within its limitations. Nobody grew rich, but nobody starved, and supplemented by homecrafts and hunting, it eenabled the pioneer to live pretty well at just above the subsistence level—hence the intense nostalgia the old pioneers would have for the old days when all were equal and none cared for riches and finery and material things. Under such a system nearly everyone grew enough for his family, and the few artisans and shopkeepers had their food grown for them, in exchange for the goods and services they provided. Such a system could support only a limited number of nongrowers, however. Which is to say it could not support towns of any size. By the same token, a barter economy could not consume any large surplus—that had to be sold elsewhere.

So the typical pioneer town consisted of a few cabins huddled together. A gristmill, tavern, or store usually formed the nucleus of such towns; there were often a number of craftsmen—a blacksmith, a tanner, a cooper, a wheelwright and cabinetmaker (who made spinning wheels, wagon wheels, and furniture), a hatmaker, a cobbler—and perhaps a doctor and a lawyer. When it achieved any size at all, the town would have a post office, and of course if it was a county-seat designate, there would be a rude log courthouse and adjoining jail—but that was the extent of a governmental presence. Education was not generally regarded as a necessity, but there might be a one-room subscription school, paid for by fees from the parents and holding classes about three months out of the year. Nor would there be a church, although one of the hardy circuit-riding Methodist preachers would arrive at irregular intervals to hold services in a private home, and missionaries of other faiths passed through as well. The town may have been platted, or shortly would be, by the man who had title to the land; but the existence of a plat did not imply neatly laid-out houses and lots along regular streets. Rather, there would be a bunch of log cabins scattered about like children's toys along muddy, rutted, or dusty (depending on the season), public pathways in and around which cows and hogs freely wandered. Of course, there were exceptions to this type of settlement. The settlers of Galesburg, Illinois, for example, lived in temporary shelters away from their townsite until they had amassed sufficient lumber to build fine frame houses on the site. But most towns grew haphazardly, with frame houses coexisting alongside log cabins.

The transition out of the barter economy was a difficult but necessary one for obvious reasons. Drastic, jerry-built measures to inject more cash into circulation were tried, mainly the encouragement of state and private banks with the power to issue notes of credit. But these institutions were unstable, often chartered by a group of stockholders who put up mere pledges to pay rather than actual money. They loaned far in excess of their liquid assets to land speculators, who in turn redeemed the notes for land and borrowed some more. Anyone could set up a bank and did; such enterprise fitted in with the speculative temperament of the West. A circuit-riding minister described the bank fever that overtook Ohio in the 1820s: "A money mania seemed to have seized, like an epidemic, the entire people. Everybody went to banking. Within the bounds of our circuit there were no less than nine banking establishments, seven of them within the county of Jefferson, and one of them said to have been kept in a lady's chest. . . . But it did not stop here. Tavern-keepers, merchants, butchers, bakers—every body seemed to have become bankers. This fever not only raged in this vicinity, but throughout the entire west."[49]

The currency of such banks passed through wild fluctuations in value; it was "cheap money" with a vengeance—so cheap it was often worthless. A reaction set in, and the states attempted to regulate the local banks. An even greater blow was delivered by the Jacksonian hard-money economists. The West awoke to find that its generous support of Jackson had boomeranged. Land sales plummeted, and a severe depression set in. Jackson's successor, Martin Van Buren, did liittle, and in 1840 voters turned to the Whigs, the party of the eastern capitalists who with a shrewd political cynicism nominated the hero of the West, William Henry Harrison. The Whigs threw in measures popular in the West, such as high tariffs and internal improvements, and won the election. Harrison, an aging Cincinnatus lured from his Ohio farm, who died after one month in office, was a political neuter whose chief virtues were military prowess, a certain nobility of temperament, and an absence of political enemies.

National politics would do little to solve the fiscal problems of the West (indeed unsound policies back east in Washington and on Wall Street would trigger national panics which the West suffered as fully as did the rest of the country). Only trade would bring money into the region, and trade depended upon access to the eastern markets. Beginning in the 1820s, the main efforts of western visionaries were dedicated to forging transportation links to the East, while, concomitantly, the eastern businessmen became increasingly aware of the western population as a market for their manufactured goods.

The early settlers of the Northwest Territory had crossed the formidable mountain barriers that separated it from the East and had drifted down the broad highway of the Ohio or had tramped on Indian traces through the forest. But the Ohio flowed westward toward its junction with the Mississippi, and until the advent of steamboat travel (inaugurated by the voyage of the *New Orleans* in 1811) sailing upstream was impossible. The coming of the National Road helped but was only a bare beginning. Ohio men hauled their grain in great wagons to market at a high cost in money and time; cattle and the tough, little razorback hogs had to be driven all the way to the slaughterhouse on foot.

In Illinois and Indiana, where the road system was largely forest trails, the journey east was even more prohibitive, and the farmers looked south, to the port of New Orleans at the mouth of the great Mississippi. The usual method was for a man to build a large skiff or flat-bottom boat on the shore of a river or creek, load it up at high water with his corn, flour, bacon, or whatever he had to trade, and let himself be borne downstream into the surging brown waters of the Mississippi. Assuming he successfully negotiated the snags and sandbars and treacherous currents, he arrived in New Orleans, there to meet a hazard in human form—the traders who hung about the docks ready to cheat him of a fair price. If the dockside sharpers didn't get most of his money, the gaming tables at Natchez might; or if he virtuously passed these by, he still had to walk back through Indian country. New Orleans was largely a local market in those days, and there was stiff competition from farmers in the area. The market became glutted in season and prices plummeted. And the length of the journey meant that farms lay neglected while their owners were in transit and would produce nothing the next year.

New Orleans was clearly an unsatisfactory outlet for western goods, until the heyday of the paddle-wheel steamboats in the 1840s and 50s made the city an important transit point for middle western produce being shipped by coastal steamer to Baltimore and New York. It was estimated that in the 1830s most of the West's wheat, wool, and hemp went east, but 70 percent of the flour, practically all of the corn, pork and whiskey, and 87 percent of the tobacco went to New Orleans. Dissatisfaction with the port remained, but there was little alternative. Historians doubt, however, that the New Orleans trade returned any significant amounts of money to the currency-starved West. And since merchants got most of their manufactured goods from the East, it was more sensible economically to link up with that region directly. A water route was the most feasible in the 1820s and there were two possibilities: up the Ohio River by steamboat to Pittsburgh and then overland to

Baltimore and Philadelphia; or across Lake Erie by schooner to Buffalo then overland to Albany and down the Hudson to the port of New York.

The state of New York turned out to be the most enterprising. Its visionary governor, De Witt Clinton, caused a canal to be built between Buffalo and Albany at a cost of $13 million. Completed in 1825, the Erie Canal linked Cleveland in Ohio with the Hudson River and eventually New York.

The successs of the Erie Canal touched off a canal mania in Ohio; there had been proposals for canals as early as 1817, and in 1825 an enabling act was passed that authorized the state to borrow money to build two canals. The Miami Canal was projected to connect Cincinnati and Dayton, and the Ohio Canal would join Portsmouth on the Ohio River with Cleveland on Lake Erie. Soon two thousand laborers were at work digging the Ohio Canal. Part of the work force was immigrants—Irish and Germans mostly—many of whom came straight off the Erie Canal project; but local labor was also involved. Farmers mainly, they hired out as subcontractors and dug the portion of the canal that passed through their lands. Contracts were let for 110 such sections south of Portage Summit alone, and over six thousand bids were submitted. Laborers worked twelve-hour days for fifteen dollars a month. The prescribed dimensions of Ohio's big ditch were at least six feet deep with sloping banks twenty-six feet wide at the base and forty feet wide at the top. The water was four feet deep, and there were ten-foot-wide towpaths on either side, for the horses or oxen which would pull the big boats. Such dimensions hint at the onerousness of the task. The land twenty feet on either side of the ditch had to be cleared of all stumps. Locks had to be constructed (there was a four-hundred-foot difference in elevation between Akron and Cleveland alone); rivers and streams that were part of the route had to be widened and deepened; the banks had to be lined with pavement or loose stone to prevent erosion. The entire canal was constructed of dirt, wood, and stone, without the benefit of concrete or steel. The huge project tied up the credit of the state, the labor of many of its people, and the hopes of all of them. When the Cincinnati-Dayton waterway—the Miami Canal—was opened in 1829, and the Ohio Canal in 1830, the jubilation was pandemic.

The celebrating started as soon as ground was broken and was sustained over the completion of each section of the canal. When a segment of the Miami Canal was ready in 1827, a huge crowd turned out to witness the water being let in; unfortunately the amount mustered for the occasion was sufficient only to dampen the bed. When the section of Ohio Canal from Portage Summit to Cleveland was completed, Governor Allen Trimble and his party boarded the packet *State of Ohio* on July 3, 1827, and proceeded to Cleveland, where they were met by a cheering crowd, after which there was a parade, banqueting, prayers, and oratory.

Governor Clinton himself did the honors at the ground-breaking ceremony held on July 4, 1825, at Licking Summit south of Cleveland, and it was he who perhaps expressed best the pride that Ohioans had in their canals. After turning over a shovelful of earth and listening to the orator of the day, Thomas Ewing, perorate about "the grand work, which is this day begun, . . . the effort of our infant state, yet in the cradle of her prosperity,"[50] the governor rose and advised the ten thousand people assembled what every Ohioan should be saying to himself:

> See what my country has done in her juvenile state! And if she has achieved this gigantic enterprise in infancy, what will she not effect in the maturity of her strength, when her population becomes exuberant and her whole territory in full cultivation. And your sister states, and the civilized world, will be astonished. It will exhibit a spectacle, unprecedented and amazing. An infant wielding the club of Hercules, and managing the lever of Archimedes with irresistible power. When the eagle, in its first flight from the aerie soars to the heavens, looks at the sun with an unfailing eye and bears in its talons the thunderbolts of Jove, who will not admire this sublime sight.[51]

It is unlikely that the average Ohio farmer went forth to his fields muttering to himself about the club of Hercules and the lever of Archimedes, let alone the thunderbolts of Jove. Instead, he may have been doing a few sums and anticipating some profits. For economically, the canals were a boon to all within range of them. A few figures will demonstrate: Shipping by wagon to New York cost $25 a ton; shipping by canal lowered the cost to $3 a ton. Flour sold for only $3.50 a barrel in Cincinnati ($1 a barrel in the panic of 1819); but in New York it was $8 a barrel. The opening up of the eastern market also meant a quick rise in prices in Ohio. Corn and wheat prices in interior Ohio doubled between 1825 and 1832. Higher prices meant higher land values; land values in Newark, Ohio, rose 50 percent the moment the Ohio Canal was started; towns sprang up along the projected route—Akron being a notable example—while Cleveland became a city. Finally, the canals lowered the cost of goods imported from the East, thus righting the West's balance of trade with the East. The all-water route from New York to Dayton lowered costs of imported goods by two thirds.

Soon the low-slung, ungainly barges were plying the waterways loaded to the gunwhales with goods—wheat, stone, coal, wool, and homespun in greatest volume; followed by pig iron, lumber, ashes, flour, butter, lard, pork, cheese, tobacco, and whiskey. The canal brought industry too; coal from the mines near Youngstown could now be cheaply shipped to Cleveland. The city's first ironworks was built in 1840, starting her on the road to industrialization.

All told, between 1825 and 1840 the western states spent $125 million on three thousand miles of canals. But even as Illinois and Indiana were breaking ground for their own canals (with somewhat spottier success than Ohio;

these states ran athwart money problems and they lacked the natural routes that Ohio had), the bell was tolling for canals—a locomotive bell as it happened. News of experiments with such locomotives as the *Tom Thumb* and the *Stourbridge Lion* elicited a buzz of enthusiastic comment from western editors' pens. The idea that *rail roads*, whether with horse-drawn carriages or with steam engines, were the solution to the West's transportation problems became a commonly accepted article of faith even before they were tried.

In the vanguard of prorailroad opinion were the large absentee landowners (who saw them as a faster way to increase property values than canals, which served limited areas) and the newspapers, which also had a stake in land sale advertisements—as well as mortgage foreclosure notices. One editor contemplated with groveling awe the vision of a single railroad joining the Atlantic Ocean to the Mississippi River. "We suspect this to be the most magnificent project that was ever proposed, in the sober conviction of practicability, in any age or country. It actually made our head ache, to stretch our thoughts from one extremity of this proposed chain to the other," wrote Timothy Flint, editor of the *Western Monthly Review* in 1829.[52]

The main argument for railroads was the horrendous condition of most of the existing roads in the West. The National Road was macadamized and comparatively passable, but experiments with corduroy roads had failed because the planks rotted and fell apart after a few years. Otherwise rock-strewn, rutted, stump-filled dirt roads which turned into quagmires in the spring were the rule. (In the 1820s, Cleveland boasted that its gravelly soil meant that its streets needn't be paved; ten years later, when the Ohio Canal made the little village a boomtown, the streets were paved.) Traveling by stagecoach could be a species of refined torture for the traveler who was jounced about mercilessly, often had to get out to push the coach free from a mire, and rarely arrived on time. The Reverend Isaac Reed, a widely traveled Presbyterian missionary, described his journey by stagecoach on the clay road between Columbus and Sandusky in the 1830s. They were caught in a pouring rain which cascaded through the doors; the drain on the coach's floor was clogged, and so water sloshed over the passengers' feet throughout the journey. Saying that it had taken the coach seven hours to cover twenty-three miles, Reverend Reed lamented: "All that had been intimated about bad roads now came upon me. They were not only bad, they were intolerable; they were rather like a stony ditch than a road. The horses on the first stages could only walk most of the way; we were frequently in up to the axle-tree, and I had no sooner recovered from a terrible plunge on one side than there came another in the opposite direction. I was literally thrown about like a ball."[53]

The roads were so awful that the westerners sometimes took a perverse pride in them, making them the subject of tall tales. On one road, it was said, a team of horses drowned in a mudhole. And the story was told of a man who was proceeding along a road when he spied a fine beaver hat in the middle of a large puddle. He waded out, at considerable risk, to retrieve it, only to discover when he plucked up the hat that there was a man under it. When he started calling for help, the man protested, "Just leave me alone, stranger, I have a good horse under me, and have just found bottom."[54] (This story was told widely and also applied to city streets.) It was also said, whether apocryphally or not, that people who lived along the road took a proprietary interest in nearby mudholes because of the money they could make extricating stuck travelers; they were even said to water their holes in dry weather. And it was reported that a tavern keeper who was selling out included his interest in a formidable local mudhole in the deal.

Like towns, the first roads grew up more or less naturally along Indian trails and migratory routes. Among the initial actions of the county commissioners or township trustees in newly settled areas was provision for roads, which they contracted for with private parties who built and maintained them and charged tolls. Similarly the county fathers licensed private ferry-operators who collected fares. Bridges were usually financed by individuals or stock subscriptions, rather than out of town or county funds. So roads grew up rather haphazardly, wherever the biggest profit could be extracted from them. The Fountain County, Indiana, historian described how this laissez-faire system worked out in practice. "The roads were laid out from one 'improvement' to another, and from one settlement to another, without much regard being had to the future growth and development of the county. The points of the compass and dividing lines were not considered, and the roads were made to run in all directions."[55]

Although serving primarily as main trunk routes, the canals were a considerable improvement over road travel. Canal boats were slower than coaches, but not much, and were certainly smoother, although a canal trip was singularly lacking in scenic diversion since the passengers gazed out at the sloping banks for much of their journey (one could get out and walk a spell of course). Inclement weather caused no delays, and the large boats could carry a greater volume of cargo than wagons, for less money. A "line," or ordinary canalboat, made about two miles an hour and charged about two cents a mile for passengers; the luxury or packet boats had more oxen or horses pulling them and made a steady five miles an hour.

But the slow-moving, brightly painted canalboats had other drawbacks in a country that was in a hurry. You could increase literal horsepower only so much; railroads however, once friction was overcome, could increase their speed almost indefinitely—to thirty or even forty miles an hour, said the writers who had looked into the physics of the situation. Canals also froze tight in winter. Then too, even after all the canals were completed, there were still many regions in the West they did not reach. For farmers in these areas, the rivers remained the best highways of commerce, as they had been from the opening of the West. So, while large parts of Ohio established ties with the East, other parts of the country continued to follow the traditional downriver flow to the Mississippi and New Orleans. Finally, railroads were cheaper. They were cheaper to build—about 40 percent of the cost of an equivalent canal—and they were cheaper to ship on—estimates ran to the same 40 percent of canal shipping costs per hundredweight.

Of course, despite these rather telling economic arguments, railroads had their opponents. There were those who thought that traveling at twenty miles an hour would place a fatal strain on the passengers' hearts, not to mention discombobulating them in other physiological ways. It was said that they would be expensive to maintain and would last only fifteen years. One newspaper warned (prophetically it turned out) of monopolies. Railroads were also dirty and noisy and a distinct fire hazard, both to the surrounding countryside and to the passengers themselves, at least in the days of open coaches. The canal stockholders who had their own pocketbooks to look to also formed a pocket of opposition.

Such objections were only nips at the heels of Progress, for the West was bound to have its *rail roads.* State legislatures began chartering railroad companies with abandon; some of them never laid a mile of track, but most listed on their charters the state's most substantial citizens. By 1840 Ohio had its first railroad—a thirty-mile section of track belonging to the Mad River and Lake Erie road, which was chartered in 1835 to connect Springfield and Sandusky. Another venture about this time demonstrated the uncertain state of the railroad-building art. Called the Ohio Railroad, it was built entirely on stilts. To avoid the expense of grading and graveling the roadbed, the rails were fastened with iron straps to parallel rows of tall poles, which had been driven into the ground by pile drivers and cut to proper, uniform height with a circular saw. About fifteen miles of the road on stilts were built, but a portion collapsed in 1843 during a test run. The stilts stood rotting for the next half century, a reminder of a $2-million investment gone aglimmering. Such expensive failures did not daunt the railroad boosters, but it was not until the 1850s that construction was begun in earnest.

The first year of the dynamic decade saw the passage of the momentous land-grant bill by the Congress, ceding two and a half million acres of public domain land to the state of Illinois for financing the Illinois Central Railroad, linking up Cairo and the Mississippi with Chicago. During the rest of the decade more than twenty-eight million acres of land were turned over to the states to stimulate railroad building, a practice that was carried out on an even grander scale in the Far West. As a result of this boost and of the returning prosperity after the panic of 1837, railroad building boomed and the West was effectively joined to the big cities of the East. Hand in hand with construction went consolidation of the various trunk lines into east-west through lines from New York to Chicago. The latter city became the hub of eleven railroad lines and had a population of 109,000 by 1860. Now the flow of produce from the West's fertile soil was largely northeastward; nearly 90 percent of the region's corn, wheat, and flour was shipped to the East and much of this went to Europe, especially to Great Britain, which became more dependent upon middle western wheat than southern cotton. Exports of wheat to the East had grown from 2 million to 29 million bushels between 1839 and 1860; of corn, from 1 million to 24 million bushels; and of flour from 800,0000 to 5.5 million barrels. With the accelerated mechanization of farming during the Civil War, in response to a labor shortage on the farms, production rose even more, and the dependence of the British upon middle western wheat was a telling weight in the arguments against intervention on the side of the South.

Improved transportation and farming methods, the fertility of the soil, migration, and the sheer physical labor of the settlers caused the West to become the breadbasket of the nation. Subsistence farming was replaced by specialization in a single crop; the hog-and-hominy economy grew into hog and corn production on a major scale; and farmers raised crops not for themselves but for a distant, impersonal market—a market influenced by national and even international supply and demand pressures and manipulations.

Agriculture was the West's business, the foundation of its prosperity, but there was also from early times a potential for industry, which the settlers did not neglect. Thus, as early as 1811, Steubenville in eastern Ohio boasted "a steam woolen mill, an iron foundry, a paper mill, a steam flour mill, a brewery, a cotton factory, nail factory, two earthenware factories, a wool carding machine, and a tobacco factory."[56] As this list suggests, much "manufacturing" actually involved processing of raw materials—the grain, wool, cotton, wood, tobacco, clay, coal, and iron ore that abounded in the region. Unlike agriculture, industry did not provide significant exports for a long time; still it played its role in the growth of towns and cities. This can be seen in the growth of Cincinnati, which was primarily a mercantile and trading center because of its strategic location on the Ohio River. In 1815 the little river town had twenty-three cotton-spinning mills, and a woolen mill featuring a twenty-horsepower steam engine which could produce sixty yards of broadcloth a day was scheduled to open that year. By 1825 Cincinnati was a small city of sixteen thousand with a manufacturing plant that included fifteen steam engines and industry representing a capital investment of $1.8 million. By 1832 the city was the industrial capital of the West, supporting "type foundries, book binderies, machine shops, tin-plate and sheet-iron works, machine carding establishments, rope walks, coachmaking shops, saddletree factories, tanneries, tobacco factories and plow and ax shops."[57] With the coming of the canal and the economic boom of the early 1830s, Cincinnati was manufacturing machine tools including "more than 100 steam engines, about 240 cotton gins, 20 sugar mills and 22 steamboats" annually.[58]

The contribution of industry—in its broadest sense—to the growth of the average middle western town in the pre-Civil War period was much more sporadic and small-scale. Towns were not founded around an industry as a rule (as they were coming to be in New England, beginning with Lowell,

Massachusetts); the typical promoter chose his site and touted it as a transportation hub, seat of government, center of industry, or whatever interested purchasers wished it to be. The potential of the site, in terms of natural deposits such as iron and coal in the area, was of course celebrated in blue-sky language, but development of this potential was left to the enterprising man with the capital and know-how to do so.

The most common exceptions to this rule were the towns that grew up around a gristmill. Even in a subsistence economy the gristmill was a necessity, and since farmers brought their grain from miles around, the mill was, along with the crossroads, the tavern, the ford, or the bridge, a natural cynosure of a widely scattered population. Not surprisingly there were a goodly number of towns with "mill" in their names—or the surname of the miller himself. Mills were largely of two types—the horse mill and the familiar water-driven mill. Horse mills featured an upright shaft turned by the horse and attached by a system of pulleys to the grindstone. The water mills employed either undershot or overshot wheels. They were of course required to be located near a vigorously flowing steam; the stream was usually dammed and the water's flow channeled through a wooden millrace, rushing against the wheel at either top or bottom and back down the flume. Some mills grew to imposing dimensions and were constructed of stone for added solidity. If the mill prospered, a sawmill was often added to the site, followed by a general store and a blacksmith's shop. Thus was the nucleus of a village formed, and other shops and artisans followed. The blacksmith was a one-man factory in his own right, as well as a repairer of a wide variety of pioneer implements. He made nails and horseshoes for a starter, but he also fashioned chains, tires, reaphooks, bullet molds, yoke rings, axles, animal traps, files, shears, locks, keys, adzes, plowshares, hackle teeth, bits, saws, and the metal parts of a variety of implements for home and farming such as spinning wheels, looms, and flails. Expert smiths made axes and guns and, if they had additional equipment, even stoves, skillets, pots, and pans. Gun- and ax-making were the most demanding arts, because they were difficult and because these two items were the pioneer man's most highly prized tools.

The smith imported the soft bar iron or cast steel he worked with from Pittsburgh or Europe. Taking advantage of abundant iron and coal deposits in Ohio, men founded combined smelting and factory operations that were elaborations of the smith's work. Such operations did sometimes become the basis of towns. Niles, Ohio, was founded in 1806 by James Heaton (and renamed in 1834 after the *Niles' Weekly Register*, a popular western newspaper) around a combined gristmill, sawmill, and iron furnace he had erected on the banks of the Mahoning River. Heaton made the first bar of pig iron in Ohio and later began manufacturing the iron into stoves and kettles. In 1842 James Ward built three more furnaces in Niles, producing bar iron, horseshoes, tire iron, and sheet iron; Welsh ironmongers were hired to man the factory.

Youngstown was another town founded on proximity to iron ore; its first crude smelter was erected in 1802, and in 1826 a coal mine was opened, setting Youngstown on the road to becoming the steel town it is today.

Another of the early town industries was the textile mill. These employed waterpower and at first performed specialized operations such as spinning, fulling, or carding, rather than turning out finished clothing; later, assuming the mill prospered, weaving machines would be added. These mills also harnessed the power from the streams, although this was a fluctuating—depending upon the rains—and ultimately dwindling source of power. For as more settlers came in and cleared the trees, the water table lowered and the streams became shallower and more sluggish. Thus most of the old mills down by the stream gave way to steam-powered mills in the town.

Such mills more directly challenged the pioneer way of life than did the gristmills, and there were those who deplored them. Making clothing for the family and others was a major pioneer cottage industry, always done in the home by the mother, who performed all the functions of carding, spinning, and fulling herself, or with her neighbors, and turned out rough, scratchy tow linen shirts which all the little boys wore (with excruciating discomfort the first time they were put on) and linsey-woolsey garments, not to mention the clothing made from animal hides. There was something about nights snug in the cabin, mother spinning or working her loom, that touched a sentimental chord with the pioneers. "Then it was that the hum of the wheel, the noise of the loom and the flax-break made the family music of the evening, instead of the mellow, molten notes of the organ,"[59] one chronicler recalled. One mother turned out seven hundred yards of woolen cloth in a year, another as many as two thousand. The opinion of the women who did the work was not solicited, but no doubt they welcomed the carding mills which ended the laborious task of hand-carding wool.

Perhaps it was the sentimental memories of mother at the distaff, the center of the pioneer household, that caused the hog-and-hominy folks to express their disgust when manufactured clothing appeared in the stores. Governor Ford wrote that "from such were heard complaints that the spinning wheel and loom were neglected, and that all the earnings of the young people were expended in the purchase of finery."[60] Why waste money on such newfangled stuffs, the old-timers thought, when good old linsey-woolsey was all a man needed? There was also a belief that if people took to buying imported goods, all the money would flow out of the state. As for the products of local mills, the objections became both economic and moral. When a carding mill was opened in Newton Falls, Ohio, the *Chronicle* warned that "idleness is destructive to every social as well as moral principle. If family fabricks were made of better material, with more care and pride, foreign stuffs would soon be out of fashion and of course out of use."[61] By "foreign stuffs" the paper was referring to goods bought at the store; and if folks bought goods at the store *that* meant idleness at home with moral decay sure to follow.

But the younger generation won out; they wanted to look nice, even stylish (Governor Ford attributed this desire to the growing habit of church going which called for civilized finery and which, not incidentally, was an occcasion for the young unmarrieds of both sexes to display themselves to each other in their most elegant plumage). Thus the Crawfordsville, Indiana, *Record* could brag in 1831: "Our hats manufactured here are good, made quite to a point at the top like they are in the east, and our boots are square-toed. The ladies dress cap-a-pie in the costume of the east, with the exception of tight lacing."[62]

Tanneries were another local industry that replaced the cottage variety. The early pioneers turned out their own animal-skin clothing, and although such leather clothing went out of style, the tanning process was performed to make leather for shoes, harnesses, and a variety of other things. In those days tanning was a smelly business involving long soakings in lye and then manure—taking a year in all—and the quality varied drastically. Hides of wild animals were tanned as well as those of cattle, sheep, horses, and goats.

And so as the area became more thickly settled and farming left the subsistence stage, the small shops in the towns appeared, taking over functions previously performed by the farmers themselves. In the towns small businesses were engaged in making bricks and tile, furniture, candles, ropes, wagons, harnesses, saddles, earthenware and tinware, cutlery, flour, tools, farm implements, and so on. These shops could not be called factories of course; they generally employed one man or at most a few workers or apprentices. Nor were all or even most of them represented in every town. They were limited by the lack of transportation to trade with the town's immediate environs and enjoyed a monopoly in their area, but some would grow and expand their trade to surrounding counties and neighboring states. The mere fact that they existed, however, meant that the surrounding farms now provided an economic base for a town with a more or less permanent population of artisans and businessmen who did not grow their own food.

That same increased farm production was directly responsible for the appearance of another ubiquitous town merchant—the grain buyer. His function was a natural one to take over from the farmer the job of transporting the grain to market and selling it there. In prerailroad times, the buyer would haul it himself in huge land schooners to one of the larger shipping centers such as Cincinnati, Cleveland, or Chicago, and return with his wagon full of goods for the storekeepers (or he might engage in storekeeping himself). These merchants soon operated out of warehouses, where they could store the grain and which were the precursors of the grain elevator—but these belonged to the railroad age. Similarly, meat-packing operations in the towns took over the farmer's home-curing task.

In addition to manufacturing for local consumers (and providing services such as repairing tools) and exporting grain, the third function of the town—and perhaps its most important economically—was mercantile trade. In pioneer times this trade was almost entirely centered in the general store, which offered a wide variety of necessities and luxuries (luxuries that in time became necessities) that the rural folk could not make or raise for themselves. The general store was the social center of the early settlements, its front porch the habitat of loungers, gossipers, political discussants, and mail readers. There might be another kind of store that also served a social function—the groceries or doggeries or traps, which were permitted to sell liquor by the drink or by the gallon, as well as other goods. They were in essence taprooms cum liquor stores, and their prevalence attested to the pioneers' fondness for whiskey. The general store too might offer whiskey as a sort of grease to the wheels of commerce; in the back was the ever-present barrel of whiskey (replacing the New England storekeeper's rum of earlier days) along with a pitcher of water, maple sugar, and a tumbler of ginger in cold weather. Every male customer was invited to partake by the storekeeper.

As its name implied, the general store was an all-purpose store purveying staples, dry goods, hardware, and myriad other items. As early as 1816, Eben Marian of Zanesville was advertising "GOODS—hardware, crockery, groceries, dye stuffs, paints, drugs, books, stationery and shoes"[63] and offering to take in payment wheat, rye, corn, oats, whiskey, hogs, lard, butter, tallow, beeswax, country sugar, cheese, rags, ashes, black salts, furs, boards, clapboards, shingles, lime, and barrels. A store in early Indianapolis listed among its wares: "cloths, cassimeres, baize, cassinetts, flannels, blankets, bombazetts, robes, dress shawls, calicoes, cambric, muslins, shirtings, vesting, hosiery, nankeens, handkerchiefs, umbrellas and parasols, plaids, stripes and chambrays, linen, hats, combs, bonnets, shoes—black, coloured and morocco,—spoons, knives and forks, saws, files, saddlery, school books, butcher, shoe and pen knives, chisels, gouges and plane bits, hammers and hatchets, hinges and screws, padlocks, latchets, spades, shovels, tongs, cotton and wool cards, augers, &c., &c. Also, queensware and glassware, groceries, powder, lead and shot, iron, steel and nails, chalk and Spanish whiting, tinware &c., &c."[64]

The pioneer store was likely a log structure, a front porch its only amenity. Inside, a long counter of rough-hewn boards, where dingy, shopworn goods were displayed, stretched the length of the room. The first ten feet of counter space was covered with bolts of cheap cloth, the next with hides (here sat the cobbler, ready to work up a pair of shoes for a customer); farther back were groceries and hardware—mainly nails and bars of iron; in the rear was the table bearing the barrel of whiskey. On crude shelves were packages containing knives, with a sample torn open for display, sheep shears, sickles for harvesting wheat, chains, bridles, and so on. For the women there was calico, cap stuff, pins and needles, and fine cambric, from which were made some of the first wedding garments for the settlers' daughters. A man who wished a fashionable broadcloth suit with yellow metal buttons, high collar, and forked tail could, if he had the money, be outfitted. A smell of drying herbs and hides (not to mention unwashed pioneer bodies) permeated the close atmosphere.

The stores were dark, gloomy, and poorly ventilated; the only light and air entered from the front, the walls on either side were covered with shelves of goods. Merchants did not curse the darkness—it made their goods less visible; much of their stock would not, alas, stand a close look. Some merchants even blotted out the light entering through the front windows and door by draping them with shawls and other goods. This insured that a person who had bargained for a piece of cloth might be surprised at its actual color and quality when he or she got it home. Sharp practices were not uncommon. An apocryphal but not untrue-to-life story was told of a deacon who called out to his clerk: "John, have you watered the tobacco?" "Yes, sir," the clerk replied. "Have you watered the rum?" "Yes, sir." "Have you sanded the sugar?" "Yes, sir." "Then come in to prayers."[65]

Later stores were a bit more elaborate and their merchandising methods more aggressive. One such store, ca. 1850, was described as follows:

> There was one counter that ran from front to the back. There was no window for displaying goods, such as all stores have now, but the front of the store was made so that when the weather was favorable the entire front was thrown open. The two wooden horses were placed on the walk in front of the store, some boards laid across, and on those boards the goods would be piled for display. Our store sold silks, calicoes, prints, etc.
>
> When the goods were displayed out front in warm weather, the boss or one of the older clerks would stand near the front of the store and if a person came along and looked at the goods he would step out and try to make a sale. A great many remnants of prints were sold at sixpence, eight and one-third cents a yard or twelve yards for a dollar. . . . Customers would usually try to beat down the price. . . .
>
> Farmers drove to town and hitched their horses on Main Street, hitching posts being provided for that purpose. They also hitched their horses to the awning posts which were in front of every store. The awning was a wide piece of canvas stretched to poles that extended horizontally out from the building and fastened to upright posts at the edge of the sidewalks.
>
> There was no delivery team in those days. We used to try to have customers take their parcels when ever they could, but when they would not do it we used to have to carry their goods to their homes in wheelbarrows. . . .
>
> We had three gas lights, one in front, one about the middle of the store and one further back. Then, for the very back of the store, where the umbrellas were kept, we had to use the candles or small oil lamps—not kerosene—to light the way. We did a great deal of umbrella-repairing; in

> fact the boss made umbrellas and parasols right in the store. Whalebone was often used for the ribs.[66]

The more elaborate general store might display on one side its dry goods—ribbon, thread, silk, corsets, bustles, fans, gloves, handkerchiefs, shawl pins, and artificial flowers for the ladies, and paper collars, cuffs, and shirtfronts, ready-made neckties, suspenders, and red flannel underwear for the men. Across from these, near the front, would be a section devoted to hard candy in jars, tobacco, cough drops, and patent medicines such as Perry Davis' Pain Killer, Radway's Ready Relief, Log Cabin Bitters, Hostetter's Bitters, Ayer's Cherry Pectoral and Beecham's Pills. Here too might be a stationery section with pens and papers and valentines in a case, and perhaps even books. The post office with a glass window and pigeonholes for mail might also be located in the front of the store. Then, on shelves, would be displayed crockery, tableware, washbowls, and pitchers, glasses, lamps, and earthenware crocks and jugs. Next would come the grocery section with its spice grinder and tins of spices and tea and coffee; the cheese and cracker barrels and sugar barrels and boxes of dried fish, as well as hogsheads of molasses, barrels of oil, casks of rum, brandy, gin, and cider. And at the rear the farming implements—pitchforks, rakes, hoes, scythes, snares, whetstones, and a circular rack of horsewhips suspended from the ceiling. Now the pervasive aroma was the acrid smell of kerosene (replacing whale oil), mingled with food odors and the aroma of heavily oiled leather harnesses.

Not only did the country storekeeper sell food and merchandise; he also acted as a bank, keeping customers' money in strongboxes. He gave credit, wrote letters, subscribed to periodicals, guided travelers, acted as postmaster, and, from his vantage point in a small community's central meeting place, became a leader in political affairs (most storekeepers were Whigs).

His economic functions were complicated by the shortage of currency, and his dispensation of credit at high interest or markups was a necessary service in the money-starved pioneer economy. His acceptance of farmers' produce in barter provided an early, if small, market for these goods.

The merchant himself often bought his goods on credit extended to him for six or nine months or even a year. Many merchants made an annual trip east or to Pittsburgh, Buffalo, St. Louis, New Orleans, or Cincinnati to acquire their stock—with which they were, of course, stuck for another year, so they had to be canny about gauging their customers' wants. Customers who bought on credit were charged a high markup and paid their debts once a year; New Year's Day was the traditional time in many areas for settling up.

Counterfeit money was a problem, and one storekeeper recalled that a young boy was put in charge of taking money and making change. With a face that the innocence of youth cleared of all suggestion of guile, he would freely pass off counterfeit bills to the customers; the storekeeper recalled, "And what is very strange, I do not believe that we ever lost a customer by such a procedure; it being my practice, at least . . . always to take the bad bill back without hesitation or delay."[67]

The general store was a victim of specialization as the town and surrounding area grew in population and prosperity. It actually combined three main kinds of merchandise—dry goods, hardware, and groceries—as well as a host of minor ones—pharmaceuticals, stationery, books, ready-to-wear clothing, and so on. Eventually, separate stores selling these items were opened. But the general store was long a fixture of the country town.

A town economy of something like the diversity and specialization that we know today did not come overnight, but gradually the subsistence-farming-barter economy of the pioneer day gave way to one based on money and a surplus-producing agriculture, plus trade with the outside. Truth to tell, the early pioneer towns were erected on shifting economic sands, which is why so many of them disappeared as casually as they were founded, while others stagnated. Governor Ford diagnosed the cause of the sluggish growth of country towns in his own state as the farmers' refusal to sell their grain at the going market prices. After setting aside enough food to subsist on and with few other immediate expenses, they held out in hopes of forcing prices up, even if it meant letting their crops rot in the fields. The upshot of this practice was that the farmers were chronically money short and so bought on credit, which meant that the town merchants charged them higher prices. At the same time, the merchants had trouble paying *their* debts and went out of business or eked out a subsistence. This meant that the towns did not prosper and remained small. Ford compared this system unfavorably with that in New England, where farmers always sold at market price and paid cash for their goods. The merchants could pay their debts and keep a turnover of goods on their shelves. As a result, Ford said, it took only three or four years to build up a New England town, while in Illinois it took twenty years.

This was part of the truth (New England merchants went through their credit stage too, as we have seen). Another element in the picture was the sheer backwardness of business techniques. Pioneer artisans and merchants dealt with a small, fluid market and labor supply; people came and went. The products they made or sold were old-fashioned and ill-adapted to the changing needs of the consumers; their market was too limited and chancy to offer the latest gadgets. The merchant had little capital as a rule, and there were no banks to provide credit resources. The pioneer merchant or tavern keeper was also a prisoner of the cash shortage; he could not demand money of people who did not have it, and so he extended them credit. If times became bad and they could not pay, he could not get any money out of them, let alone hire a collection agency to squeeze them. A debtor who fell too far in arrears would most likely pick up and move west. Thus the businessman in the town was vulnerable; he was sailing close hauled, and a sudden unfavorable breeze might keel him over into insolvency.

An obvious cause of the sluggish growth of towns was the slow pace of settlement in some areas and the scatteredness of the population. This latter could be blamed on the farmers' practice of claiming larger plots than they could effectively farm. They hung on to their land as long as they could, hoping its value would rise, but the large expanses of unproductive land meant that the necessary agricultural prosperity was slow in coming and kept out improvements such as schools, roads, and railroads. And the shortage of good transportation to market kept towns small. Then too, there was a high turnover in population associated with the pioneer period. This turnover was a repeated pattern, occurring in each newly settled area, and generally its effect was that during the first twenty years turnover was high, followed by a period of relative stability.

Whatever the reasons, the average town in the Northwest grew slowly, and its businesses had a high rate of failure. A preindustrial town had its close ties to the land, and business failure didn't count for much, since a man could still take a subsistence from his farm—or move on west. But such conditions encouraged a transient population, with eyes constantly cocked on a better chance somewhere else. Towns, to be permanent, needed a kind of postpioneer personality—the conservative types who wanted to stay put, build up a good farm, or, if they tilled the field of commerce, a paying business. The women in particular wanted the amenities of *civitas*—of a town—the law and order, schools for their children, churches in which to worship together, intercourse with their fellows, regularized social and economic exchange, permanence. These types were the natural town-dwellers; but having come west, they were also out to make their fortune, believing that with industry and righteous living (although this did not necessarily exclude sharp practices in trade), they would realize the dream of prosperity that had brought them here. They were inveterate believers in self-made success, even though the businesses they started failed repeatedly.

Consider the career of J.J. (Jerry) Barber, who arrived in Rochelle, Illinois, in 1855 and stocked a dry goods store he had built with his own hands. Probably he financed it by the sale of a section of land bought at $1.25 an acre and sold for much more to a later arrival. Like most who came west he arrived with little in his poke, and invested that little into farmland. But it was a good time to go into business in Rochelle; twenty years before there had been only a handful of settlers in Flagg Township, but a railroad line came through, linking the town with Chicago. Jerry's store did a rushing business, and he entered into partnership with John R. Hotaling. The partners, dreaming big, erected a "corner brick" in the choicest location in the little town and christened it the Republican Block. (A "brick" was a brick building. A block—an English term meaning a building containing flats or offices—was a brick structure of three, four, or five stories in a prominent location, built as a speculation in the hope of attracting tenants, just as the town itself was a speculation, laid out in the hope of attracting townspeople. On the first floor of a typical block were stores and offices, on the second perhaps a lodge or town hall, opera house, or library, and on the upper floors rooms for rent or a hotel.)

The Hotaling-Barber partnership was dissolved, however, before they moved into their new building, with Jerry keeping the goods and Hotaling taking over the block. Jerry built another block called Oak Front, which he sold to Bruce & Coon before it burned down in 1860. Besides his store and real estate transactions, Jerry began wheeling and dealing in coal and furniture, got into grain buying, and had his own warehouse. But something, it is not clear what, went wrong. The county historian makes a cryptic reference to "eastern creditors," but that is all. Probably Jerry overextended himself—buying a large stock on credit, selling to his customers on credit—and his suppliers foreclosed during a panic before he could collect what was owed him. At any rate, the historian eulogizes him:

> No man in the commercial history of Rochelle ever enjoyed the confidence of the trading public more completely than "Jerry." Early in trade, his genial manner and well-known probity commanded an immense patronage. Had his conscience possessed the elasticity of the modern tradesman, with ordinary parsimony he would have amassed a princely fortune, and, instead of resting in a grave unmarked by the simplest tablet, he might have reposed beneath the shadow of an imposing monument. As it was he met with financial disaster, failed in business, and the last years of his life were spent in comparative poverty. He died in 1872 and was laid to rest with Masonic honors. He came to Rochelle, and for awhile was successful beyond all reasonable expectation in accumulating wealth and multiplying friends; and the two seemed to disappear together fully as readily as they came.[68]

Jerry Barber may have been unwise—no doubt caught up in the speculative contagion of a temporary booomtown—and too genial when it came to extending credit, but he was not atypical. That his reputation for honesty was cited as an outmoded virtue that contributed to his downfall also says something about the way trade was being conducted in the post-pioneer era small towns. And the simultaneous disappearance of wealth and friends is a comment on the naked individualism of small-town business practices: leading citizen one day, a poor man's grave the next—albeit with the best funeral his Masonic burial insurance could buy. Where, Jerry Barber might have asked, were his lodge's "honors" when he was alive?

The pioneer idea of reciprocal help did not apply to trade; there a man was on his own. Small-town life would cling to the pioneer ideals of neighborliness and sociability, but in the business sphere economist Thorstein Veblen's "self-help and cupidity" were the ruling virtues. As the town passed out of the pioneer stage, competition among the merchants for the farmers' dollar grew, and the tradesmmen lost their former comfortable monopolies. It was no wonder then that small-town businesses, short of capital and their managers lacking rudimentary business skills, were unable to survive competition.

Undoubtedly the system weeded out some unqualified businessmen, although many a man's failure was no fault of his own but rather attributable to untoward downturns in the national economy. The system encouraged the practical, innovative, flexible types, who could scratch and scramble and, if one thing ddidn't work out, could try another. Indeed, some men engaged in a bewildering variety of careers during their lifetimes, more or less succeeding at all of them. Consider Isaac G. Naylor, of Darlington, Indiana, who was in his time teacher, printer, editor, miller, merchant, druggist, and doctor. Just as some early tradesmen kept a farm to fall back on, others acquired a skill, which they parlayed into businesses of their own.

The career of Elijah C. Brown, an early settler of Crawfordsville, Indiana, combines both a trade and ties with the land—plus a deep philosophical interest in religion. Brown was apprenticed to the cabinet trade (carpentry) at sixteen, because his father's small ninety-five-acre farm offered him no future in agriculture. He entered Wabash College, which, like many middle western denominational schools primarily founded to educate future ministers, had courses in manual trades for needy young men. Brown set up in the furniture and undertaking business (the combination was not unusual; a cabinet maker easily turned his hand to making coffins, which inevitably opened up the sideline of selling the coffins, putting the deceased in them, and both of them in the ground), which he pursued successfully for fifteen years. The historian clearly considers Brown's business career an exemplary one: "He accumulated considerable town property, and from the sale of this made some permanent investments in land. His savings have amounted to $20,000. Mrs. Brown owned eighty acres of forest land when she was married to Mr. Brown. He has divided over $10,000 of his property equally among his children. From his domestic affections and associations he derived his highest enjoyment, and his earnest and calculative care for his family induced him to toil hard to accumulate property, so that he might have enough to endow his children comfortably during his lifetime, and a competence left for himself and his wife."[69] He obviously succeeded in both these goals, because in his biography he is listed as "retired" and a son is described as owning 220 acres of land worth twelve thousand dollars. But not only did Brown achieve a modest business success; he also followed through on a childhood interest in religion (stimulated, he recalled, by his father's telling him that the massive blocks of stone littering the earth near his birthplace in Putnam County, Indiana, were the result of a violent upheaval at the crucifixion of Christ). He became a Methodist minister in 1865 and was ordained a deacon in 1875. He also had been an active abolitionist, when this was not a popular course, and had once been threatened by a mob. He spent his later years studying the natural sciences and harmonizing their findings with the biblical account of the Creation. The results of his studies he planned to set down in a book which would be called *God and the Ages.* Several characteristics stand out prominently in Elijah Brown's life: frugality, shrewdness in land investment, hard work, acquiring and pursuit of a craft, piety, and a speculative interest in science and theology. His advocacy of abolition, at a time when this course was not popular, reveals not only a social conscience, but an unwillingness to downplay his politics out of fear of losing trade.

Men who entered the mercantile business often had little opportunity to learn the trade except through on-the-job training. The early storekeepers were often true entrepreneurs, men who took a little money made through land speculation, bought into a stock of goods, and were in business. The second-generation route into the business usually meant starting off as a clerk, working one's way up, by diligence and loyalty, Horatio Alger-style, and winning a partnership after one of the original partners died.

Reading the biographies of these small-town businessmen, one notes that the careers of many were shadowed by temporary reverses, often in times of financial panic when their debtors could not pay up. Yet most pulled through and built up businesses over their lifetimes. (Of course the county historians tended to list only the eminent long-time residents who had survived business vicissitudes, a practice that insures omission of the failure stories.) But in the average small town, a half dozen at most showed any real business talent and ended up with substantial property.

Every growing town managed to throw up a rich man or two. Frequently the fortune was made—or at least begun—in land speculation; but trade—wholesale, retail, commodity brokering, and the like—and banking were also routes to wealth; manufacturing, the professions, innkeeping, or other service businesses were of minor significance in the rise of fortunes. The career of Isaac C. Elston of Crawfordsville, Indiana, can serve to stand for the select few who made small fortunes, while operating in a small-town milieu. Elston—who bore the honorific "major"—started out with a general store in 1823. At that time, Crawfordsville was a young county-seat town, population four hundred, consisting of a busy United States land office (its main enterprise), jail, courthouse, two general stores (the other was owned by a man named Smith, who quickly disappeared from trade—and history as well), two cabinet shops, a tavern, blacksmith shop, gristmill, shoe shop, and tannery—a typical pioneer town. Elston had started up his general store in the traditional manner, by freighting in a supply of goods and putting them up for sale. As a storekeeper, the major took in various pioneer produce in barter, and at some point along the line he grew beyond the traditional storekeeper's role and became a wholesaler. Indeed at one level he was performing the same function as the fur traders did with the Indians. He would stock up with powder and shot, dry goods, coffee, tea, spices, salt, and tools and exchange these for furs, ginseng, smoked pork, hides, and grain. Further, he arranged to ship these to the river towns of Madison and Cincinnati. He might make the grain more portable by feeding it to livestock, which could be driven to market on foot, or distilling it into whiskey. But meat and grain prices were depressed, and the major apparently dealt most heavily during the years from 1825 to 1830 in the pioneer's most readily cashable crop—ginseng. This was gathered wild and then dried and cured; pound for pound it brought the highest return and was shipped, via Cincinnati, ultimately to China, where the chief ginseng users were.

By 1830, however, all the ginseng in the county was "rooted out," and Elston concentrated on other crops. After a brief hiatus in commercial activities while he served as postmaster (a reward for being a Jacksonian Democrat), he expanded his activities. By 1835, he was conducting a wholesale business that extended into the upper Wabash Valley. As a wholesaler, Elston was the middleman between the local storekeepers and the merchants and commodity dealers in Cincinnati, New Orleans, Pittsburgh, New York, Philadelphia, and Montreal. The latter bought wheat, corn, pork, and lumber, either on commission or outright, and Elston, as their buyer, shipped it by land to Madison and Lafayette, whence it went via the Wabash River to the Ohio and thence down the Mississippi to New Orleans or upriver to Pittsburgh. At the same time Elston imported hardware, furniture, salt, coffee, tea, and dry goods. All the while Elston accumulated capital and acquired expertise in financial dealings with local producers. As a result of the latter, he was appointed agent in place for several large eastern firms and charged with collecting from western debtors. The major's reputation for financial acumen and probity was sealed during the panic of 1837 when, the historian says, "he judged his customers' credit so correctly that he lost very little in the panic and survived when scores of his competitors were foreclosed."[70] His currency dealings—involving the bills of exchange and the often questionable private bank notes endemic in the West—led him inexorably into the banking business, and in 1853, with a local lawyer named Henry S. Lane (who later became a United States senator), he founded Lane and Elston Bankers and Exchange Dealers. Even though fifty-one banks failed in Indiana between 1852 and 1857, the Lane and Elston Bank was a success and still exists as the Elston Bank.

In addition to his currency dealings, Elston was deep into land speculation, owning property in seven counties and involved in promoting two Indiana towns, Lafayette and Michigan City, which "took" and thrived. Finally, the major was a leader in railroad building in the area; he had received the call early on while trying to ship farm produce on the atrocious pioneer roads. The major built the biggest and finest house in town; his daughter married the town's most famous son, General Lew Wallace, author of *Ben Hur;* and his fortune was handed down and expanded through the generations. Elston was a dealer and a middleman; he transacted in every pioneer commodity from ginseng to land to livestock to debts to money (a speculative item in its own right, which fluctuated in value). The multiplicity of irons he had in the fire was not unique among the restless individualists on the frontier; Major Isaac Elston, however, had the shrewdness and talent for turning his various enterprises and speculations into money. But for every Elston there were many Jerry Barbers, and a similar ratio of success to failure obtained for the towns in which these entrepreneurs had their base of operations.

The typical middle western town was founded by men who shared a dream of prosperity based upon steadily rising land values. Achieving this dream often necessitated fierce fights with nearby, and therefore rival, towns over such economic bones as the farmers' trade, county seats, canals, railroads, state institutions, and the like. As a result, for nearly every town that succeeded, there was another town with similar great expectations that sank into village somnolence or disappeared altogether. This sense of rivalry, primarily economic but also the product of local chauvinism, reflected the individualism of the West, and it held sway from the earliest days of the territory. Jacob Burnet wrote of the three earliest settlements in the Old Northwest that "although they had one general object, and were threatened by one common danger, yet there existed a strong spirit of rivalry between them—each feeling a pride in the prosperity of the little colony to which he belonged."[71]

The earliest rivalries were often based on competition for designation as county seat. A county-seat town could expect to attract a nucleus of judges, lawyers, court functionaries, and county government officials and support them modestly with its power to tax the surrounding countryside. Perhaps more important—because the economic perquisites of the county seat weren't really that large—were the psychological dividends of the county-seat designation—the intangible cachet of solidity and permanence it conferred on a struggling young town, which would attract to it trade and money. Many of the early county-seat designates did not last, for the same economic reasons other towns failed; nonetheless the citizens of a potential seat wooed the prize with ardor—and with every canny pioneer stratagem and political dirty trick at their command.

When counties were new and the population sparse and rough-hewn, this conflict was conducted at an elemental level, a sort of variation of the trial by combat used to settle personal scores. This was exemplified in the rivalry between Mount Vernon and Clinton, Ohio, both newly laid out in 1805. In Mount Vernon, it was the locals' wont to assemble in town on Saturday and work at clearing the stumps from the projected streets. This rite always concluded with copious libations of a drink called "stew"—a mixture of water, maple sugar, allspice, butter, and two or three gallons of whiskey—accompanied by gossip, wrestling matches, footraces, shooting contests, and the inevitable fights. The commissioners charged with making the momentous decision between Mount Vernon and Clinton were duly appointed by the state legislature. On the Saturday they chose to inspect Mount Vernon, they found the citizenry industriously occupied grubbing stumps. After the commissioners had parted, impressed by the Mount Vernonites' civic-mindedness, some of the boys hatched a plan in the midst of the customary convivialities. Several of the roughest looking (and most *stewed,* one might imagine) were delegated to proceed immediately to Clinton. When they arrived, they found the commissioners making their rounds. The Mount Vernonites accosted the magistrates, identified themselves as citizens of Clinton, and started shoving them around and berating them. The commissioners beat a retreat and later handed down a decision favorable to Mount Vernon. That was the last that was heard of Clinton, which vanished from history, as did many such defeated towns.

Sometimes the commissioners were plied with liquor and bribed, a less imaginative but often effective ploy. Both of these lagniappes were proffered during the complex machinations connected with the establishment of a county seat in Darke County, Ohio. There were two challengers for the title, both named Greenville. The first Greenville came into existence in 1808 when John Devor purchased a half section on the site of old Fort Greenville and laid out a town partly within and partly outside the boundaries of the fort. Then two brothers named Terry and Billy Wilson platted another Greenville nearby. Unfortunately for the Wilsons, they gave a town, as it were, and nobody came. Actually, one man committed himself to buy two lots from the Wilsons, but Devor immediately lured him away with the offer of two presumably better lots in his Greenville free of charge—"to purchase his acquiescence in the measures taken to remove the seat of justice of the county to the southeast side of the creek,"[72] as the historian delicately puts it. In 1809 the Ohio legislature had formally created Darke County and appointed commissioners to divine a proper site for the county seat. The Wilson brothers quickly launched a two-pronged attack, with Terry promising each commissioner a choice lot in the new seat if their Greenville were chosen, and Billy applying quantities of whiskey and money. These overtures had the desired effect, and in 1810 Greenville was anointed. But that did not end the story. Perhaps word of the commissioners' impropriety got out; at any rate new commissioners were appointed in 1811, and their decision went to John Devor's Greenville, the only consideration being a promise by the proprietor to donate one-third of the town lots to the county.

It became a common practice for the proprietor of the soil to turn over one-third of his lots for public use, as sites not only for the county courthouse and jail but also for a town square, churches, schools, burying ground, and other public facilities. What apparently started out as a lure ended up as perhaps the only public-interest consideration that went into the planning of such towns. The willingness of the landowners to go along with such an arrangement showed how eager they were to win the prize, since such donations meant that there were fewer lots they could sell for profit. The county officials might even play an active role, like a planning board. In Madison County, Ohio, for example, the commissioners settled upon land owned by John

Murfin. Murfin in turn offered a tract of two hundred acres, which he would plat at his own expense, "the streets and alleys to be made commodious for the public good, a convenient public square shall be laid out, which, together with one-half the in and out lots shall be for the use of the county."[73] The Court of Common Pleas then came up with its own plan, which called for appointing a director to search the title and then purchase 100 to 125 acres at four dollars an acre and "pay for same out of proceeds of sale" to the general public. Thus the profits from the sale would go to the county, and Murfin would receive a flat rate. The director would then lay out lots and streets and alleys at right angles and 120 "even" lots (i.e., lots in the town), with the remaining land to be divided up into two-acre outlots. One lot was to be reserved for a courthouse and public square at the intersection of Main and Main Cross streets, two lots for "churches and academy," one for a jail, and one outlot for a burying place. The streets were to be named, the plat recorded, and the lots sold at public sale with certificates of sale to purchasers in return for a contract of payment which called for one-third down, one-third in nine months, and the remainder within eighteen months from the date of the contract. The town was to be named London, and Main Street lots were not to be sold for less than fifty dollars. Ultimately Murfin actually deeded 103.75 acres to the director and received $415—a 332 percent profit if he had bought his land at land office prices—and the town, more orderly in inception than most, was on its way.

Sometimes the selection of the county seat would drag on for so long that a better location emerged from the pack to overtake the original front-runner. In Woodford County, Illinois, Versailles was made the temporary seat in 1840, with the proviso that it furnish a suitable building for holding court. At the end of two years an election would be held in the county to determine the permanent site. This plan was devised by a prominent personage in the county whose pocketbook lay with Versailles; his assumption was that during its two years as acting county seat, Versailles would attract a large population and so win permanent designation. Before the two years were up, however, the town of Hanover began bustling ominously. The new rival evidently made Versailles' champion nervous, because he attempted to bypass the election, lobbying in the state capital for the appointment of a commission (presumably one "greased and swallowed" by him) to settle the matter. He failed, and the election was held, Hanover winning. This was a fatal blow to Versailles, which soon vanished from the map. Hanover went on to change its name to Metamora (there was already another Hanover in Illinois), but not to greater glory; its seathood was in turn usurped by Eureka in 1896.

Obviously, only a limited number of towns could be county seats; furthermore the mere designation did not always ensure survival. Many an early seat at some wilderness crossroad never got beyond the stage of a log courthouse, jail, general store, tavern, and a few cabins. A sort of negative determinacy principle was at work, under which a town that was designated did not necessarily survive, but on the other hand a town that *lost* the designation inevitably languished or disappeared—unless, of course, it had some other economic base.

A major factor in the relative prosperity of towns was a strategic location along a transportation route—whether it be a trace, a river, or a lake or, later, a canal or railroad. River ports were the first towns of any consequence in the Old Northwest, obvious examples being Pittsburgh (both a staging town for settlers going west and a terminus for goods being shipped east overland and on the Ohio River), Cincinnati (a hub for trade between the interior and the East), Louisville (a port linked to the Kentucky and Indiana interiors), and St. Louis (a port for Mississippi River trade with New Orleans and eventual gateway to the Far West). Lesser ports on these routes also grew up, such as Madison, Indiana, and Cairo, Illinois, despite its clouded beginnings. With the completion of the Erie and Ohio canals, Cleveland became a great lake port, as did Chicago, after railroads linking it with the southern interior were built, although its heyday coincided with the age of railroads and it made its mark as a railway hub.

Numerous lesser towns owed their initial existence to their location on some river or tributary creek that was optimistically envisioned as navigable. But as the land was cleared by settlers, many of these lesser streams grew shallower by the year and dreams of steamboats plying them faded quickly. One such town was New Salem, Illinois, where Abe Lincoln spent his young manhood. The town grew up, as did so many others, around a mill that attracted farmers from the area; soon a general store and a grocery were opened. Then, in 1829, the miller platted a town and offered lots for sale. By 1831 New Salem had a post office, a cooper's shop, a ferry, and a doctor. The prime selling point was the town's location on the Sangamon River, which the proprietor confidently believed to be navigable by light-draft steamboats. This hope lasted until 1836, when a steamboat attempting to reach New Salem ran aground, and New Salem's hopes with it. By then other towns had sprung up in the area and were drawing trade away from New Salem. Its main rival was Petersburg, which Abe Lincoln had helped plat; within a year lots that had originally sold for $10 and $20 were going for $50 and $150, and the town had obviously gained the confidence of the region. New Salem soon lost its post office and the deathblow came in 1839 when Petersburg was made county seat. By 1840 it was deserted; eventually its buildings—all but the cooper's shop which was moved to Petersburg—moldered away and New Salem vanished from the face of the earth.

Physically, yes; but as the years passed, New Salem acquired a new existence in history, legend, and poetry. For it was the town where Abraham Lincoln had spent his young manhood, where, according to the poetic legend—unanimously doubted by historians—he had courted Ann Rutledge, wrestled with Jack Armstrong, ran after a woman who had forgotten her change, and educated himself by reading, feet up on a tree, in front of the general store he ran for Denton Offutt. Nearly a hundred years after New Salem's demise, the publisher William Randolph Hearst (an unlikely Lincoln acolyte) bought up the site and helped finance the restoration of the town as it looked in Lincoln's day. As for Petersburg, New Salem's vanquisher, it is today a small place of twenty-six hundred souls of which a guidebook says, "Its chief distinction is as part of Lincoln land and gateway to New Salem State Park."[74]

The coming of the canals gave an impetus to a new kind of port town, located along the artificial waterways. The present industrial city of Akron owed its birth to a canal. Akron was promoted by two speculators—General Simon Perkins, who was a member of the canal commission, and one Paul Williams, whose identity is lost in the mists of history. Obviously trading on inside information acquired through General Perkins's position, they bought up for a song one thousand acres on the projected route of the "Cross-Cut" or "Beaver" Canal through the Cuyahoga Valley. The town was laid out in 1825, and its first inhabitants were Irish laborers imported to dig the canal. With the completion of the waterway, industry came in, including a factory that made stoneware and sewer pipes from the rich clay deposits near the town, a match factory, blast furnaces, and grist and sawmills. As for Perkins and Williams, they became rich men.

Akron's success soon spawned a rival, Cuyahoga Falls, which was laid out in 1837 by a promoter named Birdseye Booth as a deliberate challenge to Akron. Cuyahoga Falls did indeed prosper, as it offered good waterpower (the river fell two hundred feet in two and a half miles before reaching the town). Within three years Booth was bidding for the county-seat designation and almost won. By 1847, Cuyahoga Falls had a population of twelve hundred; paper, saw, and flour mills; two blast furnaces; two tanneries; a fork and scythe factory; and a starch factory. But it was never able to usurp Akron's place and eventually became its satellite.

The coming of the railroad brought about the eclipse of some of the port towns created by the canal. The state of Ohio had started abandoning sections of the canal in 1863, and by 1872 it turned over to Cleveland three miles of canal running through marshland. The city handed this land over to the railroad, which drained and filled it and laid tracks. Not so auspiciously located as Cleveland, which was a booming Lake Erie port, was Milan. The Ohio Canal had made Milan a prosperous grain-shipping port, and its streets were clogged with great grain wagons, or "land schooners." Then the Lake Shore and Michigan Southern Railroad began building a route through the area and proposed a right-of-way through Milan. Instead of welcoming the railroad, as many towns did, Milan businessmen saw it as a threat to their canal traffic with Lake Erie and forbade the road entry to their town. It was a futile gesture; the railroad went ahead and laid its track farther south, and Milan went into decline.

Between 1844 and 1864 Spring Bay, Illinois, was a thriving river port.

Offering the best landing on the Illinois River, it became the grain center for the whole of Ogle County—a place where fortunes were made, one hundred wagons a day in its streets. But the railroads preempted its business, and by the 1870s the town had settled into sleepy mediocrity with a small grain business, three general stores, three saloons, two blacksmith shops, two wagon shops, one harness shop, two shoe shops, one physician, a school, and a town hall, but no lawyers or churches. Then there was Charleston, located at the mouth of the Black River and incorporated in 1836. One of the early shipbuilding centers on Lake Erie, it was bypassed by both canal and railroad and all but disappeared until the 1870s, when it was reborn as Lorain.

A lesson of the railroad's capacity to build and simultaneously destroy may be read in the tale of two Illinois towns, Buffalo Grove and Polo. The Illinois Central Line was originally routed to pass through Buffalo Grove, but objections were raised by some big landowners, who did not want it on their property. So the route was diverted one mile east of the town, where it crossed Zenas P. Aplington's farm. Aplington did not object to the railroad on his land, or at least he was persuaded not to, for he formed a partnership with the chief engineer of the Illinois Central and a prominent citizen of Dixon. Aplington moved some buildings from Buffalo Grove to his land in March 1853. A town was platted with the three partners as proprietors and given the name Polo (after Marco). Lots were sold in May and the railroad track was laid by December. The "instant town" of Polo grew rapidly after that, while Buffalo Grove declined until, by 1878, there was no store left in its limits.

By 1857 Polo had a population of one thousand people and fifty-five buildings valued at thirty-five thousand dollars. It grew to twenty-five hundred people in 1878 and boasted six general merchandise stores, three dry goods stores, six groceries, two druggists, five physicians, two dentists, four attorneys, one restaurant, two barbers (no waiting), one billiard parlor, and no saloons (the town was dry). It was also the locus of the Polo Manufacturing Company, which made the King-Fink Polo Harvester (invented by King and improved by Fink, both Polo boys), the Polo Harvesting Company, which made the Porter Harvester, and the Buffalo Mutual Insurance Company. At that point, though Polonians were perhaps unaware of it, the town had crested; in 1970 its population was still twenty-five hundred, while Buffalo Grove had swelled from one thousand to eleven thousand, a beneficiary of the exodus to suburbia from Chicago, which was twenty-seven miles away. Over the long haul, Buffalo Grove, nearly done in by the railroad, had won—saved (if that is the word) by the automobile.

The Illinois Central directly spawned no fewer than thirty-three towns along its route. Needing towns along its right-of-way, and forbidden by law to do so, four directors of the railorad formed a subsidiary, the Associates, that platted the towns and sold the lots at auction. First, however, the Associates bought up federal land along the right-of-way in places where, as directors of the railroad, they knew depots would be located. The depots attracted settlers, the towns grew up around them, and the Associates grew rich. The towns were identically laid out in a grid patttern with the railroad line bisecting their centers (this saved surveying costs). The street names were patterned after those of Philadelphia, with the streets running east and west named after trees and those running north and south numbered. In 1855, the Illinois Central was authorized to develop towns, and laid out twenty-nine of them. This "railroad town" pattern would be followed by towns farther west along the transcontinental lines.

The nineteenth-century shortsightedness of the Buffalo Grove citizens was not emulated by most towns, who saw the railroad as their salvation. The usual behavior was to put out the welcome mat in the form of a hefty subscription to the railroad's stock. The railroad companies financed themselves on a pay-as-we-go basis and would go where they got the best offer. Another practice, designed to induce competition among landowners and drive down the price of land to be acquired for right-of-way, was to project several routes, then sit back and wait for the lowest bid. Towns also organized railroad companies of their own to connect them with the terminus of an already going line. This is what the town of Crawfordsville, Indiana, did in 1850, when it organized the Crawfordsville and Wabash Railroad, projected to cover the twenty-eight miles between the town and Lafayette, which was on the New Albany and Chicago line (later the Louisville, New Albany, and Chicago Railroad, and, still later, the Monon). The county commissioners bought one hundred thousand dollars worth of stock (the money was raised by a bond issue), which never paid any return and was written off as a donation to the line. When the Lafayette merchants got wind of these plans, they realized that Crawfordsville might draw away some of the trade that they had built up in that area, so they put up money to build a plank road that would run within one mile of Crawfordsville and then stop (a "spite road," one might say). The plank road eventually rotted, while Crawfordsville's railroad was successfully completed to Lafayette in 1852 and three years later was consolidated into the New Albany and Chicago.

When a railroad was completed through a town, it was an occasion for great rejoicing and magniloquence (the driving of the first spike might also call for celebration). Typical was the scene in Wooster, Ohio, on August 10, 1852, when the first train on the new Pittsburgh, Fort Wayne, and Chicago Railroad was scheduled to arrive. The day began with a "national salute" fired at sunrise. At two in the afternoon people from all over the county began assembling at the depot; by three, there were between fifteen and twenty thousand of them. A telegram arrived assuring the eager welcoming committee that the train with six hundred passengers, including five hundred invited guests from Pittsburgh and Allegheny City, had passed through Massillon. Promptly at 4:10 the engine with its gleaming brass work, belching black smoke, arrived—but let the local paper describe the ensuing excitement: "The scene was magnificent; the people shouted, cannons boomed thunderingly, whirlwinds of gladness swept over acres of clapping hands, and on faces young and aged a 'grand Homeric jubilation was radiant.' It was the Pentecost of gaiety. The fire companies never looked or behaved better; the martial music was inspiring and heroic, and the guests were happy and hilarious, both by choice and by compulsion."[75] The gaily dressed party from the East disembarked and were directed to the American House for a banquet, at which copious and flowery toasts were offered. At night there was a parade of the fire companies, their engines drawn by matched horses caparisoned with flowers, plumes, and floating banners. Fireworks followed, and the evening reached its crescendo with the launching of a hot-air balloon; rising with it into the hot summer night were the hopes of Wooster.

The ceremonies at Rochelle, Illinois, in 1854, held at the Lane Hotel (and marred, unfortunately, by the failure of well-wishers from Chicago to arrive because their train broke down) were climaxed with an ode by a local bard:

The steam-horse is come to our grove in the West
Our joy at his coming cannot be expressed.
Untiring he moves from Chicago to Lane
To haul in our lumber and draw out our grain.
The sound of his snorting is heard on the gale,
He'll never be contented until the long rail
Has reached the Pacific and then mingling lay [*sic*]
Will be music to those who are far, far away.[76]

The railroad boom began in earnest in the 1850s, authoritatively ushering in the postpioneer period. Since the need for railroads in the small towns was obviously often a life-and-death matter, for perhaps the first time in their histories they called upon their local governments, whether city, town, or county, to raise large amounts of public funds. (The state governments similarly encouraged railroads by a variety of fiscal measures ranging from tax concessions to direct financial aid. The local municipalities followed this state example, but the important point is that they became aggressive investors in railroad stock in their own right. A state could be reasonably certain that railroads would be built somewhere within its borders; a town, however, had a desperate need for the railroad to route itself specifically through the town. Consequently, it had to go out and get the railroad.) The railroads did indeed bring prosperity by easing access to such natural resources as timber, by providing transportation to market of local agricultural products, and by bringing raw materials to the local manufacturer and goods to the local merchant more cheaply. At the same time, as the case of Crawfordsville shows, the town rarely made any money directly from the railroad. In other words, the stocks were worthless, while towns frequently defaulted on the bonds issued to raise the subsidy or tried to avoid payment. (Some, however, like Cairo, Illinois, were paying off nineteenth-century debts well into the twentieth century.) Another unforeseen long-run development was that the railroad might actually jeopardize local industry by introducing cheaper, competing products manufactured in the cities. A town with a monopoly over a large trading area might boom for a while, only to watch this shrink as other competing local lines snaked out from other towns. The financial exertions necessary to attract a railroad might overstrain the town's economy—more specifically the banks which often put up the money and which were often built on sandy economic soil in the first place. So a railroad by itself was not always salvation; at times it would be only a temporary boon, stimulating industries that later were to go under, giving the town a few bracing breaths of prosperity before it returned to somnolent stagnation.

In truth, the odds against any town undergoing an economic boom commensurate with the extravagant promises of its early boosters were tremendous. For every Cleveland, Chicago, Cincinnati, and other towns that "took off" and grew into cities, there were hundreds of small places that remained stamped forever with the identity of "small town"; yet they had been founded with high hopes that they would become cities. The average town grew slowly, was vulnerable to distant economic currents, had frequent local business failures, and gradually settled into an economic role that locked it in an uneasy symbiosis with the surrounding countryside, from which it took the farmers' surplus and to which it supplied goods and services. Because its prosperity rested on an agricultural base, its merchants were vulnerable to the same fluctuations in the commodity markets as the farmers were. The absence of construction activity and industry in London, Ohio, was commented upon by a sojourning Irishman: "Bedad, this is the first town I ever saw that was entirely finished!"[77]—and there were many like it.*

The negative influence on towns' growth rate of the scatter-gun pattern of settlement of the West by farmer-speculators whose reach exceeded their grasp as tillers of the soil has already been described. Another baneful influence, especially in the prairie areas, was the absentee speculator. Playing a similarly negative role were the large individual landholders and land companies, with holdings of several hundred thousand acres. The absentee speculators, as has been mentioned, withheld land from cultivation, while the large holders, who actively managed their spreads, sought to turn them into "bonanza" farms. They used tenants to work their lands and engaged in intensive mechanized cultivation and wasteful farming that exhausted the soil. The results were high land prices demanded by the speculators, which discouraged smaller farmers, and widespread tenancy at high rents on the

*Of a more livewire town, St. Paul, Minnesota, Mark Twain said, "It is a very wonderful town, indeed, and it is not finished yet. All the streets are obstructed with building material, and this is being compacted into houses as fast as possible, to make room for more—for other people are anxious to build, as soon as they can get the use of the streets to pile up their brick and stuffin."

bonanza farms. The farmer-speculators who could not keep up their high mortgage payments and were eventually foreclosed also ended up as tenants. It was estimated that 20.5 million acres of land were held by speculators in Indiana, Illinois, and Iowa alone. Senator William M. Stewart of Nevada charged in 1871 that of 447 million acres of government land sold, fewer than 100 million acres were owned directly by farmers. This last figure may be exaggerated (and the percentage of speculator-owned holdings was higher in the states west of what was originally the Old Northwest), but as Representative Henry D. Moore of Pennsylvania told the House in 1850, there was a New York speculator who owned an entire county in Illinois. On this land he would settle at most a hundred tenants. The effect of absentee ownership in Iowa was described by Senator Jim Lane of Kansas to the Senate in 1862: "I have travelled days over . . . Iowa without seeing a house, and on asking the reason, the answer was it was because the land belonged to non-residents."[78]

Paul Gates, an authority on American land policy, summed up the effects on community growth of scattered settlement—effects that would be magnified several times over in areas with absentee landlords or large tenant farms:

> On every frontier the settler-speculator was present. He rarely learned from experience. By claiming 320 acres instead of 160 he separated himself that much more from his neighbor. He had to bear a heavier proportion of the cost of road construction and maintenance; his school costs were increased or the establishment of schools was delayed and his children were denied educational opportunities; the expense of county and state government, in a period when the land tax was the principal source of government income, was burdensome. Other social institutions like churches, granges, and libraries came more slowly because the population was so dispersed. Furthermore, railroads, which all settlers wanted in their vicinity, could not be pushed into sparsely settled areas without large subsidies. State and county subsidies required special assessments upon the already overburdened taxpaying farmers, and land grants, whether by state or federal governments, created a near land monopoly.[79]

Yet the towns grew in the Old Northwest, the majority of them successfully making the slow transition from pioneer hamlet to preindustrial trading center. In the early New England towns, communal values and religious control were preeminent; in the Middle West, economic factors dominated. The New Englanders who emigrated to the Middle West played an important role. As Page Smith has pointed out, they were traditionalists or conservative dissenters seeking to revivify a religious purity they had lost in New England.

Thus they formed islands of stability in the heterogeneous stream of immigrants. Their communally settled towns were more likely to "take" since the citizens in such towns had ties of mutual dependence upon each other and shared faith in a religious ideal. On the other hand, what we might call the laissez-faire or purely speculative town was less stable, yet also more open, and better adapted to mingling the heterogeneous population of the West, although the white, native American element remained the dominant group. And it offered values of sociability and law and order, as well as economic opportunity. On the frontier the town had a necessary role to play—a conservative, stabilizing one of concentrating economic and social relations in one place; of harnessing and directing the volatile energies released by the frontier situation; of serving as trade, financial, and distribution centers for the surrounding countryside; tied to the land, the pace of their commerce was in step with the rural rhythms of growth and harvest.

Although no middle western town is typical, the story of Greenville, Ohio, which we have already alluded to in connection with the Devor–Wilson brothers battle over the county seat, is as commonplace as any, so we will tell it here as prosaically as it happened.

Every small town is lapped by the currents of history, however slightly, at some point in its career, and Greenville was no exception. In its first incarnation as Fort Greenville, it was the site of the signing of the treaty with the Indians that opened up the Ohio Territory. After receiving the county seat designation in 1811, the Greenville founded on land belonging to John Devor and his aunt had a temporary influx of population during the War of 1812, when the fort was regarrisoned. When the soldiers and their followers left, the town was once more a tiny hamlet with a handful of people. This handful, the historian reports, tripled between 1814 and 1817, but economic growth was slow. The first enterprise, and main building, was a two-story log tavern. Somebody started a tannery, but in the vernacular of the time, "it didn't come to shucks." The local shoemaker entered a sideline—operating a pottery kiln. And two doctors arrived—not to mention two "root and yarb [herb]" quacks, who provided an exotic plant for every disease, which occasionally may have been as effective as the regular physicians' universally dispensed calomel. Terry Wilson is heard from again in an economic connection, when he tries to start a mill, but this was destroyed by fire, the luck of the Wilson boys holding true to form. The town had another grain mill and a sawmill, both of which were going concerns, but there was little else. The roads were so bad that nothing on wheels could move for nine months of the year.

In 1816 the founding Devors had suffered a slight legal setback involving a clouded title to their land, which they had claimed before the county was officially organized by the legislature. This was settled, and Darke County officially came into existence on December 14, 1816. The first sale of Greenville town lots was held that year, under the supervision of the sheriff of

Miami County, out of which the new county had been carved. Five lots were sold by "partition" sale—one-third down and the rest in deferred installments, the customary mode of selling town lots. Among their first acts, the commissioners of the new county (who were, of course, the only government in the area) ordered a road surveyed and appropriated funds for the erection of the first public building in Greenville—the county jail. Trials were held in the schoolhouse, which was also used as the grand jury room and located on the lot donated by the Devors for the burying ground; a circuit judge rode through once a year to preside. The first trial held in the county involved a man accused of selling whiskey to the Indians, which all peace-loving pioneers regarded as a serious offense, not out of concern for the Indians' health but because drunkenness produced violence. Jury duty in those days provided a test of civic-mindedness because the county was not authorized to pay for the jurors' food while they were deliberating. One jury deliberated for sixty hours without food or drink, proving that some of the pioneers respected the law even over the claims of their stomachs.

Education in Greenville began with the usual pioneer school—a drafty puncheon-floored cabin with rough benches where squirming, frigid scholars sat unwillingly for at most the three winter months and were taught the rudiments of reading and writing and sums by, more often than not, a slightly scapegrace scholar who had fled some peccadillo back east and who kept warm by frequent pulls at the whiskey jug and vigorous whippings of his unruly pupils.

Education in Greenville took its first step forward after the Ohio legislature passed the first state education act in 1827—and promptly fell flat on its face. Greenville Township was carved up into school districts according to the law, and the township trustees appointed three school directors (precursors of the school board). These worthies, "no two of whom by reasons of feuds and ill-feeling"[80] would speak to each other, had some difficulties transacting business, and a year passed with no action whatsoever on schools. A new and more sociable board was elected the following year, and it swung into action, ordering that the old schoolhouse on the burying-ground lot be disassembled and moved to another lot, which had been acquired by the town from Bill Wiley in lieu of a fine he owed on an assault-and-battery conviction. A public subscription was solicited to build a new school to replace the one that had been moved; unfortunately two would-be contractors got into an argument one night over their bids on laying the floor for the school, the upshot of which was that one snatched the subscription paper and angrily cast it into the stove. So much for the new school. As in most pioneer communities, funding for education—despite the noble words of the Ordinance of 1787—was slow in coming. About all the town fathers did was to tear down the old school and sell the logs as firewood. Classes on a fee or subscription basis were held in two makeshift schools that served the town for many years.

Meanwhile, the town economy was not exactly booming. In 1824 a wool-carding mill and grain mill were erected along a nearby stream. These lasted until 1835, when they were put out of business after a doctor whose land had been flooded by backed-up water from the mills brought suit. In 1826 another combined grist and saw mill was built a mile and a half below town; it survived until the 1840s "with little profit."[81] There were two other sawmills around this time, said to be busy about one third of the time at best. Another grist and saw mill built in 1826 was frequently idled when its machinery broke down, although it remained in business, more or less, until the 1880s. A tannery erected in 1826 pursued a checkered career through numerous hands, never turning a profit. Another tannery, built the same year, lasted three or four years and "turned out a commodity which they said was leather, but by other people was called horn; a side of it might be bored or cut when moist, but in the dry state defied awls and edge-tools."[82] Yet another tannery, located within the town on Water Street, also changed hands several times.

Still, there was enough of a Greenville in existence for the town to be incorporated by act of the state legislature during the 1832–33 session. In the 1830s Greenville was a backwater town of two stores, a blacksmith's shop, two doctors, a whiskey shop, one frame church, a schoolhouse, and a brick courthouse and jail. Its metamorphosis from the pioneer chrysalis probably followed the usual progress. At first there would be a few cabins set in a clearing; then these would give way to cabins built of hewn logs, some double cabins with a connecting second story. With the establishment of sawmills, the first frame house would appear, then another and another, and the wealthiest citizen might indulge himself in a more substantial brick house. Still the town had a raw and shabby look, the streets were rutted and repositories for garbage, dishwater, and dung, which in summer gave off a pervasive reek.

By 1840, the town was definitely passing into the postpioneer stage. The population had increased from one hundred in 1824 to eight hundred in that year. The town boasted a newspaper—the Greenville *Journal*—which was not at all unusual for a county-seat town; towns of one to two thousand frequently supported three newspapers, though not handsomely. The small-town editors were a breed apart. Most started as printers, and their editorials resounded with the autodidact's rococo phraseology, heavily seasoned with commas. Most were mouthpieces for one political party or another (in exchange for which they got all the legal notices when their party was in power), and they carried on vitriolic *ad hominem* feuds with rival editors representing the other party. These vendettas enlivened the otherwise stale and trivial columns of news that filled their pages. Nonetheless, the papers stimulated the lively concern with politics that characterized most county-seat towns.

The town itself had acquired a more orderly shape. There was a square in the center with the usual second-generation courthouse—a square brick structure with a peaked roof capped by a cupola. A distinct business district could now be discerned, featuring six mercantile stores purveying a wide variety of goods—in contrast to the early days when, as the historian put it, "every dealer had nearly a little of everything, but very little of anything."[83] Still there was no separate hardware store, no drugstore, no clothing store (the absence of which the historian explains with the laconic statement, "No Jew had yet appeared in the town"[84]; first-generation Jewish pioneers often started out in the clothing business in middle western towns), no boot or shoe store, and no proper grocery store, with the exception of "traps called groceries" which sold liquor as well as provisions. There were, however, two lawyers, four doctors, two hotels (which in pioneer times would have been called taverns; by a similar acquisition of refinement, the "traps" or "groceries" became saloons), four churches, a flour mill, and a printing shop, connected with the newspaper. The only town industry producing for export was a small shop that turned out hoop poles, slender hickory or oak poles used for barrel hoops. Farmland in the surrounding area was selling for prices ranging from two dollars an acre, unimproved, up to twelve dollars an acre for improved land. This latter was, of course, partially or wholly cleared, the girdled trees and stumps burned and grubbed out, and there were probably a hewn-log or even frame farmhouse, with glass windows and spires of smoke rising from brick chimneys, and a barn on the property. Now wooden "worm fences" snaked across the rolling, green, cultivated fields—a sure sign of prosperity since the cost of fencing an eight-acre farm—$356—was considerably more than the land had originally cost, and most farmers started out with scarcely enough cash to pay for their claims, even at land-office prices. Fencing also reflected the new "herd laws" which for the first time required the farmer to keep his animals penned up, rather than letting them wander on roads and into the town.

Gone too was the wildlife that once had roamed the land, the bears, wolves, deer, elk, and wild turkeys and the rattlesnakes too, probably exterminated by the hundreds in mass hunts, as were other such "pests." No longer did dark, rumbling clouds of passenger pigeons darken the sky for hours at a time. There were other changes too, marked now only by some grizzled elder as he rambled on about how once the river had run high and fast, how the nights had been cool in summer because the great "butts," or trees, that blocked out the sun prevented the ground from soaking up the heat, and how the wetlands once lay idle for more than half the summer, covered with water. But probably the bustling townspeople in their factory-made clothes were too busy to listen to his maunderings.

A new middle class was forming in the town, bounded above by a few wealthy men and at the bottom by the poor—in Greenville mainly Negroes and Irish immigrants. The middle class included grocers, merchants, tradesmen, artisans, shopkeepers, clerks, doctors, lawyers, dentists, ministers, teachers, bookkeepers, petit officials—respectable, industrious, God-fearing, early-to-bed-and-early-to-rise, heedful of their neighbors' good opinion, bent on making money and avoiding alien ways.

By 1848 Greenville was perceptibly bustling and the population had taken a marked jump to two thousand. Now there were three dry goods stores, four groceries, three hotels—the Broadway, the Buckeye, and the King House—and three churches—Methodist, Presbyterian, and New Lights (United Brethren). The historian notes, however, that parts of the town were still covered with forest or water. By 1850 more specialized merchants had made their appearance—a tailor, a druggist, a hardware purveyor, a milliner, a bookseller, and an insurance agent. Five three-story "blocks" had been erected in the business district, and there was a steam-powered flour mill, capable of producing 150 barrels a day. The town's bright future was further buttressed when the railroad boom of the 1850s made it the hub of not one but three railroads; four turnpike roads as well entered the town. Now there were two newspapers, each claiming eight thousand subscribers in the county. Improved farmland was selling for $40 an acre; between 1853 and 1878 the average price of good farmland had risen from $11.35 to $30 an acre.

A photograph taken ca. 1870 would probably depict a blur of activity. Sixty new buildings were in the process of construction; and there was industry—a foundry and machine shop and a steam planing mill—as well as finance—a building and loan association. The streets were graded and lined with shade trees, and more beautification in the form of parks was in the offing. Schools were in permanent buildings now, and Greenville High School, completed in 1868, accommodated one hundred students. By 1874 a gasworks was in operation, illuminating interiors and streets, and the fire department had purchased a bright red, brass-trimmed Silsby steamer, christened "Greenville," and two hose carts at a total cost of seventy-two hundred dollars. By 1880 the population stood at four thousand—an increase of 500 percent in the space of forty years. Fraternal organizations abounded—the Pioneer Society, the Sons of Temperance (the rise of temperance in the Middle West went hand in hand with the disappearance of pioneer ways), the Masons, the Women's Christian Temperance Union, the Y.M.C.A., the Darke County Bible Society, and the Patrons of Husbandry. It was a stable town, if the divorce rate was any criterion. In 1877 there were 334 marriages and 41 suits for divorce; grounds for divorce included absence, neglect, drunkenness, and cruelty. Seduction and illegitimacy were rare, the historian reported, attributing this to the fact that "family honor was highly estimated."[85] There had been only one execution for murder since a soldier was hanged at old Fort Greenville, and regarding the man sentenced to hang in 1880, "no inconsiderable portion of the better half are opposed to hanging." [86] The poor Greenville had with it, and they were consigned to the new poor farm, which had replaced the old New England practice of boarding out poor people at county expense with whoever made the lowest bid. The population of the poor farm increased from 15 to 106 between 1856 and 1880.

Such was Greenville in the 1880s, a pretty, peaceful middle western town that had weathered its economic setbacks and was on the whole well satisfied with itself and optimistic about the future. Hardly any of the old pioneers were left. Some perhaps would, if they were given to garrulity, echo the words of the pioneer-mother heroine of Conrad Richter's trilogy of novels, *The Trees, The Fields,* and *The Town.* Sawyward Wheeler had lived to see the town of Americus grow up and had waxed rich from her land investments. She now sat alone in her fine brick house, longing for the trees—the "big butts" she had once hated because they choked out sky and sunlight—and for the pioneer life of her girlhood with its simple joys and self-reliance:

> What was the world coming to and what hearty pleasures folks today missed out of life! One bag of meal, her pap said, used to make a whole family rejoice. Now folks came ungrateful from the store, grumbling they had to carry such a heavy market basket. . . . Folks in Americus today seemed mighty tiresome and getting more so. If you saw one, you saw most. If you heard one talk, it's likely you heard the rest. They were cracked on living like everybody else, according to the fashion, and if you were so queer and outlandish as to go your own way and do what you liked, it bothered their 'narve strings' so they were liable to lock you up in one of their newfangled asylums or take you home where they could hold you down to their way of doing. . . .
>
> [It was] the pride and greed and great shakes of these town bodies that bothered her. Nothing was good enough for them any more. Twice had her own church been rebuilt during her life time and still they had to make it bigger, with a new steeple so high no workman for less than four dollars a day would risk his neck on it. . . .
>
> That wasn't half of it. Merchants were spoiling the Square, buying up houses and making them over into shops. They even tried to buy the old cemetery and put up a new bank and hardware store on the graves.[87]

The pioneer days were gone in the fictional Americus, and they were gone in the real-life Greenville, and so were most of the people who had lived them. Perhaps we can pinpoint the watershed day when Greenville emerged from the pioneer era. It was a day remembered in 1880 by a dwindling few, the next greatest day in Greenville's history, after the signing of the treaty that ended the Indian wars. It was a rally held in honor of the visit of William Henry Harrison, adopted son of Ohio, hero of the West, soldier, politician, drinker of hard cider, candidate for president on the Whig ticket. On that day over one hundred thousand rugged sons and daughters of the Old Northwest assembled in Greenville. They came from Kentucky, Indiana, and Michigan, as well as Ohio, to honor the first man of the West to run for the presidency.

The delegations, some dressed in pioneer buckskins and homespun but most in store-bought finery, were met by the Greenville bands—the most popular of which consisted of William Morningstar riding a horse while playing on his fiddle such campaign airs as "Hail to the Chief," "Bonaparte's March," "Soldier's Joy," and "Money Musk." Once assembled in town, they marched in a great parade with floats and bands. One delegation pulled a log cabin on wheels; another accompanied a great canoe, symbolizing the hero's victory at Tippecanoe, drawn by ten prancing white horses and carrying twenty-seven young women who represented the twenty-six states and the Goddess of Liberty.

Then, to the martial music of the fife and drum corps, the swelling, good-natured throng marched west of town to a natural open-air amphitheater formed by the hills overlooking the speakers' stand on three sides. They listened to the first orator, Tom Corwin, argue with much vehemence that the reelection of Martin Van Buren would mean ruinously lower prices for labor and goods. At last it was the old general's turn, and as he rose to speak, still tall and lean, the woods and hills of Ohio rang with the frontiersmen's cheers. Harrison delivered a brief talk emphasizing his support for republican institutions, flavored with personal reminiscences of his long service to the West, and then the meeting broke up.

That night Andrew Scribner, the local Democratic leader, became thenceforth a Whig, for the general himself was a guest in his home. A pioneer merchant, who had arrived in Greenville in 1811, worked at various jobs until he had the eighty-dollar entry money to take out his quarter section, sold the land two years later for sixteen hundred dollars, and bought a stock of goods to open his first store, Scribner had tasted the fruits of the West's promise. No doubt in the heat and hysteria of the day, the symbolism of Harrison's campaign—with its deliberately flaunted pioneer trappings and its aggressive assertion of the candidate's western identity—had awakened a dormant sectionalism in Scribner's heart. No matter that Harrison's advertised penchant for hard cider and log cabins was largely a campaign tactic devised by the eastern Whig party leaders after a Van Burenite had made a snide remark casting doubt upon this Virginia aristocrat's frontier ties. In any case, although the pioneer symbols already belonged to history and legend, out of them had been molded a political figure suitable for the national stage—a homespun westerner backed by eastern money. Still, Harrison's advent established that the West was part of the nation. As Jessup W. Scott would write in *De Bow's Review* in 1853, "The west is no longer the west nor even the *great* west. It is the great centre. It is the body of the American eagle whose wings are on two oceans."[88]

The frontier had moved on; there was another West out there.

4
The Great West—Mining Camps and Cow Towns

The populating of the nearly one billion acres of empty land west of the Mississippi and across the wide Missouri occurred in a series of peristaltic waves, beginning in the 1840s and continuing for the rest of the century. First to arrive was the advance guard, the trailblazers—explorers, trappers, and mountain men, hide and tallow traders, free-lance adventurers, the military. Then the settlers in their wagon trains lumbering over the Oregon Trail to the lush meadows of the Oregon Territory and the inland valleys of California. Next, the gold-seekers, bowling across the plains and deserts pell-mell in 1848, working up and down the California mountain ranges, then backtracking to the gold and silver country in the Rockies and the Southwest. And finally, a last great wave, first by wagons, then by the railroads, to mop up the leapfrogged Great Plains. By 1890 the great movement west was over, ending in a final hurrahing stampede of boomers into the Oklahoma Territory, a rush of humanity that created entire towns in an afternoon.

The vast, empty land demanded new tools, new social organizations, new men and women. And it produced a new canon of myths and heroes—the stuff of countless dime novels, Wild West shows, movies, and television series for later generations. The heroes are familiar enough—the cowboys, the lawmen, the gamblers, the gold-hearted dance-hall girls, the bad men, too, for heroes need evil to conquer. The western town played a part, too, mainly as backdrop and chorus, before which the central figures enacted their agon. The fictional western town was as rigidly formalized as the set for a Japanese No play—the false-front stores on a dusty street lined with hitching rails, the saloons with bar, gambling tables, and stage for the dancers, the general store, the jail, and the church. The people of the chorus had a stereotypical form—women in crinolines and the men in frock coats and string ties, their striped pants tucked into boots. Their lives were projected as dim, ordinary, law-abiding shadows, against which were contrasted the bold-hued dramas of the principals. These were the "decent folk," whom the heroic lawmen died for; they were the meek who would inherit the set after the leading actors left and the last wild cowboy was interred in Boot Hill. Colorless, sober, conservative, salt-of-the-earth, they represented the future—and a dull one it was. Occasionally, as in the film *High Noon*, their passive virtues were transmogrified into hypocrisy and timidity, mocking the lonely courage of the marshal they had hired to risk his life for them. The implication was: Are these dull, cautious folk really the worthy heirs of the noble cowboy? In Stephen Crane's short story *The Bride Comes to Yellow Sky*, the last cowboy is a drunken anachronism, wearing his nobility in tatters, yet not to be scorned.

The recurrent themes of many a western drama did, of course, have a basis in reality; they were gross, even cynical heightenings, foreshortenings, and oversimplifications of situations of which many living people in America had firsthand memories—at least through the 1920s and 1930s (indeed, some of the earliest westerns were filmed on location at towns that were contemporaneous with the story). Neither the Puritan towns of New England nor the pioneer towns of the Middle West generated the same body of drama and myth. Further, by the time the West was being settled, the eastern towns had settled into stability and order; the frontier that was moving west, like the vacuum created by a twister, sucked up all the flotsam and jetsam, the rootless and dissatisfied, those seeking a second or third chance, the aggressively ambitious, and the rootless sociopath. These driven, risk-taking spirits included many of the lawless, but also many more who wanted law, order, houses, churches, schools, trees, and all the rest but whose hope for something better and lack of opportunity had led them to plant shallow roots. They were basically conservative souls who still were free of a vested interest in a particular social organization. They were innovative enough to improvise the institutions they needed. They encountered conditions of terrain and climate radically different from what they had known east of the Mississippi, so they quickly adopted the new tools invented by eastern industry especially for the unfolding western market. The railroads rolled forth across open country, unfettered by narrower confines, conquering the West's endless flatlands, girdling its mountain ranges; barbed wire enclosed the open land for farming, penning up the herds of cattle which in the earlier grazing economy had trampled the plains; windmills provided water in an arid climate; and various farming implements cleaved the tough grass mat covering the plains and turned over the semiarid soil.

The conditions in the West were so novel and demanding that the towns which grew up during various stages of settlement had a slapdash, improvised look that enchanted visiting writers from back east and the readers there who devoured their empurpled descriptions. There was a romance of newness and wonder about the West that never faded; the swift change and hullabaloo of life was reflected in the populaces of the towns. The harsher realities of nature did not figure so much in the romance, of course, although nature, and the technology imported to tame it by the waves of immigrants, deeply influenced the ultimate shapes these towns took. The West was innovative and disorderly, yet its uninhibited way of life harbored latent viruses of stability and order that ultimately brought about its demise. Towns that teemed with brawling, prosperous men might be empty a year later—or settled into droning respectability. Yet a legacy was handed on, for the innovations that evolved into more stable institutions were often tinged with some of the color of the wild days. Towns that had lusty, misspent youths sank into comfortable middle age; yet memories of the old free spirit remained.

The early town-planters represented differing groups. Each came to exploit a different natural resource, and each clustered into a unique kind of settlement. First there were the Spaniards who settled California and the Southwest; then the mountain men, the fur trappers who roamed up and down the Rockies, wherever there were pelts to be had; then the freight haulers who forged trading links between the westernmost frontier along the Missouri River and the distant Mexican outposts in and around Santa Fe; then the miners of 1849 who chased their El Dorados in California and elsewhere; then the cattlemen out of Texas who drove their herds north to the first primitive railheads; and lastly, the immigrants, American and foreign, who put down their brave little farms and towns in the rolling green immensity of the Great Plains. Each of those groups created settlements and towns or at least temporary gatherings for exchange and society—uniquely adapted to their economic and social needs.

The towns in early Spanish California had only a peripheral influence on the American urban styles that supplanted them, yet these essentially Spanish innovations shared a common European folk-village heritage with the early New England towns. The Mexican hegemony was not a brief one, of course, but to the acquisitive, go-getting Americans who flooded the state during its brief independence in 1848 and after its annexation by the United States, the period was quickly a memento tucked away between the scented leaves of a dusty tome. Only the few mission churches that still stand serve as a reminder of the alien past. As the historian Charles Howard Shinn wrote in the late nineteenth century, "Protestants and Catholics alike treasure these memorials of the dreamy, romantic childhood of California, of conditions of society that have forever departed from the American continent, and of an ecclesiastical rule more powerful and more exclusive than existed elsewhere in North America."[1]

Although the Spanish and Mexican governments had in theory a quite enlightened and liberal policy toward the California Indians, according them many rights, in practice they made them childlike wards of the church. The vehicle for this was the mission system. The first mission, founded in 1769 by Father Junípero Serra, was called San Diego; Father Serra subsequently founded six others. The mission Indians lived in a state of benign peonage under the priests and a small garrison of soldiers. Discipline was strict, flowing out of the church's stern purpose of indoctrinating the heathen. The Indians were also taught various trades and methods of farming and were fed and clothed by the friars. The missions were virtually sovereign city-states, independent of the Mexican government. They flourished and grew into rich domains of vineyards, fields, cattle, and sheep. By 1813 over seventy-five thousand California Indians had been converted through them. They were constructed of adobe bricks around a large, cool, shaded courtyard, with a stream running through it; on one side was the church, with workshops, storerooms, monastic cells, kitchens, and the like on the other three sides. Mission life seemed to have been frozen in time, its days following venerable medieval rhythms, keyed to the seasons and punctuated by the regular tolling of the bells which called the inhabitants to prayer. After the revolution of 1822 in Mexico, which resulted in a liberal government, the missions were placed under secular authority, and the lands reverted to the state. After two decades they fell into decay and desuetude, the Indian serfs long since freed.

In their heyday the missions effectively ruled California, with the cooperation of the weak civil authorities; small villages grew up near the missions but remained sparsely inhabited, for the priests discouraged immigration and granted land titles with a niggardly hand to the few who came. The missions were governed by the chief Franciscan friar, who was called *presidente;* theoretically, he enforced Mexican law, but in practice he meted out a rough frontier justice, grounded in local customs. That the mission system was at bottom founded on simple compulsion, however enlightened were the motives behind it, was demonstrated when the Indians were freed and quickly reverted to primitivism. Chanting, "We are free. We do not choose to work," they slaughtered the herds of cattle and looted the buildings; then they returned to the hills and a life of indolence. Under the (often corrupt) civil authorities the missions' once prosperous economies fell apart.

By 1834 California's population was about five thousand, among whom there were forty Americans and Englishmen living at the sufferance of the Mexicans, involuntary converts to Catholicism. The Spanish citizens had built up a prosperous, leisurely way of life centered around their ranches in the fertile valleys. Life was halcyon. It was a sleepy, easygoing civilization; plenty of food for all, proud hospitality to strangers, no fences, and few roads. A romantic, doomed way of life, dominated by the dashing cavaliers who sat superbly on their fine horses. Shinn quotes an old yaquero on his deathbed in 1874, who sat up to cry out with his last breath a vision of comrades long gone: "I hear the ringing of their spurs on the mountain, the trample of their horses!"[2] By then the ringing of spurs and the trampling of hooves had been drowned out by the miner's pick, the pioneer's plough, and the gabble of commerce.

Yet along with the ranches and the missions and the military posts known as presidios, another type of settlement grew up in California, less glamorous perhaps, yet surprisingly democratic in its institutions. These were the pueblos, or free towns. The purpose of the pueblos was to house a farming population that would raise food to supply the soldiers stationed at the presidios; in 1777 the Spanish viceroy ordered the first two to be established at San Jose and Los Angeles. Another pueblo had been founded at Branciforte, near Santa Cruz in 1795. All of the subsequent pueblos were outgrowths of mission towns and presidios.

Pueblos bore certain resemblances to the early New England towns; the land systems in both had their origin in ancient European practices. The colonists who settled the pueblos were given a yearly wage for the first five years and were also supplied with horses, mules, sheep, cattle, tools, seed, wheat, and other necessities. The pueblo's lands were divided up according to four uses. There were the common lands, which supplied common pasturage, water rights, timber, firewood, and the like; municipal lands for governmental use; house lots, which were distributed among the colonists, who were required to improve them within a certain time; and sowing lands—the individual farm plots of the colonists.

The pueblo government consisted of a council and a chief executive called the alcalde. During the first two years of the pueblo's existence, these officials were appointed by the viceroy, but once the pueblo had become established, they were elected. The alcalde served as both chief executive and chief judge, while the council carried out duties similar to those of an American municipal body, such as authorizing road repairs, laying out streets, and providing other municipal amenities used by the people in common. Later laws provided for land grants by the alcalde to each colonist, for which the landholder would pay annual rent or taxes.

When the Americans took over in California, the alcaldes were often continued in office, or else their powers were transferred to a justice of the peace; the alcalde's powers to grant town lots remained in force until 1950, and land titles conveyed by him were recognized by the new government. Moreover, during the interregnum between the proclamation of California as a republic and its amalgamation into the United States, the military government kept in force the alcaldes' judicial powers as judges of the courts of first resort, handling everything from minor offenses to murder (sometimes with a jury). Just as the most important pueblos were Yerba Buena and San Francisco—which were later united as the city of San Francisco—the alcalde in San Francisco was among the most powerful, and during the tumultuous years of 1848 and 1849 he presided over hundreds of trials.

In 1848, dissatisfied with the incumbent alcalde and the anomalous legal situation with its mixture of Mexican and martial law, a group of San Franciscans formed a rump government and appealed to the military governor. The provisional governor ignored their manifesto, declared their government illegal, and reaffirmed the powers of the alcalde. The unpopular alcalde eventually resigned, a new one named J. W. Geary was elected, and then, when a city government was duly established under the new California state constitution, Geary was elected San Francisco's first mayor. Thus the symbolism of continuity between Old and New California was preserved—symbolism affirmed by the title of "ancient and honorable pueblo" which San Francisco retains to this day.

Symbolism aside, the now quaint Mexican ways survived only in a pleasant haze of memory, a nostalgic Edenic dream, even though the Mexican culture was alien to the newcomers, who discriminated against its descendants who lived in the state. The people who swarmed into the state during and after the gold rush of '49, and who stayed, founded their own towns, which turned out to resemble nothing so much as the towns of the East and Middle West from which they came.

By the 1860s and 1870s, when the state was entering a new golden age of agricultural prosperity (based, then, mainly on wheat), the town boomers set to work in earnest laying out their gridiron towns. The settlers who took up lots gave a stamp of transitoriness to these towns. They erected simple, prefabricated frame houses imported from the East to provide shelter until they made their fortune in real estate or whatever gilded dream had brought them, meanwhile providing small-business services to later immigrants. The result was that the California country towns evolved into what historian John Brinckerhoff Jackson has called "half slum, half service and administrative center.[3] In one section were the homes of the wealthy—the big landowners and farmers and other holders of economic power—while all the rest was dreary rows of frame houses, hotels, and rooming houses for the large transient population, and slums on the outskirts for pariah groups—Chinese, Indians, Mexicans. In the countryside were the great wheat fields, worked by the itinerant labor, while in the town the few who profited from their labor resided in grand houses with well-watered lawns.

Such towns were characteristic of Central Valley; in the south lived the people of southern origin, known as "Pikers," (a sobriquet allegedly derived from Pike County, Missouri, and applied to forty-niners from that region; another version has it that Pike was a euphemism for "puke," as in vomit). After leaving the goldfields, these people got down to large-scale cattle ranching, which was more congenial to their migratory temperaments; the existence of their large spreads discouraged and obviated the need for towns.

To the north was the Bay Area, set with its jewel, San Francisco. First a port for the American hide and tallow trade that brought New England clipper ships to the state in the Spanish days, San Francisco became the entrepôt for the forty-niners and grew at a prodigious rate, a rough, buoyant city of pleasure, lavish wealth, and flamboyant vice, with ornate theatres, over three hundred restaurants, palatial hotels, a business district where the banks and mining companies, growing rich off the state's gold, had their offices in grandiose masonry buildings. There was always a large floating population, first of miners and later of foreign immigrants, while the despised Chinese were huddled into their scabrous Chinatown along Sacramento Street. A visitor to the city during the 1870s wrote, "A large portion of the people have no homes. They live, or rather they exist, in hotels, in boarding houses, in lodging houses, eat at restaurants, spend their days at their place of business, and their evenings at resorts of amusement."[4]

San Francisco's saving grace was first of all its site, and second (paradoxically) its topography. The city's gridiron pattern gave it its unique roller-coaster streets, along which rows of small houses marched up and down. These came in the seventies in response to a burgeoning population of middle- and working-class San Franciscans who wanted homes they could afford—the equivalent of the workers' homes in Philadelphia, the row houses of Baltimore, the small, narrow brownstones on the West Side of New York. Rather than being provided by "developers,'" they were the result of cooperative financing through homestead associations, of which there were at least thirty in San Francisco by 1868. The members of the associations pooled their savings, part of which were used to buy a tract of land. The tract was subdivided into house lots, and the individual members borrowed money to build from the association. The houses were simple two-story frame types, taken from standard plans in builders' manuals of the day. The San Francisco touch was provided by "gingerbread," which could be bought separately and affixed to the house by the contractor, and by bay windows, providing a view of same, and also prefabricated. The result was block after block of these small wooden houses, which took on considerable charm in their setting. Los Angeles, meanwhile, was going the way, on a larger scale, of the Central Valley towns—a central business district ringed by slums where the poor lived, and suburbs with manicured lawns, palm trees, and plashing fountains as settings for the grand houses of the rich. The inclinations of the relatively well-off middle western people who moved to Los Angeles beginning in the late nineteenth century dictated an acceleration of this suburban sprawl. They demanded in their turn single-family dwellings with neat, shrunken lawns, protected by jacaranda trees and restrictive covenants. So Los Angeles was set off on its metastasizing growth, a city designed for anti-urbanites with ever-increasing circles of suburbs in distance directly proportional to affluence, leaving the enclaves of the poor behind, clustered around the abandoned core.

Such were the urban patterns that California spawned in the post–Civil War years, but one other kind of community, considerably more unconventional, played a role in the state's history—the mining camps and towns.

These hurly-burly settlements were towns of the moment, rising and vanishing almost overnight, providing temporary housing and a measure of law and society for the restless breed of miners who swarmed into the state following the discovery of gold at Sutter's Fort in 1848. Their span was measured by the availability of gold in the area; when the accessible veins played out, the miners, men to many of whom the itch for gold had become a form of addiction, moved on to some other strike, the big bonanza just over the next ridge.

The truly gold-infected, whose fever was never cured, simply dormant for a time like an old Far Eastern hand's chronic malaria, were perhaps the minority; the majority of the forty-niners, although equally smitten by the fever, would, if they did not strike it rich, as was likely, settle into other jobs (often in a corporate mine) or return home, their youthful dreams of wealth chastened by the hardships of the miner's life. They came in every hue of the American social spectrum, from all parts of the country; they were predominantly young, without women, and sufficiently dissatisfied with prospects back home to stake their all on the chance of gold. As many as one hundred thousand of them came in 1849 alone, some by sea all the way around Cape Horn or to Chagres in Panama, across the isthmus then by ship to San Francisco, but the majority came directly cross-country because it was cheaper simply to borrow the family wagon and convert it with some canvas and hickory lathes into a prairie schooner. Then they stocked up with food and read up on the routes west in the immigrants' guides of the day—which were predictably inaccurate, describing tortuous desert trails as verdant boulevards or prescribing "shortcuts" that led straight up sheer mountain faces.

The first wave left in December of 1848, most of them by ship, fearful that if they delayed until spring all the gold would be gone. Those who went overland headed to the jumping-off towns on the banks of the Missouri River, where the natives extracted their pounds of flesh and more before passing them on to the tender mercies of the ferry operators who charged exorbitant fares to cross the wide river. The initial rush was a mob scene with men fighting each other to the death for places on the ferries; later the crossings were better organized and lines stretched for miles. Even though the ferries ran twenty-four hours a day, the wait could be as long as two weeks. Once extricated from the larcenous natives' clutches and across the Big Muddy, the men set forth in wagon trains across the Great Plains. For the bulk of the migrants, it was by then spring of 1849—the rainiest spring in memory, turning the trail into a quagmire, making cooking fires and dry beds impossible. On top of all this came disease—colds, malaria, diarrhea, and, most deadly of all, Asiatic cholera. Perhaps five thousand, out of the estimated fifty-five thousand who went overland, were struck down by disease before the wagon trains reached the High Plains. There the cholera was left behind but in its place came other hardships—the climb to the South Pass through the Rockies and the alkali deserts, where thirsty, starving men had to be forcibly turned away to their deaths by the more fortunate, who were carefully husbanding their own dwindling rations—and finally the rugged Sierra Nevada, made even more hazardous by a late snow that year.

Some of the other routes—the Santa Fe Trail, or directly west from Fort Smith, Arkansas, or across northern Mexico—were perhaps easier but still provided fearsome hardships of their own. Many of the groups that crossed the continent had organized themselves into mining companies in their hometowns before they left (these bodies could be elaborate; one had rules calling for "a president and vice-president, a legislature, three judges, and a court of appeals, nine sergeants as well as other officers;"[22][5] others featured gaudy uniforms and bristling armories). Such groups held together on the long crossing, providing mutual succor, but once in California they quickly fell to quarreling and broke up. Similar associations were organized to charter ships, selling stock to finance the passage (single passage ran as high as one thousand dollars), but many of these, too, did not survive the stupefying boredom of the six-month voyage around the Horn. These associations presaged the miners' penchant for organization of their affairs that flowered in the goldfields—a uniquely western Mayflower Compact.

To understand the remarkable miners' society, we must backtrack to the early days of 1848, when the territory of California had its own private (as it were) gold rush before President James Buchanan's December 1848 message to Congress confirmed the strike officially, and set thousands of men to singing "Oh, California! That's the place for me!" The first gold was discovered in a stream feeding the millrace of John A. Sutter's new sawmill, by a contractor named James W. Marshall while making an inspection. Marshall's eccentric ways caused him to be known, at the age of only thirty-five, as a "queer old codger,"[6] and his discovery never brought him great riches. (He claimed supernatural powers, eventually harbored the delusion that all the gold in California belonged to him, and died a derelict.) Sutter's Fort was already a prosperous operation, catering to and providing shelter for the early bands of American pioneers arriving in California; in the days of Spanish rule Sutter had fed them well, paid them for farm labor, then charged them five or ten dollars for a "passport" to go on their way. When Sutter learned of Marshall's discovery, he first thought of finishing the new sawmill before the workers threw down their tools and ran off to dig for gold. Sutter's mill was finished but then the men took off, and Sutter, who had tried to keep the discovery a secret, started leasing promising sites. Such a secret could not be held for long. A Mormon merchant from San Francisco named Sam Brannan visited the gold site and took back a bottle of gold dust. He rushed to the center of town and began shouting, "Gold! Gold! GOLD from the American River."[7]

Such was the story anyway; however they heard about the gold near Sutter's Fort, the men of California dropped what they were doing and headed for the area, leaving army barracks empty, ploughs standing in their furrows and San Francisco (which had a population of two thousand) a near ghost town. The first arrivals made tracks for the vicinity of Marshall's find, but given the primitive mining technique in use—"crevice mining," which involved scraping up the soil or gravel in a dry streambed with whatever implement one had—the readily extractable supply was soon exhausted. But the new men were gold-addled. Up and down the Sierra Nevada, discoveries were being made; news of each new find spread quickly, and the miners rushed about from one to another. Techniques became more sophisticated by the end of the year; wet digging came into favor—the fabled shallow washing pan in which the miner swished the "pay dirt" underwater, allowing the heavier nuggets, flakes, or gold dust to settle as the lighter soil floated away. A bit more complex, and certainly more efficient, was the cradlle, an oblong box on rockers which was shaken violently until the dirt was separated out. There seem to have been no big strikes, but recoveries assayed at ten or fifteen thousand dollars in a few days were not uncommon.

The later-arriving forty-niners had their own modest bonanzas, too, but most found hardscrabble. Of a company of 120 men who had sailed together on a clipper, none, reported an observer, found anything. Weeks of work might yield a bare two or three dollars; one miner estimated after three months that his earnings had averaged a penny a day. Now they sang:

> My cradle I can rock at home, if ever there I get,
> And there I'm bound with empty purse and pockets all to let.[8]

Although the total output in 1849 was valued at $10 million, the rub was that in hunting gold the prize went to the very few. The stories of the few big killings served as propaganda to fuel the avaricious dreams of the rest. Many men stayed and perhaps became infected with a permanent case of "aurimania." Others returned to San Francisco and profited from the trade of the gold-seekers who continued to pour into the state (as a result the city's population grew from two thousand to fifteen thousand during 1849). The post-forty-niners arrived at an accelerating rate so that by 1853 the state, which just eight years before claimed five hundred Americans, now boasted three hundred thousand, and the U.S. geographical center of population had shifted eighty-one miles west. The later miners employed even more sophisticated methods, such as damming and diverting streams to expose auriferous sands beneath or coyoting—sinking shafts to bedrock. They used great "Long Toms"—coffinlike boxes more than twelve feet long placed on top of one another, the dirt shoveled into the top one and water sluiced through to wash away the soil and allow the gold to sink, through perforations, into the bottom box. These methods demanded cooperative effort, so the men would sometimes organize into mining companies and share the profits; those companies that had been formed back east and survived the trip were also adapted to this sort of mining.

Such working arrangements reflected the technological genius of the miners; their political talents were equally impressive, for, beyond the pale of all government, they "legislated" on the spot a body of criminal and property law. At that time, before it was proclaimed federal land, most of California belonged to no one. So a miner asserting his claim to a patch of creekbed did not have to contend with any prior owners. But this meant that by the same token there was no established legal authority to arbitrate conflicting claims or peace officers to enforce judicial orders; the miners were on their own in a kind of state of nature. The overwhelming majority of the miners were native-born Americans; they were a law-abiding lot who found themselves without laws to abide by. Though most were perhaps farm boys, there was a goodly sprinkling of lawyers, doctors, ministers, schoolteacheers, college boys, and the like.

Whatever their background all found themselves in a state of equality—all started off the same, and in the primitive conditions of life in the Sierra Nevada there was no basis for any distinction of class. Further, there was considerable fellow-feeling among them—or at least among those of similar stock; a man started with ties to his "pard," with whom he shared a tent or a claim, and the ties radiated to the others working in his vicinity. Even though many miners worked in obsessed solitude while panning a stream, they retained a sense of cooperation. Later foreigners came so that there was indeed a pungent ethnic stew—the Pikes from Missouri and the Mississippi Valley, Yankees from the East, Negros from Jamaica, Sonorans (Mexicans), Sydney Ducks (Australians), Kanakas (Hawaiians), Limies (English), Paddies (Irish), Coolies (Chinese), and Keskydees (Frenchmen—the name supposedly derived from the Frenchmen's recurrent question, "*Qu'est-ce qu'il dit?*") Still, native-stock Americans made up 70 percent of the population, and where they held sway they treated the other foreigners with varying degrees of intolerance, the Chinese and Mexicans universally relegated to the bottom of the ladder. The most frequent conflicts were thus of racist origin, and the greatest hatred was directed against the Sonorans, who were the largest foreign group and who admittedly numbered some outlaws among them. There was fighting between Mexicans and the Americans in some areas. The Americans also employed racial covenants to exclude the Mexicans from prospecting in areas they claimed. Another practice was the "foreign-miners" tax, which was imposed on any foreigners attempting to work in an American-controlled district. The Chinese were excluded under the principle that a white man had a prior right to a claim, and after he had done with it, the Chinese could have what was left.

Among themselves, the Americans were more community-minded. As men poured into likely areas, they realiized early on that some sort of *ad hoc* law was necessary to prevent eternal squabbling over claims. Most of the miners grasped that it was in their interests to divide up the claims equally among all who showed themselves in an area and then let each man make out the best he could on his allotted portion.

The military government in San Francisco, fearing trouble from the disorderly bands that were pouring into the state, made some feeble stabs at setting up mining codes, but soon gave up, for there was not sufficient military manpower to enforce a code, the soldiers stationed in California having left their regiments decimated to search for gold. What grew up instead was a loose division of mining areas into autonomous self-governing districts. A district was defined as an area larger than a camp, which was the cluster of tents to which the miners working an area of adjacent claims returned to sleep. It was small enough to embrace a group of camps within hailing distance of one another. There were no official boundaries but a district incorporated a large, natural gold area—a valley, say—in which a number of men were working claims. In practice, the camps, the sleeping places of the miners working the clusters of claims, were the irreducible social unit; when there were enough of these, they organized themselves into a district. Although a district generally included several camps, it could comprise but one.

It was in the camps that the seeds of mining law took root. A number of men agreed among themselves on the size and location of each man's claim; perhaps they might assign every prospector ten square feet of streambed. If there were later strikes in nearby sections of the stream, those whose claims had played out or yielded nothing would transfer to the new area; new men would also come in until several camps dotted the area. By then the need would arise for a uniform claim system for all the camps, and a meeting of all the miners in the area would be held, at which time the district was organized and its fundamental mineral law drawn up. These regulations would differ from district to district, depending upon the terrain and prevailing mining conditions. Once the "laws" were promulgated, the need for enforcement naturally followed. The utopian days of '48 had passed; pay areas became more crowded, and hardened criminal types—as well as "undesirables"—began to arrive. Or there were simply disputes over the boundaries of claims. At any rate, claim-jumping cases as well as more serious crimes arose, and the district evolved quasi-judicial bodies to handle those.

According to Charles Howard Shinn, who had been a miner, three forms of government evolved among the miners. The first was the miners' court, which Shinn compared to the folkmoot of the early Teutons. Actually, it bore a more immediate resemblance to the New England town meeting, and the New England background of many of the miners is a more plausible source than Shinn's postulated "race instinct." All miners in the district, regardless of age (there were more than a few sixteen-year-olds among the miners) or class or education, voted in the election of the miners' court. Such courts were first organized by the men of '48, and they continued through the years; although inefficient and given to wrangling, they had the advantage of involving everyone in the district in their deliberations. In some matters there seems to have been a requirement of unanimity before a decision was taken, as was the case with the town meeting; in criminal cases, though, a voice vote of guilty or not was usually taken. And sometimes, when a serious crime had been committed, a judge was elected, a jury impaneled, and arguments heard before a decision was reached.

The second system, according to Shinn, was the alcalde system, a borrowing from the office familiar to California natives. Perhaps this borrowing had its origins at Sutter's Fort, for John Sutter was the legally elected alcalde of that area. At any rate under this system, the miners in a district would choose an alcalde, who was granted the considerable powers of the civil alcaldes. In some areas, the alcaldes might be given the American title of justice of the peace, but the idea of vesting the judicial powers in one man was the same.

The third way was the justice committee, a standing committee elected by the district's miners as a body and delegated powers to try criminals and arbitrate disputes. The number of members varied from district to district, but the committee handled all cases independently of the miners who had elected it.

Despite (or perhaps because of) the fluid frontier society out of which they sprang, the miners' courts and alcaldes were a step more formal in structure than lynch law or kangaroo courts; they were closer to town governments on the scale of evolution. Many miners' alcaldes, for example, were paid and had elected sheriffs to enforce their decisions and recorders to take them down. In capital cases, the alcalde might preside over the jury trial, and in many camps the miners were on call to serve as defense or prosecuting attorneys.

The miners' governments operated in complete independence of the civil authorities, and there was usually no appeal from their decisions. Justice was often stern, with penalties ranging from forfeiture of a few ounces of gold to whipping and banishment to death. Despite its rarity in the early days, theft was always regarded by the miners as a serious crime, and the death penalty was widely prescribed in the mining districts, though the frequency with which it was imposed depended upon the degree of the theft—horse thievery, for example, usually drew a hanging because of the scarcity of the animals in the gold regions, while lesser thefts were usually punished by a fine of an "ounce" or two, or, more severely, twenty to thirty lashes.

Punishment was swift: A man to be flogged would be taken out immediately, while those sentenced to be hanged might be allowed a few days to make their peace with their maker, assuming feeling against them wasn't running too high among the assembled miners. The line between a rudimentary system of law fairly applied and outright vigilantism or mob rule was frequently crossed, for the mining camps were populated by a rough-and-ready element of womanless men whose only recreations were drinking and gambling. If the boys at the "folkmoot" happened to be liquored up, and passions were aroused, God help the poor defendant, especially if he were Mexican, Chinese, or Indian. Shinn himself remarked on the prevalent nativism and hatred of the colored races and noted that most of the worst trouble occurred in the southern California camps, which, as it happened, were predominately settled by men from the American South and Southwest, who had a tradition of resorting to revolvers rather than the courts to settle a grievance. Perhaps it was understandable that the "Americans" would band together to appropriate the good claims for themselves and kick the foreigners out, but the cruelties practiced on racial out-groups exceeded the bounds of normal acquisitiveness under frontier conditions. Especially vulnerable were the Mexicans, who were also the most competitive group. As Shinn noted, "This tendency to despise, abuse, and override the Spanish-American, may well be called one of the darkest threads in the fabric of Anglo-Saxon frontier government."[9] The innate "conservatism" of the miners, especially those from New England, expressed itself in the establishment of democratic, quasi-governmental institutions to protect life and property; but it also erupted in a jingoistic racism which denied equal treatment to all.

Shinn describes a happening at the Sonora camp which symbolizes the transition from miners' justice to the relatively impartial kind administered by legally constituted judicial institutions. The trouble started in the southern camp of Sonora in June 1850, when the state collector of the foreign-miners' tax arrived to receive his tribute from the foreigners in the area, mostly Mexicans. The tax came to thirty dollars a month at the time, which was no inconsiderable sum to the average miner, Mexican or American, who had yet to make his strike. The Mexican miners held meetings protesting the tax and decided to refuse to pay it. Rumors circulated that the Mexicans (who outnumbered the Americans) were arming themselves, so about two hundred American miners picked up their guns and marched to Sonora, where they set up patrols and guard posts and volunteered their services to the local alcalde as a posse. A number of Mexicans fled into the remote mountain country and began conducting bandit raids on local miners. Most of the Mexicans remained peaceably in their camps. Stirred up by the banditry, the citizens of Sonora met on July 3 and authorized the formation of a rifle company of "twenty-five men good and true,"[10] supported by subscriptions from the surrounding camps.

Then on Wednesday, July 10, four Mexicans were caught in the act of burning the bodies of two American miners on piles of brush. They were taken to Sonora, and an angry crowd gathered. But the miners' court procedure was set in motion. At the trial the defendants contended that the bodies had been dead for several days when they came upon them, that no one knew who the real murderers were, and that, following Mexican custom, they had cremated them. This defense cut little ice with the jury, and the four were quickly sentenced to death. But just as the ropes were being thrown over the nearest stout limb, Judge Tuttle, a pioneer of the region, arrived, accompanied by two other civil judges and other citizens. Judge Tuttle courageously intervened and in a "thrillingly earnest appeal"[11] reminded the mob that the town of Sonora was now under state law and a court of sessions existed which by rights should try the case. The judge evidently played upon the local pride of the new town of Sonora by pointing out that since the county was legally organized, an irregular trial would be an indelible blot on its record. His plea cooled the mob, and it agreed to allow a formal trial the following week, at the first session of the county court.

On Monday, July 15, armed miners descended upon the town to see justice done. Rumors that a nearby Mexican camp was in a state of insurrection provided a diversion, and the sheriff and a posse of thirty were dispatched there. They rounded up 110 of the Mexicans and clapped them in a corral in Sonora. The next day they were questioned by an interpreter and freed when their innocence of any hostile intent was readily established. By Tuesday, the day of the trial, the town was swarming with two thousand armed men come to cast a skeptical eye on the procedures of the newfangled court. By late Wednesday the jury had reached its verdict: "There did not appear a tittle of evidence against the prisoners and the jury acquitted them."[12] With that, the men in town dispersed quietly, ashamed, perhaps, of their previous bloodlust.

Although the following year there was a resort to vigilantism in response to a crime wave, which resulted in some whippings and banishments (but no hangings), the trial was a milestone in Sonora's passage from mining camp justice to legally constituted authority. It was no coincidence that at this time Sonora was also making the transition from mining camp to municipality, as were several other such places. It has been said that mining is a good way to pioneer a territory, but a poor way to hold it, meaning that miners will rush in where others fear to tread, but will move on when an area is played out. Without a doubt, the rush of 1849 did open up California and, aside from populating the state within a few years, had a lasting effect on its institutions—its schools, its government, its law—not to mention the effect on its economy of the total of $1 billion in gold mined there between 1848 and the 1880s alone.

The gold fever that swept back east was a more florid form of the "Ohio fever" of the late eighteenth century which had populated the Ohio Valley; the dreams of riches which had sparked the Spaniards of the sixteenth century remained a potent lure to the men of the New England towns and middle western farms. By the mid-1850s, the hard-core miners were heeding other siren songs and leaving the mother lode for Oregon, the Rockies, and the Great Basin in the Southwest. But many others remained to exploit the state's fertile agricultural valleys. The old-style miner could no longer extract gold with his primitive methods, so in his place came industrialization, the use of mining machinery financed by eastern capitalists to exploit the still-rich California earth. The miners thus did not hold the country, but they made it possible for others to, and one of their legacies was the towns that grew up from rugged, brawling mining camps, of which Sonora was typical.

Sometimes the terms mining camp and mining town are used interchangeably and, indeed, there is no hard-and-fast definition of either. Generally, however, a mining camp rated lower on a scale of permanence; it was a collection of tents to sleep in with perhaps a primitive saloon and place to gamble. Yet inevitably in mining regions where there was a substantial miner population and consequently plenty of gold to be had, the need for a town with more permanent facilities asserted itself. In some areas, a small place might be already in existence; in others shrewd speculators rushed in to plat a town and sell lots; and in still others a cluster of miners' tents was the nucleus for a town.

However it began, the mining town existed to serve—or exploit—the miners by selling them food and tools and providing them with amusement as a respite from their lonely hours on their claims. One might say that the purpose of some mining towns was to give the miner a place to drink, gamble, or whore away his "poke," then send him off to the mines again dead broke—a crude but efficient way to accelerate the transfer of money. As Shinn points out, these early towns were "but overgrown andd permanently settled camps."[13] About fifteen or twenty such mining camps received town charters from the state government—names such as Weaverville, El Dorado, Auburn, Shasta, Oroville, Grass Valley, Nevada City, Jackson, and Placerville. Some of these survived, while others became ghost towns—the miners' contribution to the scenery of California. Those that failed were founded on nothing more than gold, and when that ran out, the miners simply abandoned their claims and the merchants immediately followed, walking away from their houses and stores. Others, such as Nevada City, rode the waves of several booms and busts. In the spring of 1850 it consisted of a few tents, but by that August, following a rich strike, it mushroomed into a town of two thousand. But that winter the miners left again, leaving the region's first newspaper, the *Alta California*, to pronounce it a "frost-work city"[14] i.e., as transient as the frost on a windowpane. The following spring the miners drifted back, and the town was once again bustling—actually, a number of gravel hills near the town were rich in gold, deposited there by streams of the Tertiary period. Yet these placer mines were soon picked clean, and Nevada City was again in jeopardy, until subsurface quartz mining resurrected it once more. The underground mines at nearby Grass Valley produced more than $100 million in a little over a hundred years. Nevada City drew wealth from these and from its Miner's Foundry, which made the heavy machinery needed in quartz mining (in quartz mining, shafts were sunk deep in the ground, the quartz rock bearing veins of gold was blasted, and the rubble carried to the surface, where great stamping machines crushed it; the gold was extracted from the gravel by passing it over quicksilver). Still other towns became modest trading centers after the gold had played out, county-seat towns whose occasional mansions, theaters, or hotels of Victorian opulence stood as reminders of flush times past.

Physically, in their early stage, mining towns were hardly promising. They were mainly tent towns, the tents placed haphazardly about, with sometimes more permanent structures of canvas or even blankets on board frames (the cost of imported lumber was prohibitive) and perhaps a wooden building or two of dubious architectural provenance and equally dubious soundness. The main street, if any, meandered between the tents, a sea of mud or a deep carpet of dust, depending on the season. Around the tents the miners had scattered their litter—broken picks, empty sardine tins, steak bones, whiskey bottles, battered tinware. The squalor in which the miners lived attested to the transitoriness of their habitations; here today gone tomorrow when the gold played out; certainly rudimentary sanitation was one area the miners' courts neglected. The men patronized the "hurdy-gurdy girls," who did business in the more permanent mining towns. In one camp the men paid a dollar for the privilege of gazing on an exhibit of a woman's boots and shawl, and in another, when a man's wife arrived, the inhabitants formed a long line for the privilege of gawking at her for a brief moment, after which a generous collection was taken and presented to the husband. Drinking was heavy, especially on Sundays, the miner's day off, when it began in the morning and continued on into the evening; professional gamblers were everywhere, and some, it was said, took in as much as $17,500 a month. Where there were more permanent saloons, boasting an "orchestra" (a fiddler) and a wooden floor, Saturday night dances would be held, the miners often dancing with each other. The miner's outdoor life involved long hours of working alternately immersed in freezing streams or exposed to the hot sun (during the winter free-lance mining shut down); further, the diet consisted mainly of pork and beans, vile black coffee, and bread leavened with saleratus which was then baked on a hot stone or in a skillet. Scurvy and various stomach disorders were, not surprisingly, common; more serious were the epidemics of malaria, cholera, and other diseases that swept through the camps. Despite their impermanence, ugliness, and pestilence, the mining camps bore jaunty, defiant names—sobriquets like Rough-and-Ready, Mad Mule Gulch, Hell's Half Acre, Murderer's Bar, Shirt Tail Canyon, You Bet, Lousy Level, Gomorrah.

Everywhere a febrile restlessness was in the air, a pent-up kinetic acquisitiveness, sublimated by day into the lonely hours standing hip-deep in icy streams with the washing pan, then exploding at night as restless men wandered about talking gold, gold, gold, or fighting, or throwing away their hard-earned dust on the turn of a card. Complementing the almost palpable gold lust was the riotous inflation of prices, due in part to the scarcity of goods in a state where they had to be imported nineteen thousand miles around the Horn from the East Coast and in part to the avarice of the merchants. Prices fluctuated wildly and varied with the locale. At Gold Run, near Nevada City and Grass Valley, in the early days a miner reported that at the one "store" (a square canvas shanty) moldy biscuits went for a dollar a pound, pork was two dollars and flour one dollar a pound, and boots were six ounces of gold dust per pair. Gold dust was the favored currency and the monetary unit was a pinch, which was just that. (With miners carrying the stuff around, it got in their clothes and hair, and so saloonkeepers "panned" the night's sweepings methodically, and barbers saved the day's hair trimmings for later sifting.) In other camps the prices were equally high—potatoes a dollar a pound, chickens four dollars each, apples at two for seventy-five cents (1849–50 prices). Canny John Sutter was one of the first to attempt to profit; prices at his store, as jotted down by a visitor in 1849, were as follows: "Two white shirts, $40; one fine-tooth comb, $6; one barrel of mess pork, $210; one dozen sardines, $35; two hundred pounds of flour, $150; one tin pan, $9; one candle, $3.20."[15] The law of supply and demand functioned like an engine missing on half its cylinders and in need of a ring job; one day lumber would be four hundred dollars per thousand and a month later would bring a price less than the freight charges; the humble but necessary saleratus might be twenty-five cents a pound and it might be fifteen dollars a pound; tobacco one day would sell for two dollars a pound and a week later would be so plentiful it was tossed out into the streets. Interest rates ran constant, though—10 percent a month.

For the miner who had yet to pan out, these prices could be onerous, and for those whose grubstake ran out before they made a find it was go home or find a job locally. The miner's life-style dictated high living and flamboyant consumption (for it was only gold, wasn't it?)—if he squandered his poke, tomorrow he could go back to the diggings and find some more. Indeed, many miners developed a phlegmatic fatalism, a stoic acceptance of the fickleness of the god of chance (for the discovery of gold was largely dependent on chance and certainly not on superior virtue or effort) that made them perfect marks for gambling games. They would watch fascinated as their fortune rode on the wheel or monte card, and when they lost, they would shrug and go off into the night—perhaps the gold was not real anyhow. Gambling was honest, one miner wrote; certainly there were few quarrels in the gambling dens, and the professional gambler, with the house odds in his favor and the abundance of wealth around, had little need to cheat. Shinn describes the miners' psychology:

> Men, who had been brought up to keep sober, and earn sixteen dollars per month, and save half of it, went to California, found rich claims, earned several hundred dollars a month,—of which they might have saved three-fourths,—but spent every cent in riotous living. Men who had been New York hod-carriers paid out ten dollars a day for canned fruits and potted meats. But only a few years later, when the surface placers were all exhausted, these same unkempt sybarites returned to beans and pork, strapped up their blankets, and made prospect tours to other regions, taking their reverses more placidly than one could have thought possible.[16]

Such were the true miners, taking the ups and downs calmly, pursuing, ever pursuing the new strike, the better "prospect." As Shinn observed, "The habit of following with swift feet each new excitement became as much a part of the Argonaut's nature as the habit of running after a fire is a part of the healthy boy's organization."[17]

The more permanent mining towns became seats of a rather bizarre nouveau riche culture—schools without teachers or pupils (every proper town had a school), literary societies founded by illiterates (the activities of one consisted of "spinning the hat" to see who would buy the next round of drinks), and theaters presenting Shakespeare as well as the vaudeville of the day featuring the female performers. For the actors it was bonanza time, too; it was not unusual for a miner to rise up after a performance and with gruff shyness ask if the company would honor him by accepting a small gift of five hundred dollars' worth of gold dust in appreciation for their fine performance. Newspapers, beginning with the famous *Alta California*, proliferated to such a degree that in the 1850s California had the highest number of newspapers per capita of any state in the Union.

During the mining-camp era in California, conventional towns grew up in several ways. There were first the speculative or paper towns, founded by real estate promoters seeking to serve (exploit) a mining population. As Shinn writes, "Speculation in promising town-sites soon reached as extravagant heights as it ever did in the Mississippi Valley or in the Pennsylvania oil-region. Every cross-road, river landing, and ferry had its 'corner-lot speculators,' who prophesied its future greatness."[18] Most of these towns probably remained paper towns, so unstable was the mining population they served, and such names as Oro, Linda, Eliza, Fetherton, Kearney, and many more had lives as evanescent as mayflies.

Others of these supply towns grew and flourished, carried forward by the momentum of growth that received its initial impetus from mining. After the mines ran out, they became agricultural trading centers. Both Sacramento and Stockton were such towns. The latter was, in 1849, a single ranch house; three months later it had ballooned into a tent town with a population of one thousand. Sacramento became a bustling supply depot of canvas dwellings, its streets, hastily laid out in a monotonous gridiron, littered with great piles of boxes and bales and teeming with drivers cursing at their oxen, their wagons filling the air with choking dust. A single, small frame building was the town's only hotel. It was called the City Hotel, and its operator paid an enormous thirty thousand dollars a year in rent to the owner and filled every inch of floor space with arriving miners who needed a place to stay for the night.

Then there were the towns, already mentioned, that grew directly from mining camps. That they achieved permanence is probably because of the minority of miners whom Shinn called the "home-hungry, home-creating few,"[19] who were determined to make a go of them. One such town, Sonora, had its genesis in an untypical concern for the miners' welfare, particularly their health problems. Sonora Camp was erected in 1848 by a few Americans but mainly by Mexicans and Chileans. By 1849 the population in the area had reached five thousand, and the Americans, though still a minority, were in charge. They seem to have been an uncommonly decent sort. When the rainy winter of 1849–50 arrived, miners in the area—many of them Mexican—were stricken by scurvy, because of their exclusively salt-pork diet. It became apparent that the sick miners required hospital care and a diet of fruit and vegetables. To accomplish this, all agreed, a town government was needed to organize a hospital. The camp's alcalde was made mayor by common consent, and a council of seven (five Americans and two Frenchmen) was elected. A hospital was built with money contributed by miners; the alcalde also donated his fees.

But the treatment was enormously expensive, given gold-rush prices. Lime juice was $5 a bottle, potatoes $1.50 a pound, and canned fruits and other antiscurvy remedies of the day cost twenty times as much as they did back east. The hospital's orderlies drew $8 a day, which was about half what the average miner made but many times the going wage for such work back east. Because of the high overhead, a new source of revenue was needed, so the inhabitants voted to plat the land and sell the lots.

To the miners, such a disposition of mining-camp land was unprecedented. To them, land was valuable only for the minerals lying on top of or underneath the soil. On open federal land, mineral rights could be claimed anywhere, except where a bona fide land purchase had been made from the land office, which was rare in gold-rush California. In the state's early days the miner was supreme; the law recognized the superiority of his claim over all others, and the state court ruled that "the right belongs to the miner to enter on public mineral lands, although used for agricultural purposes by others and whether enclosed, or taken up and entered under the Possessory Act."[20]

Thus the owner of a town lot could not forbid a miner from digging up his property, so long as no injury was caused to the house or store on it. Hydraulic or sluicing operations sometimes washed away roads, orchards, and even houses. Under the miners' rights of eminent domain whole towns were moved; in other towns mining within the town limits often extended to coyoting under the streets, making them vulnerable to later cave-ins. The state was, for a time, literally turned over to the miners.

As with most mining camps, the land Sonora occupied belonged to nobody and everybody, save for the mineral rights below the surface. Any miner could take up a lot and live on it for nothing. Hillside land not claimed for mining was considered common pasture, unless someone wished to build on it, in which case more power to him. The streets simply followed natural topography and old pack-mule trails. Under the miners' land socialism, each took what land he needed and worked it according to his luck and ability. But when the need for money for the hospital arose, the Sonoran miners performed the unprecedented act of subdividing the land into salable parcels.

Soon after this was completed, the first state legislature met and did its own dividing up of the state into twenty-seven counties. Unlike the state legislatures back east, it found itself hard up for county seats in some areas, including Tuolumne County, where Sonora was located. Thus did Sonora become a county seat without the slightest bit of hustle or chicanery on the part of the local residents. Indeed, a legislator versed in the ways of the world tipped off the Sonora town council that the town's accession to county-seathood was imminent and advised them to "take some of the boys and secure possession of just as many town lots as possible."[21] Naturally, the legislator expected to be cut in on the profits that would result from the land sale. But the councillor to whom he wrote lacked the necessary worldliness (perhaps he had been off in the hills too long); he reported the letter to the council, which promptly adopted a resolution forbidding any private citizen from acquiring town lots since "all such unoccupied lands do belong to this town in its corporate capacity."[22] The resolution was enforced, and when the lots were sold off to the highest bidder from time to time, the proceeds of the sales went to the hospital, for the good of all.

Sonora's subsequent development illustrates the transition from mining camp to a proper municipality. One step involved the office of alcalde. This was abolished by the state legislature in 1850, leaving the town with no equivalent officer with judicial powers. Further, around this time the legislature also apparently invalidated the town government then serving and ordered the town to apply for a new municipal charter. During the hiatus of authority the town elected a "miners' justice of the peace"—an office used in some mining camps instead of an alcalde with roughly similar functions. The justice of the peace remained the effective government until a proper slate of town officials could be elected in 1852. This pantheon of officialdom proved too expensive for the little town to support, so the government was simplified in 1855 to a board of five trustees, a setup similar to that of many pioneer towns in the Middle West. Thus Sonora traveled from an alcalde to an alcalde-mayor to a justice of the peace to a town government. But it remained at heart a mining camp with all the faults (including the near lynching of the Mexican miners previously described) as well as virtues of the breed.

Nevada City was another town that began life as a mining camp and somehow survived the vicissitudes of a gold-based economy. Unlike Sonora, Nevada City seems to have sprung up in an eruption of enthusiasm, akin to traditional town-booming, after the revival of the mines in 1851. The local citizens straightaway procured themselves a charter and elected a grandiose slate of city officials which would have done for Chicago, including nine aldermen and a "president of the council."[23] They acquired a building for a city hall, put up a jail, and erected a hospital, for the miners there were likewise afflicted with scurvy. The town government soon ran aground on the shoals of fiscal irresponsibility, however. No provision had been made for taxes or selling town lots, and license fees were minimal. By paying off its creditors with scrip, the town ran up debts totaling eight thousand dollars. A town meeting held to deal with the problem favored throwing in the towel, which was accomplished by ordering the aldermen to fire all the town officials. The legislature then canceled Nevada City's charter, setting it adrift in legal limbo until 1853, when it was reincorporated with a more austere town government. Then came the industrialization of mining, and Nevada City manufactured the mining machinery that exploited the deposits around Grass Valley. A photograph taken in 1873 shows Grass Valley's Main Street, which has been newly macadamized. Picking through the rocks that cover the street are thirty or so men, all looking for traces of the yellow metal, a last gesture of once-independent placer miners now working in factories for wages.

The photograph also gives a glimpse of the substantial, if ugly, town Grass Valley had become. It boasted, in addition to its macadamized Main Street, plank sidewalks under the overhanging roofs that jutted out from the downtown stores, some of which were brick blocks. Nevada City developed a more attractive business area and added some graceful homes and churches, many with New England motifs such as widow's walks. As Shinn observes of all the mining towns of the gold era, "It must be remembered that a great deal of capital went into permanent investments in these thriving and energetic towns. Brick blocks, three-story hotels, stores, banks, and fine residences embowered in blossoms and surrounded by lawns, were not infrequent long before 1856 in all the towns."[24]

For those miners who spurned the life of the townsman, of clerking in a general store or working for another man underground in the quartz mines and coming home at night to hearth and wife (women of the respectable sort were becoming more in evidence, many of them wives from back east come to join their husbands), there were new prospects opening up elsewhere after 1853, when placer mining had played out in the mother lode. First came the Fraser River strikes in British Columbia in 1857–58. Most of the miners who rushed there in leaky, jammed-to-the-gunwhales coastal ships or overland met disappointment, however. The river was in flood, the gold-bearing regions were difficult to reach, and only a few areas—mainly in sandbars, twelve to eighteen inches beneath the surface—produced much gold. Then too, the autocratic rule of James Douglas, head of the Hudson's Bay Company, was alien to the miners' democratic ways, and they pulled out.

The miners who returned to California from British Columbia were soon pursuing other prospects. There were the rushes in Idaho that moved east to Grasshopper Creek in Montana. Dubious legends of the "lost mines" of the Spaniards, plus a few contemporary strikes, drew others to Arizona. But the young territory was, in 1853, arid and forbidding; further, the Apache under the military genius Cochise were riding high. In contrast to Montana, where farmers and ranchers followed the gold miners and built up a permanent economy, the Arizona miners left few traces. The first mining camp was Gila City, which became notorious. As one observer put it, "It opened up with a saloon to supply the necessities of life and later added a grocery store and a

Chinese restaurant for the luxuries."[25] The Gila City mines played out by 1863, after yielding gold worth about $2 million. Better gold, silver, and copper strikes were made in the Tucson area. The town was a hellhole even before the miners came, populated by about five hundred Mexicans, Indians, and Americans, of whom a traveler said, "If the world were searched over I suppose there could not be found so degraded a set of villains."[26] Everyone carried (and used) a gun, and in the cemetery were buried only two men who had died of natural causes. Ironically, the tough little town of Tucson could not stand up to the Apache; most of its residents had checked out by 1865, when Cochise's raids reached their zenith and U.S. military protection was scant. The clearing out of Tucson's dregs, courtesy of the Indians, gave the town a chance to start over on more equal terms with vice.

The late 1850s saw the gaudiest rush of all—the fabulous Comstock Lode, which produced $300 million in silver and gold over the years, was discovered in Nevada east of the Sierra Nevada in the Washoe Mountains of the Great Basin. The first prospector to see gold in those hills was a whiskey-soaked old reprobate named James Finny, universally known as Old Virginny. Finny in his soberer moments—and perhaps his drunken ones as well—was, however, a good judge of placer country, and his diggings in the hill he ebulliently christened Gold Hill convinced him that the territory was promising. His discovery caused little excitement, however; it was not until later the same year when two other prospectors, Peter O'Riley and Patrick McLaughlin, discovered what would be called the Ophir vein of the Comstock Lode that interest began to build. O'Riley and McLaughlin worked their claim more assiduously than Finny had until it was easily yielding three hundred dollars in dust for every cradle wash. By then a miner named Henry T. P. Comstock rode in on his mule and announced that he and Finny and a man named Penrod were laying claim to the area as partners. Rather than argue, O'Riley and McLaughlin formed a partnership with the three. Comstock promptly bought out Old Virginny for a blind horse and a bottle of whiskey, and another man, Joseph D. Winters, joined up.

Soon the miners had sunk shafts, which were yielding an unusual dark blue quartz. This "blue stuff" turned out to be three-quarters silver and one-quarter gold and assayed at an incredible $3,876 a ton. This was the Ophir Mine, the richest ever. News of these finds brought some seasoned gold men to the area, including George Hearst (father of William Randolph Hearst) and Judge James Walsh of Nevada City. They were a new breed of capitalists and they sized up the Washoe situation correctly: Large amounts of investment and advanced mining techniques, rather than hoards of independent prospectors, would be needed to exploit this treasure. They bought out the five partners, paying McLaughlin $3,500, Comstock $10,000, and O'Riley, who held out longer than the others, $40,0000—very little, indeed, considering the great wealth the mines produced, but at the time the prospectors could reasonably argue that they had got the best of the bargain. In the first place, the full-scale mining necessary to exploit the lode called for a good deal of capital, which was probably available, but which would have required the partners to become businessmen with lawyers, stock certificates, incorporation papers, and the like—something a true prospector with gold fever in his blood shied away from.*

Virginia City was a town energized by hope, on the electric optimism a crowd of miners could generate when rubbing up against one another. True, for everyone who stayed, hundreds more returned to California. It was the usual gold-rush mass hysteria that had brought them in droves to the little jumping-off town of Placerville, California, to clog with their bodies the narrow, precipitous trail across the mountains, on foot or in stagecoaches, buggies, or whatever conveyance could be commandeered at staggering prices. When they arrived, most became aware of what Judge Hall had already warned about when he brought the news back to Nevada City in June: This strike was limited to the few claims centering on the Comstock Lode, which had already been taken. As a result, when winter set in in 1859, only three hundred miners remained at the spot; in February ten thousand more came but of these only about four thousand remained at the end of the year. This was no country for the little man, yet there would be jobs in the mines and endless opportunities for speculation.

The quartz from the Ophir vein had indeed been rich, but no one knew how much of it there was or, even if the wealth was boundless, how much could be taken out. The excavations in Gold Hill and neighboring mountains were the deepest ever attempted and called for more sophisticated techniques than employed in the California "coyote holes." The men on hand hired out to the owners of the Ophir, Mexican, Central, Belcher, and Gould & Curry mines and attacked with picks the hard rock. Shafts, rather than tunnels, were sunk, and cave-ins were frequent. In 1860 a vein two hundred feet wide was discovered, yet it could not be tapped because of cave-ins which resulted

*Indeed, the typical miner either panned dust from a placer site or sought out potentially valuable properties that he sold to others. It was really the buyer, rather than the discoverer, who bore the risk, since only a madman—or a conman—could say with any assurance how long a vein was or how much good ore it would produce. Later prospectors did do better than the Comstock men, though. Charlie Adams, discoverer of the King Mine in 1893, received $150,000; and Felix Mayer, who discovered the North Star in Arizona, sold out for $350,000. Both of these men died broke, the money squandered—as happened with the Comstock five, and most prospectors, for that matter. With $350,000 one could start a bank, but what right-thinking prospector would want to become a banker? No, they were like Old Bill Baer, who made and lost three fortunes in his lifetime. Still, Old Bill reformed in his later years. As a miner who knew him named Fred Rhodes recalled: "When he died, he had some money left. He got tired of bein' a tramp, you know."[27] Old Bill's last sale brought him only $2,500, but he held on to this money, and it was enough to keep him in his declining years.

in the loss of many lives. A German mining expert saved the day by inventing a system of "square-set" timbering to shore up the walls. This involved heavy timbers joined in mortise-and-tenon joints and forming a honeycomb of hollow cribs which together supported much more weight than could individually placed timbers. This improvement enabled the miners to go even deeper, but now the heat was so hellishly intense that, even with ventilation shafts, the men could only work a few minutes at a time. This problem eventually gave rise to the Sutro Tunnel, a four-mile ventilation tunnel sunk into the mines, begun in Carson Valley. The tunnel was actually completed by 1870, but by then it was too late to cool any miners; the ore had nearly played out.

With engineering feats (or follies) such as these, Virginia City's fortune was assured; mining shares shot up in value and the population grew from four thousand to more than fifteen thousand in 1863. Men worked the mines around the clock in three shifts; 5,000 men were employed in the mines, 675 in the Gould & Curry Mine alone; wages averaged five dollars a day.

For the rest—the speculators who did not own shares of the fifteen or so claims (or *leads* as they were called) that tapped the Comstock—gold fever was replaced by stock fever. In the early years most of the town lived on a gaseous future expressed in shares in a mine. Known in common parlance as "feet," they derived from the measure of one's underground claims, which were expressed in the number of feet one owned in, say, the Washtub Mine. Mining being an industrial enterprise now, the speculators and prospectors laid claim to a certain number of feet, incorporated their mining company, and sold shares. These shares changed hands at a furious rate, often bought and sold without the slightest knowledge about the actual claim being represented. (A mine, Mark Twain remarked, was a hole in the ground owned by a liar.) The streets of Virginia City were a peripatetic stock exchange, with the local citizens, the "brokers," wheeling and dealing with frenetic abandon. Indeed, "feet" was the chief item of commerce in the city's early days.

Perhaps the heady air of Virginia City's altitude had a tonic effect on its bustling inhabitants; still there were more propitious sites for a town than the side of a seven-thousand-foot mountain (Mount Davidson). Nonetheless, the miners of '59 planted a town there, hard by the putative lode, as though they wanted to be able to keep their eyes on it day and night, lest some rival spirit it away. Mountainside mining towns were not, by then, entirely unknown and would become commonplace in the Rockies. Their serpentine streets were so narrow that in one, with tracks right on Main Street, the shop awnings had to be raised whenever a train passed through.

Virginia City in its early days seemed to have been put where it was out of caprice or perverse willfulness; its plan seemed to derive more from the addled maunderings of Old Virginny than any sensible human thought. Lacking any lumber for building, those first settlers in the winter of '59 sheltered themselves as best they could. J. Ross Browne, a visiting journalist, described the scene:

> Frame shanties, pitched together as if by accident; tents of canvas, of blankets, of brush, or potato-sacks and old shirts, with empty whisky barrels for chimneys; smoky hovels of mud and stone; coyote holes in the mountain side forcibly seized and held by men; pits and shafts with smoke issuing from every crevice; piles of goods and rubbish on craggy points, in the hollows, on the rocks, in the mud, in the snow, everywhere, scattered broadcast in pell-mell confusion, as if the clouds had suddenly burst overhead and rained down the dregs of all the flimsy, rickety, filthy little hovels and rubbish of merchandise that had ever undergone the process of evaporation from the earth since the days of Noah.[28]

There was, of course, a saloon—a tent. The "bar" was a sluice box, and the stock consisted of two barrels of flavored raw alcohol labeled, in a prime example of western tall-tale humor, "brandy,'" and served in tin cups. The "streets" were filled with milling crowds of rough, dirty, unkempt miners in which mingled a few San Francisco swells in boiled shirts and stovepipe hats. Over there, a running argument was taking place, for which, periodically, a knot of fistfighters peeled off to elaborate the discussion in a flurry of blows, while yapping dogs snapped at their heels. A number of hard-eyed men watched quietly, their hands resting on their revolvers, ready to intervene if a pard was getting the worst of it or the debate did not go to their liking. But, as Browne observed, "These dangerous weapons are only to be used on great occasions—a refusal to drink, or some illegitimate trick at monte."[29] The dispute was probably over a town lot, which one man had staked out and another had "jumped."

Farther on, in what was apparently the center of the town, if such a perpendicular town could be said to have a center, other knots of men stood around discussing in passionate tones the hot stock issues of the day. Prospectors from the hills, rough men in red flannel shirts, offered for inspection sample rocks ("croppings" or "indications") taken from possible mines already optimistically christened with names such as the Rogers or the Lady Bryant or the Mammoth—names that, their owners claimed, would soon be spoken in the same reverent tones as the Ophir, the Mexican, the Gould & Curry. If the buyer hurried, he might have a piece of this valuable "lead" for only seventy-five dollars a foot. As for the rest—

> Jew clothing-men were setting out their goods and chattels in front of wretched-looking tenements; monte-dealers, gamblers, thieves, cutthroats, and murderers were mingling miscellaneously in the dense

> crowds gathered around the bars of the drinking saloons. Now and then a half-starved Pah-Ute or Washoe Indian came tottering along under a heavy press of fagots and whisky. On the main street, where the mass of the population were gathered, a jaunty fellow who had "made a good thing of it" dashed through the crowds on horseback, accoutred in genuine Mexican style, swinging his *riata* over his head, and yelling like a devil let loose.[30]

The people in the streets stayed out as late as they could, for they had no homes to go to. Sleeping accommodations were supplied by a few enterprising innkeepers who rented out floor space in tents, shacks, or huts; in "sleeping-houses" (as Browne accurately denoted them) men "sought slumber at night" jammed together in twenty by thirty foot rooms—a dubious privilege for which the sleeping-house keepers extracted a dollar a head. There was one euphemistically dubbed "hotel"—"a tinder-box not bigger than a first-class hencoop"[31]—which slept three hundred men. "Slept" was the wrong word, for the next morning the bleary-eyed men emerged into the incessant dust-whipping wind, cursing their host, and headed for a bar where they stood about pretending to observe the festivities while catching a few winks leaning against the wall or a post.

In its first year of life, Virginia City perched on the shifting sands of speculation, and this condition was reflected in the makeshift, temporary state of its architecture—rather like the sidewalk pitchman's display case which could be quickly folded up and spirited away at the first sign of the law. Nobody owned anything, but everybody traded. Town lots were acquired by bare physical possession in a kind of king-of-the-mountain game that invited claim jumpers to try to take the territory for themselves. "Nobody had any money," Browne noted, "yet every body was a millionaire in silver claims. Nobody had any credit, yet every body bought thousands of feet of glittering ore. Sales were made . . . at the most astounding figures but not a dime passed hands . . . silver, silver everywhere, but scarce a dollar in coin. The small change had somehow gotten out of the hands of the public into the gambling saloons."[32] "Feet" were the universal currency; miners exchanged their exaggerated finds for someone else's hollow claim; feet were used to pay the grocer—if he would take them.

By the spring of 1860 the town started taking shape, even though the mines were not in production. Streets were laid out, and corner lots were going for one thousand dollars each; a supply road was opened and lumber imported; more permanent buildings went up. By the year's end, Virginia City boasted a theater, thirty-eight stores, eight hotels, nine restaurants, and twenty-five saloons. Talk of money pervaded the air, but most of the populace ate pork and beans, drank the cloudy alkaline water, and breathed hope. Through 1861 immigration slacked off. Most of the miners entering Nevada were sidetracked by the nearby Esmeralda and Humboldt strikes. Congress's faith in the area was demonstrated when it created the Nevada Territory that year by lopping off a large chunk of land from Utah, the domain of Brigham Young and his Mormons, who officially frowned upon gold rushing as not a fit occupation for saints, although the storekeepers in Salt Lake City took their tithe through the dizzying "mountain prices" they charged transient gold-seekers. The capital of the new territory was at Carson City, where that year arrived the new governor's secretary, Orin Clemens, accompanied by his brother Samuel (soon to become known under his pen name Mark Twain).

After a period of fruitless prospecting, Sam moved out to Virginia City, where he had been offered a job as a reporter for the *Daily Territorial Enterprise.* He found the town just beginning its flush times. He gawked at the streets, climbing up the mountainside like the terraces of a tea plantation; the whole city was slanted like a roof, he decided. The "street-terraces" went up the mountainside at fifty-foot intervals. The houses were built away from the mountain so that they fronted on the street and their backs jutted out on high support stilts. A person looking out his or her rear window thus would look directly down the chimneys of the houses on the street below.

Law and order in Virginia City were, theoretically, in the hands of a large police force, but every man carried a gun (reporter Sam Clemens discarded his; he had never used it and only wore it because he did not like to appear conspicuous), and the twenty-six graves in town were all occupied by men who had not pulled theirs fast enough (or too fast, but with fatal ineffectuality). In the western society of that day there was a pecking order, at the bottom of which were immigrants, or easterners, dudes, or tenderfeet, meaning someone who had arrived a few months later than you did. Dudes were identifiable by their back-east attire. The quickest route to distinction, Clemens decided, other than shooting somebody, was to become a saloonkeeper. The saloonkeeper was at the pinnacle of Virginia City society; he was widely deferred to and constantly in demand to serve as alderman or state legislator. In mining-camp society, Clemens noted, the "rough element predominates;"[33] thus members of the traditionally honored professional groups back east—the lawyers, doctors, editors, bankers—found themselves socially on a par with the gambler, the desperado, the speculator, the miner who had struck it rich.

Wealth's conspicuous display was the chief end of Virginia City's gold-rich aristocracy. Social life was gay and frenetic. Mary Mathews, a widow with a small child, who boldly came west in search of her brother's legacy, eventually landed in Virginia City, where she supported herself by taking in laundry, running a boardinghouse, and "baby tending." On this last, she could make five dollars a night, and her services were much in demand. There were balls every night, she recalled, and the "ladies were very fashionable."[34]

The capitalists who owned the mines and mills would eventually emerge as the true aristocracy of wealth and power, but in the early days every man considered himself on the sure road to riches. For who among them had not heard of the men who had been lifted overnight from the valleys of poverty onto the peaks of wealth by a strike? Such as the two cousins with a small freight-hauling business who took some feet in a silver mine in payment for a debt. Ten months later the mine paid out, and each cousin was said to be collecting one hundred thousand dollars a year. Or the man who lived off a strike providing sixteen thousand dollars a month, who was fond of reminiscing how he used to work for five dollars a day in the same mine that had yielded his strike. Or the poor Mexican who occupied a patch of land in a canyon near the Ophir Mine. When the land became valuable—there was a tiny stream on it, which the mining company needed—they traded him a hundred feet of the mine for his land; the hundred feet turned out to be the richest section of the mine, and four years later its value was $1.5 million. Telegraph operators were particularly well placed to trade on inside information, and several became rich buying stocks. Small investors like Mary Mathews made more modest fortunes. She bought small blocks of stock when she could; eventually her investments were paying her two hundred dollars a month—though later the companies folded and the annuity stopped. Even the "failure" stories perversely reinforced the dream—the Curry of the Gould & Curry claim, who owned two thirds of its twelve hundred feet, sold his share for twenty-five hundred dollars in cash and a spavined horse; four years later the mine was valued at $7.6 million in the San Francisco market. Or Old Virginny and the other finders of the Comstock wealth. There were daily stories in the newspapers touting some new find; such tips were routine, Sam Clemens recalled, and the reporter who wrote the story was always rewarded with several feet in the newest El Dorado—he himself acquired so many feet in this manner that he lost track of them.

Because of the remoteness of the area and the compactness of its veins of treasure Virginia City was more than a mining camp. It was its own supply base. It was the seat of government for the area and the shipping point from which the quartz was sent off for processing. By the 1870s it was processing the ore in its own stamping mills and exporting bars of the pure precious metals. These mills transformed Virginia City into a dirty, smoky industrial town, its chimneys smudging the crystalline sky and laying a black pall over the surrounding countryside. The beast had been born; mining had moved into the industrial stage; Virginia City had become a little Pittsburgh; in time other ores—copper, tin, lead, coal—were being mined in place of the depleted gold and silver.

With mining becoming an industry, the prospects for towns were improved, and town-site speculation became popular. The town boomer had to promote a site that offered some permanence, which meant that there had to be sufficient ore in the vicinity to keep several thousand miners on the job. Since the long-term potential of any given strike was difficult to assess, the boomer was in as risky a profession as was the prospector; still his initial outlay was small and there was the chance of a nice windfall from sales of fifty-by-one-hundred-foot town lots to erstwhile merchants, plus whatever business enterprises he could build up from his ground-floor vantage point. Near potentially rich strikes a brisk and often unscrupulous competition raged among rival claimants of the same land, or between rival towns striving for economic dominance over the territory.

A case of the latter occurred at the outset of the fifty-niners' rush to the Pikes Peak area. The played-out mines of California and the disillusionment of the Fraser River run, combined with the panic of 1857, which loosened the ties to land, home, and job of a lot of men back east, set off another wild rush. This time town boomers added their misleading puffery to the siren song that crossed the plains to lure the gullible.

A prospector named John Beck, who remembered a strike made in the area in 1850, worked the South Platte River area with William Green Russell, a friend from Georgia; they found "color" near the mouth of Cherry Creek. This claim played out, and after an unsuccessful foray to the north, Beck and Russell returned to the Cherry Creek area, where they met a group of men from Lawrence, Kansas, led by J. H. Tierney, who were also prospecting the area. The two parties joined forces and agreed that town planting looked to be a more promising enterprise than gold seeking. They formed the St. Charles Town Association, and platted a town east of the junction of Cherry Creek and the South Platte, then settled back to await the arrival of the first wave of eastern dudes drawn by the news of the strikes.

By fall, over a thousand hopefuls had arrived; some, however, were put off by the steep prices the St. Charles Town Association was charging for home sites and so organized the rival Auraria Town Company with a site west of Cherry Creek. Then, in November, still another party from Leavenworth, Kansas, under Willian Larimer, arrived to look into the town prospects. Realizing immediately that the best sites were already taken, Larimer's group spread around plenty of whiskey and shares in its own company, which was known as the Denver City Company, and bought out the few remaining agents of the St. Charles group. The new proprietors of the soil then laid out their own town, Denver City, and got down to some serious booming. Agents were dispatched to the depressed farm towns of Kansas and Missouri and farther east to spread the good news of riches to be had in Pikes Peak country. Newspaper editors in the jumping-off towns in Kansas and Missouri, which stood to make some business, took up the cry of gold, printing entirely fanciful stories of prospectors who had struck it rich. Strategically placed near these stories were ads proclaiming the virtues of Kansas City or Leavenworth as a place to buy equipment for prospecting expeditions.

Soon, practically the entire Mississippi Valley had succumbed to gold fever; a new breed of prospectors was born, the majority of them small shopkeepers who had gone bust, farmers who had lost their farms, or callow youths like the one soliciting meal sacks at Council Bluffs, Iowa, who explained that he intended to pack them with all the gold he expected to find at Pikes Peak. Few of these men were versed in the skills needed to survive the journey across the Plains. They expected to kill their food along the way, of course, and sleep in promised but nonexistent barns. Many starved, and a few resorted to cannibalism, the most famous case of which was that of a man named Blue who lived off the flesh of his two brothers who died along the way. When the newcomers arrived in Denver in April 1859, they took one look at the inflated prices of necessities and the paucity of mining sites and turned tail. Thus were the fifty-niners transformed into "stampeders" and the "Pike's Peak or Bust!" signs on their wagons amended to read "Busted, by Thunder."[35] Thus ended the ill-starred gold rush of '59.

But Colorado gold was no flash in the pan; it was there—lots of it, and silver, too—if you knew where to look. The town jobbers who had laid out Denver City had got themselves a profitable piece of real estate. In the spring of 1859 John H. Gregory, another of those unkempt wanderers upon whose prospecting skills whole towns and even states would be built, made a strike on the north branch of Clear Creek. A few days later, haggard from the sleeplessness that is a side effect of the gold drug, he made for the assay office with what turned out to be nine hundred dollars' worth of dust and nuggets deposited in the miner's "bank"—his frying pan. When the news reached raw, struggling Denver, there was joy in the streets; Denver was saved.

Gregory's veins soon played out—or rather "drifted" into the hills, meaning that underground mining would be necessary to get out the gold that was probably there. Gregory himself sold his claim for twenty-one thousand dollars and was sensibly working for one hundred dollars a day prospecting for more substantial capitalists. But now the assurance was doubly sure that existence of gold in the Rocky Mountains was a near certainty. Another, more temperate rush began, this one attracting seasoned prospectors from the California fields and farmers with trail skills. These men began to hit with monotonous regularity—Russell Gulch and Spanish Diggings and Jefferson Diggings and Twelve Mile Gulch and Fairplay Creek all yielded reliable "color." Miners were arriving at the rate of five thousand a week; the eastern newspaperman Horace Greeley came out to learn if it was worthwhile for more young men to go west. He proclaimed that it was, and the good word he put in for Colorado country drew more easterners. Denver became the hub city of the state, a supply depot for the surrounding mines; but there were other settlements as well putting down roots in wealthy regions beyond Denver's ambit—Boulder, Golden, Canon City, Colorado Springs, Pueblo, Leadville, and numerous smaller mining camps that had their day in the sun before the miners left their unpainted frame buildings to bleach in the summer heat and weather the fierce winter blizzards.

In their camps the Colorado miners adopted the mining law devised in California. In fact, three out of every ten miners, Horace Greeley estimated, came from the California fields. The more conservative and businesslike mood that had replaced the colorful frenzy of the earlier rushes was evidenced by the names these miners gave to their districts—often they simply bore numbers. Boundaries were drawn with greater exactitude, and government officials' powers more clearly delineated. Claim law was set down in sufficient detail to encompass all eventualities. For example, Sec. 73 of the Russell District code read: "Females have the same right as males. Youths under the age of ten shall not be allowed to hold claims."[36] Criminal penalties were drawn up in precise detail—hanging for murderers and horse thieves, ten to twenty-five lashes on the bare back for other thieves. The Russell District code provided very precisely for trial procedures—even including payments to witnesses ($1.50 when summoned and $1.50 a day for each day at the trial). According to the historian Ray Allen Billington, the laws were enforced so promptly that crime was almost nonexistent in the goldfields, with the result that the shadier types fled to the wide-open quarters of Denver. But Denver was rapidly becoming "citified." Among the signs of urbanity: an Irish schoolmaster, two newspapers, a library, a debating club, a barber who told grizzled old prospectors to "get your beards mowed,"[37] and a bartender who ordered the boys either to cut out the potshots or be gunned down. The bad element that came in from the goldfields was dealt with by the People's Government, a body similar to the Citizens Committee that cleaned up San Francisco.

Perhaps Billington overstates the degree of public peace in the mining towns. There continued to be pockets of wildness, towns where the "bad element" was in control. Such were Tin Cup (née Virginia City) and its rival, Hillerton, which had been hastily laid out three miles east on Gold Hill. By 1880 both towns had populations of about fifteen hundred and were thriving. By 1881, however, Hillerton had "evaporated," as the local newspaper editor put it. One has the picture of the entire population suddenly picking up and moving out, and indeed that was a common procedure with mining camps. The Montana town given the pseudonym of Crystal in Albert Blumenthal's sociological study of "Mineville" in *Small-Town Stuff*, for example, experienced such an exodus. An old-timer recalled that the town had been about to close down in 1882, but silver was discovered just before the telegram giving the order arrived. Crystal went on to prosper—until the panic of 1893, which emptied it completely within a month. The old resident recalled that the people were living in typical mining-town style, saving little, spending it all on the pleasures of the moment. Then, one day, completely unexpected—the end of the world, some called it—came the announcement that the mines were closing down. The word "hit me like a thunderbolt. Nobody's credit was any good and nearly everybody was 'broke or nearly broke.' Most of the people were gone in a week and nearly all were gone in a month. Most of them made no attempt to take any more of their belongings than could be stuffed into trunks or suitcases or carried on the back. Houses almost completely furnished were left. It was terrible to have things so suddenly quiet. All that noise and excitement was gone. The houses were empty and the people who remained were downcast."[38] The announcement had come at 10:00 A.M., and within an hour the four miles of dusty road to the depot were filled with people hurrying to catch the 1:00 P.M. train.

A Tin Cup's survival was not due to the superior virtue of its citizens, who were a depraved lot, but to its better access to the mines. The town was controlled by a rough element who profited from saloons, prostitution, gambling, and other devices, not excluding murder, for siphoning gold dust from the miners' pockets.

By 1882 Tin Cup's population had risen to six thousand, and it boasted a dozen stores and shops, several hotels, and twenty saloons, which was probably almost enough. In 1880 the rough element had elected a tractable mayor and town council and a marshal who was warned that should he attempt to arrest anyone or otherwise interfere with the swindles of the town's leading businessmen he would be removed to a lonely spot on a dark night and shot. In other words, he was a kind of legal shill, a figurehead of lawfulness, set up to lure in the sheep for the shearing. Subsequent marshals seem to have occasionally exercised their authority to the extent of rounding up drunken miners and gamblers, taking them to the jail, and then releasing them. Evidently the "good element," which was present in small numbers, asserted itself, because in 1882 a marshal named Harry Rivers decided to lower the boom on a ruffian named Jack Ward, whose idea of a lively Saturday night's doings was to come into town and pick fights with inoffensive miners (and offensive ones, too). These were not fistfights; in one battle over one hundred shots were fired. At any rate, Rivers challenged Ward, and both drew and fired. Neither man was hurt, but Rivers disarmed Ward and locked him up. Such was the salutary effect of this chastisement on Ward that he decided to get religion; two years later he was a two-fisted preacher in Glenwood Springs, drawing copiously upon his former evil ways for the texts of fire-and-brimstone sermons.

The days of the reform administration were numbered, however—as were Rivers's. One night he arrested Charles "Frenchie" La Tourette, owner of the notorious saloon Frenchie's Place. While Rivers was leading him off to jail, La Tourette pulled a concealed pistol and shot the marshal dead. Rivers's successor went insane; the one after him was killed, the historian tells us, leaving off scorekeeping at that point. Apparently the only thing that could purge Tin Cup's iniquitous life-style was a dose of economic depression. When the surface gold at Gold Hill disappeared, so did the rowdies. By 1884 it had a population of about four hundred, although the Gold Cup mine continued to produce a respectable amount into the 1890s. By 1900 even this had played out and Tin Cup was a ghost town; however, in 1903 an eastern syndicate pumped in more capital, and one tunnel was extended sixteen hundred feet under Gold Hill. This activity revived the town for a while, as did another effort in the area between 1908 and 1912, but at last the Gold Cup closed down in 1917. The town of Tin Cup survived for a while as a summer resort, and fishermen still use its cabins.

Tin Cup's ability to have brief remissions from its terminal decline was not an uncommon trait of the Colorado mining towns. They waxed and waned and waxed again in rhythm with improvements in mining techniques, capital infusions, and demands for new kinds of ore. Initially, the camp might go through the placer period—mining the gold washed down in streambeds. Placer rushes were the most democratic, and anyone with a washing pan could theoretically participate. After that came float mining—the search for exposed ore in the hills and mountains. Then there was the lode or quartz mining stage, involving shafts sunk deep in the ground. This last method, of course, required a large capital and labor investment, as well as machinery for extracting the ore. Further, the deeper ore could not be separated by the ordinary stamping method, so that new processes involving smelters, chlorination, lixiviation, and reduction were introduced, which enabled mining companies to rework already worked ground, as happened at Tin Cup. Further, different metals were mined at different times, the usual sequence being gold, silver, lead, zinc, fluorspar, and uranium. Colorado underwent a series of booms, coming in ten-year cycles, from the 1860s through the early 1900s, and the mining towns' fortunes ebbed and flooded.

Within the duration of a single strike, the Colorado mining towns also passed through several architectural stages. First there was the tent or "rag city" stage, when, in the flush of the boom, there was no time to build permanent structures and no wood or brick with which to build them. If the town lasted a year or so, log cabins for the miners began to appear, and on the main street wooden stores with ubiquitous false fronts, along with the wooden sidewalks which were often overarched by porchlike roofs extending out from the buildings and supported on wooden posts.

The false-front store was not, of course, endemic to mining towns, but appeared in every kind of western town from the Great Plains to California. This rather brazen facade was certainly not a case of form following function, for the false front had no function. Nor was it an eastern heritage, since in their early stages the New England towns and their descendants, the pioneer towns of the Middle West, did not employ such fronts. The false front was a Potemkin-village device designed to present the illusion of an eastern main street, with its rows of two- and three-story blocks. Vincent Scully explains its use as a "reaching for urban scale, for a shape in the vastness."[39] Although "vastness" suggests a town lost in the immensity of the plains, mining towns were often dribbled out along valleys or perched on mountainsides. Still, perhaps, the urge was similar on either flat or rugged topography—a need for instant "townness" amidst a geographical and psychic lostness. The false fronts proclaimed that here was a lively business street of a live-wire town—that it was a going concern—and they announced it instantaneously, without drawing any longer looks that would go behind the facade. They also created an instant building line, defining the main street, giving it more substantiality than would the alternative of leaving the gabled roof edge exposed or of building flat-roofed buildings (which were impractical in a rainy climate).

The commonest false-front style was a simple full rectangle shape that added a "second story" to the building, though many were not even that high. Elaborations of the basic false front were of course possible, beginning with the simple two-step facade and going up to more elaborately designed fronts capped by a half-circle silhouettte in the middle. The final cosmetic was paint—the letters of the store's or saloon's name against a spanking white backdrop; behind the facade, though, the basic building frequently remained unpainted, as though the sense of permanence was proclaimed out front while uncertainty huddled in back. Add to the false fronts the store porches, providing galleries where people could gossip and shelter from the sun, and the wooden sidewalks, echoing with the ring of heavy boots, and one had a quick, economical business and social center—an instant Main Street. Although Mark Twain speaks of Carson City's square with its "liberty pole," the town square does not seem to have been a popular feature in the "instant" western towns. The mining and cow towns had little need for a square. The mining towns were often in the mountains, so there was no room, and the cow towns kept their chief "import," the cattle, penned up on the outskirts for obvious reasons of space, efficiency, and hygiene. These were one-street towns—wide streets in the lowland towns for the bustle of freight wagons bringing in supplies to miners who were so starved for flour and canned goods that they crowded about and bought them off the wagons when they arrived, or carrying out gold and silver. As for the cattle towns, the railroads were their reason for existence and they invariably ran right through the main street.

There was behind the false fronts a good deal of jerry-built ugliness about these western mining towns—muddy or dusty streets, raw wood and shingles, debris scattered about, unloaded supplies piled up in vacant areas, smoke and dust and the teamsters' curses singeing the air. Away from the business district the town streets ran at odd angles or made serpentine climbs up mountainsides. The miners' abodes—tents, shacks, cabins—were scattered around the edges, emanating an odor of frying bacon, burned pan bread or beans, discarded garbage, and unwashed men. And perhaps a stamping mill's roar contributed to the din in the daytime, while at night the sounds of shouts, music, and the restless movement of homeless men in a febrile search for distraction punctuated the air. Surrounding the town were hills scalped of their once fine stands of timber, which had been cut down to provide lumber. Such towns were towns in a hurry to make money and spend it; there was no time to pause to erect amenities, no time even to clear away the garbage scattered in the wake of their frenetic exploitation of the land. Fires frequently raged through them, burning their wooden buildings to the ground. There was no fire-fighting equipment (other than barrels of water along the sidewalks); indeed the water table was so low in many places that fire was inexorable; the only defense was to rebuild, if by then there was sufficient accumulated wealth about the place.

Fire or not, those towns of some permanence did eventually build stone and brick buildings in their business districts, and the newly affluent managerial, mercantile, and professional classes erected their fine homes around the outskirts. It has been said that a mining town had not made it until it had a saloon, a church, and a community center—to which should be added a cemetery, a hospital, a railroad station, a Masonic lodge, a school, a bank, a hotel, an express office, an opera house or theater, and a courthouse. Any or all of these might be candidates for more permanent building material, for, in their varying ways, each embodied important community purposes.

The bank, as the repository of the community's wealth, obviously had to project, however crudely, a sense of affluence, as well as a solidity that affirmed the safety of the wealth stored within. The town's main hotel often served as both a commercial center, where visiting buyers and sellers conducted their business, and a social center, the watering place of the town's *haut monde.* It was also the place where the town made its impression on outsiders coming in to do business, so the finer its appointments the better; though privately owned, hotels were often financed in major part by community stock subscriptions, involving appeals to town pride.

Then there was the town cemetery—not a building, of course, but expressing in its own way the town's climb to respectability. In the early days, the grave markers were merely wooden boards, with names and dates painted or burned on them. The class of people interred there was distinctly on the undesirable side, being made up to a considerable extent of men who had died violently in various affrays. The western phrase "he died with his boots on" was coined to contrast such violent deaths with a peaceful death in bed. The first Boot Hill was supposed to have been in Dodge City, where there was a sizable population of rootless men prone to violent ends. There being no undertaker or embalming facilities, the unclaimed dead were buried with dispatch and little ceremony, dressed in the clothes on their backs and the boots on their feet (these were sometimes removed and placed under the deceased's head as a pillow). The cowboy who had a saddle blanket for a shroud was considered fully prepared for burial. Mining camps, as well as cow towns, had their Boot Hills. In Tin Cup, there were four different cemeteries—one for Protestants, one for Catholics, one for Jews, and one, inevitably called Boot Hill, for presumed infidels. In Tombstone, the town's Boot Hill accommodated everybody, which led the respectable folk—churchgoers, members of fraternal organizations, and the like—to form their own cemetery rather than consign their earthly remains for an eternity in a bad neighborhood of gamblers, gunmen, and prostitutes. Such were the subtleties of even mining-town societies, however, that some of the leading families who had already reserved their plots in Boot Hill decided that *it* was the superior place after all. The two schools of thought kept up a running argument.

With the transition from mining camp to more or less established town, the Boot Hills were hastily swept into the dustbin of the disreputable past; the new cemeteries had artistically carved markers of marble or stone with prim, lugubrious, or euphemistic epitaphs (it looked bad for a town to have too many gunshot deaths flaunted in its cemetery; hence "killed by lightning" was often given as the cause of death). Such epitaphs, Muriel Wolle discovered after studying thirty cemeteries near Colorado ghost towns, overwhelmingly resembled the inscriptions on graves in the region back east from which the deceased had emigrated.

Similarly, the architecture of the permanent homes was imported from the East. In the seventies and eighties, when many of the Colorado mining towns were in their heydays, the Victorian style was dominant and its locutions could be found adorning palatial homes, mingled with dollops of Gothic and Greek revival. Gables and elaborately carved bargeboards were especially popular manifestations; a distinctly New England influence could be seen in carved wooden posts on porches and picket fences.

The genteel Victorian spirit in morals as well as architecture reached a kind of apotheosis in Georgetown, Colorado, one of the handsomest of all mining towns. Georgetown started out as a hustling mining camp, then entered its golden—or rather silver—age with the discovery of the fabulously rich Anglo-Saxon silver lode; over $200 million was taken from the mines there until the repeal of the Sherman Silver Purchase Act in 1893, which resulted in the demonetization of silver. With that blow Georgetown, like "Crystal" and many other silver towns, went into decline, and never recovered.

Almost from the beginning, Georgetown was a city of homes, settled by easterners who brought their families along. The stability of this element, plus the town's prosperity, made it a place of considerable quiet gentility, despite its unforeseeably brief life span. There were several imposing mansions, and even the lesser houses boasted elaborate Victorian exteriors, painted a special shade of pink, etched in gingerbread, green lawns surrounded by wrought-iron fences, iron-lace balustrades, cupolas, hitching posts, and mounting steps. There was also a block-square park or green, reflecting the New England influence. The town had five fire brigades, with the twice-state-champion Alpine Hose Company the most famous. Whether as a result of this or its three churches, Georgetown never had a major fire (the main casualty was the opera house, whose boards were trod by all the famous touring companies fresh from Denver; it burned down in 1892, despite the efforts of fourteen fire companies to save it). It was also the locus of two of the most famous hotels of the West—the Barton House, where General Grant stayed three times, and the Hôtel de Paris, the creation of Louis

Dupuy, an eccentric Frenchman who transplanted lovingly detailed Gallic *luxe* to the Rocky Mountain state.

The image of Tombstone, Arizona—at least as it has been cultivated in this century—stands in strong contrast to that of Georgetown. But despite its current tourist image of a rowdy, "shoot 'em up" town, site of the gunfight at the O.K. Corral, Tombstone could as well stand as an example of the maturation of the mining camp into a relatively stable, prosperous industrial community with churches, homes, families, and law and order. It evolved—over the space of a few years; time works faster in the West—into a county seat and financial, processing, and trading center for a large area of land, where mining was the main industry but which also had some ranching, although this population was too scattered to support any sizable town after the mining played out. When the county seathood eventually passed to another place in the 1920s, the town was on its uppers and had to exploit a mythical version of the old days to keep going.

Tombstone's Columbus was a prospector named Ed Schieffelin. Schieffelin was so typical of the breed that he might have been turned out by a mold. Born in Pennsylvania in 1847, he was brought west by his father in the 1850s; the elder Schieffelin came to pan for gold in Oregon and transmitted the fever to his son. By the age of thirty Ed was living the roaming, lonely life of a prospector, questing after a bonanza while barely making enough to eat. He was an anchorite of gold, living in the desert, touching civilization only to resupply—or, if things were very bad, to work at a job long enough to make a grubstake. Schieffelin differed from his fellow gold-seekers in one major way, though; he had no taste for high living and was a teetotaler. This personal ascetism, plus a shrewd, if untutored, business sense, enabled him to profit handsomely from his big strike.

In the late 1870s Ed's hunch-radar had homed in on the San Pedro Valley in Arizona. There he dug up some promising samples which he took back to show potential backers in the hopes of interesting them in financing further explorations. Nobody was interested—most already owned more feet in promising but nonproducing mines than they needed—but Ed stubbornly clung to his vision.

The long and short of it was that Ed Schieffelin's hunch that the area was a rich one was amply proved out. In February 1878 he and his partners (his brother, Al, and Dick Gird, an assayer) struck ore that assayed out at $12,000 to $15,000 to the ton in gold and $12,000 to $15,000 to the ton in silver. Their discovery was christened the Lucky Cuss Mine because after Gird had assayed the rocks Ed brought him he said, "Ed, you lucky cuss—you have it."[40] Ed had christened his earliest discovery Tombstone because when he was prospecting out of Fort Huachuca, the soldiers stationed there thought he was crazy for venturing out into Indian Territory alone. They considered his hopes of finding gold equally daft, and each time he returned to pick up more supplies, they laughingly told him that all he would find in that dangerous country was his tombstone. Ed liked the defiant irony of the name Tombstone so well that he called another of his claims the Graveyard; but it was the first that gave its name to the mining district and to its major town.

Before the Schieffelins and Gird had even registered their claims at Tucson, the county seat, prospectors were entering the country, guided by a sixth sense that something big was opening up; one of these, Hank Williams, discovered the Grand Central Mine, which turned out to be the richest in the area. Williams had an agreement with Gird that he would share all discoveries in exchange for the latter's assay services. He tried to back out of this, but the three partners remonstrated with him, and he agreed to cede them a section of the Grand Central ledge. This the partners promptly named the Contention Mine, in commemoration of the dispute. As it turned out, the Grand Central, the Contention, and the Tough Nut, a Schieffelin-Gird discovery, were the richest lodes in the district; the Lucky Cuss yielded only a small pocket of ore—albeit rich ore.

But by the time the first bar of bullion was poured from the smelter in the summer of 1879, Ed Schieffelin was already getting itchy feet. The Tombstone district was now the new Comstock and swarming with people. To Ed it smacked too much of civilization, of crowds; besides he hated the life of the businessman. So he turned over the running of the company to his brother and Gird and in November 1879 hit the trail. He dedicated the rest of his life to the prospector's calling, and when he died in 1896 in Oregon, alone in his cabin, a sack of ore that assayed out at two thousand dollars to the ton was found near his body. Just before his death he had written to a friend that he was thinking of moving on; in the letter he came as close as he ever would to stating his credo: "I like the excitement of being right up against the earth, trying to coax her gold away and scatter it."[41] In his will, he asked to be buried in the "dress of a prospector, my old pick and canteen with me on top of the granite hills about three miles westerly from the City of Tombstone."[42]

Ed Schieffelin's Tombstone—the mine and the town—were by then almost played out, but what a time he had given them! The mine produced $7 million in gold and silver; the town a legend. Actually, in the beginning, several towns sprang up around the Tombstone district mines, but most of them ephemeral, and Tombstone proved to be the toughest.

It had first to overcome legal squabbling over the ownership of the townsite, however, and then a tangled welter of suits between mining companies and individuals over various claims, making Tombstone a lawyer's paradise; the populist miners' courts of California days now belonged to a bygone era. Despite all the litigation, though, Tombstone grew apace. By October 1879 it had a population of about one hundred and forty structures, including tents; in the surrounding area lived even more people, mostly miners in camps with hastily slapped-on names like Hog-em, Gouge-em, and Stick-em. A stage line provided service once a week to Tucson, carrying in miners at ten dollars a head, one-way. In 1880 the federal census put the town's population at 973, but the floating population of miners who lived on the outskirts, yet shopped and took their meals in the town, was two thousand; by 1881 Tombstone's population was estimated at seven thousand, and these energetic souls were beginning to agitate for a county-seat designation (the town had been incorporated early in its career, the citizens having successfully argued that incorporation would enable them to provide their own peace officers, thus saving the county authorities this expense).

The Tombstone folk were no slouches at playing county-seat politics in the territorial legislature. There were rumors that some of Tombstone's most famous local product—silver—found its way surreptitiously into the pockets of some of the legislators, but the town's most effective tactic was exploiting the rivalry between Tucson and Prescott for designation as territorial capital. Tucson had been the capital for ten years before being supplanted by Prescott in 1877. The Tucson folk were pressing a new bill that would reestablish their town as the capital. Tombstone's representatives allied themselves with Prescott in the voting, and, in return, when the bill creating Cochise County came up, Prescott voted with Tombstone. Once Cochise County had been created out of the original Pima County, of which Tucson was the seat, the next step of making Tombstone its seat followed as the night the day, for Tombstone was the biggest and most prosperous place in the new county. The bill, passed in February 1881, also incorporated the city of Tombstone and chartered its government, which would consist of a mayor and four councilmen, elected from the city's wards.

In two years Tombstone had risen from a collection of shacks and tents huddled together on a dry, mesquite-stubbled mesa to an autonomous county-seat town. Its dusty streets now swarmed with miners, and a chorus of hammers ringing against wood celebrated the town's growth, as new businesses were erected. There were already 110 saloon licenses outstanding, and the most elaborate such establishment was the Crystal Palace Saloon, located in the Wherfritz Building on Allen Street. This block also contained the Golden Eagle Brewery (every mining town needed at least one brewery, for demand was high and the product too bulky to ship) as well as the offices of U.S. Marshal Virgil Earp, brother of Wyatt, and the medical offices of Dr. George Goodfellow and his next-door neighbor, Dr. H. M. Matthews, who also happened to be county coroner—a proximity that provided the stuff of humorous comment among Tombstone folks. The Crystal Palace, however, for all its grand mirrors and crystal stemware, had grown out of a humble free-lunch parlor cum saloon, which the Golden Eagle Brewery had opened on its premises in 1879. Although there were nowhere near 110 saloons in Tombstone, there were plenty of them (plus fourteen round-the-clock faro games), many rivaling the Crystal Palace in luxurious appointments such as carved mahogany bars, long mirrors, chandeliers, and velvet and plush rococo decor. There were also two hotels (the Grand and the Cosmopolitan); fine stores with the latest ladies' and men's fashions from San Francisco; two solid banks; numerous restaurants and boardinghouses (necessities in mining towns), ranging from the luxurious with imported chefs to establishments like the Cancan, named, it was said, not for its *gaieté parisienne* but the source of its food; three newspapers (the *Nugget*, the *Independent*, and the famous *Epitaph*); the obligatory miner's hospital; a handsome brick county courthouse; and several "theaters" (some merely saloons with entertainment) ranging from the notable Schieffelin Hall—the largest adobe structure in the United States, with a seating capacity of seven hundred—as well as the notorious Bird Cage, where a resident troupe, abetted by pretty waitresses, performed bawdy sketches and songs. Top vaudeville entertainers, like Eddie Foy, also appeared at the Bird Cage, and from time to time plays were presented—such as a memorable performance of *Uncle Tom's Cabin*, during which a drunken cowboy shot the (live) bloodhound pursuing Eliza over the ice floes. The cowboy had, of course, been emotionally caught up in the drama, but the rest of the spectators were so angered that they beat him up; the next day the remorseful, hung over cowboy offered his horse and money in payment for the dog. The entertainment at Schieffelin Hall was more respectable, including plays and lectures; it was also a meeting place for the local fraternal organizations, such as the Masons, Knights of Pythias, G.A.R., and the like, which were springing up. There were at least two other community halls, which were used for dances and union meetings as well as entertainment. There were also schools and four churches—Catholic, Methodist, Presbyterian, and Episcopal (whose first minister was an energetic young man named Endicott Peabody who, if he did not tame Tombstone, cooled it down a bit before going back east to become the first headmaster of Groton, where he had more success with the sons of the aristocracy). Other cultural activities included debating and literary societies, amateur theatricals, and a glee club whose debut performance at the Oriental Saloon was hailed as "immense!" by the *Epitaph*'s reviewer.

The town was plagued by fires, and twice the business district was burned down, only to rise again. Fire companies were organized, but the real problem was the shortage of water, which had to be carted in by the barrel, until a pipe was laid to bring in water from a reservoir in the Dragon Mountains eight miles away. This was not enough, however, so the Huachuca Water Company was set up, financed by eastern capital. Twenty-one miles of wroght-iron pipe were laid to a reservoir in the mountains, and soon water was flowing in at a pressure sufficient to jet a stream 260 feet in the air from the mouth of a hose. With this water supply, plus a business district completely rebuilt in brick and adobe, the threat of fire to Tombstone was ended; the concurrent arrival of such modern devices as the telegraph, the telephone, and gas lights on the streets and in homes signaled that civilization had fully arrived, within the space of only three years.

Still Tombstone retained the feverish ambience of a mining town. The lonely men flocked to the saloons and dance halls at night, and the air was rent by tinkling music and drunken shouts and laughter. Though the miners had their drinking, wenching, gambling, horse races, wrestling matches, and cockfights for amusement, they worked hard—sixty-hour weeks for most, with little time for getting into trouble more serious than a drunken spree; some had their families settled in town, and others participated in the cultural activities.

The town churches did not bar the rougher element, because, like many western churches, they had a strong missionary strain and felt obliged to convert the sinners as well as the bankers. Thus dance-hall girls might attend Sunday services and then return to work hustling drinks. Many a congregation held services on the premises of a local saloon, lent by a friendly saloonkeeper, until their church was completed. Miners tended to be at least boozily sentimental about religion, if not religious, and were generous in their responses when the hat was passed. Vice and virtue lived in an easygoing truce in Tombstone—the locals even boasted about the high-class prostitutes the town offered—and there seems to have been no great waves of antivice fever, nor any attempt to confine the vice area to "across the tracks," as was done in some towns. There was at least one professional gambler in Tombstone who maintained a double life; in Tombstone he was known as Napa Nick and also Judge because of his distinguished air and white chin whiskers. Once, the historian Odie B. Faulk recounts, two men arrived from Napa City, California, looking for the Judge and were surprised to find him dealing faro. They explained that back in Napa City, the Judge lived an exemplary life in a large house and his wife and daughters were socially active. Despite his frequent absences on unexplained "business trips," the Judge was an esteemed citizen of Napa City, whose many charities and benefactions had won him the gratitude and respect of all.

Curiosities like Napa Nick and his sometime partner, a nameless beauty who "seemed by her manner to have come from a good family" and who always was tastefully dressed and adorned with "magnificent diamonds,"[43] as well as respected madams like Cora Davis, who practiced such strict honesty with all her patrons that when a customer became drunk, he was requested to check his valuables and given an invoice; when he sobered up, the valuables were returned—such people were regarded with respect or at least tolerance by more conventionally employed Tombstone citizens. They were, after all, good for business, in their way. But there was also another element that was not so tolerable—the hard-core thieves and killers who plagued the town and gave it its exaggerated reputation as a den of cutthroats.

From its earliest days, Tombstone had had a sense of law and order, with miners sometimes meting out a form of justice that was closer to that of the California mining camps than a properly incorporated village. The carrying of guns was prohibited in the town, though the gamblers retained their concealed derringers. But there were a lot of tenderfeet to be fleeced in Tombstone—miners, cowboys, soldiers from nearby Fort Huachuca—so it was no surprise that some wolves moved in, along with the more conventional shearers—the gamblers, saloonkeepers, prostitutes. Beyond that there were the regular bullion shipments on the stagecoach, which could carry twenty thousand dollars a trip. Located in easy proximity to four different jurisdictions—two U.S. territories and two Mexican states—Cochise County was also an ideal base for rustlers and smugglers. Some of these—notably the Clanton gang—operated outside the town, but they often became embroiled in the criminal schemes of the town gunmen.

The precipitating factor, though, was the arrival in town of the Earp brothers—Wyatt, Virgil, Jim, and Morgan—plus a tubercular dentist named Doc Holliday, his woman, Big-Nosed Kate Elder, William Barclay "Bat" Masterson, Luke Short, and Buckskin Frank Leslie. Wyatt, Masterson, and Holliday had become friends in Dodge City, where Wyatt was a city marshal and gambler, Masterson the sheriff, and Holliday a gambler. When Masterson lost his campaign for reelection as sheriff, the group decided to try Arizona, where Virgil was living. Virgil wangled a commission as a deputy U.S. marshal, assigned to assist L. F. Blackburn, a deputy marshal stationed in Tombstone. Although early histories hail Wyatt Earp and Masterson as sterling lawmen—echoing the popular mythology—later revisionist works have depicted them as murderous opportunists who looked upon the lawman's job as a cover for their gambling and more brazen illegal activities.

Thus when the chance came, Virgil ran for city marshal (Wyatt was working as a bouncer at the Oriental Saloon, while Morgan Earp, Luke Short, and Buckskin Frank Leslie were dealing faro there; Jim Earp continued his career as a bartender and stayed out of the subsequent violence—he had received a disabling wound in the Civil War). Virgil lost, but this was the "reform" election, provoked by disputed townsite claims, that swept in John Clum, editor of the *Epitaph*, who represented the "law and order" Republicans. Clum, it happened, was an admirer of Wyatt and appointed him city marshal at the first vacancy. In the meantime, though, there had been a stagecoach robbery in which Doc Holliday was directly implicated and other members of the Earp gang suspected by some. Accused of the murder of one of the guards, Holliday was subsequently acquitted, despite Kate Elder's hostile testimony (she was later driven out of town by Marshal Earp in revenge).

At any rate, Wyatt continued his feud with the county sheriff, Frank Behan, of whom he was jealous both because he had wanted the job—worth thirty thousand dollars a year in tax-collection fees—and because they both fancied the same dance-hall girl. Another stage robbery occurred and again suspicion was strong that the Earps were implicated. Also involved were some of the remnants of the Clanton gang, whose ranks had been recently decimated by Mexican troops in an ambush avenging a Clanton raid on a Mexican packtrain. The Clantons may have carried out the actual holdups; at any rate, according to the theory advanced by Odie B. Faulk in his history of

Tombstone, Wyatt Earp planned them and, fearing the remaining Clantons would talk, used his marshal's position to instigate a fight with them. The fight was the famous shoot-out at the O.K. Corral in Tombstone (October 26, 1881) and resulted in the deaths of three of the Clanton gang; Virgil and Morgan Earp were seriously wounded but survived. The three Earps and Holliday were arrested for the killings, but a partisan judge turned them loose on grounds of insufficient evidence. To most of the townspeople, however, it was obvious that Wyatt had gunned down the cowboys in cold blood after they had been disarmed by Sheriff Behan. All sympathy was with the cowboys, who were buried in a big public funeral with a banner draped over their coffins reading "Murdered in the Streets of Tombstone." A vigilante group called the Citizens' Safety Committee, organized by the same "law and order" Republicans who had once regarded Wyatt Earp as their champion, warned the Earps that if there was any more trouble from them, they would be hanged without benefit of a friendly judge.

With this blow the Earps' fortunes went into decline. Wyatt had to give up his gambling concession at the Oriental, and Virgil was gravely wounded and Morgan shot dead in two separate shoot-outs. The remnants of the gang quietly sold off their extensive and mysteriously acquired town real estate, and when Wyatt was warned that he would be held for the revenge shooting of Frank Stilwell, Morgan's killer, he and his band rode off into the sunset for good—and into the hearts of America, for years later their considerably embellished and sanitized stories would be told in the popular press and they would become heroes.

During their brief stay there, the Earp gang gave the town a certain notoriety; their peccadillos, coupled with the widespread rustling and smuggling in the area and the running brushfire war between the outlaws and the Mexican army, led President Chester A. Arthur to issue a proclamation threatening Arizona with martial law unless it behaved. The Tombstone people were outraged at this slander, and the *Epitaph* editorialized self-righteously: "There is not a State or Territory in the Union more peaceable than Arizona, nor one in which the law is more promptly obeyed or thoroughly respected."[44] This kind of protest was predictable, for Tombstone's lawless reputation was bad for business and real-estate values, as well as involving meddling outsiders in local affairs. Like any small town, Tombstone had developed a xenophobic streak. Years later, of course, after the gold and silver were gone, its citizens annually reenacted the gunfight at the O.K. Corral, which had become good for business.

Tombstone's mines were doomed because the shafts were sunk so deep that water was discovered; this was tamed by better mining methods and elaborate pumps—and was indeed regarded as a boon—but labor troubles, the declining price of silver after 1893, and the exhaustion of the silver lode made the mines a losing proposition economically. Although a railroad came in in 1903, it was too late; mining continued through World War I, then petered out completely. In the twenties Tombstone suffered the indignity of being replaced as county seat, and it became a half-empty ghost town, living on its memories. But it was these memories that provided the raw material for Tombstone's rejuvenation as a tourist town, celebrating the notorious past that more successful towns wanted to live down.

At the first Helldorado celebration in 1929, two old-timers, editor John Clum and rancher Billy Fourr, were on hand. Clum wrote a sardonic pamphlet about the event, noting that any resemblance between it and the Tombstone he knew was entirely coincidental. He and Fourr recalled that there had been only one serious gunfight—the O.K. Corral shoot-out—and one lynching in the town's fifty years (the lynching actually took place in nearby Bisbee, later to succeed Tombstone as county seat); further, only six men had died violently during 1881, the worst year of the town's existence. After the two old-timers watched the trumped-up Helldorado events, Clum has Fourr turning to him and saying, "Don't you remember that away back there in 1881, when you were mayor, a man seldom grew anything but a mustache [a reference to the lush beards the Helldorado celebrants had grown], and there was a city ordinance forbidding anyone but a peace officer to carry firearms within the city limits?" To which Clum replies: "Well, Billy, you remember that we were not giving a HELLDORADO show away back there in 1881."[45]

To those who had lived there, Tombstone had been no religious retreat, but still, as mining towns went, not a den of lawlessness either. Closer to that perverse ideal was Dodge City, Kansas, whose boosters called it "the biggest, wildest, happiest, wickedest little city on the continent."[46] This burst of civic pride came when Dodge's days as a wide-open cow town were numbered, however, so perhaps a similar nostalgia to that of Tombstone was beginning to haze over recollection. And no doubt, too, the respectable citizens of Dodge, who did not make their money off the cowboys' end-of-the-trail sprees, were glad to be rid of this troublesome element, who gambled away their pay in Dodge's halls of chance, bought watered champagne from her soiled doves, patronized her brothels, fought and shot each other on the slightest pretext of injured honor, annd galloped their horses up and down Front Street—and sometimes on the board sidewalks and into saloons—like a wild, whooping hoard of barbarians from an alien land.

The cow towns of Kansas, however, were all of a piece, with the railroad going right down Main Street. On one side lived the permanent residents, and on the other—the "wrong side"—were the cowboys' palaces of sin. This geographic division became also a psychic one between the settled folk and the cowboys. Many of the former came from the eastern states, went to church every Sunday to worship their glum Puritan god, and made money from their small businesses; aligned with them were the farmers and sheep ranchers—the grangers and nesters—who were filling up the empty plains, wrenching a straitened living from the arid land of Kansas. The Puritan influence was strong in Kansas—dating back to the pre–Civil War days when groups of

New Englanders heeded the godly call to come out and expel the proslavery element, then platted their gridiron-pattern speculative towns, owned by stockholders back east, on the flat prairies. They represented the correct Puritanical mix of piety and Yankee business sense. These people, along with the less pious émigrés from the Middle Atlantic states, were willing to make money off the cowboys to a point, but when their economic interests began to diverge from the cowboy trade their faith was handy to anathematize such trade as the devil's work.

Against these sober, hardworking folk were the cowboys, those colorful vaqueros of the Great Plains, rootless men who were equally hardworking, putting in eighteen-to-twenty-four-hour days during the cattle drives up from Texas, dirty, miserable, existing on a monotonous diet of meat, beans, coffee, and bread, earning thirty dollars a month. Most of the cowboys were raised in a southern heritage; they had their own biblical code, formed by another, long-ago nation of herdsmen who believed the land should be open to all, rather than fenced up into neat little farms. Their mental horizons were as broad and empty as the Plains itself, and their code was the Code of the South, which enjoined the violent redress of wrongs by the injured party. These men had a hair-trigger sense of honor and "face," and they carried guns as extensions of their touchy machismo. And nothing pleased them more, it seemed, when they were hurrahing a town, than firing off those guns in the air. Drunk, they were quick to take offense, quick to use their guns on the offender. The mix of their hypersensitive individuality with alcohol was a highly volatile one, and little in the way of pretext was needed to touch it off.

Then, too, the cowboy was an itinerant laborer (like the miners before him) who on the job lived a seminomadic existence, traveling from his employer's ranch on the long trail drives to market and back. His home was the male world of the bunkhouse and the saddle; his possessions were his immediate equipage—saddle, blanket, chaps, boots, hat, gun—and the bank he put his money in was the faro bank. So when he arrived at the cow town, tired, dirty, womanless for months, it was inevitable that he would cut loose. This cutting loose was launched by the rite of "taking the town"—galloping up and down the streets firing his guns, riding into the saloons. The possession was symbolic, in the sense that the conquest did not ordinarily involve the townsfolk, except as they got underfoot, and was concentrated on the section that had been ceded to the conqueror in the first place—across the tracks where the saloons and bordellos and gambling dens were. Once this transient cavalry had made its "conquest," its riders could settle in to occupation duty, paying extravagant tribute to the locals—who were themselves mostly itinerant professionals who followed the action from cow town to cow town along the westward-reaching railroads in their "hell on wheels" cars. But the cowboy had the consolation of being exploited not as green outsiders but as men who had flaunted their temporary rights of possession.

The cowboy's behavior was in a way an assertion of his "rights"—not the rights of deeds and mortgages and fences but of usufruct, bought with his hard-earned pay collected at the end of the trail drive. The lawful citizens had their own code, which they occasionally tried to enforce on the cowboy, but he believed it did not apply to him and flaunted his contempt for it. But this was a quixotic gesture, for in the long run the permanent settlers were slowly choking the lifelines of the cowboy culture. They would take his money and tolerate his sprees—keeping him to his own quarter of town—but all the while they were occupying and fencing off the open range that was the cowboy's true empire.

The clash of these two cultures—the cowboy and the townsman—has provided endless themes for western movies; while it was real enough and recurrent in the Kansas cow towns, there is no need to oversimplify it, as the movies did, awarding glory to one side or the other, romanticizing the cowboy and the lawmen hired to keep the peace in the towns. The cowboy has been sufficiently demythologized so that we have seen the brutish side of his life. Yet he also had his panache and rough chivalry. While on the trail he would eat and sleep in the same dirty, sweat-stained clothes, but when he hit town he would become a dandy—going to the barber to have his hair cut, his mustache trimmed, curled, or dyed. He would then don his town finery—kid boots with high heels and a suit of corduroy or fringed buckskin—and sport a derby and a cane. He often was, indeed, a bit of a fop, and this, too, was an expression of his high-living life-style.

And his character often mixed elements of his southern heritage—courage, honor, weakness for gambling, love of sport and competition—with frontier, and specifically western, virtues of self-reliance, courage, hardihood, endurance, skill at one's trade, and a kind of wary consideration of others. As Walter Prescott Webb wrote, "Such men take few liberties with one another; each depends upon himself, and each is careful to give no orders and to take none save from the recognized authority. There is no place for loquaciousness, for braggadocio, for exhibition of a superlative ego."[47] The cowboy's speech was pungent and direct, yet laconically picturesque. And, when he was not mean drunk, he had an engaging youthfulness, an exuberance, a generosity of spirit. He was sentimental and protective about women, even though most of the women he met were whores. If his job was hard and mean, he retained a sense of pride and of adventurousness about it; like the Confederacy, it was a doomed way of life, yet all the more romantic for that.

As for the townsfolk, they were not uniformly hardworking and respectable. For one thing, the most powerful men in the town often made most of their money from the cattle trade, so they were not eager to offend the cattlemen and their employees by strict law enforcement. In unholy alliance with these pillars of town society were the itinerant professionals—gamblers, saloonkeepers, prostitutes, and madams—who, if they did not actively run the town, at least used their money to buy immunity from all law. Then there were the lawmen, the Wyatt Earps and Bat Mastersons, who, as we have seen, were frequently hired guns willing to work both sides of the law, passing easily from sheriff to gambler, clearing the flagrantly obnoxious cowboys off the streets but all the while skimming off their share of the action. And lastly the ordinary folk of the town, who lived out dull lives and never went near the cowboys' fleshpots. Stuart Henry, who grew up in Abilene during its heyday as a cow town in the 1870s, recalled how the hot summer days droned on for most: "In dog days the men sweat profusely while figuring in their little stores or offices. Between sales or trades you behold them idling there, longing for something to occur. A bunch of Indians skirting through, a string of prairie schooners passing, a train an hour late, even a change in the wind, afforded subjects of extended interest. Godsends in the way of news were a dogfight, a swearing quarrel between two residents, the broken limb of a neighbor tumbling off a new roof."[48] In other words, just another small town. As for the farming people who were beginning to cultivate the land around the town, there were many of these who were the same breed of restless forerunners we saw in the Middle West—who built a shack, scratched a crop or two out of the soil, then sold out and moved farther west.

The town of Abilene, Kansas, was the first of the cow towns, and its speeded-up evolution was recapitulated by the later ones. To understand its history, we must understand the nature of the cattle business as it grew up immediately following the Civil War. The postwar cattle business in its flush times—roughly from 1867 through 1882—was a bonanza business, not unlike gold mining in its preindustrial era. The resource—cattle—of course did not need to be discovered, for they existed, five million of them, running wild in the southern region of Texas between the Nueces River and the Rio Grande. These cattle—tough, mean-tempered, hardy longhorns of Mexican origin—were threatening to become pests. They would charge a man without fear (there was even a story about the bull which charged General Zachary Taylor's column during the Mexican War and scattered several regiments); their meat was tough; and, in herds, they were skittish and easily prodded into stampede. Nonetheless, they represented beef on the hoof, too good for the starving Indians on the reservations but good enough for the northern laboring man.

Now, after the Civil War the situation was simple; though undevastated by the conflict, Texas was nonetheless impoverished by it. On the local markets, the cattle were worth three or four dollars a head—but there were few buyers. Up north, however, they were worth up to fifty dollars a head, delivered. Putting it another way, the Texans had no money but were rich in cattle; the North needed this cattle and had the money. The cattle were there for the taking; the problem was to get them to the North and specifically to the closest railroad, from which they could be transported to the eastern markets. By this time, the railroads had crossed the Mississippi and touched the edge of the Great Plains. To the Texans, the best point to aim for seemed to be Sedalia, Missouri, which was connected by rail with St. Louis. Accordingly, in 1866 herds set out by the shortest route across the Red River and on to Missouri—and trouble. As though the hardships and unfamiliarities of driving cattle were not enough, the Texans ran into armed Missourians who attacked them and confiscated their herds on the pretext of preventing Texas cattle fever (which the longhorns carried but were immune to themselves) but actually to appropriate them for their own sale. So the Sedalia route was a disastrous one, and later drives either tried to go through the timbered country east along the Missouri-Arkansas boundary or else headed west around Kansas, over the grassy plains north and then east to St. Joseph, Missouri. This latter route was circuitous, but it had the virtue of reminding the Texans, who came from plains country themselves, of the preferability of flat, open country over bandit-infested timber. What was needed was a market and transportation depot at the end of this route where the herd owner would sell his cattle to reputable dealers without the intervention of thieves.

This was precisely the idea of a visionary buusinessman named Joseph G. McCoy, who operated a livestock-shipping business in Illinois. McCoy carried his dream around to officials of the several railroads that served the general area. The Kansas Pacific, although skeptical, did not say no; the president of the Missouri Pacific, which connected with St. Louis, however, threw McCoy out of his office. McCoy then went to the Hannibal and St. Joe, which could link up with Chicago, and talked them into a contract granting favorable freight rates. Thus did Chicago, rather than St. Louis, become the hog butcher of the world. At any rate, McCoy next searched for a town located on the Kansas Pacific and, after some turndowns from towns that did not want to be cow towns, fastened on the tiny settlement of Abilene, which alleged itself to be the seat of Dickinson County, although its one hundred people and about a dozen dirt-roofed log huts belied any such pretensions.

Within the space of a few months, however, McCoy had imported the necessary lumber to build pens for the cattle. The next step was obviously to get the actual animals, and since the cattlemen did not know of Abilene's existence, McCoy hired a man to beat the bushes for wandering droves. The man went two hundred miles south and finally spied a herd uncertainly making its way through Indian Territory (later Oklahoma). He described the new deal waiting for cattlemen in Abilene and, McCoy later wrote, found a sympathetic ear: "This was joyous news to the drover, for the fear of trouble and violence hung like an incubus over his waking thoughts alike with his sleeping moments. . . . They were very suspicious that some trap was set, to be sprung on them; they were not ready to credit the proposition that the day of fair dealing had dawned for Texan drovers, and the era of mobs, brutal murder, and arbitrary prescription ended forever."[49] Swallowing their doubts, though not completely, the Texans wheeled their cattle toward Abilene, and the first of the wicked cow towns was on its way. In 1867, thirty-five thousand cattle were driven to Abilene; the next year the number more than doubled and kept increasing until the figure reached seven hundred thousand in 1871.

Up the old Chisholm Trail, which McCoy had laid out, the cattle came, colored like a Navajo blanket—gray, white, brindle, buff, black, and mottled white and red—and driven by whooping, swearing cowboys. Once at Abilene the weary animals fattened up on the grass around the town, to the annoyance of the growing farm population, and then were sold and put on trains for the East. Some, however, were sent to the ranges farther west and north, providing the nuclei of other herds. The discovery had already been made by a party going to Oregon that, like buffalo, cattle could live off—indeed thrive on—the rich green grass of the Great Plains, even in winter. It was truly a Kingdom of Grass, and ranchers came in increasing numbers, culminating in the boom years of the 1880s, when men rushed to the plains to buy "range rights" (which were unrecognized by law) and set up great spreads. Foreign capital entered in particular abundance, as the English papers fueled avarice with highly colored reports about cattle bought for four to five dollars bringing sixty to seventy dollars' profit a head at market. The country was prosperous, there was plenty of investment capital, the waves of immigration were creating a large population in the East, while the stockyards along the Great Plains at Chicago, Kansas City, and St. Louis were growing, and the use of refrigerator cars and people's acceptance of canned meats meant that Texas and northern range cattle could be processed close to home and shipped east profitably. Meanwhile the Great Plains were still sparsely settled, although with the invention of barbed wire in 1874, homesteaders were moving in and fencing their land—with the encouragement of the railroads, which were jobbing towns and transporting people to them.

All these elements combined to create a speculative frenzy that sent investors rushing to get in before the good land was all gone. The bubble quickly collapsed, though, as the land became overgrazed, making herds vulnerable to the droughts of 1882 and 1883. Coupled with the loss of herds was the decline in prices, so that profits fell to five then to nine dollars a head. More homesteaders took up land and the supply of free grass dwindled correspondingly. Soon the old way of cattle raising based upon an open range, plenty of grazing land for all, and ever-rising demand back east was gone. The cattle business passed from a bonanza business into the era of closed pasture, scientific breeding that produced less hardy but fatter breeds which could not survive the trail and the practice of transporting cattle to feeder ranches in the north. The spread of the railroads west and south eventually eliminated entirely the need for long drives from Texas to railheads such as Abilene.

While it lasted, though, the cattle bonanza was a booming, gaudy era both for the men who raised the animals and for the cow towns they took them to. In its five years of prosperity, Abilene quickly grew into a sin city epitomizing the raw West, and it was taken to heart accordingly by reporters sent out by editors back east who wanted some colorful copy. The town's Texas Street became a midway of brightly painted false-front stores and saloons, and a febrile, round-the-clock ambience reminiscent of the mining towns took hold. But inevitably the culture clash between the cowboys and the locals escalated. By 1872 the surrounding farm population had become more substantial; their interests were more directly in conflict with the cattlemen's. They wanted to fence off their land, and the town merchants, coveting their steady trade, sided with them; real-estate speculators eying the potentially rich farmland around Abilene added their considerable weight. That winter, when the cowboys had gone back home, the citizens of Abilene sent out a circular to all known cattlemen in Texas which read: "We the undersigned . . . most respectfully request all who have contemplated driving Texas cattle to Abilene the coming season to seek some other point of shipment, as the inhabitants . . . will no longer submit to the evils of the trade."[50]

The Texans did not try to force themselves upon the reluctant folk of Abilene. The Kansas Pacific began promoting Ellsworth, which it had left on the vine when it moved its terminus farther west. The Ellsworth people, realizing that they no longer had a privileged end-of-the line status, had been busy too; they persuaded the Kansas legislature to lay out another cattle trail from Fort Cobb in Indian Territory (later Oklahoma). But the herds did such damage in the winter of 1871–72 to the ranges they were foraging around Ellsworth that the local farmers organized a protective association and ot the quarantined area increased. The trade then moved to Wichita, but again the farmers expelled it with quarantine laws.

By 1872 the Sante Fe Railroad had pushed farther west, and at its terminus stood the little town of Dodge City, Kansas, which was eager for the business. Dodge was already booming as a supply camp for buffalo hunters during the great slaughter of the early seventies. Buffalo having been wiped out in Kansas and driven north, Dodge's businessmen were looking for another set of live ones who could compare favorably with buffalo killers earning as much as one hundred dollars a day. So the torch was passed to Dodge, and the movable blackjack games, bars, and brothels—the "hells on wheels"—were not far behind.

Actually, although some cattle arrived at Dodge in 1872, there were no cattle pens, and the town's real cattle boom did not get underway until 1875. The town started as a collection of tents and shacks devoted mainly to the business of selling whiskey and other pleasures and necessities to the soldiers at nearby Fort Dodge, as well as to the buffalo hunters (after whom the camp acquired its first name—Buffalo City) and the drivers and bullwhackers of wagons passing by along the Santa Fe Trail. The fort and Dodge existed in an uneasy parasite-host relationship in those early years. The soldiers would come to town and get drunk and skinned, or mix it up with bullwhackers and buffalo men, whose enormous .50-caliber Sharps rifles made them formidable foes—as did the bullwhackers' twenty-foot whips.

The county in which Dodge was located—Ford—was not organized, so there was no local government. Aside from brief forays to claim a corpse, the army did not participate in local law enforcement, because the commandant, Major Richard L. Dodge, did not feel he could exercise civil authority without resigning his commission. As a result, the town was run by a group of thirty or forty vigilantes, whose identities, as was customary with vigilantes, were supposedly known only to each other. They were most of them probably town businessmen, plus some toughs who were handy with a gun; the law they dished out was capricious at best, mainly designed to keep the rest of the town under the vigilantes' thumb. The vigilantes revealed their true colors in 1873, when several of them killed an inoffensive black orderly from the fort who was buying supplies and who had run out to protest when the locals made off with his wagon. The killing of another black soldier in the town suggests a racist origin for the murders, although they were passed off as simple drunken bullying by the town bravos. Major Dodge confined himself to protesting to the governor, calling the soldier's murder "the most cowardly and cold-blooded murder I have ever known in an experience of frontier life dating back to 1848."[51] A provost guard was posted in the town with orders to arrest any soldier attempting to patronize the bars, but he quickly succumbed to Dodge's temptations himself and had to be forcibly retired in disgrace.

In his letter to the governor, Major Dodge said the Dodge vigilance committee, like others he had observed on the frontier, had been "organized by good men in good faith," but then, not being strong enough to do the job, had inducted "some of the roughs" and was well on its way to becoming "simply an organized band of robbers and cutthroats."[52] Consequently, the governor was caught in a dilemma: "In selecting a man from Dodge City to execute the laws, you risk appointing a member of the vigilantes (all the members being known only to themselves), who would use his power for the benefit of the vigilantes; or you appoint a man well disposed to carry out your views but paralyzed by terror and utterly powerless to do anything."[53]

Major Dodge's point was probably well taken, and his description of the decline of an initially well-meaning vigilantism into an alliance between the town's leaders and their hired guns to divide up the spoils, stifle citizen protest against corruption and crime, and bullyrag blacks, aliens, or any other elements or individuals deemed a threat to their rule. There was, in other words, the same element of know-nothing nativism that sometimes besmirched the mining-camp governments. The stationing of a contingent of black soldiers at Fort Dodge may have bestirred the locals into "teaching them a lesson" by killing two of their number who had intruded into town: or perhaps it was simple bullying. At any rate, shortly thereafter rumors spread through Dodge that the black soldiers had been ordered by the War

Department to burn the town to the ground. Historian Stanley Vestal searched War Department records, however, and was unable to find any such order. At any rate, Major Dodge apparently arrested the white men who had abetted the killing and was later sued for false imprisonment. The governor of Kansas, Thomas A. Osborn, wrote to the secretary of war in 1874 in defense of Major Dodge's action ("Life and property was endangered by the desperadoes temporarily in possession of the town[54]) and recommended that the U.S. district attorney in Kansas represent the major in court. Dodge emerged from the trial with a verdict of innocence, already promoted to a colonelcy; the killers were later punished.

With that the vigilantes seem to have disbanded. To keep the peace the town hired a series of city marshals who had reputations for prowess with a gun. None of these lasted, and if Stanley Vestal's somewhat overcolorful account is to be believed, the presence of renowned gunmen in the town seemed to stir up trouble by attracting eager challengers desirous of unseating the town's reigning and legally designated killer. At any rate, after the last marshal retired hastily from the fray, the town's temporary council met on Christmas Eve, 1874, in an attempt to bring the law to Dodge. The council's first accomplishment was to draw up a body of town ordinances regulating such things as tenure in office and salaries, licensing, and crime. The criminal statutes singled out for opprobrium such matters as indecent exposure, profanity, committing a public nuisance (which was later used to arrest cowboys who rode their ponies into saloons and dance halls), and the discharging of firearms within the town limits (except on Christmas, New Year's Day, the Fourth of July, and Lincoln's Birthday). Most crucial for Dodge, though, was Section 7, Ordinance 4, which prohibited all persons from carrying any deadly weapon, including pistol, bowie knife, or slingshot "concealed about his or her person."[55] Later amendments called upon visitors to Dodge to check their firearms. Realizing that such strictures would be regarded as downright inhospitable by the cowboy element, who felt undressed without a gun, the council only narrowly voted to enforce them.

The attempt to curb violence and keep the peace by regulating weaponry stimulated a controversy within the town at large. As in most western towns, national party labels did not mean much in town politics (most voters voted Republican in state and national elections); instead there was a "law and order faction" opposed by other groups who, while not necessarily against law and order, were reluctant to offend the cowboys and cattlemen. The law-and-order faction included saloonkeepers as well as soberer citizens, for even though the saloonkeepers' trade came from the cowboys, they also bore the brunt of their drunken outbursts or hung over vengeance the morning after, when they awoke with empty pockets and furred tongues, dimly remembering where all their money had gone. So these merchants, and the gamblers as well, needed strong protection and favored gunless cowboys (no doubt the gamblers would retain their concealed derringers).

The non-law-and-order faction was dominated by the wealthy merchants of the town—the cattle dealers and the store owners who supplied the cattlemen with food, clothes, guns, and ammunition. They had no fears from cowboy high spirits or morning-after recriminations. The gun dealers, whose number, evidently, was legion in Dodge, profited indirectly from this violence, supplying its instruments (the sign of one arms merchant consisted simply of an enormous wooden red revolver hung prominently over the street). Siding with the big merchants were representatives of the Santa Fe Railroad, which had made the town and which could break it by upping freight rates or even rerouting their line; along with this stick the railroad held several carrots such as a new roundhouse, more tracks, enlarged cattle pens, a hospital, and other fringe benefits. The Santa Fe's role in Dodge was summed up by a citizen talking to a visiting reporter: "Everything that happens is the Santa Fe. The Santa Fe giveth and the Santa Fe taketh away. I reckon they own half this town anyway."[56] So long as the cowboys' activities did not injure its property, the railroad favored giving them the run of the town and anything else that would keep them coming to Dodge with their cattle.

Despite the Santa Fe's considerable weight, however, it did not command the votes, and the winner of the first mayoral election was George M. Hoover, a leader of the law-and-order faction. Hoover hired more gunslingers, including that tarnished paladin, Wyatt Earp. Earp later boasted in his biography that he cracked down on the cowboys, enforced the gun laws, and even put away a wealthy cattleman. Some find Earp's recollections in the realm of fantasy (the book, *Wyatt Earp: Frontier Marshall,* was actually written by Stuart W. Lake after Earp's death, based on a draft by Earp but considerably embellished). Certainly his later career in Tombstone suggested that he was far from a white knight. Still Earp claimed that it was under his regime that Dodge's Dead Line was put into force. This was the policy that, as in Abilene, consigned hell raising to the south side of the railroad tracks running in the center of Front Street and reserved the north side for law abiders. According to Earp, across the tracks it was anything goes, and he and his deputies were content to let the cowboys kill or maim each other in that sector as much as they liked, so long as the trouble didn't spill over to the north side. Likewise, the cowboys could keep their guns on the south side, but let them cross the track with their guns and it "was justification for shooting on sight, if an officer was so inclined," or at the very least "certain arrest."[57] Like much Earp said in his dotage, that assertion seems open to question and part of his attempt to whitewash his past by portraying himself as a stern and resourceful champion of law and order who rid the West of its bad men. Nonetheless the Dead Line idea seems to have been Dodge's compromise solution to the cowboy problem—a solution that allowed the visitors to raise all the hell they wanted, the merchants to profit from them, and the ordinary citizen to walk the streets unmolested.

But could Dodge exist half-Gomorrah and half-Methodist? Apparently it could, thanks to that talent for creative social innovation Webb says characterized those who settled the Great Plains. A social note in the town's newspaper unintentionally expressed the official satisfaction with this informal zoning policy: "The boys and girls across the Dead Line had a high old time last Friday. They sang and danced and fought and bit and cut and had a good time generally. Five knockdowns, three broken heads, two cuts, and several incidental bruises. Unfortunately none of the injuries will prove fatal."[58] The key is in the use of "unfortunately." The paper's tone maintained a kind of racy cynicism mixed with boosterism that was generally devoid of all crusading zeal or piety. It presumably reflected the prevailing opinions. When the editor felt like unlimbering a little boosterism, he was inclined to extol Dodge's reputation as the wickedest little city in the West. He did, however, lump this unique civic accomplishment in with the usual citation of Dodge's prosperity, its assured place as the most live-wire little burg in the West, where the rigors of go-getting were leavened by fun and high jinks and practical jokes, in the robust spirit of the West. Just as other small towns prided themselves on being the wheat or azalea or ball-bearing capital of wherever, so Dodge trumpeted its preeminence in sin. It was a cow town and proud of it. If there were a lot of shootings, well, the only way to stop the mayhem beyond the Dead Line would have been to burn that part of town to the ground.

Actually, subtract the violent fracases that took place across the tracks, and you have left a rather peaceable, orderly town. Vestal searched the crime reports and found them dominated by crimes of passion, such as fights over a woman, barroom quarrels, and grudge killings by, say, a disgruntled employee. The dominant crimes in Dodge were assault and battery, mayhem, highway robbery (horse thievery was big in that part of Kansas), drunkenness, gambling, and fornication. But what Vestal calls "bestial, cruel, and unnatural crimes" were lacking; there was little cruelty to animals, brutality, sexual perversion, abuse of children, wife beating, dope peddling, kidnapping, extortion, or rape. A respectable woman could walk the streets at night without fear of molestation. And theft by the transients upon the homeowners was exceedingly rare, a pattern that prevailed in other cow towns. For example, Stuart Henry wrote of Abilene: "Our houses stood between the jaws of Texas Street, and no cowboy ever entered the yard nor paid the slightest heed there to members of our household. Crazily drunk, they raced past, filling the air with shots and curses, while our doors stood always open or unlocked."[59] Unlocked doors were nigh universal in the West, and in part the security of ordinary people in their homes owed something to the cowboys themselves, who for the most part were, with all their obstreperousness, an honest bunch. Perhaps in part this was because of their peripatetic way of life, requiring few possessions. Also, in Dodge they drew their accumulated pay, so they were by their lights rich—until, of course, they had squandered it. But then, although they might hang around town for a while, they did not need to steal to eat, or look to charity. They would simply shrug and go back to work on a job that provided them with free meals and open-air lodging. Finally, honesty was traditional in small southern towns, where owners left their stores unattended for hours. One store in the cowboy town of Colorado City, Texas, was described this way:

> In warm weather the merchant did not even close the front door of his store before going home at night. The next morning when he came to work, as apt as not, he would find a group of freighters or cowboys who had arrived in town during the night asleep on the counters or floor, or perhaps someone passing through during the night had helped himself to a pair of California pants or a plug of chewing tobacco; but if he did he left the price of the item where the merchant could find it.[60]

The Mississippi country store of Flem Snopes in William Faulkner's novel *The Hamlet* is described in almost the same terms, though the novel is set forty years later. One further example of the cowboys' fabled honesty. At Dean's store near the heavily used Red River ford, where millions of cattle crossed on their way to the Kansas and Nebraska cattle towns, the owners, the Dean brothers, gave almost limitless credit and loans without collateral to the cowboys passing through. During the two decades the cattle drives lasted, the brothers never lost a cent from their customers, and cowboys would ride hundreds of miles out of their way to clear the books.

Even the crime of murder in the cow towns may have been exaggerated. Robert Dykstra made a careful study of newspaper records of homicides in the five most important Kansas cattle towns (Abilene, Dodge, Ellsworth, Wichita, and Caldwell) and concluded that there had been a total of 45 during the period 1870–85, an average of 3 a year or 1.5 for each period when the cowboys were in town. The most killings in one year were five, registered in Ellsworth in 1873 and Dodge in 1878. Of course these were small towns with populations of one to two thousand, augmented by another one thousand or so cowboys during the cattle-trading season; but with such a large and armed population of transients in the mood to raise hell, more might have been expected. Vestal's study of killings in Dodge indicates that many of them involved feuds between locals; cowboys, gamblers, and peace officers made up the rest of the statistics. Dodge's law officers for the most part tried to avoid gunplay, preferring to give an unruly cowboy who had strayed across the Dead Line a knock in the head or to "buffalo" him.

In sum Dodge was no better than it should have been—a wide-open town that still had as many churches per hundred people as any other western town and one year spent $400 on Bibles, and that had started up a school as far back as 1873, when the vigilantes were still running things. There were two newspapers, theaters, a famous cowboy band, a fire company, myriad sporting events, and a roller skating rink. There were obviously people living normal lives in Dodge, growing up and getting married and raising families, and they apparently struck a *modus vivendi* with the roughneck elements. True, occasional waves of reform erupted, but they never amounted to much until after the cowboys stopped coming. The town actually had laws on its books prohibiting gambling and dance halls but no one expected them to be enforced. Instead, periodic fines were levied as the traditional sin tax. Public opinion, as expressed by the local newspapers, merely called for the maintenance of "square games" so that there were minimal arguments between the pros and the cowboys, and as little gunplay as possible.

As in other western towns, gamblers were accorded a social ranking equivalent to bankers', and sporting types like William H. Harris, who dealt out of the Long Branch Saloon, and Bat Masterson were popular, respected men. In an election in 1885 Masterson was indeed voted the "most popular man in Dodge City."[61] As Masterson put it, gambling "was not the principal and best-paying industry of the town, but was also reckoned among its most respectable."[62] When temperance advocates began moving into Kansas in the late seventies, the local paper was alarmed, and when a temperance leader actually visited the town, a delegation of armed townsmen was on hand ostensibly to provide him an escort. He left unscathed and Dodge was left unconverted, although fist fights between local wets and dries later broke out from time to time. The state of Kansas went dry in 1880, but Dodge judged rightly that the law was not intended to apply to it, and the saloons remained open until 1887, after which speakeasies and "blind pigs" flourished. But by then the cowboy trade was gone.

The official knell of doom tolled in 1885 when Kansas passed the Herd Act, which prohibited Texas cattle from moving through the state, supposedly as a health measure to prevent Texas hoof-and-mouth disease, which could decimate herds of northern cattle. Actually the cattle from the south were grazed separately, and the measure's main purpose was to pacify farmers who complained about the herds trampling their crops and eating their own pasturage. The Dodge people tried to stall off the inevitable by proclaiming a special trail, leading to Dodge by a circuitous route, with the town agreeing to indemnify against damage to any farmer's land, but there were few takers. By then the barbed-wire fences of the homesteaders formed a more formidable barrier than any law. The powers of Dodge had been siding with the cattlemen in their hostility to the farmers and so regarded the influx of settlers with mixed apprehension and hostility. In the bad winter of 1879 the townsmen's spite threatened to abrogate all frontier traditions of helping one's neighbor. The wheat crop that year was a poor one and the farmers were extremely hard up. But the men of Dodge refused to give them a scrap of food, though they could well afford it. Finally the women of the town rebelled and formed a benevolent society to help the hungry farmers and their families. As conditions grew worse on the farms, the men relented, and the county commissioners were authorized to provide the hungry with cornmeal, flour, bacon, and other food. That did not greatly alleviate the mutual animosity, but when the crop of 1880 failed, Dodge again provided succor. Eventually the state took over relief efforts, and with better crops, meaning an increasingly lucrative farm trade, the two groups became more accommodated to one another. By 1885 more than one hundred thousand acres of Ford County were being farmed, and eighteen thousand of these were fenced. There were sheep in the county now, and the local paper published a rather pathetic story on the possibility of making blankets from cattle hair.

The leaders of Dodge saw the handwriting on the wall as far as the Texas cattle drives were concerned and relinquished the title of cattle town. It gladly passed the honor to Caldwell, Kansas, whose citizens were so eager that they goaded the Santa Fe into extending its tracks to their town by offering a rival line a subsidy. Caldwell declined as a cattle town after 1886 because the railroad it had lured with the subsidy that went to the Santa Fe instead—the Kansas City, Lawrence, and Southern Railway—laid tracks to Hunnewell, enabling it to take away part of Caldwell's business. Then, in 1889, the Boomers occupying Oklahoma Territory blocked off further cattle drives from Texas on the three main trails, which passed through their land.

As it happened the ranchers around Dodge City were raising blooded stock of their own and were as fearful of Texas fever as the other ranchers; moreover, Dodge had become a considerable horse-trading area, as well as a service center and supply depot for the surrounding countryside. And so on New Year's Day of 1886, the men celebrated as usual with Tom and Jerries given away by the Front Street saloons. Already the newspapers had been twitting Dodge on its new decorum, and the editor of the local paper had written that he regretted "the quiet and orderly condition of Dodge City on Christmas day." [63] The gunfighters—the Earps, Hollidays, Mastersons—had gone to wilder climes, and many of the sporting crowd had headed for newer cow towns such as Trail City, which was supposed to have a great future on the proposed National Cattle Trail (which never materialized; farewell, Trail City). Bat Masterson, however, did return to Dodge in 1886—leading a temperance crusade. Not long after this incident he gave up the gambling life and went to New York to become a sportswriter. As for the cattlemen, let one old trail captain sound the epitaph for the days of when the plains were open, unfenced, a sea of grass, and a great broad highway from Texas to Kansas:

> Now there is so much land taken up and fenced in that the trail for most of the way is little better than a crooked lane, and we have hard lines to find enough range to feed on. These fellows from Ohio, Indiana, and other northern and western states—the "bone and sinew of the country," as politicians call them—have made farms, enclosed pastures, and

> fenced in water holes until you can't rest; and I say, D—n such bone and sinew! They are the ruin of the country, and have everlastingly, eternally, now and forever, destroyed the best grazing-land in the world.[64]

What the old trail captain could not or would not see was that it was not the farmers alone who ultimately destroyed the "best grazing-land in the world," but also the ranchers themselves. The farmers at least farmed the land—sometimes destructively—but the cattle raisers had practiced systematic overgrazing since the earliest days throughout the Great Plains from the 100th meridian to the Pacific, from southern Colorado to the Canadian border. This overgrazing, which has continued to the present day, reduced much country that was once covered by rich green buffalo grass to bare stubble, overgrown with sagebrush and other tough vegetation. Overgrazing put an end to the speculative boom of the 1880s; drought and harsh winters brought about the "Big Die" in the High Plains, resulting in thousands of cattle carcasses choking up the Yellowstone, Powder, Belle Fourche, and Platte rivers. They were piled up along the barbed fences the cattlemen had put up to keep out homesteaders, by the roadsides, and in gullies and gulches. A miasma of carrion stench hung over the country in the spring of 1887—the result of speculation, greed, and mismanagement in the summer of 1886. Some of the land cropped to the bare ground eventually recovered, but other land turned into desert and never recovered—land laid bare to the ravages of flash floods that gouged out erosion gullies, as though some giant claw had raked the soil. So weep not for the cattleman, for he did his share of destroying the "empire of grass."

5
The Great Plains—Homesteads and Prairie Junctions

The original cattle ranchers belonged to a pastoral era, when the land was free to all and its riches for the taking. Many ranchers acceded to the farmers when the railroads came through; some even platted a town on their spreads, sold off the land, became president and chief stockholder of the town bank, and lived out their days in quiet respectability as the town's leading citizen. Their lives, as Walter Prescott Webb pointed out, had spanned the entire history of the cattle kingdom. Yet before the rancher and the miner there were others—the fur trappers, the mountain men who blazed the trails of the West, living off the land in their own style. And before them, of course, the Indians, who created a colorful, nomadic culture around the buffalo—a culture that died when the buffalo was killed off, and the hunters driven farther and farther off their hunting lands and herded onto reservations. All of these inhabitants lived in a state of closeness with the Plains, exploiting the varied wealth that nature had placed there millennia ago.

The mountain men were inveterate loners, living a half-Indian existence and scorning civilization. They were obviously not town planters and avoided human society for months on end. Yet they had their own form of community—the trappers' rendezvous, the gatherings of trappers bringing their pelts to sell to the fur traders, an occasion for orgiastic drinking and wenching. The itinerant traders gave way to the trading posts, often small forts run by private individuals where the trappers and the Indians traded their furs for civilized goods. Sometimes these forts grew into towns, especially if they were on a trading route—some of the scattered military posts the United States set up across its new empire did likewise. Non-gold-seeking settlers headed for the Northwest via the Oregon Trail in the 1840s, and a few intrepid men who had preceded them set up forts and trading posts to temporarily house them when they arrived. The gold frontier stimulated more settlement, and the need for communication back east grew. The freight companies had been in the West almost from the beginning, starting with the Santa Fe Trail expeditions to Mexican territory. They continued at great hazard and difficulty to bring supplies out, aided by government subsidies. Stage lines and the brief-lived pony express brought mail and passengers to the new settlers and carried the gold and silver from the mines. And along these stage routes were small stations that sometimes grew into towns. All of these modes of transportation had their day and played their part, but it was the coming of the railroad after the Civil War that opened up the West to agriculture and mass settlement; for it was the railroad that forged ties of steel between the West and the urban centers of the East, which provided a market for the West's produce. The coming of the railroad also heralded the introduction of the industrial age to the West, in the form of mass-produced technologies, without which agriculture on the Great Plains would have been impossible. So, unlike the reign of the mountain men and the forty-niners and the cattlemen, the conquest of the Great Plains by the farmers was a product of industrialization.

In the Middle West the towns preceded the railroads. But in the Far West the railroads preceded the towns. In the Middle West towns grew up along trails and wilderness roads and rivers, streams, and canals, and then wherever a town boomer decided to create one. But the railroads did not become an economic force until the 1850s, and so they connected already existing towns. The harbingers of the future were those first railroad towns laid out by the Illinois Central in the 1850s. With its 2,573,800 acres of land, the Illinois Central was the biggest land baron in the state, causing a British visitor to say, "This is not a railroad company, *it is a land company*."[1] It was good rich, prairie land, worth twice as much, one of the Central's founders estimated, as all the farmland in Ohio. And Illinois grew so fast that the price of this land exceeded the railroad proprietors' wildest dreams. Between 1854 and 1857, the company sold half its land for over $15 million, at an average price of $13 an acre. In the middle of the alternate, six-square-mile checkerboard sections interspersed with sections of public-domain land on each side of its right-of-way running the length of the state, the Central strung a series of monotonously laid-out towns, and gave them names that ran in alphabetical order. Thus it profited several times over—from the sale of the land and from the produce the farmers to whom it had sold the land brought to the towns it had platted and shipped on the trains it owned at freight rates it fixed noncompetitively. Owning a railroad was a license to print money, in short—or so it seemed at the time.

The railroad and right-of-way acts of the 1850s set the direction of the postwar railroad boom. The big difference was that the West afforded opportunities for plunder that made Illinois look like small potatoes. Eventually the western railroads would be given more than ninety million acres of good western land, with the four largest (Union Pacific, Southern or Central Pacific, Northern Pacific, and Santa Fe) receiving over eighty-eight million of those acres.

The misuse of government monetary subsidies by railroad managements through devices such as the Crédit Mobilier of America, the construction company that reaped profits of 100 percent, was a national scandal of the Gilded Age. The land grants to the western railroads were also criticized as a great land grab, directed toward enriching the railroad entrepreneurs while removing public lands from the reach of the common man. There is a great deal of truth to this, although the argument can be made that, given the decision to entrust railroad building to private enterprise, the public-lands subsidy represented a transfer of the enormous risks involved in building transcontinental railroads from the government, which could ill afford them, to private contractors, who were "paid" in land that had cost the government nothing. Finally, even more tellingly criticized was the tremendous waste involved in the construction of the western railroads because of the haste with which they were laid down, necessitating that most of them be completely rebuilt as little as fifteen years after they were completed. Add to this waste the excessive debt structure erected upon the railroads, the governmental graft that they encouraged, the subsidies from state and local governments that were never redeemed (which placed an onerous burden of interest charges on the taxpayers), and the anarchically competing railroad systems that burgeoned and collapsed into bankruptcy in the nineties.

Yet the driving of the Golden Spike on May 10, 1869 at Promontory, Utah—the junction of the Union Pacific and Central Pacific railroads—was an event of immense symbolic importance. This jointure of the Atlantic and Pacific coasts by a frail-seeming pair of tracks crossing vast plains, deserts, and mountains meant to the people that the American East and West were at last one; the Civil War had preserved the constitutional union and now the transcontinental railroad had forged a geographical union across the continent to the shores of the Pacific. Little wonder that there was national jubilation on the day of the ceremony.

The railroads laid 22,885 miles of track in the West between 1865 and 1873—32 percent of the mileage in the entire country—at a cost of $1.2 billion (an amount equal to about half the national debt as it stood in 1873, still swollen by the costs of the Civil War). Most of these lines were extended in section after section of track across uninhabited lands by the straightest route possible, with no population centers to detour them. Unlike the East and the Middle West, where tangled skeins of railroads, financed by small companies, joined up towns and consolidated into larger systems that were merged with trunk lines linking the heartland with the coast, in the Far West the trunk lines were put down first, in a single giant stride that took from eight to fifteen years of effort, with the only witnesses the grim-visaged Indians. The capital this great effort demanded was colossal, the return low once it was completed; in 1873 the return on investment in the West was about 2 percent compared with 6 percent in the East. Poor's *Manual of Railroads of the United States* for 1873–74 explained the reason for the disparity: there was "an excess of mileage to population"[2] in the West. Because of overconstruction the annual earnings of western railroads declined from $12,615,846 in 1869 to $11,402,161 in 1872. Poor called for a stop to this "suicidal" policy which was "working more mischief to the railroad interests of the country than all other causes combined."[3] Undoubtedly, the burst of railroad building overcommitted western financiers such as Jay Gould and was the main cause of the panic of 1873.

The panic slowed down but did not stop the railroads' growth, and it may have stepped up immigration by the unemployed. This was all to the good for the railroads, who desperately needed people in their empty domains. As one executive capsulized it, "No people, no trains." To get these people the railroads found themselves cast by history in a major role in the West's settlement. They fell heir to the role of organizing parties of settlers, transporting them to their home sites, and distributing land among them—roles previously played by the New England colonies and the land companies and town boomers of the Middle West. They too organized themselves into land companies to sell off their lands on attractive terms to settlers. They laid out towns along their rights-of-way; they subsidized immigration societies that propagandized the virtues of the West to settlers, and put out the guides advising them where to go, what to bring; and they ran immigrants' trains with special reduced fares.

The first settlers after the war came by covered wagon, of course, often a long line of them abreast (rather than single file, because of the dust) sweeping across the level prairies. The lure that brought them was land, but what set off this migration from past ones was that *some* of the land was free. For with the withdrawal of the South from the Union, Congress was able at last to pass a real free-land act—the Homestead Act of 1862. The act provided that, upon payment of a small entry fee, a settler could take up as much as 160 acres of land for his own use. If he erected a dwelling on this land and lived there for five years, the land was his for nothing; if he wished to exercise preemption rights he could, after six months, buy the land at $1.25 an acre. That was the act in essence; it was later subjected to numerous amendments, with variances for mineral, timber, and desert land, large parcels reserved for the states to sell, as well as other laws requiring irrigation, out-and-out payment, or other preconditions for occupancy.

The law was imperfectly administered by inadequate personnel who were often corrupt; it was evaded widely by ranchers and others who needed larger acreage to profitably graze their animals and who hired dummy entrymen to claim land for them. At most the act affected about 80–100 million acres out of the nearly 500 million acres of western land open to settlement. Between 1862 and 1882, 552,112 homestead entries were filed, but only 194,488 of these claims were "proved up" either by the claimant fulfilling the five-year residency requirement or paying the preemption rate of $1.25 an acre outright. The rest of the land—more than two thirds of it—went to speculators or large owners. And so the act that seemed to fulfill at last the Jeffersonian dream of a nation of small holders; of which Abraham Lincoln said: "I am in favor of settling the wild lands into small parcels so that every poor man may have a home,"[4] and which Horace Greeley called "a reform calculated to diminish sensibly the number of paupers and idlers and increase the proportion of working, independent, self-subsisting farmers in the land evermore,"[5] was at best only a partial success.

Yet, this "common man's land law" did stir the yearnings of thousands of immigrants—the tenant farmers and renters of the Middle West, the incorrigibly restless who always saw hope just over the horizon, the Civil War veterans with their land warrants looking for a new start, the landless sons of farmers, and the urban proletariat seeking escape from the satanic mills (a small number, actually; the immigration was twenty times as great from the country to the cities than the other way), and the foreign immigrants who may have been handworkers (tailors, locksmiths, carpenters, fishermen) rather than farmers in the old country but who all single-mindedly equated the New World's promise with a plot of land, free and clear and theirs alone.

The Homestead Act was a greater boon to the early settlers than to the later ones. The best land was the rich black soil of the prairie plains east of the 98th meridian. Although it had some timbered areas, this land was mainly treeless, level as a billiard table, its sticky black loam inviting to the plough. Rainfall was adequate and corn, wheat, or almost any other crop the farmer put in would thrive. (The relative abundance of rainfall demarcated the region from the more arid High Plains west of the parallel.)

The men in Congress who had passed the Homestead Act had based their estimates of farm size on the experience of the Middle West, where 160 acres of land—a quarter section—was more than adequate and indeed abundant. Thus plots of 80 and even 40 acres were permitted to be registered. These sizes would provide a living for a man and a small family and were the most workable size in terms of labor and machinery available to the ordinary homesteader. Larger farms were often taken up in part for speculation and not worked in their entirety. The level prairie land did, however, favor large-scale mechanized farming, and so in the treeless parts of Indiana, Illinois, and Iowa, known as the Grand Prairie, large numbers of "bonanza" farms worked by laborers or tenants appeared. Still, in the immediate postwar period there was opportunity for the small farmer, for he could take up the land and, without the need for clearing out the stumps, put in a crop.

Consequently, rural life in the prairie region lost some of the pioneer diversions that arose out of cooperative labors. The prairie farmers lived lives of lonely toil, unlivened by the social sharing, the mutual help, the common bonds of being in the same boat. They worked hard, made money (some of them), and lived the boring, unimaginative lives chronicled by Hamlin Garland in his novels, stories, poems, and sketches. Garland wrote of the "main-travelled road" that provided a title for one of his books of short stories, which "has a dull little town at one end and a home of toil at the other."[6] Walter Prescott Webb observed that Garland and others who wrote of the prairie agricultural regions became realists, pointing up the grim side of life, the narrow, provincial cast of mind that dominated. The chroniclers of the Plains—the Wild West—on the other hand, emphasized romance, unpredictability, extremes of nobility and evil. The romance of the Wild West missed, of course, the grimness of life there, but the life that Garland saw had all color and romance leached out of it. The pain and dreariness and loneliness of prairie life demanded to be told, as though eastern readers must be deliberately disabused of any sentimentality they might have about the region. The Far West, on the other hand, inspired novels steeped in color, exoticism, adventure. The Far West literature was the literature of the frontier and the cattle kingdom and the mining camps while that of the Prairie Plains was the literature of the farms and "dull little towns"—the literature of the ordinary, of monotonous hardship, of a milieu from which many Americans, like the authors, had escaped with relief and loathing (yet with a residue of nostalgia and inarticulated loss).

Those prosperous small farms of the Prairie Plains were by no means within the reach of all. Much of the best land (the now familiar story) was taken by absentee speculators or large landholders. This was possible because large areas of public-domain land were assigned to the railroads, or to the states for resale, or kept off the market by the U.S. government to prevent speculators from buying it up. This land was often ultimately sold for prices beyond the reach of the immigrant.

Further, as mechanization increased productivity, the small farm of around a hundred acres was becoming less competitive with the larger farm. The census figures from 1880 on showed a steady decline in farms of fewer than one hundred acres. There was a growing trend toward tenancy among two groups—the small farmer who lacked the capital to buy up good land and the former smallholder who had lost his farm because he could not meet the payments to the bank or loan shark or simply could not make a go of his land. The smallholders had to struggle to keep their heads above water. Those without enough money to buy land were forced to work as farm laborers, while others rented; but farm workers tended to be an itinerant proletariat, unable to save enough to buy their own farms, while the tenants often had to deal with harsh landlords who took their entire crops in payment of rent, then threw them off the land. Other tenants had it better, but still they were often in a situation of being required to make their own improvements of the property and once they did so, finding that the owner had raised their rent because the farm had become more valuable. These landlesss farmers—who numbered from 25 to 40 percent of the total in some areas—had shallow economic roots and were prone to have another go farther west rather than eventually buy and work a profitable farm where the good land was.

Indeed, the railroads in their proselytizing for new settlers did not ignore this landless tenant class. In 1879 the Burlington Railroad, a big holder of Nebraska land, took out ads in Illinois papers urging young men to come west: "Life is too short to be wasted on a rented farm."[7] The Santa Fe also advertised its lands in Kansas, claiming that there were "no lands owned by speculations"[8] in its grant. That was only partly true, for the speculators had already bought up the railroad lands in eastern Kansas, where the best soil was; one of these buyers was a foreign-born landlord whose large holdings in Illinois had made him the focal point of the tenant agitation. In Ford County, Illinois, which had the largest amount of tenancy and tenant unrest, as early as 1872 the people began organizing homesteading groups, which migrated to Kansas.

So the Prairie Plains—the richest agricultural region in the entire country—were soon filled up and developed or held by speculators. Consequently, the homesteaders' march was quickly pushed farther west, across the 98th meridian and into the High Plains. The High Plains area was flat and treeless and had a semiarid climate, with annual rainfall averaging from twenty-five inches in the east to fifteen inches or below in desert regions. This vast area comprised most of North and South Dakota, Kansas, Nebraska, Oklahoma, western Texas, eastern Montana, Wyoming, and Colorado and a thin slice of New Mexico. The eastern parts of many of the states the 98th meridian crossed were good farming regions; but generally the meridian marked the beginning of a significant decline in rainfall. This semiaridity made farming in the region precarious—subject to the vicissitudes of alternating adequate rainfall and drought. There were other hostile environmental factors in the region—high winds, extremes of climate with frigid winters and burning summers, plagues of insects, shallowness of the soil, toughness of the matted grass, and absence of trees except in river bottomland. The exiguousness of this land made new demands of those who settled there—in some ways a revolutionary way of life, as Webb claimed in his classic study *The Great Plains.* If the plains brought out resourcefulness and innovation, they put such a high price on success that a cruel toll was exacted from the many unable to meet this price. The area that represented the last dream of the landless, of those seeking a new life, turned into a nightmare for many. Here there were no hostile Indians to unite against, no forests to clear away in cooperative labor—here the enemy was implacable Nature and a cruel isolation that turned many inward and set them down the route to madness.

Until the railroads began their drumbeating, the Plains had no propagandists to sing its praises. Far from being another Garden of the Universe, on most American maps through the 1850s it was identified as the Great American Desert. Explorers over the course of centuries had found it an inhospitable place, with little promise for farming. Some thinkers decided its hostility to settlement was a good thing: The G.A.D. would serve as a barrier to curb the native restlessness of Americans, thus stopping emigration once and for all. Of course, some saw the beauties of the prairie—the endless rolling grasss like a great green ocean; the bright-hued flowers which grew up in riotous colors after the rains; the overarching blue dome of sky. Others noted its utility for grazing—a prediction that the Coronados of the cattle country took up when they staked out their kingdom after the Civil War. Brigham Young was alerted to the potential of the Salt Lake area by John C. Frémont's reports. But given the agricultural methods of the day and the experience with the forested lands and rich soil east of the Mississippi, few envisioned the area patchworked with farms. The essentially agrarian mind-set of the day lacked a sense of how industrialization would revolutionize farming. The railroad technocrats and robber barons supplied the cutting edge of this industrial vision, motivated by the need for people and profits, capable of bringing to bear all the latest technologies against the enemy, Nature. Fittingly, the railroad men, who had forced their rails across this hostile land, were the first believers in its future. They had to believe, for they needed people, towns, farm produce; inexorably committed to growth, groaning under crushing debt, they knew a Plains devoted to cattle was not enough. A few Abilenes and Dodge Cities located on a few trunk lines sufficed to handle the cattle trade; but large-scale freight and passenger operations shuttling from east to west required a population base—people growing grain, people consuming the manufactured products of the East, people living in towns and on farms. In their briskly efficient vision, they divided the land into a great checkerboard of sections extending out from twenty to one hundred miles on either side of their right-of-way. These squares had to be sold off for farms and towns if any immediate profit was to be made from the land alone; after that, would come the steady, long-range return from freight.*

Without the railroads the people would have probably come anyway, only more slowly. Certainly the promise of the Homestead Act and the increase in immigration from Europe were sufficient to insure that. The early wagon-borne settlers confronted a prospect that affirmed the Great American Desert

*The railroads bear a substantial share of the blame for the uncertainties of farming and town-planting on the Plains. They sought to settle a large population scattered on small farms, producing for the urban market back east. Thus, the farmers were more vulnerable to economic cycles, and towns lacked industry and marketing relations with the farmers. The farms themselves were isolated economic units, each in competition with its neighbors. See *Garden in the Grasslands*, David M. Emmons (Lincoln: University of Nebraska Press, 1971).

appellation, but still they came, their very innocence of what they would find perhaps their strongest impetus. The new settlers saw an endless vista, a horizon unbroken by trees and overhead a burning sun in a vast cloudless sky. An eerie stillness surrounded them; it was due to the absence of any birds on the Plains. There were few game animals, other than the herds of buffalo (gone by the 1880s), but an overplenitude, it seemed, of dangerous rattlesnakes. The lost babe in the woods of the early colonists' tales had his or her counterpart in the child of the wagon train who wandered off in the tall bluestem prairie grass and was not seen again until winter when the grass was withered by frost and the pathetic little corpse was found, dead of a rattler's bite or starvation. In the monotonous vastness of it all, one could easily lose one's bearings, for there were no landmarks, no trees, no rocks—it was especially easy to become confused at night or on a cloudy day, when there was no sun to point out east and west.

One of the most terrifying hazards of the plains was prairie fires, set by lightning or perhaps a campfire. These would sweep over an area, driving all the animals before them and leaving bare, black stubble. Such a burned-over area was one woman's most vivid memory of her arrival at her new home in Adams County, Nebraska:

> I shall never forget the black prairie as I saw it in 1872, just after a prairie fire had swept over it. To me, coming from southern Michigan with her clover fields, large houses and larger barns, trees, hills, and running streams, the vast stretches of black prairie never ending—no north, south, east, or west—dotted over with tiny unpainted houses—no I can't say barns—but shacks for a cow, and perhaps a yoke of oxen—that picture struck such a homesick feeling in my soul it took years to efface. [9]

Even the crude shacks relieving the emptiness of the land were rare at first, because there were no trees and imported lumber was prohibitively expensive. Most of the settlers either made dugouts in the sparse hills or, more frequently, employed the native building material—the sod of the plains matted with the tough wiry roots of the grass. To quarry this "Nebraska marble," the settler hired a man with a grasshopper plough to cut foot-wide strips of soil. Rectangles two feet long were then cut from these strips. A clearing sixteen by twenty-four feet was made, and the pieces of sod were piled up on top of one another around its outline, making walls two feet thick and still covered with grass. Space for a door and a window would be left open, and a ridgepole laid along the top of the peaked roof, with brush for rafters and more sod placed on top to make a roof. The naturally insulated sod house—or "soddie"—was cool in summer and warm in winter, and since it was built low to the ground, it was resistant to tornados. And it cost nothing to build. It was also dark inside, and its roof leaked so that the dirt floor became a bog when it rained. Displaced snakes and mice would crawl out of the sod unless the builder had taken care to chink their holes when he removed the sod.

One sees contemporary photographs of the soddies with families seated outside squinting in the bright sun, the farmer often standing squarely by his plough, the tool of his trade, and a weapon of his survival like a Kentucky woodsman's long rifle. In the windows were often potted geraniums or begonias which the women had brought, as slips, from back east, the only reminder of the homes they had left, undoubtedly with considerable regret, to live on this godforsaken prairie. The chroniclers of the Plains have shown how hard the life was on a woman (with the significant exception of Willa Cather, who extolled the strength of pioneer women in characters like Alexandra Bergson in *O Pioneers* and Antonia Shimerda in *My Ántonia*).

The classic figure of the suffering woman of the Great Plains is Beret, the Norwegian immigrant in Ole Rölvaag's saga of life in the Dakotas, *Giants in the Earth* (a novel based closely on immigrant accounts). While her husband, Per Hansa, a robust, genial, optimistic man, revels in his new farm and builds it into a profitable enterprise, despite vicissitudes of drought, blizzard, and plagues of grasshoppers, Beret slowly is driven mad—not just by the harshness of life, the lack of amenities, the emptiness of the vistas—but by a sense of some profound guilt that haunts her. There was something unwholesome about life there, Beret found; the absence of civilization made her vulnerable to her inner demons. She is gripped suddenly by an unnameable fear: "*Something was about to go wrong.*" She views the flat, empty land and thinks, "Why, there isn't even a thing that one can *hide behind*!"[10] She grows worse until a preacher comes to the small settlement, starts a church, is kind to her, and succeeds in exorcising her oppressive sense of looming evil. But her sanity is won at the cost of becoming a religious fanatic. In the depths of a raging blizzard, when one of their neighbors is dying, she develops an *idée fixe* that he must have a minister; she nags Per Hansa until he fatalistically sets out in the storm to find a preacher; he never comes back. His body is discovered the following spring, sheltering by a haystack: "His face was ashen and drawn. His eyes were set towards the west."[11]

Rölvaag pits the Old World superstitions and guilts, as well as the deep ties to the little villages with their rhythms and community, against the pioneer's westering urge. Beret has brought a heavy baggage of sin, like her father's old trunk which she cherishes and plans to use for her coffin. Her guilt transforms the vast indifferent land into an ominous presence. The guilt she feels—what Per Hansa cannot understand—is for the hubris that leads a man to cast off the settled ways of the village back in Norway and go forth into the wild godless land, beyond the reach of custom and tradition. It is the woman, with her conservative, old-country notions, who brakes Per Hansa's dream. He is the optimist, oriented in the future, a pragmatist. For the man, then, the Plains represented freedom, opportunity, and a rejection of the old ways, and

Beret, as Rölvaag depicts her, must instinctively fight this and hate it until her hate seeps into her own system, poisoning her.

Webb considers the tragedy of women of the Plains and concludes that the region "exerted a peculiarly appalling affect on women" if the fictional characterizations were any indication, and his own upbringing convinces him there is much truth to the fiction. "Imagine a sensitive woman set down on an arid plain to live in a dugout or a pole pen with a dirt floor, without furniture, music, or pictures, with the bare necessities of life! . . . The wind, the sand, the drought, the unmitigated sun, and the boundless expanse of a horizon on which danced fantastic images conjured up by the mirages, seemed to overwhelm the women with a sense of desolation, insecurity and futility, which they did not feel when surrounded with hills and green trees."[12]

Webb is not saying that women were spiritually inferior or hinting at darker psychopathologies as Rölvaag does; rather he is describing the result of the social role of many women of the day, who were conditioned to finding meaning in keeping a home, who were used to the amenities and the "finer things." When such accoutrements of civilization as they had known it were absent, many women had trouble adjusting. Fortunate were those who at least had other women to commiserate with. Mary Ballon, who kept a boarding house while her husband prospected in California in 1852, described in a letter to her son back east how she and the few other women in a little mining town longed for home: "I would not advise any Lady to come out here and suffer the toil and fatigue that I have suffered . . . Clark Simmon's wife says if she was safe in the States she would not care if she had one cent. She came in here last night and said, 'Oh dear I am so homesick that I must die' and then again my other associate came in with tears in her eyes and said she had cried all day, she said if she had as good [i.e. bad] a home as I had got she would not stay twenty-five minutes in California."[13]

Whatever the causes, the fact remains that most women courageously survived the grim life in the lonely sod huts. Elinore Pruitt Stewart, a young widow, went west in 1909, determined to homestead. With the help and advice of the Wyoming rancher, whom she worked for as housekeeper and then married, she proved up her claim. In one of her letters published in *Harper's Magazine*, she avers that she is "very enthusiastic about women homesteading. It really requires less strength and labor to satisfy a large family than it does to go out to wash"[14] (she had been a "washlady" in Denver before moving to Wyoming). But she added that "temperament has much to do with success . . . and persons afraid of coyotes and work and loneliness had better let ranching alone."[15] Later, when towns grew up, with opportunities to pursue their own interests, rather than laboring unremittingly for their husbands' dreams, they blossomed—like those slips of flowers they had carried west. In the rough mining and cow towns, "respectable" women were often put on a pedestal and given deference and protection because they were so scarce; at the same time, the truly independent women were in the shady part of society for the most part—the madams, actresses, and roughneck females of the West who kicked the traces of Victorian gentility and managed to become financially successful and even win the grudging respect, if not social acceptance, of their fellow townspeople. The western woman was still, on the whole, a more independent, self-reliant article than her sisters back east, and in the freer air of the region various women's causes, ranging from prohibition—a preeminently women's cause on the frontier—to voting rights, flourished. When the Nineteenth Amendment to the Constitution, giving women the right to vote, was ratified in 1920, only two states east of the Mississippi (New York and Michigan) had woman's suffrage laws while thirteen states west of the 98th meridian had given women the vote—Wyoming had granted it as early as 1869 and Colorado in 1893.

Women did not play a leading role in founding towns on the Plains; it was men who platted the towns, laid them out, sold the real estate, built the buildings. But the acute loneliness of Plains life and the absence of amenities for her and her children surely made many a woman a staunch backer of urban as opposed to rural life, yearning for a town nearby, not to live in, but for the trading, the schools, churches, and above all the sociability as an antidote to loneliness.

Many settlers came in groups to begin with—family groups, neighborhood groups, groups from the same town, and, of course, ethnic groups of foreign immigrants from the same village in the old country. Some of the groups formed the nuclei of towns; they made up a little settlement on adjacent claims and claimed town status themselves or, by their presence, encouraged a promoter to come in and plant one nearby. The small party of Norwegians in *Giants in the Earth* clung together in their adjoining homesteads and organized schools and a township government with a justice of the peace as more settlers joined them. On the farthest outposts of the frontier, a group of wagons on the distant eastern horizon was a welcome sight and any company was welcome. And, if the newcomers took up homesteads, it was proof that the country was "settling up"—that it was becoming a going proposition. The appearance of the railroad in the area was an even more welcome harbinger. These settlers were not the kind of loners who fled as soon as a neighboring chimney sent a plume of smoke up against the big sky; for a complex of reasons, beyond relieving the monotonous isolation of their life, they longed for a crossroads, a group of houses, a post office, a store or two, a depot—a village with a name, a bare minimal urban presence. This yearning stemmed from their cultural heritage, their origins in some town back east or the Old World. But most of all, a town was a guarantor that this wilderness, a wilderness not of trees but of empty spaces, was surrendering to civilization and progress.

There is a section in Rölvaag's novel when the settlement is plunged into great excitement by the arrival of five wagons carrying Norwegians. Per Hansa, the area's most effective booster, is away, but Tonseten makes a passionate plea to convince them to stay. When the newcomers jibe at the lack of trees, he tells them that a lack of trees is a positive virtue—it makes the ploughing easier, makes it possible to plant for yourself the size of wood lot you need, and so on, forgetting the cold winters when the only fuel was twisted strands of dried grass. After painting the future of his own region—the churches, schools, and town that would grow up—Tonseten warns them against going elsewhere: "Suppose they went to a place where no one had come yet? Couldn't they understand that all of Dakota Territory would never be peopled? Why, there weren't enough folks in the whole world for that, and never would be either! . . . Or if they should be so unfortunate as to choose a location where no one followed after? . . . What then?"[16] Tonseten is a gifted booster; the people decide to stay. And eventually, one fine day, "a strange monster came writhing westward over the prairie, from Worthington to Luverne; it was the greatest and the most memorable event that had yet happened in these parts. . . . People felt that day a joy that almost frightened them; for it seemed now that all their troubles were over, that there could be no more hardships to contend with."[17] Such optimism, at the mere coming of the railroad, was obviously a bit steep; still Rölvaag has captured the yearning of early settlers for neighbors and for a town and a train which would bring them the goods of civilization.

For those who had none, the desire for the railroad paralleled, became indistinguishable from, the need for neighbors. Promoters, aware of this need and the possibility of profiting from it, were not long in appearing on the scene. These individuals often represennted smaller companies and promised a spur line between the settlement and the main trunk line, thus insuring that it would grow into a town. Naturally, the settlers would be required to subscribe to the railroad's stock. In short it was the same game that the local railroads had played back in the Middle West, a game that had the power of making or breaking a town. Wherever a group of shacks or soddies clustered together and called itself a town, wherever a county had been organized, the railroad promoters were not far behind.

State governments too were hit up for their share, and here the lobbyists working the legislature spread out the bribes with a lavish hand. The Union Pacific, for example, doled out four hundred thousand dollars between 1866 and 1872, while the Central Pacific spread around a half a million dollars annually between 1875 and 1885. That these systematic lobbying campaigns paid off is obvious from the rich returns in state land grants the railroads raked in. Frederick A. Cleveland and Fred W. Powell calculated that the railroads were granted "one fourth of the whole area of Minnesota and Washington; one fifth of Wisconsin, Iowa, Kansas, North Dakota, and Montana; one seventh of Nebraska; one eighth of California; and one ninth of Louisiana." Congressional land grants between 1862 and 1872 handed over more than 200 million acres of public-domain land to railroad companies.

Land, of course, was not cash in hand, nor was it sufficient to pay off the railroads' costs. The land was converted into ready cash by the device of floating land bonds—bonds with the land as collateral. Other capital was raised by mortgages on equipment, and other bonds and stocks. Union Pacific issued bonds with a par value of $110 million—for which they received only $74 million in cash, because investors considered railroads a very risky investment with a low return. In addition the U.S. government lent the roads $64 million, most of this to the Union Pacific and the Central Pacific. This amount—plus $114 million in accumulated interest—was almost miraculously paid off in the 1890s. Total land sales, one estimate has it, brought the railroads $440 million by 1940. At any rate, the railroad promotors managed to enrich themselves personally by stock watering or forming construction companies, billing their own railroads exorbitantly and skimming off fat profits, rather than by profits from operations.

The desperation with which the western towns sought railroads was probably far more intense than the competition in the Middle West. A couple of examples will suffice to show how much of their resources some towns and cities were willing to pledge. In 1872 Los Angeles was handed a take-it-or-leave-it demand for six hundred thousand dollars by the Southern Pacific and paid up; this was the equivalent of a one-hundred-dollar assessment on every man, woman, or child then living in Los Angeles County. In 1880 Superior, Minnesota, turned over one third of its "lands, premises and real estate,"[18] as well as right-of-way land, to induce the Northern Pacific to pass through. In Nebraska, where settlement was thin, forty-three counties between 1867 and 1892 made a total of $5 million in subscriptions to railroad companies, some of which never laid any track. That comes to more than one hundred thousand dollars a county, a considerable burden of debt on a populace of newly-arrived settlers, many of whom had little money. Yet without the railroad their areas' economic potential could not begin to be realized. Without towns nearby, farmers were isolated from their markets, and had no idea of the going prices for their grain. If there were no competing lines in their area, the local dealers who bought their grain and shipped it to market had to pay inflated shipping costs, meaning they paid the farmer that much less for his crop. Nor could the town merchants survive without a railroad, for the farmers would be compelled to take their grain and do their shopping where the depot was.

In Adams County, which began to fill up in 1870, the Burlington and the Union Pacific had large land grants. The Burlington, or its agents, had energetically promoted the virtues of Adams County in Michigan, and many people from that state, especially Civil War veterans, emigrated. The railroad carried them by train to the end of the line, after which the passengers debarked and walked to the first town in the county, Juniata. The railroad had planned Juniata as its first depot in the new county, and to get it underway had brought four settlers to the location where Juniata was to be. The four men took out four adjoining homesteads in their own names and built the requisite dwellings on each of the adjoining corners, using wood that the railroad had furnished. A railroad surveyor then laid out the town's streets, and when the first settlers received their patents from the government, they sold the land to the railroad, with two of the men receiving one quarter of the town lots in payment for their services as group leaders. The Burlington also drilled a well for the settlers.

Juniata grew and became the first county seat of Adams County. Meanwhile, in 1872 a representative of the St. Joseph and Denver City Railroad, which ran north-south, asked the county commissioners to authorize seventy-five thousand dollars in bonds so that it could lay tracks through the county, making a junction with the Burlington at Juniata. The taxpayers voted the proposition down; many felt that the St. Joseph and Denver City would have to come through thee county anyhow, bonds or no. They were only half right; the railroad did lay tracks through the county by the end of the year, but it made the junction with the Burlington at a point several miles east of Juniata, where there was a cluster of three or four houses. This settlement was christened Hastings, after Major Thomas del Monte Hastings, a railroad construction engineer. The custom of naming a town—or even its streets—after a railroad employee was common enough, but the name was also chosen because it started with "h," and like the Burlington (and the Illinois central before it), the St. Joseph and Denver City was naming the supply stations at the end of each completed section in alphabetical sequence—thus, Hastings was the end of the sequence running Alexandria, Belvidere, Carleton, Davenport, Edgar, Fairfield, and Glenville. Juniata, named after the river in Pennsylvania, followed Archer, Burks, Crete, Dorchester, Exeter, Fairmont, Grafton, Harvard, and Inland and was succeeded in its turn by Kennesaw, which was founded in 1872.

As the county was settled, every new town was founded by one of the railroads. There was Prosser, laid out by the Missouri Pacific in 1887, on land purchased from a homesteader by railroad agents who passed themselves off as representatives of eastern capitalists looking for cheap land for sheep grazing. The Missouri Pacific was the recipient of a $175,000 subsidy from the county, which Juniata (by now more wary about railroads' locations) almost did not support until it received assurances that Prosser would not be located too close to it. The town was named after the superintendent of the construction crew that laid the track, and its streets were named for his children. The town reached its peak in the early 1900s when it had a grain elevator, a roundhouse, stockyards, a state bank, and other small businesses. Thirty years later the bank was merged with one in Hastings, other businesses moved out, and the Missouri Pacific tore down its depot and roundhouse and took up its tracks, leaving only a tiny village. The railroad gave and the railroad—and time—took away.

Then there was Hansen, a stop on the Grand Island and St. Joseph, successor to the St. Joseph and Denver City. It was founded in 1879 and named for a civil engineer working on the railroad at the time. Since it biggest business was a blacksmith's shop, one could have predicted the future of Hansen. When the automobile came, it dwindled away to some homes and grain elevators serving the area's farmers. Thee railroad remained but trains only made irregular freight stops.

The four men who preempted the land for Kenesaw and sold out to the railroad promptly moved away, leaving an empty town. Others came, however, and the town did well. Before the turn of the century, it boasted a general store, a hotel, a grain business, two lumberyards, two hardware stores, a billiard parlor, a restaurant, a physician, a newspaper, and a bank. In its heyday, Kenesaw had a municipal electric plant, an opera house, and two hotels, and four westbound passenger trains and three eastbound stopped daily, plus many freight trains. The Ray Bash Players gave regular performances, and Walter Schultz's Kenesaw motion picture theater was another favorite entertainment; Schultz was famous in the area as the inventor of "Walt's Disc Talking Equipment Company," which was sold to buyers as far away as Mexico and Puerto Rico. Hit hard by the Depression in 1930, Kenesaw survived as a village of seven hundred or so souls, thanks in part to federal relief projects. In the 1960s, eighty new homes went up, and town businesses such as the Kenesaw Cafe and Supper Club, Larmore's Jack and Jill Grocer, the Silver Dollar Tavern, the Holiday Coin Laundromat, Sharon's Beauty Shop, Sheila's Beauty Shop, Shurigar Brothers Land Leveling, Custom Combining and Grain Drying, Beals Care Home and the Jackson Funeral Home prospered. But while once a considerable railroad yard bisected the center of the town and the Burlington employed forty men in the town, now only one passenger train a day ran through, no boarding.

So it went. Towns and villages, all drawing sustenance from the umbilical railroad. Most of those that lived by the railroad, died, or rather stagnated, by it. With the coming of the automobile, the towns no longer served as trading centers for the surrounding farms; the farmers drove to the county seat or the city, and the trains no longer stopped at crossroads to pick up farmers—or the towns they had gone to, for that matter. The one exception was the town of Hastings, for on that fateful day when the people of Juniata voted down the bond issue for the St. Joseph and Denver City, Hastings was on its way. Two other railroads later came in, making Hastings a small but considerable terminus. Feeling its oats, it began to petition for the transfer of the county seat from Juniata. There ensued several years of petitions and votes, with the Juniata townspeople staving off the challenge by every legal means. So many such battles were going on in Nebraska at the time, as town fortunes ebbed and flooded with the locations of the railroads, that the Nebraska legislature passed a law requiring a petition of three fifths of the voters in the last election; if this was achieved then a general referendum on the question was held. Juniata first sought to gain approval for an allocation of funds to build a courthouse, on the theory that such a commitment would strengthen its hold on the seat, but a Hastings partisan at the meeting jumped on his horse, rode to Hastings, and galloped back in the van of an army of Hastings men. According to the county historian, they came "in wagons, on horses, on whatever conveyances they could muster [and] some brought shotguns, revolvers and other weapons with which to defend what they considered to be their rights."[19]

The county commissioner adjourned the meeting but later accepted a bid for construction of the courthouse in Juniata, at which point the one Hastings man on the scene, A. E. Cramer, the county clerk, protested that the procedure was illegal and refused to put his official seal on the document. The commissioners promptly declared the office of county clerk vacant. Cramer took it to court, and the judge ultimately ruled in his favor. Another petition was got up by the Hastings forces, who, while the Juniata-dominated county commissioners stalled, kept adding names with such vigor that when the commissioners finally got round to the petition they suggested that some of the signatures must be invalid, inasmuch as their total number exceeded the entire population of the county.

Finally, an election was held in 1877. Poll watchers from Hastings were posted in Juniata and vice versa. Crowds of angry men milled about in both places, and in Juniata the local partisans attacked and drove away the Hastings men, who were convoying a poll watcher. The poll-watcher—the same Mr. Cramer who as county clerk had fought off the Juniata courthouse—quickly realized that the Hastings escort was badly outnumbered. He hightailed it back to Hastings, leaving the victors busily augmenting Juniata's vote total. When Cramer arrived home, he found that word had preceded him on the telegraph, and a mob of Hastings men armed with "whips, clubs, scythes" and other weapons had already mobilized. The Hastings army, led by Cramer, returned to Juniata and successfully retook the polls from Juniata.

The upshot of the victory was that Cramer and another Hastings loyalist were allowed to supervise the Juniata vote count. The ballots had been made up in rolls, with perforations around each one so that it could be torn off and given to the voter. The poll watchers noted that in some cases the voters had not even observed the nicety of tearing off individual ballots, so that long, unseparated strips of pro-Juniata votes festooned the ballot boxes.

When the votes were at last tabulated, Hastings was adjudged the winner by a comfortable margin. Juniata promptly cried foul, and the court appointed a referee to supervise the recount. The referee found irregularities on both sides (including long strips of unseparated pro-Hastings votes) but decided that more Juniata votes were tainted by fraud. As a result, although Hastings's final vote was decreased, its margin of victory was increased.

This did not end the melodrama. On the day the judge announced the referee's decision, a Hastings man was dispatched to Juniata to secure the county records; he was accompanied by a cowboy named Smith, "a thorough westerner and an excellent shot with the revolver,"[20] who happened to be working at the local livery stable. The two men entered Juniata at dusk, when the local folk were eating supper. They quickly proceeded to the office of the county clerk, still Hastings's man in Juniata, A. E. Cramer, who had all the records piled on his desk ready to go. The Hastings emissaries swooped them up, stacked them in the wagon, and sped off for home, while the burghers of Juniata were obiviously chewing their suppers.

Later, Hastings also added the county jail to its booty. A Juniata townsman recalled the bitter gall of that moment:

> The rapid growth of Hastings took from Juniata the county seat, and along with it the only building we had that in any way suggested that we were the honest legitimate county seat of Adams county. It was the Adams county jail. Such an addition to our town! About as large as a good-sized dry good box, but our hopes were built on nothing less than that every man, woman and child in Hastings would find in it an abiding place. So with wrath in our hearts, and tears in our eyes, we watched it disappear toward the east, and poor Juniata was no more the metropolis of Adams county.[21]

Diminutive as it was, the jail was sturdily built and considered impervious to jailbreaks. The small wooden building that had served as the county courthouse was another matter, though; the Hastings people let Juniata keep that. The county treasurer, a Juniata man, moved the building to his own yard, where it stayed, a reminder of the town's glory days, along with the town windmill, the wooden bandstand at the downtown intersection and the public bell in front of J. J. Williams's restaurant, which served both to call people to meals and as a fire alarm.

With the capture of the county seat and the completion of the railroads, Hastings enjoyed a rapid growth, from a population of zero in 1870 to more than 3,000 in 1878, while the entire county was increasing from 19 to 10,235. Immigration was to be even greateer in the next decade, as more railroads came in to carry the immigrants and rainfall increased abnormally throughout the Plains area, creating the illusion that this condition was permanent. The early settlers of the seventies might have raised a note of caution out of their own harsh experiences. Adams County had better agricultural conditions than most, with reasonably good rain, a considerable pool of underground water, and fertile soil. The first settlers sought out a conjunction of fertile soil, level land, and water for their homesteads, with land along the Blue River especially prized. But by 1873 more than half the land of the county—and all the best land—was taken up, leaving less desirable locations for the rest.

In 1873 the people got their first taste of Plains weather when on Easter Sunday a blizzard struck. It had been a warm, sunny day, and indeed spring had arrived so early that many farmers already had their crops in; however, since the winter had been unusually dry, the ground was hard, and birds ate most of the seeds. Then at about four o'clock an eerie stillness settled in, as though the whole world was holding its breath. Huge, churning clouds billowed up on the horizon to the northeast, while in the southwestern sky an inky blackness appeared. The silence grew more ominous, and people sensed something bad was coming. A roar was heard growing louder and louder until it was like a thousand freight trains. The two storms, barreling in from opposite directions, collided above Adams County and the sky became a maelstrom of the elements. The wind snatched up trees, barns, and houses and hurled them about; the air was thick with dust and the roar was deafening. The heavy winds were followed by snow, and although the temperature never went below freezing, the wind was so fierce that a few hours' exposure to it meant death. Some people did die, others huddled in their flimsily built houses and soddies. The soddies survived but many wooden houses were blown away. One family, just recently arrived, had thrown up a temporary shack, twelve by sixteen feet. When the storm came, seven of them crowded in to wait it out; later they brought in their four horses: "Their tails were a foot in diameter, filled with snow so firmly packed that it was a difficult task to remove it. Every muscle in their bodies quivered like a man shaking with the ague. They were so hungry that they soon began gnawing at the 2 × 4 scantling in front of them. To prevent this we had to fill the scantlings with shingle nails."[22] The family survived in their little shack—probably because they were in a relatively protected area. By Wednesday afternoon the storm finally abated, but many settlers had lost not only their crops but the animals upon which they depended for food. Cattle starved because the snow had covered the buffalo grass in the draws where they fed.

The following year another kind of blizzard struck—a blizzard of grasshoppers. This biblical horde waited until the end of July, when the wheat was waving thick and green in the fields, and the new settlers watched proudly as the wind sent shimmering silver waves across it. Then seething masses of black clouds blotted out the sun. The clouds were alive—a swarming, shrilling ravening mass of insects which descended upon the grain. In forty-eight hours it was over, not a green thing was left standing. They even ate green paint, later legends had it. The fish in the streams and the fowl in the barnyards had gorged on the insects so that their flesh tasted of it for weeks. So severe were the effects of the grasshopper plague that local relief societies were organized to help the destitute. Congress appropriated $180,000, allowed homesteaders to delay their loan payments, and temporarily waived the requirement that they must occupy their claims continuously. In many areas the grasshoppers deposited their eggs in the soil; their progeny were back the following year, eating the seed corn as soon as it had been planted.

The tide of immigratiion was slowed but not stopped by these disasters. Many settlers stuck it out. They had no choice, having sold everything to come; they were situational optimists with a pragmatic faith that their situation would improve in time. They had engaged in a radical leap, and were loathe to admit defeat, to skulk back to their hometowns, tails between their legs, to hear the "I-told-you so's" of friends and relatives. They had a stubborn pride—and also fancied a visit to the homeplace in a state of greater prosperity than when they left. They continued to write cheerful letters to their friends back east, and the immigration societies kept up their propaganda din. The claims in their brochures were moderated, but, as Walter Prescott Webb remarks about a similarly subdued description of the cattle industry during the boom of the 1880s, it was "the sort of moderation that makes the thing discussed more desirable."[23] It was the last great American land rush, and its numbers were swelled by the European immigrants arriving at Ellis Island. Recruited both at home and abroad by the railroads, the immigrants were assisted from their point of embarkation by the railroads, herded onto special immigrants' trains, and sold land on "easy" credit terms by the railroads once they arrived west. Gone were the great lumbering, jouncing covered wagons, replaced by the speed and efficiency of the railroad cars, on which people were human freight. *Harper's Magazine* christened the immigrant cars "the Modern Ship of the Plains" and described a typical one:

> An immigrant sleeper is now used, which is constructed with sections on each side of the aisle, each section containing two double berths. The berths are made with slats of hard wood running longitudinally; there is no upholstery in the car, and no bedding supplied, and after the car is vacated the hose can be turned in upon it, and all the wood-work thoroughly cleansed. The immigrants usually carry with them enough blankets and wraps to make them tolerably comfortable in their berths; a cooking stove is provided in one end of the car, on which the occupants can cook their food, and even the long transcontinental journeys of the immigrants are now made without hardship.[24]

Whether it was truly without hardship, the journey was undoubtedly a long one for people who probably had few "blankets and wraps" to make them "tolerably comfortable," and who had just arrived in a strange land.

Another special accommodation for immigrants was the zulu car—a freight car with bunks and a stove, in which a single family or small group traveled with all their possessions stored alongside them in the car. The traffic in people and their goods was so much a part of the railroad's business that as late as 1972 the Burlington and Northern (formerly the Burlington and Missouri) Railroad's schedule of freight charges still listed "emigrant movables," which included not only household goods but also agricultural implements and even livestock. For the immigrants, train travel had not only the advantages of special low rates and greater speed, it also enabled them to bring with them all the goods and equipment necessary for starting a new life, without having to buy the extra equipment needed for wagon travel.

One of the largest groups of foreign immigrants to come to Adams County, Nebraska, was the German-Russians; though these immigrants had cultural problems of assimilation unique to themselves, their story is similar to those of many other foreign ethnic groups who went west. (Foreigners played a larger role in the early settlement of the West than is commonly realized. In the early 1870s three of ten westerners were foreign-born. More than half the men in Utah, Nevada, Arizona, Idaho, and California were immigrants. After 1880, however, cities exercised a stronger lure, and the proportion of foreign-born fell to one in twenty. The great majority of them threw off their ethnic identification much more rapidly than their compatriots in the cities.) The German-Russians' story also shows how farflung were the railroads' efforts to attract settlers. The German-Russians came from the Ukraine and Crimea; they were Germans who had migrated to Russia in the early 1800s, settling at first along the Volga, north of the Black Sea. With the upwelling of nationalism under Czar Alexander II from 1868 on, the expatriated Germans lost their former special privileges under Russian law and began to consider emigrating. Alert American railroads and steamship lines spotted the opportunities for revenue this group offered and began cultivating them. The Burlington and Missouri transported a delegation of German-Russians to Nebraska, where they were lectured on the virtues of the state and the ease with which they could purchase railroad land. The delegation returned to Russia, and by 1876 the first German-Russians began arriving in Hastings. One man, Pastor Neumann, a prominent American Lutheran but also an agent for the railroads, was an influential force in settling the early immigrants on the journey to America. He traveled up and down the Ukraine, speaking to the German-Russians in their home villages, urging them to make the move. Neumann met one party (they often traveled in communal groups, and many were Mennonities) in New York and sent them on to Dorchester, Wisconsin; at some point in their journey they were met by Burlington representatives, who offered them free passage to Lincoln, Nebraska, on the theory that if one group settled there, then other German-Russians would follow. In preparation for these later groups, the railroad built immigrant hostels in Lincoln and Sutton. These served as halfway houses for new arrivals until they could find land or jobs. Since the majority did not have enough money to buy land, they often ended up working for the railroad during the period it was pushing its tracks westward. Still another effort by the Burlington involved persuading already arrived German-Americans to write their friends back in the old country and tell them of the glories of Nebraska; the railroad provided them with a circular to send along entitled *An unseren Verwandten und Freunde im Russland (To Our Relatives and Friends in Russia).*

These efforts paid off, and an ever-increasing number of German-Russians—mainly Protestants from the Volga region—came to the town of Hastings in the 1880s. The attitude of some of the native Americans in the town toward the arrivals was perhaps summed up by a news item in the Hastings *Gazette Journal* in 1886: "A carload of Russians was unloaded today."[25] The reference might as easily have been to cattle, and there was no further identification of the individuals who came, where they went, or how many of them there were. Like other immigrant groups, the German-Russians met prejudice; in the town they were commonly referred to as "Rooshians"—until World War I when their German heritage was suddenly recollected and they became the object of anti-German hysteria. Some Hastings people did help, though; a member of one immigrant party recalled that a lumberyard gave them boards to build shacks with and that the mayor of the town visited them and sent them food. The mayor was Jacob Fisher, an immigrant from Germany.

Because of the common language, the German-Americans provided more help than others in the town, but the German-Russians gradually formed their own self-help organizations, centered around their churches. The majority, who had no money with which to purchase farms, worked for the railroads and in the town's brick and cigar factories. They all lived on the south or "wrong" side of the Burlington tracks, and even their ghetto was subdivided, with immigrants from Norka living on one side of Burlington Avenue and those from Frank on the other. In Hastings they served their time as a low-wage labor pool. Many men worked for fifteen dollars a week in factories or, with their families, as migrant workers in the beet fields. Perhaps the greatest contribution the German-Russsian wheat farmers from the Steppes made to the Plains was their introduction in the 1880s of hard red or winter wheat, which they had smuggled in in their luggage and which was admirably suited to the Plains environment because, being ready for harvest in the spring, it did not depend upon the uncertain summer rain to bring it to maturity.

Some 115,000 German-Russian immigrants came to the United States between 1873 and 1914, and another 150,000 to western Canada—a majority of them frugal-living Mennonites. Most came to Nebraska in the 1880s, as did the other foreign immigrants—Germans, Irish, and Scandinavians in the main. In the seventies it had been the American-born, from Illinois, Iowa, Michigan, and New England. The Hastings newspaper had remarked in 1878 that "the B & M aims to put a settler on every 80 acres in Southern Nebraska,"[26] and by the end of the 1880s they—and whoever else was responsible—had probably accomplished this. By 1890 there was little good land left to be homesteaded in the eastern part of the Great Plains. In that year the director of the Bureau of the Census announced that the frontier was over: "The unsettled area had been so broken into by isolated bodies of settlement that there can hardly be said to be a frontier line."[27]

Actually, good land remained farther west and in Oklahoma and four times as many acres were taken up by homesteaders after 1890 than before. But the tide of humanity had washed over the Great Plains until it lapped the foot of the Rockies; the land that had been leapfrogged by the Oregon parties and the forty-niners was now engrossed by the later arrivals. Between 1870 and 1890, 430 million acres of the Great Plains to the 100th meridian had been claimed by various parties and 225 million were under cultivation. (Only 80 million acres of the West's land had gone directly to homesteaders under the Homestead Act of 1862, however.) By 1880 Kansas had 850,000 people and Nebraska 450,000; by 1885, 550,000 people lived in the Dakota Territory east of the Missouri—an increase of 400 percent over five years. Smaller numbers had moved into eastern Wyoming and Montana, where the cattle kings put up a determined resistance in the famous, if exaggerated, "range wars."

The last frontier in the classic meaning of the term was the region to the south known as Indian Territory. Here, by treaty, lived twenty-two tribes that had been driven off their lands both east of the Mississippi and in the southern plains. Their treaties with the U.S. government had granted them the right to live there "as long as the grass shall grow and the waters flow," or words to that effect, a legal phraseology popular in broken treaties with the Indians. Will Rogers, the vaudeville satirist who had Cherokee blood, was later to write of this treaty: "They sent the Indians to Oklahoma. They had a treaty that said, 'You shall have this land as long as grass grows and water flows.' It was not only a good rhyme but looked like a good treaty, and it was till they struck oil. Then the government took it away from us again. They said the treaty refers to 'water and grass; it don't say anything about oil.' "[28]

Actually, Rogers may have been telescoping history, because the first interest in the land came before oil was discovered there. In 1880, caught up in the homesteading fever, a group of frontiersmen began making forays into Indian Territory and more specifically into the triangle of two million acres of unassigned land known as the Oklahoma District. These men were lawless types who styled themselves "boomers." The army tried to chase out the renegades, but it was an impossible job keeping up with them. Further, in the manifest-destiny spirit of the times, congressmen took up their cause, asking rhetorically how good red-blooded Americans could be denied this land in favor of a few scrawny redskins living under some sort of outmoded treaty. Why, it was a waste of good land to keep it out of the hands of white men who knew how to make it worth something. Bowing to the popular mood, Congress sold out the Indians once again and passed an act opening up the Oklahoma District to homesteaders. The president set the date of entry for noon, April 22, 1889.

In the few months remaining before the day, thousands of people gathered along the borders of the district, joining the boomers already there. Temporary towns had sprung up all along the border. They had names such as Beaver City and Purcell and populations up to fifteen thousand, yet there was not a permannent building in any of them, with the exception of the single plastered house where the railroad agent lived. The inhabitants lived in dugouts, sod houses, shacks, and tents; many of them were dressed like Indians, an observer noted, because "clothing is the most difficult thing to obtain."[29] Soldiers patrolled the border, trying to keep back the gun-jumpers. It was estimated that nearly one hundred thousand people were poised at the border.

At last the day arrived. A young man named Hamilton Wicks participated in the rush and set down his experiences for *Cosmopolitan* soon afterward. Observing from a more detached vantage point, aboard a chartered train bound for Guthrie, the nascent capital of the district, Wicks saw all manner of people edging up to the starting line. There was a "tatterdemalion group, consisting of a shaggy-bearded man, a slatternly-looking woman, and several girls and boys, faithful images of their parents, in shabby attire, usually with a dog and a coop of chickens" sitting in their covered wagon. Nearby he saw "a couple of flashy real-estate men from Wichita . . . driving a spanking span of bays, with an equipage looking for all the world as though it had just come from a fashionble livery stable." Others proceeded forward in all manner of vehicles, horses and on foot. "The whole procession marched, rode, or drove, as on some gala occasion, with smiling faces and waving hands. Every one imagined that Eldorado was just ahead."[30] All lined up as the hour of noon approached, while a troop of cavalry restrained them with difficulty. At least a bugle sounded, and with a great shout of exultation, the crowd rushed headlong toward the promised land.

Wick's train kept pace and then outdistanced the rest with a rush down the last grade and across the bridge near the Cimarron River, where the town site of Guthrie swung into view. The town—the first, perhaps, of many American towns to bestow on itself the proud sobriquet "Magic City"—had already been roughly laid out. There was a water tank, a station, a Wells Fargo office and, the cynosure of all desires, the Government Land Office, a hastily erected structure twenty by forty feet, where land claims would be filed. As soon as the train stopped, Wicks bundled his blankets out the car window and jumped after them. He joined the thousands of others milling and rushing about, all bent on claiming a valuable town lot. Since there were no markers, it was difficult to tell where the best spots would be—whether one had a desirable corner lot or merely a less valuable section of street. The object of this surreal game was to select one's lot and then, before anyone else, drive a stake and erect some sort of dwelling, in conformity with the Homestead Act. Wicks scuttled about until he saw a man who looked like one of the deputies posted on the site to keep order. The man had taken advantage of his assignment to stake an early claim. Playing a hunch, Wicks asked him if the spot he was standing on might perchancce be a street. "Yes," the deputy replied. "We are laying off four corner lots right here for a lumber yard." "Is this the corner where I stand?" Wicks pursued. "Yes," the deputy said, beginning to catch Wicks's drift and eyeing him ominously. Jamming his stake in the ground with his heel, Wicks shouted, "Then I claim this corner lot! I propose to have one lot at all hazards on this town site, and you will have to limit yourself to three, in this location at least." An "angry altercation" followed, but Wicks stuck by his claim and buttressed it by sticking a folding cot into the ground and draping it with a blanket. "Thus I had a claim that was unjumpable because of substantial improvements," Wicks noted.[31]

His brother later arrived by train with a proper tent and other equipment. They hired a man to plough around their corner lot and set up their tent. Feeling secure at last, Wicks strolled around the new town. Ten thousand people had squatted upon that square mile of prairie within the space of an afternoon, and the array of white tents looked as if "a vast flock of huge-white-winged birds had just settled down upon the hillsides and in the valleys." Here indeed was *a city laid out and* populated in half a day."[32] Soon thousands of campfires were winking in the dark bowl of the prairie, and "there arose from this huge camp a subdued hum declaring that this almost innumerable multitude of the brave and self-reliant men had come to stay and work, and build in that distant Western wilderness a city that should forever be a trophy to American enterprise and daring."[33]

For all the frenetic excitement of that day and the acquisitive emotions aroused, not a single killing or serious fight took place in Guthrie, even though many were armed. Wicks himself speaks of the people rushing about, "each solely dependent on his own efforts, and animated by a spirit of fair play and good humor."[34] It was a spirited race to drive one's stake in first, and the losers acceded more or less graciously to a prior claim. Disputed claims were often resolved by a flip of a coin. And as for those luckless ones who landed in a place that turned out to be the middle of a street (it was rather like playing chess on a board without squares), they accepted the luck of the draw with a shrug.

Thirty-six hours later, the citizens of the new town of Guthrie, who hailed from thirty-two states, three territories, and a half a dozen foreign countries, and few of whom knew each other, formed themselves into an electorate and chose a mayor and a five-member city council, adopted a city charter, and authorized the first tax, a simple head tax. Within a week, permanent buildings were going up and church services were being held. The West had seen many forms of innovative social organizations among those who settled there, but Guthrie represented the first "instant city." Or perhaps not so novel, after all, being the latest in a western lineage that went back to the ex-Revolutionary War soldiers in Marietta, Ohio, nailing their by-laws to a tree—or even further to the Pilgrims drawing up their Compact in the tossing *Mayflower.*

6
Apotheosis of the Small Town

"The Good Years" the historian Walter Lord called them, meaning the last decade of the nineteenth century and the first decade of the twentieth century. To Henry Seidel Canby this period was the Age of Confidence: "the last era in the United States when there was a pause, and everyone, at least in my town, knew what it meant to be an American."[1] Canby's town was Wilmington, Delaware—a small city, actually—autonomous, stable, prosperous, conservative, dominated by a solid Quaker bourgeois class with an admixture of southerners, who were hereditary but not ideological Democrats in politics and traditional Episcopalians in religion. Canby's class set the tone for the town, and it believed wholeheartedly in the future, in Progress, in the benevolence of technology, in God, and, above all, in America. No matter that the confidence was an illusion; it was an illusion that life did not openly challenge, though subterranean forces of change were stirring. It was the time, in the Middle West that Sherwood Anderson evoked in his novel *Poor White*, when the slumbering little villages were poised and waiting. It was a time when—in the nostalgic memories of some at least—life was lived out in the soft light of a tree-shaded street on a summer afternoon, to the soft clip-clop of horses, the drone of the bees and cicadas, the clink of ice in the lemonade pitcher, the creak of the porch swing—a time of pause and prosperity.

Canby's town derived its stability, he thought, first from its geographic location, "facing Europe across a narrowing sea, yet not near enough for ominous responsibility, drawing wealth for its rising factories from the great dynamo of the West, its streets still not too congested for pleasant shade, its countryward roads still quiet to walk upon, its population mentally homogenous, yet with too much racial admixture to be tame, its spirit as of young middle-age when nothing seems to stand in the way of an increasing success."[2]

The comfortable life-style of the upper- and middle-class people set the tone; the threats or contradictions to that life were still segregated off some place—across the tracks, in Polish town (or Italian Town or Nigger town or Irish town) where the new immigrants lived, or off in the cities. The discontents of mill and factory were still far away, like the soft rumble of distant thunder and the flickering fluorescence of heat lightning on a still July night. Indeed when Canby wrote his book, in the early 1930s, the economic storms had broken; but this apparently served to intensify the radiance of memory. For him, the past emerged in heightened contrast to the present. He felt compelled to defend this confident era and take heart from it: "The time has come to think of the nineties as something more than a bad small-town joke."[3]

Others felt this nostalgia in the 1930s—some in reflex to the social crack-up; some, like the critic Edmund Wilson, who became a Marxist in the thirties, were not nostalgists. Wilson wrote in a letter to his friend, novelist John Peale Bishop, who had sent him his latest novel *Act of Darkness*: "I began by being enchanted by your evocation of the American small-town-and-country life of thirty years ago. What you describe in West Virginia is very like what I remember myself up here [Red Bank, New Jersey, where Wilson was born], and I have never read any book which brought me back as yours did into that world of large old houses away in the woods and fields or in little countrified towns where rather a high degree of civilization flourished against a background of pleasant wildness."[4] Even Wilson was not immune from a trend in the thirties that sought to celebrate values in the American past which the intellectuals of the twenties had dismissed with contempt. Sinclair Lewis, his career beginning its long downward arc, extolled middle-class small-town folk in *The Prodigal Parents*, and Sherwood Anderson became a small-town editor for a while in Marion, Virginia, and wrote his books *Hello Towns* and *Home Town*. The peak of nostalgia for the small town was reached in Thornton Wilder's play *Our Town*, produced in 1938 and set in a small New England village modeled upon Peterborough, New Hampshire, by the Wisconsin-born Wilder. Wilder's play sought to portray the universals in the humdrum life of a specific small town, on certain specific, seemingly randomly selected days. But the year Wilder "randomly" chose, 1901, was a year that surely carried overtones of turn-of-the-century tranquillity and nostalgia for the audiences of the time. Wilder's conceit was that war, politics and depressions were irrelevant, and so he artfully chose a year when the audience thought this was so. With social problems muted, Wilder could focus on the quotidian of Grover's Corners, a place where nothing ever happened—except the really basic, timeless, fundamental things—birth, love, and death.

Thus the audience could escape from the turbulent political and economic mess of the thirties into a sheltered harbor of nostalgia. They were shown that daily life has its tragedies, too, but the play was essentially comforting. It evoked an era when boys took their girls to the ice cream parlor to propose. The use of the archetypal New England small town of American memory also removed the locus to an idealized sphere with patriotic connotations. The people were old American stock, hard-working, frugal and decent (for the most part). Finally, Wilder located his town *sub specie aeternitatis.* Or as the little postcard addressed to a little girl in the play puts it: "the World, the Solar System, the Universe, the Mind of God." Not only was this little town timeless, a synechdoche for the universal experiences of mankind; it was also located at the center of a stable cosmos, like the ancient astronomers had located the earth in the center of the solar system—a cosmos of which God was fully and eternally mindful.

In this God's-eye-view of life—a convention beautifully carried forth in the staging of the play without scenery—"Daily Life," "Love and Marriage," and "Death" (the titles of the three acts) are the only important matters. The reduction of life to a few simplicities was another kind of artful artlessness, a philosophical sleight-of-hand that enabled Wilder to ignore the complexities of society and focus on, in Arthur Miller's words, "the indestructibility, the everlastingness, of the family and the community, its rhythm of life, its rootedness in the essentially safe cosmos despite troubles, wracks, and seemingly disastrous, but essentially temporary, dislocations."[5] No matter that these "universals" of family and community had already receded into the past by the 1930s; Wilder so effectively evoked them, so touchingly portrayed familiar situations, that the audience accepted the illusion.

But all that this really says is that *Our Town* was a deliberate, stylized work of art. Its dramatic situations were genuinely affecting, and if people were no longer simple, good-hearted, and innocent like the characters of the play, and if small towns were subjected to larger social forces, no matter. For the play's truth lies in the residuum of memory, in its evocation of a common dream that, if it never really existed in quite that form, in fact certainly did in the ideals of Americans. The gap between what we were and what we dreamed was all the more poignant, because it was located in the plausible, real-life hopes of a large number of Americans.

At a less realistic level, the popular fiction of the 1930s also pursued the small-town dream. Such a shift was evident in the heroes and heroines of the popular stories. In the 1920s *The Saturday Evening Post*, which had extolled the values of business since its most famous editor George Horace Lorimer took over in the 1890s, had changed the nature of its businessmen heroes. They were no longer small entrepreneurs, but had become big-city tycoons of industry. In contrast, the magazines with a mainly rural audience, such as

Country Gentleman, continued to emphasize the virtues of life on a small farm, thus sentimentally preserving a way of life that was beset by modernization. But in the 1930s, as a study of popular magazine fiction by Patrick Johns-Heine and Hans H. Gerth shows, the writers began locating "the soul of American life" in the small town:

> As for locale, there is no mistaking that the farm and with it the small town is exalted as representative of a whole way of life. It is significant that the typical conflict within the story is between the essential human goodness of small-town types as opposed to a metropolitan moneyed elite; unpretentiousness against pretentiousness, and littleness versus power. In short, those values lacking in the metropolis are the ones capitalized upon in the depiction of small-town or farm life, and the latter become personifications of good while the city remains the vessel of evil. We may assume that this is gratifying not only to those who live in towns and villages, but also to those persons who have recently migrated from farm or town to city and who have sentimental associations which find fulfillment here.[6]

For its part, *Country Gentleman* responded to the move away from the farms with more small-town or village settings in its stories and more small-town-businessman heroes, as though the small town had replaced the farm as the repository of American virtue, with the city remaining the locus of all modern-day evils.

Thus the mass magazines had guided their readers toward the city and its values by emphasizing the success fantasy; but by the 1930s this fantasy had broken up on the shoals of the Depression, while the anti-small-town cynicism of the twenties had exhausted itself. And so the pendulum swung back to small-town values, in an echo of the popular fiction of the turn of the century, which also reacted against the labor strife, Middle-Border populism, and financial panic of the late 1880s and early 1890s. In the magazine fiction of the 1930s, the obligatory happy ending embodied "recognition or deference from others. Its characteristic basis is moral virtue which is rewarded by love and esteem from others, sometimes even by a tangible reward; but never does it result in upward mobility marked by 'wealth,' 'success,' 'status.'2 22 [7] The tycoon hero was replaced by the honest, decent, "little man," who cares more for doing good than making money. Similarly, the metropolis, as the goal of ambitious young men, gave way to the small town, where the real "soul of America" remained intact.

For Canby's generation a turn-of-the-century small-town boyhood was a common experience: "Life in America began on the farm and was continued in the small city or town. In the eighties and nineties of the last century the fathers and mothers of most families had been born in the country, but we who are middle-aged now, prevailingly owe our provenance to the town. It is the small town, the small city, that is our heredity; we have made twentieth century America from it."[8]

In 1890, for three quarters of the nation, the small town was Mecca, Athens, Rome, and Babylon all rolled into one—on a much humbler scale, of course. It was the urban place where people met, gossiped, bought, sold, bartered, exchanged, learned. Next to the individual farm, it was the irreducible social and governmental unit of American society, the economic and political center that was closest at hand to most of the people. Down all those Main Streets flowed the quiet main stream of American life; the town's ideals were America's—or so its boosters thought. The small towner could afford to be smug and complacent and observe the city with mixed distaste and bemused superiority—like the depot loafers in Booth Tarkington's novel *The Gentleman from Indiana*, who watched the city people in the big trains whizzing through their villages "with the languid scorn a permanent fixture always has for a transient and the pity an American feels for a fellow-being who does not live in his town."[9] But the sheltered assumptions of this world were invisibly eroding, as big-city influences seeped through cracks in the provincial dikes. While solid burghers made invidious comparisons of their life with that in the cities, their upwardly mobile sons and daughters were flocking to these cities. "Local Man Takes Lucrative Position in Chicago"—or Duluth or Pittsburgh—the headline in the town paper always read. The "lucrative position" might be as a clerk or mill hand, but no matter: When one moved to the city one rose in the world, it was universally assumed.

One New York editorialist, John Habberton, knew better and grappled with the meaning of this "rush to failure in the city." He rejected the "old explanation" that the "rush" was made up solely of farm lads and lasses weary of the dull life on the farm, who "had heard of city pleasures some of which were said to cost nothing while others were very cheap" and of "city wages, payable always in cash and at stated dates." These farm youths were part of it, he wrote, but so also were "mechanics and artisans of all kinds . . . for in the villages and country districts employment is irregular and pay uncertain. The more aspiring of them hope for the larger opportunities and recognition that the country dares not promise; they know, too, that such of their children as are inclined to study may become fairly, even highly educated in the city without special cost to their parents. Of the 'seamy' side of city life they know nothing, for their acquaintances who 'went to town' have not returned to tell of it; few of them could return if they would. The few who go back to the old homesteads are the men who have succeeded, and in any village such a man in effect resembles a gold-laden miner from Cape Nome or the Klondike; his example threatens to depopulate the town."[10] Habberton saw a countermovement to the country, though, by "city brains" with "city money," who were introducing scientific farming and amenities into country life and who, if asked, advised aspiring emigrants to stay where they were.

But in the meantime the small towns and cities could afford to be a little smug, for life was good, and its promise seemed as benign as a hot summer afternoon along a quiet street, with the little girls in their white dresses, the mothers in their long skirts and shirtwaists, the men coming home in dark suits and high, stiff collars, the little boys in knickers rushing out to greet them. There were hitching posts and a horse step out in front of many houses; but the first automobile had appeared in town, purchased probably by the local doctor, or maybe the banker. It had made a dusty, noisy debut on the town streets, chased by a crowd of boys and dogs and laughed at by courthouse-square idlers. But mainly horses clopped patiently along the streets, pulling their big wagons or trim, elegant barouches and victorias.

Our small town is a horse-drawn economy, a horse culture. Most of the larger houses on our street would have a horse barn out back; a man regarded a good horse and fine buggy, trimmed with brass lamps and a patent-leather dashboard, as his finest possession. But he had to beware of flaunting his rig. As the Indiana writer Meredith Nicholson observed: "A man who kept a horse and buggy was thought to be 'putting on' a little; if he set up a carriage and two horses he was, unless he enjoyed public confidence in the highest degree, viewed with distrust and suspicion. When in the eighties an Indianapolis bank failed, a cynical old citizen remarked of its president that 'no wonder Blank busted, swelling around in a carriage with a nigger in uniform'!"[11]

In the town, the great dray wagons creaked and groaned over muddy or dusty streets, carrying farm produce to the local elevator, or goods from the depot. Lighter spring-wagons, bearing a store's name in large letters and driven by young clerks with as much recklessness as they could get away with, made deliveries to customers. There were hitching chains around the courthouse square, if the town had one, or a series of rails, like one-rail fences along the main street or simply rings attached to the board sidewalk. In the heat of the summer, the manure dropped by the waiting horses drew seething clumps of bluebottle flies and its stench hung in the air. In the winter the horses were draped with blankets, or else stabled, for men were adjured to be kind to their animals; the farmer who got drunk and left his team out all night might receive a public reprimand in the paper. On market days, when the farmers came to town, the horses and wagons would be parked chockablock, perpendicular to the sidewalk, all along Main Street.

The farmer had no other way to ship his livestock and produce to market but to take it to the nearest country town with a railroad station, a stockyard, a grain elevator. During shipping seasons, the congestion of farm wagons in the street could be fearsome. In Algona, Iowa, wagons and teams would at these times be four or five abreast on the town's main street, forming a line that stretched nearly a mile from the depot to the City Hotel in the middle of town. In towns still closer to the soil, pigs and cattle might still be driven through the streets, without the formality of loading them in a wagon.

The horse culture supported a variety of businesses. There were, of course, stores where the farmer stopped off to pick up supplies before the trip home and the saloons where he wetted down the dust in his throat. There were livery stables, carriage makers, blacksmith shops, harness makers, feed shops, the establishments that made horse troughs, hitching racks, and town pumps, and the assembly place for the commerce to and from the farm—the depot, stockyards, elevators, restaurants where farmers and teamsters caught a meal in midjourney. The average country town with a population of six thousand easily supported six livery and feed stores, four harness-and-saddle dealers, and twelve blacksmiths.

Craftsmen like the blacksmith or the harness maker had standing in the community, and were known as independent, at times cantankerous businessmen, and as versatile, skilled artisans who made a wide variety of tools and implements. The livery stable was also a unique social institution in the horse-and-buggy towns of the nineteenth century. It was here that the drummer came to rent a rig in which to make his calls on local merchants, the bachelor for transportation to squire a girl on a Sunday ride, or the family to rent a horse and sleigh for a winter sleighride. It also stabled and fed animals brought in by transients.

The livery stable served as a social center and loafing place, for men only. Typically, they were two-story boxlike structures of unpainted wood, the walls covered with tin signs advertising various patent remedies for ailing horses. They exuded the stable smells of horses, manure, feed, and hay. There was a rude office with wooden chairs, a desk, a cot for the night man, and a potbellied stove, around which loungers gathered in winter; a blackboard on the wall kept track of which horses were rented; and there might be signs admonishing the hirer to—

Whip Light,
Drive Slow.
Pay Cash
Before You Go.[12]

Horses—often near worn-out old nags—and appropriate rigs were hired for weddings and funerals, so stable owners were likely to be the first to know about marriages and deaths, or which of the town's young bucks had hired a rig to go on a spree in a neighboring town—and in what condition he returned. All the earthier town gossip could be heard at the livery stable. William Allen White, Louis Bromfield, and others recalled learning about sex while eavesdropping on the men at the livery stables. Sherwood Anderson worked in one for a time, sleeping there at nights on a cot under a horse blanket. He had a coworker, a man named Ed, who boasted incessantly about his sexual conquests. Young Sherwood guessed that the tales involving local matrons "were a pack of lies," but the talk "inflamed" him and he couldn't sleep. One night Ed brought a local prostitute to his cot and offered her to Anderson, who was so disgusted by this "crude manifestation of human lust" that he "went home to sleep." Another time Ed and some friends brought him a glass of "beer;" it turned out to be pure whiskey, and Anderson became sick when he gulped it down.

The owners of these establishments were independent, profane, sloppily dressed, caring little for respectability. On Saturday market days the farmers and men of the town gathered at the livery stable to discuss the crops and local politics. In smaller towns, the blacksmith's shop might still serve a similar social function. In the village of Halifax, Massachusetts, for example, Guy S. Baker recalled that his father's shop "provided a meeting place for the menfolk. Situated at the crossroads and unavoidable . . . princes and paupers, generals and politicians, governors and, in one case, a future president, stopped to visit my father. . . . Much settling of the world's problems took place in the village blacksmith's shop."[13]

A farm wife might drive a horse, but in town the establishments of the horse culture were an exclusively male preserve. At the livery stable a man could bet on horse races, play checkers and cards, smoke or chew tobacco, and even take a drink. Stallions were often kept at the livery stables to service mares. On such occasions, many a wide-eyed small boy got a functional education in sex and reproduction. But if the women of the town heard about what was going on (this was, after all, a Victorian era, when bulls were referred to as "gentlemen cows"), they would rise up and order such spectacles halted, requiring the gentlemen horses to perform their services in privacy. But their efforts to shield their sons from the facts of life were in vain: The forbidden fruit had already been tasted.

Another male sanctuary was the barbershop, which by the 1890s had acquired a look of tone and elegance, at least in the larger towns. Some had baths in the rear; in front there was a line of polished wood chairs with rich-hued velour upholstery; on shelves were aligned the customers' shaving mugs, some embellished with initials or a design, like a coat of arms, which reflected the owner's occupation. There was a smell of soap, steaming towels, bay rum, and cigar smoke in the air, and the place was a hive of gossip on Saturday afternoons when men came in for their shaves and haircuts. An idea of the barbershop's popularity is suggested by the large number a town supported. In 1890 Crawfordsville, Indiana, with a population of six thousand, had eleven barbershops (and nineteen saloons and eleven pool halls).

The general store had long been a favored loafing place in the small town, although by the nineties, it was either on its way out, replaced by more specialized operations, or else so packed with goods and crowded with the Saturday farmers' trade that there was little room for loafers around the stove or cracker barrel. Prohibition forces and specialization combined to transfer the storeowner's hospitality barrel of whiskey to the saloons. The saloons too were not immune from the prohibitionists, especially in those towns with an active group of churchwomen, but usually they existed in a sort of truce with the forces of respectability. Sherwood Anderson recalled a German saloon-keeper who lived across the street from his house, whose wife and son never went out. He thought the family was ostracized. "It was an age of temperance societies and there were two churches on one street. To sell liquor, to run a saloon was to be, I am sure, the devil's servant."[14] Male-dominated city governments favored, and patronized, them, of course, taking the statesmanlike attitude that it was best to have vice licensed and conducted out in the open. As a sop to the forces of temperance, saloon license fees were often earmarked for schools. In some towns the saloon district might be located "across the tracks," western-style, or in a special district—which, by making drinking furtive, had the effect of encouraging rapid and heavy consumption.

More commonly, the saloons established themselves right on Main Street, to catch the farmers' walk-in trade. Even then, they often had a closed-off, forbidden air to conceal the inner goings-on from the eyes of respectable folk walking the streets. Inside, though, they could be opulent. A saloon in Hastings, Nebraska, proudly announced that it had spent three thousand dollars on new fixtures, including a mirror behind the bar that was fourteen feet long and seven feet high. Bars were long and solidly constructed of dark wood, echoed in the paneling on the walls. The decor included prints of racehorses, prizefighters, and voluptuous nude women. Yet for all its sometimes sleazy aura of sin, many town saloons were orderly places. In towns with sizable German or Bohemian populations in the area, the saloon was a place to quaff a stein of beer and partake of the bountiful free lunch. In *My Ántonia*, the hero, Jim, hangs out at one of them, listening to the talk, until the proprietor asks him not to come in anymore: " 'Jim,' he said, 'I am good friends with you and I always like to see you. But you know how the church people think about saloons. Your grandpa has always treated me fine, and I don't like to have you come into my place, because I know he don't like it, and it puts me in bad with him.' "[15]

The saloons existed in a shaky truce with the prohibition forces, but the darker forms of vice—gambling and prostitution—were suppressed or operated on the basis of payoffs to police. Still, in the 1890s most towns had a red-light district. In Muncie, Indiana, there were more than twenty bordellos operating openly, compared with two or three clandestine establishments in 1923. In Hastings, in the 1880s, the newspaper viewed with alarm the thirty or forty gamblers and six bawdy houses: "They are in the suburban parts of town as well as the best business streets. Vice is on the increase."[16] For years, town politics were a battlefield between the "reform" forces seeking to clean up vice and the politicians who drew considerable, if discreet, financial support from saloon owners and the brothel operators—not to mention the town businessmen, who believed saloons stimulated spending.

In Everett, Washington, a lumber boomtown, a reformist police chief who attempted to clean up the town was opposed by local businessmen. As one said, "What's the difference if a logger comes in and spends $50 in a dive? Doesn't the money finally get into circulation in more respectable places?"[17] The conflict was similarly fierce in the western cow towns, as we have seen, but it was present, in a less flamboyant degree, in other towns of the Middle Border—and in towns with a strong Puritan-Yankee heritage, like Clyde, Ohio, where Sherwood Anderson grew up.

In Hastings, Nebraska, the newspaper, as newspapers are wont, could not resist reporting upon the colorful and violent doings of the "soiled doves" or "scarlet women"—such as the time that the police had to be called to a G.A.R. encampment to clear out the prostitutes from the tents, or the time an irate wife brought the police to raid a house of ill repute where she believed her husband was taking his pleasure (he escaped through the back door), or the shootings involving prominent citizens. Suppression of open prostitution was a measure of a town's level of civilization and distance from frontier days; eventually the flesh traffic shrunk to a few ordinary looking houses with perhaps a light (not necessarily red) burning on the porch and scantily clad women lounging in the parlor. In smaller places there would be a single woman, usually old and blowsy, known to accommodate gentlemen callers ("Hatrack," the heroine of a notorious short story of the 1920s, dispensed her favors in the cemetery, a favorite small-town trysting place).

Most small towns of the 1890s had their demimondaines. They served as an outlet for natural instincts during the Victorian era, but also reflected the schism in sexual attitudes. Sex was, of course, officially reserved for marriage, and the old pioneer rite of the shivaree, which included bawdy, sometimes cruel, jokes on newly married couples—painting chamber pots (in hopes the user would sit on one while it was still wet), beating tin pans outside their window on their wedding night—continued as a kind of communal celebration of the sexual aspect of marriage. Although its cruel side betrayed unconscious male hostility toward women, the shivaree served as an outlet for the young bachelors to express both their jealousy about the girl's being removed from circulation and a ribald rite of male potency, in counterpoint to the religious celebration's public proclamation of the bride's putative virginity.

It would be wrong to say that because female premarital chastity was demanded, the marriages that followed were lacking in erotic love. But the ideals of womanhood carried over from pioneer days, when women were scarce and when men lived in theoretical compliance with the code of chivalry and courtesy toward women, had given women a kind of sexual inviolability. Alexis de Tocqueville had marveled at the way an unmarried American girl went about unchaperoned; he observed that chastity was preserved by placing "more reliance on her free will than on safeguards which have been shaken or overthrown." Rather than being "over-scrupulous of the innocence of her thoughts," her parents preferred not to hide "the corruptions of the world from her." Tocqueville thought there was a danger in this practice because "it tends to invigorate the judgment at the expense of the imagination and to make cold and virtuous women instead of affectionate wives and agreeable companions for men."[18] Here the usually objective Frenchman betrays his preference for upper-class European ways, which called for the sequestering of young girls until marriage. He could not grasp that American girls' "judgment"—their placing head over heart—was not necessarily inimical to their being "affectionate wives" and "agreeable companions."

Still, American girls had to be more wary. They had lost the protection of arranged marriages, as in Europe, and the Puritans' contractual marriages. Thus, despite the supposedly frowning, watchful eye of society, an unmarried girl was still vulnerable to seduction and abandonment, and it was no wonder the theme of the jilted girl, with or without child, was a recurrent one in Victorian melodramas and sentimental songs. In Puritan times, couples got officially betrothed, and if there was premarital sex it was tolerated, so long as they publicly confessed their sins and got married. A new middle-class morality made the girl independent but also severely condemned her sexual mistakes. The seducer, being the man, could flee wrathful parents by going West, but the girl was stuck. It was no wonder that she had to encase her feelings in the protective armor of "judgment." By the same token, men of an honorable stripe must honor chastity, and place unmarried girls on a pedestal of inviolability. As Lewis Mumford put it: "The American woman . . . learned to preserve her freedom and power by keeping sex at a distance. It was on the assumption that 'nothing could happen' that the sexes came together so easily."[19] Mumford adds, "The ideal maiden of adolescent America was a sort of inverted pariah: untouchable by reason of her elevation. In defiance of Nature, her womanliness and her untouchability were supposed to be one."[20]

As a result, unmarried boys and girls inhabited separate, only furtively overlapping, sexual worlds. The girl may have been warned of the wickedness of the world, but she was told precious little about sex and procreation; learning by trial and error was forbidden, for the "error" could result in the ruin of her reputation through gossip or the ultimate stigma of unwedded motherhood. For their part, boys grew up believing there were two kinds of women—"bad girls" with whom secret sex was permitted, and "good girls," who were pure and inviolable and with whom sex was out of the question until marriage. They married the latter, after conducting their youthful experiments with the former. Sherwood Anderson recalled the kissing games of his youth—"post office"—which went no further than a pecking kiss: "She was a nice girl, that was it. You didn't attempt to go too far with her. Nice girls didn't go too far."[21] A boy was also barraged through the church and various crusading organizations by propaganda against "impure thoughts." The town boy lived between the official sexual morality inculcated by a church and home and the worldly wisdom picked up from the traveling salesman's smutty stories at the local hotel, the scandalous gossip at the livery stable, the farm boys' earthy sophistication about animal reproduction, and his own peers. The Iowa novelist and lawyer Herbert Quick wrote in his autobiography *One Man's Life,*"I have often wondered what city boy ever had more evil associates than did I out there in the prairie."[22] Quick compared the crude sexual knowledge he picked up in an Iowa town to walking through "a fiery furnace" and attributed his emergence without "scorching of the garments" to "the inflexible moral rectitude" of his parents.[23] William Allen White described his own lubricious education less apocalyptically. This education included "the slaughterhouse and the livery stable . . . the romantic woods where the peripatetic strumpets made their camps" and the sex education "from Saxon words chalked on sidewalks and barns [and] Rabelaisian poetry [on] the walls of backhouses."[24] Such an education was not necessarily warping, but it was poles apart from that of most girls. The result was that sex and romantic love occupied two separate spheres, which, if things worked out for the best, would be fused in marriage. Henry Seidel Canby put it this way: "Romance suffused the American nineties, and romance was incompatible with our quite realistic knowledge of sex. A thrilling imagination sometimes suggested the possibility of joining the two, but that was to be later. The girl must be won first and won romantically."[25] Canby was speaking as a "nice boy" from a middle-class family who was most deeply exposed to the official morality. The distinction between sexuality and romance produced a "good–bad" girl syndrome, reflected in the popular fiction of the day. Female characters were presented as either "good" or "bad." "The bad girls represented sexuality," Page Smith writes, "the good girls purity of mind and spirit, unclouded by the shadow of any gross or vulgar thought."[26] Even in Ed Howe's *The Story of a Country Town,* a realistic novel, the subplot involves the sturdy, upright Jo Erring's idealistic passion for the cloyingly innocent, sweet Mateel. A town layabout and remittance man makes advances to Mateel—out of small-town boredom and spite—driving the naive Jo to unreasoning jealousy, murder and suicide.

Others, small-town boys like Sherwood Anderson, Floyd Dell, and Edgar Lee Masters criticized small-town prudery, while describing in their autobiographies the widespread illicit sexual experimentation that went on.[27] Both Masters and Anderson were initiated into sex by lower-class girls. In Masters' case they were hired girls in his home. Anderson tells of two local girls who were known as "Shetland ponies" in Clyde, because of their promiscuity. A rendezvous he had with one is broken off when a boy follows him to the trysting place in an empty boxcar and throws stones at them. "There were in our town, as in all towns, what were called 'the nice girls,' " Anderson wrote in his memoirs, "and there were others not presumed to be nice. They were perhaps the daughters of poor men. They did what was called 'making out.' They were hired girls, servants. If you wanted to go about with nice girls, you were to stay away from them, or, if you did go about with one such you did it in secret."[28]

The compartmentalization of "nice" boys' and girls' sexual educations was ended with marriage; in the privacy of the bedroom their conflicting interests and attitudes were supposed to fuse and ripen into love. Once the marriage vows had been said, society washed its hands of them, caring only about the proprieties and the preservation of the marriage. What went on in the bedroom was sequestered from view, at most a subject of veiled gossip. But in their new roles of husband and wife men and women were also consigned to mutually exclusive worlds. The man's was business, getting a living, making money, rising in the world. The wife's is well summarized by Lewis Atherton:

> She prided herself on being a good cook and housekeeper. Company dinners with lavish quantities of food demonstrated her ability as a cook and her husband's success as a "good provider." While guests crammed themselves with food, she bustled about the table to see that all were properly served, and not until the last guest had finished did she permit herself to eat. As an angel of mercy to neighbors in distress and an avenging instrument of gossip, she maintained her family's influence in society and church affairs. She was economical of her husband's worldly goods, condemned the vanities of rouge and the sin of cigarettes, and got her washing on the line at an early hour on Monday morning. Most of all, she sought "advantages" for her children, and operated as a matchmaker in behalf of her marriageable daughters.[29]

The job of housewifery had dawn-to-dusk hours, and the only laborsaving devices were hired girls or children old enough to help out. The great cast-iron wood-or-coal-burning range in the kitchen (a few gas-burning stoves were appearing) had to be fired up before dawn to cook a big breakfast for the family, and women were up at four or five o'clock in the morning. The fire was kept going no matter how hot the day—cooking always had to be done, and water heated for laundry and baths.

The housewife's week followed a prescribed cycle. Monday, of course, was washing day, when women raced with their neighbors to see whose lines would be the first to billow with sheets and clothes. On Tuesday the ironing would be done, and on Wednesday the accumulated mending and sewing. Thursday was a more or less free day for reading and embroidering; Friday was cleaning day and Saturday baking day. Saturday was also the day for going to the store, though when telephones became common, the housewife would call up and place her order, which would be delivered the same day. On Sunday the housewife was supposed to rest and go to church, but there was a big Sunday dinner for family and visiting relatives to be prepared at some point. And there was a seasonal rhythm to her tasks, even in towns. Spring meant cleaning the whole house, top to bottom, beating rugs, turning mattresses, washing the company dishes which had sat all winter on the top shelf, and so on; the chores might last ten days to two weeks. Since most women kept gardens out back, spring was also planting time; families might have their own chickens too—perhaps even pigs to be butchered when the weather first turned cool—but milk was delivered by the milkman or by the farmer himself. The coal and ice men, and other specialists like the scissors-sharpener and the yeast man (with new yeast for bread) made their rounds too. In summer there was the garden to care for, and in fall, in addition to the fall cleaning, there was the harvest of fruits and vegetables to be canned and root vegetables to be stored in bins and barrels in the cellar. These canned goods helped to liven the monotonous winter fare of meat and potatoes—especially the pickles, relishes, jams, and jellies the women preserved. Store-bought canned goods were rare, and as late as the 1920s, in some places, women flattened empty store-bought cans and concealed them at the bottom of the garbage, so the neighbors couldn't detect their "laziness." In winter there were children to be gotten off to school on icy mornings—rousted out of warm beds into frigid rooms, which they fled to dress before the warmth of the kitchen fires.

Easing the wife's burden was the availability of cheap help. Most middle-class families had a "girl"—usually a farm girl or an immigrant girl who lived in as a maid. The children had their chores too; the boys had the job of splitting logs for kindling and filling the woodbox, or bringing in the coal. Girls helped in the kitchen and with other domestic tasks, as an apprenticeship for their own eventual assumption of the housewife's role.

Although her day was long, the woman of the house managed to break it up with gossip over the back fence with her neighbors, or visiting. Wealthier women with increased leisure on their hands organized social activities, participating in whist clubs or playing the other popular games of the day, such as hearts, high five, or finch—but only in those towns where the prejudice against card playing had abated. There were also teas and afternoon functions, reading and study groups, and various clubs for good works such as the Women's Christian Temperance Union and church groups. Despite their avowed dedication to Christian charity, women's groups sometimes developed rivalries. In one New England village the Wide Awake Club and the Village Improvement Society feuded over which would sponsor new street lights. During a particularly tense period in the rivalry, when a member of the Wide Awakes arrived at church one Sunday, every member of the Village Improvement Society present rose up from her pew and walked out. The following Sunday the Wide Awakes came early, and when the first Village Improver arrived they walked out en masse.

During the W.C.T.U.'s heyday, local chapters not only agitated against liquor and tobacco and harassed saloonkeepers, but also urged social reforms, such as a new orphanage to replace the county poor farm, visited the sick, and donated food and money to the destitute. Chapters held oratorical contests with speakers declaiming on such subjects as "Prohibition, the Hope of Our

Country" and "The Rumseller's Legal Rights." The wide-ranging concern for the town's moral well-being was exemplified in the activities of a Thorntown, Indiana, branch, which took up a collection to send a local prostitute to the hospital for treatment of her narcotics addiction and encouraged a man with syphilis to undergo the then standard treatment with bicholoride of gold. Although perhaps regarded as busybodies by some, the staunch Thorntown ladies seem not to have been unduly inhibited by squeamishness or Victorian decorum.

The close link between respect for women and temperance is shown by the pledge taken by members of the White Cross, a temperance society for men. They promised "by the help of God to treat all women with respect and endeavor to protect them from wrong and degradation; to endeavor to put down all indecent language and coarse jests; to maintain the law of purity as equally binding upon men and women; to endeavor to spread these principles among my companions and help younger brothers; to use every possible means to fulfill the command: Keep Thyself Pure."[30]

Many idealistic men embraced temperance out of conviction, and in the reform era of the early 1900s, temperance became a standard ingredient in the progressive prescription for a better society. The rough timber town of Everett, Washington, had a community-rending debate over prohibition by local option, with the businessmen and industrialists against it and many workingmen in the union movement for it. Clarence Darrow, the lawyer who had defended union men like Eugene Debs, came to town to speak against temperance, denouncing it as a "movement of the rich to deprive the poor of certain pleasures they enjoy."[31] But George Cotterill, a prolabor legislator, spoke out in favor of prohibition. "Close the saloons, Cotterill believed," wrote Norman H. Clark in his history of Everett, "and the workingmen would march to the union hall in a fierce, wide-eyed sobriety to demand their share of the world's wealth."[32] To Cotterill, reforming public morals was one of many reforms paving the road to a better society.

Women's historic role in the pioneering days had been primarily economic—performing her share of the labor necessary to clear and work a farm in the wilderness or the Great Plains. She was a "civilizing" force mainly in maintaining the home and nurturing the children. Such cultural life as there was in pioneer society was promoted by men as frequently as women. It was only as the rough days fell behind that women began devoting themselves to promoting "society" and advancing moral, cultural, and spiritual values. Men came to be considered too busy, too practical to concern themselves with art, literature, and culture. They had their own clubs—fraternal orders like the Masons and the Odd Fellows, which provided ritual, fellowship, and social activities; they had politics, including direct participation in the running of the community. And they had active debating and scientific and philosophical discussion societies. Increasingly, however, the book clubs and art groups became women's domain. In Muncie in the 1890s there was an Art

Students' League, an outgrowth of art classes taught by a local artist, whose study abroad had been subsidized by the town businessmen (in exchange, he copied European masterpieces for their homes). During the league's first years, its members did indeed seriously study painting, and annual exhibitions of their work were held, which were reviewed with unflagging enthusiasm by the local paper's critic. The ladies' monopoly of artistic matters reflected a commonly held attitude that "art had nothing to do with the realities of life and should be left to the women. The men were too busy."[33]

Some cultural activity was undertaken in a spirit of boosterism and rivalry with other towns. Thus the town of Waterloo, Iowa, officially proclaimed that its Library Association had been founded "to gratify the demand for some kind of recreation, to extend the knowledge of our city, and to gain the reputation we claim to merit as being the best city in central and northern Iowa."[34] It was often emulation of urban ways combined with moral uplift that inspired such organizations as the W.C.T.U. The Cedar Falls Reading Circle, founded in 1876, was directly inspired by an article in *Scribner's Monthly* on village improvement societies, in which the author decried the "barren and meaningless lives" so many lived in American villages and prescribed greater interest in culture: "There are multitudes who never dream that their village . . . can be the center of a culture as sweet and delightful as a city possesses."[35] The Cedar Rapids ladies took this exhortation to heart and formed the Reading Circle, which, significantly, was open to all walks of life in the town, though its membership was limited to sixty—men, women, business and professional people, housewives, workingmen, and farmers were all invited. The circle listened to readings of passages from novels and then disscussed the author. History, science, philosophy, contemporary affairs were also discussed, and the president of the normal school later boasted, "We venture the assertion that no city in the state, large or small, can furnish as many actual readers of Carlyle, of Emerson, of Macaulay, of Ruskin, of Prescott, of the English and American poets and prose writers as can [Cedar Rapids]."[36]

Despite the increase in social and cultural activities, woman's work and woman's pride still centered around the home. Home in the Wilmington middle class to which Henry Seidel Canby belonged was a separate world, with its own seasons, weathers, and a "daily rhythm, in which each hour had its characteristic part, in a house where change came slowly and which was always home, nourished, if it did not create the expectancy of our generation that the norm of life was repetition and therefore security." Canby adds, "Life seems to be sustained by rhythm, upset by its changes, weakened by its loss."[37] A variation on that sentiment was later played by the journalist Eric Sevareid in a nostalgic piece about his hometown in *Collier's* magazine. The town, he wrote, "was, simply *home*—and *all* of it home, not just the house but all the town. That is why childhood in the small towns is different from childhood in the city. Everything is home."[38] So to Sevareid the secure rhythms of home reverberated through the entire town. The emotions of security and belonging, which their memories held for so many small-town boys who left to make good in the city, had their living heart in the home they grew up in. And presiding unquestioned over that domain of the heart was the woman, the mother.

In his book *As a City Upon a Hill,* Page Smith contends that the towns passed from patriarchies to matriarchies. The founding fathers were admired, even revered for their progenitive role; but then the economic vicissitudes that buffeted the next generation of males toppled them from their patriarchal pedestals. Smith points to the myriad descriptions in fiction of the father as a comic, failure-prone figure, from Sherwood Anderson's portrait of his father in his novel *Windy McPherson's Son* and his autobiographical *Tar: A Midwest Childhood* to Thomas Wolfe's of his in *Look Homeward, Angel.* These characters believed boundlessly in the success myth, but lacked the talent, the shrewdness, the brains, the ruthlessness, or the luck to grasp their dreams. Windy McPherson leads the Fourth of July parade, on the strength of his boasted prowess with the bugle, but when he raises it to his lips, the sound that issues forth is a "dismal squack." "Windy looked about him with troubled eyes. . . . The thing he felt, was in him, and it was only a fatal blunder in nature that it did not come out at the flaring end of his bugle.[39]

Many men, like Windy, felt "the thing" was in them but somehow it did not come out. They had, in other words, the prescribed dreams, but could not realize them, however they tried. Was it "only a fatal blunder in nature," as Windy comically believes, or was it a failure in character—a lack of the virtues of industry and application that were supposed to guarantee success? If making money was an outward token of virtue, wasn't the lack of it a sign of inner weakness? As Smith puts it, "The man, the perpetually optimistic architect of new enterprises, was better suited for establishing communities than for making them thrive. Far more town ventures failed than succeeded, and the man who still believed that failure was personal, that it was due to one's inability to measure up to the ethic, had no defenses against defeat."[40] He was daily reproached by the success of the town's founders—the real-estate speculators and promoters who were in on the ground floor, the bankers and merchants who built up their businesses in a time of rising property values and growth. Their success may have been largely luck and timing, but it transformed them into solid, substantial citizens—weighty men, whose words counted—while the failure could only flail about in various enterprises that, if they did not founder, won him a small living, at the cost of long hours and deference to his customers. The figure of Eugene Gant's father in *Look Homeward, Angel* looms as a larger-than-life caricature. Gant, artist, dreamer, carver of tombstones, and drunkard, hurls defiance at the town during his periodic binges, then returns home sick and defeated, to be affectionately bossed and fed soup by his daughter, Helen. His wife, Eliza, is grasping and shrewd; she hoards their money, runs a boardinghouse on her own, and buys up land. The elder Gant is a hurler of Shakespearean rodomontade, a failed artist; to him a house represents the labor he has put in it, but to Eliza it is a piece of property. Gant loves money and spends freely, carrying large sums in his wallet; with Eliza to steady him he makes some, but it is through her investments that their fortune grows. He hates owning property; she has the speculator's eye.

Eliza Gant gains the upper hand by outdoing the men of the town at their own game—something few women did. Most confined their power to the home, and it was because of this, Smith says, that the town became a matriarchy. The town was the "tomb of the man's ambitions,"[41] but the proscenium of the woman's triumph. In a time when motherhood was exalted and mothers consigned to a pedestal of virtue, she looked after the town's morals, its children, its all-embracing home. In the growing cities, women's roles became more circumscribed; as the husband devoted more time to business, the raising of the children was left to her but little else. In the small town, the wife, "married to a man of diminished potency and power, took over the responsibilities of the father," while in the city she made the child—especially the son—"a substitute for an absent or inattentive husband."[42] And so small-town boys grew up with an identification with their mothers ("All I am I owe to my mother"), while city boys were more emotionally oriented toward their fathers. The small-town man chose to flee into masculine pursuits, most of which drew the reproachful eye of the female-dominated forces of morality—the home, church, W.C.T.U. The woman triumphed, in Smith's words, "finally subduing the town, making it into a larger mother, the place where trust and love and understanding could always be found, making the town one of America's most persistent and critical symbols—the town as mother, comforter, source of love."[43]

Sherwood Anderson often wrote of his hometown as a protective, loving place—a kind of surrogate mother, with kindly townspeople (male and female) replacing his dead mother. Before her death, Anderson's mother, Emma Anderson, kept the family together by taking in washing. Irwin Anderson, Sherwood's father, worked irregularly as a house painter, drank, and had affairs with other women. A persistent image in the crusades of the W.C.T.U. was the sodden male, defeated by drink, cursed by his ravening sexual desires, ruining his health through his vices of drink and tobacco.

A more equable observer of small-town life, like Lewis Atherton, might argue that Smith overstates his case—look at the happy, loving marriages. Smith's insight is difficult to demonstrate, and sexual behavior within marriage was a closed book in those days. The small-town boys who wrote of their own discoveries of sex could not fathom or describe their parents' sexual lives and did not even want to try. Whatever the private behavior among married couples, there was a change in small-town sexual attitudes in the late nineteenth century. The Suffield, Connecticut, historian recorded the changes wrought by Victorian prudery in that old Puritan-founded town:

"The freewheeling days when one confessed openly in church to fornication had given way to an unhealthy reticence regarding anything physical."[44] Illicit sex was punished legally, impersonally: "Even one Chloe Woodworth, who in the space of a few months was brought into court several times for committing adultery with four different men, loses character. She was dealt with and dispatched in an impersonal manner our forefathers would not comprehend."[45]

Prudery bred private prurience and public reticence. The controlled but direct carnality of the Puritans was replaced by the more diffused emotions of romance. As Canby said, the girl must be won romantically, then sex would come; the courtship rituals must be followed. At least the walking out, the buggy and sleigh rides, the ice cream sociables, and the dances and card parties had fun and charm and enabled young people to get to know one another, with sex kept in the background. Further, the courtship might draw upon a long growing-up together. Canby observes that "one met one's girl, not in the transitoriness of a weekend, or at the end of three hundred miles of auto road, but for long acquaintance. She would be there and you would be there next week, next year. She was one of a family, and that family part of a community which was yours. She carried with her the sanctions and refusals of Society."[46] Marriage or the disgrace of illegitimacy was the penance Society demanded for youthful ardor.

The ultimate onus of inchastity fell upon the woman. Lewis Atherton describes a news story in a midwestern paper about a pregnant girl whose lover jilted her. The editor took the occasion to warn women against men's false blandishments and exhort mothers to instruct their daughters accordingly, for "shame could not be covered up no matter how long one lived or how good one became in later life. A woman's entire life could not atone for such a sin."[47]

The sexual side of marriage might also be blighted by female ignorance and male insensitivity. Women who wanted no more children had to try to impose continence upon their husbands, in the absence of other birth-control measures, which men were generally reluctant to resort to. The kinds of marital beds people made for themselves were as various as the people lying in them, but if Victorian prudery engendered sexual tensions, it at least had the advantage of not unduly elevating expectations.

Certain sexual tensions were not to be aired in the courts, and the divorce rate remained low. In Muncie, Indiana, in 1890, for example, there were 9 divorces for every 100 marriages. The crude divorce rate per thousand population was 1.0—and that was high; for the entire United States the crude rate was 0.3. By 1929 this figure for the entire country increased six times to 1.7, and in Muncie it had quintupled to 5.0. The low divorce rate in the nineties was largely due to the stigma attached to divorce, but also even though a trend towards marrying at a younger age was underway, couples were still relatively more mature and settled when they married than newlyweds in the 1920s. With divorce a comparative novelty affecting only one tenth of all husbands and wives, there was less thought about it as an escape. This undoubtedly made for a more stable home, whatever the private tensions between husband and wife, but the marriages that sometimes resulted could be bizarre. In his memoir *Plain People*, Ed Howe tells of a married couple who had not spoken to each other for fifteen years; yet during that time, four children were born—all "excellent people," Howe claims.

Most women preferred an unhappy marriage—considering the alternative. Being jilted in courtship was a severe blow, and spinsterhood was a state not to be borne. The life of a spinster was at best a half-life, and rather than face it, many women hitched up their courage and went West or to the city. The unwed woman's fate was usually to live with her relatives as an unpaid domestic or to find social redemption in caring for an aging mother. Her position might require the invention of a tragic love, for it was considered "normal" for a woman whose lover has died in her youth to assume the estate of a kind of virginal widow. More drastic was the tactic of a woman Ed Howe knew who put unremitting pressure on her boyfriend to marry her. She at last succeeded in setting a date for the wedding, but when it arrived, her fiancé had fled. She nonetheless took his name, moved to a far-off town in the West, and lived as his widow for the remaining forty years of her life.

The spinster was odd woman out in the small town, living somewhat outside the pale; there were few careers she could devote herself to—school teaching being the main one—and indeed the idea of a career was frowned upon, for it implied that the spinster had chosen work over marriage. Rather, she was tacitly released from her duty to marry and selflessly serve her husband on the condition she selflessly serve others. Zona Gale's *Miss Lulu Bett*, published in 1920, is a portrait of a small-town old maid, who lives as a poor relation in the home of a smug, boorish, petty tyrant. But Miss Lulu Bett revolts against her station and finds happiness in marriage.

Bachelors had their own image in the town. It was assumed there was some flaw in their makeup, but at least they had a job and self-sufficiency. They were also free to participate in the male social world, including the demimonde of the town. Yet the male side had its share of odd men out—recluses, hermits, tramps, eccentric, even dotty, men escaping from some mysterious disgrace in their home place or the loss of their true love to another man. Issues of the *Badger State Banner* of Black River Falls, Wisconsin, were full of news items about unhappy grotesque bachelors:

> Henry Johnson, an old bachelor of Grand Dyke, cut off all the heads of all his hens, recently, made a bonfire of his best clothes, and killed himself with arsenic.

* * *

Tuesday last, A. Snyder, a man about 35 years of age and a bachelor who resides at Morrison's creek, was found wandering in the streets of this city in an insane condition.

Henry Lloyd, a bachelor, who resided 5 miles and a half from Janesville . . . was found dead in his bed on Sunday. . . . He was 83 years old. . . . Disappointment in love had made him a recluse. . . . It is said Henry fell in love with a girl from New York, years ago, but never confessed . . . he determined to go east and ask her hand in marriage. He made the trip only to find she had married another man the day before his arrival. He returned to Wisconsin brokenhearted, and from that time to his death, he avoided female society. No woman ever crossed his threshold, and when he rented a pew in the Congregational Church at Emerald Grove, it was with the understanding that no woman should ever enter it. He devoted his attention to horses and farming.[48]

These lonely spinsters and bachelors were often portrayed as grotesque or tragic in novels and stories with a small-town setting, and ordinary townspeople regarded them slightly eccentric while affectionately joking about them. In small towns, marriage was the sovereign cure for loneliness and the only approved state for men and women. The nuclear family was the primary social unit of the town. George Hillery's definition of the "folk village" as "a localized system of families cooperating by means of mutual aid"[49] is apposite here. By the 1890s many towns had passed beyond this stage to what Hillery called "the vill"—"a localized system integrated by means of families and cooperation,"[50] but the family was still at the heart of life. The impersonal institutions of government, factory, business, and public education were increasing in importance, but none of these institutions had as yet usurped the family's central position.

Theodore Dreiser in his travels through Indiana in 1916 saw the family as flourishing but nonetheless doomed; he believed that the city was the future, and the ideals upon which the family was founded were becoming anachronistic. "Have we made the ten commandments work? Do not these small towns with their faded ideal homes stand almost as Karnack and Memphis?" And "It seems to me as if I myself have witnessed a great revolt against all the binding perfection which these lovely homes represented."[51] In complete contrast to Dreiser, Sarah Orne Jewett apostrophized the old ways of the rural coastal Maine she knew so well in "The Country of the Pointed Firs." A striking and central image in her story is the Bowden family reunion, which draws the Bowdens and their in-laws in droves to the old family homestead. Over different footpaths they came in "straggling processions walking in single files, like old illustrations of the Pilgrim's Progress." All the visitors assemble in the meadow, where they are organized into ranks of four, and march across in a long procession to the grove where the family picnic will be held, like "a company of ancient Greeks going to celebrate a victory; or to worship the god of harvests in the grove above. . . . We carried the tokens and inheritance of all such households from which this had descended, and were only the latest of our line."[52]

At the contemporary end of Jewett's procession lay the amoral city of Dreiser, a congeries of whirling, isolated atoms of humanity driven by chemic forces. And on the way were the rootless wanderings of Hamlin Garland, unable to settle his own family in a place or find a church where the memory of their ancestors was still sanctified. "Deep down in my consciousness is a feeling of guilt, a sense of disloyalty to my ancestors, which renders me uneasy,"[53] Garland wrote. A poignant but probably irrelevant lament for most Americans, except in the South and parts of New England, and among the rich. Americans who moved west were nomads who shed their ancestors, and their pasts, like locusts discarded their shells.

Like Ed Howe, many came "of a long line of plain people." Beyond that he knew little: "I know the addresses of none of my relatives, except a brother who lives next door, and of his children and my own. In visiting homes, I frequently see old pictures, silver or furniture coming down from ancestors. I have nothing of this kind. The only relic I have of my father is an old spectacle case. I have no picture of my mother, nor anything touched by her hands."[54] He did not know where his father had been born; there was a shadowy uncle and aunt, but they were more family rumors than people; there was a girl in the family Howe always thought of as his half sister, a daughter of his father's first marriage, until someone told him much later that the girl had been the daughter of his father's first wife by another marriage. Blood relatives or not, "we cordially disliked each other,"[55] Howe recalled.

Sherwood Anderson was known to misstate the facts of his life, but his vagueness about his father's and mother's early lives, and that of his grandmother too, seems real enough and probably encouraged him to invent the stories he did about them—he described his grandmother as an evil-looking Italian woman (she was of German origin and a respectable Presbyterian), and he gave his father an exotic war history. As William Maxwell wrote in his book *Ancestors*, "With a Middle Western American family, no sooner do you begin to perceive the extent of the proliferation of ancestors backward into time than they are lost from sight. Every trace of them disappears, through the simple erosion of human forgetfulness. They were in movement in a new country. . . . In the mountains of Virginia they listened thoughtfully to tales of how easy life was in Kentucky, and from Kentucky, when they had to sell out, or were sold out, to pay their debts, they moved on into Illinois. With their minds always on some promised land, like the Old Testament figures they so much resembled, they did not bother to record or even remember the place of origin."[56] And elsewhere he notes, "Apart from their gravestones, which their descendants soon lost track of, the people who settled in the wilderness did not leave lasting memorials; they left stories instead."[57] But the ideal of family as identity remained; it conferred love and self-esteem by simply being born into it; and by extension, one's home town was a community to which one belonged by birth—"one big family," in Anderson's words and Booth Tarkington's too. Or, as Lewis Atherton wrote, "In the nineteenth century especially, people were born into the small town as they once were born into the church. They 'belonged' by their very presence, and they had something larger than themselves to which to cling."[58]

Most towns were, then, made up of streets of homes—of houses on neat rectangular yards, always one to a family, lining the tree-shaded streets marching out in orderly grid pattern from the business district. To every family a house, and these houses in their collectivity made up the town and gave it its look.

Home architecture in the late nineteenth century had its purely practical aspects, but its social functions were to provide refuge for the family and proclaim the tastes and standing of its owner—one might almost say, to protect the woman while proclaiming the man. The latter function became more pronounced in the years between 1870 and 1900—corresponding to the emphasis during the Gilded Age on conspicuous consumption.

Certainly there was a trend toward the more elaborate in home design—from the classic and simple to the baroque and fancy. The prevailing style in many towns in the 1830s and 1840s was Greek Revival, which reflected ideals of egalitarianism and democracy. American builders (there were few architects) played multiple variations, keyed in with a client's pocketbook, but all on the basic theme of the low-pitched, gable-ended roof—the classic Parthenon facade. Simplicity, in the relative sense anyhow, continued after the Civil War. In the wittily observed opening pages of *The Magnificent Ambersons*, Booth Tarkington, recalling the section of Indianapolis where he grew up, described the houses of most of the people as being "of a pleasant architecture. They lacked style, but also lacked pretentiousness, and whatever does not pretend at all has style enough. They stood in commodious yards, well shaded by leftover forest trees, elm and walnut and beech, with here and there a line of tall sycamores where the land had been made by filling bayous from the creek. The house of a 'prominent resident,' facing Military Square, or National Avenue, or Tennessee Street, was built of brick upon a stone foundation, or of wood upon a brick foundation."[59] These placid architectural waters are roiled by the advent of Major Amberson, a wealthy merchant prince, who erects an enormous stone mansion with turrets and the town's first porte-cochere on the largest and most prominent lot of a two-hundred-acre tract known as "Amberson's Addition." This area was landscaped and set with fountains and statuary, giving it a splendor that one local reporter saw as outstripping Versailles.

Like Major Amberson, the merchant princes of growing midwestern cities sought to emulate the merchant princes and robber barons back east, who erected grand palaces along the Hudson. Looking down his nose a bit, Sydney George Fisher, a snobbish Philadelphia lawyer, observed all this new building in 1864: "Countless country houses cover the right bank [of the Hudson] all the way down. They are in every variety of style, some costly and grand, all comfortable and well kept. They are the summer abodes of the rich men of New York, therefore many of them, of very vulgar and common people and their beauty and expense imply neither taste nor cultivation on the part of their owners. Upstart wealth, often enormous wealth is the characteristic of New York."[60]

Those of ample means could afford to spend money lavishly on the exterior and interior of their mansions, like Major Amberson with his black walnut woodwork—"Sixty thousand dollars for the woodwork *alone.*"[61] Men of lesser wealth and more circumscribed tastes could not, of course, look to these mansions as direct models, but they could imbibe from them the notion of the house as an expression of themselves, their self-esteem and social aspirations, their consumption. If their tastes needed guidance, there were the architectual plan books that were widely circulated in the nineteenth century. These books, some in large folio size selling for ten dollars a copy, were aimed at architects, builders, and their clients and contained detailed drawings of a wide variety of houses, with interior plans and specifications of plumbing, woodwork, and the like with estimated costs of each. With these books—and the cheaper magazines that later replaced them—the aspiring homeowner could find a model that appealed and lay in his price range, then hire an architect or, more likely, a local builder to erect it, incorporating his own suggested variations, along with the builder's modifications.

In one of these plan books, *Victorian Home Building,* written in 1875 by E.C. Hussey, the philosophy of the house as home is expressed in the flowery language of the day: "It may not immediately appear, to every one, that a house is not necessarily, in any true sense of the term, a 'Home.' It is however, the shell, the hive in which busy hands and anxious hearts combine their toil and hope.[62]

Given that Hussey's book is in part an exercise in salesmanship, in which a large number of manufacturers of household items are openly plugged, presumably as quid pro quo for their advertising, the vaporous sentiments do suggest the maternal side of the home ideal—the home as sanctury of the family, quietly blending into a neighborhood of "high-minded, sober, industrious, refined Christian people," and exemplifying taste and economy, the quiet middle-class virtues, while avoiding eccentricity or ostentation. As in all these books, the houses come in a wide range of prices, starting with a basic simple house for $750 and going on up to one costing $18,000. The social range to which the book is directed encompasses the clerk or small shopkeeper at the lower end of the scale and the moderately wealthy small-town banker at the high end. Although some of the houses are ornate, they are not excessively so, and Hussey seems to favor restraint and proportion.

He also frequently stresses the interior plan—how the layout of the rooms will contribute to family happiness. In the course of describing a fairly modest house ("Cost at New York, $3,500"), he establishes that the home is woman's domain: [A house] is not only the home center, the retreat and shelter for all the family, but . . . it is also the workshop for the mother and her helps' [sic]. It is not only where she is to live, to love, but where she is to care and labor. Her hours, days, weeks, months and years are spent within its bands; until she becomes an enthroned fixture, more indispensable than the house itself."[64]

Hussey was unusual in the amount of philosophizing with which he embellished his books. Many plan books gave details and nothing more. Undoubtedly, however, they influenced styles by disseminating the designs of contemporary architects into the farthest reaches, the most remote small towns of the nation. The architect's job was to please the client, but he still had the role of subtly suggesting styles he thought would appeal. Where Hussey employed the middle-class Victorian, religious approach—he invokes the divinity frequently—others might make a more direct appeal to the rising status-consciousness of the newly wealthy.

When the Italianate style first came in, Samuel Sloan's *Homestead Architecture* described the ideal villa: "Though not remarkably ostentatious, its appearance at once bespeaks it the abode of the wealthy and refined."[65] Italian villas usually came in two styles—"regular," or cube-shaped, and "irregular," or L-shaped. Their distinctive features were a cupola and dome-arched windows, and they ranged from the austere to the elaborately laid out with wings and protrusions at various angles. The ideal, though, was a country villa inhabited by a man of cultivation and leisure; and this ideal could be shrunk for a much smaller suburban lawn.

Style, then, began to make a statement, or as the modern architect John Maass put it: "Each style contained a distinct 'message.' A Gothic Revival house usually signified that the owner was proud to be of old English stock. An Italianate villa did not mean that the owner was of Italian descent but 'This is a cultured and artistic household' and a French style house proclaimed 'This is a stylish and fashionable home.' "[66] Maass adds that in expressing the virtue and character of the owner, the nineteenth-century house also expressed his financial worth: " 'Fine men build fine houses' was accepted as a true statement. Hence it was but a short step to reversing the proposition: 'If you own a fine house you will be taken for a fine man.' Nineteenth century America usually equated affluence with virtue."[67]

This philosophy percolated down to the middle class. The Victorian homebuilder could express his own tastes—or rather what the prevailing modes in the builders' plan books told him his taste was. With less money to spend on ostentation, he resorted to cheaper methods of building made possible by advances in technology. The balloon frame, which replaced post and handhewn beam construction, employed massproduced lumber—two-by-fours nailed and studded into a frame for the walls and roof of the house. Upon this skeleton was applied a "skin" of wood or brick. The development of jig and scroll saws enabled the production of a vast range of scrollwork ornamentation, making possible the familiar Victorian "gingerbread." Metals, especially tin, were also widely used for roofing and ornamentation. Finally, architects, coming into their own as professionals, increasingly wrote the rules of the game; in searching for styles that would appeal to their clients, they became eclectic—borrowing, transforming, reviving, and combining. All these developments reached their apotheosis in the Queen Anne style of the 1880s—popularly known as "Victorian."

Actually the Queen Anne style had nothing to do with Queen Anne (reigned 1702–14); it was, rather, an American imitation, inspired by pictures of English country houses of the period. It was an eclectic style, combining elements of Tudor, Gothic, and English Renaissance in its steep-pitched roofs, assymetrical gables, towers, and turrets, and gingerbreaded porches (also haphazardly called verandas or piazzas) and eaves. It took its inspiration from the past, yet it employed modern balloon-frame construction and massproduced ornamentation; it even could be scaled down to a simpler model, sometimes called the Queen Anne cottage. It was a distant kin of those vulgar millionaires' mansions along the Hudson, suggesting in a more modest and actually standardized way that the owner was expressing his personality and standing. A rich variety or ornaments could adorn it; similarly, the shape of the house could be freely varied by placement of turrets and eaves and bay windows. From the builder's point of view, the style was almost foolproof, since any sort of proportion was workable. Each house could be made different from the one next door by changing the mix of elements—yet not *too* different. The basic style remained, identifiable, acceptable, indeed the fad—*Carpentry and Building* magazine dubbed it "the modern craze,"[68] and in the mid-1880s every plan in the magazine was a variant of the Queen Anne Style.

Kalamazoo, Michigan, in the 1880s was in the midst of a boom, as it successfully evolved from a trading center to a manufacturing center, and in the 1887 special trade edition of the Kalamazoo *Telegraph*, there is praise for the grand new Queen Anne homes rising up on the more affluent streets. So strong was the pull of fashion that Frank Little, a resident on one of these streets, decided his beautiful thirty-five-year-old Greek Revival cottage was dated: "It has no architectural grandeur or beauty—turrets, domes, battlements, cock-lofts or multitudinous gables," he complained.[69] In order to keep up with the neighbors, he tacked on a Victorian veranda to the front of his house, which obliterated the temple facade.

Perhaps Mr. Little was too easily swayed by the crowd, but his surrender to the new style shows how novelty and status consciousness could override the traditional. The Queen Anne style represented an "instant past" for a nation of nomads. Americans were searching for a past—any past; as Peter Schmitt observes, "Now, with horse cars and telephones and electricity, they wanted their houses to look old. They wanted to feel they'd always been there—moments after they unpacked the last barrel in the newest suburban development."[70] Thus, things old—Tudor shingles, English oak, stained-glass windows, fireplaces (supplemented by central heating)—became the new rage.

It is noteworthy that much of the new building in Kalamazoo in the 1880s was being done by the rising professional and managerial class—the white-collar clerks, executives, engineers, bookkeepers, businessmen. They had the arriviste's need for a house that proclaimed instant status, as well as allowing the owner some individual display. With its aura of permanence and age, the Queen Anne house served as an appropriate family sanctuary—a romantic castle (some even had moats); a display of the master's prosperity on the outside; a place of formal public pleasures on its large lawn and wide veranda and in its formal parlors within; a retreat with narrow halls, private nooks and crannies, and odd-sized rooms. As the machine age loomed, the Queen Anne house seemed to suggest the old workmanship, though its gingerbread was all machine-made.

To the acerbic Thorstein Veblen, all this unfunctional gingerbread and useless detail was an expression of the new canon of taste—"conspicuous waste." This taste eschewed simplicity and serviceability in favor of novelty and idiosyncrasy. The ideal was to show "wasted effort," which in turn attested to expensiveness, proclaiming that the owner could afford to lavish his money on "evidences of misspent ingenuity and labor, backed by a conspicuous ineptitude."[71] It was, in short, "the substitution of pecuniary beauty for aesthetic beauty."[72] Veblen pointed to the architecture of the 1890s as a conspicuous example of conspicuous waste, an example of "the human proclivity to emulation," which seized upon "the consumption of goods as a means of invidious comparison, and has thereby invested consumable goods with a secondary utility as evidence of relative ability to pay."[73] Thus in architecture, egalitarianism gave way to status seeking, and the new houses of the aspiring, anxious middle class in towns all over the country struck a further blow at the earlier egalitarian ideals expressed in the frontier log cabin and the Greek Revival house.

By Veblen's theory, the pecuniary aesthetic dictated that "goods are humilific, and therefore unattractive, if they show too thrifty an adaptation to the mechanical end sought and do not include a margin of expensiveness on which to rest a complacent invidious comparison."[74] Recall Mr. Little of Kalamazoo, who felt compelled to add Victorian excesses to his classic house. The Victorian plan books are full of basic, cheap, square or L-shaped frame houses which were perfectly functional, and it was just this simplicity that placed their owners lower down on the class ladder. The best that owners of such houses could do, if they possessed a modicum of upward aspiration, was to embellish them with useless ornamentation. The smaller Queen Anne "cottages" employed wooden flowers, sunbursts, or elaborate brackets.

The resulting small white frame houses, with their small porches and attenuated columns, rails, and ornaments, were ubiquitous in the Middle West. In Sinclair Lewis's *Main Street,* the new bride Carol Kennicott casts a cold eye upon her new home: "A square smug brown house, rather damp. A narrow concrete walk up to it. . . . A screened porch with pillars of thin painted pine surmounted by scrolls and brackets and bumps of jig-sawed wood. No shrubbery to shut off the public gaze. A lugubrious bay-window to the right of the porch. Window curtains of starched cheap lace revealing a pink marble table with a conch shell and a Family Bible."[75] Sensitive souls like Carol found a meanness in this architecture; it connoted narrow, thwarted lives to the village rebel. Similar emotions are experienced by the narrator of Willa Cather's *My Ántonia:* "On starlight nights I used to pace up and down those long, cold streets, scowling at the little, sleeping houses on either side, with their storm windows and covered back porches. They were flimsy shelters, most of them poorly built of light wood, with their spindle porchposts horribly mutilated by the turning-lathe. Yet for all their frailness, how much jealousy and envy and unhappiness some of them managed to contain! The life that went on in them seemed to me made up of evasions and negations; shifts to save cooking, to save washing and cleaning, devices to propitiate the tongue of gossip."[76] How many middle western writers came out of those white or brown frame houses! Cather, Lewis, Masters, Anderson. Make of it what one will, none of the critics of village life in the teens and twenties grew up in those turreted mansions on the hill.

So the aspiring middle class had its gingerbread, while the less affluent middle class lived in simple, functional frame houses. At the bottom of the scale were the workingmen, who occupied anything from shacks of their own devising to company houses that were single-story sheds, enlarged to three or four rooms. These sheds were often located "across the tracks," or, rather, next to them. The workers' houses at their best offered a little land out back for a garden, no front porch, thin, uninsulated walls, and small, cramped rooms. In such a house lived the American poet Carl Sandburg of Galesburg, Illinois, amongst the other Swedes who, like Sandburg's father, worked on the railroad. Such houses at least offered the pride of a little plot of earth (though probably the occupant did not own the land but rented it from the company), in contrast to the dormitories of the New England mill towns—an amenity that reflected the greater space available in middle western towns of that day.

Probably over 90 percent of all families in towns like Muncie or Galesburg lived in single-family houses; yet every town had its "shacktown" where the very poor lived. Their "ownership" was strictly by squatter's rights, and their "homes" were hardly worth the lumber in them. Shacktown was the bottom of the heap, the end of the line; its inhabitants were nonpersons, the invisible poor, excluded from the community. About the only social services they received were blows from a policeman's club when they were obstreperous and baskets from the Ladies' Aid when they were hungry.

By the 1890s towns of any size were developing neighborhoods with visible economic similarities among those who lived in them and differences from other neighborhoods. The larger, the more urbanized the town, the more elaborate its social topography. In Canby's Wilmington, "each neighborhood outside the slums was a little town in itself, with a store or two, a livery stable, wooden houses tucked in behind for the darkies, vacant lots held for speculation, solid dwellings of the quality, raw built mansions of the new rich, and rows of little houses for the plain people."[77] Symbolically, the town's founding father lived in a big house on the highest hill, selling off his remaining lots to support himself and finally shooting himself when the tide of new houses reached his lawn.

There grew up a variety of names for the wealthy section of town—"the Hill," "Quality Street," "Elm Street," "the Northeast"—used generically to mean both a geographical area and a social class with power in the community. Similarly, the names of other neighborhoods had negative connotations because of the supposedly less desirable people who lived in them—"Shacktown," "Shantytown," "the Canal," "the other side of the tracks," "Back Street." For the climber, the arriviste, who was confronted with a "no vacancy" sign on the neighborhood to which he aspired, there was nothing for it but to move to the suburbs—the "additions" that developers platted around the town borders, which were made accessible by trolleys and then automobiles. These additions were first identified by the name of the developer—"Amberson's Addition," or Smith's, Jones's, whoever's addition, conveying the sense of a pioneering trailblazer and shrewd entrepreneur who had opened still another parcel of wilderness to land-hungry townspeople. But by 1910 or so they were acquiring the standardized quasi-rustic names we know today; in Kalamazoo, for example, additions were christened "Home Acres," "Idlewild," "Woodlawn," "Rose Hill," and "Parkwood."[78] The age of the pioneers had ended, the frontier had vanished, replaced by the suburb, and the speculator's role as town father was no longer honorific. Instead, the town was entering the age of urbanization; now people were buying a pseudo-pastoral life-style, escaping the small cities that towns like Kalamazoo had become. The Indiana romantic novelist Meredith Nicholson, who tended to see things *en rose*, observed the inhabitants of these new additions in his book of essays *The Valley of Democracy:*

> Cruising through the West, one enters every city through new additions, frequently sliced out of old forests, with the maples, elms, or beeches carefully retained. Bungalows are inadvertently jotted down as though enthusiastic young architects were using the landscape for sketch-paper. I have inspected large settlements in which no two of these habitations are alike, though the difference may be only a matter of pulling the roof a little lower over the eyes of the veranda, or some idiosyncrasy in the matter of the chimney. The trolley and the low-priced automobile are continually widening the urban arc, so that the

acre lot or even a larger estate is within the reach of city-dwellers who have a weakness for country air and home-grown vegetables.[79]

Nicholson peoples these additions with young couples—"the product of the high schools, or perhaps they have been fellow students in a State university."[80] Nor do they "lead starved lives or lack social diversions." The wives "gather on one another's verandas every summer afternoon to discuss the care of infants or wars and rumors of wars; and is there not tennis when their young lords come home? On occasions of supreme indulgence the neighborhood laundress watches the baby while they go somewhere to dance or to a play, lecture, or concert in town."[81] Nicholson seems to be describing a Levittown with maples and hollyhocks, ca. 1910.

But on most quiet, town streets the only harbinger of the flight to the suburbs to mar the peace of a summer afternoon was the clang of a trolley bell. Electric-powered cars had still not replaced those horse-drawn trolleys of only yesterday, which moved at a slow pace, ready to stop when a lady waved at the driver from her window, and wait for her while she put on her hat, came downstairs, gave the maid her instructions, and proceeded decorously out the front door (in Booth Tarkington's recollection). Electric trollies, on the contrary, observed schedules, made regular stops, and hurried along at ten miles an hour or so. The interurban trollies plied their way along the main streets, providing fast, clean transportation to neighboring towns, stopping anywhere en route to pick up a hailing country man or woman. Townspeople welcomed these trains when they were first introduced, but local merchants either looked upon them to boost their trade with the countryside or saw them as a menace, shanghaiing potential customers and spiriting them to rival cities nearby. In some places they forced the railroads to make more frequent stops and pick up passengers at crossroads. But like canals in an earlier day, the interurbans were soon made obsolete by another mode of transportation—the automobile. Introduced around the turn of the century, the interurbans were gone by the 1920s or 1930s.

There is another innovation along our street, one that is far less obvious than the trolley car. It is the addition of street numbers to the houses, a minor but important watershed in the town's development. In some places there was an instinctive resistance to the numbers, because they signaled the passing of the era when everyone knew where everyone else lived. In the quieter village era, people hardly paid attention to street names, so what difference would a number on the house make? They spoke of "the Smith place" or "over at the Browns'." The editor of the Gallatin, Missouri, paper chided some local women for being "taken in" by an itinerant seller of metal house numbers. The women were putting on city airs, the editor said; why, not one in ten folks in Gallatin even knew the street names. That they could be criticized for this minor ornamentation on their houses was a commentary on small-town conformity, but also an unconscious last stand against the invasion of urban ways. In the town of Hastings, Nebraska, a rapidly growing trading center, there was no such resistance. "In January, 1885," the local historian reports, "citizens began agitating for street numbers on houses; the town was growing so fast it was hard to tell where people lived."[82] And so a subtle duality crept into people's thinking: A house might be "the Smith place," but it was also 64 Kensington Avenue.

Other urban touches, however, our street lacked—notably paving. Even in Wilmington in the nineties, Canby recalled, only the main streets had cobblestones; the side, residential streets were a yellow-clay morass in spring and fall. Town services came slowly in the 1890s, so the home remained the provider of many things that we take for granted. Water came from cisterns or wells in the backyard and was, in the most advanced houses, pumped by hand with a small pump on the kitchen sink. The lack of a city water system meant vulnerability to fire. Sewage lines were nonexistent—hence the "necessary" or "privy"—both Victorian euphemisms—in back. But in many houses the W.C. was beginning to appear, although it simply drained into a vault or cesspool out in the back. The best homes employed soil pipes for drainage and lined the pits with stones. The W.C. was frequently located on the first floor, in the back of the house, as though it had been reluctantly admitted into the house proper; the tradition was that wastes should be disposed of outside, and the problem of odors—"sewer gases"—was something the architectural plan books dealt with. Some located the W.C. by a chimney area, so that the gases could escape through it. The irrepressible E.C. Hussey warns solemnly of the dangers of "death laden gases" flowing through the house due to the increasing number of W.C.s "more or less centrally located within the house walls."[83] Hussey, ever ready to plug an advertiser, recommends Jenning's Sanitary Specialities "designed for the shutting off of sewer gas" and adds that "the matter of expense cannot, by civilized people, be allowed to interfere with the use of the very best appliance that can be obtained for such purposes; a plea of a few dollars more first cost can never justify an act which holds in its issues the health and frequently the lives of our children and ourselves."[84]

As for electricity, it spread slowly to the home. Early electric plants of the eighties and nineties served primarily business customers and downtown streets; incandescent lamps were replacing the gas or kerosine lamps which the lamplighter, pulling a handcart, lit nightly. The Hastings Company—a privately owned local business, like most early utilities—started out with forty-five "subscribers" in 1885; by 1901 a new electric company—the old one had gone bust—was announcing that it had one circuit available for businesses needing light all night. And not long after that, the *Tribune* was suggesting that the fifty-nine new arc lights downtown (which supplemented existing gas lamps) should be kept on until at least one A.M. because most parties did not break up till then and people needed the lights to get home by. It was not until 1912 that the entire downtown area was lit up by locally manufactured lightoliers; by then electrical conduits were buried and more and more homes were having electric lights installed. The more conservative town fathers and householders resisted the new age for years.

Lighting in most towns proceeded at a leisurely pace. There were major problems with faulty dynamos and lack of trained people to maintain them. Athens, Illinois, introduced its electric lights in 1892 with a parade; but by 1897 the dynamo had gone on the blink, and service was not restored until the early 1900s. In 1903, the electric plant owner in Cassville, Wisconsin, had twenty-eight subscribers in the business district and advertised for an engineer to run the plant from sunset to midnight—except on moonlit nights, when there was no service. No trained engineer could be found who would work for thirty dollars a month—and soon the dynamo broke down. Letters to the manufacturer took several months to produce repairs, for emergency service was nonexistent.

Townspeople undoubtedly joked about the poor service, and regarded the electric light as a promising novelty; businessmen, however, saw it as adding to their downtown shopping hours and proclaimed "great white ways" of lit-up streets in the local papers with considerable more fervor than Genesis devotes to God's illumination of the universe. But beyond all the hoopla, there was something magical and beautiful about that original incandescent glow in the streets. A sense of awe and wonder is implicit in a newspaper account of the first incandescent lamp in Kalamazoo's Bronson Park in 1882:

> The park was thronged last evening till nearly 10 o'clock by people from all parts of the village. The great attraction for all was the electric light which robed everything in a magic effulgence, and seemed to idealize all surroundings. It was a source of unfailing wonder and admiration for old and young. The splashing waters of the fountain, the dew on the heightened green of the sward, the trees, the walks, the faces and dresses of the promenaders, everything within the wide radius of the lustrous beacon were seen under a new, strange and lovely glamor. As one crowd withdrew, taking lingering looks of the brilliant meteor transfixed above the scene, and noted the effect upon the surroundings, other multitudes gathered at the fountain to experience the same pleasure and wonder. Many who came to the park last evening witnessed the electric light for the first time.[85]

These public displays aside, householders made do with coal-oil lamps, or, more commonly, the soft glow of gaslight. If they were fortunate enough to live in a natural-gas boomtown like Muncie in the 1890s, where it was thought that the supply of the stuff was inexhaustible, subscribers had only to pay for the installation of the fixture; there was no attempt to meter the gas and charge for the amount used. It was considered cheaper to have the gas on all the time—opening windows and doors when it became too hot—than to waste a match relighting it. (Such practices, the state geologist estimated, caused the entire state of Indiana to waste about one hundred million cubic feet of natural gas per day.)

Telephone service in small towns was also started as a local business, and it was confined to the town limits. Edgar Lee Masters recalled working for such a lone operator one summer and helping him bottle cough medicine, which the communications magnate sold on the side to supplement his income. It took small-towners a while to get used to giving numbers to the operators—known as "Central," of course—when placing their calls; they tended simply to ask for "Mrs. Jones, please" or "Spencer Hardware, please." The newspapers ran items reminding subscribers to consult the listings of numbers, even though the operator might well know the number of everybody in town, at least in the early days. Certainly, the operators were reputed to know everything else about everybody and acted as a kind of answering service, telling callers that "Mrs. Clayton isn't home. I just now seen her walk into the Bon Ton." (Owning a telephone in a small town was also considered a bit snooty and citified in the early days, and in the words of one woman, "It was not until about the time of the Spanish War that phones became common enough so you thought of feeling apologetic at not having one."[86] By the mid-1900s there were four million telephones in the nation, but free enterprise posed problems. A town of ten thousand might have as many as three phone companies, and businessmen were compelled to subscribe to all of them, listing the separate numbers in their advertisements.

Eventually, the phone companies, like the trolley companies and electric companies, would merge or divide up the territory, or else the competitors would be driven out of business. (Physical force was sometimes resorted to. In Hastings the two rival trolley companies tore up each other's ties and track.) Then large utility companies began buying up the local power and telephone companies that were not municipally owned, and in later years the towns found themselves with more efficient service, but vulnerable to disasters or strikes in far-off places that interrupted their own service, not to mention monopolistic rate-setting.

But in the 1890s the impact of the telegraph and telephone, like the automobile, the electric light, and other wonders, was still muted. People still visited instead of making a telephone call, and along our street on that bygone summer afternoon, the women who have finished their daily chores have put on their good clothes to call on neighbors or to sit on their front porches. There was some ambivalence about the wisdom of front porches; one home-building book advised that above the 35th parallel they were probably unhealthy, and were best suited for more southerly climes. Then, too, in a time when it was thought "poor-folksy" not to have a yard, the porch was an afterthought; only when population pressures and rising real-estate prices forced smaller lot sizes for houses, did porches become the rage. Still, call it a veranda or piazza or just a porch, most houses had them, along with a porch swing or glider, in which the housewife could rest and take the breeze on a hot day, and at night a young couple could sit out of earshot, yet within chaperoning range of parents.

Of yards, there is little to add; most middle-class houses, located on lots 25 feet wide and 125 to 150 feet deep, stood close to the sidewalk, with most of the space allotted to a producing garden in back. It was considered bad form to seek privacy behind trees; people would think you had something to hide. Thus, Carol Kennicott's aversion to her bridal home's lack of "shrubbery to shut off the public gaze" was a violation of the unwritten code of Gopher Prairie.

The inside of the middle-class house was cluttered and crepuscular typically, an arrangement of small, dark rooms, filled with heavy furniture of the Mission or Moorish style. The standard line-up on the lower floor was parlor, dining room, and kitchen, and on the upper floor, there were three or four bedrooms (or "chambers" as they were usually denoted in the planners' books, "bed room" being a term reserved for a tiny cubicle for a servant or poor relation and containing a bed and little more). However large (or small) the house, a parlor (living room) and a kitchen were indispensable. The formal parlor served for ceremonial entertaining of visitors or occasions of courtship among the young. It contained the family's best furniture, a Bible on the table, pictures on the wall, a scattering of books, beaded lamps and curtains, family albums, and various bric-a-brac and hideous objets d'art, depending upon the period. The furniture was rigidly uncomfortable and thus eminently suited to family state occasions; it also discouraged use and so lasted forever. The longevity of the parlor furnishings was enhanced by the practice of shutting it off and closing its drapes when it was not in use.

In contrast to the stuffy formality of the parlor, the kitchen was a center of work and life. Here, as we have seen, was the domain of the mother, a workshop for food preparation, cleansing of clothes and bodies, laying up of supplies for the winter months, and, in less affluent houses, eating. Most middle-class homes, however, had a dining room, and larger houses added a sitting room or library or both, where the family read and played the misnamed parlor games. Beyond that one expanded into servants' quarters, pantries, bathrooms, W.C.'s, conservatories, greenhouses, billiard rooms, and so on. There might also be a carriage house and shed in back, and a cellar below, in which more and more frequently was appearing a furnace that heated the whole house by means of hot air piped up through registers (a less expensive substitute was a register located above the kitchen stove so as to admit its heat into the upper chambers and bedrooms; the stove could also be attached to hot-water pipes).

From the innards of the average family's home one could deduce a pattern of life: kitchen, the wife's place of work; dining room where the family gathered for meals; sitting room, with a coal-fueled base burner for warmth, where the family took their leisure, culture, recreation; and parlor for formal intercourse with the outer world. The parlor was usually the front room of the house, presenting a face of stiff formality and materialistic display of family totems and precious objects to the world, yet buffering the more informal family life inside. When one paid a call, one was directed to the parlor and did not penetrate further.

The average middle class home was a kind of hive of small boxlike rooms, narrow corridors, sharp angles, dark polished woods, velvet and fringes, cool darkness in summer, red-glowing warmth of the stove in winter—a mix of functionalism and banal ornamentation, propriety, privacy and claustrophobic closeness. The house stood in a standard-sized yard and in a block of standard-sized yards with alleys and back fences and hedges bordering them. It faced a street, front-porch forward, a place to sit and feel the breeze on a hot summer afternoon and watch the people on foot and carriages passing by, just as others were sitting on their front porches on their streets. On this particular street the summer dust has been recently dampened by a passing sprinkler-wagon. The sidewalks are a bit rough underfoot, being made of boards, which come loose and they are loosened further by idle boys with nothing better to do. Trees line the street, their overarching leafy canopy providing pleasant shade. Such trees were the first act of beautification in most towns. Planting a tree inspired thoughts of one's posterity, of the generations that would come afterward. Even in old New England towns, which might have two hundred years of existence behind them, the arboreal urge was felt. In Suffield, Connecticut, for example, the architect Henry Sykes said in a public address in 1868 on the town common, "Let those public grounds be adorned with trees, that when a few years hence you may assemble to commemorate the two hundreth anniversary of this town, you may have before you the promise of future beauty, and when your children's children may assemble to commemorate the three hundredth anniversary, they may rise up and call you blessed."[88] Suffield had the traditional elms lining its streets which were the glory of New England streets, dating back beyond memory. Theodore Dwight wrote in the 1830s that "I have not yet been able to ascertain whence arose the ancient practise of thus decorating the streets and high roads, but from my earliest recollections, the fine elms, spreading their noble branches over my head, excited my admiration. . . . In many places, particularly in some of the villages, the finest trees, of extraordinary growth, form two, three, or four lanes, andd overshadow the broad path."[89] Sykes and others transformed the town common from its natural unkempt state by landscaping it and planting elms and maples around it. Sykes was an early pioneer in a town beautification movement that gained momentum in the 1890s.

This movement had as its first project tree-planting, as though in emulation of the New England aesthetic. In Great Plains, where trees were sparse, towns held tree-planting days, during which everyone helped out in planting imported elm or oak saplings along the streets. In the 1880s the Nebraska legislature created Arbor Day to encourage the practice, and so many states followed suit that it became a national holiday. Trees, of course, were also functional, providing shade in the summer. In the Far West and the clay-soil, piny-woods areas of the South where trees were sparse and the sun hot, shade was created in the downtown areas by roofs, awnings, or decorative cast-iron balconies overhanging the sidewalks.

Tree planting and parks were the chief community expressions of beautification, and a New York newspaper urged the nation's towns to accelerate their efforts before it was too late: "In a few years hundreds of towns will become cities. Now they have the country in their very streets; soon it will be gone—unless the parks are set apart and space for trees is left on either side of the new streets and extensions of streets. No town is too small or too far away from the present lines of swift development to take the necessary precautions; and the way to begin is for some public-spirited citizen—man or woman—to stir the matter up."[89]

But early community beautification efforts were concentrated on trees and parks; they rarely extended to the business district. Aside from the occasional centrally located park or square, as in Kalamazoo, Main Street was generally left to grow anarchically—a proliferation of stores and buildings of varying shapes, sizes, and materials with little relationship to one another. Carol Kennicott is struck by this hodgepodge on her first walk around Gopher Prairie in Sinclair Lewis's *Main Street.* The description in the novel is based upon the Main Street of Lewis's own hometown of Sauk Centre, Minnesota, and derived from a visit he made there in 1916 with his then wife, Grace Hegger Lewis, a woman of urban sophistication who came from a background of faded gentility. Mrs. Lewis later claimed that her husband had seen the town anew through her eyes and that he had used this vicarious view in setting down Carol Kennicott's initial reactions to Gopher Prairie. Carol is depressed by "Main Street with its two-story brick shops, its story-and-a-half wooden residences, its muddy expanse from concrete walk to walk, its huddle of Fords and lumber-wagons";[90] there is no restful beauty for the eye, no park, no courthouse square. There were trees, but "at best they resembled a thinned woodlot."[91]

Carol's dreams of bringing beauty to the prairie vanish; what she has beheld was "not only the heart of a place called Gopher Prairie, but ten thousand towns from Albany to San Diego."[92] Main Street is a national eyesore: "It was not only the unsparing unapologetic ugliness and the rigid straightness which overwhelmed her. It was the planlessness, the flimsy temporariness of the buildings, their faded unpleasant colors. The street was cluttered with electric-light poles, telephone poles, gasoline pumps for motor cars, boxes of goods. Each man had built with the most valiant disregard of all the others."[93]

Much of the ugliness Carol Kennicott saw was attributable to new technology—the automobile and its noise, the telephone and electric wires. In towns that had, unlike Gopher Prairie, some manufacturing, the soot and pollution of soft-coal smoke could be added to the indictment. All these developments came in the 1890s and 1900s, further contributing to the chaotic look of many towns. Citizens of real-life Main Streets, who were less disaffected than Carol, may not have noticed the clutter, or perhaps they regarded it as tangible evidence of Growth and Prosperity.

But was Gopher Prairie a stand-in for every American small town from the Atlantic to the Pacific? What of the New England towns with their elm-shaded streets, their village greens, their old colonial homes, their white-spired churches? Or the languid-paced southern towns like Lexington, Virginia, whose Main Street is described by town historian Henry Boley: "A quiet country-town street, with rows of chairs and benches under the shade of the trees, where the village gentry could rest and enjoy leisure and comradeship, far more important to them than buying and selling."[94] The energies of commerce were muted in towns like Lexington, and their streets showed it. There were quiet stores, where one met "unbounded hospitality for all, which seemed the prime reason for the store's existence. Clerks and proprietors alike were solicitous as to the comfort and entertainment of the callers, and upon seeing a lady enter, an easy chair was immediately offered and accepted."[95]

Lexington was redolent of the traditions of the Confederacy, which were kept alive by the members of the Never-Sweat Club—former Confederate soldiers who held forth daily from easy chairs on the courthouse balcony. It was cultured and genteel, home of Washington and Lee University, and indeed home of General Robert E. Lee himself in his declining years. More typical was the Missouri town described by a visiting journalist as "a genuine southern town, surrounding a hollow square with a court house in the center."[96] Nearly every southern town, it seemed, had its square, a convention that flowed up north, merging into the New England village green tradition. Other familiar aspects of southern towns were: "Streets gullied by water and overgrown with weeds, frame houses, log houses and stucco houses, with deep porticos and shade trees; negros trudging with burdens on their backs; deserted buildings, tumbling fences . . . "[97] Unlike Lexington, many southern towns resounded to the hustle of commerce. Some became ghosts, too, when the economic base shifted—from tobacco to cotton, say—and the action moved elsewhere. The slow-paced elegance of the old Confederacy existed only in such places as Lexington; elsewhere it was either decay and poverty or growth and bustle, with a new generation of businessmen in the saddle.

The older, traditional towns that had resisted industry retained a mellow beauty because they had grown at a leisurely pace, in contrast to the Gopher Prairies that were thrown up in a new land. In the traditional towns, business was not king; there were, to be sure, canny merchants living in them who knew the value of a dollar—and clutched each and every one of them they made. But the town aristocracy did not let upstart businessmen get out of hand; they clung (selfishly) to an older sense of beauty and fitness that clashed with modernity and served to prevent its excesses.

Still, in the larger, more prosperous towns, commerce and aesthetics were not always in opposition. Large buildings were erected that had style and inspired genuine community pride. The county courthouses were elaborate, imposing, domed structures, many built in this period. New commercial buildings or "blocks" benefited from the new architecture. The Italianate style was frequently employed in the 1880s, and was well adapted to producing an elegant facade on a row of buildings, with bracketed, overhanging cornices, rows of arched windows, occasional columned arcades, raspberry-brick fronts, and stone trim and ornamentation (which later gave way to cast iron and pressed tin). These blocks had the name of the owner carved into a prominent corner, as well as the date of their completion, as though he were proudly signing the work his money had wrought. The Queen Anne style was not as adaptable to stores, although its turrets and brick fancywork were in evidence—most prominently in courthouses and clock towers. Sometimes a stylistically unified "block" would occupy a large section of a square, lending beauty and elegance. There were, of course, cheaper brick buildings of little distinction randomly mixed in, but sometimes they could combine along a section of street to create at least an uncluttered effect, a pleasing low line against the sky. The increased use of plate glass and the restrained store signs, painted in gilt letters on a black background or employing brass letters and block calligraphy, added an atttractive element to the general picture. One sees these brick stores and blocks of the eighties and nineties today on Main Streets through the Middle West; they have endured and in their time were the characteristic, vernacular American architecture. Not as lovely perhaps as an old English town's Tudor timbers or unified rows of stone houses and stores but, in their modest way, attractive—and durably so, as modern restorations reveal. Often there is a unity of style because in periods of prosperity whole new sections of buildings would go up on Main Street—or, in some cases, after devastating fires, the chief impetus to urban renewal in the nineteenth century.

And even when Main Street lacked uniformity, it was being most true to itself. It was the central axis of the town's grid pattern, the main artery through which the lifeblood of the town flowed—its commerce, its parades, its ceremonies. Its people met, talked, shopped along it. It was totally pragmatic in design, its character dictated by no prince or patron or philosopher-king architect; it was, in other words, democratic, reflecting the free play of the marketplace, a hundred decisions of individual entrepreneurs. It grew by increments to meet new needs; it might even change drastically as the town changed in function from a trading to a manufacturing center. "Neither a sense of history nor a sense of obligation toward the future trammeled its youthful vigor,"[98] wrote the architectural historian Carole Rifkind. It reflected the philosophy of the town builders, who put practicality and development first; Americans "will habitually prefer the useful to the beautiful," Tocqueville wrote, "and they will require that the beautiful shall be useful."[99] And so there was a unifying, if haphazard, aesthetic at work that is discernible in hindsight. It was a kind of embellished practicality, created by anonymous local builders who were inspired sometimes by designs of distant architects in the plan books and builders' magazines or else by purely functional and pecuniary considerations.

In part the problem of Main Street was spiritual, a sense of deadening civic apathy reflected in the dirty streets and unkempt layabouts. The Carol Kennicotts dreamed of romantic European villages; like Hamlin Garland, they hungered for the charm and excitement of distant places and escaped to Europe only to find the life there alien and remote. The aversion to Main Street was more than to "beef-red brick and faded clapboards,"[100] as novelist Glenway Westcott put it, more than distaste for the ugly architecture per se; it was a hunger for wider vistas, whether aesthetic, cultural, or career, than Main Street offered. Main Street itself was not malign in its ugliness; it only seemed so: The solution to its ugliness was really nothing more complicated than the will to pave it, clean it up, and mute the cacophony of commerce, thus revealing a humble practical beauty (and Main Street, it must be admitted, had much to be humble about). The venerable charm of a European village was not there, but instead a plain American character that needed emphasizing and, above all, time to mellow it. But the rebels did not have time, just as the builders of Main Street did not, and so time did its work at its own pace without them.

Even back in the 1890s amenities were appearing on Main Street. Paving, for one thing. In the evolution of the art, town Main Streets passed through the dirt into the cobblestone or macadam (crushed rock) stage, followed by an oiled surface over macadam, followed by brick or Belgian blocks or even cedarwood blocks, which was the quietest surface in the carriage days. Each of these materials had early flaws, but advances in the art made them more practical. By the 1900s many towns had smooth streets of vitrified brick, which avoided the ruts and grooves of earlier paving in which water and horse urine would collect, and was reasonably quiet when heavy carts passed over it. Of course the pavement might stop abruptly at the edge of town, where the streets reverted to the primal dirt.

Regular street cleaning gradually followed hard-surfaced streets; it was inadequate at first, often merely spreading the horse dung around; eventually, though, farm animals were banned from streets in many towns, and besides the automobile had replaced them. Another sign of progress, small as it may seem, was the passing of ordinances against spitting in the street. Such sanitary ordinances were the work of the village improvement societies that sprang up after the Civil War, usually sparked by the women of the town.

They agitated for further clean streets and sidewalks, placed litter baskets around, demanded regular garbage collection, planted trees and flowers in parks, and called for benches, horse troughs, drinking fountains, rest rooms, and similar facilities. Women were behind most of the civic-improvement activities of the nineteenth century; beauty, after all, was woman's domain, like the moral crusades. The town fathers were constitutionally averse to spending town funds on such luxuries. During the Progressive Era, reformers urged city and town governments to provide street-cleaning, garbage collection and other services that the women had fought for and that the town fathers had thought unnecessary and too expensive. Progressivism and economic self-interest among downtown merchants also helped bring municipally provided services into being. Such common benefits elevated the importance of the town government, but resistance to higher real-estate taxes among the businessmen kept beautification from getting out of hand—or off the ground.

Traffic, however, was getting out of hand, even in the horse era, with all those carts and drays going to and from the station. It was no wonder that the automobile in its early innocent days seemed by comparison a rather benign apparatus. There were complaints about the arrogance of the owners, who, as one commentator put it, "think that [the automobile] gives them not merely the right of way, but all the way there is,"[101] and towns sought to limit speeds to twelve miles per hour. In some places automobilists banded together in clubs, like the motorcycle clubs of today, though without their hoodlum image, for these were the well-off respectable folk of the town. They would meet and embark upon long excursions on a Sunday through the countryside, monopolizing country roads and scaring the horses. As to the latter problem, Professor Frederick R. Hutton, who taught engineering at Columbia University School of Mines, had this advice: "I always examine the horse coming towards me, and if he seems nervous or shy, I stop at the side of the road and speak to him."[102] Most drivers were undoubtedly less kind; after all, as Dr. William Howard wrote, many were suffering from "speed mania," which was the irresistible desire to dash along public highways, an "objective symptom of the high nervous tension" of modern life.[103] For all the drivers' speed mania, what would be short trips today were then major expeditions because of the primitive state of country roads. Drivers fitted themselves out for trips as though they were going to Afghanistan—women in linen dusters and large hats with a sheer silk veil or even goggles, men in dusters, fur-rimmed goggles, and a large, flat, brimmed tweed cap. There was an etiquette of the road, which ordained that two cars meeting one another exchange salutes—gentlemen touching their caps, ladies bowing slightly but perceptibly. No matter that one could not recognize the occupants of the other car in their goggles and veils, "it was quite simply assumed that anyone encountered en route, also in an automobile, must certainly be an acquaintance or, if not an acquaintance, someone one should *know*."[104] Automobiles were the playthings of the rich, and so fellow owners were bound to be of one's own social station.

The days of noisome fumes that fouled the air, threatening to strangulate Main Street itself, were still in the future. At the turn of the century local transportation still had charm—bicycles silently passing in the night, their lamps winking like fireflies, Booth Tarkington recalled; the crisp hoofbeats of a spirited animal pulling a swain and his girl in a trim buggy, the solid clop-clop of a heavy-footed dray horse. At night the streets were leisurely places, and in summertime strollers took the air or sat in the park under the bright gas lamps. Men gathered at some central place—in front of the drugstore, in the back room of a hospitable store, along the curb in front of a saloon, at the courthouse square, to talk politics, crops, religion; women sat on benches gossiping; boys and girls whizzed around on roller skates, the metal wheels whirring and clacking against concrete. On Saturday nights, when the farmers came to town, shops were open and streets were crowded with the country people in their town clothes, while women shopped and children walked about starry-eyed at the urban wonders. "When the weather permitted, all the inhabitants of the village would . . . be 'down town' as the main street was known on Saturday nights, shopping, gossiping, mothers with infants in arms or pulling small children along by hand on the rough board-walks,"[105] as Mark Schorer recalled Sauk City, Wisconsin. Saturday night, wrote Glenway Westcott, was to the farm people "the sweet reward of the long week's labor; it is their opera, drama, their trip to Zanzibar."[106]

Another center and loafing place was the depot, where people gathered to see the trains come in, or just watch the huge black locomotives exhaling steam in great explosive sighs, while they took in water from the water tower. Local reporters were assigned to the depot "beat," interviewing those coming and going, like the shipping-news reporters in the big cities who met ocean liners. The depot area might be the town's alternate vital center, where hotels for traveling men, with their flashy sophistication, were located—a secondary hub, a link with the outside world, a place of dreams of distant places and banshee train whistles in the night, the steady roar and clicking of the wheels, the pistons chanting "You are missing something missing something missing something . . . something . . . something. Out there."

On Friday and Saturday nights there would likely be band concerts in the new pavilion in the park, and the people would move in close, sit and listen to the men in their natty, colorful uniforms play Sousa marches and Strauss waltzes and "After the Ball" and "In the Shade of the Old Apple Tree." "What does a band mean to a town? Better to ask what is a town without a band,"[107] said Sherwood Anderson. The town band was a typical product of town pride, an object of rivalry with other towns; but it was also entertainment and the exemplar of unity and morale. The town band traveled to other towns as official emissary and in its own town played at ceremonial occasions, parades, reunions, fairs, lodge picnics, or in the pit for visiting *artistes* at the opera house. But a band's gold-braided uniforms and silver instruments could be costly (silver was thought to have a better tone than brass, and so "silver cornet bands" were preferred to brass bands). The town allotted some financial support, but it was minimal and often had to be supplemented by fund drives. Revenue from admission charges at concerts helped, but band members (who, of course, worked at other jobs) paid their own way on trips. Town bands had their heyday at the turn of the century, but went into gradual decline, to be replaced eventually by the local high school's aggregation.

Singing was popular in an era when families still gathered about the piano. Mark Schorer recalled that "it was the piano that unlocked the double doors" of the family's prim parlor "and let some warmth into that room."[108] His mother, who had had ambitions to become a singer, played and sang in a pure soprano, and his father joined in with his "strained tenor," while Schorer and his brother listened "in that seldom-used room" looking through the "strange, seldom-examined books" kept in the parlor. There was sheet music for the popular tunes of the day—the morbid, lugubrious ballads of Victorian inspiration, like "In the Baggage Car Ahead" and "She's More to Be Pitied than Censured," or romantic love and courting ballads, like "Oh Promise Me" and "On a Bicycle Built for Two," which stayed well within moral bounds with their descriptions of at most a kiss or a chaste embrace; however, the urban temptations of ragtime were appearing on the scene—and were promptly denounced by moral guardians. The ballad—a secular adaptation of the hymn—was designed for parlor singing. It had a standard melodic line that was kept within the bounds of an octave and so was easy for untrained voices to sing; the simple chord structure also made it easy to play.

Paralleling the interest in parlor songs was the popularity of choral singing. Muncie had four men's choral societies in the 1890s. One met every Sunday afternoon and Thursday evening to sing, with the inspiration of a keg of beer and a hired instructor. In Hastings, a fifty-voice chorus, sixteen-piece orchestra, and four soloists (two local and two imported from Omaha) presented the oratorio *The Holy City* in 1902; and in other towns similarly ambitious programs were presented by choral societies with a professional director. There was also in nearly every town a male quartet, available for weddings, funerals, and other occasions.

Among the younger set, serenading was a popular pastime, with groups going from one house to another to regale the occupants with song. A young baker's diary shows how music was an intimate part of bachelor doings in Muncie, Indiana ca. 1890. One night he goes to a house to serenade; on another the "gang" assembles for "singing, guitar, mouth harp, piano, cake, bananas, oranges and lemonade" and another day a fellow union member "set up cigars and a keg"[109] at the union hall and all present sang and played cards till eleven. At lawn fetes and family reunions there was song.

Women singers, sometimes professionals, were on hand to sing in church, at weddings, and other occasions. Mary Wilkins Freeman's story "A Village Singer" tells of a singer, paid by the local church, who is displaced by a younger woman when the congregation decides her voice has faded with age. The ousted woman, who lives next door to the church, retaliates by playing her organ and singing whenever her successor is performing. After the new singer's sweetheart—the older woman's nephew—angrily tells her to stop, her resistance collapses. She takes to her bed and languishes away—but not before making a poignant speech to the minister about callously discarding old people.

By the 1890s the church was no longer the center of song; singing had spread to the home, to the choir societies, and, on Main Street itself, to the town's opera hoouse, which every town with any pride had erected. Of course, the term "opera house" was something of a misnomer, since grand opera was rarely presented. The opera house (sometimes called "music hall" or "academy of music") was primarily a theater, where traveling theatrical and vaudeville companies appeared, lecturers spoke, and local talent events were held. The word "theater" had a connotation of urban sin, a prejudice deriving from Puritan days, but "opera" sounded high-toned and cultural, so the proprietors used the name in deference to local public opinion and good morals. Occasionally a Gilbert and Sullivan troupe might play the opera house, but that was generally as close as it got to opera. Hastings's Kerr Opera House opened in 1894, but it was not until 1917 that the San Carlo Opera Company came to town to present *Rigoletto, Cavalleria rusticana,* and *Pagliacci.*

Like hotels, railroads, and other civic improvements, opera houses were often financed by stock subscriptions; prominent townspeople bought shares out of civic duty, in order to furbish the town's cultural reputation. Sometimes a wealthy local citizen put up all the money, in exchange for the honor of having the opera house called after him. Whether a civic enterprise or a private one, opera houses were not notably profitable investments, and most lived a precarious existence after the initial novelty and glamor wore off.

In many towns the opera house was located on the second floor of a new block, which had a bank, offices, shops, and even apartments on its other floors; bigger towns might even erect an entire building solely for the opera house, which was the town's palace of culture, its center of entertainment. Such structures represented a step beyond the bare wooden stages in churches or lodge halls where visiting troupes had to perform. In one town the audience had sat on planks resting on nail kegs, with two patchwork quilts serving as curtains.

From these rough beginnings, it was a giant step to the opulent palaces erected in Iowa, as described by Lewis Atherton:

> During the late 1870s and early 1880s many Iowa opera houses contained elevated dress circles, which curved in horseshoe fashion to boxes

> on both sides of a proscenium arch. Ornate Corinthian iron posts supported enormous balconies. Garishly decorated side walls and ornate gilt scrollwork on boxes, on the railings in balcony and gallery, and sometimes on the proscenium arch itself, impressed audiences with the rich abandon of their surroundings. A dome of gas jets in crystal globes gave off a dazzling display when lighted by ushers with tapers on long poles before audiences assembled and again between acts. Advertisements of local mercantile firms bracketing the sides of the stage were dwarfed to proper size by competition from stage curtains of rich blue or red, caught and draped back in gorgeous folds by painted gold ropes with enormous tassels. Iowa's elite occupied the better seats in such opera houses—men with sideburns, walrus moustaches, or full beards, only a few smooth shaven. They wore stylish clothes—long-skirted coats, trousers from which the crease had been carefully removed [creased trousers were considered plebeian, because they had lain on the haberdasher's shelf; hence, they were "ready-made" and also known, invidiously, as "hand-me-downs"], straight, stiff collars, and wide four-in-hand ties. Their feminine companions were partial to bangs and dressed in funny little bonnets, tight waists, voluminous skirts, and enormous bustles.[110]

Not all opera houses were so luxurious. The Concert Hall in Beaver Dam, Wisconsin, was simply a ninety-foot-long room, with a stage and proscenium arch at one end and folding chairs for the audience to sit on. One reached it by climbing the stairs to the second floor of the block in which was located, walking past a tavern, a lawyer's office, the office of the Beaver Dam *Citizen*, and thence up to the ticket window. After purchasing a ticket, one then climbed another flight of stairs and found one's seat in the auditorium. There were kerosene footlights, a curtain with a standard view of the Bay of Naples, and a few basic flats that were used over and over no matter what play was being presented.

However luxuriously or shabbily appointed, the opera house also served as a community center, political forum, lecture hall, little theater, concert hall, and recital hall for young students of dance, music, elocution, or whatever, with their proud parents serving as a paying audience; it was used as a roller-skating rink, vaudeville theater, movie theater, and auditorium for high school commencements and band concerts. Through the years, the range of entertainment, education and inspiration was staggering—cliff-hanging melodramas like *East Lynne* with virtue-triumphant heroes and ultimately defeated villains, whose earlier standard red-lined capes gave way to a cooly-puffed cigarette as a distinguishing prop; slide shows and travelogues; acrobatic troupes; minstrel shows; Shakespearean tragedians; temperance lectures by Neal Dow, Susan B. Anthony, and Frances Willard; lectures on phrenology; speeches and lectures by such celebrities as P.T. Barnum (who spoke on "The Art of Money-Getting, or Success in Life," but did not forget to anathematize smoking and drinking whiskey); Ralph Waldo Emerson; Theodore Tilton, a Negro known as "the infant Hercules of American freedom" who was a popular speaker on the subject of Negro suffrage; Mark Twain; Josh Billings; Frederick Douglass; William Jennings Bryan; humorists like James Whitcomb Riley and Bill Nye; and many more. It was, on the whole, a lively show which gave small-town audiences clean, unsophisticated, and uplifting entertainment and instruction tailored to their tastes—as well as a frisson of melodramatic thrills, a glimpse human oddities, echoes of faraway places, and the excitement of having sinful showfolk in town (although in earlier days visiting players sequestered themselves in their rooms, rarely venturing out except to perform; in this way they believed that by not mixing with the public they retained an aura of mystery). There was even a little decorous sex (like the dance of the seven veils in a production of *Salome* that scandalized folks in Louis Bromfield's boyhood Ohio town, although the actress who performed the dance wore flesh-colored long johns and was of an advanced age). The dominant impression one gets is that the average opera house owner had to hustle to keep his head above water, renting out his hall to anything that moved, talked, sang, danced, or otherwise publicly exhibited itself in a manner not lewd or offensive to local taste. The surefire draws—star performers such as Walter Keene or Mrs. Fiske or Sarah Bernhardt—could be had only for a substantial guarantee, which could make engaging them risky in small places; the same was true of elaborate stage or musical productions. Hence, the owner had to book the seedier acts and the charlatans too. At any rate, with the coming of the motion pictures, radio, and phonograph the opera house's cultural preeminence in small-town life rapidly faded, and the American theater, which had, through its touring companies, become the mass entertainment of its day, receded to the big cities.

The history of the Kerr Opera House in Hastings recapitulates the ups and downs of the opera house business in general. It began in a fanfare of trumpet blasts and went out with a whimper fifty years later. In the early 1880s, when Hastings was in the midst of a building boom, a local banker named William Kerr, who was appropriately Scotland-born and had arrived in town with sufficient thriftily accumulated capital to start his bank, announced that he was erecting an opera house at a projected cost of sixty-one thousand dollars—far more than the town's previous grandest structure, the Masonic Hall, which only cost thirty thousand dollars. The Kerr structure was a block, however, and also contained offices, a saloon and Kerr's Adams County bank. The opening night audience marveled at its gilt trim, chandelier, and thick velvet curtain—not to mention its gaslights and the two steam boilers in the basement which were proudly claimed to provide "summer heat" in the middle of winter. Still, with all the attendant ballyhoo, on opening night, December 23, 1884, the operetta *The Queen's Lace Handkerchief* did not draw a full house. After that, the opera house survived through the years, presenting traveling troupes in popular stage plays, local theater groups, musical programs, political conventions, and eventually movies, as it spanned two entertainment eras. Popular stars in popular vehicles, like Walter Whiteside in *The Typhoon* in 1913, sold out the newly remodeled house; the three operas presented by the traveling San Carlo Opera Company in 1917 drew good audiences.

But despite these individual successes the opera house seemed unable to engage a loyal following; its presentations probably fell iinto some kind of vaguely high-brow never-never land. There were never enough prime theatrical spectacles on tour to draw continuing large audiences, and Kerr seemed unable to tap the low-brow audience. The Scotsman nonetheless devoted all his spare time to the opera house—he and his wife even performed janitorial duties. Perhaps because of such thrift, when Kerr died in 1907, he left an estate of three hundred thousand dollars to his son, Tom, in addition to the opera house. But, for reasons that aren't clear, Kerr's widow had Tom declared mentally incompetent, and took over the opera house until her death in 1913. Others managed it while poor Tom drifted in and out of institutions until 1928, when a cousin successfully petitioned to have him declared sane. Reluctant to live in Hastings because of the stigma of his past and unwilling to spend the necessary money on refurbishing the now seedy palace of culture, Tom told his cousin to convert the building into shops and offices. In a rundown part of town, the building failed as an office, and its final curtain was demolishment.

The opera house provided a window on the essentially urban world of theater and music—but a small one. Imported entertainment remained the icing on the cake of small-town culture in the 1890s. Much of the leisure-time activity was still homegrown. Young people had their hayrides and sleigh rides, their ice-skating in winter and swimming in summer, their dances, and ice cream sociables and boating parties. Families went on camping trips in the summer, or to the increasingly popular lakeside homes, if there was a lake nearby. There were excursions by train or interurban to nearby cities for shopping or entertainment. Little theater groups proliferated in the 1900s. Men had their lodges and discussion groups, their saloons and sporting houses. Women had church work and reading and sewing clubs.

Many towns in the nineties took pride in their town baseball team, which had fierce rivalries with other towns; it was not unheard of for the home team to fire an umpire it was displeased with in the middle of the game and replace him with a more sympathetic arbiter. Sunday baseball became a crucial moral issue in many places. At first banned, it was so popular that the town fathers began to bend the rules. One compromise was to allow Sunday games, so long as the band played hymns between innings. The old Puritan prohibitions against Sunday activities were falling away, and it was increasingly becoming a day of games, as well as meetings, rallies, picnics, and speeches.

There was an astonishing tolerance for oratory in those slower-paced times.

There seemed to be no public occasion, however minor, at which a speaker or two did not hold forth. An ice-cream sociable and a funeral called for oratory; it might take six or eight speakers to dedicate a new building properly. Such civic occasions were well attended, and the people expected to sit back and listen to an inspiring speech, and a long one. During his travels in America during the 1880s, James Bryce noted that no gathering was complete without someone "offering a few remarks . . . upon anything in heaven and earth, which may rise to his mind."[111] If there was no occasion, well, the speech itself could serve as one. People would show up to hear a speaker even if his subject was not announced in advance, and conversely, popular speeches could be repeated at a later date with no diminution in the house. Meredith Nicholson recalled the all-day political rallies in the Middle West, "where one or two hundred people of all parties gather, drawn by an honest curiosity as to the issues."[112] The people would draw up before the speakers, stand in a grove and sit in their buggies or Model T's, listening to a day of oratory by candidates of both parties. The old political barbecue of pioneer days with its free food, copious whiskey, and fiery oratory (known as "shell the woods" or "burn the grass") was on its way out, Nicholson said.

Among laboring men there were socialist clubs where the ideas of Marx or Henry George or Edward Bellamy's *Looking Backward* were discussed. In his novel *Moon-Calf* Floyd Dell describes a rich variety of political thinkers—socialists, atheists, agnostics, and cranks—among his town's workingmen and craftsmen. Meredith Nicholson noted how industrialization stimulated the discussion of the new problems it created: "I remember my surprise to find not long ago that a small town I had known all my life had become an industrial center, where the citizens were gravely discussing their responsibilities to the laborers who had suddenly been added to the population."[113]

Talk itself was a primary form of amusement among small-town people, who loved to pass the time of day gossiping at the store or post office or depot. Gossip was a daily sustenance as well as a form of social control; it kept news circulating through the town's vital system, informing as well as evaluating. It concerned personalities, rather than ideas, and meted out praise and condemnation. "Gossip served as informal judge and jury, and it sat daily to pass on every individual in the town,"[114] Lewis Atherton remembered. Ed Howe said villagers heard the gossip about their sins on the way home from committing them—and said the omniscient eye of gossip made them behave. Gossip was a quintessential small-town avocation. For its full savor, it required firsthand knowledge of the person gossiped about—his or her quirks, beliefs, place in town society—even ancestors: it presupposed a continuity over time and ample moments of leisure.

Another oral tradition was the camp meeting of the pioneer era, where people assembled to listen to lengthy and usually gloomy predictions about their posthumous fate and to debate religion. These continued in more subdued form. Ministers' sermons, while not so long as in early Puritan towns, were still an hour or so in length, and people were expected to stay awake. Then there was the tradition of political oratory, of politics as a spectacle, with its torchlight parades down Main Street and campaign speeches and Fourth of July orations. At any rate, from gossip to oratory, small towns were oral cultures, and on public occasions the people liked speeches of moral uplift or patriotism, which repeated to them the simple pieties embedded in their own hearts. But they also liked debate and controversy, and turnouts for imported lecturers of national reputation was good. By the 1890s the earlier lecture circuits, such as the Lyceum movement and its epigoni, gave way to the chautauqua movement, which for a few brief decades brought speakers and performers to small towns all over the country.

Chautauqua derived its name from Lake Chautauqua, New York, where in 1874 a summer institute for Sunday-school teachers had been organized by Rev. John H. Vincent and Lewis Miller, a businessman. The institute began to present secular as well as spiritual speakers, while retaining an aura of religious uplift and morality. Soon a pavilion had been erected by the lake, and people came by the thousands to sit in the shade and listen to a variety of speakers holding forth on subjects in which they had expertise. It was adult education fortified by a religious sanction. The idea spread; by 1900 over two hundred communities in thirty-one states had their own permanent pavilions by a lake or in the park. Then Keith Vawter, who ran a lyceum bureau in Cedar Rapids, Iowa, and J. Roy Ellison, who had one in Omaha, Nebraska, teamed up to book chautauqua speakers into small towns that lacked a pavilion. The idea was to have a traveling circuit of speakers and performers, like a vaudeville circuit, going from one town to the next on a regular schedule. Vawter and Ellison's troupes carried their own tents—used circus tents the partners had bought up—and seven tents and performers were on tour through the summer, each performing seven days in a town, then moving on. With seven shows every day drawing an average audience of a thousand apiece, the profits were high. The speakers and other members of the "troupe" had guaranteed employment throughout the summer.

Vawter and Ellison had added a wrinkle to their scheme that made it a guaranteed money-maker. They sent out advance men who would, by appealing to local pride, persuade town businessmen to put up a guarantee of $2,000 to $2,500 a week. Such guarantees had been the bane of opera house owners when demanded by theatrical stars from the big city, but Ellison and Vawter got them, for they understood the small-town mind. The historian William L. Shirer, who grew up in Cedar Rapids and worked for Vawter and Ellison, described the technique. The two impresarios hired ministers as advance men, and they pitched their appeal to community pride: "No mention of any profits the Redpath-Vawter chautauqua might be interested in. Not a word about the local committee taking all the risks and Vawter taking all the profits. With a zealousness he had learned in the pulpit he would convince these local Babbitts that as the 'leaders of the community' they owed it to their town to bring again next summer this marvelous institution of uplift, culture and inspiration." Should the prospects begin having second thoughts when it came time to put up the money, the advance man would say: "I will be frank with you. We have a long waiting list. There are dozens of towns in this part of the state, some of them not far, which are awfully envious of you. If I offered them this contract I'm now presenting you, they would sign it in a minute. They're dying to have chautauqua in their community."[115]

The tactic usually worked, for chautauqua was considered a wholesome, educational diversion for the entire family which also attracted business to the local merchants. During the quarter of a century it flourished, chautauqua thus managed to acquire the patronage of local businessmen, who in turn received the plaudits of the civic and religious-minded for presenting this unique mixture of education and uplift. In one town, the chautauqua got started after a revival meeting had drawn a good crowd; the transition from one to the other was considered a logical one evidently, for the next year a chautauqua came in.

In its heyday, chautauqua occupied the town's prominent people for an entire week. In some places people would set up tents on the chautauqua grounds; stores would deliver groceries for cooking out, and the local newspaper published a list of tent numbers so families could find each other and visit. A typical program might include Dr. Robert McIntyre and Sam Jones, ministers; the iron-constitutioned, leather-lunged, silver-tongued William Jennings Bryan; Robert M. La Follette, the Progressive party leader; the Slaton Jubilee Singers; the Dunbar Quartette and Bell Ringers; the First Regiment band and local bands. There might also be religious travelogues and slide shows, pipe bands, all-women orchestras, troubadours, an Italian band, speakers on health and government, movies, Bible talks, and programs especially for the children.

By World War I, however, chautauqua was already fading; it too would fall victim to movies, radio, and other twentieth-century distractions—not to mention the advent of a more sophisticated generation that found the familiar formula rather old-fashioned. But in its prime, chautauqua mirrored small-town values perfectly; it was a kind of earlier, traveling *Reader's Digest*, successfully mixing information, entertainment, and inspiration. It had elements of the old camp meeting, but its comfortable middle-class pieties reflected the local churches, which were beginning to become more secular and loosening their moral stays just a bit, while quietly consigning the hellfire old-time religion to the evangelical sects patronized by the poor people in town. In Wilmington, Canby noticed that religion was increasingly a matter of ritual, rather than spiritual conviction: "We went to church neither to be social, nor to be good, nor, save for brief intervals, to be uplifted, but because of something much deeper than any of these motives, a taboo against staying away that had kept its power although its inner significance was lost. . . . It was custom, which is a step deeper than use and wont, that sent us to church after church began to be meaningless."[116] In less traditional communities, the attitude was blunter—religion was primarily good for real-estate values and business. As Page Smith put it, "In the drive to 'socialize' the churches, less and less attention was paid to the doctrinal and theological side of the churches' life and more and more to 'activities.' There was a growing emphasis on music and on liturgical aspects of church services. Sermons became, in many instances, tepid moralizings."[117] These changes occurred over the long haul, but they suggest why chautauqua, with its mixture of music, homogenized social and political thought, uplift, and religiously inclined entertainment, plus its patronage by the business establishment, was in the mainstream of small-town attitudes. It was, in its way, a transitional form of entertainment, locally sponsored yet involving imported live talent—a link between the local, oral culture and a "packaged" national one.

More direct and elemental in its appeal was another great event—this one brazenly proclaiming its exoticism, its glamor. This was the circus, a pageantry of exotic sights and sounds that crowded the memories of every child who grew up in those days. As Lewis Atherton firmly puts it, "Of all attractions, the circus held first place, its popularity being so great as to place it in a class by itself."[118] In his latter days, when he took a sour view of much of the world, Ed Howe wrote: "There have been a few wonderful events in my life, and heading the list is the performance given by Miles Orton's circus in Bethany, Missouri."[119] William Dean Howells, Mark Twain, Hamlin Garland all accord it similar fond tributes in their memoirs. Garland wrote in his memoir of growing up in Iowa in the 1870s, *Boy Life on the Prairie*, "No one but a country boy can rightly measure the majesty and allurement of a circus. To go from lonely prairie or the dusty corn-field and come face to face with the 'amazing aggregation of world-wide wonders' was like enduring the visions of the Apocalypse."[120] His reference to the "amazing aggregation" is, of course, a quotation from the inimitable assonant, alliterative, hyperbolic prose of the circus handbills, which in Garland's area the advance man would fling over fences into cornfields where farmers were working and also post prominently in the town. Circuses usually came in June, and their arrival was the greatest of all events, eclipsing even the Fourth of July celebrations and the county fairs.

Early on the long-awaited day, Garland and his family would pile into their wagon and join a stream of other wagons heading to the town, where early arrivals were already jostling through the streets. Town boys had spent every waking moment hanging around the field where the roustabouts were erecting the tents, the lucky ones helping out with odd jobs like carrying water to the elephants. But one more preliminary event remained: the big parade through town. To Garland—

> this was not a piece of shrewd advertising. . . . It began somewhere—the country boys scarcely knew where—far in the mystery of the East

> and passed before their faces. . . . It trailed a glorified dust, through which foolish and slobbering camels, and solemn and kingly lions, and mournful and sinister tigers, moved, preceded by the mountainous and slow-moving elephants, two and two, chained and sullen, while closely following, keeping step to the jar of great drums and the blaring voices of trumpets, ladies, beautiful and haughty of glance, with firmly-moulded busts, rode on parti-colored steeds with miraculous skill, their voices sounding small in the clangor of the streets. They were accompanied by knights corseletted in steel, with long plumes floating from their gleaming helmets. They, too, looked over the lowly people of the dusty plains with lofty and distainful glance. Even the drivers on the chariots seemed weary and contemptuous as they swayed on their high seat.[121]

While the more sophisticated town boys capered about at the edges of the parade, "the country boys could only stand and look, transfixed with pleasure and pain—the pleasure of looking upon it, the pain of seeing it pass."[122] Garland goes on in this vein, his memories mixing the fabulous and the real so that the parade seems half dream, as perhaps it was. After the bright red-and-gold wagons and the piping steam calliope had at last made their way up Main Street and around the square once or twice, they departed, leaving the appetites of onlookers whetted. Hamlin—or "Lincoln" as he calls himself in the book—is jostled out of his reverie by his father's proposal of dinner, and the family goes off to have a picnic meal.

After the meal, the family ventures to the midway, a riot of flags, huge white tents, colorful signs advertising the "ossified man" or the "cigarette fiend," who smokes a hundred packs a day, or Madame Ogoleda, the snake-woman, or "the fattest boy in the world" or Professory Henry, "court wizard of Beelzebub himself . . . magician of Mahomet," the air alive with the tumultuous cries of the barkers. The boys cling to their father amidst the clamorous entreaties and lures assaulting them from every quarter. The whirl of sensations in Lincoln's brain is stilled for a time when the staunch town sheriff's arrest of a card sharp diverts him. As he enters the big top, "the breathless interest of the morning was gone. The human drama before the sideshow had put the wonders of the menagerie on a different plane,"[123] but gradually the powerful spell of the circus reasserts itself. Entranced, he watches the graceful equestrians and acrobats; he finally departs: "The day had been too exciting. His head was throbbing with pain, and the smells of the animal tent were intolerable. . . . His brain was a whirling wheel, wherein all his impressions were blurred into bands of gray and brown and gold and scarlet."[124] The memory of the circus will stay with this prairie boy always. "Lincoln had a dream now, that the world was wide, and filled with graceful men and wondrous women as well as with innumerable monsters and glittering harsh-throated birds and slumbrous serpents. Some day, when he was a man, he would go forth and look upon the realities of his dream."[125]

In Garland's novel *Rose of Dutcher's Coolly*, the heroine is inspired by the graceful beauty of an acrobat to flee her hometown. One can hardly say that in real life circuses precipitated a mass migration to the city, or even that there were many young people affected like Rose was. But the popularity of the circus and the vivid impressions it made on so many is a testimonial to the power of its appeal. The glamour and excitement of its spectacle was heightened by the contrast to the drabness and boredom of country life.

The circus was splendid and alien, a bacchanal of exotic impressions, beauty and sin and spectacle all intermingled. But by the 1890s the circus was in decline—or at least the small traveling circuses that stopped in prairie towns. Big circuses, such as Ringling Brothers or Barnum and Bailey, had simply too much overhead for a sojourn in a small town to be profitable; the large shows traveled by rail and could play only the towns located along the line.

Realizing the lure of the circus, the sponsors of county fairs and fall festivals borrowed some of their attractions. Sideshows, games of chance, and other amusements were added to the traditional cattle-judging contests, farm implement exhibitions and displays of home-canned peaches and strawberry preserves. Later, local merchants might simply import a carnival alone, which would set up its attractions in the downtown area and stimulate business. But most county fairs tried to carry forth the tradition of the agricultural fair, while adding entertainment and sometimes spice in the form of risqué attractions not normally permitted in town but helpful in insuring a profit for the midway.

Throughout the Great Plains these agricultural fair-carnivals became fall festivals, and there arose a vogue for dubbing the event with an Indian-sounding name which was actually tthe name of the county spelled backward; thus the Adams County, Nebraska, festival was called Yt-Nuoc-Smada (Omaha had already preempted Ak-Sar-Ben). The 1910 Yt-Nuoc-Smada was held from October 10 through 15 and included a stock show, farm products exhibit, farmers' institute, domestic science and corn shows, parades, floats, decorations, and balls with kings and queens and their courts. The county historian does not mention the midway attractions, but perhaps they were similar to those of the Mardi Gras Carnival Company, which traveled about the Middle West with a bill that included the Amaza show (woman on a flying trapeze and magician); the Electric Theater (motion pictures, which were still a touring attraction and wonder, but being domesticated into local theaters); the Old Plantation tent with minstrel acts; plus a Ferris wheel, a penny arcade, a merry-go-round, a snake pit, and "a show picturing the bombardment and surrender of Port Arthur,"[126] among other amusements. Adams County's event unleashed nocturnal revelers, and the local paper reported: "Everybody was out for a good time and nobody allowed his dignity to interfere with the process. Tons of confetti were showered on unsuspecting spectators. Whistles of all conceivable kinds were used to keep up a continuous pandemonium. But withal, it was an orderly, good-natured crowd, bent merely on fun. There was a prospect of a disturbance when a score of young folks got into the middle of the street and began giving an imitation of an Indian tribe on the way to battle. Police Chief Widmaier took the leaders to one side and gave them a lesson in carnival etiquette which caused the immediate disruption of the bank."[127]

In the late nineteenth century most county fairs had their climax in hotly contested, eagerly awaited harness races, which drew the best animals and drivers on the state circuit. Those smart-stepping trotters and pacers, with drivers in their fragile sulkies and colorful shirts, provided grace and excitement. The center of many a town's fairgrounds was a wooden grandstand and race track, where races were held in spring, summer, and fall, with the county fair meet the world series of the season. On the final day, families brought picnic baskets and arrived early to pack the gray, weathered-lumber grandstand, with its splintering wooden seats, or else crowded close by the track so that, when the horses came pounding into the stretch, the marshals had to yell at them to get back and give them room. As the horses neared the finish line, the entire grandstand stood and cheered; plenty of bets were riding. The horses had been specially bred and trained, some on farms in the county; they were the cream of local horsedom. For lovers of the breed—and the bet—the county fair was merely an adjunct to the racing; indeed, in one stuffy New England town a smart horseman organized an agricultural society, so that it might have fairs, at which, not incidentally, there would be horse racing. He knew that the local bluenoses would not stand for horse racing alone.

The county fair was perhaps the earliest communal event in many country towns of the East and Middle West; but its original purposes got lost along the way. Where once it had had an educational function for the farmer, it became increasingly just another event sponsored by town businessmen to boost trade—like all the various "days" in honor of some local product, such as sauerkraut day, or the Wild West Festivals in towns that had not known a cowboy, or Old Settlers Days in towns where the relics of the pioneering past had been cast aside to make way for Progress. Country boys who would ultimately leave the farm to work in a factory had less interest in agricultural exhibits anyhow, and were looking for more citified attractions. The merchants obliged with the meretricious glitter of the midway, where sharpers fleeced country boys with rigged wheels or stacked decks, where gambling and drunkenness replaced the innocent revels described at the Adams County Fair. There was increasing competition from the state fairs too, which became expensive extravaganzas. The advent of the Model T meant that country folk could drive to them. The small towns fought back with increased midway attractions, until the agricultural part of the fair became the sideshow, and the sideshow became the main attraction—and eventually the whole show. University extension services, the Department of Agriculture's county agent, and the Farm Bureau would take over the fairs' educational mission to the farmers, and Future Farmers of America and Four H

Clubs would work with the young people. The county fair's decline was another reminder that little remained of the town's ties with the land but the cash nexus. (In fact, many towns took to holding trade fairs, devoted to celebrating the local industries.)

But small-town life in the nineties retained many traditions, rites of passage, ceremonies, and festivals. These carried in them, however diluted by modernity, a residue of more ancient village ways. Folk ceremonies, imbued with magic, superstition, religion, had once provided communal ritual—a sense of public occasion bearing deeper social and psychological meanings—in village life since time immemorial. These rituals, associated with planting, harvest, religious observances and ancient pagan ceremonies, gave rhythm and punctuation to daily life, and provided a sense of cohesion and continuity with the past. Only vestiges of the old ways remained, and other, newer occasions had been invented that served parallel functions. Their passing of the old ways marked a decline in the ties and continuities of the folk life; but the persistence of half-forgotten traditions, distorted out of all recognition, and the reinvention of substitute rites serving similar functions, though in a more attenuated, artificial way, showed that a perdurable core of emotion and custom remained, even as the towns entered a newer era marked by industrialization, urbanization, education, legalistic norms of behavior, and all the other symptoms of modernity.

And so there were still rites of passage marking birth, marriage, manhood and womanhood, death, each celebrated in ritualized ways before the whole community. And there were the holidays, with their accumulated baggage of lore, habit, and tradition, some centering around the family, some providing for public release of pent-up high spirits or somberer emotions.

All the high points of a person's life in a small town usually drew the notice of all of the community. When he or she was born, a doctor probably presided, except in the more backward areas, but the birth was usually at home, and neighbors were hovering in the wings to provide direct assistance or covered dishes and baked goods for the family; food in a small town was the universal coin of neighborliness. It served at deaths too, when bereaved families were overwhelmed with pies and cakes and casseroles, and invited the neighbors in to share the neighbors' own largesse. It was a time when most things were cooked in the home and were gladly given in the knowledge that others would do the same when the donor's time of trouble came.

The birth was duly announced in the local paper, which everybody read. After that, birthdays of both young and old would be celebrated with a party, or at least friends and neighbors looking in, as well as family. No presents were expected though.

The next great moment in the young man or woman's life was high school graduation. These had evolved into elaborate ceremonies, often lasting several days and closely covered on the front pages of the local paper, which also printed the pictures of each graduate. In 1906 the Crawfordsville, Indiana, high school commencement spanned ten days, during which a broad program of scholarly, social, and ceremonial activities took place. The formal occasions included the "promenade" or ball, followed by the baccalaureate, literary-society contest, class play, and graduation exercises. During the literary-society contest, the Polymnian Society defeated the Clionian in declamation and debate events; the class play was *As You Like It*. Then came commencement. The girls, their cheeks flushed with excitement, were dressed in crisp shirtwaists and long skirts, their long hair cut short in bangs in front or swept up in a pompadour, with the ample excess cascading down their backs. The boys wore dark suits and the throttling high collars of the day, which perhaps accounted for the pop-eyed look young men often have in contemporary photographs. The commencement ceremonies included musical selections and declamations by six seniors. The topics in 1906 were: "American Diplomacy," "A Neglected Bulwark," "Hysteria of Reform," "The Passing of a Nation," "The Rue We Wear," and "The Senate." It was a time for the deepest thoughts and grandiloquence these products of the local education system could summon up. In those days when there was no minimum school-leaving age and teachers flunked out the poor scholars, graduating from high school was a formidable peak of achievement. At last the diplomas were presented, and the seniors marched out two-by-two to the strains of "Pomp and Circumstance," their faces quicksilver studies in adult gravity alternating with uncontrollable adolescent grins.

Carved above the door of their school were the words "Enter to Learn. Go Forth to Serve." High school had become a training ground for college or getting a living in ways that often would draw the graduate away from his hometown. The days when McGuffey's *Eclectic Readers* taught industry, frugality, piety, and morality to every small-town boy and girl were passing; McGuffey's strictures against pomp and wealth seemed old-fashioned. McGuffey had carried the credo to the Puritan village into the nineteenth century, and within the limits of his world view he served small-town life well. McGuffey taught that "village and country life surpassed the cities"[128] and that one should be contented with one's lot, however meager, and one's town, however small:

Then contented with my State,
Let me envy not the great,
Since true pleasures may be seen,
On a cheerful village green.[129]

But the world of McGuffey's *Reader*—a world of village smithies, horses and buggies, small merchants, town pumps, watering troughs, and village greens—had passed; McGuffey made no mention of factories and cities, except in cautionary tales where their evils were pointed out. Although the *Readers* were still in use in 1900, the world they depicted had gone; the high school graduate was trained, his footsteps aimed for wider worlds. As Page Smith points out: "Of 299 high school graduates [in Aton, Indiana] in the years from 1877 to 1910, ninety percent left the community. The high school did not provide the town with leaders; it simply encouraged migration to the cities. It brought in city ideas and city values. It loosened the ties of community; it gave the small-town boy or girl a kind of cosmopolitan contempt for the town with its pokey ways, its narrowness, and country manners. It encouraged restlessness as it discouraged ambition."[130] Smith contrasts the secular, modern values of high schools around the turn of the century with the ideals of latter-day covenanted communities like those of the Shakers and Mennonites, who fiercely resisted public education, sensing that it was a threat to their community. The modern educational system increasingly accentuated preparation for a job and adjustment to life, rather than traditional values. As a result, high school classes were like seedpods that ripened over the school terms, then opened at graduation and scattered to the winds.

But not only the schools were at fault; opportunities lay increasingly in the outer world, in the cities, where a host of managerial, bureaucratic, academic, and scientific jobs were opening up. A study by R.H. Knapp and H.B. Goodrich called *Origins of American Scientists* found that the small denominational colleges, so ubiquitous in the Middle West, did at first produce mainly teachers and ministers, but as years went by they became more secularized, their curriculums more specialized. As a result, science became more popular and, still later, law and medicine and managerial occupations. Other studies show that while the large universities and large cities produced the greatest number of business leaders, the small colleges and small towns produced a higher proportion of scientists. Noting that a striking number of scientists were grandsons of ministers and came from towns that had a strong early Puritan influence, Page Smith theorizes about the role the small town played: "Protestant orthodoxy and the psychology of the small town engendered an ideal of professional 'calling,' fluidity of social organization, and an ethic of service to the larger good that, in an increasingly materialistic and secular society, made science a most attractive field for young men from thousands of small-town communities.'"[131] Science, in other words, combined a Puritan sense of vocation, austere worship in a laboratory-church, and a self-abnegating devotion to a higher, impersonal, cooly implacable truth—a type precisely embodied in the hero of Sinclair Lewis's novel *Arrowsmith*.

Later, the small towns would produce a markedly high proportion of engineers; they did not, however, as popular myth had it, produce most of the nation's business leaders, for these increasingly came from big cities and suburbs. But for ambitious, inner-directed, upward-striving small-town boys, the next logical step up the social ladder would take them inevitably to the city. The pattern was as Canby suggested: the earlier generation of farm-born people moved to the towns, and the following generation sought its fortune in the cities. The town served as a kind of "staging area," a transitional point for the move from farm to city, over succeeding generations. To the farm boy, the city was still distant; but the town provided a stepping-stone. Smith comments that "as the farming population contracted, the importance of the town as an intermediary between the farm and city grew. The town, with its essentially rural tradition and its relatively sophisticated and complex social and cultural life, prevented the development of a rural peasantry in America and bridged what in most cultures has been a wide gap between farm and city."[132]

Smith's insight is acute, but the act of growing up in a small town in the 1890s was still a process of fitting into a coherent society grounded in a place, which had requirements and expectations that one in time met, resisted, evaded, or fled. The town was a little world with visible boundaries; it was made up of people whom you had known all your life and who knew you (and continually appraised you) in turn. Canby expresses this well:

> To us [the town] was a unity, indissoluble and unchangeable, like the Union. It was a culture with mores, it was a life in which one quickly knew one's place, and began that difficult weaving of one's emotions with experience that is called growing up, in a set of circumstances which one could not and did not really wish to alter. . . . The town waited for you. It was going to be there when you were ready for it. Its life seemed rich enough for any imagination. . . . You belonged—and it was up to your own self to find out how and where. There has been no such certainty in American life since.[133]

That certainty was ebbing. The life of Wilmington was ultimately not rich enough for Canby's immagination, for he studied at Yale, taught there, and then moved to New York, where he was cofounder of *The Saturday Review of Literature* in the 1920s. But even Thornton Wilder echoes this theme in *Our Town*, when he has Editor Webb say, "But our young people here seem to like it well enough: 90% of 'em graduating from High School settle down right here to live—even when they've been away to college."[134] This was the small-town dream; but even in New England it had never been true, from William Bradford's elegy to the "old town" of Plymouth whose citizens deserted it to the mass westward migrations in the nineteenth century on through 1901, the year in which *Our Town* is set.

And so graduation had an underlying poignance, which even the graduates in their moment of triumph felt in the back of their minds and which accounted for the tears that joined the laughter. Something was over; it was youth, of course, but also youth in that town for many of them. Such nostalgia was forgotten as they eagerly looked ahead, but it huddled down quietly in a corner of their minds and would never leave them.

In Grover's Corner (*Our Town*), the Stage Manager says that just after high school commencement "most of our young folks jump up and get married."[135] Since the percentage of young people under twenty-five who were unmarried was actually greater in the 1890s than it was thirty-five years later we must again make Grover's Corners an exception. Young men often lacked the money to get married, and their sweethearts waited for years before the time came. Marriage traditionally required a house, and that required a young man to raise a good deal of money. There was no such thing as paying a small part down on a lot and a house and borrowing the rest; he had to have the full purchase price, and this had to be saved up slowly, over the years. If the young man had an adequately paying job, the couple might get married and save up for a home, but it took discipline. A series of articles in *The Ladies' Home Journal* in the 1890s called "How We Saved for a Home" gave case histories of couples who saved up to buy splendid homes; in one case by saving *half* of the husband's weekly salary, the goal was accomplished in five years. The other stories were similar, with salaries in the range of fifteen to thirty dollars per week.

When at last the couple did get married, they might make it a simple ceremony, after which they went right back to work. But those who could afford it had a formal church wedding or, as was popular in some areas, a ceremony at the bride's home, complete with minister (and it would have been incomplete without him; civil ceremonies were rare). The people of the town attended the wedding feast vicariously through lengthy descriptions in the local paper, which went on for at least a column and were front-page news. World news was less pressing then, and local events were in the forefront; the small-town editors had given up their partisan feuds and now filled their columns with local social doings of the most trivial sort. Thus a wedding was a major event; the local society reporter described in lavish detail, tricked out in prescribed clichés, how the rooms were decorated—"southern smilax and white chrysanthemums were displayed from the chandeliers"—and what the bride wore—"a becoming gown of white d'esprit over white organdie with stitched white trimmings. It was made demi-train with high neck and long sleeves."[136] This continued through the bridesmaids, mother of the bride, groom, and so on. The prominence given to weddings shows not only a different perspective on what was news, but emphasizes the gravity with which this event was regarded. "Almost everybody in the world gets married—you know what I mean?" says the Stage Manager in *Our Town*. "In our town there aren't hardly any exceptions. Most everybody in the world climbs into their graves married."[137] To such a momentous (and irrevocable) event in a person's life, the proclamation of a decision that the bride and groom would live with the rest of their lives, great attention should be, and was, paid. A wedding far outweighed in importance the Russo-Japanese War or what the king of England said.

After the wedding, life was, as the Stage Manager says, "The cottage, the go cart, the Sunday afternoon drives in the Ford, the first rheumatism, the grandchildren, the second rheumatism, the deathbed, the reading of the will."[138] Death brought the community into play for the last time: the food discreetly left in the kitchen; the condolence calls; the preparation of the corpse in the bed in which it had died—and perhaps slept in for many years—without benefit of the mortician's cosmetics; the laying out in the parlor; a stream of people filing softly by throughout the day paying respects to the family; the old friends who sat up with the body through the long lonely night; and then the funeral the next day, with family, friends, numerous townspeople, members of the husband's lodge, ladies of the burial society who had decorated the grave site. Funerals were long and doleful; the minister droned on interminably about the virtues of the deceased and hymns were sung; then the black hearse with white-gloved pallbearers in attendance and a black-plumed horse drawing it made its slow progress to the cemetery. It was not unusual for town businesses to close down completely for a funeral, and nearly everyone joined the procession to the burying-place, where at graveside a few last words were said, before the finality of the earth raining down on the coffin. Back at home neighbors had cleaned and dusted, leaving a neat—and empty—home for the grieving family to return to. There they sank down wearily and talked in numbed voices and at last went to bed, to try to get some rest in preparation for the new day.

Death in Victorian times, like many of the other facts of life, was overladen with black veils and extravagant, morbid sentiments; one need only read the doleful laments of the poems on the tombstones. Newspapers would even report in somber tones that Dr. Smith had visited Mrs. Jones and pronounced her illness incurable—which meant he either did not know what the sickness was or that it had progressed beyond the remedies in his limited armamentarium. The life expectancy at birth in 1900 was about 50 years and the average death rate per thousand was 17.2, meaning that in a community of 2,000, 34 people would die in a year. But the infant mortality rate was eight times what it is today, and in the one-to-four group, the death rate stood at nearly 20 per thousand. So death was frequent and close, and the loss of children struck keenly at nearly every home. It was no wonder that the sentiments of death were so extravagantly expressed, or that bereavement was such a public spectacle. But at least those who died did not die ignored; their deaths unlocked a freshet of community concern and detailed personal memories. Obituaries, like wedding reports, were long and fulsome, and the deceased's life was described at great length, his virtues exaggerated almost beyond human capacity.

Sarah Orne Jewett caught the tender concern for an individual soul in her story "Miss Tempy's Watchers." The two watchers sitting up with the body of Tempy Dent are old friends, and they pay her tribute through the long night, then have a late supper from her cupboard. Their talk drifts around to their own deaths. Sister Binion comforts Mrs. Crowe, who is feeling stirrings of dread over "the great change." "I know that old Dr. Prince said once, in evenin' meetin'," she tells her, "that he'd watched many a dyin' bed, as we well knew, and enough o' his sick folks had been scared o' dyin' their whole life through; but when they come to the last, he'd never seen one but was willin', and most were glad, to go. 'Tis as natural as bein' born or livin' on,' he said."[139] Later the old women doze, and "overhead, the pale shape of Tempy Dent, the outworn body of that generous, loving-hearted, simple soul, slept on also in its white raiment. Perhaps Tempy herself stood near, and saw her own life and its surroundings with new understanding. Perhaps she herself was the only watcher."[140] Jewett anticipates the dead Emily's return to a day in her life in *Our Town*, and her poignant cry: "Oh, earth, you're too wonderful for anybody to realize you. Do any human beings ever realize life while they live it?—every, every minute?" "The saints and poets, maybe—they do some," the Stage Manager replies.[141]

Death was the black thread woven into the fabric of the town's life, but there were bright threads too. The year was punctuated with the traditional holidays, which provided welcome relief from the dull routine of the days. The premier holiday of all in a small town was Christmas, a time of the smell of the Christmas dinner and of the piny tang of a fresh-cut tree in the parlor; of carol singing and popcorn strands and brightly wrapped presents; of family closeness when family members returned and relations visited. Each family had its Christmas ritual, and each drew on the customs that had grown up around the event, changing little over the years. Christmas was—almost suffocatingly—home.

Christmas had barely ended when New Year's Day was at hand. New Year's Eve was spent by some in revelry and by some in religious observances at watch parties in the churches. Revelry ranged from bells and oyster suppers to carousing in the local saloons by idle farmhands and laborers who were seasonally unemployed and who tossed away their last money on drink. On New Year's Day, the custom of calling on one's friends was popular. These could be informal rounds, often fueled by liberal helpings from the punch bowl at each stop; but the practice of leaving calling cards—touted by the local printers—added formality to the ritual. The more socially minded held open houses, which were preceded by announcements in the local paper that so-and-so would be "at home" New Year's Day.

After the New Year's festivities, life settled back into the routine of battling snow and harsh weather and cabin fever in the more isolated northerly villages. Men and boys might get out to do some hunting, and young people had their taffy pulls and sleigh rides. Every fourth year, February provided an excuse for a Leap Year dance, with the ladies choosing partners; or a Valentine's Day dance, accompanied by the exchange of cloying sentiments on lace-bordered cards. The coming of spring brought with it the profoundest Christian holiday, Easter. But along with the church observances, which culminated in sunrise services on Easter morning, there were also the vestigial pagan rites exclusively for the children—coloring Easter eggs, egg hunts, and egg rolls on spring-greened lawns. April Fool's Day was a kind of day of license during which children could play practical jokes without suffering any retaliation. On May Day boys and girls clandestinely placed baskets of flowers and cookies on each other's doorsteps; the old English custom of the maypole dance, which had been carried on by some early colonists, had died out though: the Puritans had never approved of it.

Summer meant the closing of schools and the unleashing of hundreds of barefoot boys to roam fields and woods, skinny-dip in local creeks and ponds, and engage in such illicit pleasures as smoking corncob pipes and chewing tobacco. Girls played more decorously, though there were always a few tomboys who joined the boys in strenuous activities, once they had survived the initiatory tests. The days melted into one another like a golden, vernal dream, until suddenly it was fall, time to gather nuts and pick berries and go back to school. Soon would come Halloween, a riot of sanctioned mischief—ticktacks on old maids' windows, grinning gap-toothed pumpkin faces, and the ultimate outrage of decency, the overturning of the backyard privy, a test of fortitude that was spiced by the danger of an angry householder catching the perpetrators and the fears aroused by the boyish folklore about "someone who fell in," a fate that set off hoots of mingled scatology and disgust. Halloween pranks often became sheer destruction for the sake of destruction, and the line between the prank and nineteenth-century juvenile delinquency was never clearly drawn.

Two celebrations of profounder impact for the adults occurred in the spring and the summertime. The first was Memorial Day, or Decoration Day as it was universally known then. The holiday had been proclaimed in 1868 by General John A. Logan, commander of the Grand Army of the Republic, the Union veteran's organization. The day was devoted to eulogizing the war dead, and decorating their graves. Every northern town had a large contingent of veterans, and so the ritual was universally observed; the South, of course, had its own day for honoring the Confederate dead.

The cast and props were different in each town, but the basic script was remarkably similar. There might be a sunrise cannon salute to start the day, and then people from town and surrounding countryside would congregate along Main Street and the parade would begin. Among the marchers would be the inevitable town band, a complement of present-day soldiers, veterans in their old uniforms, wagons and carriages bearing local citizens, politicians, and schoolchildren carrying bunches of flowers or sprigs of evergreen to decorate the graves. Children had an important part in Memorial Day observances. In one town fifty girls in white marched in pairs representing peace, liberty, and other virtues; another fifty girls in red, white, and blue costumes executed drill maneuvers, and small boys marched too, wearing white stockings, red sashes, and blue caps with brass buttons. That was undoubtedly one of the more elaborate parades, and it was said to be nearly a mile long; smaller towns would simplify the rite, but the veterans, flower-bearing children, bands, and politicians were usually on hand. On the parade continued to the cemetery, where the children decorated the graves; there were prayers, songs by vocal groups and the firing of a rifle salute. After that the crowd repaired to the courthouse or park or grove for picnic suppers, pugnaciously Republican oratory, band music, singing, and socializing.

Beneath the politics and old-soldier reminiscing deeper psychological currents flowed. There was, in 1890, a sense that the country was forever at peace, that the great national trauma of civil war had healed, that the enemies of the Union had been forever repelled. The Civil War was still a living memory for the veterans—even for those who had not actually fought, had perhaps even paid a bounty, but who had over the years come to believe that they had taken part. The veterans, as veterans are wont, often sat around the livery stable telling stories of their exploits, some of them perhaps true. As years passed these memories had lost their sting and mellowed into nostalgia, and now it was a "time of waiting" in the country towns Sherwood Anderson recalls in *Poor White*, when "the Civil War having been fought and won, and there being no great national problems that touched closely their lives, the minds of men were turned in upon themselves."[142] Decoration Day was a festival celebrating this triumph and the days of peace and progress that lay ahead.

But there was also a deeper collective affirmation in Memorial Day—a kind of communal ceremony for the dead, with the vestal girls in white carrying their flowers and sprigs of evergreen. Flowers on a grave juxtaposed death and life—death and resurrection in the Christian belief; the act of placing them there by the community's young symbolized remembrance by the new generation of each man lying beneath the earth. The sociologist W. Lloyd Warner termed Memorial Day a collective rite of the dead, a "sacred symbol system functioning to integrate the whole community." He continued:

> In the Memorial Day ceremonies the anxieties man has about death are confronted with a system of sacred beliefs about death which give the individuals involved and the collectivity a feeling of well-being. Further, the feeling of triumph over death by collective action in the Memorial Day parade is made possible by recreating the feeling of euphoria and the sense of group strength and individual strength in the group's power, which were felt so intensely during the wars when the veterans' associations were created and when the feeling so necessary for the Memorial Day's symbol system was originally experienced.[143]

And so Memorial Day was Main Street's rite of the dead, an occasion both solemn and joyful, bunches of flowers neatly laid by small hands on graves with G.A.R. medallions, followed by cold fried chicken and "bloody shirt" Republican oratory and the oompah-boom-boom of the town band. A collective tear for old soldiers few knew, but whom once long ago someone loved better than their country did. A town in white dresses and straw hats and ice-cream suits celebrating its own life amidst memories of their dead on a warm afternoon of spring flowers and grassy tombs.

On Fourth of July the symbolism was different—proud patriotism, we-can-lick-anybody-in-the-world chauvinism, firecracker-banging and pride, mingled with the solemn reading of the most sacred and totemic of American writs, the Declaration of Independence. There was patriotic music from the bandstand, oratory, large picnic dinners, and small boys in sack races. Here the rituals affirmed the national collectivity through brash patriotism and exploding gunpowder. But even by the 1890s strident Fourth of July patriotism was melting into the pleasures of a summer day. In Hastings, where once three thousand G.A.R. veterans had assembled for an encampment and a parade was held, the day became simplified over the years, and the newspaper talked of "supervised play" for the children as an antidote to dangerous firecracker orgies. People spent the day fishing or picnicking, then after sundown gathered at the bandstand to hear a concert and watch the fireworks. The day's program emphasized contests such as running, jumping, catching a greased pig, wheelbarrow races, and the like. In many towns it was the same—the strenuousities of patriotism muted, and the dangers of untrammeled firecracker firing curbed by law. Old Glory was contemplated in a more relaxed way, with time devoted to lying beneath a shade tree, watching the cottony clouds drift in the hot blue sky. There would be freezers of homemade ice cream and perhaps a keg of beer. The women would stroll with their parasols or sit and gossip, the men would pitch horseshoes or play catch, and the boys and girls would wade in the pond or play hide-and-seek, then return exhausted for lemonade and a fresh peach ice cream. On such green summer afternoons under an overarching blue dome of sky one could well believe that one's town and one's country were good places, that life itself was good, that the same slow rhythmic heartbeat of the days would continue down through the years.

7
Town, City, and Factory

"In America in the eighties urbanization for the first time became a controlling factor in national life," Arthur Meier Schlesinger wrote in *The Rise of the City*. "Just as the plantation was the typical product of the antebellum Southern system and the small farm of the Northern agricultural order, so the city was the supreme achievement of the new industrialism. In its confines were focused all the new economic forces: the vast accumulations of capital, the business and financial institutions, the spreading railway yards, the gaunt smoky mills, the white-collar middle classes, the motley wage-earning population. By the same token the city inevitably became the generating center for social and intellectual progress."[1] In 1880 the United States was still a nation of farms and small towns. More than forty million people—nearly 70 percent of the population—lived in rural areas or in villages of less than twenty-five hundred people; 42.5 percent of the labor force was engaged in full-time farming. But forces were in motion that would tip the balance toward the cities.

Just as Frederick Jackson Turner was proclaiming the end of the frontier—the westering dream he thought was the key to the American character—a new frontier was in place and beckoning to young men seeking to better themselves. At a time when foreign immigration was attaining record levels and providing an urban pool of cheap labor to man (and woman) the pullulating factories, emigration from the farms and villages to the towns and cities was also taking place. This exodus would, in the long run, be the greater one, for it was the beginning of a continuing migration from the farms that has continued to the present day. Its prime cause over the long haul was the technological revolution in farming technique which enabled fewer farmers to produce more food, converting farming from a labor-intensive to a capital-intensive industry that required large investments for equipment and land. Back in the 1880s this technological revolution was just taking hold, however; then the main reasons for the migration from the farm were economic and social.

Homesteaders in the Great Plains were racked by the great droughts of the eighties, and in all parts of the country, the lot of many farmers continued to be hard. Charles B. Spahr, an agricultural scholar, estimated that the average wealth of rural families in the 1890s was only a third of that of urban families (defined as living in towns of four thousand or more). "The people on the farms and in the villages in the East," Spahr wrote, "have shared no more in the advancing wealth of the past quarter of the century than the people on the farms and in the villages of the South and West."[2] As late as 1916, a time of relative farm prosperity, only 14,407 farmers out of 6 million—one fourth of one percent—filed tax returns under the new income tax law, which limited filing to those making over three thousand dollars a year. One in 400 farmers were above the cutoff line compared with one in 200 teachers, one of every 80 ministers, one of every 22 salesmen, and one of every 5 lawyers and bankers.

The eighties had been a decade of growing agrarian discontent, which exploded into demonstrations and spawned the Populist party. Many farmers were deeply in debt, and the sickening drop in farm prices added to this burden. A study by Allen G. Bogue of mortgages in four Illinois counties showed that most farmers had been involved in paying off a mortgage—83 percent of them taken to purchase land and/or build houses, fences, barns or other improvements on the land. In a Nebraska township 77 percent of the resident owners were paying off mortgages. Land prices were inflated in the 1880s, when many of these farmers bought—as high as $6,000 for 80 acres—and interest rates were 8 to 10 percent. Then came drought, and financial panic. Wheat plummeted from $1.05 a bushel in 1870 to 49 cents in 1896. If nature allowed him a crop, the farmer could not sell it; or if he could sell it, the prices paid did not cover his costs, let alone enable him to pay off the high interest on his debt. "Ten-cent corn and ten percent interest"—the bitter phrase spread among farmers on the Middle Border like a prairie fire. They had no choice about the usurious rates of interest they paid; farming was always a gamble, but for the many who came West with hearts full of hope and empty pockets, their desperate, long-shot bet needed ever-rising farm prices to pay off. These did not come.

The farmer's worst enemy was his success, which resulted in overproduction; the settlement of the Great American Desert had been so rapid, and the homesteaders had so successfully made it bloom, that they had produced more than the country could consume. Drought often turned their corn and wheat to dust, but when the crops came, low prices turned their hopes to dust. The farmer was at the mercy not only of the weather, but also of exploitive middlemen who gouged him every step of the way—the railroads with their high shipping rates that wiped out any profit; grain speculators and manipulators who kept the "buy" price the farmer got low and the "sell" price *they* got high; and merchants who charged the farmer exorbitant prices for equipment, clothes, and groceries.

The struggles of the farmer in the political arena, which culminated in 1896 in the Democratic-Populist candidacy of William Jennings Bryan (who thundered in his "Cross of Gold" speech, "Burn down your cities and leave your farms and your cities will grow up again. But destroy your farms and the grass will grow in every city of the Union."[3]), are beyond our scope. But for every farmer who fought back, one or two—how many no one knows—simply gave up.

For there were other difficulties that had little to do with the price of wheat. The isolation, the grinding labor, the lack of amenities that characterized the farmer's life in the late nineteenth century compared unfavorably with the lure—stronger because it was still novel—of the towns and cities. There the promise of new inventions glittered—electric lights, telephones, streetcars, new skyscrapers. There dim, lofty peaks of glamour and wealth beckoned; there a young man might have a clean job as a clerk or at least work a twelve-hour day in a factory, which, compared to the long hours on the farm, seemed relatively paradisiacal, however it turned out in practice; what's more the pay was regular. And, after all, as the most popular writer of the day, Horatio Alger, preached, with pluck and luck this neat young clerk might rise in the world, although it helped if he happened to be on hand when the boss's daughter was about to be run down by an onrushing carriage. But it was not only farm or town boys; the women were almost equally eager to achieve some financial independence before eventually marrying; farm wives longed to escape the drudgery of their life too. The Iowa lawyer Hubert Quick wrote in 1913 that "the drift to the cities has largely been a woman movement."[4]

Disillusionment with the farm was powerfully expressed in the writings of a new group of agrarian realists—notably Hamlin Garland, Joseph Kirkland, Harold Frederic, and Ed Howe. Garland's family had lived in several places in the West, wandering restlessly like so many others who were in search of a prosperity that ever eluded them. Garland knew well the blasted hopes, the dark side of the pioneer's dream. (Much later he wrote, of his family's odyssey: "I clearly perceived that our Song of Emigration had been, in effect, the hymn of fugitives!"[5]) He undertook to tell as much of the bitter truth as he could about farming life in a collection of stories of country life called *Main-Travelled Roads.*

William Dean Howells, the influential editor of the *Atlantic Monthly*, was quick to discern the import of Garland's book. "If any one is still at a loss to account for that uprising of the farmers of the West which is the translation of the Peasants' War into modern and republican terms, let him read *Main-Travelled Roads*, and he will begin to understand. . . . The stories are full of those gaunt, grim, sordid, pathetic, ferocious figures, whom our satirists find so easy to caricature as Hayseeds, and whose blind groping for fairer conditions is so grotesque to the newspapers and so menacing to the politicians."[6] Although occasionally sweetened by an upbeat ending, most of the stories in *Main-Travelled Roads* portray a life of bleak, unremitting, dead-end labor in which people are trapped, like Grant McLane in the story "Up the Coulee" who says, "A man like me is helpless. . . . Just like a fly in a pan of molasses. There ain't any escape for him. The more he tears around, the more liable he is to rip his legs off."[7]

Garland became a reformer and saw hope for the farmer in the new populism, but Harold Frederic in his novel set in upstate New York, *Seth's Brother's Wife*, seems to opt for escape. Frederic's grim portrait of rural life—"a sad and sterile enough thing, with its unrelieved physical strain, its enervating and destructive diet, its mental barrenness, its sternly narrowed groove of toil and thought and companionship"[8]—is somewhat softened by the happy ending when the hero marries a nice country girl and has the hope of happiness. Nonetheless, Frederic has another of his characters say, "The nineteenth century is a century of cities; they have given their own twist to the progress of the age—and the farmer is almost as far out of it as if he lived in Alaska. Perhaps there may have been a time when a man could live in what the poet calls daily communion with nature and not starve his mind and dwarf his soul, but this isn't the century . . . get out of [farming] as soon as you can."[9]

Ed Howe's *Story of a Country Town* is shot through with gloom and a sort of weary contempt for the futility and provincialism of his fictional Twin Mounds, but his portrait, based on his hometown of Bethany, Missouri, was an accurate one, as fellow Missourian Mark Twain attested in a letter to Howe: "Your picture of the arid village life is vivid, and, what is more, true, I know, for I have seen and lived it all,"[10] Twain said. Later, in his autobiography, Howe recalled the region: "I doubt if there is in the world today a neighborhood as melancholy as ours was about the time of the beginning of the Civil War."[11] Howe's story is set during the pioneering days, but he anticipates the quality of desperation, the aimless boredom and suppressed despair, the discontent in many small towns and on the farms in the 1880s.

A documentary history of Black River Falls, Wisconsin (*Wisconsin Death Trip*), by Michael Lesy found grotesque behavior, insanity, suicide, poverty, and despair rife in the 1880s and 1890s, a time of economic and psychological collapse in the nation. Hard times had spread from the cities and farms to the small towns, in the form of bands of tramps, farm wives driven insane by hard times, unemployed men who chose an agonized death by swallowing carbolic acid. A deep malaise had gripped the countryside, a social breakdown and anomie that was the counterpart of the evils of the city slums, only rural isolation and loneliness made it cut more cruelly. Failure was the American dream turned into nightmare. "Since rural and country town culture was primarily an elaboration of secular Calvinism and [Adam] Smithian egoism, a man's success and a man's failures were judged to be reflections of his soul. When confronted by such a judgment, many men committed suicide."[12] Similarly, disease took an inordinate number of children, leaving their parents racked by guilt and grief. Some chose suicide—"overcome by foreboding, [they] killed themselves and their children so that they might at least master the time and conditions of a death that seemed inevitable."[13] Still others went mad, gripped by a paranoia that was fed by the furies that seemed to pursue them; some became compulsive neurotics, obsessed with inventing perpetual motion machines. (Christopher Lasch holds that the compulsive neurotic was the dominant character-type of nineteenth-century laissez-faire capitalism, just as the narcissistic type is of today's consumption and service-oriented capitalism.) "By the end of the nineteenth century," Lesy writes, "country towns had become charnel houses and the counties that surrounded them had become places of dry bones. The land and its farms were filled with the guilty voices of women mourning for their children and the aimless mutterings of men asking about jobs."[14]

Lesy's picture is distorted, yet the accounts in the Black River newspaper, insane asylum admission forms, county records, and other contemporary documents offer powerful proof that the hardships of country life did exact a harsh toll—that realists like Howe and Garland were not exaggerating. The indictment was echoed by Ole Rölvaag, who had described the joy with which his Norwegian settlers greeted a new town in *Giants in the Earth.* Later Rölvaag called life in these new prairie towns, "uniform and without nuance," lacking the "heartfelt spontaneous joy"[15] of European villages—especially those of his native Norway, where each had its unique customs and traditions.

Harold Frederic's advice—"get out of it as soon as you can"—reflected the views of uncounted young men ("young" is a presumption, since Department of Census figures of the day reveal little about the migrants to the cities; however, the traditional pattern is for the young to leave, while the middle aged and established stay behind). For the women, leaving home was more difficult, but there were precedents. In New England, the Lowell mills in the 1820s drew many young farm girls, but they were later replaced by foreign labor, who would work more cheaply. Those early farm girls who participated in the Lowell Experiment had hoped to save some money and then go home and get married; but when they came home, they found that the marriageable men were no longer about. "Gone west," in a phrase, because the exodus from New England, as we have seen, began early—a precursor of things to come. These women turned to teaching school and became that archetypal character, the Yankee old maid. Yet, not all these women stayed home, repining for some real or imagined sweetheart who had migrated or died young, and to whom their troth was eternally pledged. Some went west too. The historian Stewart Holbrook remarks that "from the ranks of the Yankee Old Maid came largely the schoolmarms of the American West, for the old maids, often in sheer desperation, joined the migration even before the railroads had appeared to remove the uglier aspects of travel west of the Berkshires and Lake Champlain."[16]

Holbrook estimates that five hundred thousand Yankees, male and female, emigrated before the Civil War, and thousands more followed afterward—most to the West but also, as the days of cheap land ended, to cities of their own region. In the 1880s, 932 out of New England's 1,502 townships declined in population—two thirds of the towns in Maine and New Hampshire and three fourths of those in Vermont declined. The hills, which the early settlers had favored for their farms, had long since reverted to forest or were closely grazed by herds of merino sheep; and the same happened to the richer lowlands, which were not nearly as rich or productive as the level, gunpowder-black lands of the Middle West. Whole towns were either abandoned or inhabited by only a few old people. "The proportion of abandoned wagon shops, shoe-shops, saw-mills and other mechanical businesses had far outstripped the abandonment of farms,"[17] one traveler wrote. The same was true in upstate New York, the goal of the earliest Yankee emigrants.

Yet in just forty years, between 1860 and 1900, New England's population doubled; it increased 20 percent in the 1880s alone. The growth was all in its rising industrial cities, where shoes, textiles, and hundreds of other finished goods were manufactured for the western settlers (urban populations were swollen by immigrants from abroad as well as home).

It was to a New Englander, Josiah Grinnell, that Horace Greeley had first directed his famous remark about going West—or so Grinnell claimed. Greeley was indeed a friend of the young abolitionist minister, whose sermons against slavery lost him pulpits in Washington and New York. The editor of the New York *Tribune* not only advised Grinnell to head west, he gave him an assignment to report on the 1853 Illinois State Fair for his newspaper. (Grinnell went on from there to Iowa, where he founded the town of Grinnell and Grinnell College.) Fourteen years later in 1867, when the tide was running the other way, Greeley wrote, "We cannot all live in cities, yet nearly all seem determined to do so. Millions of acres . . . solicit cultivation . . . yet hundreds of thousands reject this and rush into the cities."[18]

New England had always been a poor place for farming by American standards, so the desertion of its rural areas was inevitable. But the Middle West, the breadbasket of the nation, was also experiencing sufficient emigration to cause concern. Most of it was to the Far West—more than a million middlewesterners had moved to Kansas, Nebraska, and the Dakotas by 1890, and 600,000 more lived in the states and territories farther West. Articles prophesying the death of small towns began appearing, such as the one in the

Forum in 1895 entitled "The Doom of the Small Town." The writer cited the loss of population in 3,144 out of 6,291 townships in Ohio, Indiana, Michigan, Illinois, and Iowa in support of his doom-saying; yet, again, all these states were gaining in population. Between 1880 and 1900, the number of Americans living in towns of 8,000 or more grew from one in four to one in three—and half of these lived in towns of over 25,000. The largest cities showed the most spectacular growth—24 million people, or 80 percent overall—in the first two decades of the twentieth century. New York had grown from 2 million to 3.5 million between 1880 and 1900; Chicago from 500,000 to 1.5 million over the same period. In the Far West and the South, Los Angeles increased from 5,000 to 100,000 in 1900, Denver from nothing to 134,000, and Memphis from 23,000 to 100,000 over the years between the Civil War and the turn of the century. About one third of this growth consisted of rural emigrants to the city. Between 1900 and 1910, the nation's cities grew by 12 million people; 30 percent of these were from the country, 41 percent were foreign immigrants and 22 percent were natural increase—the excess of births over deaths.

Most of the urban growth was concentrated in the northern states of New York, Pennsylvania, Massachusetts, Illinois, and Ohio, where over half the entire urban population lived in 1890; only 7.7 percent was in the South. By 1900 six out of ten people in the North Atlantic states and three out of ten in the Midwest lived in cities, while only one out of ten in the South did so.

Yet the South too was changing, emerging from the ruins of war and from its plantation system which had militated against both industrialism and town building. After the Civil War, many of the cottage industries which had been located on the plantations moved to nearby crossroads, forming village trading centers for the surrounding area. Industrialization came in the form of the cotton-mill towns which were popping up along rivers in the 1870s and 1880s. Schlesinger describes them: "The typical mill village possessed but a few hundred people, mostly laborers and their families gathered for the purpose of working in a particular factory and living in unpainted shanties along a single street ankle-deep in dust."[19]

A boom in railroad building during the Reconstruction did much to stimulate industry and also shaped the rise of new towns. The historian T. Lynn Smith wrote, "By 1900 important towns were aligned along principal railways like beads on a string."[20] Hustling cities like Atlanta (not nearly so devastated by General Sherman as popular memory had it) owed much of their postwar growth to the railroads; the railroad made possible the rise of Texas cities such as Houston and Dallas. Birmingham, Alabama, was practically a railroad town, founded by northern real-estate speculators in 1871 to exploit the rich iron deposits in the area and supported by the Louisville and Nashville Railroad, which brought in track to form a junction with the Alabama and Chattanooga at the new town site and invested in town real estate and iron mills. Initially slowed by a cholera epidemic and the panic of 1873,

Birmingham soon grew rapidly, to 26,000 by 1890 and an astonishing 132,685 by 1910.

Yet, C. Vann Woodward showed that industrially the South was merely running fast to stand still, compared with the North. In 1860 the South had 17.2 percent of the manufacturing establishments in the nation and 11.5 percent of the capital; by 1904 those figures stood at 15.3 percent and 11 percent. Total value of manufactures was 10.3 percent of the national total in 1860 and 10.5 percent in 1900. The percentage of the southern work force engaged in manufacturing lagged far behind that of the north, and commercial and service jobs predominated. Cotton and tobacco growing and dirt farming in the countryside remained the chief occupations. Woodward summed up: "The southern people remained throughout the rise of the 'New South' overwhelmingly a country people, by far the most rural section in the country."[21] The key to urban growth was expansion of manufacturing—and the census figures again reflected this. In the fifty largest American cities 42 percent of the work force was engaged in manufacturing; in the southern cities the average figure was 10 to 12 percent lower.

With the exception of the South, then, the nation was rapidly urbanizing, the population of the cities being swelled by the rural exodus, foreign immigration, and an increased birthrate. The broader trends, if correctly reflected in the census figures, seemed to support the prophets of small-town doom, for a decline in the number of farmers would erode the economic base of the country towns, which depended upon their trade for their livelihood, and the declining economic opportunities in the small towns and the lure of higher-paying jobs in the cities would deal the towns a second blow—a sort of demographic one-two punch. The statistical watershed often cited by historians is the 1920 census, which revealed that for the first time in the nation's history more Americans lived in towns of twenty-five hundred or above than lived in rural areas.

Yet the situation was a bit more complex. In the first place, many of the towns with populations of twenty-five hundred to ten thousand remained country towns, spiritually and geographically far from the big cities. Furthermore, the smaller places, the hamlets and villages, did not for the most part turn into ghost towns; they continued to grow, albeit at a diminished rate, for they too served as catch basins for the surplus population of the farms. Finally, the disappearance of towns has, as we have seen, been going on since the birth of the United States. During the period of settlement, when town booming was all the rage, towns died left and right. In Iowa, between the 1840s and 1930s, 2,205 towns, villages, and hamlets were abandoned—an average of 22 a year. This in a prosperous farming state that was growing rapidly in population.

Actually during the years from 1880 to 1920, most small towns and villages grew in population—though not so rapidly as the cities. Over the same period the *number* of villages and towns from less than a thousand to up to 10,000 in population also increased—nearly doubling. The rural population continued to increase absolutely, even while it fell drastically as a percentage of the total population of the United States. More refined studies, which included incorporated towns not covered by the census and were limited to towns that were not suburbs or satellites of cities, supported the proposition that most small towns and villages held their own or grew modestly. A somewhat more significant change in the years of urbanization was the slow decline in the *percentage* of the total population living in small towns. In the Middle West, for example, country towns of less than five thousand population had 18 percent of the region's total number of people in 1903, but this had fallen to 16 percent by 1932.

At a time when the buoyant optimism of the pioneers and the town founders was turning into doubt and ambivalence in the face of larger social and economic forces, a movement arose to revive rural life. Known as the Country Life movement, it had at its core a curious amalgam of idealistic progressives and profit-minded businessmen, both of whom were concerned about the flight from the farms, although for different reasons. Some reformers felt that something precious and vital to America's survival would be lost if the nation's small towns and farms were allowed to disappear; they also saw a movement back to the land as an antidote to urban poverty. Among the most articulate and idealistic of these was Liberty Hyde Bailey, an agronomist and philosopher. Bailey extolled farmers—the "land-people," he called them—as "the fundamental fact of democracy."[22] "As the land-people live and have their being, so will our civic and social life be conditioned and sustained,"[23] he wrote. To him, farming represented a simplicity and a closeness to nature that was ennobling; cities were parasitic, battening on the blood of the country's young people, and could be easily dispensed with.

Beginning by idealizing the life of the tiller of the soil, Bailey came to see the drawbacks of that life. As chairman of the influential Country Life Commission appointed by President Theodore Roosevelt in 1908, Bailey heard firsthand from farmers who responded to the commission's questionnaire about their problems. He later wrote that "one of the greatest insufficiencies in country life is its lack of organization or cohesion, both in a social and an economic way. Country people are separated both because of the distances between their properties and also because they own their own land. . . . There is a general absence of such common feelings as would cause them to act together unitedly."[24] The American dream of independent farming had its costs, and Bailey was one of the first to see this.

Yet Bailey did not advocate collective action—farmer's unions for economic purposes, say, his sentimental attachment to the farmer's individuality made him oppose both organization and government regulation. Economic betterment was low on his list; the farmer should make a living of course, but an important part of his compensation was psychic, the satisfaction of living close to nature. Agriculture was far more than a business; it was a civilizing force.

The other group interested in improving the farmer's lot believed precisely the opposite—that farming *was* a business and that the farmer should learn more efficient methods and employ improved technology. This group included businessmen whose trade depended upon the farmer, and many farmers themselves. Enable the farmer to earn more money, they said, and his problems will be solved.

This view was the more narrowly realistic one, and this hardheaded, dollars-and-cents approach was more appealing to the farmers, who regarded idealists like Bailey as big-city do-gooders. The farmers themselves were too conservative and cantankerously independent-minded in that era to accept some of the reformers' ideas, such as consolidated rural schools and churches; yet they were not averse to taking government money, grudgingly paying the price of greater regulation in return. The idealistic faction of the Country Life movement was simply out of touch with the realities of life on the farm; they could not see that technological change, high land prices, and higher wages in the city were causing the rural exodus. They sought to preserve a Jeffersonian ideal in a time of industrialization and urbanization. But they were right in seeing that farm life should be made more attractive. Their advocacy of more amenities for farmers paved the way for an acceptance of technological changes on the farm; yet other of their proposals bordered on the impractical, such as their advocacy of the quarter-section (eighty-acre) farm at a time when consolidation of farmland was improving productivity (a man with a family could just get by on eighty acres in the 1910s) and their suggestion that country roads should be made narrower so that more land could be put into cultivation. Some of their reforms even had effects opposite to those intended. The push for better roads in rural areas did not result in increased solidarity among farmers through improved communication among them; rather it enabled them to go to town, for Henry Ford's Model T would soon appear on the roads in increasing numbers, revolutionizing the farmer's life and ending his rural isolation. Rural free delivery also diminished socialization among farmers by ending their trips to the village post office where they met their fellows and gossiped as they picked up the mail. But some of the reformers' efforts bore fruit. They helped stimulate regulatory legislation that controlled railroad shipping prices, for example, and the Progressive movement adopted many of their ideas. The more practical school of reformers also stimulated farmers' organizations—notably the Farm Bureau—and the reformers' heavy emphasis on education lead to the state university extension services devoted to informing farmers on new techniques.

The romantic strain in the Country Life movement was less fatal to it than was its timing. Its heyday was 1900 to 1910, a time of rising prosperity on the farm and myriad improvements in the farmer's way of life, from the Model T to the party-line telephone to the Sears Roebuck catalog. While in the 1880s and 1890s populist orators were urging the farmer to "raise less corn and more hell," in the early 1900s a speaker could say that "from the beginning of Indiana to the end of Nebraska there is nothing but corn, cattle and contentment."[25] In 1909 wheat prices of ninety-nine cents a bushel were at the threshold of the farmer's symbolic goal of dollar wheat, and farm income was more in line with costs. With the galloping growth of the cities, which provided consumers for the farmer's produce, overproduction was less of a problem. The era of overexpansion on the farms was also drawing to an end, with the closing of the frontier and unavailability of cheap land. Between 1870 and 1890 the number of farms had nearly doubled, but from 1900 to 1920 the increase was less than 20 percent. New land brought under cultivation was also correspondingly less, and since it was poorer land, it did not contribute any new glut of agricultural produce.

At the same time, opportunities for the young farmer were shrinking; farm tenancy increased, and the difficulties of moving from tenant to owner status were all the greater. A major reason for the difficulty—and a condition that further enhanced the contentment of the established farmer and the speculator-landowner—was spiraling land costs. Farmland prices overall increased by 118 percent between 1900 and 1920; in the wheat lands of Kansas, Nebraska, and the Dakotas, the rises were even more spectacular—377 percent in South Dakota, for example. By 1900, the cost of starting an average farm was $3,000, and the largest proportion of the cost was land. This was thirty times the cost of a quarter-section in the homesteading days, and it was prohiibitive to all but a few.

Mobility on and off the farms could be seen in microcosm in the Oklahoma county surrounding the town Angie Debo calls "Prairie City." Between 1900 and 1907 the farm population decreased by 25 percent. About half the farmers who sold out moved to the town, where they worked in grain elevators, stores, or produce houses or at selling real estate; others moved on to what remained of the frontier—unclaimed land in Oklahoma and the Texas Panhandle, irrigated land in Arizona, and even Mexico. Most of the rest were northerners, who hated the climate. They stayed the five years necessary to prove up their claims, then sold out and moved to California. The stable elements in the population were the farmers from Kentucky, and the Germans and other immigrants, who bought up land from the sell-outs. This pattern was not atypical; in other parts of the country much of the migration from the farms was to the nearby small towns, or else farther west. The foreign immigrants who came in were generally excellent farmers and were bound to stick it out, but they were looked down on by the native Americans and tended to associate only with one another.

The countryside was further depopulated by improved transportation which regularized and broadened the farmer's market. This made specialized large-scale farming feasible, necessitating the use of expensive machinery on large tracts of land. Far from providing an arcadian alternative to the evils of industrialization, farming was starting to become an industry and a business too, the difference being that one did not work at it in factories under the smoke-palled skies of the cities, but out in the fresh air, under the big skies of the West.

For the country towns and villages, rising agricultural prosperity seemed to offset the exodus from the farms. Farmers with more money in their overalls, their tastes whetted for new gadgetries, flocked to the towns on the traditional Saturday shopping day and bought out the stores. And the towns, with their monopoly of the trading area, prospered accordingly. So it went, but in his Swiftian essay "The Country Town," the iconoclastic economist Thorstein Veblen found cracks in the structure of the small-town businessman's monopoly of the farm trade.

According to Veblen, the town businessmen have one common bond—real-estate values—and their interest is in keeping these inflated as high as possible. The town is "managed as a real estate 'proposition.' "[26] The townsmen thus have a common cause: increasing the farm trade. And upon the volume and profit of the farm trade real-estate values depend. The town's virtual monopoly on the farm trade means that prices will be based upon "what the traffic will bear," a figure that is always subject to readjustment but invariably represents the maximum overcharge possible. This price sometimes goes beyond what the traffic will bear, in which case the farmer must give up and move out or else shop elsewhere; usually he does the latter. In the case of money lending, however, the "critical point is not infrequently reached and passed. Here the local monopoly is fairly complete and rigorous, which brings on an insistent provocation to over-reach."[27]

At the heart of Veblen's analysis is the contention that these high profits attracted more merchants than were needed. Businessmen are motivated by the twin gods of "self-help and cupidity" so they can hardly do otherwise, but the result was that "while the underlying farm population continues to yield inordinately high rates on the traffic, the business concerns engaged, one with another, come in for no more than what will induce them to go on, the reason being that in the retail trade as conducted on this plan of self-help and equal opportunity the stocks, equipment and man-power employed will unavoidably exceed what is required for the work by some 200 to 1000 percent."[28]

Competition, then, did not lower prices; it lowered profits, keeping the businessman in a state of continuing insecurity; he was at once in competition with and in collusion with his fellow businessmen. To cut prices would be to risk ostracism. He had to depend, instead, on "salesmanship"—"largely a matter of tact, patience and effrontery," "a matter of buying cheap and selling dear," and "pusillanimity."[29] Town merchants found themselves in a competitive standoff, and one result of this, which Veblen does not mention, was the growing prevalence of cut-price sales, loss leaders, "dollar days." The merchant no longer could "buy cheap and sell dear," for he had competitors doing the same; in such a situation someone had to lose. So a merchant resorted to cutting his profit margin on some items in order to attract customers into his store and away from his rivals. William Allen White, the shrewd, business-minded editor of the Emporia, Kansas, *Gazette*, deplored these loss leaders in his editorials, saying that businessmen must make a profit and that it was foolish of them to cut prices on staples like bread, sugar, and potatoes—they should confine their price-cutting to fancy articles like canned goods or ready-made noodles. When the bakers in Emporia had an all-out price war, White arranged a meeting of the bakery managers and persuaded them to set a uniform price on a uniform loaf of bread, even though a chain store continued to sell its bread at a lower price.

"Stick together, keep your prices up," White constantly counseled the town merchants. He also deplored the growing tendency to sell "cheap stuff at cheap prices" and the obsession with making a "quick dollar." "Carry quality goods, advertise quality goods—goods that you can stand back of as represented—make a low profit above overhead expense, but make a profit," White said in one editorial.[30] "Cheap merchandising makes a cheap community," he went on, pointing to the example of Atchison, where ten stores had closed in the past year. "Why? Because merchants thought they could make money on leaders priced below cost and they got something started they could not stop. When everybody prices a different leader, the whole merchandising structure of a town is on a minus cost basis and sooner or later the bats fly in at the windows of that town, the coyotes run in the streets, and the sheriff's auctioneer is the town's merchant."[31] The results of cheap merchandising were vacant buildings, which brought lower rents, which in turn depressed real-estate values. "Up come the cloth [going out of business] signs and down goes the town."[32]

Fixed prices, good quality—that was William Allen White's prescription for the small-town businessman; but it was not the philosophy of the chain stores, which began proliferating after 1910 (the A&P grew from 1,726 stores in 1915 to more than 10,000 in 1923). The chains were national organizations; they could afford price-cutting and low margins; they could, indeed, drive merchants who were unable to match their low prices out of business—and that is just what they did. White's theories belonged to an older day; he celebrated small business but did not realize that big business was breaching the fair-trade walls of the closed economy of the country town. Veblen saw it, though. The autonomy of the small businessman had been eroded by the rise of large firms which manufactured the goods he sold, Veblen said. These firms controlled the businessmen's profit margins, making them mere local distributors—"tollgate keepers for the distribution of goods and collection of customs for the large absentee owners of the business."[33] Nonetheless the small businessman clung to the pillars of his faith—self-help, cupidity, and salesmanship; what is more, these same values were co-opted by the big businesses "whose public men and official spokesman have come up through and out of the country-town community, on passing the test of fitness according to retail-trade standard."[34] The ideology of salesmanship reigned supreme; it stressed avoiding offense and cultivating goodwill on the one hand, while secretly collecting evidence of one's competitor's shortcomings for use against him on the other. Thus the country town remained conservative, holding to beliefs of the last century, which were comfortable, accepted, and inoffensive to all, while rejecting any new and alien ideas which would disturb the town's peace, good order, and intellectual torpor.

It can be seen that Veblen had more on his mind than the economic situation of the small-town merchant; he was guying the small-town ethos, and his indictment echoes H.L. Mencken's gleeful attacks on the booboisie and Sinclair Lewis's satiric shafts against Main Street. The pettiness of the small-town merchant's soul, Veblen said, was writ large in the nation, and its chief prophets, Warren Gamaliel Harding and Calvin Coolidge, sat consecutively in the highest seats of power in the land.

As a polemic—as satire—"The Country Town" was brilliant; as descriptive sociology and economics, it was less satisfactory, and short on facts. Lewis Atherton offers much evidence contravening Veblen's premise that the country town had a monopoly. In their early days, perhaps, when towns were expected to serve a trading radius equivalent to the distance a farmer's team could cover in a day (to town and back), there was a kind of monopoly. The farmer did appreciate the convenience of a town close by in the days of poor roads that were impassable in bad weather. Studies showed that the average farmer would travel twenty miles to town, at the maximum. But then came the railroads, which enabled the farmers to take their custom to other towns along the line, even to the cities. Hard-surfaced roads and the automobile enhanced the farmer's shopping mobility even more. So the farm family did shop around, at least for goods other than necessities, where style and price weren't factors.

Then too, the town stores changed in two important ways. First, the custom of extending credit atrophied, thus ending a farmer's ties with one particular store. And, second, as goods were packaged and standardized and made in greater varieties, price competition had more meaning. Local merchants (as opposed to the chains) resisted such competition with "fair trade" agreements, but as Veblen pointed out, the small-town merchant lost a good deal of price discretion when he handled items manufactured by large companies elsewhere and shipped in. With such tight margins, "salesmanship" and "pusillanimity" was all the merchants had going for them. Although the picture those words summon up, of a toadying, calculating figure, was too harsh, the storekeeper was a generally unheroic figure, operating on a close margin, and spending long hours in his store. He tended to blend in with the goods—bland, friendly, agreeable, taking care to say the things to people they wanted to hear. He kept his violent opinions to himself or expressed them away from his store.

Atherton does criticize the small-town merchants for their backward ways. They had little merchandising flair and tended to place orders with their favorite traveling salesman rather than getting the best quality items. The old-time town merchant—indeed often a retired farmer—maintained his store with goods ordered from distant suppliers and felt himself lucky if his flyspecked stock turned over twice a year. This haphazard style of merchandising worked well enough with unsophisticated farmers, like the immigrant families depicted in Willa Cather's *O Pioneers!* or the lonely, toilbent farm woman in Hamlin Garland's story "A Day's Pleasure" who looks on a trip to town with her husband as an escape from her dreary life on the farm, even though the town's only pleasures for her are a walk up Main Street and a chance to sit and rest in the grocery store. But farmers had become more sophisticated consumers.

In his autobiographical *Boy Life on the Prairie,* Garland himself recalled the sense of adventure he felt as a boy when the family went to shop in the county-seat town of Osage, Iowa, and he was immersed for the first time in the sights and smells of a large, well-stocked general store, where his father supervised, with close scrutiny of quality and price, the purchases of major necessities such as high-topped boots for the winter, schoolbooks, caps, and slates. Shopping was an event to farm families, and those that could afford it did not deny themselves the pleasure of going to the best places. And they made sure that plenty of study and comparative shopping went into their purchases. They knew which merchant's prices were too high, and they avoided him if they could.

Imagine then, the wonderful world opened up by the mail-order catalogs, with their pages and pages of goods at low prices. Montgomery Ward, the first of the great mail-order houses, was founded in 1872, followed by Sears, Roebuck, and Company in 1886. If mail-order catalogs took away the pleasure of going to town for shopping, they offered, through mass-merchandising and low-profit-margin operations, prices that the farmer could afford. The rise of the mail-order houses sent shudders through small-town merchants all over the country; there were predictions that country towns were doomed, that all that would be left of them would be a post office and a railroad depot. Rural free delivery was a boon to the farmers, but local merchants opposed it because they feared it would increase the incursions into rural areas by the mail-order houses.

This was another instance of the merchants finding their economic interests in conflict with the farmers'. From the point of view of preserving good relations with them, they would have been better off accommodating themselves to the competition (which they did, eventually, anyhow), rather than making such a show of fighting it. Thorstein Veblen's indictment of the country town, despite its coolly satirical tone, was written out of his own embittered childhood memories of the treatment Norwegian immigrants like his parents received from the Yankee storekeepers in the Minnesota town near the farm where he grew up. Many farmers did feel they were overcharged; the mail-order houses arrived on the scene at a time of agrarian discontent, when the Grange was active in setting up cooperatives among farmers to enhance their buying power and when the farmers and town merchants came close to open warfare. Grange co-ops made bulk purchases from manufacturers and thus could undercut the town stores; but their variety was limited.

The town businessmen retaliated with social snobbery, especially to foreigners, but also to farmers in general. Their attitudes comprised a mixture of nativism and the urbanized outlook of small-town elites, requiring them to look down their noses at farmers and classify them, in the urban parlance, as "hayseeds," or "jays," or "reubens." However, the well-off farmers, with large holdings, received the respect and envy due men of their means. Meredith Nicholson remarked that "the owner of a big farm 640 to 1,000 acres . . . is a valued customer of a town or city banker; the important men of his state cultivate his acquaintance. . . . Farmers of this class are usually money-lenders or shareholders in country banks, and they watch the trend of affairs from the viewpoint of the urban businessman."[35] But most farmers did not fall into this superior category. Indeed, in some towns there was a rising country-squire class of wealthy landowners, who owned large tracts of farmland as an investment and hired tenants to work them. Owning land without working it oneself gave one a cachet of aristocracy.

With such attitudes, it was little wonder that many small towns were so dilatory in encouraging the farmer's trade. Lewis Atherton deplores the callous treatment of farmers by the merchants in many country towns of the Middle Border. Rather than shore up their relations with farmers by fair prices, good-quality merchandise, and common courtesy, merchants came up with "buy at home" campaigns, an unwitting assertion of their desire for a monopoly. When towns did make an effort to provide a comprehensive range of goods and services—stores of many kinds, lawyers, medical care, entertainment, transportation, educational resources, as well as simple considerations like benches and comfort stations for shoppers—they gained the enduring loyalty—and business—of the farmers. Atherton's message was that this was the desirable path for country towns to take.

But many towns had begun to feel the stirrings of the industrial revolution in the cities. They were looking beyond the farmers' trade to industry. A change was taking place in small-town attitudes—they were becoming mesmerized by the big-business success ethic emanating from the cities. The city was still considered Sodom and Gomorrah, a sink of sin and iniquity, a pestilential warren of slums inhabited by swarthy foreigners. The small-town life, like the agrarian life, was superior; townspeople were friendlier—they "cared whether you lived or died." Yet at the same time the towns had never been immune to the winds of change in the greater society around them; and in the 1880s and 90s, they harkened to the Gilded Age ideology of rugged individualism, of acquisitiveness as a positive—perhaps the highest—virtue. Money was proof of superior strength in the capitalistic jungle.

Yet running counter to the new ethos was an older belief that great wealth was derived from exploitation of the laborer, the farmer, and the small towns. The rum-soaked cities were sinks of vice, while the small towns were centers of the old-time religion—a reflexive Christian fundamentalism stripped of its fervor—and prohibition. Foreign immigrants were diluting the superior pure American stock. (This belief was one of the premises of the Country Life movement; the reformers believed that the country was the last bastion of "American stock" and must therefore be preserved. It also became the central plank of the platform of the revived Ku Klux Klan.)

These tenets found a champion in William Jennings Bryan, a leading spokesman for agrarian reform in the Democratic party and three-time Democratic candidate for president. Bryan kept a chaste distance between himself and the true radicals of the Populist movement, but his jeremiads against the Wall Street bankers and big capitalists lay farther to the left than the beliefs of the Democratic leadership. His embrace of religious fundamentalism—which lead to his humiliation at the 1925 "monkey trial" in Tennessee by Clarence Darrow—and prohibition, however, warred with his Progressive side. But he remained a radical-reformist voice in the Democratic party until his death. Bryan's high point in his three runs for the presidency came in 1896, whenn many observers believed that McKinley's *éminence grise* Mark Hanna had defrauded him of the election (Hanna had also raised an enormous campaign fund by naked appeals to businessmen's fears of a populist government). But Bryan's strength lay in the New West and the South; he did not carry a single industrial state; the conservative farmers of the Middle West (all the radicals had moved farther west) opposed him. Louis W. Koenig points out that Bryan "did better in the cities in the more urbanized and industrialized sections of the nation than in the cities of the less populous and more agricultural states."[36] One could easily add small towns to those cities of the agricultural areas; Bryan appealed to workingmen and western farmers; but conservative areas, such as the rural Northeast and the South, rejected him, and the traditionally Republican small towns of the Middle West as far west as Kansas and Nebraska followed suit.

If Bryan was the silver-tongued orator of the Progressive cause, his imitator, William Gibbs McAdoo, another power in the Democratic party, was sounding brass. The "plastic" McAdoo, in Arthur Schlesinger Jr.'s phrase, spouted populist, antiurban rhetoric, even though he had practiced law in New York City for many years. When he arrived in that city in 1924 from his adopted state of California as candidate for the presidential nomination, he delivered a ritual populist blast at "this imperial city . . . the city of privilege, the seat of that invisible power represented by the allied forces of finance and industry which, reaching into the remotest corners of the land, touches the lives of people everywhere . . . reactionary, sinister, unscrupulous, mercenary, and sordid . . . wanting in national ideals, devoid of conscience . . . rooted in corruption, directed by greed and dominated by selfishness."[37] McAdoo, the Klan, and the Anti-Saloon League blew up small-town values into political slogans—thus caricaturing them and reinforcing the nativism, racism, and provincialism that represented the worst instincts of the rural areas.

By the end of the nineteenth century, Page Smith claims, "the older ethic of self-denial, of 'character,' of unremitting labor gave way slowly to the cities' values of aggressiveness, of enterprise, of deference to riches. Suspicion of those who prospered too much was replaced with admiration for the tycoon. If to the surviving pioneers the millionaire was 'no better than the sneak thief who robs your granary or hen roost,' their sons admired and envied the few entrepreneurs who brought capital into the community."[38]

This shift in values encouraged "a calculating shrewdness," and "the ability to drive a hard bargain took the place of the earlier emphasis on cooperation and mutual helpfulness."[39] Community spirit was replaced by rugged individualism, which "was not a product of the towns and farms but rather of the depersonalized life of the cities."[40]

Sherwood Anderson remembered the changes that began taking hold in his hometown of Clyde, Ohio in the 1890s: "The day of the hustlers is at hand, the houses of the town pushed up quickly, people swarming into the town who have no notion of staying there—a surprising number of them will stay, but they have, at first, no intention of staying."[41] He contrasts these new people with the New England settlers in an earlier day, when the growth of towns was slow and measured. These people of the older generations "had come drifting in slowly, bringing traces of old customs, sayings, religions, prejudices. The young farmers came first, glad of the rich free soil. . . . A slow culture growing up . . . growing as culture must always grow—through the hands of workmen. In the small towns artisans coming in—the harnessmaker, the carriage-builder, the builder of wagons, the smith, the tailor, the maker of shoes, the builders of houses and barns too."[42] A new spirit of speculation and gain was in the air—not the old boomerism of the land speculators, but a new ethic of success. A local storekeeper invested money in the oil interests of John D. Rockefeller, then operating out of Cleveland—and became rich. The dream of riches and ease spread like a fever through the little town of Clyde.

Like other towns in that era, Clyde also had high hopes of finding natural gas deposits, and Anderson tells how the men stood around the street corners and the drugstore talking sotto voce of stocks and drilling schemes. Finally, an explosives expert comes, who will set a charge that will unlock the natural gas beneath the soil and pour riches into the pocket of every man. The bang goes off, but Clyde's boom is a bust: Nothing comes up but water and soil.

Anderson uses the great gas exploration comically, to ridicule the febrile dreams of ease and riches. In contrast, Plattville, Booth Tarkington's seat of small-town folksiness in *The Gentleman from Indiana,* has a promoter drilling for oil—a former bunco artist who was reformed by the noble hero. This now-honest wildcatter does indeed strike oil, among the many happy endings in which the book abounds; and Plattville seems on the verge of moving to some vaguely defined higher plateau of prosperity—without, of course, losing any of its deeply ingrained folksiness. Whether Tarkington's novel had any basis in fact is beside the point; its author, as an accomplished sensor of the popular mind, knew that his middle-class audience needed to believe in the happy ending of wealth frrom striking oil.

In his generally nostalgic portrait of Wilmington in the 1890s Henry Seidel Canby recalls being repelled by a new spirit of commerce that was creeping into his upper-class milieu. Evoking the traditional, gracious terrapin suppers his mother gave, he interjects: "In a community growing year by year more commercialized, more cut-throat in competition, where speculation was beginning to dominate industry and they themselves [the male guests] in daily intercourse put business first, such evenings as this were . . . the last stand of the old order where a man was a gentleman first and a lawyer or banker afterwards, or he did not entirely belong."[43] (This rejection of businessmen from above, from the high ground of the "gentleman," was a vantage point from which Tarkington also aimed his most critical volleys.) Business had become "much more than an occupation—it was a philosophy, a morality, an atmosphere . . . the dominating object and chief subject of thought."[44] In contrast to the ways of the old aristocracy, Canby thought, the new business class cared only for profits and had no code of responsibility to the community.

With the success ethic in the ascendancy, the small towns became the strongest supporters of the business ideology of the Republican party in the 1920s. A turning point was the appearance on August 15, 1896, of an editorial by William Allen White, who was then the young editor of the Emporia *Gazette* and not yet the sage of small-town America he was to become; the editorial, however, set him well along that road. It was called "What's the Matter with Kansas," and in it White charged that the people of Kansas were like "a spavined, distempered mule . . . we don't care to build up, we wish to tear down. . . . Give the prosperous man the dickens! Legislate the thriftless man into ease, whack the stuffing out of the creditors."[45] He was inveighing against the radical, antibusiness, anti–Wall Street proogram of Populism, which implied, he said, that "we don't need population, we don't need wealth, we don't need well-dressed men on the streets, we don't need cities on the fertile prairies; you bet we don't!"[46] Of course, White was saying that's just what Kansas did need. He had thus placed himself squarely in opposition to Bryan, who, he said in a kinder moment, "stood as much for the idea of socialism as the American mind will confess to,"[47] and whose Democratic party was "the party of emotions, the party of 'feeling,' the party of classes, the party of revolution."[48]

"What's the Matter with Kansas" was noticed by the Republican party boss, Mark Hanna, who saw that it was distributed all over the country, in time for the 1896 presidential election. Kansas went for Bryan, but White's ideas were blown up into a sweeping repudiation of Populism by a common-sense small-town editor of the West, right in the heart of Bryan country. But White's views were not then the apostasy from the old small-town values that his critics said; he was not embracing the standards of big business and the financial interests, the "invisible powers" that Veblen accused of making the small-town businessman a pawn, a "tollgate keeper."

White was at heart a singer of praises of small-town life, which he saw as the highest expression of American democratic ideals. Yet he was also enough of a newspaperman to be aware of what was going on. The small-town booster side of him was compelled to cheer investment and growth; he was still close to the pioneer values of his parents, their struggles to re-create civilization and prosperity in this difficult country. But White also sensed the threat of the centralized capital and industry based in the city—"Wall Street." He feared that the friendly, equable middlewestern small town would be overwhelmed by the forces of big business, a theme he developed in his 1918 novel *In the Heart of a Fool.* Not that business was bad, however; it must simply be made to comport with the village ideals of honest dealing and fairness for the little man. Most of all, White was the voice of small business, which—against its better interests it could be argued—remained allied with the big-business forces in the Republican party.

The town gradually, subtly capitulated to the city by turning its back on agrarian radicalism and solidarity with the farmer. The town's quarrel with the city lost all political content; it shriveled up into a mean-spirited negativism, bigotry, and nativism. Small-town morality came to mean not a possible humanization of social Darwinism and opposition to business monopolies but rather the narrow morality popularly characterized by the terms "puritanical" and "bluenose." The town came to stand for opposition to Reds, radicals, labor unions, foreigners and immigration, saloons and liquor, Catholics and to some extent Jews—all ills of the big city. Indeed, the opposition extended to all fun in general, it almost seemed, though many of the vices such as card playing, dancing, drinking, and sex that small-towners condemned they engaged in on the sly, in their own style, like the farmers Mencken later accused of opposing wine and cocktails for city people while guzzling moonshine and legal hard cider during Prohibition. City sophisticates could add another count to their indictment of small towns—hypocrisy. Small-town moralists perverted ideals that had a core of validity. Antisaloon sentiment grew out of the real problem of drinking on the frontier. But it was carried to excess in a system of national Prohibition, for which a vocal minority agitated during World War I, when a spirit of idealism and sacrifice was abroad. Walter Lippmann saw that Prohibition was "a test of strength between social orders. When the Eighteenth Amendment goes down, the cities will be dominant politically and socially as they now are economically."[49] "Small-town morality" became the butt of sophisticated and influential urban commentators like Mencken, as well as the novelists who attacked it in the teens and twenties.

Exhausting its moral capital in negativism, the small town widened the gap between it and the cities; yet to the Republican politicians and big businessmen it suddenly had become the repository of true American values—which were, to be sure, equated with the values of the Grand Old Party. Warren Gamaliel Harding of Marion, Ohio, who dallied with his mistress in the White House and played poker with his cronies in his off-duty hours at the house on H Street, extolled the small town as the cornerstone of the American way of life; his successor, the taciturn Calvin Coolidge, had imputed to him by voters the shrewd common sense of a Yankee general storekeeper combined with the tightfistedness of a small-town banker. Both men were seen by their admirers as personifications of small-town America but actually they embodied its worst qualities—the Veblenesque triumvirate of self-help, cupidity, and salesmanship. American business had found its champion in the weak, easygoing Harding, who looked the other way as his corrupt subordinates did business with the oil companies in the Teapot Dome scandal. It had found in the laissez-faire Coolidge the counterpart of the village constable who looks the other way when the banker's son is committing criminal mischief.

And so small-towners knelt before the god of business, and small-town editors and politicians sang its praises. Wall Street and chairman of the boards of large corporations approvingly read the simple commonsense pronouncements of White and of Ed Howe, whose words were echoed by hundreds of obscure and less-talented small-town editors. Howe was an odd, embittered man, a misogynist and something of an eccentric. He was a village atheist, who had rebelled against his preacher father's unforgiving old-time religion; he may have been harboring a deeper psychological wound inflicted when his father deserted his wife and children to run off with a parishioner. He wrote antireligious editorials in his newspaper, scarcely orthodox fare in a family journal. Like his father, he deserted his wife, though not for another woman, and he didn't go very far, setting up bachelor quarters in a little house in his neighbor's backyard. His son recalled that his father was a gloomy man, unhappy 80 percent of the time and subject to spells of melancholia that lasted for weeks, during which he would not speak to his son. Perhaps because of his role as the village infidel and his attacks on farmers as "'wolves," he numbered H.L. Mencken among his fans; Mencken, championing literary realism wherever he found it, also admired Howe's plain, blunt style, his "resolutely relentless honesty, sacrificing every appearance, however charming, to what he considers the truth."[50] Howe composed a series of maxims that were reprinted in newspapers nationwide and that were a mixture of shrewd, cranky observations on small-town life, and life in general, and praise for free enterprise:

> There must be poverty to punish the shiftless, and encourage industry. If you can forgive the magnificence and vanity of a successful politician, why are you unable to forgive a successful businessman? Every time I strike a match or turn an electric button, or use the telephone, I am indebted to businessmen, but if I am in debt to any politician I do not know it. Every business establishment is in danger of ruin because of the clamor of employees for shorter hours, and their victory would ruin it."[51]

Howe had gone from debunker of the small-town myth to a small-town sage, who was quoted approvingly on Wall Street and in the boardrooms. After he retired from editorship of his newspaper, he published a personal newsletter called *E.W. Howe's Monthly,* full of maxims like those above, which were widely reprinted and quoted. John D. Rockefeller once ordered two hundred copies of a single issue. In the 1920s, when, as Frederick Lewis Allen wrote in *Only Yesterday,* "business had become almost the national religion of America,"[52] when indeed, *The Man Nobody Knows,* a book by advertising man Bruce Barton, portrayed Christ as "the founder of modern business," and when Columbia University was using door-to-door salesmen to flag its business courses—Howe was just as attuned to the *Zeitgeist* as Horatio Alger had been in his day. Alger was the voice of the young, ambitious country boy in the big city; Howe was a voice from the village, celebrating urban big business. He was a self-made man, a former printer who had bought a small-town newspaper, fought off competitors, and became a success, making twenty-five thousand dollars a year from his paper. Stories in the mass magazines such as *Liberty,* the *Saturday Evening Post,* and *Collier's* also extolled business success and made the businessman a hero. These contrasted with warm, optimistic stories set in a small town, often featuring a shrewd rural philosopher, in the lineage founded by Edward Westcott in his novel *David Harum,* which appeared in 1898 and sold three quarters of a million copies within two years.

Other writers of the era of considerably more skill apostrophized the small town itself as the embodiment of friendliness and neighborliness. While Howe extolled the virtues of unfettered capitalism, transmuting them into small-town terms and thus giving them legitimacy as fundamental American values, literary defenders of the small town recreated it as a sanctuary of goodnesss and folksiness, a refuge from a hostile world. This hostile world was urban, industrialized America—the world created by the business ideals that Ed Howe celebrated. But the sentimentalizers' message was not critical of these values; it was rather an escape from them into the idealized town, where the battered soul from the city was therapeutically bathed in love, fellowship, and egalitarian acceptance.

Prominent among the small town's literary defenders was Zona Gale, who wrote two books of stories, published in 1908 and 1909, about a middle western town called Friendship Village. Gale used the term "togetherness" to describe village friendliness. She has a character in one story exclaim after a social event, "I declare, it wasn't so much the stuff they brought in, though that was elegant, but it was the Togetherness of it. I couldn't get to sleep that night for thinkin' about God not havin' anybody to neighbor with."[53] Gale's characters are quite capable of saying things like, "If you want to love folks, just you get in some kind o' respectable trouble in Friendship, an' you'll see so much loveableness that the trouble'll kind o' spindle out an' leave nothin' but the love doin' business."[54]

Booth Tarkington sounded similar sentiments in his novel *The Gentleman from Indiana,* published in 1899. Plattville, his fictional Indiana town, is inhabited by people who seem "one big, jolly family"[55] to the eastern-educated hero, John Harkless, who chucks a newspaper career in New York to become editor of the local paper. Indeed they are a homogeneous bunch—all white and middle-class; the "trashy" element is segregated in a nearby hamlet called Six-Cross-Road. That is, they are segregated until they nearly kill Harkless, who has crusaded against them in his columns. The town rises up, and kicks out the Six-Cross-Roaders. Harkless, a dropout from the city rat race and self-condemned failure, finds contentment and the love of a beautiful, modern woman in this small town inhabited by the "beautiful people."

Even a committed realist like Hamlin Garland could not completely abstain from contrasting small-town kindliness with the impersonality of the city, though not without ambivalence. In Garland's story "God's Ravens," a reporter returns to his hometown in Wisconsin to escape from Chicago, the "great grimy terrible city."[56] His initial impressions are critical, but then one day he faints in the street. The people of the town rush to his aid and lavish kindness on his family. Garland's happy ending is forced and sentimental, and a complete break with his harsh description of the townspeople's hypocrisy and petty-minded gossip that preceeded it.

In Willa Cather's *O Pioneers!*, the heroine, Alexandra Bergson, worries that she has missed something in her hard life and cries out that she would rather have the freedom city folk have than her prosperous farm. But her childhood friend, Carl Linstrum, who lives in the city, tells her, "Freedom so often means that one isn't needed anywhere. Here you are an individual, you have a background of your own, you would be missed. But off there in the cities there are thousands of rolling stones like me. . . . When one of us dies, they scarcely know where to bury him."[57]

There was a common theme running through the "just folks" school of small-town literature—the small town as haven from the anxieties of economic and social change. As Anthony Channell Hilfer puts it, "The village myth itself served readers of such fiction as a temporary refuge from the supposedly peculiarly urban complications and tragedies of life."[58] The myth was needed to provide escape from a society of cities packed with poor people and grimy factories, under an inhumane industrial system that made working men and women interchangeable tenders of machines and an economic system that extolled predatory amoral competition. In *The Gentleman from Indiana* John Harkless tells of becoming disillusioned with "the rush and fight and scramble to be first, to beat the other man."[59] He saw his classmates "growing too busy to meet and be good to any man who couldn't be good to them." And there was "the cruel competition, the thousands fighting for places, the multitude scrambling for each gingerbread baton, the cold faces on the street."[60] Harkless finds he must go back home to Indiana because "the people out in these parts knew more—had more *sense* and were less artificial . . . and were kinder and tried less to be somebody else than almost any other people anywhere."[61] Plattville, then, is a place "where people are kind to each other, and where they had the old-fashioned way of saying 'Home.' "[62] In short, Tarkington protests against the coldness and superficiality of the city in contrast to the common sense, genuineness, and deep friendliness of small-town folks. But his novel is ultimately an empty protest, an escape into the warm womb of "home."

Zona Gale's narrator in the Friendship Village stories only hints at her past, but we learn she too has fled the big city and (like Gale herself) had an unhappy love affair; at the end of the book her lover rejoins her, providing a final happy ending in a book that is well-larded with them. Friendship Village is not remote from modern developments. The main street is macadamized; the rich widow, Mrs. Proudfit, owns a motor car; there are telephones. But the improvements blend into the "medieval" qualities of the village, its customs and folksiness: "With us all the Friendship idea prevails: we accept what Progress sends, but we regard it in our own fashion"[63]—which is to say with a kind of quaint eccentricity. The people in Friendship Village are not without faults but they are always brought round by kindness, love, and faith in God. Mrs. Proudfit, as her name implies, is a bit proud, snobbish and sanctimonious; she is also rich and takes frequent trips to Europe. Well, she rescues a local girl who has returned to Friendship after ten years, in seeming disgrace because she had run off with her stepsister's boyfriend. Indeed, the whole town embraces the prodigal daughter. A sanctimonious church deacon (as it must be in heaven, sanctimony is the most prevalent sin among Friendship Villagers), refuses to let the women of the town temporarily house and feed a group of orphans stranded by a train wreck. But just let him see their rosy cheeks and hear the organ played divinely in the background and he melts—and anyhow "he's an awful tender-hearted man in spite of being so notional."[64] There are no poor or sick in Friendship, only those who, like the narrator and various widows, are "soul sick an' soul hungry."[65] A surprise Christmas dinner fixes them up nicely. In the world of

Friendship Village, the happy ending is as common and pervasive as the Monday washing on the line.

Friendship Village is a town of womenfolk who do good works, gently bully their shadowy menfolk into doing nice things, and cultivate happiness, even though they all have some sorrow in their past. The strongest male figures are two clerics—one, kindly old Dr. June, and the other a more manly rural preacher, who ends up marrying his old love, the fallen woman who returned in disgrace and is redeemed by togetherness. Gale's two male heroes are tailored to the tastes of the pietistic female readers whose tastes dictated sentimental character of the popular fiction of the era.

This view of life distantly echoed William Dean Howells's call for literature to present the "more smiling aspects of life" and extol the "large cheerful average of health and success and happy life,"[66] though Howells had in mind a truly American literature that would echo this country's optimism and prosperity, not the sentimental pieties of Gale and Tarkington. Certainly pre-industrial American life had its smiling aspects and these endured amid the upheavals of the Industrial Revolution. Van Wyck Brooks describes the older America that still survived in—

> the old settled West, the prosperous communities of Ohio for instance, with Indiana and Illinois, that were often allied to New England in origin and feeling . . . [where] one felt the genial atmosphere of the horse-and-buggy age, warm, kindly, tranquil, neighborly, unhurried. Leisurely homekeeping people jogged about in their phaetons and surreys, perhaps on some 'little drive around our town' to show their cousins from Topeka the cast-iron statues of the mastiff and the deer that one of their prosperous friends had set up on his lawn . . . [the] unquestionable signs of the modest wealth of some Civil War general or colonel whose most intimate friend was perhaps the local harness-maker. For virtually all wealth was still modest in these villages and towns, where there were always men sitting on fence-rails, whittling, in alpaca coats and loungers in tilted chairs in front of the hotel.[67]

Here was to be found what Howells praised as the "large cheerful average of health and success and happy life" that makes up the dominant American experience.

Gale, Tarkington, and even Jewett were convalescents from the wounds inflicted by the city; small towns had been their quasi-sanitariums in periods of depression in their lives. What they expressed in their stories sounded an answering chord in Americans who, although they might live in the city, saw the small town as an idealized refuge from urban complexities—a place, as Robert Frost defined home, where when you have to go there they have to take you in. Garland was the archetypal wandering American who longs for some lost home and never finds it. He tried the small town, he tried the city, and he tried Europe, but none really satisfied his hunger. Life in West Salem, Wisconsin, had yielded up the disillusioning knowledge that the people were obsessed with the new and forgot the old (he might have appreciated more the Maine towns Sarah Orne Jewett describes, where the old widows paid regular visits to their deceased husbands and ancestors at the burying ground and meditated upon the past). Like many wandering Americans, Garland ended up in California, the terminus of the American westering dream—the place where his wandering father had longed to go.

Theodore Dreiser wrote of the tug of small-town life even as he rejected it in his autobiographical *A Hoosier Holiday*, anticipating his fellow Hoosier, the coiner and proponent of "sweetness and light," Meredith Nicholson. In *The Valley of Democracy*, published in 1918, Nicholson extolled "the real 'folksy' bread-and-butter people who are, after all, the mainstay of our democracy"[68] and located them in the farms, villages, and small towns of the Middle West. Dreiser rejected the placidity of small-town life as antithetical to his vision of literature. "Out of its charms and sentiments," Dreiser wrote, "I might have composed an elegy or an epic, but I could not believe that it was more than a frail flower of romance."[69] He turned his back on the town and in his heroic and pioneering novels broke the trail followed by realists of the teens and twenties who perceived the sentimental view of small-town life in the ruling genteel tradition as a falsification of the small-town life they had experienced growing up.

The real import of the small-town myth was that it flowered in popular literature at a time when whatever grounds it had as an accurate reflection of life were fading from the scene; perhaps that is why its literary propagators fastened such excessive praise upon it. The town was becoming increasingly urbanized in outlook as it sought to survive in the new industrialized nation; its people clung to ideals that were preserved by its insularity and nurtured by its ties with the land, but twentieth-century social change made those ideals increasingly empty. When Gale and Tarkington spoke of "togetherness" and "the folks," they had a vision of stable, homogeneous, conflict-free communities—a watered-down version of the New England founding fathers' vision of covenanted towns—Christian utopias in the wilderness. But that vision had, in an age of a national industrial economy, become obsolete.

Even so, the early forms of industrial production caused a minimum of disruption of traditional village life. In the early nineteenth century, industry in the United States meant mainly the textile mills, although Eli Whitney practiced a rudimentary form of mass production at his arms factory near New Haven, Connecticut, when he was making rifles for the War of 1812. Most manufacturing was done by individual craftsmen, each of whom made the entire shoe or suit or gun or whatever. The industrial centers of textile manufacturing were in New England, where the factories in Lowell and other towns had been financed by Boston capitalists. These New England factory-towns were initially run in a spirit of benevolent paternalism, grounded in the Puritan ethic. The farm girls who came to work at the Lowell mills worked under conditions regarded as a model of enlightened concern for their welfare (the millowners knew that if conditions had been otherwise, their parents would not let them come). They were chaperoned and exposed to education and moral instruction. Their hours were long and their pay low, but they were able to save something and were expected eventually to return home and marry that fine farm boy next door. This rosy picture, which entranced even the dyspeptic Charles Dickens on his visit to America, soon clouded over; working conditions deteriorated, the girls went home, and a proletariat of immigrant workers earning subsistence wages was spawned. In short, all the evils of industrialism—as well as its successes—were born in Lowell and its sister industrial cities.

Such mill towns were different from most small towns. Their plants were based upon large concentrations of capital infused from outside, and they employed masses of unskilled workers. They quickly were blighted by the by-products of uncontrolled industrialism—disease, poverty, noisome slums. Benevolent paternalism lingered in the relationship between owner and workers, but it had been transformed into a system for enforcing the rigid discipline of mass production. Workers and their families lived under the thumb of the company, but the company had no obligation to them—as did the master to the apprentices in his home workshop. The paternalism of the craft system was replaced by a system of free labor, but vestiges lingered. Workers' lives were regulated, ostensibly in the interests of morals and Christianity, but actually in order to get more work out of them at lower cost. The fierceness of competition in the textile industry and its vulnerability to national economic cycles further lessened the workers' economic security. These mill towns became small cities, with their economic base the profits and wages of industry, in contrast to smaller places where farmers were in the majority, and the craftsmen or small-factory workers might work part-time on their farms.

The Lowell factories represented one kind of industrialization, but there were others. Another early type which might be called nonurban or "grass roots" industrialization also arose. Here the town remained small, and the industry was locally capitalized and often shaky. Products were made for a home market, and the emphasis was on local labor and craftsmanship. Often the "industry" mainly involved processing local products of agriculture or of the mines and forests. In a few cases, a specialty achieved a wider market, but frequently, as the town became linked to the urban centers by better transportation, the local industries died off, and the goods they had once produced were shipped in. The virtue of locally owned industry was that it remained responsive, to a degree, to a community of which its owners were a part.

A variant of nonurban industrialization was small-scale rural manufacture of textiles, a product of the age of waterpower. The mills were loccated in hamlets and specifically founded to manufacture textiles for a wider market, rather than process the local agricultural products for the use of the farmers. There were many of these mill hamlets in eastern Pennsylvania and Delaware. An example was the cluster of mill hamlets around Rockdale, Pennsylvania. Anthony F.C. Wallace described a typical setting in his book *Rockdale.* Each hamlet resembled an English village, with the millowner living in the great house, high on the hill, and the workers close by the mill below. The factories were typical textile mills of the early nineteenth century, three-story structures of Pennsylvania fieldstone, sometimes covered with yellow and white stucco. The workers lived in tenements provided by the millowner, constructed in the same way. The mills were built along a creek, which supplied their power. "The mills themselves, powered only by water, whispered and grunted softly; the looms clattered behind windows closed to keep moisture in the air; even when the workers were summoned, it was by the bell in the cupola and not by a steam whistle."[70] The setting was predominately rural, there were farms about, and many farmers worked in the mills in slack times. There was no pollution or noise—railroads would not reach Rockdale until 1856—and the source of power was constant. The number of workers in each mill was small; their wages, except for the simplest jobs (which were usually performed by children) were relatively good. The owners' rents for the housing were low, and workers raised food in their own garden plots. The owners themselves were usually not wealthy men, although they generally came from socially prominent families. With borrowed money they went into business for themselves in order to make a fortune appropriate to their station. Their attitudes were paternalistic, shaped by the evangelical Christian movement of the 1840s and 1850s.

In sum, Rockdale in 1841 "was almost a self-sufficient rural community, like a plantation or a commune, tied economically to world markets and financial centers by the buying of raw cotton and the selling of yarn and cloth, and linked intellectually and spiritually to the wider culture by the participation of its citizens in migration, travel and reading. Its social structure of caste and class, its style of family life, were for the moment not seriously in question, and the deeper dilemmas inherent in its way of life were not yet fully realized by its citizens."[71]

Rockdale represented a kind of pastoral small-town industrialization, a harmonization of town and country, worker and capitalist; the relationship between the owner and the employee was almost feudal, like that between master and serf—or in more modern terms, between farmer and farmhand. It was not an ideal system and was of its time; but it did stand for the best kind of enlightened industrialism and retained at least a simulacrum of the village virtues. The workers' villages were really dormitories, from which they trudged daily to their jobs. Still they were encouraged to have a family life (a significant proportion of the Rockdale families were headed by widows, whose only support was the labor of their children and who were thus drawn by the availability of jobs for women and children in the mills). Their children were, after the passage of the public education laws of the 1840s, educated, and the owners' pious wives tended to their souls. Each community was self-sufficient, yet there was mobility among them, as well as intermarriage; artisans, tradesmen, storekeepers, doctors, and ministers were scattered about the area, providing their necessary services in a manner that resembled the rural South more than New England. But each village was run by the resident millowner; there was no self-government. These company towns did not maltreat the workers, but they were as devoid of democracy as an army barracks.

The hamlets of Rockdale then might be classified as specialized towns—rural worker-barracks, set up and benevolently maintained to service the mills with a stable, orderly, powerless labor force. The workers were, in Marxian terms, a landless proletariat (except for their rented cottages and gardens) without any effective organization or status other than that bestowed upon them by the owners. Certain of the more skilled mill operators, such as the mule spinners, might have qualified as craftsmen, but they never organized. In nearby Philadelphia there were several handicraft unions—carpenters, cordwainers, handloom weavers, house painters, printers, pharmacists, and more—but they were religious and middle-class in their aspirations, and looked down upon the kinds of people drawn to the mills—women, children, and Irish and other immigrants. The crafts, which were outgrowths of the old medieval guilds with their apprentice-journeyman-master system and control over training and quality of work, did join together in a Workingman's party for a while, but this fell apart. They then abandoned politics and concentrated on economic issues, and their strike in 1835 won them the ten-hour day. The textile workers remained unorganized and worked a twelve- to fourteen-hour day for nearly eighteen years more (five of these years under a state law mandating a ten-hour-day, which the Rockdale owners defied), until their employers decided it was the better part of Christian virtue to give them a ten-hour day. But whatever the different skills involved in the textile workers' jobs, they were interchangeable, unskilled machine-tenders, and only those performing foremanlike duties could hope to rise in wealth and status. In the relatively idyllic system of communal industrialism practiced in Rockdale, the workers remained content with their lot; for many the job was a way station to a farm in the West. When this escape hatch was shut, the idyll ended. Rockdale's decentralized industry was based on waterpower; a more conventional, urban factory system came into being in nearby Chester, made possible by the use of steam power.

In the pre–Civil War period the craft system flourished, but the presence of the factory system and assembly-line production was being felt. Richard P. Horwitz looked into industrialization in Winthrop, Maine, between 1820 and 1850 and found a remarkable stability in the popular terminology for the various jobs, even though working conditions were evolving toward an industrial pattern. There was a general class of "workingman," which included both the "manufacturer," the man who ran the mill or shop, and the mechanic or artisan—a skilled craftsman who rose out of the apprentice system and who possessed skills and a greater responsibility for the quality of the product. An "operative" was someone who tended a machine, but operatives might be called mechanics too. "Laborers," however, never were. They were the lowest level, performing unskilled tasks and ranking with the farmer's hired hand. Mechanics were respected, but not as much as those in business or trade or the professions; the highest ranking was the antique rank of "gentleman," a man of wealth who did not need to work, but nonetheless busied himself with important affairs. "Capitalists" were also looked up to, because they were men of wealth who had the awesome power to found large enterprises. There were no capitalists in Winthrop; the closest thing was an "entrepreneur," who started a small business or trade, risking his own or borrowed money. Professional men, because of their college education and important work, were highly regarded.

The keys to status were the kind of work one did and the amount of money one earned; the wealthy young layabouts who tried to fob themselves off as gentlemen were scorned by the community, because they challenged its fundamental values of hard work, "character," skill, trustworthiness, and other Yankee virtues. Mechanics, because they worked with their hands, could never be the equal of businessmen and professionals, who worked with their heads, as the accepted division had it; professional men, because of their college training, were considered scholarly and wise and were therefore ranked above most businessmen. Thus, mechanics were encouraged to "better" themselves by becoming manufacturers or businessmen, although such was the respect for the good mechanic's skill and industry that there was criticism of this downgrading of honest manual labor. Being apprenticed out to a craft was an honorable course for a young man; he might also be sent to learn business skills from an established shopkeeper. The term "mechanic" meant any skilled manual worker (including barbers) who was not a farmer (though farmers might become mechanics by starting small handicraft businesses on the side). There was no distinction made between "craft" and "industrial" workers. Whether or not the mechanic worked with a machine made no difference; "the 'mechanic' who tended a power loom was just a more productive 'weaver' than his . . . predecessors [who operated handlooms]."[72] Introduction of new, expensiive machines capable of turning out twice as much as the old ones had no effect upon their operators' status.

Similarly, division of labor—the change from one man making an entire product to several men each performing one operation in a process—had no great effect on status. Shoemaking was an important industry in Winthrop, and although it remained a handicraft, a division of labor arose with workers performing different operations in assembly-line fashion. The transition from old-style shoemaking to a rudimentary assembly line did not have the effect of lowering a worker's status from mechanic to operative—or laborer.

Technological changes in farming, in contrast, did produce two kinds of farmers—the self-styled "practical farmer," who followed the old ways proudly, and the "book farmer," a pejorative term for the farmer who read up on and tried to apply the new advances in farming techniques. Each saw himself as superior to the other, but the practical farmer had the weight of tradition on his side.

Horwitz concluded that the absence of rivalry in the industrial arena "could have contributed to Winthrop's rapid industrialization. Unlike the 'practical farmer' the 'mechanic' did not have to face a change in identity with the modernization of his duties. Though some people might begin to consider him an 'operative,' he would quite properly continue to think of himself as a 'mechanic.' " And mechanic was an honorific state. In other words, if industrialization had threatened self-worth and identity, its impact might have been more disruptive to the social order. But in pre-Civil War Winthrop, the old-style Yankee work ethic applied to all workingmen equally; the labor of no man who worked with his hands was held above that of any other man and he had a sense of belonging.

What we see in Winthrop is a gradual change in the social relationships of the work place engendered by new technology. The community's values could accommodate to these changes by ignoring them. What was happening though was fundamental: a breakdown in the master-apprentice system, the only social distinction that workingmen recognized. It embodied the ethos of paternalism, training, and a body of skills that all might acquire who underwent the necessary period of training. When this system broke down, other distinctions, imposed by the factory system, sprang up; workers became "operatives"—as they already had in Lowell, and to a lesser degree, in Rockdale. The operative was essentially a machine-tender, who was easily replaced, and whose skill was limited to the operation of that machine.

But in small towns, this loss of status was cushioned by a sense of community; the stubbornness of old ways, the reluctance to change, preserved the old relationships among workers, and the ways of doing the work changed slowly, almost imperceptibly. In larger, more rapidly industrializing towns and cities, such resistance to change had to be swept away; a new ideology rose up to justify the discipline of the factory system. For the paternalistic controls of the home workshop operated by a master craftsman was substituted the contract system of "free labor"—meaning a worker must meet the conditions laid down by his employer or be fired. At the same time, the churches preached a new gospel of temperance, discipline and good order—the key virtues of an obedient, hard-working, steady workforce. This early gospel of industrialization implied at least a complementary duty by the owner to look after the welfare of his workers. But this obligation was not good business and was soon sacrificed to the pressures of competition-engendered cost-cutting. And so, in its place, came a more compatible doctrine—which preached absolute rights of property and survival of the fittest. By 1890 these streams of change had merged into a mighty river of industrialization.

The effects of the new industrialism on the town of Muncie, Indiana, were studied by a group of sociologists headed by Robert S. and Helen Merrell Lynd. Middletown, the pseudonym the Lynds gave to Muncie, was the title of the book they published in 1929, summarizing their findings in rich and voluminous detail. They focused on the changes in Muncie during the watershed years between 1890 and 1925, when it grew from a quiet country town into a highly industrialized small city, with both locally owned and absentee-owned factories, employing modern high-speed mass-production techniques. "This narrow strip of thirty-five years," the Lynds wrote, "comprehends for hundreds of American communities the industrial revolution that has descended upon villages and town."[73]

The Muncie of 1890 was in the midst of a boom and awash with visions of ever-ascending prosperity. Huge quantities of natural gas had been discovered in the area, and the burning flames on the uncapped wells were like election-night torches celebrating a glorious victory that would usher in a new era. The local boomers christened Muncie "Magic Town" and rubbed their hands over rising real-estate values; it was the answer to every small-town prayer. Factories came in to use the natural gas—so cheap and plentiful, it seemed, that it was almost like the air you breathed. One of the most notable businesses was the Ball family's glass jar factory, which made the famous Ball mason jars, a name that became generic, like Kleenex, for probably the best receptacle ever devised for home canning and preserving.

In the Muncie of that era, the Lynds discerned two main classes—which they denominated the business and the working classes. The criterion for this simple breakdown was the old one of working with one's hands, with things, versus working with people. The striking fact about those two classes at that time was their relative equality. The working class was made up of skilled craftsmen—notably the glassblowers who made the Ball jars. They had an apprentice-master system and active fraternal organizations such as the Knights of Labor. They mingled democratically with lawyers and businessmen in the active, well-attended debating and study groups of the day. Noted labor leaders came to town to speak and received warm public receptions. Economically the skilled workingmen were as well-off as most businessmen, and their incomes were more secure than the businessmen's. In short, they had respect and status.

By 1924 it had all changed, however, and the cause was industrialization—or, more specifically, the advent of mass-production machines which replaced skilled craftsmen. No longer were the glassblowers needed at the Ball plant; their place had been taken by machines which could be operated by the rawest farm boy after a few weeks training. Indeed, young men were more adept at operating the machines than older men; thus the veneration of age and hierarchy built into the apprenticeship system withered away. The "mechanic" had become an "operative"—indeed, almost a "laborer"—doing a boring, routine, repetitive job. There was no way he could move up in the factory, except by becoming a foreman. But the foreman's job had changed too. It required administrative skills, as well as the ability to manipulate people; mechanical skills were secondary. As a result, some businesses hired foremen directly out of colleges where they had studied management skills.

Social life was affected too. In the old Muncie, the workers lived near their places of work, but the coming of the automobile and public transportation enabled them to live anywhere; old neighborhoods were broken up and people made their homes among strangers. "Visiting" or "neighboring," once ritual pastimes among the working class, fell off, while social isolation increased. The loneliness and alienation of the city had entered the gates of the small town.

While the workingman was losing his former perquisites of status and self-respect, the business class was on the rise. Their values were in the saddle by the 1920s. As the workingmen's associations lost ground, Rotary, Kiwanis, the Boosters, and the other sanctums of Babbittry became the citadels of power and prestige. Deprived of prestige and satisfaction in his work, the worker had to find new ways to achieve status; the only way that was open was the middle-class way. Consumption—and the acquisition of money. And so the mass producer became a mass consumer, taking satisfaction in acquiring possessions—a car, a radio, and all the other goods that national advertising trumpeted to him. The consumption ethic was already familiar to the business class, so they had fewer problems in adjusting to the new ways.

The worker, having lost his traditional path of upward mobility within a craft, was forced to accept the businessman's success ethic. If, as was likely, he could not achieve business success, at least his children could, so giving them a boost up the educational ladder out of the working class became a major aim of solid working-class people. But the schools with their cliques and fraternities aped the class values of the business class, and so the easiest road to recognition for a working-class boy was through athletics (for the girl it was marriage, but her only negotiable assets were looks and charm). Businessmen devoted their leisure to cultivating contacts that would be helpful to them in making more money, but workers had no such opportunities, so their leisure was devoted to escaping from the deadening routine of the job.

Such, in simplified form, was the story of what happened to Muncie. The public proclamations of the emergent businessmen and merchants sometimes sound as though they had been written by Sinclair Lewis; their values echo the aphorisms of Ed Howe. The Lynds, however, maintain their scientific detachment—and their liking for the people of Muncie. The cardinal tenet of the local faith was still friendliness, and the people took as much pride in it as a housewife in her angel food cake, serving it up to strangers with that shy pride middle western folk have; or else with the booming bonhomie of the businessman, which foreigners find so repellent and which is actually a kind of over-anxious social kindness of the sort that dreads the initial silences between strangers and blunderingly patches them over. Middletown was a livewire, friendly burg, as one of Lewis's characters might have said, and if it was distrustful of Reds, atheists, foreigners, bohemians, Negroes, highbrows, pacifists, "knockers," and other "outsiders," it would let alone those who were "different"—even show a patronizing fondness for them—so long as they didn't represent a threat to the fundamental values of the town.

The sociologist W. Lloyd Warner in his study of "Yankee City" (Newburyport, Connecticut) found similar effects of industrialization, along with an elaborately described class system. In 1930 Newburyport was an old New England town with a population of seventeen thousand. Its principal industry, shoe manufacturing, had undergone the same radical transformations that the manufacture of glass jars in Muncie had. As in Winthrop, shoemaking had progressed from families making their own to individual craftsmen in home workshops (which also served as retail stores) to masters with small shops of apprentices, performing specialized operations, with other entrepreneurs marketing the shoes. Then the entire process of shoemaking was mechanized, and the old craft system was wiped out. A crucial variable in Newburyport was the absentee ownership of the factories. The original owners, three native sons who founded the businesses and built them up into successes, had sold out to large chains. These three patriarchs knew their workmen by name. Because of their involvement in the town life and their emotional commitment to its welfare, they were sensitive to local public opinion. After they sold out to large chains based in New York, this personal, local touch was gone. Outsiders came in to run the plants, and they were correct, but remote and bureaucratically oriented.

A decisive event occured while Warner's team of sociologists had Newburyport on the examining table—the strike of 1933. There had been other strikes but none so militant, so traumatic. Warner concluded that the deeply divisive strike was a symptom of the crumbling of the old Newburyport way of life—not only its paternalistic, craft-oriented factories but also its social hierarchy. In the past, efforts by union organizers had been futile, but in 1933 the workers welcomed the unions and, what is more, extended their solidarity to their brother shoe-workmen in other towns. The big-city absentee owners—several of them Jewish—became scapegoats for the workers' resentment against their loss of status. The new managers actually running the factories were regarded by the workers as mere errand boys, carrying out the unpopular policies of the owners. In comparison, the old owners were part of the community, their wealth and ancestry had placed them at the top of the town's social, economic, and political hierarchy. The men nostalgically associated the reign of the old owners with the time when their jobs had status and they had self-respect.

Since the old hierarchy had broken down, there was no longer a system of reciprocal rights and obligations between workers and owners, no feelings of "a common way of life in which each did what he had to do, and, in so doing, worked for himself and for the well-being of all."[74] The union thus filled a vacuum: "The workers of Yankee City were able to strike, maintain their solidarity, and in a sense flee to the protection of the unions because the disappearance of craftsmanship and the decreasing opportunities for social mobility had made them more alike, with common problems and common hostilities against management."[75]

The workers had been melted down into an undifferentiated mass and were increasingly driven to act out of common interests. "There is no doubt," Warner wrote, "that each worker's uneasiness and reasoning about what was happening to the status of his family and himself—a situation which he meagerly comprehended and which was almost beyond his ability to communicate coherently to his fellows—whipped him into attacking the owners, who provided visible targets and could be held responsible for the loss and degradation of the worker's cherished way of life."[76]

It might be charged that Newburyport, with its old-style Yankee social hierarchy, was a rather unique community. Still, Warner and his team had laid open the living bone, tissue, and nervous system of a traditional New England city in which the upper economic classes and the people "who ran things" coincided. By the 1930s this hierarchy, founded fifty years before, was dying; yet it cast a clear shadow over the present; its breakdown intensified the feelings of loss of status the workers felt. Outside forces had taken over the community, but not in a clearcut way; their authority was bureaucratic and not moral, economic but impersonal and lacking the emotional bonds and weight of tradition. Newburyport was entering a new era: Its institutions shivered and creaked, like an old house settling after it has been moved to a new location. Life in the new era went on, but something irretrievable had been lost.

An elegy for the small-town ways that vanished with the coming of industrialization appears in Sherwood Anderson's novel *Poor White*, published in 1920. The novel dramatized the destruction by industrialization of the old values of closeness to the land, craftsman's pride, the ties of community. The hero, a practical dreamer named Hugh McVey, drifts around the towns of the Middle West, searching for something. He observes, from the outside, the "undercurrent of life" in those small middle western towns, where, in even the smallest, "a quaint interesting civilization was being developed. Men worked hard but were much in the open air and had time to think. Their minds reached out toward the solution of the mystery of existence."[77] Country lawyers read Tom Paine; farmers talked of work, God, and America's destiny.

And "the people who lived in the towns were to each other like members of a great family. . . . A kind of invisible roof beneath which every one lived spread itself over each town. Beneath the roof boys and girls were born, grew up, quarreled, fought, and formed friendships with their fellows, were introduced into the mysteries of love, married and became the fathers and mothers of children, grew old, sickened, and died. Within the invisible circle and under the great roof every one knew his neighbor and was known to him. Strangers did not come and go swiftly and mysteriously and there was no constant and confusing fear of machinery and of new projects afoot. For the moment mankind seemed about to take the time to understand itself."[78]

To Anderson, the roof was a metaphor of community; the town was a substitute family—"walled in, isolated, the one big family feeling that did prevail."[79] Bidworth became a metaphor for all the little towns of preindustrial America at the time when *Poor White* is set, a pastoral of families working in the fields, men gossiping on street corners, craftsmen at work in their shops, taking pride in their work.

Then industrialization comes; its catalyst is the lonely dreamer, Hugh McVey. To avoid the idle dreams of his boyhood, he attempts to busy himself with practical things, as the New England–born stationmaster's wife who raised him taught him to do. He invents a mechanical planter, and a local entrepreneur invests in it, raising money by selling stock. A factory goes up; it fails, but another comes—and the "invisible roof" is breached.

Anderson's own hometown of Clyde, Ohio, was in the foreground of his mind in writing *Poor White*. The town had become a small railroad terminal of north-south and east-west lines. The railroads shipped the area's raspberries and cabbages or sauerkraut to the nearby cities. Small local industries had sprung up, such as the Clyde Cooperage Company, which made barrels for the sauerkraut. In the 1880s there were also an underwear factory, a granite and marble company, and several nurseries and greenhouses. Then a large parlor-organ manufacturing plant was built outside town along the railroad. It later made furniture, then pianos, then bicycles, and then, in the early 1900s, Elmore automobiles. Anderson's theme in *Poor White* was suggested by the coming of industry to hundreds of small towns like Clyde, and the effects of the loss of the humane contemplative agrarian ways and the pride and independence of the craftsmen. "Something was in the air," Anderson wrote in his autobiography, *A Story Teller's Story* (1924). "One breathed a new spirit into the lungs."[80] The factories were coming in—into Ohio and all the middle western states, "and no town was without hope of becoming an industrial centre."[81] His feckless father had talked of years of apprenticeship and becoming a craftsman: "It's something at your back," he told his sons, "something that can be depended upon. It makes a man able to stand up as a man before his fellows."[82] But when Irwin Anderson imbibed the spirit of the new age, he changed his dreams to quick riches. The town's authentic craftsmen—Vet Howard, a wheelwright; Val Voght, an old white-bearded merchant; Thad Hurd, a storekeeper—spoke to the boys more soberly: " 'Things are on the march,' they said, 'and the new generation will do great things. We older fellows belong to something that is passing. We had our trades and worked at them, but you young fellows have to think of something else. . . . Get into the manufacturing business if you can. The thing now is to get rich, be in the swim. That's the ticket.' "[83] Anderson observes that "learning a craft was a slow business and one was in a hurry. 'Hurry' was the battle cry of the day."[84]

Anderson went to work in the factories—first in a nail factory and then in a bicycle factory, as an assembler: "With some ten or twelve other men I worked at a bench in a long room facing a row of windows. We assembled the parts that were brought to us by boys from other departments of the factory and put the bicycles together. There was such and such a screw to go into such and such a screw hole, such and such a nut to go on such and such a bolt. As always in the modern factory nothing ever varied and within a week any intelligent quick-handed man could have done the work with his eyes closed. One turned certain screws, tightened certain bolts, whirled a wheel, fastened on certain foot pedals and passed the work on to the next man."[85]The workers talked endlessly of money and sex—"futile fellows, ever more and more loudly proclaiming their potency as they felt an age of impotency asserting itself in their bodies."[86]

In the bicycle factory he had a foreman named Rice, an old craftsman who used to make carriages by hand. He had been a friend of the owner of the factory and was given the job of supervising the dipping of the bicycle frames into paint. Rice added the final touch: a hand-painted decorative line on the frame, which he unerringly made straight. No one else could do it; Rice was a craftsman—"Every man to his trade,"[87] he said. But he felt contempt for what he was doing. "The dipping of bicycle frames in tanks of enamel is all right for you boys but for a real workman like me. . . . Bah."[88] Striping the bikes was the only job that took skill, but he hated it. He had to work, though, for he had a son who lost a leg in an accident and a big doctor bill to be paid. Rice cursed the coming of the horseless carriage—"the same as with these goddamn bicycles—all alike, all alike."[89] He gets drunk, then takes off running down the street: "I'm scared I'm going to cry or something so I run."[90]

What the workingman had lost was his rapport with his materials and with the end product of his labor. "To the workman, his materials are as the face of his God seen over the rim of the world. . . . Ford factories cannot kill the love of material in the workmen and always and in the end the love of materials and tools in the workmen will kill the Fords. Standardization is a phase. It will pass. . . . If the machine is to survive it will come again under the dominance of the hands of the workmen."[91]

Anderson didn't have the answers but he brooded over the questions. He wrote with the authority of one who had once held the values he now criticized. Part hustler, part dreamer as a boy—known as "Jobby" because of his incessant work at one job or another—he pursued business success energetically, getting out of the factory, becoming an advertising copywriter, founding his own paint-supply business in Elyria, Ohio, for which he wrote punchy mail-order copy. He was successful in business—always spoke of himself as a "slick businessman." After he had two nervous breakdowns from overwork, he left his wife and children and went to Chicago. There he worked in advertising, but declared himself a writer. He fancied that to counter the sterile forces of industrialism one must embrace a craft—in his case, writing. In *A Story Teller's Story*, he tells of reaching down "through all the broken surface distractions of modern life to that old craft out of which culture springs" and exults in finding his writer's vocation: "I sang as I worked, as in my boyhood I had often seen old craftsmen sing and as I had never heard men sing in factories."[92] "I had become a writer, a word-fellow. That was my craft," he proclaimed. "The arts are after all but the old crafts intensified, followed with religious fervor and determination by men who love them and deep down within him perhaps every man wants nothing more than anything else to be a good craftsman. Surely nothing in the modern world has been more destructive than the idea that man can live without the joy of hands and mind combined in craftsmanship, that men can live by the accumulation of monies, by trickery. In the crafts only one may exercise all one's functions. The body comes in, the mind comes in, all the sensual faculties become alive. When one writes one deals with a thousand influences that motivate his own and other lives. There is . . . the respect of what had gone before, for the work of older craftsmen."[93]

But the old ways were irretrievably gone, and only a few poet-dreamers like Anderson were there to eulogize its passing; most people living and working in towns were too busy or were not aware. Opposing industrialism was like standing on the tracks and crying "Stop!" at a huge, speeding locomotive named Progress. The question now was not stopping it but controlling it, humanizing it, keeping it a servant rather than a master. In his later life, Anderson became a socialist and spoke at union rallies in southern textile mills. He was a good speaker too, easy with the working men and women because he had been a factory hand himself, wandering among those little Ohio towns, living in lonely rooms. While he was editing his country weekly in Marion, Virginia, he went to Washington and interviewed Herbert Hoover, who was at the time secretary of commerce. Hoover was surely the man of the age—an engineer, a self-made millionaire, and smart to boot. Anderson asks him about industrialization and standardization and boredom among the workers. "When I go to ride in an automobile," Hoover tells him, "it does not matter to me that there are a million automobiles on the road just like mine. I am going somewhere and want to get there in what comfort I can at the lowest cost."[94] Anderson realizes that Hoover has capsulized his philosophy; he disagrees but remembers Hoover's talk about controlling the great floods of the Mississippi. "What happens to the age in which a man lives," he decides, "is like the Mississippi, a thing in nature. It is no good quarelling with the age in which you live."[95]

But a group of southern poets (of the "Fugitive" school) and teachers, historians, and novelists did quarrel with the age, raising a concerted agrarian protest in a collection of essays published in 1930 entitled *I'll Take My Stand.* It was a kind of last stand against industrialism by southerners who cherished the agrarian traditions of their region, traditions that nourished a civilization that was humane and affirmative of the spiritual and artistic values that industrialism ignored. The humanism they espoused was not an abstract or dilettantish one but was "deeply founded in the way of life itself—in its tables, chairs, portraits, festivals, laws, marriage customs."[96] Industrialism, they said in a collective manifesto, is out of control. Laborsaving devices are invented, which throw men out of work; a new industry comes along to sell a new commodity—which no one desires but which consumers are cajoled into buying—putting the men back to work. The cycle continues, for industrialism necessitates new machines and more consumption to keep the machines turning. The agrarians denied being nostalgists, or even against industry per se; most of them believed that the agrarian peoples of the South—who should ally with the populist farmers of the West—must preserve their way of life (a way of life that included subordination of the Negro; here, the Fugitives' humanism broke down with a crash).

I'll Take My Stand was an articulate cry from the Old South against the hustling promoters of the New South. Herman Clarence Nixon, a political economist, showed that the South had moved slowly into the industrial era and such industries as it had—those of Birmingham aside—were mainly devoted to processing agricultural products such as cotton or tobacco and could remain decentralized. Nonetheless, the exodus from the land was accelerating, and time was drawing short. Look at your past, the Agrarians said to the South and to all Americans, see what you stand to lose. Do you want to lose all of it? As Robert Penn Warren, the novelist, later wrote: "The past is always a rebuke to the present; . . . it's a better rebuke than any dream of the future. It's a better rebuke because you can see what some of the costs were, what frail virtues were achieved in the past by frail men."[97] Even though by now the South has become industrialized and urbanized, *I'll Take My Stand* endures as a strong critique of industrialism. The Agrarians were not trying to turn the clock back; they were simply demanding that men be sure they knew what time it was.

The effects of industrialism—and its sometime outcome, urbanization—on small towns from the 1890s through the 1920s were profound. Many of the towns were caught up in the fever, believing that if they did not join they would die, others fretted and tried to conceal their static population figures by inflating them. A faith that equated growth with progress seized them. Like the man who reaches middle age and suddenly realizes that he will go no further in his job, that he will remain married to the same woman the rest of his days, that the fires of youth are quenched—so did many towns, born in a boomer's optimism and sustained by the vision of ever-rising real-estate values and the hope of eventually becoming at least a small city, fear in their maturity that they would probably remain static. Like many middle-aged men, most did not accept their fate gracefully but developed roving eyes. The object of their ardent searches was often a fresh, young industry, which they hoped to lure to their town by using the older man's only remaining bait—money.

As early as 1882, Ed Howe had described the insatiable itch for industry of the people of his fictional Twin Mounds: "People were always miserable by reason of predictions that, unless impossible amounts of money were given to certain enterprises, the town would be ruined, and although they always gave, no sooner was one fund exhausted than it became necessary to raise another."[98]

Such was the behavior in Brookfield, Missouri, early in the twentieth century, which wooed and won, after great difficulty, a shoe factory. Brookfield's suit began when a crusading local editor launched a campaign to "stand up for Brookfield" and called for the formation of an improvement association of concerned citizens to bring in industry. After some casting about, it developed that the Brown Shoe Company of St. Louis was ready to open a branch factory devoted to the manufacture of fine ladies' shoes and employing five hundred well-paid skilled workers. Brookfield's civic leaders leaped into action and set about raising a subsidy of forty thousand dollars, which, along with free land for the plant site, would be the shoe company's if it decided to locate its factory in Brookfield.

The shoe company remained coy and said it was considering other towns. Eventually, Brookfield's only remaining rival was Taylorville, Illinois; two Missouri towns—Chillicothe and Macon—had dropped out to a heartfelt "Thank you, Sisters" from the Brookfield newspaper. Employing a polite form of extortion, the shoe company was holding out for the highest bidder, a practice that was commonplace in Missouri (only a few months before, Mexico, Missouri, had called for an end to such competition; it had lost out on its bid for another branch of the Brown Shoe Company when its rival, Moberly, had found out the amount of its bid and upped the figure by ten thousand dollars).

Finally, with a fattened bid of sixty thousand dollars, plus free land, water, and sewage, Brookfield won and the company actually built its plant. The factory, however, proved to be a mixed blessing, offering low wages and part-time work to unskilled labor to make cheap work shoes. Many of the workers were not local people, but outsiders drawn by the erection of the plant; at their low rates of pay they probably added more to the town's burden than they contributed in taxes and trade.

Town after town in the Middle West fell into the subsidy trap and found themselves with similar low-paying industries on their doorsteps. The promoters of such arrangements, of course, reaped the subsidies and benefited from a docile (nonunionized) small-town labor force. The local factories benefited too from a nonunion policy, since it meant that they did not have to compete with higher-paying factories for workers. The threat of such higher-paying new businesses, whether unionized or not, might indeed rally a town's business establishment against the newcomer—and usually they were successful. Such collusive monopolies limited job opportunities and pay in many towns. The nonunion newcomers also kept wages low by brandishing the threat to go elsewhere should the workers start listening to the subversive words of "outside agitators." When such a threat came, the town establishment usually rallied behind the industry and against the workers. The announcement that appeared in the Warsaw, Illinois, paper was a typical wounded cry by civic fathers who saw a dearly bought new industry in jeopardy:

> After several months of negotiation and investigation, the Mirror Leather Goods Company of Chicago had been induced to move its plant to our community. . . . Unfortunately agitation and intimidation is being attempted by paid organizers who care nothing for our community and who are schooled and trained in the art of creating unrest. The citizens of Warsaw are capable of handling any situation that may arise without the aid of outside paid agitators, who do not have the best interests of Warsaw and its people at heart.

In the small towns, the lust for growth was not without pathos, for their purses were small and their vulnerability to sharpers large. Not that the bringing in of outside industries was always a bad policy. If gone about prudently, with care taken to select stable firms that were appropriate to the town and to avoid excessive subsidies, the new industries could provide jobs that would keep the town's work force employed and absorb the surplus farmers. But it was a dilemma that continues to the present day.

At the dawn of the industrial era, businessmen and politicians saw only Progress, even as the ills of industrialism afflicted their towns. In Kalamazoo, Michigan, the new village president, Peyton Ranney, asked in his inaugural address in 1881: "What means the double and triple capacity of the workshop; what means the crowded tenements, the bursting houses, and the clamor of many for a habitation except that Kalamazoo is being lifted out of her passive condition."[99] The town's monopoly as a trading center was breaking up, as nearby villages along the railroad began dealing directly with the farmers. So Ranney was applauding the social upheaval as symptomatic of a new era for Kalamazoo as a manufacturing center. Had the railroad ended Kalamazoo's monopoly? Then the town would use the railroad to ship out the products of its new industries.

Kalamazoo's first great leap forward was successful. In 1882 Ranney was boasting that "evidences of general thrift are seen on every hand, from the busy and extensive shops to the man who furnishes the muscle to carry them on . . . our general business was never more flourishing than today. Our crowded streets and the clatter of the freight wagons are city-like; surely indicating the great increase in our commercial interests."[100] The city's population had doubled since 1870 and tripled by 1900. Factories sprang up, some producing for local consumption but the larger ones for wider markets—sash and door makers, paper companies, a foundry making ploughs and other farm implements, a manufacturer of spring-toothed harrows. Workers were paid one to two dollars a day, which was low for the times, but that did not matter to the boosters. As the local newspaper put it: "A city is the men who make it. Are they pushers, hard-workers, industrious, ever at it? The city shows it at once."[101] The editor also pronounced Kalamazoo "one of the most beautiful towns in the Union if not the most lovely of all."[102] As evidence for this claim he pointed to the mansions of the new, wealthy white-collar class, rising up on West Main and Woodward and Stuart avenues. But a local reformer named Caroline Bartlett Crane saw it differently. Kalamazoo, she wrote in a national magazine, "had all the big-city problems with few of their solutions."[103]

In his novel *The Magnificent Ambersons* that shrewd chronicler of the passing of the old order, Booth Tarkington, evoked the metamorphosis of a town (much like his native Indianapolis) into a city:

> New faces appeared at the dances of the winter; new faces had been appearing everywhere, for that matter, and familiar ones were disappearing, merged into the increasing crowd, or gone forever and missed a little and not long; for the town was growing and changing as it never had grown and changed before.
>
> It was heaving up in the middle incredibly; it was spreading incredibly; and as it heaved and spread, it befouled itself and darkened its sky. It's boundary was mere shapelessness on the run; a raw, new house would appear on a country road; four or five others would presently be built at intervals between it and the outskirts of the town; the country road would turn into an asphalt street with a brick-faced drug-store and a frame grocery at a corner; then bungalows and six-room cottages would swiftly speckle the open green spaces—and a farm had become a suburb which would immediately shoot out other suburbs into the country, on one side, and, on the other, join itself solidly to the city . . . But the great change was in the citizenry itself. What was left of the patriotic old-stock generation that had fought the Civil War, and subsequently controlled politics, had become venerable and little heeded . . . the old stock became less and less typical, and of the grown people who called the place home, less than a third had been born in it. There was a German quarter; there was a Jewish quarter; there was a negro quarter—square miles of it—called 'Bucktown'; there were many Irish neighborhoods; and there were large settlements of Italians, and of Hungarians, and of Rumanians . . . But . . . the almost dominant type on the streets downtown . . . was the emigrant's prosperous offspring; descen-

> dant of the emigrations of the Seventies and Eighties and Nineties, those great folk-journeyings in search not so directly of freedom and democracy as of more money for the same labor. . . .
>
> For as the town grew, it grew dirty, with an incredible completeness. The idealists put up magnificent business buildings and boasted of them, but the buildings were begrimed before they were finished. . . . They drew patriotic, optimistic breaths of the flying powdered filth of the streets, and took the foul and heavy smoke with gusto into the profundities of their lungs. "Boost! Don't knock!" they said. . . .
>
> They were happiest when tearing down and building up were most riotous, and when new factory districts were thundering into life. . . . They had one supreme theory; that the perfect beauty and happiness of cities and of human life was to be brought about by more factories; there was nothing they would not do to cajole a factory away from another city; and they were never more piteously embittered than when another city cajoled one away from them.[104]

Not all towns were so profoundly affected by industrialism in the late nineteenth century, but those that weren't wished they had been. Such was the contagion of Progress. Those frontier boomers and town jobbers turned out to have been more than mere real estate salesmen; they were prophets in the wilderness; their early gospel of Growth had become scripture, and the industrial city had become the magnet of the twentieth century, while the old village with its clopping horses and whittling loafers around the courthouse was excess baggage to be discarded by the army of young men and women in headlong flight to the city of their dreams.

8
The Village Rebels

"Chicago! Chicago!" went the last line of Floyd Dell's autobiographical novel *Moon-Calf*, the name tolling in the mind of the protagonist, Felix Fay, like a summons of destiny. Felix, who is Dell's alter ego, is the prototypical sensitive young man; he has served his newspaper apprenticeship, experienced his first bittersweet love, assimilated all that the intellectual life in the small town of Port Royal, Iowa, has to give, written his beauty-smitten first poems. It is time to move on to the city.

Thousands of artistic young men and women of Dell's generation in the Middle West heard the call and plunged into the larger stream of emigration from the farms and towns to the city—Chicago. Carl Sandburg, born in Galesburg, Illinois, vagabond, socialist, newspaperman, apostrophized the city in a harsh new unpoetic language that was far from the villanelles and roundelays Dell had shyly read to the small artistic set of Port Royal: "Hog Butcher for the World,/Tool Maker, Stacker of Wheat,/Player with Railroads and the Nation's Freight Handler;/Stormy, husky, brawling,/City of the Big Shoulders."[1] With a trace of the country boy's dazzlement, Sandburg celebrated the raw energy and business vitality of this boomtown-made-good on the inland sea, this "monster brain" of the Middle West's economy, which had grown from half a million to over a million souls between 1880 and 1890.

Theodore Dreiser, a tall, skinny, buck-toothed teenager, had made his initiatory journey to Chicago from Warsaw, Indiana, in 1884, at the age of thirteen, and would use his impressions sixteen years later to describe a similar journey by Caroline Meeber, heroine of his great naturalistic novel *Sister Carrie.* Indeed, he was to base Carrie's story on that of his sister Emma Dreiser, who came to the city, was seduced by a married man, and ran off to New York with him, after he had stolen thirty-five hundred dollars from the safe of the elegant saloon where he had been the trusted manager. All the pretty, soft Dreiser girls seem to drift into illicit love affairs in the city; the object of Dreiser's passion, however, was the city itself. Chicago, he wrote his friend H.L. Mencken much later (praising Mencken's book on Nietzsche), was a place "where the weak must go down and the strong remain."[2] This frail, clumsy, dreamy boy himself nearly drowned in the urban maelstrom, trying to earn his way at menial jobs he was not dexterous enough to perform. Ever afterward the city, with its imperious indifference to the weak and its prizes for the strong, remained the crucible of his literary vision. Dreiser's restless wanderings from Chicago (where he spent five years) to St. Louis to Toledo and Pittsburgh and Buffalo and finally New York only affirmed the metaphoric city in his mind. He once compared the city to a great plant—its flowers were the gaudy wealth and luxury of the rich and, feeding these flowers, making them bloom, were the roots sunk deep into the poverty of the masses. His own impoverished childhood had taught him, through the example of his pious father, that the essential force in the lives of the poor is not morality but necessity. He was mesmerized by the awesome gap between the rich and the poor in the city; he had known poverty and wrote articles about it, but he also wrote approving profiles of the successful businessmen of the day. In Pittsburgh, Dreiser had imbibed Herbert Spencer's philosophy of Social Darwinism—the survival of the fittest—and it made a deep impression on him. Spencer posited a natural "law of segregation," which drove men to herd together in the city, in accord with the law of social evolution from simplicity to complexity. "There is something in nature to make the many wish to be where the many are,"[3] Dreiser wrote, and the operation of this law resulted in these great agglomerations of human atoms, mindlessly swirling about like swarms of bees. Some sank exhausted to the bottom of the hive, and a few lived in royal luxury, like the queen bee, off the efforts of the workers and drones. "Here were huge dreams and lusts and vanities being gratified hourly."[4] Religious morality, the conventional Christian God had nothing to do with it, and indeed the vaporous pieties of the church merely blinded men to their fundamental self-interest.

Dreiser's early years in Chicago made an indelible imprint upon him, and he later described the waves of young immigrants like himself who came there in the last years of the nineteenth century: "To it, and at the rate of perhaps fifty thousand or more a year, were hurrying all of the life-hungry natives of a hundred thousand farming areas, of small cities and towns, in America and elsewhere. The American of this time, native, for the most part, of endless backwoods communities, was a naive creature, coming with all the notions which political charlatans of the most uninformed character had poured into his ears. He was gauche, green, ignorant. But how ambitious and courageous!"[5]

In his Spencerian period, when he wrote *Sister Carrie, Jennie Gerhardt, The Genius* and *The Financier,* Chicago was the primary city for Dreiser; on its image were grafted his later experiences in New York in his maturity—New York, where he achieved the pecuniary success he craved as editor of a group of genteel, idealistic ladies' magazines published by the Butterick Company, and where he had first arrived as an unemployed newspaperman, achieving a precarious job on the *World* by storming the editor's office, and where he felt the terror of poverty. He used these last memories in describing Hurstwood's decline in *Sister Carrie.* After the failure of *Sister Carrie* in 1900—his publisher, Doubleday, had found it too daring and in effect buried the book, although it had received some praiseful reviews—he had a nervous breakdown and touched bottom in the urban depths almost in emulation of Hurstwood. But it was to the career of the Chicago transit magnate Charles Yerkes that he turned for the model of his hero of *The Financier,* Charles Cowperwood, the ruthless exemplar of the success ethic. Where better to find a capitalistic freebooter than in the City of the Big Shoulders?

When Dreiser returned in 1912 to research the crooked financier's Chicago career, one of the people he talked to was Edgar Lee Masters, a lawyer and sometime poet, who had come to Chicago from Lewistown, Illinois, in 1892. By then everyone in Chicago's literary world knew of Dreiser, for *Sister Carrie* had been reissued by another publisher in 1907 and had become as much a battle cry as a book among the younger generation. They saw it as the shock force of a new wave of literature that would speak the truth and sweep away the sentimental pieties that had dominated American letters. To Masters, *Sister Carrie* had proved that it was possible to write an honest novel about a woman without genuflecting to the prevailing cant that she must be punished for her transgressions. "You cleaned up the country and set the pace for truth, and freed the young, and enlightened the old where they could be enlightened,"[6] he told Dreiser. Floyd Dell championed Dreiser in the pages of the Chicago *Evening Post's Friday Literary Review,* of which he was then assistant editor under the catalytic Francis Hackett, (he later became editor). Sherwood Anderson chanted a hymn of praise to Dreiser the literary pioneer: "The feet of Theodore are making a path, the heavy brutal feet. They are tramping through the wilderness of lies, making a path. Presently the path will be a street with great arches overhead and delicately carved spires piercing the sky. Along the street will run children, shouting, 'Look at me. See what I and my fellows of the new day have done'—forgetting the heavy feet of Dreiser."[7]

The sun of Dreiser's small but dazzling reputation warmed the brief, gaudy flowering that came to be known as the Chicago Renaissance. The major writers in this renaissance, which lasted roughly from 1910 through 1916, were all small-town youths who had fled to the city, but unlike Dreiser and

Sandburg, their vision turned back upon the towns they had come from, rather than primarily upon the city (although the city inspired and infiltrated their work—and indeed made it possible). The books they wrote were, in their day, incendiary, striking at the heart of the village ways that the purveyors of folksiness and togetherness had celebrated. Galvanized by Dreiser's realism, as well as other aesthetic currents swirling in the Chicago air—*vers libre*, post-impressionism, modernism, translations of the works of Emile Zola and other modern Europeans—they perpetrated a small but lively literary movement.

A central stream of this movement was dubbed by the critic Carl Van Doren in 1920 "The Revolt from the Village." This revolt was not exactly new, as we have seen, for writers such as Ed Howe and Hamlin Garland had written realistically of small-town ways in the late nineteenth century. But Howe had become a country editor-sage, and Garland was considered a mossback writing sentimental novels, and perhaps worse, protesting Dreiser. Nor was the revolt solely the work of the Chicago Renaissance writers; its most widely audible outcry was Sinclair Lewis's *Main Street*, and Lewis was not a Chicago figure. Other writers of the period had reached independently the same conclusions about the cultural aridity of the village—notably Willa Cather in her 1910 short story "The Sculptor's Funeral" and in *My Ántonia* and other books that drew upon her memories of Red Cloud, the small Nebraska town where she grew up. And then there were the partial recanters—most visibly Booth Tarkington, who looked down a gentlemanly nose at boosters in *The Magnificent Ambersons* in 1918, and Zona Gale, whose *Miss Lulu Bett* in 1920 turned Friendship Village upside down. But to Van Doren, the germinal test of the revolt was Masters's *Spoon River Anthology*, which appeared in 1915. Most of its poems had been first published in clusters over a period of six months in *Reedy's Mirror*, a St. Louis paper edited by William Marion Reedy. Reedy was a follower of the economist Henry George and propagated George's single-tax gospel in his paper; but he also published literary criticism, poetry, and fiction. Reedy, described by Masters as a man of "huge corpulency," with a massive head and "large dark mirror-like eyes,"[8] had a sharp eye for literary talent.

Masters first met Reedy not at a literary salon but while undertaking a law case in Missouri. He asked Reedy to recommend a St. Louis lawyer; he was impressed by "the orotund eloquence of [Reedy's] fluent talk" and they "became friends at once."[9] Thus it was that Masters's early work never appeared in the two famous little magazines of Chicago's *belle époque*—Harriet Monroe's *Poetry* and Margaret Anderson's *Little Review*. But Monroe, publisher of Vachel Lindsay's "General William Booth Enters into Heaven" in 1913, Sandburg's "Chicago" in 1914, as well as poems by Eliot, Pound, Yeats, Sassoon, D.H. Lawrence, Amy Lowell, and most of the other important or soon-to-be important poetic voices of the day, did invite Masters to the informal luncheon parties at the offices of *Poetry*, where there was usually a prominent poet "from afar" present, such as Siegfried Sassoon or Wallace Stevens, as well as Monroe, her co-editor Alice Corbin Henderson, and Eunice Tietjens and other local poets. These "happy affairs" and "new friends" revived Masters's chronically sagging spirits "enormously"[10] and brought him into the vortex of the Chicago poetry scene. It was Monroe who corrected the proofs of *Spoon River Anthology* in 1915, while Masters was laid low by pneumonia brought on by his exhaustion from turning out the Spoon River poems by night and trying a difficult labor case during the day.

Monroe's devoted effort was in spite of her disappointment at being denied the chance to publish the Spoon River poems in *Poetry*. She had, apparently, not known of Masters's poetry in 1912 when she founded her review, and by the time Masters started writing them in May 1914, he was committed to his mentor, Reedy. Thus they appeared in the weekly *Mirror*, at the rate of two to four each issue, a tremendous outpouring that found Masters drawing upon previously untapped springs of memory. Sometimes he seemed to be in a "clairvoyant" or trancelike state. "Sometimes I think I didn't write it," he told Dorothy Dudley. "It passed through me, I was only the medium for it."[11] Something had unlocked memories of twenty years in a small town and big city, and the people he had met in the course of his workaday life. *Spoon River Anthology* was a miraculous outburst in Masters's hitherto desultory poetic career; he had grasped his true subject—or rather his subject had seized him—and his life was irrevocably changed. The book was a sensation, damned by the guardians of morality and praised by the urban intellectuals. It became that rarity, a best-selling volume of poetry.

By then Masters was forty-seven years old, not the usual age for a rebel. Born in Garnett, Kansas, in 1869, he was taken while still an infant to his beloved grandfather's farm near Petersburg, Illinois, a small county-seat town. Then the family moved to town. His father had tired of farming and took up the law and became county attorney. For most of his life he was the opposite of Sherwood Anderson's father—a success, an effective country lawyer, and a powerful local politician. Masters admired him and let him guide him into the law, though he had developed an inchoate interest in literature. But there were traces of resentment in his recollections of his father, who, he sometimes felt, never really cared about him and had helped his other children more than he had helped Edgar. But the elder Masters was a practical man, as well as possessing a great deal of charm, by his son's account, and seemed to direct his efforts toward placing each of his children in a good career or marriage. Without the experience painfully, drudgingly acquired during Masters's twenty years practicing law, there might not have been a *Spoon River Anthology*.

Masters's first job in the city was as a collector for the Edison Company (Dreiser worked in a similar job and enjoyed it, while the gloomy Masters found it grubby, monotonous work). He went into partnership with some shady lawyers, then with the great Clarence Darrow, with whom he didn't get along (he does not even mention him by name in his autobiography), and then practiced on his own, with some success. He circulated among Chicago's leisure class on the *laissez-passer* of his sister's marriage to a playboy who was heir to a comfortable Chicago fortune, and he had usually disastrous affairs with a number of women while married to a genteel girl. He mixed with the poor and working class as a labor lawyer. An ardent Democrat like his father, whose parents had come from Virginia and North Carolina, Masters was a loyal supporter of William Jennings Bryan and a political liberal, despite his choleric view of life.

After Masters had spent a year at Knox College and had read for the law, his father offered him a partnership in his own firm as well as a political plum, the job of master in chancery, which paid two thousand dollars a year and which the elder Masters, as Democratic political boss and four-time mayor of Petersburg, could easily pick for him from the patronage tree. But the usually dutiful son rebelled. The proximate cause was an unhappy love affair, in which the girl dropped Masters for a clerk in a dry-goods store. The incident was doubly galling because the owner of the store belonged to the town's puritanical, antiliquor Republican set, which had sabotaged his father's political career whenever possible. Masters's identification with his father and his paternal grandparents was such that he adopted their party politics, retained a sympathy for the South (he always referred to the Civil War as the War Between the States), and even concocted one of the few debunking books about Abraham Lincoln ever written. Masters's soul mirrored the schism in the two small towns where he grew up between the Democratic party "wets" and the puritanical, New England Republican "dries," whom he regarded as hypocrites. In Petersburg the prohibitionist set included many of the town bankers and merchants and controlled one of the newspapers. Masters paid them back in his bitter references to the scheming, sanctimonious merchant "Thomas Rhodes," among others, in *Spoon River Anthology*.

Masters had also been finding life at home claustrophobic, and there were quarrels with his strong-willed New England-born mother, who had, late in life, taken up writing herself. Beyond these immediate dissonances, he had a long and deep-seated resentment against "the village spites, the melancholy of the country, and . . . the bad will that followed me everywhere."[12] He would sit in his father's office, which overlooked the square in Lewistown, and watch the farmers come to town, tie their horses to the hitching racks around the county courthouse, and go off to do business with the various merchants and lawyers on the square. This spectacle depressed him with its "vast futility"; he accumulated a "soul fatigue."[13] He recalled the awful Sunday afternoons in Petersburg—he associated Sundays with frightening tornadoes that swept in from the West, the organ of a nearby church playing lugubrious hymns—and the Saturdays when the rowdy Spoon River backwoodsmen came to town. Inclined to melancholia, Masters found small-town life made it worse: "There was a loneliness in this town and the surrounding country which could not be borne many years longer. It was this loneliness and an introspection produced by the country that gave me melancholy."[14] The only medicine for this malaise was the city, Chicago; Masters went there in 1892.

Characteristically, his first impressions were more ambiguous than were Dreiser's. To the latter, the sights, sounds, and smells that bombarded his ardent senses conjured up exotic images. Chicago was "the pulsing urge of the universe," crying out to Dreiser—"All that life or hope is or can be or do, this I am, and it is here before you! Take of it! Live, live, satisfy your heart! Strive to be what you wish to be now while you are young and of it! Reflect its fire, its tang, its color, its greatness! Be, be, wonderful or strong or great, if you will but be!"[15] To Dreiser, the city was the life-force itself; it pandered to desire and the dreams of luxury and beauty that arose out of the drab poverty and rootless existence of his childhood; the city was change, flux, desire, people on the way up or on the way down, snatching riches or dying as ciphers, unremarked, unremembered, ignored; it was thousands of people jostling, fighting, desiring, but never connecting. Dreiser's childhood had been rootless; moving from one small Indiana city to another, he had felt the numb shame of being poor and the lash of malicious gossip. But nowhere had he formed strong bonds, and so he grew up without forming any strong resentments. He was like Carrie who breaths "a pathetic sigh" as her village passes by through the Chicago-bound train's windows "and the threads which bound her so lightly to girlhood and home were irretrievably broken."[16]

The Chicago Masters saw was a sprawling place, its rapidly spreading borders engorging the prairies; its raw, half-finished subdivisions, the apartments and houses, rising in anticipation of the World's Columbian Exposition of 1893, were intersected by future boulevards which were mere ploughed strips with half-finished curbs and newly planted trees struggling self-consciously to grow in the alien setting. When at last his train drew into the center, he too felt the noise and bustle, heard laborers shouting, switch engines crashing, the dull boom of dynamite explosions where the new drainage canal was being dug; and finally he saw the city streets lined with countless saloons, dives, flophouses, and hotels and one "wanton" street which resembled closely the brothel section of Peoria and other smaller places. The streets teemed with people of every race and nationality, the air was miasmic with coal smoke and gas fumes, huge trucks rattled the cobblestones. "Chicago thus began for me as a mist rising from the sea, in a sense without a beginning,"[17] Masters wrote; he could never romanticize it as Dreiser or Sandburg did. He lit briefly in a boardinghouse run by his uncle and inhabited by strange old ladies who seemed as though they might lurk behind the curtains and leap out at him at night. He crisscrossed the streets stalking a job, lived in a succession of lonely boardinghouses, and gradually built up a successful law practice.

He kept doggedly writing poetry when he had the energy, and after unhappiness in his marriage and a destructive affair with Tennessee Mitchell, who later became Sherwood Anderson's wife, he was uplifted when he met Dreiser and Harriet Monroe and other figures in the Chicago Renaissance. The ideas of Ibsen, of Shaw, of the Irish Theatre, of advancing science, of a rearisen liberty were in the air, "and nowhere more than in Chicago, where vitality and youth, almost abandoned in its assertion of freedom and delight, streamed along Michigan Avenue carrying the new books under their arms, or congregated at Bohemian restaurants to talk poetry and the drama. All this came to my eyes as though I had been confined in darkness and had suddenly come into the sunlight."[18]

In 1914 Masters represented a group of striking waitresses, "an emotional experience that revived all my slumbering humanism."[19] Politically, socially, aesthetically, then, Masters was having his own psychic renaissance: Wilson was president, and the New Freedom promised liberal measures that would curb the domination of the trusts and disown the imperialism of McKinley and Teddy Roosevelt. Floyd Dell marked the year 1912 as the year of the birth of "a New Spirit"—in that year Edna St. Vincent Millay's "Renascence" was published, *Poetry* was founded; Vachel Lindsay was chanting his barbaric folk-poetry; the Irish players toured America; Maurice Browne started his Little Theater in Chicago.

For Dell, 1912 was the birth year of a new era of consciousness; Masters's birth as a poet came in 1914, the year he wrote *Spoon River Anthology.*

"About the 20th of May my mother came to visit us," Masters recalled, and they talked of the past in Lewistown and Petersburg, about the people they had known and how they had turned out. "The psychological experience of this was truly wonderful." After he put his mother on the train, he returned to his home "full of a strange pensiveness."[20] He went straight to his room and wrote "The Hill," the first poem in *Spoon River Anthology,* beginning with the lines—

> Where are Elmer, Herman, Bert, Tom and Charley,
> The weak of will, the strong of arm, the clown, the boozer, the fighter?
> All, all, are sleeping on the hill.[21]

All dead of various causes; all buried in a cemetery of memory. And so Masters had found his metaphor—a graveyard, where the village's dead rise up and speak their epitaphs in terse free verse (inspired most directly by Masters's reading of the epigrams from the Greek Anthology, a book that Reedy had lent him). Masters's brilliant compression of whole lives into short poems resulted in part from his working methods, which were dictated by the small amount of spare time he had for writing poetry and by the habits of intense concentration he had formed. The talks with his mother had triggered his memories, but the germination of *Spoon River* went back even further. Eight years before, Masters had told his father that he was going to write a novel—and one only, for the law was taking all his energies, while his wife was drawing him into a kind of enervated, droning domesticity. The idea for the novel, as he somewhat cryptically described it, arose out of his perception that "the country lawyer and the city lawyer were essentially the same; that the country banker and the city banker had the same nature; and so on down through the list of tradespeople, preachers, sensualists, and all kinds of human beings."[22] What Masters apparently meant was, first, that he could freely draw upon the people he had known in both town and city for his Spoon River cast of characters and, second, that Spoon River would serve as a microcosm for the larger world. Masters was unable or disinclined to make the city a theme, as Dreiser had done, and so instead he created the people of this mythical village, the Lewistown and Petersburg of his memories, some of whom languish or shrivel up into meanness, some of whom go to the city and some to Europe, meeting their various tragic fates. Masters never wrote his novel; instead, he wrote a poem-novel, *Spoon River Anthology*.

Perhaps most revealing of Masters's attitude toward his material was the title itself. There was, of course, no real village named Spoon River, but there was a Spoon River, a brown, sluggish creek which meandered through the countryside between Lewistown and Petersburg. This bottomland was inhabited by leftovers from the pioneer era—backwoods people, poor white trash; indeed the kind of villainous lowlifes Tarkington described as inhabiting Six-Crossroads in *The Gentleman from Indiana.* They were disdained by the respectable townsfolk of Lewistown, and Masters paints them luridly in his autobiography: "men with sore eyes from syphilis, blinking in the light; men with guns or slings in their pockets, carrying whips, and fouling the sidewalks with tobacco spit; women dressed in faded calicoes twisted about their shapeless bodies. . . . These creatures at Lewistown howled in their insane cups, they fought with knives and guns and knucks. The streets stank. The shopkeepers stood in their doorways eyeing chances of trade; they walked back and forth behind their counters serving the malodorous riff-raff from the bottoms."[23] Their presence made Saturdays "days of horror" for Masters and for his mother, who longed for the cultivation and gentility of her native New England. The real Spoon River wound its way through dismal country, its banks choked with weeds and thickets and cottonwoods, past "little towns as ugly and lonely as the tin-roofed hamlets of Kansas."[24] From this unregenerate clay he extracted "whatever beauty there is in that part of the *Spoon River Anthology* which relates to a village depiction, and is not concerned with a world view."[25] He meant the same "beauty in ugliness" that Dell praised in Dreiser and that was an aesthetic hallmark of the Chicago school. In his autobiography he recalled threading his way through the dangerous streets of Lewistown as a boy, emerging into the peace of older friends' studies where there were books and he read Shakespeare and Sophocles. Or the walks with a girl named Anne, to whom he read poetry. Spoon River comprised a negative pole—Lewistown, with its primitive, backwoods mind, violent, ignorant, and prejudiced, half sunk in the primal ooze—and a positive pole, Petersburg, which he loved. Lewistown included not only the violent men from the bottoms with their syphilitic eyes, but also the sanctimonious merchants who traded with them—the whole narrow-minded segment of the town with its "village spites," the puritanical, hypocritical merchants who had fought his father and who proclaimed virtue and secretly sinned. Petersburg, however, was inhabited by noble, cultivated, uninhibited southerners.

There was undoubtedly a good deal of malice in Masters's attitude toward the people of Lewistown, a mean-spiritedness similar to that of the townspeople he creates. And this animus mars his poems (there is, for example, the predictable church elder, an ardent prohibitionist who takes clandestine nips from a druggist's bottle of medicinal brandy and dies of cirrhosis of the liver). Nonetheless these village types were recognizable; everyone who had lived in an American small town knew them—or thought they did (and considering the popularity abroad of the play and the opera based on the *Anthology,* many in Europe knew them too). Masters had ripped the pious wallboard off the village, sending its secrets scurrying about frantically in the light. The book, of course, has its heroes, but it is the twisted, tortured lives of the townspeople imprisoned in "taboos and rules and appearances"[26] that most readers remember from *Spoon River Anthology.* Masters freed his dead to speak their own bitter, uncompromising elegies and traced the tangled root structure of their lives beneath the surface—the secret spites, envies, hatreds, loves, failures, loneliness. *Spoon River Anthology* was village gossip raised to the gravity of poetry.

Many of the characters of Spoon River were, of course, recognizable to the people of Lewistown and Petersburg. Masters had changed the names, using the names of signers of the Illinois Constitution as well as ones he invented. Similarly, he shuffled and "combined traits of individuals he had known and episodes of stories he had heard in his two hometowns. Thus in the *Anthology* there is character named "Butch" Weldy, a reformed bad boy, who is injured in an explosion at the canning factory owned by Thomas Rhodes's son and who cannot collect any compensation because of the circuit judge's narrow ruling. There was a real Weldy in Petersburg, but he was a peaceable character, who, during a dry period in the town, bought a jug of whiskey in nearby Havana. Returning home, Weldy was spotted by the town marshal hired by the prohibition forces, a large, powerful brute who carried a lead-knobbed cane. The marshal stopped Weldy and after some words between them suddenly began beating him mercilessly with his cane. In self-defense Weldy pulled out a small pistol and shot the marshal dead. Masters's father took the case, after a mob threatened to lynch Weldy and, by plea bargaining with the judge (the prototype of the notorious circuit judge in " 'Butch' Weldy"), secured Weldy a life sentence and later, backed by the prosecuting attorney, persuaded Governor Altgeld to pardon him. This story is recounted in the poems "The Town Marshal" and "Jack McGuire" (McGuire represents the real-life Weldy). In these poems, however, instead of plea bargaining, McGuire's lawyer, Kinsey Keene, offers to withhold damning information he has about the financial maneuvers by old Thomas Rhodes that wrecked the bank; the judge, a friend of Rhodes's agrees, and McGuire receives a fourteen-year sentence.

In this way, Masters rearranged true stories, added to them and recast them so that they reflected his animus toward the Republican-prohibition forces in town, personified by Thomas Rhodes, or so that they presented his political and social beliefs and hatred of injustice. Masters created a living myth—the quintessential repressive village hiding its secret sins; it was a durable myth and lived on in small-town novels fifty yearss later (*Peyton Place* being but one example). Oliver Goldsmith's 1770 poem, "The Deserted Village," which extolled "Sweet Auburn, loveliest village of the plain," as a place of peace and rest, to which the poet longs to return "and die at home at last," had been the precursor of the other village myth—the village as home, as womb. Masters was closer to another English poet of Goldsmith's time, George Crabbe, who in 1783 reacted against Goldsmith with *The Village*, a realistic rather than elegiac view of village life—"a life of pain," disease, poverty. As it happened, among the books in the Masters house at Petersburg there was a collection of Crabbe's poetry, but Masters said he did not read Crabbe until after he wrote *Spoon River*.

The Springfield, Illinois, poet Vachel Lindsay was one of Masters's earliest champions, though there could hardly be two more disparate personalities—Masters the skeptical, anticlerical lawyer, lover of women, rationalist; Lindsay, the son of Campbellite missionaries, a teetotaler, virgin, mystic, and visionary who bummed about the West, selling his poems, lecturing at schools or wherever people would listen, filled with an inchoate messianic zeal. Lindsay, who, Masters said, "looked like a Poor Pierrot" and was petted by women with the same platonic affection that "they had for the middle-aged Sunday-school superintendent of their church,"[27] wrote poetry to be chanted, poetry that drew upon the camp-meeting imagery and rhythms of an earlier America. He worshiped Lincoln (who had lived in the Lindsay home in Springfield for a time) and hated the spreading industrialism. He was a townsman to the bone—in another time he might have founded a utopian colony, but instead he dreamed of his own Springfield as a new Athens, run by poets and artists rather than businessmen and boosters. He understood Masters's twisted Spoon River villagers but wanted to free them, building for them a new town where all religions were one, with Carl Sandburg and Edgar Lee Masters parks and ethnic festivals and cathedrals whose pantheons of saints included Emerson, Lincoln, Henry George, Johnny Appleseed, and Jane Addams. There was something of the eternal boy in him—he had lived under the thumb of his strong-willed mother and once said, "I am practically the person she made of me when I was eight."[28] The energetically amorous Floyd Dell, hearing the priggish Lindsay reciting his lines, "My sweetheart is the girl beyond the Moon,/For never have I been in love with woman," observed affectionately that "some youths ought to choose poetry instead of a girl"[29] and that Lindsay had made the right choice.

Both Lindsay and Masters were obsessed with their villages in different ways; both were imbued with Illinois history—again with different results—and both rejected the city as a subject. Masters, however, did care about Chicago's past and was intrigued that Fort Dearborn had been built by the painter Whistler's grandfather. Sandburg, like Lindsay in his preoccupation with American folklore and his vagabond's love of the open road, reveled in the imagery of the big city and saw it as something entirely new, proudly unfettered by tradition. Masters admired Sandburg's Whitmanesque barbarisms, his forthright language and rude realism, and his celebration of the life on Chicago's streets. When he walked through the city with Sandburg, Masters recognized that a new Chicago had come into being. Still, he was a scrupulous poetic craftsman who had studied the traditional techniques thoroughly, and he thought Sandburg's "Chicago" "a mere piece of interesting extravagance. I felt that he did not know Chicago, except as a city of packing plants, and criminals, and dirty alleys."[30] What Sandburg omitted from his poems was the old Chicago, the city "which had always cultivated music and the drama; . . . a town of lawyers, of notable characters, of society figures, of reproductions of New York and New England culture."[31]

And so in varying ways Masters, Sandburg, and Lindsay, the three major poets of the Chicago Renaissance, touched and respected each other, though each pursued his own course. They had small-town boyhoods in common, but their attitudes towards their homeplaces was vastly different: Master's memories formed a chancre of resentment, Lindsay dreamed of Springfield as the Puritan cultural city on the hill, and Sandburg, in Whitmanesque catalogues, sang the city electric. They were like three ploughmen working different, but parallel furrows; they shouted encouragement over the rows and shared a meal and talked, but when the talk was over, each resumed his own course. Masters, however, had an influence, once removed, upon another figure of the renaissance, Sherwood Anderson. The two apparently never met, although they had loved the same woman, Tennessee Mitchell, but *Spoon River Anthology* played a catalytic role in Anderson's own *Winesburg, Ohio.*

Anderson later denied—or rather allowed his publisher to deny—that he had read Masters's book, but artists are sometimes chary about confessing their "influences"—especially when the influence is a contemporary (and former lover of one's wife). The fact remains that when he was living in a boardinghouse favored by young artistic hopefuls, a fellow bohemian lent him a copy of *Spoon River,* which Anderson read in a single night and enthusiastically praised as a true picture of village life. The book did not shape Anderson's vision of small-town life, but it may well have suggested its form—interrelated short sketches about an Ohio town. Thus, although Anderson cited more remote influences on his work—Mark Twain, George Barrow (who wrote sketches about gypsy life), Gertrude Stein—Masters's book was white-hot and immediate. He had published two novels, *Windy McPherson's Son* and *Marching Men*, both of which caused little stir outside the Chicago circle and both of which belonged to an earlier period of his development. In 1915, Anderson had, like so many others, every pore open to the New Spirit.

We have already recounted how Anderson had a nervous breakdown and threw over his paint-supply business in Elyria and came to Chicago, where he supported himself writing advertising copy. He soon fell in with the bohemian set that lived in the abandoned storefronts from the Columbian Exposition on Stony Island Avenue near Jackson Park, which provided cheap studios for young artists. "A new life began for me,"[32] Anderson said. Floyd Dell ("the literary band master of Chicago,"[33] Anderson called him), and his soon-to-be exwife Margery Currey presided over this set, which included the newspaperman Ben Hecht, the critics Burton Rascoe and Lucian Cary and his wife, Gus, the poet Arthur Ficke, and others of the cast of rebels, dreamers, would-be's, and never-to-be's. Dell recalled the life as lively, studded with cheerful, spirited dinner parties, with much talk about and some practice of free love, socialism, and the new writing. Dell himself, whom Sinclair Lewis aptly described as "a faun at the barricades,"[34] affected high collars, a black stick, an outlandish suit. A superb literary journalist, he edited the *Friday Review* with considerable skill, managing to champion the most avant-garde and outrageous, while not upsetting his extremely conservative employer, a Jew who had embraced the Baptist religion and other forms of conventional respectability. Dell had almost lost his job early on, when he wrote an enthusiastic front-page review of a book that appeared to advocate divorce—but a book, as it happened, that had been written by the scion of a prominent Chicago family. That turned away wrath, but his employer lay in wait for any misstep. It came in 1913. Dell began a review with a flippant lead sentence: "Will you have a cocktail?" As it happened, the book under review was a temperance plea, and Dell went on in his review to praise it; but the owner of the paper had been so outraged by Dell"s opening line that he was seized by the urge to fire somebody and made wholesale dismissals in other departments. Dell, whose job had been saved when the managing editor explained the book's antialcohol message, resigned in sympathy and moved on to New York and the Village.

Anderson had come to parties at Dell's place and at Margery Currey's (the couple lived in separate studios even while married) and had read parts of the manuscript of *Windy McPherson's Son* aloud. Dell was very impressed, lauding the novel's "quasi-Dostoevskian" qualities. Dell, with the sympathy to new talent that was characteristic of him, took *Windy* under his wing. He in fact took it to New York with him and tried to find a publisher; he also changed the book's ending without consulting Anderson. After American publishers rejected it, Dell gave it to an English publisher, the John Lane Company, and Anderson, who of course saw Dell's changes in proofs as Dell knew he would, let most of the alterations stand. He was always grateful to Dell for his help, calling him "a kind of literary father to me."[35]

With Dell gone, Margery Currey continued to befriend Anderson, as did Hecht, Rascoe, Lewis Galantière, Harry Hansen, Sandburg, and others who lunched regularly at a place called Schlogl's. Anderson's first wife, Cornelia, and their children had rejoined Anderson in Chicago, and Cornelia impressed Anderson's new friends; she even contributed a book review to Margaret Anderson's *Little Review,* where her husband's stories were appearing. But the marriage was doomed. They divorced in 1916, and Anderson later married Tennessee Mitchell. Cornelia moved to Indiana, where, although untrained for it, she embarked on a career as a schoolteacher. In 1915 Anderson was living in the artists' boardinghouse. The people living there, whom he dubbed "the little children of the arts,"[36] were grotesques in their own right. They found their way into the stories he began writing—the stories that became *Winesburg, Ohio.*

Many of the "little children" were small-town escapees. In *The Briary-Bush,* Floyd Dell's sequel to *Moon-Calf,* Felix Fay, fresh from Iowa, meets similar young people from small middle western towns at a settlement house. A girl at the settlement house named Rose-Ann (a character based on Margery Currey), who persuades Felix to work with her on a play the residents are producing, refers to the theater-struck young people as "freaks," explaining, "If you live in Arkansas and want to make lovely stage-pictures, you *are* a freak; or you become one trying to keep from being dull like everybody else."[37] She tells him about a scenic designer from Nevada named Dick who wore evening clothes all the time, worshiped Baudelaire, and took drugs. He had died in the slums of pneumonia and starvation. "And Dick was—just a nice boy who wanted to do beautiful pictures and poems. Nevada did that to him."[38] Felix recoils from this fin-de-siècle vision of the artist; despite his literary ambitions, he is trying to be down-to-earth, to come to grips with the Chicago of Upton Sinclair's novels *The Octopus* and *The Jungle*; he is a socialist and had worked in factories, by choice, back in Port Royal. But still he feels the tug of the artistic world.

Anderson in his artists' boardinghouse on Cass Street found acceptance and even a kind of respect. He was almost forty, an older man, after all; like the other bohemians he had a workaday job in advertising, creating ads for diarrhea remedies by day, but the important thing was that he had quit his life as a small-town businessman and dedicated himself to writing. Anderson experienced an exhilarating sense of freedom, as well as a sense of community with his fellow artists—"a feeling of brotherhood and sisterhood with men and women whose interests were my own."[39] Later would come the rivalries and jealousies, the selling out, the dry periods, the work that misfired, but now he felt his artistic life was in its full drawing. His new friends freely told him their life stories, the small-town frustrations, the sense of being misfits. Anderson formed the idea that he would "take them, just as they were, as I felt them, and transfer them from the city rooming house to an imagined small town, the physical aspects of the town having, let us say, been picked up from my living in several such towns."[40] He would take the young man who wanted to be an actor, but who was meanwhile working as a clerk, and put him—"as I felt him, some inner truth of him"[41]—into "the lonely figure of some queer man who lived upstairs over a drug store in a small town."[42] But elsewhere he mentions hearing other tales of small-town life from people he met in the city, some of them not young artists at all. An old man from Clyde, whom he describes in *A Story Teller's Story*, did double duty as Wing Biddlebaum in "Hands" and Judge Horace Hanley in *Poor White*. But, like Masters, Anderson had apparently been stimulated by the richness of the city's human typology, the multitude of human stories, and he was open to them and used them in his Winesburg tales. The starting point was the small town in his memory. As he told William Faulkner, "You have to have somewhere to start from. . . . It don't matter where it was, just so you remember it and ain't ashamed of it."[43]

He says he sat down one afternoon in November, 1915 at his desk by the window of his small room with the bed on props so he could look out over the cityscape—sat down that snowy or rainy (the weather varied in different accounts) afternoon and, on the back of an abandoned manuscript, he began writing a story, which he wrote straight through, so oblivious to the world that when he finished his bare back was wet from the moisture blown in through his open window. The story was probably either "The Book of the Grotesque" or "Hands." The original manuscript for *Winesburg, Ohio* seems to show that '"The Book of the Grotesque" was written first; it also shows that, contrary to his later recollection, Anderson did not leave the stories just as they flowed from his pencil; he altered words and generally worked the stories over, though not in any major way.

At any rate, the stories came into existence, with Anderson feeling "as though I had little or nothing to do with their writing."[44] His descriptions of writing them in a trancelike state are reminiscent of Masters's account of writing *Spoon River Anthology* and Dreiser's of writing *Sister Carrie* (challenged by a friend to write a novel, Dreiser had scrawled the title at the top of a sheet of paper and begun writing, without any conscious plan). It was as though these three pathbreaking authors had acted as literary mediums for disembodied voices floating about in the *zeitgeist*. Anderson and Masters had drawn upon people in the towns and the cities and used the village settings of their boyhoods as a frame, a stage. As Anderson put it: "It was as though the people of that house, all of them wanting so much, none of them really equipped to wrestle with life as it was, had, in this odd way, used me as an instrument. They had got, I felt, through me, their stories told, and not in their own persons but, in a much more real and satisfactory way, through the lives of these queer small town people of the book."[45]

Perhaps that was why Herman Hurd, Anderson's boyhood friend, told his son that he could recognize only a few minor characters in *Winesburg, Ohio* as actual inhabitants of Clyde. No matter; when the book was published in 1919, the village was outraged, and people did see themselves in the stories, whether they were there or not. Mainly, though, the small-town moral guardians were outraged by the book's "immorality"; it was called a "dirty book," and Anderson was damned by the reactionaries as being "sex-obsessed" and hailed by the sophisticates as the "phallic Chekhov." The Clyde librarian even burned the copies she had ordered. The storm soon passed, for *Winesburg, Ohio* was only mildly daring, its concern with sex restrained. It was soon surpassed in this area by other, more graphic books. But the furor that attended it showed, if nothing else, that any direct mention of sex was anathema to the small-town moralists (as well as the big-city antivice crusaders such as Anthony Comstock and his successor John S. Sumner).

Anderson mentions the attacks on his book repeatedly in his memoirs, sometimes denying the charges and at others flaunting his sexual rebellion proudly, like a badge of honor. When he is in an uncharitable mood about Carl Sandburg, he will inject a dig that none of Sandburg's work was unsuitable for the *Ladies' Home Journal.* At other times he observes more clinically that "sex was a tremendous force in life. It twisted people, beat upon them, often distorted and destroyed their lives."[46] This revelation is used to reproach Mark Twain, whom he otherwise idolized, for printing privately his bawdy jape *1601.* He finds the prudery of the older realists, such as William Dean Howells, and the New England writers, such as Longfellow, Whittier, Hawthorne, and Emerson, as marring their work beyond redemption. But then he explains that "it wasn't exactly free love [that the Chicago Renaissance people wanted]. I doubt that there was with us any more giving way to the simple urge of sex than among the advertising and business men among whom I worked for certain hours each day."[47] Sex must be freed from "Puritan" repression—so many marriages were "without love, without tenderness."[48] Anderson goes on, "I think we wanted to reveal something—" that is, to open up a hitherto hidden corner of human life in literature.

Winesburg, Ohio is not primarily about sex; the thwarting of that instinct is but one cause of the twisted lives of the villagers; the young men and women of the town find occasions for sexual experiences. The real problem is the thwarting of love, the breakdown of community. This was a problem of the cities too, of industrialism. In the little villages of the time, as the critic T.K. Whipple pointed out, the pioneer tradition "of fierce practical ambition" lived on, but the newer generation could no longer live by this straitened code. This change registered in literature as a pervasive sense of decline from better days, and nowhere more passionately than in Willa Cather's work. She praised the sturdy pioneers who had built the West (averting her eyes from the tragic side of the frontier, which Ole Rölvaag and Hamlin Garland had seen) and deprecated the emerging business class in the towns. In *A Lost Lady* she romanticizes Colonel Forrester, the railroad builder, and by extension all his kind: "The old West had been settled by dreamers, great-hearted adventurers who were unpractical to the point of magnificence; a courteous brotherhood, strong in attack but weak in defence, who could conquer but could not hold. Now all the vast territory they had won was to be at the mercy of men like Ivy Peters, who had never dared anything, never risked anything."[49]

Cather was instinctively a conservative, a defender of the old values, which she found written in a larger, bolder hand by larger, bolder men and women; Ivy Peters—the repellent local boy who gains control of Colonel Forrester's magnificent home and eventually his wife—and his kind are small men, miserly where the pioneers were thrifty, wheeler-dealers where the pioneers were builders—cutting up the pioneers' legacy "into profitable bits."[50] In *The Magnificent Ambersons,* Booth Tarkington contrasts Major Amberson, whose munificence is a stride into a new age of consumption and display, with his contemporaries who are still practicing the pioneer thrift of their forefathers. Even Sinclair Lewis in *Main Street* harks back to the pioneer era as a kind of golden age. In her naively earnest quest for the modest utopia of village improvement, Carol Kennicott is briefly caught up in a longing for the "simplicity" of the pioneer era, which Gopher Prairie has discarded: "This smug in between town, which had exchanged 'Money Musk' for phonographs grinding out ragtime, it was neither the heroic old nor the sophisticated new."[51]

The machine age brought not only an ethic of consumption and mass entertainment, but also a new kind of repression, which Anderson illuminated more directly in his next book, *Poor White* (1920). The tragedy of the Winesburg people was, Anderson said, that "the living force within could not find expression,"[52] and so the people were left grotesques, seething with inner obsessions, lusts, loves, and aspirations, unable to express them. They accost the reporter George Willard—the unscathed youthful hero of the book, the man who will tell the truth—hurtling themselves at him under cover of the night (Winesburg is a night town) and pouring out the queer truths bottled up within their souls. Buried deep in them is a sweetness and beauty, hidden from the light; they yearned to break out of the drab, confining streets and buildings, the moral straitjackets of this second-generation pioneer town. Anderson, through George Willard, is both a confessor and a voyager into the secret recesses of these souls. "I have gone beneath the surface of the lives of men and women,"[53] Anderson said, and in his wandering around the Middle West he had inveterately made up stories about the lives of the people he saw, and he had listened to those who poured out their stories to him. Like

Masters, he found beauty in the ugliness of these lives—sweetness in the apples—but unlike Masters, he did not judge or condemn or protest. He was content to evoke the pathos of thwarted lives.

And so in their various ways the figures of the Chicago Renaissance embraced the new realism, and portrayed the village life they knew in a way that had not been expressed before in American literature, at least with quite such precision and art. Although loosely banded together by a common desire to see realistically rather than skeptically, they were quite different individuals, from quite disparate small-town backgrounds. Dell, for example, had come to Chicago from Davenport, Iowa, a town of some culture with a large German-Jewish-socialist population, and with several writers, such as Octave Thanet (Alice French), a popular sentimental novelist, still living there. In Dell's own circle there had been the novelist George Cram Cook and his wife, Susan Glaspell, and the poet Arthur Davison Ficke. Cook and Glaspell went on to found and manage the Provincetown Players and produce the early plays of Eugene O'Neill (O'Neill's defection to Broadway was so traumatic to Cook that he gave up the theater to travel through Europe—and died at fifty-one). Once in Chicago, Dell interviewed the English novelist Arnold Bennett, who when he learned that Dell came from a small town, expressed approval, saying that he would therefore know more about life. But Dell realized that his boyhood had been a rootless one, spent in three towns, and he resolved to tell in *Moon-Calf* of the unformed, confused but questing young man he had been. Dell bore no grudges against Port Royal; it had been a good place to grow up in, and he had learned much there. Masters, on the other hand, retained a residue of bitterness against his homeplace, while Anderson was a nostalgist clinging to a sense of something having been lost, something good swept away in the coming of the modern world. And, ironically, the impetus to his leaving home had been his early success-worship, his hustling desire to make a lot of money.

Their lives belied the picture of the village as crusher of artistic inspiration, for all of them had found older mentors in their townspeople who encouraged their ambitions, lent them books, shared a love of literature. There were, of course, creative spirits who had been thwarted by the circumspection and excessive self-consciousness bred by village suspicion of the artistic. The lives of those who did not heed the call to the city provide their share of case histories, talents withering or souring into self-destructiveness or "queerness" or becoming bland in order to conform with village standards.

There was George Cram Cook, who attempted to stay on in Davenport and write novels, determined to live on a truck farm he had inherited. But the second novel was long in coming, and Cook eventually had to flee. Dell's picture of Cook at a meeting of the Contemporary Club in Davenport shows the future avant-garde impresario tamed. Dell, Cook, and a German workingman friend had been invited to a discussion of the use of injunctions in labor disputes, a practice, as good socialists they naturally opposed. A lawyer read a paper that took an orthodox, conservative position in favor. When Cook was invited to give his reaction, it was not the George Dell he knew who rose to speak, but a stranger: "It was the George who belonged to respectable Davenport, hated it, feared it, was morbidlly sensitive about what it thought of his eccentricities—the George who had been brought up as a gentleman, whose father was there looking on and wishing to be proud of his big, handsome, brainy son."[54]

George Cram Cook found that neither the superior aloofness he affected, nor the company of the Port Royal bohemian set were enough to protect him from the smothering associations of home and town; they slipped through the chink in his armor and enveloped him. The artistic young men who for some reason returned to their native place met a similar fate. Paul Barnitz, the brilliant son of a Kansas minister, was one. He went to Harvard and studied under William James. He was an acolyte of Baudelaire and wrote a book of poems which was dedicated to the French poet. But he went back home, began (or continued) using drugs, and died of them at the age of twenty-five. Or there was Willis Adams, a painter from Suffield, Connecticut, whom a Springfield physician befriended and gave money for study in Europe. Adams lived in Venice, was a friend of Whistler, and painted works of promise. But his patron died, and Adams, apparently wearying of the bohemian life, returned to Suffield to live. Although he continued to paint, he became a recluse, wryly dubbing himself "the Suffield sufficiency." He sold some paintings to the townspeople, who only "wanted something pretty and hand-painted,"[55] and roamed the fields and meadows alone. Finally, he moved to Greenfield, Massachusetts, to live out his days; when he died he left behind a large body of unsung (and unsold) work. One of the few painters who was able to go home again was Grant Wood of Cedar Rapids, Iowa, who had gone to France in order to paint the same landscapes the impressionists he admired were painting. But finally he realized that he had left his true subject behind, and one day, sitting at a sidewalk cafe with William Shirer, then a reporter for the Paris *Herald Tribune*, he confessed that "all I really know is home. Iowa. Everything commonplace. Your neighbors, the quiet streets, the clapboard homes, the drab clothes, the dried up lives, the hypocritical talk, the silly boosters, the poverty of . . . damn it, culture. . . . I'm going home for good."[56] Wood went home to Cedar Rapids and set up a studio in a coach house provided by his patron—a local undertaker who admired and bought his work. And there it was he painted "American Gothic" and "Daughters of Revolution" and other caustic portraits of angular rural types that outraged the bourgeoisie.

Or there were the stay-at-homes and the refugees from the city like Zona Gale and Booth Tarkington, who cut their artistic cloth to fit the prejudices of their home folk. Crawfordsville, Indiana, produced an unusual number of best-selling authors in the late nineteenth century for a town of six thousand, and all of them wrote in the genteel or romantic styles that were then popular. Most prominent of the Crawfordsville writers was General Lew Wallace, a Civil War general and former ambassador to Turkey, who wrote *The Fair God* and *Ben Hur*, the latter a huge best-seller that lived on in dramatic and cinematic reincarnations. There were also Maurice Thompson, specializing in historical romances and author of the best-seller *Alice of Old Vincennes*, and the Krout sisters, Caroline Virginia and Mary Hannah, one a reclusive invalid most of her adult life, a poet and author of romantic novels about Indiana history, such as *Knight in Fustian*, and the other a vigorous, pioneering woman journalist. And finally there was Meredith Nicholson, who lived most of his life in nearby Indianapolis and sang paeans to "the folks and their folksiness" in *The Valley of Democracy*. He was an observer of the smiling side of Indiana life, reflecting the state's official optimism and friendliness. There was nothing base about all this; Dreiser, after all, was an admirer of the jolly vernacular poems of Indiana poet James Whitcomb Riley. "I revere James Whitcomb Riley with a whole heart," Dreiser had written in *A Hoosier Holiday*. "There is something so delicate, so tender, so innocent not only about his work but about him."[57] Dreiser had been too "bashful" to call on Riley during his travels in the state and had "heard he didn't approve of me," but a sentimental man himself, he was reminded by Riley's poems of his own barefoot-boyhood days.

Nicholson, a prolific journalist, essayist, novelist, was the only full-time writer among the Crawfordsville school on the male side. Thompson was a prominent lawyer and politician (his one bestseller, *Alice of Old Vincennes*, was published shortly before his death), and Wallace was also a lawyer, who had married the daughter of the town's richest man, a writer of some talent who preferred to guide her husband's successful literary career. Their contributions to popular literature were considerable, but to literature itself negligible. Wallace meshed perfectly with the prevailing Victorian piety and idealism in his religious novel *Ben Hur*, which not incidentally provided a colorful, if slow-paced, historical romance; Thompson and his brother, Will, started the archery fad which swept the nation in the 1880s. He was steeped in the romantic side of the southern heritage and the obligatory canon of Sir Walter Scott; and his novels, whether set in the Old South or Indiana's pioneer past, were elegies for a lost code of chivalry.

But none of the Crawfordsville school ever wrote anything that was not safely within the boundaries of popular taste and Victorian morality; their success demonstrated, perhaps, how strongly the middle western small town had come to represent the average in the American mind, the common denominator of taste. Like Tarkington, they never left home, and they instinctively sought to please the people they lived among. Their distance from the center of the New Spirit in Chicago was indicated in a review of Nicholson's novel *Otherwise Phyllis* (1913) in the Chicago *Daily News*: "Reading Mr. Nicholson's story is like discussing Crawfordsville with some one who has lived there . . . he says he would rather please people in Montgomery County than any others. It would never occur to me to try to please the people of Crawfordsville, but I am sure that Mr. Nicholson will please them. For he can do honestly what some of the rest of us cannot—he can write a novel about an Indiana town in a spirit of mellow kindness."[58]

"Mellow kindness" toward a small town was becoming passé even in 1913; by 1920 when Sinclair Lewis's *Main Street* was published, the village myth, already shaken by the disclosures of *Spoon River Anthology* and *Winesburg, Ohio* (the latter's appeal was mainly to the intellectuals, however; it sold five thousand copies in two years, a good sale for such a book but nothing like the sales achieved by *Spoon River Anthology*) was now tottering. It remained for Harry Sinclair "Red" Lewis to give it the final push. His novel was an exhaustive catalog of every small-town shortcoming—and a few of the good points. In the book's opening lines, Lewis made a rather grandiose claim: Main Street was America—"This is America—a town of a few thousand, in a region of wheat and corn and dairies and little groves. The town is, in our tale, called 'Gopher Prairie, Minnesota.' But its Main Street is the continuation of Main Streets everywhere."[59]

Thus Lewis broadened his indictment of a middle western town to embrace provincialism, boosterism, materialism and all the other sitting targets of the intellectuals who had been raging against "the emotional and aesthetic starvation"[60] of American life. Lewis's *Main Street* and *Babbitt* two years later were the first expression of these ideas to achieve a wide audience. *Main Street* was greeted with critical joy and brisk sales. By 1922 it had sold over 390,000 copies, and millions of Americans had read it. Women in small towns all over the nation wrote to Lewis that he had told the story of their lives through his heroine Carol Kennicott. Frederick Lewis Allen called the effect of the two books "overwhelming." "The intellectuals had only to read Lewis's books to realize that the qualities in American life which they most despised and feared were precisely the ones which he put under the microscope for cold-blooded examination. It was George F. Babbitt who was the arch enemy of the enlightened, and it was the Main Street state of mind which stood in the way of American civilization."[61] *Main Street*'s coattails pulled Zona Gale's *Miss Lulu Bett* and Floyd Dell's *Moon-Calf* on to the best-seller lists. Dell was surprised to find himself a spokesman of the disillusioned postwar generation—surprised because his book was set at the turn of the century and because it was not a particularly scathing portrait of small-town life. He too received letters from readers who insisted that in Felix Fay, the dreamer, the moon-calf, the small-town intellectual, Dell had presented their thwarted lives. Felix Fay was the small-town misfit who does escape, rather than remain and die spiritually, like the characters in *Main Street*—like Carol herself. Dell's *Bildungsroman* naturally appealed to the young, who were caught up in the fads that were the leftover froth of 1912 Chicago—the short hair, the "splendid paganism" and moonlight swims, the corsetless women who smoked, the Dionysian drinking, the rejection of the moral totems of the older generation. Thus, while calling him the "most serious and ablest of the group," Vernon Parrington consigned Dell to the school "which holds that the sufficient tests of intellectual emancipation are rolled hose, midnight discussions, black coffee, and the discarding of wedding rings."[62]

Lewis mixed realism and satire, and his characters were puppets of their environment like those of the naturalistic school. His heroine was not interested in rolled hose, petting parties, or bathtub gin; she wanted to make the little town of Gopher Prairie a Better Place to Live. Lewis's talent in bringing American character types to life on the page was a marvel, his ear for American speech sure and deadly. "Yump," his men barked with supreme self-satisfaction. Who has ever heard a man say "yump"? And yet the sound caught the spirit of a type of middle western businessman. Lewis worked on the surface, heightening reality by caricature, but never losing touch with the source of his inspiration. Alfred Kazin has remarked that Lewis's readers enjoyed how well he had "hit off" the local druggist or the pompous booster. He could be devastatingly funny, yet Carol's dull terror walking down Main Street, sensing the eyes of the town upon her through the windows of the little clapboard houses, or Babbitt's near fall from Zenith grace after he takes up with the local bohemian set, were chilling. Both Carol and Babbit return home defeated; the real terror of loss of status, of being an outcast had been powerfully evoked by the profounder Dreiser in *Sister Carrie,* as he describes Hurstwood's downward slide through apathy and poverty to death. There remained in Lewis a residue of the buoyant optimism of the middle westerner, and in this he resembled Tarkington a little, although Tarkington was no mean hand at satirizing a Babbitt type when he wanted to. The difference was that Tarkington's Babbitt would turn out to be a solid citizen and win material success and happiness, while Lewis's would rebel, then return sadder and wiser to his old life, taking comfort as Carol did, in having fought the good fight. The hope remained with the younger generation—with Carol's baby ("Do you see that object [the baby] on the pillow?" Carol asks Will Kennicott on the novel's last page. "It's a bomb to blow up smugness."[63]); or with Babbitt's son, who finds integrity in working with his hands and mastering the intricacies of the Model T. Lewis was at his best poking fun at the brilliantly observed minutiae of American life. America in the twenties was weary of the sacrifices of war, of the impossible moral uplift of Prohibition, of the repression of the "Red scare" and censorship; it was ready to laugh at itself, to see itself in the distorting funhouse mirror of Lewis's satire. Or rather to see the other fellow, for as Jonathan Swift observed, in the glass of satire we always see another's face.

Main Street was the only book of Lewis's that he had *lived* rather than researched. He attended numerous Rotary Club meetings, and eavesdropped on countless smoking-car seminars to write *Babbitt,* and toured America in an open Ford to write *Free Air.* For *Main Street* he recorded his impressions of his own hometown, but he still put more of himself in the book than any of his others. He had honed his skills writing mostly inconsequential stories for The *Saturday Evening Post* and other middle-class magazines of the day—and stopped writing for them when *Main Street* was a success, for his aspirations had always been above those of a commercial hack, catering to the conservative values of George Horace Lorimer, editor of The *Post*. His mimetic brilliance was subversive; his industrious research and professional talent for carpentering a novel made him both an entertaining and critical observer of American life, until he lost his way in the thirties.

There is a lot of Red Lewis in Carol Kennicott, he admitted to an interviewer; and there was also a lot of Will Kennicott, the unsung hero of *Main Street*, who embodied the values of Lewis's own father, Dr. E.J. Lewis. The younger Lewis's wife, Grace, saw this when she accompanied him to Sauk Centre for a visit. It was "Dr. E.J. Lewis versus Sinclair Lewis," she wrote. "Not the Doctor in person but the qualities he had taken from his father: a small-town puritanism, a suspicion of city ways, and a respect for the prosperous businessman."[64] "Harry, why can't you do like any other boy ought to do?"[65] his exasperated father would say to him over and over. Never would Lewis really believe that he could live up to his father's rigid standards; yet he owed him a lot, for Dr. Lewis had set him on the road to Yale, an eastern education, and the world beyond Sauk Centre. (Lewis would never entirely get over his awe of the East; it never held for him a destructive glamor as it did for Scott Fitzgerald.) Dr. Lewis had put him to the grindstone, got him studying so that he could pass the entrance examinations. His values of hard work and making money became Lewis's too.

The aloof and stern Dr. Lewis, a man of compulsive habits who went home to lunch at precisely the same time every day, also contributed to Lewis's lonely childhood. In his later years Lewis was wont to look back fondly upon his boyhood town of Sauk Centre, calling it "a good place to grow up,"[66] but actually he was a lonely boy, who often cut up and played the fool as a defense, who trailed around after his older brother, Claude, eternally seeking but never receiving his approbation, and who had only one close friend of his own age. No doubt he did engage in the activities of a small-town boyhood, walking the railroad ties, rambling through the nearby prairie with its rich farms and distant hills which were stippled with Indian-paint colors in autumn, swimming in the creek under the Old Stone Arch or in the many lakes roundabout. But he was gangling and awkward and not good at games; instead, he read every book in the Sauk Centre library and sometimes would sequester himself in the old carriage house in back of his home and play for hours at a game in which keys and screws represented people, enacting stories he made up.

At Yale, with his skinny, ungainly body, his red hair, he was also a misfit among the smooth, tailored products of the eastern prep schools, and the story is told that at an alumni baanquet years after graduation when he was famous, he recounted in vivid detail every slight and snub he had received. After he graduated from Yale in 1907, he traveled by cattle boat to Europe, bummed around Carmel, California, joining a commune of young artistic hopefuls ("an assemblage of pot-boiling dilettantes,"[67] Mark Schorer called them) janitored at Helicon Hall, Upton Sinclair's short-lived experiment in communalism, and worked as an editor in New York, until he quit in 1915 to write full-time.

All the while he had been harboring the idea of writing a novel about small-town life. This ambition dated back to 1905, when he was spending a summer at home. He was bored and feeling more painfully than ever before the limitations of Sauk Centre. He had talks with a young local lawyer named Dorion, who, he noted in his diary, "was very well read particularly (being a socialist) in socialist writers and up to date contemporaries."[68] One night Dorion and Lewis teamed up against a young minister in an argument about socialism. Aside from such intellectual diversions, young Lewis was finding his home town "hell for dullness."[69] His animus boils over in a diary entry confessing that he had drunk too much port the previous evening—" 'The Village Virus'—I shall have to write a book about how it getteth into the veins of a good man & true. 'God made the country & man made the town—but the devil made the village.' Where in the city one could see a friend or go to the theater, in Sauk Centre there is nothing to do save drink or play poker (for those who do not read much)."[70] His talks with Dorion and that passage were the genesis of a projected novel called "The Village Virus," which evolved into *Main Street*. Dorion (who seems to have remained in Sauk Centre only a short time) became Guy Pollock, the faded, deferential lawyer, who is one of the few people of intelligence and culture in Gopher Prairie. He is a minor character, but for a brief time Carol Kennicott is half in love with him because of their shared disaffection. When she asks him why he stays in Gopher Prairie, he describes the debilitating village virus, which "infects ambitious people who stay too long in the provinces with apathy."[71] Pollock had studied in New York and loved the city, but he came to Gopher Prairie and was slowly sucked into the quicksand of village ways until he was trapped, his spirit smothered, unable even to carry on a flirtation with Carol.

Lewis never wrote "The Village Virus." Although he claimed to have put down twenty thousand words of it during that summer of 1905, his biographer Mark Schorer could find no evidence that he ever did. In his article on the revolt from the village, which appeared in *The Nation* in 1921, Carl Van Doren called Edgar Lee Masters a crucial influence on Lewis, responsible for deflecting him from writing superficial stuff. Lewis, however, disputed Van Doren, saying that he had never read *Spoon River Anthology*—although he had heard passages from it read aloud—and that he had been planning *Main Street* since 1905. One suspects that if *Spoon River* did not directly influence him, it encouraged him; it was a weather vane that showed the winds were blowing his way. Around 1916 he discussed writing a novel about a small town with his friend and later editor Alfred Harcourt, who was to cofound the publishing house of Harcourt, Brace & Company in 1920; the new firm's first list included *Main Street.* Lewis's trip to Sauk Centre in 1916 may have resulted in some actual writing, but more probably in notes and impressions and a new perspective—Sauk Centre through the eyes of his wife, Grace Lewis, who recalled that whenever the dinner-table conversation at Doc Lewis's turned to writing, the inevitable and only question was, "How much do you get for a story?" followed by silent calculations of how much a week that came to. In 1918, Lewis had begun making notes for a novel still to be called *The Village Virus.* In this version the heroine was a schoolteacher named Fern, whose "desire for beauty in prairie towns was but one tiny aspect of a world-wide demand [for] alteration of all our modes of being and doing business; . . . it was one with universal & growing desire to chuck out pompous priests, intriguing politicians & diplomats. . . . She believed that this ambition of hers was one with the world-wide inquiry into war, into that system of growing and distributing force which, since it permits hunger at one end and surfeit at the other is palpably false."[72]

One has a sense, from this inchoate portrait, of the character of Fern as more ideological than Carol Kennicott eventually was; she was a radical, a rebel against economic injustice, and perhaps Lewis still had Dorion, the socialist lawyer, in mind and was envisioning his life at odds with the conservative forces in the prairie town. Fern gave way to Carol, but she remains in the book as the schoolteacher who is hounded out of town by the sanctimonious Widow Bogart, who wrongly accuses her of leading her ne'er-do-well son astray. At any rate, after two years of work Lewis scrawled on a sheaf of manuscript "the *first* first page of MS. of Main Street Sinclair Lewis Washington D C March 1920."[73]

The first draft, Grace Lewis recalled, was completed in February 1920, and it had much of the resentful college sophomore during the boring vacation of 1905 in it. During this period Lewis did not give up magazine commitments completely as he later claimed, but he did work on *Main Street* intensively from early in the morning until late at night in a rented room, his wife and child banished for several months. He sent the final version to Harcourt in July 1920, and the publishers had high hopes of selling as many as 20,000 copies. Actually, it sold 181,000 in the first six months of 1921 alone, and by then Harcourt, Brace & Company, heeding the extraordinary demand, had three boxcars full of books ready to ship to the stores.

By making the naive but questing Carol the heroine of *Main Street* rather than the futilitarian Pollock or the radical Fern, Lewis was able to show Gopher Prairie through the innocent, quizzical eyes of a spirited girl. He also, perhaps calculatedly, avoided writing a socialist novel; the most radical characters in *Main Street* are the village atheist, Miles Bjornstam, a muted socialist, and the populist farmers, whose complaints against the town merchants echo Veblen's "The Country Town." Carol was no latter-day Emma Bovary, as some reviewers claimed; she was a typical Lewis character who registers and reacts against an oppressive environment. Carol struggles, but her efforts are all failures. Her dreams are essentially the stuff of a rather silly romance—a Georgian town hall for Gopher Prairie and "Strindberg plays, and classic dancers—exquisite legs beneath tulle—and (I can see him so clearly!) a thick, black-bearded, cynical Frenchman who would sit about and drink and sing opera and tell bawdy stories and laugh at our proprieties and quote Rabelais and not be asked to kiss my hand!"[74]

Floyd Dell recalled that he initially read *Main Street* as an exposé of Carol. But he had some correspondence with Lewis, in which Lewis assumed that Dell surely had approved of Felix just as he—Lewis—impliedly approved of Carol. Dell, who had undergone psychoanalysis, used Felix to illustrate the mistakes he had made in life, and he wrote *Moon-Calf* and *The Briary-Bush* in a spirit of self-discovery. In the end Felix gives up his bohemian dreams of freedom, a life of "being a poetic infant," and accepts "adult responsibilities"[75] of marriage and family. Dell was, in a way, searching for what Anderson called "the thing that makes the mature life of men and women in the modern world possible."[76] He wanted a wife, children, and a little cottage in the country where he could write serious books—rather pastoral ambitions when held up against his role as literary bandmaster of the Chicago Renaissance, socialist, bohemian, and editor of the radical monthly *New Masses*. Carol, however, really didn't know what she wanted, nor did Lewis, and in the end she settled for what she had. Lewis's "revolt from the village" was, as many critics pointed out—as indeed were Masters's and Anderson's—an ambivalent one; his heart was with Carol but his head was with Dr. Will Kennicott. He had caught the village ways in voluminous, precise, sometimes hilarious detail; he had teasingly waved the red flag of revolt before the noses of the philistines—and generally they loved him for it, especially the transplanted small-towners in the cities. For a year or so after the publication of *Main Street* the Sauk Centre paper huffily refused to mention his name; then the local boosters began to take notice of how famous their local boy had become and all was forgiven.

The entire revolt from the village, if it was that, was in any case aimed at a village that was already receding into the past. Anderson was the most prophetic in writing about the larger themes of alienation and loneliness; his *Winesburg, Ohio* was in part a plea for the ideals of the old village, a protest against the dislocations of the new age which had destroyed community. Lewis measured an earlier prairie village by an incompatible urban sophistication. Dell was the most urban-minded and sophisticated of the lot; as the most directly autobiographical novelist of the four, he had the fullest acceptance of his experiences. His small-town roots were attenuated, like Dreiser's, and like Dreiser, he easily broke the village's strongest bonds—nostalgia and rancor. In any case, middle western towns in the 1920s were no longer isolated backwaters; mass communications and new technology were bringing

Main Street into the mainstream—not always for the better. Edgar Lee Masters expounded on the changes when his *New Spoon River* was published. Mourning the passing of the "homely" small town of his boyhood, he blames industrialization and urbanization:

> Go into any community of the kind I am speaking of and you'll find this process going on. The town is being made a ganglion of the city. Telephone and telegraph wires make it part of the metropolis, the radio, the automobile, the airplane, the city newspaper, the magazines carrying Paris fashions, the standard cigar stores, the standard grocery stores, the standard drug stores, machine gas stations, everything that the city can boast of, the small town of today can boast of. The privately owned canning companies, lumber mills, are taken over by large corporations who run them more cheaply and more efficiently. Industrialism is in the saddle; it is America. This is a country of monopolies and the small towns long preserved from this influence are being drawn into the net. As a matter of fact, most of them like it. The slogan Watch Us Grow is a triumphant marching song to them. Our literature is full of this change and movement.[77]

The town was becoming more like the city (and the city had added the cultural flavor of the emigrants from towns to its ethnic stew)—and losing its independence and identity, which included insularity and conformity. The figures of the Chicago Renaissance had sung the city uncritically like country boys and attempted to articulate a regional culture. But the Middle West was no longer a separate region. As Irving Howe wrote, "Even the most insistently sophisticated of the Chicago writers remained small-townsmen in many ways. That, paradoxically, was why they could so readily accept Chicago. . . . No one who had actually lived his life in the city was likely to take so romantic a view of it, could so eagerly pounce on it for 'material'."[78] Howe points out that it was "town-loneliness" that had driven these writers to the big city and "when they found themselves lonely in the city, as it was inevitable that they would, they began to recreate the town, not in the shape of its reality but in the image of those ideal communities for which they had yearned. . . . The Bohemias, the Greenwich Villages are always the work of young writers and artists who, on the margin or in the interstices of the city, come together to recover the intimacy of the town while hoping to realize the freedom they had expected to find in the city."[79] Thus the somewhat parochial bohemian life in Chicago—Anderson marrying Masters's former mistress, Anderson adopting Dell's black stick, Anderson finding true community with the little children of the arts, the critics such as Dell, Hecht, Hansen, and Rascoe practicing literary logrolling on behalf of their friends' books, even the parochialism of a Margaret Anderson, who had "a kind of savage scorn of everything she did not understand."[80] The Chicago Renaissance was a communal emotional outpouring, short of ideas; it was a romance of freedom, an explosion of negative energy. As such, it achieved its main purpose of unlocking the creativity of its artists—a creativity that would have been thwarted in the villages they came from, or rather the villages that were imprinted in their minds—but it was limited, a phase when people were free to "play" at life. Similarly, the entire revolt from the village was limited by history, bounded by the era of the transitional, postpioneer country-town era which was passing. What was said needed to be said, and as a strong, critical voice in the new realism, it energized American literature considerably; Puritanism, the bête noire of the revolt, was not in any historical sense the enemy; the old Puritans had known of sex and evil. Rather the enemy was the officious latter-day Victorian puritanism that dictated what could and could not be discussed in literature (Dell went to jail to protest comstockery). In order to discuss sex or send up boosterism, but above all to restore the juices of life to the novel, the complexity of desire and good and evil, that sterile puritanism had to be overthrown. In *Sister Carrie*, after all, Dreiser had borrowed the standard shop-girl-evils-of-the-city novel of his day and divested it of the Victorian cretonne that concealed the harsh truths of life. The buried lives in the villages, which had similarly been ignored in the cheerful literature, were given their day in literary court. The very self-consciousness of the rebels, which made them revolt, making possible their writings, spread through the larger American society; it placed the small town firmly in the American mind as a place of spite, frustrated lives, conformity, middle-class morality. The Spoon Rivers, Winesburgs, and Gopher Prairies of America, however, receded into another corner of the small-town mythos, along with the Friendship Villages and Plattvilles. The former were truer literary reflections than the latter, but they harbored their own distortions. The sum of both traditions indicated, if nothing else, that America had a love-hate relationship with its country towns. The freedom and imperial wealth and cultural fecundity of the cities were powerful drugs, and thousands of real-life Felix Fays and Carol Kennicotts and George Willards imbibed them. But deep down inside they must always wonder—had something been lost?

9
Caste and Class in the American Town

The unflattering portraits of small-town life by the literary rebels of the 1920s did not put the Babbitts into flight or transform the nation's Main Streets into Parisian boulevards. The revolt from the village was most influential among eastern urban intellectuals, for whom it was one front in a broader assault on middle-class American values, and expatriates from small-town life in the cities, who had their own private rebellions articulated in it.

As the migration to the cities continued, America's "urban" and "rural" societies were no longer distant poles. Certainly there were still rural back-waters that clung to old ways, but increasingly the separate world views of city and town were shading into one another. Like two countries after a war, they opened their borders, stepped up their exchanges of people, and installed new communication lines. The town was already economically bound to the city, which provided markets for its products, and was becoming more and more a consumer of the city's goods, and its ideas as well. But the rapproche-ment was far from total, and the town, in some areas at least, attempted to retain at least the illusion of difference; they clung to the old resentment of the city and moral superiority. What the twenties intellectuals saw as pro-vincialism, conformity and smugness, the conservative forces, in small towns and elsewhere, celebrated as the last stand of true Americanism.

This cultural fissure aside, the deepening social and economic mutuality between town, village, and city continued. A statistical study of selected rural and urban areas by the President's Research Committee, published in 1933, showed that the demographic similarities between town and country increased in inverse proportion to the distance between them. Although the preponderance of influence flowed from city to town and village, the traffic was by no means one-way. The study focused solely on population characteristics such as male-female ratio, fecundity, birthrate, age distribution, and marriage ratio. The conclusion was not startling but still significant: In counties closest to the cities these characteristics were most similar, while the farther away the rural area was from the city, the wider the disparity between city and country's figures. Birthrates, for example, traditionally higher in farms and small towns, went down the closer the family lived to the city. Those large farm families of America's past were, in the city's growing ambit, disappearing. Even in the areas distant from the city the birthrate was falling, in line with the general decline for the nation as a whole. A trend that had started in the city spread slowly out to the countryside, like oil seeping out of a ship.

Changes in birthrate were the result of cultural changes, which in turn were influenced by socioeconomic forces. The trend toward smaller families reflected the growth of a consumption-oriented society in which parents limited family size in order to have more disposable income; and on the farms, it also reflected the technological revolution in agriculture, which, through the introduction of laborsaving devices, made children less useful as labor. Finally, the Great Depression hastened the trend to decreased family size; people simply couldn't afford to have as many children. Of course, among the ethnic poor and in the backward areas where birth control information was scarce and large families were prized—or at least endured—and on small farms that were still unmechanized, the practice of having large numbers of children continued.

The Depression also encouraged a small but pronounced movement from the cities back to the villages and country. These migrants were largely rural people who had moved to the city in search of higher pay in factory jobs and who had lost their jobs as economic conditions deteriorated. Many of them felt they could subsist on a small farm or find work in their hometowns—or at least a bed and meals; the movement was not, in other words, a people's return to farming, except in the narrow subsistence sense. These returned farmers would find farming no more profitable than they had before because they were unable to afford the large acreage and modern farming equipment that might have enabled them to make it profitable. Over the first five years of the decade, the migration back to the farms only temporarily checked the long-term net decrease of the farm population. Between 1930 and 1935 the net outmigration was 58,000; however, by 1935, as the economy began to turn upward, the net outmigration began climbing again and between 1935 and 1940 it was 708,000, surpassing the previous high between 1920 and 1925, a period of serious agricultural depression. Small towns—except those of less than 3,000 population—continued to increase in population during the

Depression—not spectacularly but in line with national population growth. (And even this trend was a continuation of a longer-term trend. Between 1910 and 1930 for every seven villages of less than 2,500 population that lost people, thirty increased by twenty percent. The 140 agricultural villages studied by the President's Commission all gained in population between 1920 and 1930—an overall increase of 8.6 percent nationally.)

A curious sidelight to the back-to-the-land movement in the thirties was the rising vogue for American folk culture and rural pioneer values among college students. The sociologist Carl Withers recalled that in the twenties the impact of *Main Street* caused small-town boys attending urban colleges to feel ashamed of their background and become objects of pity to their urban classmates. But in the thirties this attitude changed; small-town boys were regarded as "true Americans," exemplifying the rural traditions that had suddenly become so attractive (at a distance) to the students from the city.

We have already described how the literature of small-town life became more kindly and nostalgic in the thirties, culminating in the play *Our Town*, and in popular magazine fiction. The revolt from the village had ended it seemed; Sinclair Lewis wrote perhaps his worst novel, *The Prodigal Parents* (1938), in praise of a small-town middle-class businessman named Fred Cornplow, standing in for the heroic petit bourgeois, the salt of the earth to Lewis's mind, who purges the Bolshevism his children had caught from effete urban intellectuals. John Steinbeck wrote affirmations of simple people and the beset but abiding American land. Thomas Wolfe's autobiographical novels *Look Homeward, Angel* and *You Can't Go Home Again* sounded a threnody for the lost homeplace; the hero Eugene Gant is a young man who goes to the city to find fame but is repelled by thee Dreiserian "manswarm" and the corporate soulessness and mourns the lost home of his boyhood. At a time when the economic system was teetering on the brink of collapse, people longed for the simple verities and harkened to a nostalgia for the land and the idealized village. In *Home Town*, published in 1940, a year before his death from peritonitis while traveling in the Canal Zone, Sherwood Anderson made his final peace with the small town, like a lapsed Catholic returning to the Church. He too stressed the virtues of simplicity in a time of perplexity: "The big world outside now is so filled with confusion. It seemed to me that our only hope, in the present muddle, was to try thinking small. . . . It may be that there is a bigness every man should seek, but the world is full now of false bigness, men speaking at meetings, trying to move masses of other men, getting a big feeling in that way; there's a trickiness in that approach to others—through applause, feeling a false power and importance.[1]

When Anderson was writing this, the rise of mass movements such as communism, fascism, and Nazism were much on his mind. Sinclair Lewis also counterposed homespun American verities to foreign tyrannies in his novel *It Can't Happen Here* (1935). In this story about a small-town Vermont editor who defeats a rising would-be American führer, it was small-town,

American commonsense that provided the margin of victory. The trend continued after the United States entered World War II. It was most evident in the propaganda movies made during the war. Frequently those showing Americans coming to terms with war on the homefront were set in small towns; rarely were city families shown doing war work or facing the death of a son in the war. Perhaps the best of these was *The Human Comedy*, a close adaptation of William Saroyan's novel about a California family who lose a son but in the end are "adopted" by his closest Army buddy who has no town and family of his own. (It was not smallness, of course, that ultimately defeated totalitarianism, but rather an alliance of nation states, mass-production industry, centralized controls over civilian life, and conscripted armies, equipped with the latest weapons technology.)

While this more benign view of the small town among even critical urban intellectuals reflected a longing for the village simplicities, there was also increased harmony between rural areas and small towns, according to *Rural Social Trends* (1933), a book based on field studies by the President's Research Committee on Rural Social Trends. Field workers were asked to classify the relationships between 140 villages and surrounding country people as cooperative, neutral, or conflicting. The surveys were conducted in 1924 and again in 1930. In the earlier year, only 27 of the 140 villages were rated as being in a "cooperative" relationship with their rural environs, but in 1930 this figure had risen to 100. The authors, Edmund Bruner and J.H. Kolb, cited several factors that had brought about a new era of good feeling. The Depression itself had generated in the inhabitants of country and town a greater sympathy for each other. Merchants no longer called the farmers "lazy, inefficient and extravagant"[2] as they had in 1924; the farmers had greater empathy with the village merchants' problems, especially after seeing some of them go bankrupt.

Better roads and more automobiles had also brought country and village closer. In one town, a study showed that farmers and their families came into town at least once a week, compared with an average of once a month a generation before. Every Saturday night the entire populace of a rural township could be observed on the town's streets. Farmers had become avid consumers of a wide range of manufactured products, as their ideas of the good life were more and more influenced by education and advertising. Studies showed that farm women listened to the radio as much as city women, which meant not only that more farmers were buying radios, but also that they were hearing more national advertising. The basic consumer goods and modern conveniences were becoming widespread—automobiles, telephones, radios, electric lights, running water. The percentage of farms with automobiles increased from 30.7 to 58.0 (7.8 to 30.2 in the less prosperous South) between 1920 and 1930. In one rural community in Arkansas, the number of electric ranges increased from zero to 70 and the number of electric refrigerators from 2 to 150 between 1925 and 1930.

The farmers were also participating in more village activities, such as certain of the economic, political, and self-help organizations, which became more prominent as the old fraternal organizations met increased apathy among townsmen. More farmers were living in villages and farming on the side, while townspeople were acquiring farms through foreclosure, inheritance, or purchase and learning firsthand of the problems farmers had. In rural towns like Carl Withers's *Plainville, U.S.A.* (written under the pseudonym "James West") "the social difference by which town people *as townpeople* once outranked country people *as country people* has . . . disappeared almost completely. ('There ain't no country boys any more.')"[3] Village merchants, prodded by competition from the chain stores, had finally begun to improve their stores and in one third of the "cooperative" towns there was evidence of growing trade with the farms (the number of village stores also rose in the 1920s). Consolidated schools extended the town's hegemony over the countryside by drawing country boys and girls to the towns for education, and their parents for sporting events and other school activities; the isolated one-room rural school was on the way out, whether or not there had been any legal moves to force consolidation (there were 149,000 one-teacher elementary schools in 1930—over half of all elementary schools—and only 1,475 in 1970). In Plainville, the consolidated school had become "'a new focus of community life and ritual,"[4] Carl Withers observed. The basketball games, debates, plays, and musical contests were avidly supported because they showed that Plainville was "up to date"; graduation assumed the emotional connotations of a vital rite of passage. Rural churches were also dying off or being swallowed up by sister churches in towns.

Finally, the old rural neighborhoods—farmers who lived near one another and socialized frequently—were breaking up (these were sometimes based on natural ties such as kinship or common ethnic origin rather than propinquity). There was an increased centralization of political and social activities in the village, Bruner and Kolb observed. New and improved roads had a centrifugal effect on neighborhood solidarity. Also, the old settlers had died off; a new generation was in the ascendancy that was more town-oriented, having been educated in the town, and less parochial, because of increased intermarriage outside the neighborhood. The rural neighborhoods had thrived on isolation; with the coming of better roads and automobiles, a wider world was opened up, and the sons and daughters—the third- or fourth-generation Americans—were increasingly seeking it. Another trend that began in the post–World War I era was the decline in some localities of farmers' "change work," a vestige of the pioneer practice of helping each other with harvesting, barn raising, and the like; increased mechanization of farm work and larger-sized farms (with hired labor to help run them) did away with the economic underpinnings of this reciprocal-labor system and so indirectly weakened the neighborly ties.

The team of sociologists under W. Lloyd Warner, who studied a small

Illinois town they christened Jonesville, spotted this trend. But the sociologists also found that historically change work had diminished class and ethnic consciousness, since people tended to work with geographical neighbors; as change work passed from the scene, ethnic identification and class considerations became the main determinants of "neighboring" patterns. In the Jonesville area, where there was a strong Norwegian community which formed an ethnic neighborhood, these developments would presumably strengthen ethnic-neighborhood ties; and, indeed, many of the Norwegians clung to the close-knit community that centered around their Lutheran church. Exclusion by the dominant "old Yankee" group of farmers had historically strengthened their ties by turning the Norwegians back upon their own community for social satisfactions.

Warner's group also discovered a new generation of "acculturated" Norwegians, who were turning to Jonesville for their social life and sending their children to high school there. Among these people the patterns of immigrant life were breaking down in a number of ways, one of which was a decrease in the traditional suspicion of city people, a suspicion that had its roots in the old country. These acculturated Norwegians, along with the wealthier Yankee farmers, who were participating fully in the Jonesville social life, told interviewers they believed that the old antagonism between city and country people no longer existed. Like the people in Plainville, they felt city folk no longer looked down on country people. Ironically, it was the most sophisticated townspeople, the "high-status" people, who continued to look down on those who worked the land. The nature of Jonesville social snobbery was such, however, that this prejudice was not directed toward the town's landed gentry who owned farms—so long as they didn't work them themselves.

The detailed descriptions of the workings of small-town class systems by the Lynds and other sociologists, but primarily by William Lloyd Warner and his team of sociologists in such books as the Yankee City series, *Democracy in Jonesville,* and *Elmtown's Youth,* came as a disillusioning corrective to the myth of small-town democracy—and also a comment of the role of class in American society. If in a small town "everybody is as good as everybody else," how could there be social classes? Yet numerous studies in the twenties and thirties revealed there were, although none found such elaborate hierarchies or described them in such voluminous detail as did Warner's team of sociologists. Warner claimed that class was the organizing principle of the social structure of the small community: "The social system of Yankee City, we found, was dominated by a class order."[5] Class was based on more than income diffeerences; it depended upon one's neighbors' judgments, expressed in such phrases as "acting right" and "doing the right thing."

Class was determined not only by behavior, but also by manners, morals, possessions, the kind of house and neighborhood one lived in, family, longevity in the community, and so on. The point was that many factors went into class distinctions: Money was not always controlling; "old family" was important but not controlling either; associating with the "right people" and belonging to the right clubs and cliques were crucial but they were related to income—having the wherewithal to support such a life-style, acquiring the right manners and meeting the unarticulated but rigid standards for admission to the cliques and organizations and groups of the right people. Warner's method, at bottom, was an elaborate polling of numerous members of the community and compiling the answers to identify the top and the next-to-the-top people. The people lower down on the hierarchy exhibited the traditional middle-class characteristics of middle income, respectability, and right-living. Next, in accordance with the basic American belief in the superiority of intellectual and service occupations over manual labor, was a class of steady, hardworking, blue-collar people. Finally, at the bottom, were the "immoral" and declassed individuals—immigrants, blacks, and the chronic poor.

Such superficials as consumption patterns and manners aside, this class system had a familiar look. Class distinctions had existed in American communities since the earliest days of the republic. At the same time there was a strong strain in the American tradition condemning class systems. Its earliest expression was in the Puritans' call for a community of love and redemption, in which the Old World vanities of pomp and display were eschewed in church and daily life, in which excessive preoccupation with gain was frowned upon, and in which conditions of economic equality prevailed amid the common hardships of the early settlements. These ideals became modified—the Calvinist belief in an elect who were saved by God's capricious and arbitrary choice began to have secular interpretations; the saints of the church began to have political and economic power; "calling" became synonymous with making money. The belief that industry brought deserved rewards was broadened to the belief that those who were wealthy were obviously superior, a kind of "economic elect."

At the same time, the Puritan settlements were increasingly subjected to outside influences, and their utopian exclusivity soon broke down. The Puritans themselves brought with them the baggage of the English class system; men who were styled gentlemen in the old country were loath to relinquish that title; the difference was that in the New World rank and class were not so solidly buttressed by law. Puritan dress was not uniform and drab but colorful; their love of possessions and fine houses was not curbed; in the church itself, ownership of more desirable pews came to be a perquisite of the wealthy. And, of course, as time went on and the settlements grew out of the subsistence stage, economic differences among men grew. The New World provided opportunities for making money; some had come with money and had a head start; others, even the indentured servants or their sons and daughters, rose in the world. Their prosperity was hardly scorned; it was indeed considered praiseworthy. And so the wealth was put to work creating and displaying a commensurate life-style, and political and economic power.

In the colonial villages that became cities, such as Boston, New York, Philadelphia, Newport, and Charleston, an even more exclusive and sophisticated aristocracy grew up. In the South, the Virginia planters were fashioning their rural gentry. Trade and manufacture brought in new sources of wealth and new opportunities for setting oneself off from the common people. Money that had by this time grown old confronted newer money, whose owners eagerly sought to buy their way into the upper levels of society. Smaller merchants, craftsmen, and traders arrayed themselves more or less below the upper rungs as a respectable bourgeoisie and in turn looked down upon the laborers and farmers who worked with their hands. In the rising industrial towns, the older class values were applied as a kind of overlay, with the new breed of capitalists and entrepreneurs fitting themselves into the older patterns as close to the top as possible; the college-educated professionals, teachers, and preachers ordering themselves somewhat below; shopkeepers, wholesalers of products artisans made, merchants next; and other nascent groups of skilled craftsmen and machine operators gradually beginning to sort themselves out in a rude working-class hierarchy, with the factory laborers occupying the bottom rungs of the working class. On the northern farms, no land-owning plantation aristocracy arose, but there was a squiredom and after that a class of successful farmers, followed by small farmers, then the hardworking tenant class, and the landless subsistence-farming poor who kept moving west. The open frontier gave the landless farmers and the urban proletariat somewhere to escape to and perhaps improve their situation, if not dramatically, at least to a level of self-sufficiency. At the bottom of the system were slaves, foreign immigrants, and the chronic poor. After the Civil War, freed slaves in the South were transferred from their status of absolute dependence upon their masters into a lower economic caste, in which their labor was exploited and they were kept from competing with whites for economic benefits.

The frontier supplied a leveling force as well as an escape hatch; the people who went west arrived theoretically as equals, with equal opportunities for all. They lived those ideals of equality in the early stages of settlement, as identical hardships forced identical conditions upon them. But, of course, they did not all arrive equal in fact; some had more education and skills and were able to set up as lawyers, doctors, tradesmen, or craftsmen; others had capital for land speculation, the main route to a fortune in the West, as it had been in New England in the early days. Still others achieved varying degrees of prosperity through luck and hard work. As the western communities passed out of the pioneer stage, as the towns sank permanent roots, and as the railroads linked them with civilization back east, those with money began to spend it upon possessions and grand homes and engage in social rounds that were inspired by their memories and fancies of the upper-class life back east.

Meanwhile, an underclass of transplanted poor whites from the South began to appear. Their poverty and shiftlessness inspired opprobrium and righteous superiority in the breasts of the soberer, hardworking folks—sometimes direct enmity, as these rude holdovers from pioneer days engaged in antisocial acts against the settled folk and had to be dealt with. Towns became industrialized, attracting another kind of underclass—immigrants to work in the factories. Other immigrants who took up farming often traveled in groups and formed ethnic rural communities that absorbed their countrymen who came later. Townspeople and other farmers of "old" American stock would assume a superiority to these people, and so "old stock" became another criterion of class.

Warner's Yankee City paradigm thus had long antecedents; the class system he and his colleagues constructed reflected an older persistiing hierarchy. Warner's class system should be taken as a scientific construct based upon extensive conversations with townspeople which produced data that fell into repetitive themes.

Ask people about class in the average American small town, and they would probably be vague about its workings—at least in more innocent times, before these same studies of class as well as novels about it (such as John Marquand's set in Boston and a fictionalized Newburyport) had entered the popular mind. Yet the sociologists found that these same people would "place" people. The so-and-so family was one of the "best families," or the Smiths were "good, solid working people who live right," or the Joneses were "shiftless ne'er-do-wells" who lived in Shacktown, or the Browns were "religious, upright, honest middle-class folk," and so on. Sharp-eyed and astute local observers knew which people belonged to which clique or organization and which kinds of people were excluded. Such comparative evaluations, though not precise, were common enough. Generally unrecognized and most damning was the revelation that class perpetuated itself—that lower-class youths tended to intermarry, to drop out from school at roughly the same age, to end up in the same jobs as their parents had. *Elmtown's Youth* showed that adolescent social behavior was closely correlated with class position.

The sociologists found upward (and downward) mobility in the class structure, but they also found that opportunities were shrinking for the lower classes. Working men in the large factories found they could rise so high but no higher. The possibilities of going into business on their own were closed off, while the chances of reaching the highest blue-collar rank of foreman—the usual entrée into the middle class—were similarly narrowed. With a few exceptions, the executive positions and growing technical and administrative ranks were staffed by college graduates—often from outside the town if, as was becoming increasingly common, the factory was owned by outsiders. In Jonesville, the executives of the local mill frequently placed their sons in line to succeed them, adding nepotism to the class machinery. College was the only escape hatch for those on the bottom, but the percentage of working-class youths going to college was very small. So the class system was self-perpetuating. Class barriers challenged the American dream of upward mobility. Americans held simultaneously the contradictory beliefs that all men were equal but that "some men are superior in status, others inferior."[6] Or, to put it another way, some men were more equal than others. In Jonesville:

> The highest crust is rewarded with deference; the lowest, often with ridicule, pity, or scorn. Knowing and recognizing their superiors and inferiors, the common men of Jonesville learn how to act properly with them. Everyone in Jonesville knows that inferiors must come last in line when the prizes are being distributed and go first when there are heavy loads to carry and unpleasant tasks to perform. The etiquette of deference in the democracy in Jonesville between inferiors and their superiors more often demands inflections of speech than outspoken admittance of superiority or inferiority, lest the speaker convict himself of being a boot-licker by his superiors or a snob and undemocratic by his inferiors. . . . Social superiors and inferiors must be subtly recognized lest these American dogmas of equality be flouted, but this same code does not protect the lowly from covert attack and exploitation by their superiors. It is well for such people to know their place and to know how to act in it.[7]

That, in a sociological nutshell, was the dirty little secret of Jonesville and thousands of towns like it.

Warner's is perhaps the baldest statement by a sociologist of the insidious aspect of the small-town class system, and it conjures up visions of Russian peasants tugging their forelocks in the presence of the master. Other observers tended not to see class differences in such harsh terms. Further, there were differing criteria of class positions not only among the sociologists but also among the people they talked to in different towns. In Carl Withers's Plainville, for example, inherited wealth meant less than earned wealth; in Jonesville, unearned income gave a higher status than earned wealth. Plainville, however, could be called a rural village, while Jonesville was, at the time of the survey in the late 1930s, a small market town of six thousand or so. The upstate New York village Granville Hicks anatomized in *Small Town* had only two classes, he decided; it too was a small, static, rural village with around a thousand people. So size and degree of "urbanity," for want of a better word, were also factors. Warner's class criteria were not universally applicable to all small towns.

Geographical area also influenced class structure. The New England Yankee aristocracy had its similarities to the southern gentry, who were descended from the old plantation aristocracy; but studies such as *Deep South* by Allison Davis, Burleigh Gardner, and Mary Gardner and *Caste and Class in a Southern Town* by John Dollard emphasized the caste distinctions between white and black over class distinctions. In both these southern towns in the 1930s, the caste system was designed to keep the blacks in their place while guaranteeing the superiority of the whites; it also provided the whites with certain economic privileges and the lordly prerogative of sexual access to black women.

As a corollary, there was the notorious taboo against sexual relations between black men and white women which was enforced by lynchings. Dollard, who had psychoanalytical training, probed the psychic costs of this system, while Davis and the Gardners focused on the anomalies already appearing in the social structure: the rise of a separate black middle class with superior economic attainments to the lower-class whites; the effects on the white merchants in town of having to solicit blacks' business (the Jewish merchants won considerable success by treating blacks politely, but not violating the taboo against addressing them as "Mr." or "Mrs."); and the impact of industry, in which blacks were often preferentially hired because they worked more cheaply. (Dollard describes these factors too, but much more negatively—for example, black shopkeepers who became too successful and were forced out of business by white boycotts.) From the standpoint of class in the southern towns, both studies suggested that although the caste system was at the heart of the southern way of life, it was already showing cracks and fissures; thus, *class*, which was based upon economic differences, education, family, and the like, was coming into conflict with *caste*, which was based upon skin color and deep-seated psychological fears and scapegoating mechanisms.

It was in the rural areas that the racial caste system existed in its purest form. The countryside was still dominated by white upper- and middle-class planters, the descendants of the slaveholders. Black people lived in a state of traditional subjugation. The rural small towns displayed the most racist attitudes. In the 1920s, when the Klan was revived, blacks moved away from small southern towns out of fear for their lives. The Atlanta *Independent* reported: "Thousands of black men and women are leaving the country and coming to the cities for protection; for they have absolutely no protection for their lives and property in the small towns and rural districts." Racism existed in the cities, of course, but in the country the whites exercised more rigid control by their ability to evict sharecroppers, withhold jobs, and selectively exercise their ultimate sanction of lynching. In contrast, the city offered more economic opportunities and these encouraged the growth of a black bourgeoisie.[8]

There were similarities between the southern caste system and the northern class system in attitudes toward the underclass. In Plainville, for example, the bottom class was the hillbillies, who were known as the "lower element" and "those people who live like animals." Such people were beyond the pale and were treated with either contempt or cruel jocularity. They were the scapegoats, shamelessly flaunting all the traits—shiftlessness, ignorance, promiscuity—that the official morality of Plainville deplored. Even the lowest class of respectable working people, known as the Holiness people because most of them belonged to the same evangelical sect, would have nothing to do with the "people who live like animals," although their religion emphasized salvation and welcomed anyone who declared himself saved.

So fixed were the class positions in Plainville that even respectable lower-class boys rarely moved into the town's upper class, and any mobility upward was mainly achieved by moving to the city. And the lower-class youths who made the move were so conditioned to being inferior that they set their aspirations minimally on a factory job with good wages. Only a few of the brightest lower-class boys made it in the city, and these were the ones in whom a sense of humiliation so rankled that they were driven to excel. Some managed to go to college, or, as in the case of one man, to become wealthy by striking oil in Oklahoma. If it was so difficult for these boys (for the girls marriage was the only respectable escape route) to climb out of their class trap, it was even more so for the lower-element boys, most of whom adopted their parents' feckless ways and opted out of the system.

There were, within living Plainville memory, only two boys who had hoisted themselves out of the lower element. One, descended from "the worst hillbilly stock," took a giant step upward when he enlisted in the army in World War I and won promotion to second lieutenant. After the war he returned to Plainville and rented a room in town rather than going home to live with his family. He worked hard, acquired a reputation for honesty, saved his money, and adopted the mannerisms of the Plainville upper class. Then he passed a civil service examination and was awarded the prestigious and relatively well-paying job of rural mail carrier. Marriage to the daughter of a prosperous farmer, membership in the high-status Christian Church, and purchase of farmland completed his accession to social respectability. Two crucial factors in his rise were the relatively classless bureaucracies of the army and the civil service—the readiest route for a boy of his background—plus his own native intelligence and talent for emulating correct manners.

Another local boy was bright in school, earned money mowing lawns, and finally landed a job as a store clerk. He was then able to marry "a good moral girl" and later entered politics and won election to a county office. His route upward was traditional boyhood "choring" (proving his ambitiousness), respectable marriage, and respectable job. The job was probably a dead end, unless he went into business for himself, which would require capital; so he seized the traditional poor boy's lifeline of politics. Still another Plainville boy from the lowest class was befriended by a childless couple in town, taken into their home, and groomed for entrée into respectable society. But their efforts ended in failure; it was Huck and Aunt Polly all over again. The woman forbade him to smoke in the house. When she caught him smoking in the local beer joint, she told him it was either quit smoking or go back to where he came from. He went back, hated "the dirt," begged for another chance, was reinstated, and then ran off to the city to look for a factory job. Within two weeks he returned in disgrace and went home to his family for good. The burden of being "civilized" was too onerous, and he reverted to the old ways.

So Plainville maintained an informal caste system for its lower element. One could overcome the stigma of birth by exerting great effort and by paying a stiff price in conformity aand circumspection. But intermarriage was discouraged, if not by law, by custom; class origin had almost the stigma of race, and it was a stigma passed from parent to child in the eyes of the community. Still, no black boy in town at that time could have taken even the narrow routes open to the three boys who moved up; at best he could go to the city, where there was the black class structure, and move up in that by adopting middle-class values borrowed from the dominant white culture.

A farm boy belonging to Jonesville's Norwegian community faced still another situation. The pressure on him was to stay within his own group and adhere to its codes; but only by becoming acculturated, which meant rejecting many of his parents' values, could he rise on the Jonesville class ladder. Yet the existence of such a ladder and the rewards it led to might be just the pull that would draw a Norwegian boy out of his ethnic "caste" and into the town mainstream.

The class system in a broad sense defined the American dream; it set the rules for rising in the world. But to achieve the prizes of success one must acculturate and renounce the security and stability of the old ways. Norwegian-descended girls had the choice of marrying a Norwegian boy, as was encouraged, or marrying a "foreigner." In time, the rigid bonds of endogamy became lax, and the girls were able to become Americanized through marriage. For immigrants and the lower element, the route to upward mobility was the same: conform to the customs and values of the middle-class native American stock.

Immigrants, blacks, and backward Americans provided the bottom foundation of the small-town class system. Yet these groups interacted with the class system in a variety of ways, from providing new blood for the upper class in rare instances, thus confirming the egalitarian attitudes of the town, to serving as the underclass to which all, but especially the groups directly above them, could feel superior, as did the middle-class white in the South to the black, or the Holiness people in Plainville to the lower element.

Another factor modifying and influencing class attitudes was gender. Men tended to be freer of rigid class considerations than women in many towns, especially those of the smaller rural type. Carl Withers noted this in Plainville as did Albert Blumenthal in his 1932 study of "Mineville," a western mining town (Philipsburg, Montana). The main reason for this phenomenon seems to have been simply that men got around more; Withers reported that men "cross the lines freely in business dealings, trading, loafing, and all the other activities lying outside the 'home,' while women, confined more sharply to the home, have much less contact across the class lines."[9] In Mineville it was considered perfectly normal for the banker to go fishing with the bookkeeper, or the doctor to josh with the prospector. One would probably be safe in assuming, however, that the banker would not invite the bookkeeper to a dinner party and that the doctor would not play golf with the prospector at the country club.

Women's historical role in many towns was to form a "society" that presupposed class distinctions; this role was carried forward well into the twentieth century. Blumenthal describes in considerable detail the frenetic activities of the socially ambitious townswomen. In Mineville the center of gravity of the entire social whirl was the bridge party, and the calculation, the subtle social gradings, the pregnant diplomatic considerations that went into drawing up the guest lists for these parties would have impressed a Newport doyenne. Blumenthal eavesdropped on two women engaged in this task. Distinctions were first drawn between sit-down luncheons, and evening parties with only refreshments—the latter were for the less important women. One separate party was reserved for the social "castoffs," while another—the key party of all—would feature wives of the town's "400" (Blumenthal's sobriquet for the highest class, which actually numbered seven families). With tongues sharp as scalpels, the women dissected the social position of each of their potential guests. Each woman who received an invitation had the burden of protecting her fancied position in the community, which she did by ferreting out the names of the other guests slated to attend. If the projected assemblage was adjuged déclassé, she preferred to send her regrets rather than be tarnished by association. If her intelligence network was inadequate and she went to a "bad" party, the plaint would be, "Wasn't that an odd bunch? I certainly wouldn't have gone if I'd known who'd be there."[10] But the two arbiters drew upon a reservoir of knowledge of the social topography of Mineville and took exquisite care to ensure that each bridge party was as homogeneous as possible, both socially and by age. On the whole in Mineville, Blumenthal thought, some women were social climbers but most were more or less satisfied with their position; the controlling motive was not ambition but rather fear of becoming declassed: "Practically all women jealously guard themselves from steps downward."[11]

The floating bridge-game situation in Mineville was a bit unusual; in most small towns a bridge club with a set membership was more the rule; the members had selected themselves out as socially compatible and took care to admit as new members only women who were their peers. If it wasn't a bridge club, it might be a reading club or an art appreciation club or a "good works" club or any of a number of activities that served as an organizing pretext. Many of the informal groups reflected local cliques, and their purpose was primarily social, with plenty of time reserved for refreshments and gossip. Although some groups professed lofty aims, there was a falloff from the earnestly self-improving women's study clubs popular in the 1890s. The Lynds quote from the minutes of Muncie's preeminent literary study group, the Conversation Club, a description of a debate in 1894 over whether "the social phase of the club life should be encouraged or not" and "whether the club should have an object beyond self-culture."[12] Some clubs, such as the main Women's Club in the city, opened their membership rolls to more people, exclusivity was generally the rule and sociability had become the main reason for joining. One member of the Women's Club complained that its greater openness had "brought in many women who want the social prestige of club membership but are not willing to work for culture."[13] There was a large increase, between 1890 and 1920, in the number of informal social clubs, organized around a clique, while the most intellectual of all the women's clubs remained the most exclusive. There was a "civic" tendency in the women's clubs—which meant innocuous charitable or improvement activities—that affected even the Conversation Club, which was run by tradition on an austere policy of no refreshments, no papers, industrious study of literary subjects, and the encouragement of "the lost art of conversation."

By the 1930s the purely social clubs were dominant. These informal but exclusive associations, with names like Kill Kare Club, Friendship Club, Why Not Club, Moonlight Savings Club, or Sans Souci, met for conversation and card playing. There were also the more formal auxiliaries of men's fraternal societies such as the Rebeckahs or the American Legion Auxiliary or the Order of the Eastern Star. These tended to be uncliquish, but their membership did reflect class associational patterns.

Finally, for both sexes there were groups centering around leisure activities—horseback riding, tennis, and golf. Their membership, especially in the thirties, was most likely to be upper class, since it had the money and leisure; hence, the widespread synonym "country club set" for a town's upper class. In Middletown exclusivity was transferred to the mainly upper-class riding club—the "horsey set."

Men of course were not indifferent to considerations of class, but their preoccupation was getting a living, and so their social and recreational activities had a manipulative element. Rising young businessmen used to associate with the rich and powerful of the community, not only to be accepted and gain reflected status, but also to make "contacts" which were "good for business." Men had their own exclusive clubs for making "contacts," the self-styled "service" clubs dedicated to improving the community. Rotary, Masons, Kiwanis, Lions, Legion, Elks, V.F.W., International Order of Foresters, Odd Fellows, Woodmen, Moose—the list was long, and proliferation served to confirm the general impression of the American male as joiner. But these clubs, for all their professions of fellowship, were not open to just anybody; they too had a homogeneous class composition. The Lynds pointed out repeatedly in *Middletown* how the members of the most prominent men's clubs—Rotary, the Real Estate Board Chamber of Commerce, and the Downtown Merchants Association—ran things in town. While composition of these organizations differed, membership was by invitation only, limited to prominent businessmen and closed to blue-collar workers or small businessmen. Such groups reflected, in short, a power elite in many towns—a kind of invisible government. Only not really invisible, because most people in the town knew who the ruling group was and discussed them in resentful or irreverent tones, and local politicians of a populist stripe might even win election by inveighing against them.

Only a hundred years before, Tocqueville had declared that Americans' tendency to form groups for a variety of purposes was one of their salient characteristics as a people. He would have marveled at the number, resilience, and incessant activity of such groups in the twentieth century. In many towns, the complaint was that there was too much to do—that is, there were too many organizations taking up too much of one's spare time. Jonesville, for example, had 176 active organizations of the informal and formal (lodge, church, philanthropic, business, political, and so on) types—or one for every 35 people. Bruner and Kolb in *Rural Social Trends* enumerated the social organizations in 140 rural villages of less than 2,500 population and came up with an average of nearly 21 for each village; they too mention the "reiterative plaint" that "there are entirely too many organizations in this community."[14] Comparing the years 1924 and 1930, the authors noted a surprisingly high mortality rate for village organizations over such a short period—but enough new groups had been formed to make the total of such organizations greater in 1930 than in 1924.

Another trend in the thirties was the rise of organizations with a civic, educational, or youth orientation and the decline of the ritual-bound lodges. This finding was echoed in Jonesville, where the Masonic Lodge, once the most important group in town, had fallen upon hard times, with scarcely enough initiates remaining to perform the required rituals. The authors of *Democracy in Jonesville* speculated that the causes for this decline included the Depression (many potential members were too financially strapped to afford the dues); the added financial burdens of an older membership (many of the organizations were insurance societies paying death benefits); and, primarily, the diminution of the number of socially prominent members in the lodges, which lessened their attractiveness to younger businessmen as a place to make contacts. The Masons, although in trouble, had managed to cling to their social edge, but they were fast losing ground and "the fact of being a high-degree Mason is no longer a sure step to social success."[15] The authors further observed that the lodges that had "secularized" their activities—that is, done away with the mumbo jumbo and became purely social—were the most successful. Often the ladies auxiliary of a lodge was much more active than the men's side—notably in the case of the American Legion. The authors theorized that activities were even more secularized and social and therefore more popular (the Legion began playing up its social side for the men, providing a bar in most towns, while remaining a bastion of conservatism and "Americanism").

Tocqueville might have been shocked at the cliquishness and class bias of the towns' organizational life, though more probably he would have coolly observed the phenomenon and updated his observations on American egalitarianism and the tyranny of the majority. The clubs had their critics, both envious outsiders and dissident, if necessarily anonymous, members. The Muncie Rotarians, with their ritualistic first name mode of address ("'Lo, Bill." "'Lo, Ed."), their Couéistic sloganeering ("He profits most/Who serves the best. R-O-T-A-R-Y/*That* spells RO-TAR-EEE."[16]), their overweening devotion to business values, seemed to have stepped from the pages of Sinclair Lewis, if the Lynds' description is a fair one. But style aside, some Muncians wondered what all these competing, mutually exclusive organizations accomplished, besides a few purely charitable activities; wouldn't it be better to combine them all into one group with definite community goals? Even during the Depression, Rotary continued unchanged with little reference to the social and economic problems of the town. The main change during the 1930s noted by the Lynds was perhaps in reaction to such attacks as *Babbitt*—an increased self-consciousness and a muting off the more egregious gladhanding. Still, the Lynds thought, Rotary's main purpose was to "seek to build morale through a solidarity achieved by the reiteration of familiar slogans and the avoidance of divisive issues."[17]

Rotary was also becoming internally cliquish, and by the 1930s its partiality toward a single group in the community was so blatant that members' sons were being routinely inducted—a far cry from the organization's ideal of selecting the outstanding individual in each business and profession (the members had already gotten around this requirement by creating a class of "honorary members," thus enabling them to include as many lawyers, doctors, or hardware magnates as they wished). The Lynds predicted that a splinter group of disaffected Rotarians would secede from the organization, and already a potentially rivalrous Lions Club had appeared in the city. In contrast, the working-class lodges, such as the Eagles, were much more democratic. They provided their members with a social-club atmosphere, where they could drink and play cards; wives were brought in through auxiliaries, picnics, and frequent Saturday night dances.

The clubs answered a deeper need for belonging, as well as for business contacts and social status, but the question arises, why was this need so strong, even in the smaller places? It is interesting to note that Rotary was founded in Chicago in 1895 by five bachelors, all displaced small-town boys who were seeking an antidote to the anonymity of the city (a kind of middle class equivalent to the bohemian communities in the city favored by small-town escapees). The somewhat strained fellowship of Rotary meetings, the insistence upon a first-name basis, the jovial banter, the speeches by a different member each week about his business, all provided a kind of synthetic community. The masks of the city were supposedly removed and, as a speaker at the Muncie Rotary put it, "It isn't Edward T. Smith, President of the So and So Corporation, you're addressing but the human being, the eternal boy in Ed."[18] Rotary also enabled businessmen to get to know one another and to discover, as a Muncie Rotarian put it, that "the other fellow hasn't got horns on and ain't out to get you."[19] It is not hard to locate the source of this need in the nature of small-town business rivalries—not only open economic competition but also the sub rosa backbiting, gossip, and malice that existed among small-town merchants. The first mission of Rotary—restoration of a simulacrum of lost community—reflected the increased urbanized life-style in towns, the fragmentation of social life.

A sense of community still existed of course in the smaller, more stable places, but in the growing towns, where the ideals of growth—more people, more industry, more, more—were being achieved, this sense was being lost. The burgeoning of new organizations, their rapid turnover as older activities lost favor and were replaced, the frantic social whirl, the spread of cliques, the triumph of the purely social group over those formed for the discussion of ideas, the secularization of the ritualized organizations, the rise of "service" clubs employed mainly for making professional contacts and acquiring status—all these traits in the town organizational life were symptoms of urbanization. It had progressed furthest in small cities like Muncie, but it was present to a degree in smaller places, as "rural" and "urban" became no longer two separate and distinct cultures, but rather points on a continuum.

In contrast, during the middle and late nineteenth century the number of organizations had been relatively small; some towns had none at all as late as the 1870s; in others a few of the national lodges began appearing after the Civil War, performing a quasi-religious function through their ritual and offering mutual assistance through the various kinds of insurance they provided. The number of other organizations, notably the politically powerful Grand Army of the Republic, plus the study groups, debating societies, choral groups, town bands, village improvement societies, and athletic teams, remained small until the 1890s, and their purposes seemed substantive in the life of the community.

But with the twentieth century came the deluge. Muncie in 1890 had 92 clubs, or one for each of its 125 citizens; in 1924, there were 458 active clubs or one for every 80 people. While population grew more than threefold, adult social clubs increased sixfold, church adult social groups over twelvefold, business and professional groups ninefold, and civic clubs of the Rotary type elevenfold. Obviously the mutual-aid and self-culture aspects of these organizations had waned and had been replaced by exclusiveness and getting ahead. Belonging became a goal, in a narrower sense of finding acceptance in a clique or an exclusive group where one's social position was advanced or at last secured; organizational life represented a kind of defense against rapid change, a securing of one's status, one's place.

In the lower levels of society where status considerations were absent, clubs performed mainly recreational functions; the decline of crafts and the demise of the guild-type educational organizations of the nineties had left a vacuum in workingmen's social life. The industrial unions that replaced them provided some solidarity, but were large and bureaucratic. At all levels there was a simple "escape" element in many clubs—for the women, escape from the home (where women found themselves with increased leisure on their hands, thanks to laborsaving devices and smaller families) and for the men, escape from the rat race into exclusive, if synthetic, fellowship with one's rivals, or the beery camaraderie of the clubhouse.

In the nineteenth century, the church had exercised much more influence in many people's lives; people spent Sunday mornings and evenings at church, and probably some weekday evenings as well for choir practice or Bible study. But church had become more secularized and "social" too; one joined a church for status and social reasons rather than doctrinal ones (and doctrinally, there were not that many differences among the various mainstream Protestant faiths). The churches, hard-pressed to stimulate interest, took to imitating the social clubs with adult and youth fellowship groups for parishioners. Sin and redemption were preached about less often, and more perfunctorily—except in the evangelical "holy roller" churches that harbored the poor and drew guffaws from Eastern sophisticates like Mencken and Sinclair Lewis; instead, it was the "social gospel," which meant, in Muncie, a chastising of "radicals" on the local college campus in sermons that were instigated, it was said, by Muncie's first family, the Ball brothers.

In short, joinerism was added to boosterism in most modern small towns, replacing the informal sociability of an earlier time when people's relationships with one another cut across age, class, occupational, and organizational lines and one's knowledge of all the other townspeople ranged over their entire lives. In those days people socialized freely over the whole social spectrum, and cliques were frowned upon as "stuck-uppity." (Zona Gale's Friendship Village stories often have an anticlique moral.) Early organizations drew together people of like affinities, shared purposes, or community goals; the purpose was not to prove one's superiority; they had often idealistic objectives that were not just empty words, as were the slogans of the Muncie women's groups, and their programs were more purposeful than the faddish potpourri of topics taken up by these groups in the twenties ("Wonders of the Radio," "What Do Colleges for Women in the Orient Accomplish?" and "The Life of Paul," to name the subject range of one club).

The fact was, as Page Smith observed, that "such a plethora of organizations is obviously a disease of the body politic in communities which have lost all sense of an integrated community life. . . . Even under the best of circumstances the organizations serve to perpetuate the fragmentations of the community and encourage the formation of enclaves and cliques."[20] The sociologist Baker Brownell observed that "as the community declines in significance and holding power the impulse to make formal organizations seems sometimes to go wild."[21]

Smith contended that the towns with the strongest sense of community, in which class and cliques were least divisive, tended to be those founded by homogeneous settlement-groups, rather than speculators—in other words, "covenanted" towns. Certainly, class distinctions were inimical to the face-to-face intimacy, the rounded involvement of each resident with nearly everyone, that characterized the stable small towns of the 1890s. A class system emphasizes the social calculus, a categorization of people by abstractions based upon surface characteristics—manners, money, background—rather than the whole personality. Yet the hypertrophy of organizational life also reflected a sense of loneliness among individuals which occurred in towns that, like Muncie, had become industrialized and urbanized. In the old days every town had its "queer" people, its hermits and crazies, but common activities, neighboring, and mutual assistance acted to meld people together by the annealing bonds of face-to-face relationships, common experiences and memories, and a sense of primary ties to family and town.

Loneliness was something new. The Lynds found that one in eight wives who belonged to the business class in Muncie had no casual or intimate friends, while one in three workingmen's wives had none. The Lynds described the decline in neighboring among people who lived close to each other—and indeed the breakup of natural neighborhoods inhabited by people in similar conditions whose menfolk walked to work nearby. They also remarked the rise in importance of the church as a place primarily to make friends, rather than a place of worship. Newcomers complained of their loneliness and difficulties in being accepted; in Mineville, Blumenthal wrote, newcomers were immediately "placed" as to class ranking, then slowly accepted. With variations, it was the same in Jonesville.

In short, one was admitted into the town through church, class, or groups, rather than into some larger whole. There was an attenuated sense of belonging to the entire town, and therefore there was less participation in community affairs, except when some natural catastrophe occurred. What historian Arnold Toynbee called the "link of locality" was strained; the organic, historical, generational ties to place were fragmented and in their place was the artificial link to an idea, a Chamber of Commerce construct. People tended to run with their own packs, while maintaining the prescribed noncommittally friendly tone with others and avoiding such sins as being "uppity." They recognized more people, but knew fewer. This alienation from the whole community was especially evident in the working class; among the business classes, the proliferation of organizations substituted for community. In Muncie, the Lynds noted, the workers came to be regarded, not as folks, but as part of the "labor supply." In Mineville, people often had a kind of impersonal tie to the town; they would rather live somewhere else and, even though "it was not a bad place," it was mainly a place where one made one's living; if there was a chance of making a better living somewhere else, one moved on. People were judged by what they made and owned, rather than who they were.

Traditional town gathering places and forums like the saloon, the drugstore, and the back room were also falling into desuetude. The saloon of course closed its doors during Prohibition (in Mineville it was replaced by several pool halls that sold home brew), but even before Prohibition a Muncie saloonkeeper said that the coming of the movies had cut into his business drastically. Other technological innovations had the effect of diminishing sociability. The popularity of the radio was blamed in part for the decline in interest in lodges and civic meetings; people would rather stay home if a good program was on. The telephone discouraged visiting and back-fence gossip, though it was a boon to isolated rural women, helping them to keep in touch with friends (it was also a boon to town gossips on a party line; some would sit for hours, receivers sealed to their ears, listening to whatever conversation came on). When ownership of automobiles became widespread in the 1920s, it was *de rigueur* for every family that owned one to pile in of a Sunday and go for a drive in the country, rather than have leisurely Sunday dinners attended by numerous friends or relatives. Automobiles also altered courtship patterns among the young, removing them from the porch swing under the parental eye and taking them off to the dimly lit roadhouses that were springing up along the highways outside of town or to fraternize with the young in nearby towns. Not that some of the same things couldn't have been accomplished in a buggy in days gone by, but a buggy's range was considerably less, and there was not so much social pressure on the young to use it. A car provided speed, excitement, mobility, and an outlet for youthful restlessness.

Parental controls over the young had definitely begun to loosen in the twenties. Families became more democratic, which was probably for the better, but parents suffered vague guilt, as they remembered their own unquestioning obedience to parents' demands. Yet, the young people were not all necessarily Flaming Youth—the taboo against premarital sex, for example, was still strong; but they had developed a cool skepticism of their parents. Young men were also, at least before the Depression, able to find jobs and earn their own way by working in factories or on farms. Many of them refused to contribute their paychecks to their families, spending the money on themselves instead. Fathers in the business class traditionally spent little time with their children, being righteously preoccupied with making money; and it was generally considered proper that the wife should be the more important parent in the matter of child rearing. But the better-off wives were putting in less time with their children too, occupying their new leisure in club work and sports. Among working-class people child rearing followed old-fashioned codes—but it was difficult to control a boy who quit school at sixteen and was earning good money tending a machine in a factory. With the advent of the Depression, however, the situation changed, and school or idleness were the main choices of the teenagers. Family life centered more in the home, and the glowing orange dial of the radio served as a substitute hearth around which the whole family gathered of necessity for free entertainment.

And so family ties too had become less authoritarian and less binding in the small town; legal and contractual relationships, such as in school and job, were usurping the place of the primary ties of the farm family in the nineteenth century. The rise of social agencies to help the poor during the Depression also involved the government indirectly in family life. Federal Old Age Assistance payments, for example, served to bring aging parents and children back together under one roof; the children took the parents in and took a share of the government check—a considerable sum in rural villages during the Depression.

Mass entertainment provided urban guides to conduct for the rural young. Albert Blumenthal, who grew up in the mining town he described in *Small Town Stuff*, had never ridden in a trolley car before moving to the city, yet the first time he boarded one he knew exactly how to hold on to the strap because he had seen it done in a movie. Similarly, the Lynds described the process by which young people learned of romantic love from confession magazines and aped the mannerisms of movie stars they saw on the screen or read about in the fan magazines. Advertising influenced consumer behavior by manipulating symbols to associate prestige, social and economic success, and enhanced personal attractiveness with use of a product.

All these invasions of town life from the city, though seemingly diffuse, coalesced to foster new styles of life predicated upon mobility and impersonality, upon externals and status symbols rather than "who you are." If one aspect of community lay in the commonplace phrase that "everyone knows everything about you" (or the popular variant: "everybody knows your business better than you do") in a small town, in the new town-city, one's identity was acquired increasingly by manipulating roles, joining the right organizations, the pursuing of status symbols, and mimicking the fads and catchphrases purveyed in the mass media.* One was thus able to influence what others "knew" about one—to stage the impression one wished to convey, within limits—through symbols of dress and behavior. Money and status were linked; as one Muncie woman put it in lamenting the lack of real friendliness: "They know money, and they don't know you."[22]

Contributing to the spread of mass-culture images was the example of the town's upper class—the "400," the "country club set," and sometimes the "fast crowd." The income, composition, and social position of this group varied in different towns; it might be limited to the true upper class, or it might

*See Max Lerner, *America as Civilization* (New York: Simon & Schuster, Clarion Books, 1957): "One might say that a small town ceases to be one as soon as someone who has lived in it a number of years finds unfamiliar faces as he walks down the street and is not moved to discover who they are and how they got there." (Vol. I, p. 150)

also include what Warner and his associates called the upper-middle class. The "upper" class would be the old money, the old-stock aristocracy, and often the political and social powers-that-be. The upper class, at least in older towns like Newburyport or Henry Seidel Canby's Wilmington, would be above the status race and would avoid the more egregious kinds of conspicuous consumption and fashion-consciousness. It would probably be a conservative force, often pulling strings behind the scenes to keep the town the way it wanted it, as the Ball family did in Muncie. To be sure, its life-style would include mansions, regular trips to Europe and New York, gentleman farming, participation in high-status sports, and ownership of fine cars or even airplanes; but its sense of having made it was so strongly ingrained that the restless urge to conspicuous consumption was muted, though not completely abated since there were loftier social heights to be scaled in the cities, if one cared to. It was the upper-middles who were driven by consuming social ambition, whose money tended to be newer and who busily acquired the "right" house, car, clothes, and so on, taking care not to shock their social superiors by outré behavior. They engaged in sufficiently ostentatious display to impress the middle classes below them and publicly establish their claims to superior wealth.

Upper-middle-class behavior combined circumspection and deference to the values of the upper class with a flair for consumption and stylish behavior. But it was the upper class that held the keys of admission into the hallowed precincts. The previously ignored upper-middle-class couple in Jonesville who bred horses and thus "galloped into society" demonstrated a creative flair in the business of social climbing. As Warner put it in *Democracy in Jonesville*: "They [the upper-middle class] are anxious people, for in their eagerness to associate with those who are their social betters they are very fearful of doing something wrong and ruining their chances for advancement. They worry for fear that they will overlook some opportunity for bettering their station in life. They are constantly on the alert to enter into worthy civic enterprises particularly those in which men and women from the elite are active sponsors."[23] So the upper-middles, on the one hand, try to be *au courant*, but on the other must defer to the sometimes more conservative values of the upper class.

These anxieties preoccupied John O'Hara in many of his novels about the Pennsylvania town he called Gibbsville (a simulacrum of his own hometown of Pottsville). O'Hara selected with a jeweler's eye the outward tokens of class; he claimed to know the vast and crucial differences between a man who drove a Franklin car and one who drove a Buick, though they cost about the same. Possessions and manners revealed class, and once class position was ascribed, all of a character's actions flowed logically. In his first and perhaps best novel, *Appointment in Samarra* (1934), he told a bourgeois horror story about the decline and fall of a Cadillac dealer named Julian English, whose financial difficulties, drinking, and caddish behavior endangered his membership in the country club set. His sense of having disgraced himself drives him to suicide. But Julian English punished himself for the social transgression of throwing a drink in Harry O'Reilly's face at the country club dance—a kind of drunken, half-deliberate, half-accidental seppuku. "Don't buck the system; you're liable to gum the works,"[24] he finds himself mumbling in his last drunken hours. He is a man who has hurled his drained bottle into the Gibbsville social mirror because he can't stand the image he sees reflected there.

In Mineville, Albert Blumenthal recalled, there was a fast upper-class set in earlier years that set the pace, exercising a tutelary role. "What they do arouses comment," Blumenthal wrote, "whether approved or not."[25] They were the first to have the latest in fashions, cars, radios, refrigerators, clothes, and interior decoration, and they also encouraged fashionable vices such as smoking, drinking, and "playing bridge for money." The social leader during the town's first twenty-five years was Mrs. Swift, who set an example of liberated sexual behavior that her acolytes emulated. The result was sometimes tragedy: One man blamed the "high life" of Mrs. Swift's circle for his own divorce. His wife, he said, had "got a taste of drinking parties, dirty remarks, and the kind of people who like such things and I blame Mrs. Swift for that."[26] Blumenthal found, however, that the compulsion to emulate the 400 was not uniform; some ambitious people tried to travel with them but failed to gain acceptance; others rejected the upper class's values and refused to play its social game.

Nonetheless, in more sophisticated towns a social symbiosis existed between the upper-middle and upper classes, with the former clinging like limpets to the latter in anticipation of acceptance. In their second Middletown book (*Middletown in Transition*—1937) the Lynds placed at the top the wealthy segment of the "old" middle class, which was fast becoming a true upper class. This consisted of "wealthy local manufacturers, bankers, the local head managers of one or two of the national corporations with units in Muncie, and a few well-to-do dependents of all the above, including one or two outstanding lawyers."[27] It was the group that ran things, keeping Middletown safe for business by discouraging unions and "radicals." At the core of this group was the Ball family. Another wealthy manufacturing family was also nominally included, but it took little interest in local affairs. Below this class was "a larger but still relatively small group, consisting of established smaller manufacturers, merchants and professional folks (Middletown's outstanding 'old' middle-class members . . .) and also most of the better paid salaried dependents of the city's big business interests (the 'new' middle-class members of the favored administrative caste . . .)."[28] Economically, the latter, salaried group predictably identified with their corporate leaders, while the "old" middle class sometimes asserted its independence through the Real Estate Board and the Downtown Merchants' Association, which its members dominated (the industrialists dominated the Chamber of

Commerce); however, in a crunch the old middle class lined up with the upper class. It was the upper class that set "new and expensive standards in the use of leisure"[29] for the town, patterned after eastern society tastes, just as the equivalent group did so in Jonesville and Mineville, though on a much diminished scale. This pattern is of course not unique to small towns; indeed it first appeared in the cities and was then emulated by the rising postpioneer aristocracies in the towns, which were looking for a genteel, wealthy, leisured, life-style. The earlier generation of rich—the pioneers—held to the frontier values of frugality and maintained a more quietly opulent life-style.

These town elites were generally distinguishable by wealth, manners, display, and social and economic power. They preserved their superior status by a variety of means, ranging from exercising a negative veto over a complaisant town government (they rarely ran for office themselves), although they could not always depend upon having their men in office; controlling the local newspaper through their influence with advertisers; setting the moral tone through the churches, and shaping and elevating the cultural tone by benefactions and promotion of causes through social groups they favored and patronized. They attempted to maintain certain standards that represented their values and vetted carefully newcomers seeking admission.

Warner's researchers demonstrated how this vetting process worked with a story about a new arrival in Jonesville (a story so apt that it is repeated in slightly different language in *Elmtown's Youth*). A young lawyer named Frank Donnelley moved to town, and one day he encountered a scion of the upper class named Clay Coolidge. Coolidge hailed Donnelley, introduced himself, and then, in a friendly but unmistakably probing manner, asked him such questions as where he had gone to law school, what fraternities he had belonged to in school, and so on. In the course of the conversation Donnelley volunteered that his father had sent him to college. By this interrogation,, Coolidge learned that Donnelley had gone to one of the best law schools and belonged to the same "best" fraternity as Coolidge had, that his father was wealthy enough to send him to school, and that, as a lawyer, his income was drawn from fees, which, on the Jonesville scale, ranked a bit below inherited wealth but above salary and wages. Coolidge was also able to judge Donnelley's manners and could easily enough discover later where he lived and in what kind of house. All this data was weighed and sifted, and in due time, after their behavior had been assessed, Donnelley and his family were "placed" in an upper-middle-class position. Such vetting would not be necessary for a workingman, who obviously belonged in the town's bottom class, or for most of what Warner calls the "Common Man" group—the solid middle class above the working class and "lower element."

In an even smaller place like Mineville, where everyone was acquainted with everyone else, class position was more quickly ascribed: "Soon after a newcomer has arrived in town he is likely to find himself in the approximate place on the social scale which he will occupy permanently. . . . The different social levels of the people are very real; and sometimes quite rigid."[30] There were "countless gradations in social position from the bottom to the top of the social ladder, which have been recognized by all and yet which have always been so informal, unstable and intangible almost to defy accurate investigation."[31] The upper class was perhaps easiest to place, being most influential, in addition to having the most money. They were the people who were high up in the local mining industry or leaders in business or the professions. Each individual possessed a mix of qualities, including personal attractiveness, a modicum of culture, college education, and genteel manners, and had "the money, inclination and ability to follow the ways of the aristocrat."[32] Most of the Mineville "aristocrats," Blumenthal adds, would be middle-class in a city; their annual income was in the ten thousand dollar range and the women did their own housework.

In a smaller place like Mineville the class system was looser, more democratic; but it appeared that, as in Yankee City and Jonesville, class was ascribed on the basis of a number of factors: People were "placed high in one respect and low in another. The sum of all these ratings of 'higher than' and 'lower than' determine[d] the person's position on the social scale."[33] Thus, families had become members of the 400 "despite their having been notoriously lacking in money, big success, professional achievement, sex morals, intelligence, artistic accomplishments, pleasing personal appearance, or high nationality rating."[34]

The allusion to high nationality rating is a reminder that foreigners, however well integrated into the Mineville community (they did not congregate in ethnic neighborhoods, for example), were still handicapped in the status race. A further pecking order was applied within the foreign groups that placed British and northern European at the top, Italians or Greeks lower, and Chinese and blacks at the bottom. Usually, a family had to live in a town two or three generations before it could emerge from the chrysalis of the lower class, though rapid rises within a generation had occurred. Immigrants were generally relegated to the working class upon arrival and told in effect to work themselves out of it if they could. One way of acquiring power and eventual acceptance was through politics, a route followed by the Irish in New England, which frequently pitted them against the native-stock establishments, such as the Brahmin class in Boston.

Suffield, Connecticut, was a typical old-style New England town with a tight aristocracy floating in old money that had been made from tobacco farming in the mid-1800s and shrewdly invested in the insurance businesses that had grown up and flourished in nearby Hartford. The legend was that when the daughter of one old family was courted by Ogden Armour, the heir to the Chicago meat-packing empire, her father objected to the match on the grounds that the huge Armour fortune was new money. Suffield's old families were the classic, conservative, Puritan-descended rich; the ladies always wore hats and white gloves when they went out on the street, and the men never appeared in public without a coat, vest, and tie.

The Suffield aristocracy were nearly all descendants of the Puritan town proprietors of an earlier day, and they controlled the banks and ran the town politics. When Irish and later Polish immigrants came in to work in the tobacco fields, the town provided them with night-school English classes and other help, but they were still at the bottom of the social ladder. Finally, in 1903, a young man of Irish stock named Hugh M. Alcorn simply decided he wanted to run for the legislature and announced his candidacy without consulting anyone. He soon learned that this was not the Suffield way; nominations for town and legislative posts were parceled out by the old Yankee families on a "you take it this year I had it last year" basis. Walking through town one day, Alcorn was hailed from a carriage driven by a black servant in livery and carrying a wizened old gentleman named Edward A. Fuller, a tobacco merchant and pillar of the community. Fuller beckoned to Alcorn and said accusingly: "They tell me you want to go to the legislature, young man." Acorn agreed that he did. Fuller peered at him through gold-rimmed spectacles, then pronounced, "Well, you can't go, young man, you can't go. Drive on, George."[35] Alcorn ran anyway, won the election, and went on to become state attorney for thirty-four years, founding a small Connecticut Republican dynasty, which his son Meade Alcorn carried forward. (It took the later-arriving Polish until 1930 to get one of their number elected to the board of selectmen.)

Town establishments were not always so well-entrenched or readily identifiable—or unified. A central dynasty like the Balls in Muncie was rather unique; in other towns, a more diffusely based industrial elite ran things. A dynasty might take little interest in town affairs, like the other wealthy family in Muncie. Then too, dynasties were not immortal; the Balls moved their factory out of Muncie and developed wider financial interests. Elites were not always united; jealousies and personality clashes might well keep them divided. In Mineville the 400 did not highbrow the rest of the town but did show a preference for one another's company and maintained invisible standards to keep undesirables from claiming membership; nonetheless, at least two of the families drew all of their friends from outside the elect circle. In Jonesville, as in many towns, the country club was an upper-class preserve in the twenties, but by the thirties economic conditions were such that, as one man (upper-middle class) said: "The Country Club isn't what it used to be. The trouble is that during the depression they were pretty hard hit so they had to let down the bars and take just about anybody so they could keep going. A lot of people got in then that we wouldn't take usually. Now they are there and nothing can be done about it."[36] (The increase in public golf courses, where even workingmen could play, tarnished the leisure-class image the game of golf had.) The older families would gradually retire from the active social scene, as their sons and daughters moved away, and a new group would take over, leaving the remnants of the old guard to murmur wistfully, "I don't know anyone at the club anymore," and remember wistfully the bygone parties and good times.

As the guard changed, though, the old upper class continued to run the club, presumably with the approval of the lower groups they deigned to admit. In the four leading social organizations in Jonesville, the role of the upper-middle-class members was to "admire and envy and emulate the upper-class members and thus express the superiority of the latter group."[37] They acted as Indians to the upper-class chiefs in the latter's pet organizations. In return, members of the upper class graciously allowed their own reflected effulgence to enhance their loyal followers' social luster in the town.

But not all towns had so docile an upper-middle class. In one place, the ruling group snobbishly opposed industry and blue-collar people. They fell in with a group of wealthy and social city people who had built summer homes on the lake. The city socialites invited the locals to their parties and let them bask in their aura. Meanwhile, industry did come, bringing with it a new managerial class that was well-educated, socially ambitious, and civic-minded. Finding itself ignored by the town elite, this group turned its energies to community affairs and pushed through a number of reforms, including school consolidation; they became by default the town leaders.

In a community that through the 1920s had been dominated by a group of "first families,"' the Rotary Club, made up of younger blood, became a progressive force. The first families had vetoed plans for a new school building, the money for which was to be donated by a wealthy citizen from outside the town, on the grounds that "when any municipality stoops so low as to accept the largesse of a private citizen it has denied American democracy and sold its own soul."[38] Not long afterward the Rotary Club was formed, made up of young businessmen, most of them inheritors of their fathers' establishments. They began a series of town improvements such as organizing a chamber of commerce, conducting an economic survey and improving business, and engaging in social welfare work.

Elites were also subject to destructive forces from within. Occasionally two leading families would become embroiled in a feud that shook the entire town. In one village the feud boiled over into open economic warfare between the two families, both of which controlled important businesses in the village, and the family that owned the bank forced the other family's movie theater and hotel into bankruptcy. Demoralization ensued; the baseball team disbanded, the park was unused, business fell off, and membership in community organizations plummeted. Even Old Home Week was not held. Though rare, such imbroglios illustrated that town elites were not monolithic; they also showed the danger of the influence they exercised over vital aspects of community life. The social-business power elite in Muncie decreed opposition to unionization in the thirties because it had decided (with reason) that the town's main leg-up in the competition for new industry was cheap labor, and unions would put an end to this. As a result, union organizers were met by police and hustled out of town, while the newspaper kept up a drumfire of blatant, sometimes threatening propaganda against unions. Owing to the workers' apathy and fear of losing their jobs, organizational efforts were consistently defeated. Elites might also oppose new industry that would compete for the local labor force and possibly force up wages.

Nor should it be said that elite domination of small towns was universal. Carl Zimmerman's studies of "Yankeeville" and "Babbitt" found that class hierarchies were unpopular with the townspeople. In Babbitt, the country club had mill workers as members, and a twenty-dollar-a-week dyer was president of the rod and gun club, which was supported by leaders of local industry, professional men, and bankers. In Yankeeville domination by wealthy families was avoided.

It should also ritually be added that elites did some good things. The Ball family's numerous philanthropies added much to Middletown, not the least of which was the university that bore their name (although the family maintained an irritatingly paternalistic relationship with it for many years). Family members served on (and dominated) the school and park boards. The upper class made important benefactions and acted as conservators of things of beauty in many a town; they encouraged culture and underwrote visiting lectures and were active in literary and artistic societies. Elites could provide civic leadership, and leadership was often a commodity sorely needed in small towns; however, their dominance discouraged the development of such leadership outside their own social circle (aside from a few lonely rebels who took on the establishment—the former mayor turned newspaper editor in Muncie; the Italian mayor in Newburyport whose campaign centered on opposition to the town elite).

The elite was often in need of replenishment. The sons and daughters tended to go east to school and never return. Some families sold out their holdings and retired to lives of cultivated leisure. The sons who succeeded to their fathers' businesses provided an object lesson in nepotism, but they at least preserved local business control in the town (the social trauma that resulted in Newburyport after the old founders of the leading shoe plants sold out to outside interests was described in Chapter VII). If the elite was exclusive and tended to limit intermarriage to social equals, there were always bright young men who managed occasionally to crash the social barriers and marry the banker's daughter. The intimacy of the small town made it easier for such matches to occur, and wealthy men often looked for protégés when their own sons disappointed them. But even young people came to observe class lines in their dating and social life.

Finally, there were the families that fell from social grace. Nearly every town had them, and such comedowns, if dramatic and precipitous, monopolized town gossip. Albert Blumenthal said lively interest was aroused when a local boy of impoverished background became the richest man in town, but the most avid attention was paid to failure stories—which often as not involved juicy crime, embezzlement, or sexual scandal. There was undoubtedly, in the public reaction to such stories, a sanctioned release of all the pent-up resentment of the high and mighty by members of the middle and lower classes, who had no hope of rising to their level and who resented, however slightly, their airs, their power, their conspicuous consumption, their big-city ways. It was no wonder that some wealthy families took care to maintain an outward facade of democracy and rectitude. "One must be 'common' in Mineville,"[39] Blumenthal wrote, and this applied to the rich as well; similarly, moral conformity insured that one did not appear above obeying the rules; it also prevented the critical gossip that undermined moral authority. So long as moral lapses weren't of the magnitude that squandered a fortune—drinking, gambling, crime—the rich might defy public opinion. But violation of the town morality, given their position, opened them up to loss of respect—they became all too human. Most failure stories were unspectacular, however—gradual attrition, rather than dizzying plunges. The second or third-generation scions who maintained the old family home but lived in genteel poverty of the shrinking income of a trust fund and a sinecure job as a clerk in a bank and who might eventually be reduced to selling off the family antiques were more the rule. Such people were often "carried," as it were, in the middle class, so long as they did not lapse into moral turpitude, unacceptable eccentricities, or any other flagitious behavior inappropriate to their class, from the consequences of which wealth no longer protected them.

The Jonesville investigators traced the story of the greased slide into obscurity of the Wells family, which had lived in the country for three generations. The grandfather had been a prominent landowner—"landed gentry," in the words of a physician who knew him, the kind of old pioneer stock that provided favorable antecedents for the town's upper class. (The importance of old-pioneer ancestry and landownership in Jonesville is illustrated by the examples of the "social register" woman who was always described as a daughter of "a wealthy land-owning family,'"[40] and the family who, when they ascended into the upper class, were suddenly discovered to have sprung from an "old influential family of pioneers."[41]) The Wells family fortunes took a downward trajectory after they had lost their land. After heavily mortgaging their town house, they all moved into the family homestead in the country. The grandson, Fred Wells, was considered capable if not brilliant; "well thought of," he was active in church and the Masons. But his wife left him and his son Harold "turned out bad." Fred stopped going to church, and there were persistent rumors of his "running around with a lot of women who don't amount to much."[42] After a year passed, Harold landed in a reformatory. The Wells family, which had been treading water at the middle-class level, sank like a stone into the lower depths.

The case of a similar but this time voluntary identification with "the lower element" was reported by Carl Withers in Plainville, where the class system was rural and less complicated. Elmer Simmons's father's farm had been sold, and Elmer took his share of the money. But rather than doing something commensurate with his upper-class position as did his brother, who bought a farm on the "prairie," where the best land was and the respectable people lived, he went to live among the hill people. He adopted their live-for-today hunting and fishing life-style and married a backwoods girl. His children were automatically branded as lazy and lacking in ambition, the stereotypical judgment of all hill children, and were invidiously contrasted with their cousins who lived on the prairie.

The less sophisticated the social-stratification system, the harder it was for a person to fall. In a town like Plainville, Withers wrote, "It is more difficult to lower one's class status than to lift it because the upper class is varied enough to retain anyone who retains its 'manners.' "[43] Loss of money was a necessary but not always sufficient cause; change in manners and morals was equally important. For someone of upper-class background to descend into the lower-class depths required a combination of flagrant social apostasy and complete abandonment of effort. With the right concatenation of circumstances, however, it did not take long for the holders of a once proud name to sink into the common clay.

During the Depression, numerous examples of defalcations by bankers and illegal or at best foolish speculations with bank reserves occurred in conjunction with the wave of bank failures. Unless the banker won back the trust of the townspeople and attempted to make good the losses, he quickly fell off his once-lofty social perch. In Plainville, bank and business failures wiped out the town's small upper class, and they took with them the Methodist church, which had been the "social" church in town; it was replaced by the Christian church. Elsewhere, some of the speculators fled town in disgrace; when it was learned that a former banker was working as a bellhop in a big city, few people in his town felt sorry for him—"he got what was coming to him" was the attitude. In another town, when the first of its two banks failed, a man who had lost money in the 1920 crash went after the banker with a gun; others in the town were ready to get up a lynch party. The other bank stayed open, but resentment built up against its high checking fees and harassment of overdrawn depositors. As a result, the bank was literally talked to death; people withdrew their money en masse and deposited it in a bank in a nearby city. Nine months after the first failure, this bank went under too.

Bankers were not excessively loved—the pawky, lovable David Harum, who helped people out and spent most of his time horse-trading, was a nostalgic fiction. Bankers in general were stereotyped as sober, secretive, and cold. These imputed characteristics ran against the small-town grain. Further, they had acquired too much power over farmers with their high-interest mortgages, and there was no court of appeal to a denial of a loan. On the other hand, a certain tightfistedness was rather expected of them; the bank, with its Greek columns and granitic or marmoreal solidity, stood as an unassailable temple of the town's money, and its high priests had to project an air of probity and shrewdness, as well as unimpeachable discretion, since they had intimate knowledge of most people's financial affairs. They were also *ex officio* members of the town's power elite. This reservoir of antipathy towards the town banker was checked by people's fear of offending him. The banker's children were considered to be a bit "wild" (a reputation that, curiously, also dogged the sons of preachers), and where this happened to be true, the police hushed up the scrapes. So when a banker was caught out at financial improprieties, the resentment burst free, and it could be cruel.*

Many banks, of course, were the victims of circumstances; the drastic fall in farm prices and the value of farmland during the Depression eroded the security for their loans and contributed to bank failures (at the same time, mortgage foreclosures by the bankers contributed to resentment against them). Some bankers carried delinquent mortgagees; and those who made determined efforts to pay back their depositors succeeded in winning back the confidence of the town. But the banker was the beneficiary of an implied trust among the people who deposited their money with him (as well as enjoying a semimonopoly position); the breaking of this covenant was taken personally by many small-town people, for their bank was no faceless corporation cloaked in legal immunities.

Public opinion in a vengeful town could pass a swift and harsh judgment on a failed banker or renegade aristocrat. For those consigned to the bottom of the social ladder by poverty or race, however, sentence had already been passed. They need not court public opinion any further, unless they were attempting to rise in the world. Those in the next higher rung—the "good" working-class people, who had steady blue-collar jobs—maintained a standard of hard work and sober morality; indeed it was their deference to middle-class values that distinguished them from the lower element. They worked hard and kept their children in school and out of trouble. They were considered "nice families" but "nobody socially." They were active in their lower-class evangelical churches and were considered excessively religious; their morality was conservative and God-fearing. They and the next rung, the small-businessmen, were the backbone of the town. The somewhat lower ranking of the "good" working-class people reflected the invidious American distinction between those who work with their hands in mills and factories

*Contrast this old-fashioned morality with contemporary attitudes—for example the universal support accorded Bert Lance in his hometown, even after President Carter's deposed Bureau of the Budget chief was accused of loose banking practices. In the author's hometown, a lawyer was accused of misappropriating funds of estates of which he was executor. Many more people felt sorry for him than condemnatory, I was told.

and those who deal in services or own small businesses, a distinction that grew more marked in the twentieth century. Only a plant foreman would be placed above the working-class level; higher-class friends, organizational memberships, and manners might pull a middle-class couple towards the brink of the upper-middle class. But the bulk of the people in the middle class tended to be resigned to their lot, having given up the social climb. They "knew their place" even if they didn't admit it. The ambition they had was displaced onto their children, whom they hoped would rise by getting a college education (or an advantageous marriage in case of the girls). Mineville's average man in the 1930s did "not aspire to exceptional achievement," Blumenthal wrote, "for as long as he remains in the community, he sees little hope for advancement in his work."[44] This onetime mining camp and boomtown was now dominated by a large absentee-owned mining operation extracting silver, lead, zinc, manganese, gold, copper, and sapphires. It was a static, even listless town for which no one could see any great future; the action was in the nearby city of Goldville. The Mineville middle-class had a bit of the gold-rush mentality from the town's glory days; they bought mining stock and half-hoped to get rich. In contrast, in Muncie the middle class bet on the future; they still clung to a belief in an ever-rising tide of Progress which would lift them upward to new levels of prosperity. The durability of the belief in Progress held even during the Depression, however, the success liturgy was chanted with somewhat more desperate urgency as the dream grew more vulnerable. Disenchantment hit the small businessmen hardest; some of them committed the ultimate heresy of voting for Franklin D. Roosevelt in 1936.

Still, Muncie's depression-battered working class developed only an embryonic class consciousness. Unlike the proletariat in the large cities, the Muncie workers were mainly farm boys or sons of farm boys moved to the city. They were "thus close to the network of habits of thought engendered by the isolated, self-contained enterprise of farming."[45] The Muncie worker was, unlike his big-city counterpart, still close to the land; 80 percent of the population lived in single-family houses with a yard, trees, and flowers. The working class still did not question (except when they thought about it) the reigning business class's credo of success, of getting ahead, of status through possessions. Only occasionally, when workers were feeling particularly gloomy about life, did they give in to a sense of being "permanently licked." Being "on the county" was a psychic calamity; poverty was personal failure. But if a test of class consciousness is active support for unions, then Muncie's workers were not class conscious. Still, as the working class's opportunities constricted, its admiration for business-class ideals became increasingly hollow. Working-class aspirations were a holdover from rural life, reflecting the stubborn individualism of the farmer and the memories of pioneer days when land was the only capital and everyone who worked hard could parlay it into a good living.

Warner's team discovered a significantly smaller working class in Jonesville than in Yankee City and attributed this disparity to Jonesville's being a rural-based market town, albeit one that had some industry. In such places more people were engaged in service jobs and the working class was relatively small; class distinctions there were "less advanced," closer to rural attitudes. Another key factor was the small number of foreign immigrants in Jonesville, compared with Yankee City.

In rural towns the class system was rudimentary. As we have seen, it was usually a two-class system, consisting of those who were considered hard-working, moral, upstanding, reliable, and able to pay their bills, and those who weren't. Or, as a man in a village with a population of eight hundred put it: "There are two classes here, the really high class and the other class. If you are not in the first, well you're in the second; and that's all there is to it."[46] In Roxborough, Granville Hicks decided, "a person by and large belongs to the class he wants to."[47] There were an upper class and a lower class, and class divisions were undeniably significant. "There is not an organization in town, including the churches, in which the upper class does not constitute a majority and monopolize the offices." But the strength of community ties was such that class was not divisive: "In nine situations out of ten the class structure is overshadowed by a basic social equality that results from the smallness of the community and a sense of a common past."[48]

The most onerous quality of class systems, simple or elaborate, was of course their implied invidious moral judgment that the chronic poor were moral failures—that their status was their own fault. This was the governing ideology in places like Muncie, even though the widespread, seemingly inexplicable economic disaster that struck in the thirties mitigated the harsh judgment and it was tacitly admitted that when people were unemployed it was not always their fault. Muncie took care of its poor quietly, but there was still a prevailing faith that the economic system rewarded the deserving and that poverty was a punishment upon those too lazy to work (and as such was a necessary goad). Perhaps the stigma of being poor was as great in the cities, but in the cities one was thrust in with others in the same condition—and forgotten—while in the towns there was a greater visibility and feeling of disgrace because of the high valuation the twin Puritan-pioneer traditions placed on hard work and the concomitant belief that work was available to any man who wanted it. Blumenthal reported that a common saying in Mineville during the Depression was, "If I have to be poor I want to be poor in a city where everybody doesn't know I'm broke."[49] In the Depression much poverty was hidden behind closed doors, like a disease under quarantine. Small-town people also had a suspicion that community measures to help the poor weakened their moral fiber. This belief may have been a rationalization of the Puritans' disapproval of idleness; it also reflected a pioneer tradition that anyone who was unable to support himself was a drain on the scarce wealth of others who felt obliged to help him. But the self-help ethic belonged to an agrarian economy; it was anachronistic in a complex interdependent industrial society.

Although Muncie and towns like it did help their poor, they found their old-style methods of private charity and their puny welfare budgets overwhelmed by the flood of human need that crested in the thirties. People would aid one another in a disaster caused by the weather or help people temporarily disabled by sickness, but an economic storm was another matter. In 1929 when the Depression was spreading but had not hit home, one of the Muncie papers observed that "Muncie is prosperous." How did the editor know this? Why, by the large number of beggars on the streets. He had counted five cripples and three blind persons on a single Saturday. Why was this good news? Because beggars "don't go to 'dead' towns. They go to where the money is. So the more 'professional' mendicants you see, the more alive the community."[50] By 1931 this editor was confronted with the presence of thousands of poor who were not "professionals." And although he became editorially involved in the problems of relief for the poor, he never abandoned the official view that the Depression was "only temporary," that economic conditions were "basically sound," that "natural" economic forces, if left alone, would inexorably bring recovery, and that the real enemy of prosperity was the meddling bureaucracy of the New Deal.

Muncie's relief effort at first centered around the Community Fund, a private charity; the town's public relief efforts fell to the township trustee, who included the function of "overseer of the poor" among his duties. This city-financed relief aided, for short periods, about six hundred families, or 6 percent of those in the city. By 1933, over three thousand families, or one fourth of the total, were in dire need and crying for help. The community's agencies were swamped, and a series of reforms was instituted in the relief system. But as this system expanded so did political corruption—grocery stores and doctors who were paid from county relief funds were making money. People on relief were required to work, in accord with the Muncie credo, but it was soon found there were not enough public jobs available. An editorial suggested that "now is a good time for people who can afford it to have all their odd jobs done to help the unemployed. The best help is helping others to help themselves."[51] This lawn-mower approach to relieving unemployment relief (not unique to Muncie) did not make any appreciable dent in the situation.

Meanwhile, farmers in the county were bellowing like wounded steers over the bond issues being voted to provide additional funds for relief. They even threatened a lawsuit to set a ceiling on such bond issues, but in a stormy county council meeting their demands were defeated four to two. Both farmers and businessmen had descried a new specter on the horizon—the specter of communism, to be precise. There was a real fear that the workers would rise up in some sort of communist revolution if they weren't fed, and opposition to relief measures was muted. But the burden upon the relief system was so great that in 1935 payments were cut back from two dollars a week for husband and wife to eighty-five cents for the head of the family, fifty cents for the wife, forty-five cents for the first child, thirty-five for the second, and thirty cents each for all additional family members. (Payments were in the form of food orders negotiable at certain grocery stores; there was no money for housing, but if a family was evicted, the Social Service Bureau would set them up in a new place by paying their first month's rent.) One woman wrote an anguished letter to the editor:

> Those in charge of relief have never known actual hunger and want, never lain awake at night worrying about unpaid rent, or how to make a few groceries do for the seemingly endless seven days till the next week's order of groceries. . . . It gives me nightmares, but I'm used to it.
>
> But we are supposed to have faith in our government. We are told to keep cheerful and smiling. Just what does our government expect us to do when our rent is due? When we need a doctor? When we need clothes? We haven't had a tube of toothpaste in weeks and have to check off some item of needed food when we get soap.[52]

Meanwhile the farmers were complaining that their tax dollars were going to buy "cigarettes, malt and other unnecessitous things for those on relief."[523] And the local editorialist was worrying about the greatly increased amount of "charity" (there was no "dole" in Muncie) causing a "deterioration of morale"[54] among working people.

The overburdened relief program was wallowing and might have sunk, had it not been for federal money allocated through a variety of New Deal programs which employed men on public-works projects. Although its businessmen held to their principles and continued to berate "that man in the White House" and the bungling bureaucrats in Washington, the city nonetheless accepted with open coffers the Federal money. In a city that refused to vote public improvements in boom times, there was in the depths of the Depression a wave of new building which would have gladdened the heart of a Latin American dictator. "Good Old Santa Claus Comes to Town," headlined a local paper, going on to remark jovially: "If Muncie is not so improved pretty soon that she will not be able to recognize her 'lifted' face, it will not be the fault of good old Uncle Sam."[55] It turned out that just about every public project the Muncie city fathers could think up, the Washington bureaucrats agreed to finance. Another newspaper noted, "It has been said that, had it not been for the 'hard times,' the city would not have some of these public works twenty-five years from now."[56] The Washington bounty made possible, among other things, a riverside boulevard across the city, dredging and cleaning the polluted river, new bridges, a park and a $90,000 municipal swimming pool, repair and redecoration of the public schools, a $350,000 arts building (with a matching donation from the Ball family).

Many of these projects had been kicked around by the city government for years and were certainly needed, but local government had never been able to effectuate them. The Muncie city government had always operated on negative principles, emphasizing frugality, tax reduction, and avoidance of controversy. As the Lynds described it, the ruling belief was "do as little as necessary to keep people reasonably satisfied."[57] City government officials were timid and fearful of the inevitable rows and criticism any sort of major project would set off. So they did nothing and depended upon the munificence of the Ball family for major improvements. There were other trammeling factors, like a kind of complacent pride in saying, well, "We're just average. No better, no worse than anybody else." If this contradicted the "Magic Town" credo, so be it; boosters were distinctly reluctant to boost civic improvements that would benefit a large number of citizens, including the poor, and which were liable to cause a rise in taxes. The Lynds cited other factors—a tradition of putting incompetents into public office because of their very mediocrity, a distrust of planners and urban experts, an electoral politics that emphasized winning reelection over doing anything that might be slightly controversial, and a bone-deep complacency that regarded life through a rearview mirror, enabling people to boast about "how far we've come," without seeing where they were now.

In Muncie and elsewhere the structure of municipal government creaked alarmingly during the Depression. Only federal money, it seemed, could shore it up. These federal funds increasingly came with strings attached, but at first they looked like free money that would pacify the restless unemployed ("Full stomachs fight communism," Muncie businessmen believed), keep the city budget balanced, and eliminate the need to raise local taxes. The antigovernment businessmen were happy for their city government to accept the largesse. There were no alarms sounded in the local paper about the possible deterioration of the city's moral fiber from accepting Uncle Sam's handouts.

But the problem lay deeper than the machinery of municipal government; it included the small-town political process itself. In his description of the upstate New York village where he settled, the literary critic Granville Hicks spoke of the sheer inability to get anything done (he was describing the World War II period, when there was a mood of patriotism and widespread call for participation in war industry, community work, and civilian defense.) Hicks traced it to the surface amiability of village life: People avoided conflict and controversy, preferring to do nothing rather than risk divisive arguments. As a result, "political controversy cannot be conducted in public with acrimony or even with candor, though there is a vast amount of whispered slander and back-stabbing."[58] Small-town politics at the local level always tended to deal in personalities rather than issues, although in Hicks's Roxborough, the people ritually voted Republican in national elections and presumably embraced the G.O.P's platform. In both national and local arenas (instinctive conservatism made them distrustful of change (a word Hicks doesn't adequately define, but presumably meaning social programs instigated by the national governmment).

In Mineville there was the same emphasis on personalities. Although the county vote in national and state elections was usually split between the farmers and the miners, the former supporting the Republicans and the latter the Democrats, in local races "attitudes arising from intimate association with the candidates triumph over party lines."[59] Issues were "largely a farce,"[60] and a candidate's success was based mainly on "the friendships and antagonisms he has accumulated during his years in the community."[61] Successful candidates were judged more by the warmth of their personal greetings than their ideas for the town. Nobody expected much to come out of the town government—it had a long history of graft and ineptitude and the county government was more powerful—and officeholders found "nothing but grief"[62] in their jobs, with the city council and the county commissioners receiving a steady torrent of abuse and criticism from the voters. When the functionaries in town and county governments did make "an independent attempt to act in accordance with the best interest of all,"[63] Blumenthal said, their actions were always taken in the teeth of opposition from the "kickers and knockers." A retired mayor recalled that when he tried to lay cement sidewalks on Main Street, the storeowners on that street were the "worst kickers," not wanting to pay their assessed share even though shoppers were stumbling over protruding boards from the wooden sidewalk. A much-needed sewer system costing fifteen thousand dollars brought out more kickers and knockers, and a proposed water tank sparked an indignation meeting. (It should be said that this mayor was accused of lining his pockets on these projects, which handily illustrates another prevailing ill of municipal government.)

During the Depression the inadequacies of small-town governments became glaringly apparent. At bottom, these governments reflected the values of the conservative business establishment, which prized frugality, self-help, and laissez-faire individualism. Any public spending was suspect and public spending on the poor was regarded as downright immoral. This can be seen in the town budgets of 85 villages in the late 1920s. Fifty-five of 140 villages did not even have a separate entry in their budgets for social services, which included education, recreation, health, sanitation, and aid for the poor and elderly. They lumped whatever they spent in these areas under the heading of "general" or "miscellaneous expenses." The 85 villages that did itemize social welfare expenditures spent an average of $1,869 per village or $1.30 per capita. And of this amount only one-fifth was earmarked for care of the poor and the aged. In 1929, as economic clouds gathered, the amount went up, but not by much. These small allocations were traditional; most villages and towns delegated to the private agencies—churches, lodges, women's clubs, and luncheon clubs—as much of the job of taking care of the poor as they could. There were also funds from the county, under ancient poor laws, but in no great amounts. A small-business faith in frugality was embedded in the very structure of small-town government. And even a depression could not dislodge it. Obviously such a frail structure collapsed under the crushing weight of need placed on it by hard times. Besides, many town governments could with some honesty plead poverty, because of their shrunken tax revenues. As a result municipal defaults became an epidemic. By 1933 more than 1,000 cities and towns in the United States were in default on indebtedness totaling $2.6 billion; the number peaked at 3,250 in 1935, although by then the total amount of indebtedness was down from the 1933 high. Repayment of principal and interest was, however, generally prompt, and the Federal Municipal Bankruptcy Act in 1937 (superseding a 1934 statute that was declared unconstitutional) restored order to the situation; many states also set up administrative bodies to supervise and assist governments in local bankruptcy. By 1938, all of the 48 cities of over 25,000 population that were in default had paid their debts, and the record of the smaller units was almost as good.

For a time, though, small governments had been overwhelmed, and out of need they turned to the federal government. Thus was a federal presence established in thousands of small towns all over the land. Even in a backwoods town like Plainville, in the Ozarks, the "government man" had become a leading citizen. Carl Withers wrote that "the outside government functionaries with offices at Discovery [the county seat]—the county agent, the FSA [Federal Security Agency] executive and the secretary-director of Social Security—have begun to outrank the local officials in social importance."[64] But the welcome was not wholehearted. In Plainville it ran up against ingrained rural folkways and backwoods suspicion. The government people—whether distributing relief in cash and commodities, certifyiing eligibility in WPA, CCC, and NYA programs, supervising needy cases under Aid to Dependent Children and Old Age Assistance, or administering the sweeping farm program of the Agricultural Adjustment Administration—were not only committing daily blasphemy against the traditional individual charity but were also urging reforms in farming techniques. Hence, Withers dubbed them the "reformers." Since all of their authority and funding flowed from "outside" the community, they were also "outsiders," subject to the suspicion traditionally directed at such people in Plainville.

The main thrust of federal relief programs was direct aid with no work required to receive it. The idea of money being given to people who did no work in return shocked the conscience of people in Plainville and similar rural places. The locals also distinguished between aid that was in the form of food and other commodities and monetary aid. The former was all right, since it resembled the traditional neighborly aid in the country, where wives were constantly dropping off something they'd cooked that day for a neighbor to try or giving away some tomatoes they'd just picked in the garden. But giving money outright shocked them, largely because it was handed out with no consideration of the character of the recipient. Country people could not stomach lowlifes and people of dubious morality getting handouts—it seemed as if shiftlessness was being rewarded. Similarly, the chief criticism of the WPA was that it hired "worthless men"; true they worked for their money, but the Plainvillers got around this by scorning their projects as "made work." On the other hand, the CCC was lauded because it was "good for" the youth of the town, building them up physically and teaching them skills. Withers thought that rehabilitation programs would have been better than relief and pointed to a successful program under the Farm Security Administration, which through loans to farmers averaging five hundred dollars per farm restored over eighty families to self-supporting status.

The county agent's power was felt most, though, because he controlled crop-reduction payments and other programs of the AAA. The county agent serving Plainville was well-liked and energetic, but he couldn't reach the poorest and most backward farmers who needed him most.

The old distinction between book farmers and traditional farmers still persisted in Plainville, as it had in many parts of the country since the early nineteenth century, and many conservative farmers either refused to cooperate with the agent or did the minimum amount necessary to qualify for crop-reduction payments. The vocational agriculture teacher, who was installed in the high school by the federal government, ran into much community resistance. The poorer farmers didn't send their boys to school in the first place; others who did forbade them to take vocational agriculture. Even the boys who were allowed to take it found that the scientific knowledge they acquired about contour plowing and phosphate fertilizer was scorned as "book nonsense" by their fathers. Scientific agriculture was badly needed in the area, where half the soil was depleted, but it was difficult to get the message across because of local resistance and because the reformers could not find appropriate channels of communication through local community groups with some prestige, such as the churches.

The New Deal programs were indeed reforms brought in to combat an economic upheaval that had overwhelmed local resources. But they were sometimes far-reaching and threatened to plough under rural ways as ruthlessly as crops and young pigs had been destroyed under early (and bitterly criticized) AAA programs. Yet, change was not new to these rural people. And new technology that had direct and readily manifest advantages was the most easily assimilable. The new ploughs that broke the plains on up to the twentieth-century technology such as the car were eagerly accepted. In Roxborough when farmers talked it was mainly about "hunting and machinery," Hicks noted. Hunting was a link with the pioneer world, while "It is the interest in machinery that brings them into closest contact with the contemporary world."[65] The farmers rejected scientific farming and talked of superstition and love; yet they did not reject modern tools and machines. "People take what they can use without surrendering their way of life."[66] If an accommodation could be made with minimal stress, the benefits of change could be enjoyed. However, if innovations were accepted grudgingly and caused fissures between old ways and new, between old people and young people, between city and country, the trauma of change would be greater. Around Plainville, conservative agricultural ways were meshed with new techniques introduced from outside to the accompaniment of much grousing and complaining. But farmers who scoffed at the advice of outside experts would, if they saw a local progressive farmer who was respected and prosperous take up successfully a new method, go along with it. If a local man did it, then it was all right. Withers overheard a farmer, who was watching his neighbor haul a load of lime to put on his field, say he "would prosecute the man that put lime on my land."[67] Two years later he was using lime. Still, Withers concluded, places like Plainville were "doomed as 'traditional' communities. As their ancient value systems crumble under the blows of a new 'tradition' imposed from outside, their problem is to learn to participate more fully in the cultural rewards of the greater society."[68] Hicks also saw Roxborough's old ways dissolving in the modern world—especially the "network of personal and economic relations that once linked the members of a self-sufficient community."[69] He thought that substitute activities must be found that would bring people closer together. Perhaps this problem was not unique to the small towns, but their conservatism made them more vulnerable by making them less adaptable, just as their smallness made them more vulnerable through a lack of resources.

In Withers's time the prognosis for Plainville was not so good. The community was disintegrating. Its youths were not being readied for their inevitable emigration, though it was obvious that the community produced more children than it could provide jobs for. Yet nearly every parent had hopes that his or her own children would stay. Plainville was still living by frontier values, yet in the days when there still was a frontier, parents were less opposed to their children leaving because when they moved farther west to settle empty land, they were repeating their parents' own exodus. But when they moved to the cities, they were considered lost. Plainville's ministers preached against the "sinful cities"; new ideas and higher education were considered to be city-spawned and thus tainted. It was the small-town tragedy: the young must move on, while the parents grieved. By damning the city, they strove to keep their children at home. The young were the only product the town had to export, so, perversely, it sought to ingest its own progeny to insure the survival of the community. If the young did leave they were made to feel guilty for "deserting" their families. Yet if they stayed, they faced a straitened life with little opportunity in a countryside where the land was poor and the seductive, novel ideas of the modern world treated with suspicion. In towns of wider acquaintanceship with the world, the young were given up with an understanding that they must make their mark. But in such an insular place as Plainville, where outsiders were still regarded with suspicion, the young had little counsel from school or parents as to the wider world's expectations. That world remained threatening and divisive. Withers observed that—

> conflicts between the 'old ways' (here) and 'new ways' (here and outside) intensified. Conflict between 'old age' and 'youth' intensified. Ridicule and contempt for 'the hillbillies' intensified, and the class structure became rigid. The leadership of old-style merchants failed, and lodges ceased functioning importantly. Neighborhoods and extended families lost much of their solidarity. Only the churches remained as strong as before, out of all the old forms of social organization; they became in some ways even stronger, because the car lessened the number of churches while increasing each congregation. The power of the churches was cast in no direction, or 'backward' toward retention of the old ways..[70]

Little places like Plainville and Roxborough were rural pioneer societies struggling to survive in an urbanized world; even in a small city like Muncie, which was much farther along on the scale of urbanization, there was a growing disparity between the old agrarian and small-business values and those of the onrushing industrial civilization. Technology had hastened change in many ways, but lacking appropriate new values, people clung all the harder to the old. The Depression encouraged a kind of agrarian regression by slowing the pace of industrialization, sending people back to the land, and making subsistence farming a desirable practice while slowing down the pace of mechanization on the farms. The studies of class in the small town indicated that, if anything, class lines hardened during the Depression, while cleavages between business and working classes, poor farmer and well-to-do farmer widened. As field animals huddle together and turn their backs to an oncoming storm, so the towns hunkered down against the economic winds and held on. The mood was inward-looking with a heightened suspicion of the outside world and its threatening ways. Factories either shut down, shared out the work, or laid men off; small-town blue-collar workers were lucky to work longer hours for less money (or fewer hours for drastically less money)—the best that even the most paternalistic owners could offer them. Organizers from large national labor unions appeared and sometimes succeeded in organizing the local plant; but they introduced a new bureaucracy into the work place. New laws protected the unions and set minimum wages and hours. Small businessmen fell under a pall of economic gloom and cultivated an even greater thriftiness.

Yet so long as the majority of people were in the same boat, economic rivalries were muted. There was a drawing closer of families and neighborhoods, countering the isolation of economic disgrace, and an enhanced sense of altruism, translated into helping the poor. But the private charity and local relief facilities were swamped and gave way to the bureaucratic forms of help from the federal government, which clashed with local customs. Public works, however, boomed, and thanks to New Deal programs, many towns acquired schools and libraries and museums and roads they had long put off out of traditional parsimony. These new acquisitions, beneficial to all, shored up sagging community morale, but they were also an irrevocable admission of the federal presence and linked the small towns in new ways to the far-off urban power centers.

What these trends produced could be seen in the story of two towns in the 1950s and 1960s. Studying the town of Putnam, Connecticut, in the 1960s, Everett C. Ladd found small-town attitudes of an earlier era persisting. A hurricane in 1955 had brought a flood which left the downtown area under ten feet of water. In the aftermath, Putnamites faced a crisis. The town had already been losing industry and population, and this disaster placed it at a crossroads, where it might have to choose whether to live or die—though no one thought of it in such apocalyptic terms. Indeed the lack of a sense of crisis was one of the problems; many people could simply not become sufficiently energized to support any major action, preferring to stand pat and hope things turned out all right. The "progressive" forces in town did manage to establish a redevelopment agency, which applied for federal funds to build a downtown shopping center, the projected keystone of the redevelopment effort. Yet many were opposed to any expenditure of local funds on the project. Some were merchants who feared the competition, but many were simply resistant to change, rather than ideologically opposed to federal funds. The opposition consisted of the conservative small businessmen, who believed that "to prosper you save." They simply couldn't accept that any good could come of spending more money. Putnam eventually got its shopping center, but not until 1965. By then, it was hard to find anyone who recalled ever thinking it was a bad idea.

In the late 1950s two sociologists, Arthur I. Vidich and Joseph Bensman, studied an upstate New York town they called Springdale and published their findings in a book entitled *Small Town in Mass Society* (a revised edition was published in 1968). Both Ladd's and Vidich and Bensman's studies show that the small-business class had retained its tight hold on town affairs, even though its ideals were becoming obsolescent by the 1960s. The business class operated grocery stores, restaurants, filling stations, farm-implement and hardware stores and the like. What characterized them—except for one operator, the most prosperous and powerful man in town, who sold farm implements and feed and ran a mill, and whose business was tied to the prosperous farmers—was that they were all fighting for a limited market. They were tightfisted, spending as little as possible on advertising, redecoration of their stores, new lines of goods, and so on; instead of ploughing their profits back into the business, they bought real estate. These shopkeepers worked long hours and operated on a tight margin. Their world view was similarly parsimonious; cost cutting and saving were their twin gods.

What had happened was that these small businessmen were in a state of slippage; they had lost status and prestige, compared with other groups. Their fortunes had taken a sickening slide when they lost their previous monopoly of the farmer's trade. The chain stores, the automobile, mail-order sales—had all taken customers away. They were living fulfillments of Veblen's prophecy—"tollgate keepers" handling nationally branded and advertised products with a profit margin dictated by the producer. They had to sell more to keep up, because they made less profit per unit. This drove them into fiercer competition with each other; they had to carry a wider variety of goods, keep their store open long hours, extend credit, and do other things businessmen regard as poor business practices. All this effort amounted to running hard to stay in one place; expanding the business was out of the question.

The dynamic go-getting expanding businessmen in the community were—history's revenge—the prosperous farmers with large, profitable dairy operations. Battening off their prosperity was the town's large farm-implement dealer. Through his friendships with these farmers and knowledge of their interests, he had become a leading political power in the town. He had the dairy farmerrs' votes in his pocket, and with this power bloc behind him, he could manipulate the village and township governments in his and the farmers' interests.

He was, in short, Springdale's behind-the-scenes political boss. He worked hand in glove with two overlapping cliques of Republican party leaders who dominated the village board and the township board of trustees. These men together were the town's power brokers; they personally chose their "boys" from the ranks of malleable small businessmen to run for local offices. Once elected, these puppets did as they were told, and indeed they didn't have to be told, since they thought as the "bosses" did. Their frugal ways meshed perfectly with the governing philosophy of Springdale: Do nothing. A suffocating cloud of unanimity fogged over their every decision. If some group in the town wanted something—a new community swimming pool, say—the town fathers would delay and literally talk the proposal to death. However, if the group demanding action was determined and sufficiently strong, the council would pass the necessary ordinances or else encourage the group to go out and accomplish the project themselves. If the activists still could not be turned aside and if the issue looked to become an important one, threatening the ruling clique's political power, then, as a last resort, the clique would co-opt the project and reluctantly put it through. The purpose of this was to defuse any popular issue that might arouse opposition to the ruling clique.

The clique's program for a greater Springdale was also a simple one: Keep taxes down and property values up. This policy was fitted to the interests of the small businessmen like a custom-made suit because higher taxes would cut into their already thin profit-margins and because their savings were invested in real estate. As for the prosperous farmers, they thought tax money spent on improvements that benefited the townspeople was a clear waste of money; the only improvements they wanted were new roads to their farms or repairs when needed, which fell under the purview of the county and township governments.

Yet when it came to federal and state aid Springdale's budget watchers suddenly grew munificent. The short of it was that they cadged all they could get. Springdale received in state aid as much as twenty times what it paid out in taxes (this was at a time when New York's state legislature was dominated by upstate Republicans who favored their small-town and rural constituents at the expense of the cities). One of the town hall bunch, a lawyer, had become an expert in obtaining this money—both through the state government and the Republican party bureaucracies.

But the upshot of all this was that the local government, to keep taxes down, plugged into the state and federal troughs and became dependent upon them. At the same time, Springdale's business class was at the mercy of the large companies that made the goods it sold and its dairy farmers were at the mercy of federal government milk-price support policies. And yet the townspeople clung to a view of Springdale as a proudly independent, self-sufficient, and self-reliant small town and heaped ritual scorn on big-city, big-government corruption.

But a new middle class was rising up to challenge the ruling group's no-spend dogma. The latter had really lost their gumption in the Depression—the optimism, the old booster's faith in Progress, in growth. They snuck back into a protective shell of frugality and conservatism; they clung desperately to what they had. But now there was a new generation that was better educated, that had experienced the color and diversity of big-city life. They were managers, scientists, engineers, teachers, and they moved in the world of corporate, governmental, and academic bureaucracies. They accepted the security and perquisites of these jobs and no longer believed in self-help and laissez-faire; they achieved their psychic goals through consuming—the right foreign car or label of wine—and they preferred more leisure to the older generation's regimen of work hard, long, and save. This generation had benefited from the GI Bill, and while in college they had been exposed to new life-styles which drove them to reject their parents' ethos. They cultivated cultural and intellectual tastes and were more liberal morally, sexually, and politically. At the local level they wanted all the enlightened social services—recreational equipment, swimming pools, parks and better schools. They had thus "broken with the traditional virtues of parsimony in government and low-tax ideology characteristic of small businessmen in small communities."[71]

What Vidich and Bensman called the "middle-class revolution" was the wave of the future that would ultimately inundate the American small town.* Springdale was thus already "a backwash"; it, and communities like it, represented "the last link in America to the nineteenth century and its values."[72]

The small town, Vidich and Bensman claimed, had become an appendage. Springdale still clung to the old pioneer myths of neighborliness, equality, grass-roots democracy, self-sufficiency, and independence, while living in a real-life world of dependency. Springdale had adapted itself to mass society, but at the expense of living a lie. Or, as Vidich and Bensman put it, the townspeople had developed several defense-mechanisms that enabled them to avoid confronting the contradictions between ideals and reality. Springdalers exhibited "an almost infinite capacity of individual social elasticity and adaptability"[73] in shaping their lives so that the conflict between their aspirations and ideals and the limited ways they can achieve them in a frustrating small-town environment was minimized. The people had their myth of small-town innocence, virtuousness, and true Americanism which existed in a kind of invidious symbiosis with the durable myth of the city as the source of corruption, a place of crime, slums, dirt, and immorality. Thus Springdale could feel superior to the urban centers, where the powerful institutions that really called the tune were located, and which diffused a new, sophisticated, untraditional, abstract, bureaucratic culture that threatened Springdale's pioneer-populist values.

The town considered itself the font of common-man common sense—the vox populi of America—but it was not a democracy at all; it was an invisible government of four men, who controlled not only the village and township boards but also the school superintendent and the churches. Yet these men kept the town together, kept it running along its narrow-gauge track. They, it might be said, got things *not* done, which was the way a significant number of people wanted it. And they mediated between the town and the larger political institutions that affected the town's destiny.

In the town, people were supposed to be all equal, friendly, and neighborly. But there was a class system that mirrored unequal power and opportunity. Privately, people evaluated their neighbors on the basis of income and busi-

*There were signs, in the 1970s, that this "new middle class" was becoming an old middle class, at least on public-spending issues, but this was unclear. The political scientist Andrew Hacker questioned the usual explanation that the group's "liberal" views are traceable to a college education. (*New York Times Book Review*, 26 November, 1978, p. 5). Why, he wondered, did "majoring in comparative literature turn people against capital punishment"? Hacker suggested that the economy "emphasized occupations requiring verbal facility." This new emphasis, along with the increased leisure of the new class, meant a faster consumption of ideas and causes—which could include anti-tax referendums as well as proabortion "issue politics," both "conservative" causes, but favored by many of the new class.

ness shrewdness and constantly strove to best each other. Town gossip enforced conformity, and anyone who questioned the way of life was ostracized. People were friendly, on the surface, but five minutes before they might have been gossiping about the very person they were greeting heartily.

This was small-town etiquette, of course; one never confronted the person gossiped about with the gossip one had heard, and even people who hated one another were civil (in extreme cases they might avoid each other). But small-town gossip and the related power of ostracization had always served to enforce a more-or-less agreed upon moral consensus, and in Springdale, Vidich and Bensman said, the enforced conformity served to suppress any questioning of the status quo—to dampen criticism. This was necessary, lest people become aware how hollow was the credo they lived by. Anyone who showed signs of introspection and independent thought which might threaten this status quo was considered "abnormal"; the individual himself suppressed any temptation to the crime of thought by plunging into a ceaseless round of hard work and business. Springdalers had developed a way of thinking that Vidich and Bensman called "particularization"—that is, seeing events as separate, discrete entities rather than connecting them and generalizing from them. In other words, charged generalizations and abstract thought were avoided. Thus, the people could be aware of the facts of class distinction or the invisible government, but they simply and deliberately refused to put two and two together in order to grasp the total reality that those facts added up to.

In the description of Springdale's history, the reader is struck by one thing: how durable and clumsily adaptive the town had been as it bobbed in the changing currents of history. Indeed, Vidich and Bensman themselves say that little of the town's culture and values originated in Springdale—that it sat upon, rather, several strata of American history: the populism of the Jacksonian era, a layer of Bryan populism, a layer of 1890s popular culture, the cultures of foreign immigrants, and so on. Like Roxborough and Plainville and Mineville, Springdale was a bundle of past and present, of births and deaths, of people leaving and people arriving (only 25 percent of Springdale's population had been born there). The town adapted clumsily, even neurotically, by Vidich and Bensman's interpretation. What held it together was the autocratic, conservative leadership of the invisible government, conformity, and mind-numbing hard work that prevented all questioning and doubt, but preserved sanity. Yet the town endured tenaciously, its people clinging to illusions that, however obsolete they were, enabled them to live. Even Vidich and Bensman said that the pioneer-populist values Springdale clung to were not necessarily inferior to those of city people as a stratagem for surviving in the mass society. While in the city people were more innovative and experimental, in Springdale they held to traditions that were cherished as the true American values.

Plainville was seen by Withers as a disintegrating rural society, Roxborough by Hicks as half urbanized, half rural but too resistant to change, and Mineville by Blumenthal as a kind of economic flypaper on which people were stuck. Springdale was seen by Vidich and Bensman as a society held together by makeshift bands of conformity and quasi-autocratic political power. Plainville was threatened by the modern world, while Springdale was a backwash that held the modern world at bay as best it could. What all had in common were the stresses of social change and an incapacity to deal with change in a rational way. The modern world clashed with the most deeply held small-town values: individualism, self-reliance and cooperation with one's neighbors, a high valuation of tradition, suspicion of "new ways" and of strangers, ties to place and insularity, generational continuity through the family, and quasi folk beliefs ranging from superstitions about planting only in the full moon to the emotional fervor of fundamentalist religion.

Understanding these tensions becomes a study for the anthropologist, for the deeper roots of Plainville and Springdale stretch down into the soil of history—an unbroken chain to the primitive folk village that is a universal heritage of humankind. The anthropologist Robert Redfield saw all small communities as mixtures of older folk forms and newer urban forms—a "combination of opposites." These communities were, in other words, located on a continuum at one end of which was the small, homogeneous, collective, sacred, isolated folk village and at the other the large, heterogeneous, impersonal, secular, individualistic city. Redfield said that these antipodal ideal types must be kept simultaneously in mind by the observer studying any community, for elements of both were present: "In every isolated little community there is civilization; in every city there is the folk society."[74] Applying this dual vision to modern communities like Plainville or Middletown involves seeing them as "an interpretation of two opposite kinds of living, thinking, and feeling, as analyzable, as if we saw in Plainville or Middletown, first an isolated, homogeneous, sacred, and personal community of kinsmen, and then as if we saw in it the heterogeneous, secular, and impersonal community that we find approximated in cities."[75] Redfield's object was to see any unique community "in terms of a position relative to two kinds of human collective living, as just this local and particular arrangement of aspects of the one in relation to aspects of the other."[76]

Like Scott Fitzgerald's Jay Gatsby, the Springdales and Middletowns and Plainvilles proclaimed their all-American faith in "the green light, the orgiastic future that year by year recedes before us." Yet as they pursued an elusive Progress, their deepest instincts clung to the safe past. "So we beat on, boats against the current, borne back ceaselessly into the past."[77] Only that past was but an American version of the common folk-peasant-primitive past of the race. The towns were swept along by a force that continues well into the twentieth century in other countries, as they too industrialize, urbanize. Sometimes the conflicts between the old and new ways are exacerbated by revolution, which new secular creeds or recrudescent older religious ones seek to control. In the United States, by the 1970s the small towns and villages had survived this process, avoiding the worst social upheavals, and moved on into the post-industrial age. Yet even in the advanced American nation, the roots in the past were still visible. The continuum stretched unbroken through time. It was a great river of history that could be traced uninterruptedly back through the early American agricultural villages, back through the agricultural communes of Europe, back further in time, back to the living source—the primal village.

10
Town and Community

In the 1950s and 1960s urban sprawl and inner-city decay accelerated: the flight from the farms continued and quickened. The Supreme Court's "one-man, one-vote ruling" deprived the country towns and villages of their traditional dominance of the state legislatures and Congress; now they needed help more than ever but found themselves falling through the interstices of the Great Society's rescue net for the cities. Small-town mayors, aware that their voices were lost in the clamor raised by the disintegrating cities, began acting in concert to call attention to themselves. A movement for rural revitalization gained momentum in the late 1960s, recalling Theodore Roosevelt's Rural Life Commission in 1909.

But by the early 1970s, as disillusionment with the city grew and as the suburbs became more like the cities, small towns and rural living enjoyed a modest revival. The disenchanted young survivors of the 1960s upheavals were in the vanguard of this latest back-to-the-land movement. They professed to be searching for a simpler life close to the soil and the sense of community of a small-town environment. "Community" became a kind of rallying cry among these people; the hunger for it explained the willingness of so many young people to submerge themselves in the brackish psychological waters of the cults and pseudoreligions that proliferated throughout the country.

But apart from these latter-day utopians, there was a growing intellectual movement that rallied around the banner of smallness. Their bywords were "small is beautiful," "human scale," "no growth," "intermediate technology," "organic farming." There was a growing distrust of big government, big institutions, big cities—bigness; and conservatives and radicals alike seemed, for the historical moment, thrown together in the smallness camp. There were urban historians such as Lewis Mumford, who found big cities more and more untenable; critics of technology, such as Jacques Ellul and René Dubos; defenders of community, such as Robert Nisbet and Kenneth Rexroth; neo-Jeffersonians, back-to-the-landers, whole-earthers, communists, and neopioneers seeking to revive old country ways; right-wing anarchists such as Karl Hess; ecologists and conservationists seeking to save the land; architects who advocated restoration and preservation rather than redevelopment; "soft" energy and human-scale advocates such as Amory Loving and E. F. Schumacher—the list could continue, and while each represented different philosophical springs, there was a convergence of the streams into the idea of smallness as a positive value. Harold S. Williams summed up the smallness movement in this way: "Smallness is not so much a literal term describing anything as it is a metaphor to reflect some basic beliefs and values deemed important and related but whose connectedness is hard to articulate at a literal level."[1] Among these values were "self-mastery, rightness of fit, belongingness, personalness, self-reliance, manageability, wholeness, control, directness, integration"[2]—all clustering around "the re-emergence of the individual," the belief that, as E. F. Schumacher put it, "people, actual persons like you and me, are viable when they can stand on their own two feet and earn their keep".[3] (Williams was president of the Institute on Man and Science, a Rensselaer, New York, think tank that had directed some of its brain power to the problem of revitalizing small towns. His article appeared in *Small Town*, the publication of the Small Town Institute in Ellensburg, Washington, founded by Clayton Denman, a college professor and leading small-town spokesman.)

But without any prompting from the philosophers and the critics of mass society, a lot of ordinary Americans also were moving back to the countryside. This movement started as a trickle in the late 1950s, increased in the 1960s, and became a pronounced trend by the mid-1970s. The demographers began taking notice, and what they saw was no longer a move from the cities to the suburbs and exurbs, but from all of these to small towns and predominately rural regions.

This movement was easy to miss in its early stages. Population watchers had been mesmerized by the emigration from the farms to the cities, which had quickened during World War II, then turned into a statistical onrush. During the 1940s, more than 8.6 million people left the countryside. The exodus continued at a rate of a million a year in the 1950s and slowed down a bit to three quarters of a million people annually in the 1960s—this from an already diminished population pool. Between 1940 and 1970 more than 28 million people had moved from the countryside, leaving behind something over 50 million people in the nation's rural areas (defined by the Census Bureau as living on places of less than 2,500 population, or open country). In other words, in 1940 the rural population represented 40 percent of the national population; by 1970 it was only 26.5 percent of the total. If towns of up to 20,000 population, outside urban and suburban areas, are added, then a third of the nation lived in country, village, and small town. By 1975 only 4 percent of the total population—about 8.3 million people—were engaged in agriculture, compared with 27 percent in 1920 and 14 percent at the end of World War II. And about a quarter of these working farmers moonlighted at other jobs more than two hundred days a year; between 1967 and 1972, the total nonfarm income of American farmers exceeded the money they made on farming.

The effects of the rural exodus on small towns were only spottily measured, though not difficult to imagine. One study estimated a 30 percent loss in business enterprises between 1940 and 1970. Another figure popular among rural specialists was that for every five farmers who moved out one small business in town failed. The Great Plains area, always a precarious base for towns, was hardest hit. Hundreds of towns were dying, others in poor health. Writing in 1970, *New York Times* reporter Douglas E. Kneeland described scenes of desolation in South Dakota. Denhoff, once a railroad center, was down to 50 people, most of them old or retired; Lincoln Valley, nineteen miles away, had shrunk to a single last resident, a farm-implement dealer, who was in the hospital; Winnett, a county seat, had lost 89 people and only 271 remained; other hamlets had lost 20 percent of their population in the last ten years. Out of a total of 728 counties in North and South Dakota, Montana, Wyoming, Nebraska, Kansas, Oklahoma, and Texas, 483 lost people. There was an acute shortage of doctors; schools were run down; movie theaters closed. There had been a "snowball effect," as one resident put it. People moved away and stores and services closed down, driving still more people to seek urban-style comforts. And there were no jobs for the young—the small town's eternal plaint: They were too educated and highly skilled for the limited opportunities offered them. Small farmers were selling out to the remaining farmers, who were able to make a living only on large, consolidated farms. There was little hope of attracting industry to these windswept, lonesome, sparsely inhabited plains.

The farm population that once provided the economic base of towns such as McKluskey was vanishing; this great, long-term migration off the land was the harvest of seeds planted in the nineteenth century. But major technological advances in farming had come that were undreamed of in the nineteenth century. In 1945 one farmer could produce food for fourteen people; by 1968 he could support forty-five people. This enabled the consolidation of small farms into bigger units (there were nine hundred thousand fewer farms in 1970 than in 1960) and an increase in the size of farms, with owners able to work several smaller farms that they had bought up. Those having total annual sales over twenty thousand dollars increased by 50 percent and made up 24.4 percent of all farms, compared with 8.6 percent in 1960; in 1972, 24 percent of the farms took in 70 percent of the income. By the end of the decade, 200,000 of the nation's 2.7 million farms produced two-thirds of all crops and livestock. Capitalization costs of farming increased because of the need for expensive equipment and the high price of good land (in 1976 a four-hundred-acre corn farm in Illinois required an investment of two hundred and fifty thousand dollars for machinery and land, and cost twenty-five thousand dollars a year to run).

The chronic lower level of income in the rural regions remained a source of rural discontent. Per capita income of farm residents in 1960 was 54.5 percent of per capita income of nonfarm residents; in 1972, after emigration had culled many marginal farmers, per capita farm income was still only 82.7 percent of nonfarm. Rural poverty continued to be more common than urban poverty—11.3 percent of families in central cities lived below the poverty line, while 14.3 percent of those on farms did.

Yet entirely independent of the movement off the farms, the flow was beginning in the opposite direction—from the heavily settled areas to the more sparsely settled land. In the 1960s this was a scarcely visible trickle. Although emigration from rural to urban areas had slowed down markedly, the urban population remained stable; this was due mainly to natural increase through births and foreign immigration. Then, in the 1970s, the national birthrate plummeted sharply and unexpectedly, and the cities began to show significant losses of population. Not that people weren't still moving to the cities, but the number moving out was markedly greater than the number moving in. Between 1970 and 1975, for example, for every 100 people who moved to metropolitan areas, 131 moved out (in the five previous years, 80 had moved out for every 100 moving in). Large cities became static or lost population, while three fourths of the open-country counties registered increases (compared with half in the 1960s and two fifths in the 1950s). In the South, the smallest towns grew more in the 1960s than they did in the 1950s, while large towns of 25,000 to 50,000 grew by less than half of their growth rate in the 1950s.

The causes of this small but significant return to the small town lay in the changing attitudes already mentioned. Public opinion polls showed anywhere from 50 to 80 percent of Americans choosing life in a small town over life in the city. Many expressed the proviso that a city of more than fifty thousand population be located within thirty miles and that there be good jobs available, but an Idaho poll had a majority saying that the presence of a nearby city was not important—and was even a deterrent. Conventional, post-hippie-generation young people also preferred country living. Fifty-three percent of Brown University students polled and 76 percent at the University of Rhode Island said that they wanted to live in a town or the countryside rather than a large city or the suburbs. Asked why, the students spoke of a need for community, a simpler, "organic" way of life, and a "closeness to nature."

Rural areas looked more attractive for a variety of other reasons. The wage and salary disparities between city and small town were narrowing, and the way of life the small towns offered was a sufficiently attractive alternative to people with city jobs to compensate for the traditional disadvantages of commuting. Improved transportation—mass ownership of cars and trucks, wider access to jet planes, and the proliferation of interstate highways—was perhaps the main motive force in the movement to the rural regions (just as better highways had earlier spawned the suburbs). The location of highways played the fateful role in the life or death of small towns that the railroads once did. People who commuted over two hundred miles daily to work were not uncommon; most of them drove and were thus able to combine country living with city paychecks. Interstates were spawning a strange mutated breed of highway "towns," consisting of service centers for travelers along well-traveled routes and at key intersections. They had nightly transient populations of ten thousand or more; these service centers also provided jobs for the surrounding rural environs. Improved transportation, along with modern communications and computer networks, made it more feasible for businesses to locate in the countryside. Once cities had provided the most efficient interaction of people by assembling a large labor pool which lived in close proximity to the workplaces; but more mobile workers and a national highway network discounted this long-standing urban advantage. The rise of the conglomerate form of business organization—with its satellite units scattered nationally and internationally—both reflected and enhanced business decentralization. Instantaneous electronic communication systems linked up the far-flung units with the urban headquarters.

And, as the countryside became more attractive to business, the troubled cities were growing more unattractive. The costs of theft and vandalism directed against businesses, air-pollution controls, traffic congestion, and higher taxes had become excessive to many. There was also the "problem" (in the eyes of management, at any rate) of unions, which not only demanded higher wages and increased fringe benefits, but also decreased productivity through featherbedding, strikes, and grievance claims. The temptation of a cheap, nonunion labor pool in small towns, where belief in the work ethic was supposedly stronger, was obvious. In the South, the citadel of nonunionism, workers doing the same job as northern workers would earn 80 cents to $1.25 less an hour. There was also the good possibility that smaller jurisdictions would be more "hospitable" in matters of taxation, environmental regulations, and the like.

Finally, there were "rural growth industries" in the trade, service, and mining areas. Manufacturing jobs accounted for only one fifth of employment in the nonmetropolitan areas in the early seventies. A prominent rural growth industry was based upon catering to the needs of retired people.

Although a rising number of specialized retirement communities housed many of the aged, many others were moving to small towns to live out their days free from the crime and clamor of the big cities. There was a larger proportion of old people in the national population, as well as a trend to earlier retirement. With their Social Security and health benefits and pension checks, many had money to spend.

Another rural growth industry was recreation, a product of a more affluent society in which a larger number of people had more leisure time and more money to spend on it. Lastly, the energy crises of 1973–74 and 1979 gave coal mining a shot in the arm and brought a rush of migration back to old mining regions such as Appalachia and the northern Great Plains. Sparsely populated western states such as Colorado, Montana, New Mexico, and North Dakota were exploited for coal, oil-bearing shale, and natural gas, and strip-mining and boomtowns profoundly altered their physical and social terrain.

The upshot was that some rural areas could provide more jobs, and even high-skilled, well-paying ones, in the case of the western boomtowns. Improved highways and air travel made the city less distant from these rural places, enabling the urban migrants to continue to enjoy the cultural advantages of the city without having to live in them. State universities established branches in small towns and cities—community colleges and vocational and technical schools—enabling them to offer more cultural activities, professional training, and intellectual stimulation. As the banker in a small Minnesota city put it: "Maybe three years ago you might have heard somebody grumbling about the cultural offerings around here. But the state college has grown to 10,000 since then. We've got new leaven in this community with all those professors and students. And if we get sick of looking at each other during the week, it's only 65 miles on a thruway to Minneapolis."[4] Television had also eased the sense of isolation in rural areas by bringing entertainment, news, and, occasionally, culture to the hinterland.

There were other intangible factors at work. Among the young, the sense of disillusionment with their parents' materialism and the fear that modern industrial technology was becoming a positive hazard to life erupted into a back-to-the-land movement which was essentially an escape from technology and complexity to the simple life of organic farming or crafts and commune-style social organization. There were also the deeper, apocalyptic fears of nuclear war, world financial collapse, crippling energy shortages, and other high-technology disasters that drove people of all ages to seek survival insurance in rural retreats. Inflationary monetary conditions contributed to a rising nostalgia for owning land, whether as a financial investment, as an investment in one's survival should urban society collapse, or simply as an investment in the fancied "good life." Books on owning country property became popular in the early seventies. The *Whole Earth Catalogue,* with its descriptions of tools and techniques of rural living, and the Foxfire books, preserving country skills of old folks in West Virginia, became bibles to the back-to-the-landers; books by the goldbug Harry Browne, such as *You Can Profit from a Money Crisis*, predicted fiscal disaster, urged buying gold and setting up a country retreat well-stocked with food and guns in the event of a collapse that would send rioting urban hordes to one's door. And E. F. Schumacher's book *Small Is Beautiful*, an underground best-seller, propounded the message that human institutions had grown too big and were out of control.

These were some of the more visible bubbles on the American stream of consciousness in the seventies. Americans had become alienated from the city's tattered social web: they no longer felt in control of things; they had lost faith in the ability of the institutions of government to protect them and provide their tax dollars' worth of basic services. The reaction of some was withdrawal and flight and apparently a lingering feeling that there was safety in the countryside. Population experts Peter A. Morison and Judith P. Wheeler of the Rand Corporation also pointed to a persistent strain in the American character, unrelated to contemporary anxieties—a "wish to love one's neighbor but keep him at arm's length" which expressed itself in a "dogged predilection for neorural or perhaps pseudorural residential settings."[5] Hence the oft-expressed wish, manifested in public opinion polls, to live in a small town that was not a surburb but was still thirty miles from the city. This wish-solution masked conflicting desires: to have access to people and yet keep people (particularly the urban poor) at a distance. Americans were closer than ever before to being able to achieve their wish to escape from the city while still having it. They could live in the country and commute to work—to the newly relocated factory or the new coal mine nearby or to the city via the new limited-access thruway; they could come home to television or journey to the city for a night at the opera; they could cultivate their gardens or they could fly to London or Paris from the nearest airport. They could, in short, live on the land or in a small town, while remaining attached by mass-communication neurons to the city. Such was the dream; whether it would be an enduring one, involving a significant number of people over a long period of time—assuming the energy supply would permit such a dream—was a large question as the decade drew to a close.

One of the many ironic aspects of the influx of people into the countryside was that it came at a time when no-growth rhetoric was gaining a sympathetic response in many areas. Thus, the very smallness and putative stability of small towns that made them attractive to urban dwellers of the more affluent kind was threatened. The urban flight transplanted urban problems to the small towns, although not on an urban scale. The arrival of new kinds of people or a new industry or housing developments and strip developments that seemed metastases spreading from the city loomed all the larger in many small towns. Influxes that a larger city could absorb with minimal dislocation—even welcome, in the case of a new industry—could be traumatic in a small town, straining the fabric of community, the quality of life, the surrounding environment.

The problems of a new kind of people, for example. In their studies of Putnam and Springdale, Ladd and Vidich and Bensman pointed to the seeds of change that were being carried from the cities by a new class of affluent, middle-class, college-educated people who had opted to live in the small towns. Add to these the retired people seeking the safe and cheap life out of the cities and the technocrats who came to work in new industries—perhaps owned by a distant conglomerate—or the booming mines or oil and natural gas operations. And of course the hippies—a broad, imprecise term embracing back-to-the-landers, artists and writers, hometown returners from the city, and a large miscellaneous floating population of restless, drifting, searching young living on parental subsidies, public assistance, or their wits. These people brought the ferment of skills, brains, affluence, creativity, alternate life-styles sorely needed in small towns, yet they also imported a lack of understanding of small-town ways, urban expectations and different moralities that generated hostility in the community.

The most obvious problem group were the so-called hippies. Some rural communes were certainly resented by locals. They were charged with sexual laxity and drug use, which outraged the town elders and raised the hackles of local youths, who often turned violent. There were assaults upon the transient hippy population. Over the longer run, though, this element either left or was quietly absorbed, so long as they did not flaunt their life-style in a way that shocked the local community's conservative moral standards. New Hampshire had seen a considerable influx of the back-to-the-landers, and Silas B. Weeks, extension economist with the University of New Hampshire, found that, despite the different values of the newcomers, they were being on the whole pretty well accepted by the community. Weeks said they actually shared some values with rural New Englanders—attachment to country living, devotion to farming (although they used different techniques and indeed represented a kind of throwback to nonmechanized, "natural" methods of farming), love of physical work, and dislike of government and bureaucracy. In Vermont, the back-to-the-landers made common cause with the conservatives in opposing a bill which Governor Thomas P. Salmon introduced in 1974 and which would have divided up the state into seven land-use zones. The opposing coalitions could be called the centralists and the decentralists, Harold S. Williams of the Institute on Man and Science thought, with the latter including conservatives defending traditional rights of property and the back-to-the-landers protesting that Salmon's bill would force Vermonters off their land by attracting large-scale developers. The decentralists won, and their presence was prominent in other controversies over land use and the environment. The controversies shocked town meetings out of their twentieth-century torpor. Townspeople met, argued, and often stubbornly voted to reject the concerted financial and public-relations blandishments (and pressures) of large, multinational energy conglomerates.

Of course, the back-to-the-landers preferred isolation and poverty and were thus rather like the isolated poor people who had always lived in the shack-towns and hollows around the fringes of towns in the past. There was a tradition of letting such people go their own way, however much their life-style was deplored. Occasionally, though, outraged locals would attempt to extirpate them, as happened in Mendocino County, California. The remote hilly region had become a haven for postsixties radicals and dropouts, who were devoted to rural living. A group known as the Mid-Mountain Community lived in rustic homes they had built themselves on the side of a three-thousand-foot mountain reachable by a single, winding dirt road. Up that road one day came officers of a special task force created by the county supervisors. The officers plastered the Mid-Mountain people's homes with sanitation and zoning violation citations. Later the squatters were informed by letter that their homes were unfit for human habitation and must be evacuated within thirty days. Rather than resist or flee, the commune people organized and set up lobbying headquarters in an apartment building in Ukiah, the county seat. With the help of public-interest lawyers, fund raising, and a public-relations campaign, they succeeded in delaying the zoning board's action against them and successfully proposed a plan that would establish a special building classification for their homes.

Other countercultural groups became so attached to the small towns they settled in that they purposely blended in with the neighbors and sought to put down roots. Accusations of drug using and sex orgies still swirled about some of them, but most did their own thing discreetly or gave up bizarre behavior that challenged small-town morality. It was the drifters and the freeloaders among them, who were accused of sponging off the town's already overloaded social services, who raised the most resentment. The tightly disciplined religious cults aroused a different kind of hostility by their aloof, secretive ways and their hold upon the young. The cults, however, kept pretty much to their reservations.

Paradoxically, it was the solid middle-class and working-class arrivals who often roiled the previously placid waters of town politics. In the town of Bow, New Hampshire, for example, which had grown from a farm town of thirteen hundred people in 1960 to a bedroom community with thirty-two hundred residents and twelve housing developments in 1976, the newcomers placed their own demands upon the town services. The town administrator described the newcomers' attitudes: "People move in here who are accustomed to certain services. For a year or two they are content with low taxes, but then they start demanding snow clearance, blacktop roads, street lights, garbage pickup . . . "[6] Soon the town would have to build a high school, a sewage system, and another firehouse, the administrator complained. "City migrants who move to the country for the charm of 'smallness,' " wrote Peter A. Morison and Judith P. Wheeler, "are not enhancing that smallness. If they demand urban amenities, even more of the 'rural character' is lost."[7]

There were taxpayer revolts in small towns that were hit with a large influx of more affluent and better-educated urban people, who, for all their proclaimed return to the simple life, demanded the amenities of urban living they were accustomed to—who wanted dirt roads that seemed so picturesque in autumn paved the minute snows and spring rains turned them into ruts and mud. A dozen areas had already tried to legislate against the demands of these groups, and Plumas County, California, local officials had cut off the county's contribution to welfare costs because a new community college had drawn "longhairs and minorities" to the area. The new arrivals' political demands inevitably clashed with the usually older, more conservative, and less improvement-minded local clique who ran things. Thus was the stage set for newcomer-oldtimer conflicts.

Another problem created by the urban influx was skyrocketing land prices. Perhaps the chief villains here were the ubiquitous promoters of housing developments—developments which, when they rose up on previously vacant land, opened a Pandora's Box of social problems. The rise of land prices in itself, whether triggered by tract developments or by the individual purchases of affluent escapees from the city, had its own impact on the social system of the town. The value of farmland in the United States tripled between 1960 and 1974—but over half of that increase came between November 1970 and 1973; farm real estate rose a further one percent between November 1973 and November 1974. With land prices so high, young people thinking of going into farming or just setting up homes in town were priced out of the market; in many towns these young people once could have expected to buy an acre or two from a neighbor or a relative for a nominal amount and set up a home, but that opportunity no longer existed and so the young people were given still another reason to leave.

Large-scale land sales for housing tracts posed another kind of threat: a decrease in the nation's stock of farmland. Federal authorities estimated in 1976 that the nation lost about a half million acres of farmland a year to developers—out of a total of 385 million arable acres—and the loss was becoming more worrisome. Also in the market for land were the large food conglomerates, which were vertically integrating their operations—that is, buying the farms where their produce was raised. Agribusiness came brandishing fistfuls of dollars and made lucrative offers that pushed many small farmers into early retirement; family-owned farms were being agglomerated into large, specialized holdings (still, about 80 percent of all farms in the United States remained family-owned). Farmers had been retiring to their local towns for many years, of course, but en masse retirements could cause the slow decay Clayton Denman observed in a Kansas town he called Cornsmith.

About six hundred local farmers had retired to the town, putting their money from the sale of their farms—$25,000 to $75,000 each—in the local bank. Developers went into action, erecting new housing for them in a subdivision on the outskirts (though there was plenty of rehabilitable housing stock in the town). The banks financed these developments and the new businesses formed to service the old people. Agribusinesses had meanwhile bought most of the farmland within fifty miles of the town. Land that had been dotted with family farms—at least two for every section of land—now had few houses; the uninterrupted acres of corn and sorghum stretched to a horizon broken by the silhouettes of abandoned grain elevators in moribund villages.

In the town itself, there was a facade of prosperity, with rows of cars angle-parked at high cement curbs and once-proud old buildings downtown tarted up with aluminum siding, shake shingles, and flashing neon signs. Meanwhile the town's most prominent building, a brick office block with a turreted clock tower, dating from the 1880s, was going slowly to seed. In the old days people lived in such buildings within an easy walk to downtown, and there were offices, lodge halls, and opera houses in them as well. The prosperity created by the retired farmers had raised the population to a modern-day peak of twenty-five hundred and brought with it a new supermarket and a new post office. But there were also signs of stagnation. Schools were decrepit, and there were few young people who would carry on the town's life; in ten years, one fifth of the population would be over eighty (assuming they were still alive), residing out in subdivisions where there was no public transportation or delivery of services. The town's one doctor was an old man, untrained in the latest developments in geriatric medicine. There was a section of town inhabited by poor people, living in shacks or once fine but now run-down houses that had been abandoned before the farmers came. The Cornsmith banks had long since run out of projects to finance—even though the town's future needs, such as medical facilities for the aging population, had been ignored. There was no thought for the future, when the old would be gone and few young people would be left to carry on. Lacking new industry to employ the young and with a limited farm population on the vast agribusiness holdings around the town to trade at the stores, Cornsmith was dying.

The large corporate farm was not new—there were large-scale factory farms in the nineteenth century. Bruner and Kolb reported that there was rising concern about "corporation farms" in the 1930s—an "acute issue" in several of the 1400 agricultural villages studied. Consolidation had been accelerated by depression foreclosures of smaller farms, which were bought up by the corporations. The large-scale farming worried the small farmers because of its greater efficiency; on one wheat farm yields had been doubled and production costs halved to less than fifty cents an acre. In another corn-belt community a corporate farm aroused more negative opinion than the chain stores among villagers and farmers. A corporation had assembled a farm of twenty-four hundred acres from smaller foreclosed family farms. Boundary fences, buildings, and groves of trees were destroyed, and each tract was operated as a single field, with crops being rotated for maximum efficiency, conservation, and productivity. A large fleet of modern heavy machines, imported on huge tractor trailers, was employed. Tractors were equipped with electric lights for twenty-four-hour operation. The use of imported machinery took business away from the implement companies in the village, which traditionally supplied and serviced local farmers. The farm hired only unmarried men, who had few ties to the community. The effects of consolidation during the Depression were described with considerable power by John Steinbeck in his novel *The Grapes of Wrath*—who can forget the scene in the movie when the great "cats," driven by robotlike men in high-top boots and goggles, bulldozed away the houses and barns of the Joad family? Steinbeck, like Sherwood Anderson before him in *Poor White*, had evoked in fiction the human impact of industrialization.

A study of two California agricultural towns by the anthropolgist Walter Goldschmidt assessed the social cost of corporate farming. Goldschmidt compared the towns of Arvin and Dinuba, which were about the same size and age, but which differed in one important respect: Around Dinuba small, family-owned farms predominated, while Arvin was surrounded by corporate farms employing hired labor.

Dinuba, the small-farm community, was more democratic in terms of citizen participation in town government and the number of policy-making institutions run by the people. The farm population was 20 percent greater around Dinuba than around Arvin and had a higher standard of living; the majority of the Dinuba farms were independently owned, compared with less than a fifth around Arvin, where almost two thirds of the farm workers were hired hands. As a result of this more prosperous, numerous, and independent farm population, Dinuba had, by all objective measurements, a more vigorous community—more community facilities, such as schools, parks, newspapers, civic organizations, and churches; more businesses—twice as many establishments doing 61 percent more dollar volume, with household-goods and building-equipment concerns especially healthy; and better physical facilities, such as paved streets, sidewalks, and garbage and sewage disposal (in Arvin some of these public services were totally lacking). When word of Goldschmidt's findings leaked out, powerful agricultural interests put pressure on the Department of Agriculture's Bureau of Agricultural Economics, for whom Goldschmidt had made the study, and prevented its expansion to other California towns. Twenty-five years later Goldschmidt reaffirmed his findings in testimony before a Senate committee looking into land monopoly in California. The implications of large-scale agriculture for small farms and small towns, he said, were even more ominous in 1972 than they had been in 1944 when he made his study.

What Goldschmidt had achieved was another *Middletown*—a study of the effects of industrialization on a small town. Only this time the industrialization was not in the form of mass-production factories in a town that drew upon a native-American, agrarian labor pool in the surrounding area, but rather on the farms themselves. The large-scale practice of agriculture around Arvin utilized a large "plant"—in terms of land acreage, capital investment, and heavy machinery—and a pool of transient, machine-tending or unskilled workers. The effect of this farm industrialization was to create a constantly changing pool of transient workers, with no ties of place. The effect upon the town was an outbreak of the classic sociological symptoms of urbanization: heterogeneity replacing homogeneity; depersonalized social relations based solely upon wages rather than ties of sentiment; more rigid class system; and a centralization of power in a few hands, leading to civic apathy among the great number of the people. Goldschmidt predicted that the farm workers, "lacking any orientation to community and other sense of social belonging,"[8] would turn to unions, as had the Newburyport workers studied by Warner and his associates in the Yankee City series during the 1930s. In fact, this has been the case in California, with the large growers opposing unions, such as Caesar Chavez's United Farm Workers, and favoring less militant unions with which they can do business. Goldschmidt's conclusions were pessimistic: "If the production of agricultural goods is to become increasingly large-scale and corporation-dominated, rural communities as we have known them will cease to exist.* Instead the landscape will be dotted by what can be called company towns, made up of workers and overseers, together with such service personnel as the company chooses not to provide itself."[9]

If corporate farm towns were a futuristic vision, toward which trend-setting California was showing the way, the relationships of the small Iowa town of Odebolt with a large farm in the county provided a historical look at the long-term effects of an old-style factory farm. The spread known as the Adams Ranch had occupied six thousand acres of rich black Sac County soil ever since William Adams acquired the land at three dollars an acre from a railroad around the turn of the century. Three generations of Adamses had lived on the land and had been none too popular with the townspeople and local farm folks. William Adams was dimly remembered as a "pretty good man," but his son Robert showed signs of high-handedness, such as the time he offered to pay for paving the streets if the people would rename their town Adamsville. The offer was refused and the townspeople's attitude toward Robert's proposed beneficence can be gathered by their referring to it ever afterwards as the time Robert "wanted to buy the whole town."[10] Another acrimonious town legend related how Robert (or his son) insisted on delivering grain to the elevator on the day specified by contract, even though the town was nearly snowed in and the elevator manager had urged him to wait

*In fact, most large farming operations in the 1970s were still owned by individuals rather than large absentee corporations—farmers who bought up farms surrounding them and engaged in high-production, low-margin operations. They did incorporate themselves to enjoy tax benefits and to enable their children to inherit the land. The net effect was the same, however: fewer small farms and farmers.

until the roads were clear. Adams had his farmhands shovel manure over the entire road into town and on the town's streets as well. The manure melted the ice but predictably ran off into the adjacent ground, leaving a long-lingering odor. The townspeople took this as another example of Adams high-handedness.

After the passing of the Adams dynasty, the spread changed hands several times. Land prices rose steadily, and at the most recent sale, the acreage was evaluated at $3 million. The owner at that time, a man from Detroit who owned several corporations and donned his farmer's hat on rare occasions, intended to raise horses and perhaps settle in the area. He had bought $250,000 worth of new equipment—none of it in Odebolt; maintenance would be performed in the county-seat town. Local farmers raised their eyebrows when they learned that a previous owner had received $241,000 in crop support payments—the largest support payment in all of Iowa. The local Catholic priest, a farm boy himself, echoed the feeling of many in the town when he said that such corporate farms encouraged people to be money-hungry. "Rural people live close to God. . . . Religious attitudes are directly related to the land,"[11] he told Victor K. Ray. But large-scale farms forced them off the land, and church attendance had dropped 50 percent as a result. "The small farmer can't compete," the priest said. "The government doesn't do a thing for the small farmer."[12]

And so the creeping growth of corporate farming brought instinctive resistance among the people in rural communities. Some of the large spreads were nothing more than tax shelters for wealthy urban businessmen or corporations, which were happily run at a loss; those owned by conglomerates could be worked at a loss because of healthy profits in marketing and processing and therefore they competed unfairly with local farmers. Corporate farming insinuated a creeping rot into nearby towns, by denuding the land of homes and people and importing cheap labor—often single men or migrant labor. This underpaid, exploited help might create a pocket of poverty that could place extra demands on the town's facilities. The corporate farmers also forced up land prices, making it more difficult for local youths to go into farming and more tempting for older farmers to retire.

The rural areas have traditionally been preserves of the very young, because of the higher birthrate there than in the cities, and the very old, because of the net outmigration of the young. In the seventies the rural birthrate had fallen and the migration of the young was continuing, but there were moderating trends at work. There was a net loss from rural areas to the cities among those aged twenty through twenty-four, but there were small net gains beginning in the twenty-five through twenty-nine group and somewhat larger gains in the thirty through thirty-four and thirty-five through forty-four age groups—much more substantial gains than demographers had predicted. In the older categories—forty-five through sixty-four and sixty-five and up—however, the net influx to nonmetropolitan areas was far greater than projected—and the projections had been deliberately set high. This increased immigration by elderly retired people to the countryside brought in a relatively affluent group, but it also brought problems.

The aging population from the cities also needed and demanded city-style services. And since retirees tended to be younger, healthier, and more active than in the past, they were not always content to sit on their front-porch rockers and watch the world go by. There might be still vigorous executives or retired colonels among them, for whom the fire bells still rang, summoning them to Get Things Done. Casting about for a project, they discovered local politics, and barged in with a divisive result a bit like that posed by younger urban expatriates.

But this pattern is perhaps rare. More common, it would seem, are the old people who outeconomize a small town's governing group on pocketbook issues. The Ouachita Mountains area of Missouri, Arkansas, and Oklahoma was the fastest-growing nonmetropolitan area in the nation in the early 1970s with a 9.4 percent population rise; much of this growth was in the Ozark Mountain country of Arkansas, where living was as cheap as anywhere in the nation and where large numbers of retired people from middle western cities, especially Chicago, had settled. Illinois clubs abounded in northwest Arkansas, and a section of the town of West Fork, where fifteen retired Chicago couples lived, was dubbed "Little Chicago." But there were strains between the city folk and the Arkansas Ozark people. The big-city superiority complexes the newcomers brought didn't go down well with the latter. "It seems like Chicago must be the worst place in the world, so many people want to get out there," commented the executive vice president of the Harrison, Arkansas, Chamber of Commerce. "And they are the worst people in the world to complain. 'I can get that at Sears in Chicago for so-and-so.' " He suggested that the answer to the griper should be, "Why don't you go back to Chicago?"[13]

In the past Harrison had run ads in the Chicago papers suggesting "Retire in Harrison," but no more. Retired people made up 20 percent of the population of the county, such had been the migration, but they were no longer considered desirable: "They want to come down here and live free and not raise taxes, and I don't push to get them. We can do without them."[14] "Gerontophobia" was on the rise in Harrison, and the Chamber of Commerce was much more interested in attracting light industry. This meant that schools and capital improvements had to be kept up, which generally meant higher taxes—which retired people on tight budgets reflexively opposed; the services they needed, of course, had little to do with attracting industry. A neighboring town, whose population was 60 percent retired people, voted down by a three to one margin a new community college which the state had dangled if the town could come up with matching funds. When the offer was shifted to Harrison, it snapped it up. Harrison's prosperity continued to rise because it had diversified to attract industry and vacationers, rather than live off retirement dollars alone.

Small towns were becoming a better choice for retired people than retirement villages—there was evidence that old people were happier living where there were young people about—so long as the pensioners did not form enclaves and accommodated themselves to local ways. Such was the prescription of a sixty-one-year-old retired Chicago electrical engineer named Alexander P. Stikker, who rejected retirement villages as "places to die," settled in West Fork, and got himself elected mayor two years after he moved there. No doubt the Little Chicago vote helped, but Stikker made an effort to get along with the local people. "People who live in the big cities sometimes tend to think of small town people as a bunch of hicks," he said. "But the people here in Arkansas are very savvy people. If you treat them with respect, they'll treat you with respect."[15]

Not all old people were moving somewhere else to retire. Many were small-towners and stayed put, like the retired farmer in Pratt, Kansas, who explained, "Me and mama, we talked about buying a place in Florida, but when we sold out we didn't get as much as we thought and mama was sick and she's buried here now and all my friends that's left is around here. So I'm staying."[16] Like Cornsmith, many ordinary towns became quasi-retirement centers. Pratt, for example, had a population of 6,736 of which 1,135 were over 65. Census figures in 1970 showed that 27 percent of the nation's older people resided in towns of less than 10,000 population, although such towns accounted for only 10 percent of the nation's total population. In Pratt, 35 percent of the town's adult population was over sixty-five. At the same time, most of the town's leadership group was under thirty-six. The upshot was that the town had a lot of nonproductive old people—and children—who needed the bulk of the governmental services, and a comparatively small population of gainfully employed adults. Back in the thirties, Bruner and Kolb had noted the increasing elderly component in the rural population and called the agricultural village "the old people's home of rural America."[17] But in those days the percentage of people living in villages who were over sixty-five ranged from about 12 percent in the Middle Atlantic states, to 10 percent in the Middle West, to about 5 percent in the South. Comparisons are imprecise, but it seems clear that small towns in the 1970s had even more older people, with the majority of them living in the Middle West and the Northeast.

Small middle western towns like Pratt, Iola, Kansas (population 6,493, of whom 1,248 were over 65) and Knoxville, Iowa (1,460 out of 7,755 over 65) had come to resemble poverty areas in the cities in one way: merchants lived from one monthly "check day" to the next. "These people are on fixed incomes," complained a Pratt Chamber of Commerce man. "They're against anything that will raise taxes."[18] Nursing homes and funeral parlors were the town's boom industries. There were 4 of the former in Pratt, employing 69 people and caring for 166 patients. As for the latter, they were often the classiest looking structures in town and were doing a good steady business. "We provide a real service," an Iowa funeral director told a visitor, "and it's because we know everyone in the family. There's something really satisfying about having the family come around later and thank you for a nice service."[19] Although volume was greater, prices were lower in small towns than in cities, the director said, so he wasn't living high off the mortality rate.

The lower prices in small towns and their relatively lower crime rate were among their main attractions to the old. Their size made them easier to get around in. But most important were community ties: all the friends of a lifetime were in the town, such as were alive. And the graveyard held those who weren't. The visitor was struck by the "dominant influence in the towns of the old—the bleak burying grounds outside of town, away from the water supply. They are starkly utilitarian and the prairie winds whine against artless marble headpieces that record the names and life dates of persons who, for the most part, died young or aged."[20] Bleak they might be to some, but to others, like the old woman in Albert Blumenthal's *Small Town Stuff*, they were a last link to the past. Of Mineville's barren and lonesome graveyard, she said, "I find it to be the friendliest place in town. There are so many people I have known and loved lying peacefully about me when I am out there that I don't feel a bit lonely."[21] The long parade of the years halted there, and each of the front ranks fell out, as the old people of a generation joined the community of the dead. Blumenthal pointed out that small-town people are more frequently and personally confronted with death than the average city-dweller (whose most vivid sensations of death are murders reported in the newspapers); each death brought at least a touch of sadness to the hundred people or more who knew the deceased. Perhaps this was why most people in Mineville did not appear to fear death. Only two people had, in recent times, achieved notoriety in Mineville gossip (which focused closely on this stage of life) for showing unusual fear of death in their last hours. One of them was a butcher and the other the undertaker.

The small towns that served as anterooms to the hereafter were faced more starkly with the eternal verities of death and taxes—the latter being the major concern of the younger working people who had to pay them. Towns like Harrison, which had some choice between revenue-generating industry and frugal old people, might put a chill on their welcome to the latter. Towns like Cornsmith or Pratt or Knoxville, however, could not turn away old people who already lived there, some of them most of their lives, or retired farmers who had traded there for many years. The result of an aging population was a sense of community arteriosclerosis; the bulk of the young people were moving away. Still, small towns were such ideal places for old people to live out their days that some of them might well specialize in care facilities for the aged, letting a neighboring town play host to new industry that would provide jobs for the young of the area. For smaller places a certain specialization was inevitable; the old dream of autonomy—of every town becoming a city and serving as factory and marketing centers—was no longer valid and was even wasteful of energies. A study of a number of Midwestern towns by John Fraser Hart, a University of Minnesota professor, suggested that small-town rivalries were obsolete. Towns in an area may form a kind of "dispersed city," with each offering several successful stores or services that drew trade from the others, the net result being that all were holding their own—only 25 percent of the towns had lost population—amid apparent economic decline. A congeries of towns linked by good highways for commuting, each providing specialized facilities—light industry in one, shipping centers in another, old people's care in a third—made more sense, at least on paper. Certainly the day of the self-sustaining town lay in the past.

The rising demographic stream flowing into the countryside thus had five main tributaries: an indeterminate number of back-to-the-landers, rural homesteaders, commune people, and creative artists and craftsmen of all ages; the old people; the middle-class escapees from the city, who often kept one economic foot there in the form of dad's job while restoring that charming old house or opening that country store or inn or antique shop as a sideline; the mostly unskilled, blue-collar, over-thirty working people following the jobs springing up in relocated industries—the trade and service, and especially the coal, gas, or other mineral industries—or commuting to urban areas and perhaps farming on the side; and finally, the new exurbanites who flowed into the housing developments mushrooming on former farmland around formerly separate small towns and whose ties were more to the city (or neighboring suburb) than to any specific town. This last stream was mainly a spillover from the cities and the suburbs into the countryside—the "thirty-mile-outers," who moved to the developments and "new towns" planted in the legal interstices between city and town, the municipal tax collectors' no-man's land of wide-open-zoning spaces, where seldom was heard a discouraging word and developers could build most cheaply (and sometimes badly), untrammeled by town or city codes.

The developers were drawn by the availability of cheap, scenic open land, new interstates, rural sewer and water lines, proximity of the site to urban employment centers, and other less concrete desiderata. After the fact, their handiwork looked as inevitable as a force of nature, as though God had ordained that the American species should live in rows of little-differentiated houses surrounding and engorging small towns like a protozoa taking its dinner; but actually it was the result of a chain reaction of individual decisions by banks, developers, property owners, and town officials. Nor should the federal government be omitted from the last. The Department of Housing and Urban Development's Communities Development Corporation, created during Lyndon Johnson's administration, underwrote many new towns, through guaranteed loans to developers, until the program foundered in 1978.

The new towns were idealistically conceived as brave new alternatives to cities and suburbs, to be run by hard-headed capitalists—developers who received federally guaranteed loans. But the towns ran into economic problems. Inordinately high start-up costs—acquiring the land, developing it, paying interest on loans, and so on—precluded any return on the developers' investments for periods of up to twenty years. Many of the new towns were in terminal financial trouble long before they were completed. There were a few successes, such as Irvine, California, and Coral Springs, Florida, but these were located on land already acquired by large corporations, which had the resources to absorb the initial losses. The successful ones also contradicted the new-town idea by becoming enclaves of the upper middle class. As for the others, the developer could have made more money leaving his money in a savings account. And such privately financed showcases as Reston, Virginia, and Columbia, Maryland, were perennially in the red. Further, there was an enforced monotony about the new towns because of elaborate zoning covenants, which each new purchaser signed and which forbade the planting of even a flower bed or shrub without approval of the planning board. The absence of stores, restaurants, and other public meeting places added to the pervasive sterility, which was most keenly felt by the young people who had no place to hang out. Their parents were happy enough with the cleanliness, safety, absence of poor people, and steadily rising value of their houses.

Thanks in good measure to the prestige of the federal government's backing, private developers were planning new towns in open fields like high rollers covering the green baize with roulette bets, then going to HUD for backing. But their promotional claims began to have a hollowness similar to those of the frontier town boomers, at least in terms of accuracy. Their high-pressure land-acquisition tactics also began to get the small-town folks' backs up. Townspeople discovered that developers usually bought up land secretly, if possible, in order to keep prices from shooting up. They pressured farmers to sell—offering thousands just for options to buy, or using psychological warfare, such as telling a farmer that he was the last to sell out, when he was actually the first domino in the line of property owners, or barraging stubborn old widows with endless visits by smooth-talking agents until they were worn down, or promising equivalent land and even firewood for life to a farmer who had voiced his concern about where he'd get his wood if he moved to the other plot.

A farmer in Warren, Massachusetts, a town that was on a target list in the early 1970s, spoke of the anguish he was put through by the developer's lawyers and the town police chief and vice-president who were also working for the development: "They offered [my son] $10,000 if he could get me to sign the option. . . . They offered me $3,000 just to sign it. They came three times and each time they laid the check on the table. . . . They have spoiled my life and my home. My boy has left me. It has hurt my wife so that she'll never be the same woman; she has lost weight, and you would not know her now."[22] The farmer later recanted the option he signed and revealed the pressure tactics to the town meeting; town opinion swung against the development. Another small Massachusetts town faced by a similar threat formed a conservation commission which was empowered to buy up open land coveted by developers and reserve it for recreational use. The device of the land trust was a favored legal device for withholding land from development. Robert Limire, a Massachusetts man who was chairman of the conservation commission, warned a neighboring town that was under the developer's guns:

> As I see it the stage is set for the rapid development of your town on a piece-by-piece basis. I see no viable action plan for saving those areas that must be saved to preserve the town's essential characteristics. I also foresee a need for rapidly expanding town services to meet future needs. School, waste disposal and other increased costs of town government have a way of growing on a per capita basis as inflation persists. The real sadness comes when citizens who have shaped the town find themselves unable to remain, as taxes per household spiral to accommodate the needs of new houses. I understand, for example, that a study conducted at my prompting shows that the average new house in your town falls some $750 per year short of being self-sustaining [yielding tax revenue equal to its share of increased governmental costs]—even with existing facilities. . . . In short, it is overwhelmingly more sensible to go about building the town you really want than it is to let random forces and piecemeal thinking determine the town's destiny.[23]

Critics of development plans often cited inadequate sewers and water supplies; the destruction—for all time—of farmland or hunting, fishing, and recreational lands; the increase in tax rates to older residents because of the need for new schools and other services for the new residents of the development; evasion of density regulations and other provisions of the town's housing codes; and broken promises that new industry would come in and provide jobs for the new residents.

The developers' answer to such charges was to cite the economic spoils that would flow to the town; but these were often pie in the sky. Of course the developers were not always outsiders; sometimes local businessmen and town officials might be partners in return for a share of the action, and often the officials supported development sincerely, out of a traditional belief that growth was good—would revive their "dead little town."

The little Illinois town of Gurnee (population 3,300), halfway between Milwaukee and Chicago, awoke one day to find itself slated for a giant amusement park, courtesy of the Marriott Corporation. The company had bought six hundred acres of farmland near the town for $40 million and was planning a Great America Park, with Disneyland-style attractions including a daily Mardi Gras parade, a simulated gold rush, and, ironically, a synthetic American small town. A shopping center and industrial park would also be built on the land, and there would be a six-lane entrance where Pine Street now stood. The prospect aroused the residents, and the issue was hotly debated. "Something that big just has to affect the town's personality," one side warned. "The benefits will far outweigh the problems," answered the propark faction. Finally a tool and die maker named Ken Miller thought to himself: "Mayor Welton kept saying. 'The people of Gurnee want Marriott, but I knew I didn't want Marriott. And my friends didn't want Marriott."[24] So Miller circulated a petition calling for a nonbinding referendum on the question of whether Gurnee should annex the land on which the park would stand, thus cutting itself in on $200,000 in property taxes the facility would generate.

"They came in here with their millions and their big lawyers and their studies and graphs and charts and all those officials who are good public speakers," Miller said. "We get off work at 4:30 and we're tired and we go to the meeting when we should fix up the house and we say, 'You're going to ruin our town' and they say, 'Prove it.' It's so hard."[25] Of course, the values people like Miller were trying to protect couldn't be translated into dollars and cents. The mayor warned that if Gurnee didn't annex the park land some other town would be getting the tax revenues while Gurnee still had the problems its enormous new neighbor would create. Opponents, though, raised the question of whether Gurnee could remain in control of its destiny in any case, with a giant corporation, its headquarters in Maryland, owning one half the assessed property in the town. Miller's wife told a *New York Times* reporter, with a sigh: "I don't know. Things are changing so fast now. Why is everything suddenly so big, so rushy and got to be done overnight?"[26] With little real choice, the town voted by a large majority in favor of annexation.

More typically, development consisted of growing jigsaw-puzzle tracts around the edge of town filled with rows of ranches and split-levels built by local contractors for local people yearning for the "country," a larger plot of land, and a more modish house with a picture window and dishwasher, instead of an old but sound frame house with a front porch in town. Small towns developed minisuburbs, a kind of middle-age spread, while their centers decayed. Farmers discovered it was more profitable to plant houses on their acres than corn, and they roundly opposed zoning restrictions as abridgements of their freedom to use their property as they pleased. They could sell an acre of land for a house for quadruple the money they would get selling it as farmland. In the Middle West the word "zoning" was a synonym for communism.

Federally funded water and sewer lines transmuted many rural acres into Green Acres. The lines were installed under programs financed by Farmers Home Administration loans or community-development block grants and designed for rural areas much in the way the Rural Electrification Administration had provided electricity in the 1930s. Although these programs were calculated to meet the needs of sparsely settled areas, their effect was often to spur developers to throw up houses on the land, once the facilities were in place. Within a year or so, the lines were inadequate. Developers even worked in collusion with friendly town boards to insure that new lines were placed where their development was planned, rather than where they were needed under existing conditions.

Then there were the strip developments along highways leading into town, commercially zoned and sprouting a garish array of gas stations, fast-food restaurants, and chain stores. Towns themselves might annex the highway land and lease it to roadside entrepreneurs, the idea being that their businesses would produce additional revenues in the form of point-of-sales taxes. These "stripvilles" not only generated ugliness and clutter, they also caused traffic congestion. In some cases the congestion became so bad that the main highway had to be rerouted around them, thus cutting them off from the drive-in trade and the town from the sales taxes that were the original rationale for permitting them.

The fringe development that had the greatest impact, however, was the shopping mall. These clusters of supermarkets, chain department stores, and discount stores (which in the 1970s had fanned out beyond suburbia to forage for new markets in small towns) became popular with town and rural shoppers because they provided ample parking, convenient layouts, and large stores. They also acted as magnets, drawing away trade from the central business districts. Although downtown merchants claimed that they could provide more personal service and were more convenient, they could not provide enough parking. People were beguiled by the idea of parking their cars and doing their shopping in one large, sometimes roofed-over area to the splashing of a fountain and the strains of Muzak. Shopping in the business district, it was widely believed, was inconvenient, since one had to walk from one store to another in an area of two or three blocks. The shopping-center stores were also providing a wider range of products at often cheaper prices, and the small downtown shopkeepers had difficulty in competing.

The stripvilles and shopping malls became ubiquitous landmarks. Some towns, conscious of the creeping blight around their peripheries, demanded and got zoning restrictions that prohibited such corporate iconography as the Howard Johnson orange tile roof or the McDonald's golden arches. But at least these commercial areas contributed to the town's economy; it was the large-scale housing tracts in the countryside that often aroused the most frustration and ire. The resentment against them was well summarized in testimony before the Senate Committee on Agriculture and Forestry in 1971 by Herbert J. Bingham, secretary of the Municipal League, Nashville, Tennessee:

* * *

> We got over 2,500 miles of rural waterlines mainly built by the Department of Agriculture and in some cases by HUD. There are no urban development standards, so along a rural road and rural waterline they built houses. They can save $2,000 to $5,000 a house by avoiding putting in sewers and waterlines and adequate streets and storm drainage and sidewalks and curbing gutter and the other requirements for standard urban development, the kind which every village and every city of this kind imposes upon new development, [within] the corporate boundaries of the city, through [what] are called subdivision regulations. There are no standards in the rural areas outside municipal boundaries. So you have cut rate development.
>
> In these rural areas, the biggest crop of farmers and the Department of Agriculture is new cities. It starts along the rural roads and the rural waterlines when a farmer continues to grow a field of corn down by the creek and plants a field of houses along the road. . . . Now, there is no requirement for planning. There are no land use controls. There are no subdivision regulations. There are not any development standards at all, and there are no urban-type facilities. The only thing is a tap waterline, just enough to get tap water. You cannot fight fires with it. You have got septic tanks instead of sewers and so on.[27]

Bingham added that usually such developments had no police protection. The increased population might also require a four-lane highway to replace the country road along which the houses were sited. But the land might cost $2 million for each mile of highway; before the development, of course, it would have been worth considerably less. He said that Nashville and the smaller municipalities within a fifty-mile radius were getting little of the new industry and population immigrating to their countryside although they had room for it within their city limits. The unplanned sprawl in the countryside thus did not benefit fiscally the nearby towns and cities, but it did add to their social burdens by costing town taxpayers money indirectly through services provided by the county government and directly through town facilities the developments' residents used.

Of course, towns could annex the developments into their incorporated boundaries, as did Gurnee, but they often bumped into legal roadblocks thrown up by the townships and villages round about that were bound on preserving their own local autonomy. Many cities were using the annexation power and others were eyeing it; some states framed their annexation laws to make it easier to do. But smaller towns were often caught between a rock and a hard place—if they did annex land that was about to be developed, their taxes would go up as the costs of services for the new people rose. The net gain in new taxpayers was outweighed by their cost to the community.

For many small towns failure to grow was the symptom of a perhaps terminal disease—or so it seemed to many town leaders. This conviction could become a self-fulfilling prophecy, according to Ralph E. Thayer, director of the Urban Studies Institute at the University of New Orleans: "Small towns, as a class, too often see themselves only as places in need of change. . . . Few small towns, with the exception of those located on growing suburban fringes, will see marked economic growth in the near future. But towns have been indoctrinated to believe that '*their* town' is a failure if not chosen for development. A defeatist mentality settles onto some towns and this attitude in itself deters investment; out-migration accelerates."[28]

Some towns, Thayer said, should cultivate their smallness as a virtue and learn to live with it, rather than adopt urban planning which would commit them to city-style growth. He pointed out that the infrastructures of many small towns were probably too fragile to support the added burdens of increased development, and he warned that those towns fated to become bedroom communities should at least attempt to control their growth by planning. More towns were doing just that.

Gladwyn Hill could report in the *New York Times* in 1974 that "from coast to coast, environmental, economic and social pressures have impelled hundreds of cities and towns to adopt limitations on the size and character of their populations."[29] As people left the cities in greater numbers, first suburbs, then exurbs, and then small towns were increasingly taking a "no-growth" posture. Or rather they were opting for controlled growth, by means of a maze of legal restrictions that checked but did not forbid the construction of housing tracts around their peripheries. The township of Ramapo, New York, set up a system under which building permits were "rationed" by the device of requiring that applicants demonstrate that their construction would not overburden municipal services. Ramapo's was a phased-growth plan extending over eighteen years, and it contemplated incremental expansion rather than sudden explosion. This philosophy was adopted by numerous other towns. Petaluma, California, placed limitations on sewage and water facilities as an indirect check to growth.

Some of these plans promptly came under attack by civil libertarians, who charged that they abridged the constitutional right to move freely about the country and live where one chose. Many of the plans embodied racism and discrimination against the poor through restrictions on low- and middle-income housing. Developers and builders also fought the plans because they hurt the construction industry. And after all, people have to live somewhere. Why should some communities be allowed to refuse to accommodate their share of the working-class and minority population and industry in their region? This raised knotty questions for the courts: Just what *was* a community's fair share? How were conflicting interests in preserving farm and recreational land, historical sites, and the fabric and integrity of small communities to be balanced? There were no definitive answers, of course, as a patchwork quilt of growth-limitation plans spread over the nation. But planners became more confident that so long as a community did not limit growth solely to preserve its social and economic status quo or to exclude lower-income groups, and if moratoriums on contruction of new facilities were temporary aand justified and long-range growth plans well-thought out and reasonable, then communities did have the right to divert, delay, and channel growth.

But for many towns with populations from ten thousand to fifty thousand growth remained imperative. A study of twelve small Minnesota cities by Dr. Edward L. Henry, director of the Center for the Study of Local Government at St. John's University at St. Cloud, concluded that in order to survive and maintain quality of life these "micro-cities" needed to be near to a large city—though not so close as to become a suburb or lose trade to the city. They should also be sufficiently scattered so as not to have to compete fiercely with their satellite villages for the rural trade. Almost a necessity was the presence of a college or junior college to stimulate cultural activities and provide an antidote to the aridity of small-town life. Most vital of all was the presence of continually expanding, diversified light industry—light to avoid pollution and diversified to cushion the blow of a slump in one economic sector. Dr. Henry summed up: "People follow jobs, and no small city can progress enough to provide for its normal growth of population unless it attracts industry."[30]

But even the value of promoting growth by bringing in new industry was questioned. Studies showed the benefits were not always as claimed. Given the wide variations among individual towns, the studies yielded up some cautionary morals. First, although new industry generally did bring in more jobs to the towns studied, the expanded job market was not open equally to all. The hard-core unemployed, for example, were not hired because the industries preferred at least semiskilled workers with a high school education and preferably those of the "right" race, sex, and age. Thus minority groups always benefited least, as did the elderly and female heads of household—the three groups that most needed increased income. The town's retired old people suffered, along with the unemployed, from the increase in prices and taxes which seemed an inevitable aftermath of new industry. Ralph E. Thayer observed that new industry may not have a uniformly positive effect on small towns because of "the usual presence of a large number of elderly residents and persons with little or no relevent training for today's jobs. Attracting industry can lead to an influx of better trained and younger immigrants, who then drive up rents, land costs, etc. The original residents can be worse off except for a few lucky ones (who were often more affluent at the outset)."[31] Studies found that many of the new workers came from outside the community, some of them commuters, and as Thayer suggests, they were young family men. Most plant managers interviewed in one survey expressed a preference for the young, high school–educated man aged around thirty, with a wife and family, who was considered both a good strong worker and "steady." Women were sometimes preferentially hired in certain businesses (textiles, electronic assembly), and women's jobs did not bring in as many people, since women would not move so readily to new jobs with their families as did men. Women's jobs might alleviate the "unemployed female head of the household" situation, except that these unemployed women often had small children and needed day-care centers, which were not always available in a small town.

Another promised benefit of new industry was the multiplier effect—the creation of secondary jobs in business that provided goods and services for the new workers. A study of 700 plants in 246 towns showed that in a majority of cases the multiplier effect was less than 1.2 (a multiplier of 1.0 meant that the industry created one new job—in the industry itself; a multiplier of 2.0 meant that for every one job in the factory, one job was created in the community). Other findings varied, with multipliers as high as 3.5 being bandied about, but the most careful study, conducted by the Economic Development Administration of the Department of Commerce and published in 1976, showed that multipliers were rarely above 1.6. The reasons for such a low multiplier included the "leak out" factor caused by the large number of commuters attracted to the jobs who spent their wages near their own homes. Town businesses also were so underutilized that they could often take on the new business without hiring more help; and the new industries might get all their supplies and other services from a national network. Thus, as one study suggested, "At worst,, the local community may become little more than a labor source for the factory with virtually no indirect or induced employment."[32]

New industry did, however, raise the average income in a town. But how much it raised it was hard to pin down. The figures varied widely from town to town. Increases ranging from 5.3 percent to one of 183 percent were reported, with the average being 50 percent. But workers whose incomes rose the most tended to be newcomers to the community; the original residents, who bore the cost of the development for industry, might end up in a worse position than before because of rising taxes, housing costs, and the like.

Towns troubled about their declining population did find that new industry definitely stemmed the decline or reversed it, but the increased population usually resulted from the migration of workers into the area. New industry did not stanch the outflow of the town's young people—one of the most often-voiced reasons in support of it. (A Walpole, New Hampshire, man who favored a new, possibly foul-smelling pulp mill said, "I've raised three daughters and had to export them. We need it. We need something for our young."[33]) New young people came in, but the local young people continued to move away at the same rate.

In eleven towns studied by the Department of Commerce on the North Central, Southern, and Western states, 30 percent of the new workers were migrants—the majority from outside the county. There was also evidence that the influx was not from the crowded cities, but rather from rural areas, thus "urbanizing" or "suburbanizing" the rural environs of the town by creating a commuting population; however, most eventually moved to the town where they worked once they felt secure in their jobs.

Expectations that the new industry would mean a bonanza in added tax revenues were also dashed. Whatever benefits might have been derived from direct payments such as property taxes or utility fees were lost over the short haul because, to attract industry, towns often rewarded them with tax holidays of anywhere from five to fifteen years. There were indirect subsidies as well—free land, relaxed pollution controls, and so on. (Ironically, studies by the Rand Corporation and other groups on business decisions to move showed that the lure of tax relief played little part in the decision; the main attraction was a "probusiness" climate in the new place. Some businesses received subsidies after they had already decided to move—conversely, businesses that had already decided to stay where they were received tax abatements.) On the other hand, revenues did result from higher property-tax assessments on houses, fatter sales-tax collections, and increased transfer payments from state and federal governments because of increased local revenues such as gasoline taxes. Offsetting these added revenues, though, were the costs of attracting the new industry in the first place—the costs of land acquisition, site preparation (improvement of access roads, landscaping, and the like), increased police and fire protection, subsidies ranging from tax relief through bargain rates on utilities, expanded services for workers' families in the form of schools, recreation, and health care, and so on. When these costs were toted up, the added revenues shrank. In five Kentucky towns with eight new plants among them, only two of the plants produced net revenues above that produced by the sites before they became industrial. Other studies comparing net gains in taxes and in business activity showed the net gain from increased taxes for the town government and the school district were only $521 and $401, respectively; the private sector, however, gained $152,981 in increased wages, sales, and so on. These figures tended to disprove the cherished belief that new industry increased the tax base and thus made the town government more comfortably solvent; on the contrary, costs rose nearly as much as revenues. Finally, there was the environmental "cost" in terms of land destroyed, pollution, and a more dense population. A study of industrialization in the rural South in the 1960s concluded: "The most striking social cost to the town imposed by industry is water pollution, which in most of the towns studied has reached serious proportions. The concern for this problem shown by town governments is after the fact. Since industry is primarily responsible, the weak position taken by local government suggests that the absence of water pollution control is one form of industrial incentive."[34]

In short, the studies showed that new industry had its costs, and that towns eager to attract it often blinded themselves to the social side of the ledger, preferring to think only in terms of more jobs and added business for the downtown merchants. And so the luring of industry by subsidy and tax concessions continued, much as it had in the nineteenth century, when town services were not nearly as comprehensive and expensive. Which is not to deny that towns needed that chimerical little nonpolluting electronics factory, or other kinds of light industry. But the hard facts were that the towns could stimulate more employment with a large heavy industry, if that was their goal. There were also the upheavals in the social and political structure of the town with the arrival of newcomers, younger and sometimes more educated and liberal than the natives. Older residents fell in income and status, and some were even forced to move away.

The businesses themselves regarded small towns wiith unsentimental fondness; thus, manufacturing jobs in non-metropolitan areas grew by 22 percent between 1960 and 1970, while in the cities they increased by only 4 percent. The motives of the companies fleeing to the countryside were not always consonant with the best interests of the townspeople. These motives included escape from taxes, pollution controls, unions, and high labor costs and business's respect for the work ethic, which was still supposed to exist in small towns. But an industry seeking other benefits, such as low taxes and cheap land, might find that, since the work ethic was equally robust in many small towns, it might as well move on when another town offered better terms. Such industries were known on the small-town circuit as "footloose" industries—industries that had no particular ties in the way of natural resources, location, or labor force to any particular location, that could simply pick up and move on.

The problem of footloose industries was exacerbated by absentee and especially conglomerate ownership. In Nebraska City, Nebraska, the Morton House Kitchens had been owned by several generations of the Steinhart family, but in July 1966, the Steinharts sold out to the British firm of Thomas J. Lipton, which was in turn owned by Unilever Ltd., a giant international conglomerate with annual sales of $11 billion. At the time of the takeover, Morton House Kitchens was a profitable operation with annual sales of $20 million and four hundred employees. In eight years, however, its annual sales were down to $4 to $6 million, by the former president's estimate, and employment had fallen to sixty-five working a four-hour day. The quality of the product had allegedly deteriorated too. Employees charged that more additives were used: "They bring in carbohydrate binders by the truckload,"[35] a shipping clerk said. Morton Steinhart had once bailed out Nebraska City's hospital when it was about to go bankrupt, had promoted industry, and had donated a park, golf course, and a pool to his home town; the Lipton company did not even bank in the town. A newspaper man recalled that "you used to be able to walk in Morton Steinhart's office and ask him for something the community needed. Now any requests for donations to community activities have to be addressed to headquarters at Englewood Cliffs, New Jersey."[36]

A study of absentee ownership of Wisconsin companies by Professor Jon Udeel of the University of Wisconsin Business School discovered that prior to acquisition by a conglomerate, employment at the firms had increased annually an average of 11.6 percent; following acquisition, employment decreased 1.8 percent every year, for reasons that were not clear. Nonetheless, Udell concluded that "it is apparent that Wisconsin's economy has fared far better among those companies acquired by Wisconsin firms than among those acquired by out-of-state conglomerate corporations."[37] Willard F. Mueller, professor of economics at the University of Wisconsin and former chief ecoonomist for the Federal Trade Commission, used the city of Gary, Indiana, as a prime example of the harm absentee ownership could wreak. "Bluntly put," Mueller wrote, "although the Gary area is built on a wealthy industrial base, its absentee owners have permitted it to become one of the most blighted communities in the nation."[38]

In August, 1977, the Crown Zellerbach pulp and paper mill in Bogalusa, Louisiana, finally closed its plant rather than spend any more money on pollution-control devices. The plant was the only industry in town, and its closing meant the loss of an annual payroll of $13 million, plus the two thousand or so secondary jobs that would be lost as a result of layoffs at Crown Zellerbach. To the people of Bogalusa the villain was the Environmental Protection Agency, which had ordered the company to install more antipollution equipment after it had already spent $2 million on such devices. The issue was seen as either no pollution or no jobs, and the workers preferred jobs. Moreover, "many also see these pollution standards as an imposition of urban values on small towns and as a misunderstanding of small-town economics. In rural areas, losing a job has severe social consequences since one may have to move out of town, away from friends and into another area where employment is more readily available. Governmental regulations that upset life in a small town are sometimes seen as working *against* the public interest rather than *for* it, and admistrators are seen as being insensitive to small town peculiarities and lifestyles."[39]

Not surprisingly, polls have showed that when people in a small town are asked whether they would prefer a local polluting industry to stay or move, they overwhelmingly state that they want it to stay. The EPA had its critics, not only in Bogalusa, but also in other small towns—among factory workers fearful for their jobs and owners who saw the regulations as too cumbersome for their small plants. Similar criticism was voiced about the Occupational Safety and Health Administration (OSHA), which was seen as binding small businessmen in red tape. In small towns the pocketbook issues were still preeminent, the social-welfare ethic weak. Thus, a large company coming in to mine newly discovered minerals was opposed in a western town not because of the boomtown atmosphere it would create, but because of the additional roads, electric power, schools, sewer lines, and so on that would be necessary. Critics pointed out that although a mine might last twenty years, the cost of needed new schools and other capital improvements would take much longer to amortize.

Such was the argument in the town of Meeteetse, Wyoming, where the AMAX corporation planned to mine copper and molybdenum. But this was the argument of the town banker; the environmentalists were worried about the damage to ranch land in the area. As it happened, this faction was dominated by large ranchowners, including the heirs to the Duke tobacco and Rumsey Union Pacific fortunes. The local wranglers, oil workers, and retired people were not terribly stirred up. Their view was expressed by a waitress at the cowboy bar, who said, "Sure I don't want to go fishing and see a body on every rock. But I'm not against the mine. That's Progress and you can't stop Progress."[40] The townspeople who favored the project signed a petition expressing nonsympathy with environmentalists, who were dismissed as "newcomers" and "remittance men."

Environmental issues could take on a divisive class edge in small places. In the town of Walpole, New Hampshire, a proposed $200 million paper mill arrayed the wealthy who lived "on the hill" against the working people who lived in the drabber hamlet of North Walpole. The latter, along with a few powerful figures in the town business establishment, favored the mill because it would produce five hundred jobs, despite warnings that, like most pulp mills, it would blanket the town with the characteristic rotten-egg odor of sulfur dioxide used in making paper. As a town policeman said, "The lower classes are for it, those that have to work for a living."[41]

The issue of jobs vs. protecting the environment was not always that clear-cut. In Bogalusa, for example, the EPA's regulations may have accelerated Crown Zellerbach's departure, but the plant reportedly would have moved out eventually anyhow, because it needed to streamline its operations; the Bogalusa plant was becoming too expensive in terms of labor costs and its equipment was obsolete. Rather than spend the money modernizing, the company found it easier to close down two of its local operations, which employed about half of its Bogalusa work force. Bogalusa did receive federal and state funds to develop its languishing industrial park and attract other industry. But the deleterious economic impact of moves by footloose industries was drawing the attention of large national unions such as the United Auto Workers. A few state legislatures passed laws that required adequate notice of a move and that provided aid to cushion the blow and encouraged locally owned new industry.

Another pressing concern of many a small town in the seventies was its chronically ailing central business district. This was Main Street itself, once the vital artery of the town's lifeblood, but now sclerotic and clogged with traffic. Too many downtowns had been designed for the horse; the glut of cars choked them to death. And so, the cornfields around the towns sprouted shopping centers that were made feasible by the same auto that had overwhelmed the central business district. The downtown merchants gradually awoke to the threat and fought back with downtown shopping malls, streets closed to traffic, improved parking facilities, and renovated stores. Some towns fought the encroachment of the new by reverting to the old—restoring the old buildings along Main Street. The preservation movement was encouraged by a school of urban planners and architects who had rediscovered the beauties of Main Street's vernacular archhitecture. "*Nostalgie de la rue,*" *Progressive Architecture* dubbed it—nostalgia for the small-town America that had flourished between 1890 and 1940. This mythifying of small-town America had been encouraged by movies and television. So the merchants recreated Small-Town U.S.A. (or something like it), fighting the new with the old (which in a way looked new). The results were sometimes false gingerbread, endless candle shops, anemically stocked boutiques, saloons with sawdust on the floor, and ersatz ice cream parlors. But, when the restoration was done with integrity and there was something there to restore in towns such as Corning, New York, Medina, Ohio, Madison, Indiana, and Jacksonville, Oregon, when the patina of neon and aluminum siding was scraped away, a considerable beauty was often revealed. Towns that restored found that they also succeeded in revitalizing their downtowns.

There were also towns that deliberately transformed themselves into something else—a Bavarian village, in the case of an aspiring ski resort. The architectural results were not always felicitous, but the effort fanned the spark of life. Other towns converted abandoned buildings—town markets, railroad stations, office blocks—into art galleries and culture centers or farmers markets. There was a recovery of respect for what those townspeople of the nineteenth century had wrought—the fine old offices, the lodge halls, the opera house, the courthouse. Of course, the ravages of time had sometimes been too severe for restorative measures—or else the ravages of "urban renewal," the philosophy of destroying in order to save, had decimated old houses to make way for a bank, razed a fine old courthouse to make room for a ranch-style seat of justice. People were learning to renounce the American propensity for destroying and building anew (so prevalent in the cities) for speculation and profit in favor of preserving the old. There was, of course, the possibility that *nostalgie de la rue* was itself a passing fad—that, as *Progressive Architecture*'s Suzanne Stephens suggested, nostalgia might next turn elsewhere—perhaps to the stripvilles of the 1950s and 1960s.

Small towns may seem at a brief glance to be drab and monotonous, but they are actually full of gentle quirks and homely architectual features that were once, to some, loved and familiar (or repellent and ugly)—fixed stars by which one boxed one's life compass. Small towns are not physically all alike; a group of architects surveyed twelve "drab and monotonous" Kansas farm towns and found each laid out differently, each with some prominent and well-known feature, each with a different Main Street. The sum total of the memories of the people who had lived a long time in those towns formed an alluvium of history, a history layered with the follies and triumphs, the setbacks and muddling-throughs of the years. What hazzards of fortune hundreds of small towns had undergone! The economic vicissitudes they had weathered showed in the fading name of a forgotten merchant on a building that now housed a laundromat, or in the empty stores pocking many once prosperous Main Streets, or the abandoned plant by the tracks. But the tenacious struggle for survival continued. Now the search for that saving new industry went hand in hand with the quest for government grants—not on account of an emergency or depression but as a matter of right. Some, however, were still too proud to beg from Uncle Sam. In 1972 the village of Dennison, Missouri, down to thirty peoople from its peak population fifty years ago of six hundred, returned $322 in revenue-sharing funds the federal government had sent it. "The Federal money has strings attached," the town board wrote. "Strings are for puppets and we are not puppets, nor do we have any freedom for sale. Thanks a lot but no thanks."[42] Actually, the town was outraged because the American latter-day successor to Attila the Hun—the Army Corps of Engineers—was putting in a dam which would divide the town up into three parts. More towns had been laid waste by the Army Corps of Engineers, it would seem, than by tornadoes. The village of North Bonneville, Washington, took on the corps, which wanted to plough it under and put up a power station, and forced it to build them an entire new town two miles from the old site. The town's five hundred people could have pocketed their compensation and scattered, but they wanted their town, their friends, leaders, community groups. They wanted, in short, their town to be moved as a community, and Congress passed a special bill that accomplished this.

This power to destroy by eminent domain was the ultimate weapon in the hands of the federal government, but it was used sparingly. More commonly, its increased involvement in the affairs of small towns kept the towns in uneasy dependency. Small towns felt the shock of recession just as much as did the cities, but were often denied their fair share of aid. Unemployment relief such as public works funds, for example, was denied to small towns for several years simply because they had no unemployment statistics that the Washington bureaucrats would accept; the cities, which did have the statistics, got all the money. Small-town mayors complained that it took five different agencies to approve a tiny program or that they received grants to start programs they couldn't afford to run—and were given no money to run them. There was a growing restiveness among small-town people over the greater state and federal curbs on their independencee. In the Maine town of Bluehill, near where the writer E. B. White lived, the townspeople built a two-million-dollar hospital with their own money, only to be told by the State Health Planning Agency that it was too small to meet state standards. White thought that what most disturbed small-town people up in his neck of the Maine woods was "the discovery that no longer is a small town autonomous—it is a creature of the state and the federal government. We have accepted money for our schools, our libraries, our winter roads. Now we face the inevitable consequence; the benefactor wants to call the turns."[43] Still, the small towns went on pursuing the many pots of federal money to be had. Some hired grant specialists, who pored over the fine print in the *Federal Register* and the U.S. Code, like alchemists over arcane formulas, searching for statutory recipes that would yield federal gold.

The old self-sufficiency was dead; Federal funds were as much a part of a small-town mayor's budgetary planning as it was of the Mayor of New York's. Acts like Dennison, Missouri's, were quixotic and a permissible luxury only when the amount of fed money spurned was $322—rather than $322,000 for new sewer lines. Self help was little Gurnee "annexing" the land owned by a conglomerate, or else Metropolis, Illinois, erecting a monument to Superman (who did battle against evil in the comic-book city of Metropolis). Metropolis's town fathers, with mass-communications savoir faire, then inveigled the press into writing it up, with the result that tourists came to visit the Superman Museum. Not so successful was Kitty Litter magnate Ed Lowe, who bought up most of the town of Jones, Michigan, for $1.5 million, and reconstructed it as a turn-of-the century small town. Nobody came to Jones's town, so he auctioned it off piece by piece, building by building, for $200,000.

Metropolis was becoming part of metropolis. The problems of the small town and the big city were increasingly the same, only the small town's were a small-potatoes version of the city's. In the small towns organizations like Alcoholics Anonymous, drug rehabilitation centers, Parents without Partners flourished, and psychiatrists were on call. The myriad substitutes for community in the modern age were needed as much in the towns as they were in the cities. The rural crime rate also rose:—10 percent in 1974, compared with 6 percent for the nation as a whole (and in some parts of the Middle West it rose 30 percent). Between 1967 and 1976 it more than doubled; violent crimes increased by 54.7 percent. No longer was rural America a safe haven; people were locking their doors and farmers were spotlighting their barnyards and feedlots. Demented, twisted murderers were roaming the land, it seemed, hunting down innocent farmers. At least some of the increase in crime was attributable to professionals, who had followed wealthy urbanites to their exurban enclaves; they were also, however, stealing antiques from old-timers. Drug use was no longer quarantined in the urban ghettos; it spread epidemically among small-town youth. But much of the crime was blamed on locals—especially bored young people (rural and small-town schools were suffering high dropout rates, and sociologists were wondering if the quality of the youths exported to the cities was as high as it used to be). Some observers on the scene discerned a social breakdown and anomie similar to that in the cities. "Social controls, local attitudes about staying out of trouble, which were once a deterrent, now have disappeared," said Samuel Stellman, director of the University of Wisconsin's Criminal Justice Institute. He blamed in part country people's habit of leaving doors unlocked, but said that "social controls have disappeared, partly because of the urban influence through television. The whole value system is gradually eroding, and that's causing conflict in the rural family. There are high rates of unemployment, more women are working and supervision of kids is tough."[44] Television's influence as a direct cause of crime was, as ever, debatable, but there was no doubt that it continued to present the bucolic image of country people. Michael Schroeder, a mental health specialist in Wisconsin, criticized the "myth about rural areas perpetrated by [television programs such as] 'The Waltons'—this great extended family, an idyllic scene. This just isn't so. There is a general sense of alienation. A lot of people are isolated. There have been studies showing that depression is higher in rural areas than in urban areas, and that rural areas have a higher incidence of mental health problems."[45]

It was curious that the media, in playing up the story of small-town crime, sometimes portrayed it as a city malaise spreading to the innocent country—as though the countryside had never known depravity, as though the boredom of small-town youth was something new. Political scientists such as James Q. Wilson, who said that urban problems sprang from "a sense of failure of community,'"[46] assumed that community was still thriving in small towns and suburbs, which, Wilson said, "because they are socially more homogeneous than large cities and because local self-government can be used to reinforce informal neighborhood sanctions, apparently make the creation and maintenance of a proper sense of community easier."[47] Wilson was expressing the traditional American assumption that small town equals community. The equation, as Western Reserve professor Park Dixon Goist points out, is a cherished one in the American imagination, and its converse is that the city is the antithesis of community. Yet, small towns can suffer social malaise and anomie as much as the city, while in the city there are neighborhoods that retain the elusive characteristics of "community."

What the small town, like the city neighborhood, has is the potential for community—for direct, caring, face-to-face interaction of people, over time, and an opportunity for individuals or small groups of people to effect visible, if modest, changes, even if they must now be mindful of state and federal regulations or funding. As the intrumentality of community purposes, small-town government is a rickety structure, cautious, conservative, parsimonious, fearful of arousing controversy. In Springdale, it devoted most of its efforts to talking to death any popular sentiment for change while seeking all the state and federal funding it could get in order to keep taxes down. Big corporations too sometimes exercised a veto; the story is told of a Maine selectman who, when asked what action the town would take on a certain measure, replied that he didn't know as he hadn't talked to the headquarters of the corporation with a branch in town. Yet, in the 1970s New England town meetings were galvanized by environmental issues and opposed big corporations. Certainly small-town government could not solve all a town's problems by itself, but it at least had the potential of involving a good portion of the townspeople. The grass roots-democracy symbolism was a cherished one—so much that President Jimmy Carter employed "town meetings" as a forum for restoring rapport between his Administration and the people. But small-town government was more than a symbol, political or otherwise; as Lewis Mumford contended, towns and neighborhoods constituted the "basic cell" of democratic government: "For democracy in any active sense begins and ends in communities small enough for their members to meet face to face. Without such units, capable of independent and autonomous action, even the best-contrived central governments, state or federal, become part-oriented, indifferent to criticism, resentful of correction, and in the end all too high-handed and dictatorial."[48] A spirit of community remained the most important (and endangered) resource of small-town life; it was a pity it was so often allowed to lie dormant until some outside threat or internal crisis roused it. The survival of many towns still remained in the hands of the townspeople themselves; their ties to place and to each other, if quickened by mutual concern and mobilized by effective leadership, *could* revive a dying town. Many towns in the 1970s were choosing to live, if only by such prosaic means as reviving the central business district or, more dramatically, fighting unplanned development or rapacious industry.

"Community" indeed meant small town to many Americans—a link to place, a sense of belonging, a network of personal, primary ties to others, homogeneity, shared values, a collective belief in each individual's worth. Such an ideal could be perverted into totalistic community, which could snuff out individuality by probing into the private recesses of the human heart. The models of total community were chilling: mass political movements which subsumed the individual or tight, small religious cults rallied around a charismatic, authoritarian leader. Such "community" often actually existed in the mad hubris of these leaders. Or it could be a subtler conformity—the Gopher Prairie syndrome—reminiscent of the society of the Houyhnhnms imagined by Jonathan Swift in *Gulliver's Travels.* The Houyhnhnms lived in a state of total community and total anarchy, prompting George Orwell to observe:

> In a society in which there is no law, and in theory no complusion, the only arbiter of behaviour is public opinion. But public opinion, because of the tremendous urge to conformity in gregarious animals, is less tolerant than any system of law. When human beings are governed by "Thou shalt not," the individual can practise a certain amount of eccentricity: when they are supposedly governed by "love" or "reason," he is under continuous pressure to make him behave and think in exactly the same way as everyone else. The Houyhnhnms, we are told, were unaminous on almost all subjects. . . . There was no room for disagreement

> among them, because the truth is always either self-evident, or else it is undiscoverable and unimportant. They had apparently no word for "opinion" in their language, and in their conversations there was no "difference of sentiments." They had reached, in fact, the highest stage of totalitarian organization, the stage when conformity has become so general that there is no need for a police force.[49]

One is reminded of the total community of love that was the ideal of the early Puritan town, with its close scrutiny of the most intimate aspects of human behavior, its use of communal shaming rather than punishment imposed by due process of law, its enforcement of propriety or scripture rather than laws, its extraction of a public confession of wrongdoing from the sinner as a precondition for taking him back into the fold. Such imposed conformity was appropriate to church-communities in the wilderness, but eventually this absolute control by the church over every aspect of behavior came to be resented. As the frontier opened up, dissenters could move on individually or could form a rival congregation and migrate as a group. So the effectiveness of the Puritan controls was never absolute. In time, the church community was set apart from the civil community, and its powers were limited to the spiritual sphere. Its rituals of guilt, estrangement, and atonement became purely symbolic, as the sanction of banishment or "churching" lost punitive force. The church's morality was transmuted into criminal and civil laws, but the church no longer had civil authority. The separation of church and state had become an essential element of American life, allowing a heterogeneous mixture of sects and doctrines, none of which, in theory, imposed its codes upon the behavior of outsiders.

Yet the idealized community of the Puritans filled a need for belonging, for brotherhood and sisterhood; men and women today have a deep sense of being banished Adams and Eves in the urban wilderness. Hence, the various communes, utopias, and sinister cults which have flourished in the 1970s, attracting the most lonely, alienated, the individually powerless. At a less pathological level, ordinary Americans continue to join informal groups and organizations whose chief reason for existence is to provide a quasi-community. They create them in the cities for companionship, mutual benefit, and sharing of tasks (such as a mothers' baby-sitting communes). They flee the cities to seek the shards of traditional community in the suburbs and the small towns.

The conflict of extreme individualism and the need to belong that runs through the fabric of American life fascinated the French anthropologist Hervé Varenne. Like Tocqueville before him, Varenne saw the American propensity to form groups as a key to American culture. In the early 1970s he lived in an Illinois town he called Appleton, and he observed close up its values, as expressed in a variety of ways—a man and woman falling in love, the credo of the Farm Bureau, the ritual of the churches, the invisible government of the small-business "establishment" convening daily at a restaurant for coffee. His conclusion was surprising: *Love* was "the fundamental precept underlying the organization of social interaction in Appleton. . . . It is one of the deepest and most general principles structuring [the townspeople's] cultural statements."[50]

Love? Yes, love—in the sense of a universalized identification of human beings, and in the sense of the merging of separatenesses, the total giving away of self to another—the ideal of love between man and woman, in families, in small groups. Such a love transcends differences of background and class (when they exist) because they are inimical to it. Love presupposes one-mindedness, and Varenne theorizes: "Insofar as true humanity lies in the full psychological realization of a choice, it is believed that communication through exchange, on which small groups are based, demands full psychological—that is, in fact, ideological—similarity inside it."[51] This demand explained the much-criticized conformity of small-community life, Varenne said, as well as the communal ideals of oneness in God, for which religious groups ever strive but never achieve on this earth. (Varenne does not mention how old these communal ideals are in America—only that they were an inspiriting force of the earliest towns and the utopian towns after them.)

Varenne did not find any one-minded pervasive community in Appleton; instead he found a town of surprising diversity. The universality of love, he said, was limited; one could only love—achieve a state of like-mindedness with—small groups of people. Thus the diversity, the numerous cliques and more formal organizations in Appleton; these groups as groups could only exist separately by defining themselves as different from other groups around them. Differences among groups defined them; people had "to invent ways of emphasizing or even creating differences,"[52]—which might be as tenuous as those between the Kiwanis and the Rotary clubs, the Presbyterians and the Methodists. If the town were a totalistic, homogeneous, undifferentiated community, the demands of love and loyalty posed by the identical expectations of several thousand people would be too much for a single human being to satisfy. Diversity was necessary to individualism, homogeneity to community (something the early Puritan theocrats failed to see). Individualism and community were thus always in gravitational tension, like twin stars revolving around each other. Or as Varenne put it: "Individualism and community are thus two poles of the structure. They are integrated insofar as neither exists outside of the other. But this integration is achieved through dialectical opposition. Where there is individualism, there cannot be community, where community triumphs, individualism is destroyed. If any mediation is possible, it is achieved by love, an individual sentiment directed toward another person."[53]

Love, in other words, is the saving grace of community, the solvent dissolving the defenses of isolated individualism. Varenne saw this love as a necessary, animating ideal in American life, solving the paradox contained in the phrase *e pluribus unum*—out of many, one. Varenne said that "in the search" it was achieved, in the tacit, universal profession of it, it existed, was "real." As he writes: "What I discovered are the worn-out cliches of countless sermons and Memorial Day speeches. But maybe this is where the folk wisdom of American life lies and what constitutes its exotic beauty."[54]

The conflicts in American life were not between ideal and reality, but *within* the ideal. Young people flaunted a new life-style, and parents had to choose between interpreting their behavior as the individuality-in-diversity that was one side of the coin stamped *e pluribus unum*, or as disloyalty to the uniformity-of-community that was the other. Carol Kennicott strove to improve the community of Gopher Prairie but her values set her apart—seemed selfish, were subversive to the town's comfortable consensus. In Springdale, the "secret government" ruled in what it sincerely thought was the best interests of the community (defined, to be sure, by the self-interest of its members), and the people went along. The establishment acted as surrogate, within narrow limits, for the entire town, imposing its definition of the public good, which the people tacitly accepted. Privately, Springdalers engaged in a race for status, invidiously comparing their wealth and possessions with others while publicly paying homage to the values of friendliness, folksiness, helping out others.

Indeed it might be said that in the Springdales of America lived a parody of Varenne's Appleton—the hypocrisy of the ideal of love. But as Robert Redfield points out, two observers can come up with equally valid "positive" and "negative" reports on the same community because they are looking for different things.* In other words, Varenne might have found the same hypocrisy, the status scramble, the cruel gossip, the Rotarian conformity, the compulsive joinerism and all the rest in Appleton had he focused on it. But unlike many students of the American small town, he was not interested in the conflict between ideal and reality; he was interested, as an anthropologist, in the reality of the ideal—the necessary ideal of love as a mediating force between American individualism and American conformity. A more serious criticism would be that Verenne did not analyze the political implications of the American need for love. In the unique American situation, what are the possible social pathologies of this dependence on love to tie the individual to community? Given the attenuated traditions legitimizing community in America, is love alone enough? How is the need vulnerable to the manipulations of politicians or charlatans? Is the altruism implicit in love too difficult of realization in a larger social sense, so that it must inevitably fall back

*Vidich and Bensman admit this possibility in the second edition of their book and quote a critique of it by others of the Cornell University team that studied Springdale: "We agree with most of what these authors (i.e., Vidich and Bensman) say about the facts of community life in Springdale, but our evaluation of these facts tends to be positive rather than negative." (Small Town in Mass Society, p. 439.)

upon the lonely self as a form of narcissism, or degeneraate into cynical selfishness? Must it find its outermost limits in family or a parochial group, ethnic, geographic or economic? After all, the multiplicity of groups in Appleton—the clubs, cliques, social classes—have been seen by others as inimical to community in a small town, leading to the decline in the individual's identification with the town as a whole.

Those questions aside, we have seen the communal ideal running through American history, and seen that it is uniquely identified with the small town. But we have also seen that the pervasive view of the small town has been fundamentally ambivalent—Friendship Village versus Gopher Prairie, home place versus Peyton Place. And the essence of this ambivalence, this tension of opposites, lies in the polarities of individual and community. The tension between them generates love and need, and also hate and resentment; the individual is never completely at home and ever-longing for home. To achieve his ambitions he must wrench himself away from the consuming demands of like-mindedness imposed by love and assert his individuality. Yet he must also ever yearn for the solace of the lost home place. This ambivalence is woven through our history.

The nostalgic pull of the "old home" that tugged at the settler moving west was the archetypal assertion of it. For Americans, home and home town have had complex connotations—an anchor in the past for a people that believed in the westering future; permanance and transience; civilization, order, and comfort for those on the frontier; a place to be from, that provided identity. Yet Americans were constantly exchanging realized, settled communities back east or in the old world, for the assertion of their individual interests—to better themselves. Most of them, as soon as they arrived in the new place, formed new communities—settlements, rural neighborhoods, villages, towns. When they did not, or did not form viable communities, disaster could result, and it was no accident that the most successful settlements were those of strong communal groups—the Mormons, the New England congregations. The cruelest blows on the Western frontier were dealt by the isolation imposed by individualistic farming. Yet that too was part of the expansionist dynamic, which was energized by the conflict between individual and community. When community demanded too high a price in freedom of an individual—whether demanding that a man be content with his economic lot or that he adhere to doctrines of the ruling church, say—he broke the ties and moved off alone or with a like-minded group of others, seeking to found a better community. The towns imposed order on egoistic demands, provided religious then secular-legal convenants by which men could live together; but they were pressure cookers of competing interests for dwindling resources, thwarting dreams of a better life; the pressures built up and escaped. The small towns were pods, scattering seeds that sprouted new farms and communities on the frontier; when the frontier ended, they exported their sons and daughters to the cities. But the restless individual pursuit of happiness was shadowed by the dream that never died—the dream articulated by John Winthrop on the *Arbella* bound for America, of a New Zion, a New Israel: "We must be knit together in this work as one man. . . . We must uphold a familiar commerce together in all meekness, gentleness, patience, and liberality. We must delight in each other, make others' conditions our own, rejoice together, always having before our eyes our commission and community in the work, our community as members of the same bond."[55] Thus was the enduring ideal first voiced. Its poignant side was expressed by William Bradford in his lament over the break-up of the original Plymouth community, as men sought their fortunes elsewhere: "And thus was this poor church left, like an ancient mother, grown old, and forsaken by her children (though not in their affections), yet in regard of bodily presence and personal helpfulness. Her ancient members being most of them worn away by death; and these of later time being like children translated into other families, and she like a widow left only to trust in God. Thus she that had made many rich became herself poor."[56]

What a multiplicity of permutations the dream of community has undergone, as seen through the receding mirror of history. The religious utopias of the Puritans, the frontier outposts and forts, where people huddled together for mutual protection behind timbered palisades in the wilderness. The old soldiers on the flatboat Mayflower drifting down the Ohio River, beneath silent bluffs, to found their fort-town of Marietta with its streets named from a Latin text. The town as light of law and enlightenment in the bumptious West. The town as real-estate speculation—the boomers' and railroad men's calculating vision of gridiron plats marching ever westward across uninhabited acres. The boomtowns and mining camps of the West, where men came to hurl away on gaming tables the gold fortuitously gleaned from the earth, as though it were a curse, and share their last morsel of skillet bread with their "pard." The jumping-off towns on the Missouri River and trading-post towns along the wagon routes west. The cow towns and soddie towns and railroad-junction towns of the Great Plains; the adobe towns of the Southwest. And the somnolent, slow-moving towns of the deep South, preserved in antebellum amber. The company towns where families lived like feudal serfs on the company's land, in the company's houses, at the pleasure of the company. The rural mill towns with their creaking water wheels and clicking looms; the new industrial towns, polluted catchpools for the immigrant masses. The country towns of the Midwest, with their hitching racks and dirt streets and men hunkered down around the courthouse. The New England towns with white churches and elm-arched streets. The fugitive transient towns with their tacked-on names and mayfly lives, pulsing in brief flush times, then fading—gray-boarded skeletons, doors to empty rooms slamming in the wind, sand sifting through the cracks.

The towns of myth—the Lincoln New Salems, the towns of grassroots democracy, where all were equal, and the judge lent Shakespeare and Milton to the poor boy. The dreamy, dozing, pastoral towns imagined by Sherwood Anderson, poised on the brink of the industrial revolution. The town as the Home from which we escaped yet whose map is etched forever in our memories. The town as base, a launch-pad for the young to propel themselves from, out into the world—these young people in the cities always fated to be asked where they were from, then, what's it near: young people from Nowheres near Somewhere. The town as repose and sanctuary and the town as the home to which you can't go again. The town: good, generous, kind, helpful in trouble, cradle to grave; materialistic, insular, suspicious, set in its ways, canny, backbiting, smothering . . .

The town in our hearts.

Epilogue: Hometown Journey

In the late 1970s, well into the middle of his life, a big-city man who grew up in a small town made a sort of pilgrimage through the Middle West, visiting the hometowns of some writers he liked—rather like an uncle of his had toured the Civil War battlegrounds. He had laid out his itinerary in advance, linking dots on maps with lines of highways to other dots, like those puzzles of childhood in which one connects numbers in sequence to form a picture. Perhaps he hoped that his journey would add up to a picture too, though of what he could not even guess. Or would this elaborate route over many miles in search of some starting point merely bring him back to an already known. He had, to be sure, a lively curiosity about those Sauk Centres and Clydes and Red Clouds and Hannibals, where the writers grew up, and other towns like them that he would encounter along the way, and an itch to walk the same streets, observe whatever remained to be seen of houses and stores and trees that they saw (like his uncle strode up Little Round Top and Missionary Ridge and along Chickamauga Creek, picking up the occasional minié ball). Maybe he would catch a glancing reflection over time of what they saw; or perhaps, barging into the attic of some long-removed life, he might come upon a letter, an old photograph, a doll. At other times, he rejected that fancy as quixotic, fearing that he would either find nothing at all or, more probably, stiffly restored rooms behind velvet ropes where memories were locked away in china cupboards.

He too had grown up in a small middle western town, as did those writers;

he had left it for the city, become a writer himself, an editor and journalist of no great note. And still he could agree a little bit with Mark Twain's remark when he was in India: "All the *me* in me is in a little Missouri village half-way around the world." Not all the "me" in *him*. But the core of his self was in that town, and its map was imprinted in his mind, so that long afterward, he would traverse the great island of Manhattan, uptown, downtown, East Side, West Side, with an anachronistic sense that he was merely going from one part of his boyhood town to another.

An ideal of that town remained, a lost Atlantis of youth, perfectly preserved by the airless sea in the opaque depths of the subconscious, bright and sweet-smelling as a summer morning, complete and whole, if one could ever uncover it—which, of course, one couldn't. And so, instead of seeking out his own town (to which, in any case, he made almost annual visits; always feeling, along with the sentiment, a low-grade panic, an urge to flee some persistent counter destiny—a black hole of the past—that seemeed to be drawing him back . . .) he sought those of others, in the hope that they would send off vibrations that would activate an answering response of meaning within himself. Perhaps this long roundabout route, covering over two thousand miles and five states, would take him to the archetypal lost home that is nowhere and everywhere, always lost and always there to be found.

My first stop was Sauk Centre, Minnesota, with a population of 3,750, about a hundred miles northwest of Minneapolis. On the outskirts of town, just beyond the Hi Ho Diner ("Open 24 Hours"), was the Sinclair Lewis Motel, and across the highway, the Sinclair Lewis Interpretive Center. Driving into town, the visitor is greeted by a banner over the main drag emblazoned with the words "Visit the Sinclair Lewis Boyhood Home and Museum." The main street, once merely Main Street, has been promoted to "Original Main Street" on the street signs. At the center of town, Original Main Street bisects Sinclair Lewis Avenue beneath the only stoplight; if the traveler keeps going straight he comes to Sauk Lake (camping facilities provided at Sinclair Lewis Park). The high school athletic teams are known as the Main Streeters. And the brochures for visitors proclaim that Sauk Centre is "Main Street U.S.A., a living museum of an American institution: the Small Town." "Red" Lewis would have guffawed at Sauk Centre's unquenchable boosterism.

He would have also appreciated the transubstantiation of his indictment of Main Street into posiitive thinking. On the recorded narration accompanying the slide presentation at the Interpretive Center, the narrator recounts how Lewis exposed Sauk Centre and towns like it as "provincial, smug, and dull"; nonetheless, "he helped Americans discover themselves and lead happier, more meaningful lives."

It was too late to visit the Sinclair Lewis Boyhood Home and Museum, so I returned to my hotel—the Sinclair Lewis Motel, of course; part of a national chain, of course. Dinner was at Chick's Supper Club, also in the motel. It was decorated in that ubiquitous early-American tavern style, with dark woods, red tablecloths, and false-front kegs; the dishes were called "Bootlegger," 'Al Capone," and similar speakeasy-era names. The young waitress in a short skirt introduced herself Playboy-bunny style: "Hi, I'm your waitress. My name is Pat." I had the Bootlegger's Special—"13 ounces of Choice Top Round Sirloin." Bloody rare but excellent. The place was busy with the Saturday night crowd. At the table next to mine, there were three men with a woman, the wife of one, I assumed. The men did all the talking—mostly about hunting: "Too early for quail. You need a killing frost to destroy their cover." They talked about food: "Everything you eat nowadays is bad for you." They talked about cooking wild duck breast in cream, and of a village around here where it used to be you could take grouse you had shot to a little restaurant and the wife would cook them up for you, if you took the husband over to the liquor store and bought him a couple of pints of brandy first. The woman talked about sunflower oil being low in cholesterol. One of the men knew a farmer who had put his corn land into growing sunflowers for the oil. "They each have a patented name," the woman said, meaning the sunflowers. "That's to prevent legal trouble." They talked about lawyers, with some awe mixed with irreverence. "They've all got so specialized they only know one field," a man said. "Some of them lawyers are so dumb I wouldn't have them make my will and I'm only worth eight dollars." That got a good laugh. They talked football, which led them into racial jokes. One joke had a punchline about blacks never dropping a hubcap, which got a good laugh too. There was a weighty discussion of "jigs" and "PRs." "Jigs're scared to death of PRs," one man explained confidently. "Jigs use knives but PRs use ice picks." I remembered Kieth the black kid in my home town with whom I'd walk home every night from football practice. And Tolliver, who'd been captain the year before, and the talk about him fighting a black on a rival team with a knife. Always, the myth went, it was blacks who used knives, in that world I never knew about, the one that Kieth walked home to after we said goodbye at the corner of Wallace and Wabash and he went on to where the colored peopled lived. I wondered what hostile memories he had of me, after he became conscious of his blackness in the sixties; his mother had worked as a maid next door, as all the colored mothers worked for our parents as maids.

I guess the men at the table had noticed me writing down their remark about jigs and PR's in my notebook, because they shut up for a while. After I'd finished eating and paid my check to Pat, I drove back into town to see a Sauk Centre Saturday night. There was hardly anyone on the streets, except four kids hanging out. I remembered how, in that small town of mine, back in the forties, we'd hung out in front of the drugstore on Saturday nights, still too young to go into the saloons—or rather have older guys go in and buy beer for us. Actually, I used to hate hanging around the drugstore, drinking Green Rivers or eating gummy marshmallow and chocolate-syrup black cows; the only excitement was when one of the country kids who had a car, because they drove to school every day and could get a license at fourteen, took us bushwhacking—looking for cars with parked neckers and shining a flashlight on them. I don't remember that we ever flashed a parked car. Later, I did my own parking and remember the dry husky smell of a cornfield and the whirring of a thousand locusts and a whip-poor-will's monotonous cry, the radio playing "Those Little White Lies," and I, too scared to go all the way. Even more scared of saying the required open sesame, "I love you." There was a guy in that town whom everybody called The Wolf, who drove around in a black Olds, one of the first automatic-shift models, every Saturday night. Around and round the town he drove, one elbow out the window, insouciantly not shifting gears, never looking at anyone, alone, aloof—The Wolf, forever hunting and never finding. Since he couldn't help but be aware that everybody watched him, the drive had probably become a rite to him, devoid of purpose.

Sauk Centre Saturday night. I walked past the Palmer House; a sign in the window said wine was served with dinner. The five or six bars in town looked to be busy, and I walked into the Sportsman's Cafe. A large noisy crowd. Peanut shells on the floor, signs advertising Schmidt Strong Beer. Several of the men wore in rubber hunting boots and camouflage suits. I ordered a Schmidt and watched the group playing pool. It was apparently a bridal party, for there was a pretty girl in a white bridal gown, and the young men wore tan suits with pastel pink ruffle shirts. They were all in slight dishabille now, playing pool, drinking beer, joking and shouting. The bride looked strong and confident as she hitched up her train to move around for a shot. It looked like a modern Brueghel scene—lively country people enjoying Saturday night. God knows, like any small town, there probably Wasn't Anything to Do; but the Sportsman's Cafe seemed alive. I paid off the bartender, left a big-city fifty-cent tip, and walked out. The streets were now empty; the stoplight over the intersection of Original Main and Sinclair Lewis flashed monotonously. A carload of kids drove through; the muffler unleashed a lazy stream of farting, Bronx cheer blasts. It was a sound, a small-town Saturday night sound, I remembered so well—a rude comment on one more empty Saturday night. . . . Twelve o'clock in Sauk Centre.—Most everybody's asleep. You get a good rest too. . . .

There was no answer at the Sinclair Lewis Boyhood Home when I rang the bell the next morning, but an elderly woman soon emerged from the house across the street and came over to let me in. The modest L-shaped frame house had been impeccably restored, with much of the original furniture. It looked the prototype of a small-town doctor's house. The bathroom had the original heating pipes—an elaborate bank of them, like a church organ. As my guide recalled Dr. Lewis's extreme pride in them because they were the first in town, I was reminded of Dr. Will Kennicott's obsessive solicitousness for his furnace. My guide began her lecture with a somewhat doleful pronouncement: "This is where Sinclair Lewis spent his unhappy childhood," and the house's fussy cluttered decor and dark-hued ugliness seemed to exude a grim confirmation of this statement.

After the tour I walked through town, past John's Cafe, where the men were having their Sunday morning card game, right down Main Street, retracing Carol Kennicott's steps when she came as a young bride. Sauk Centre is now a brighter, cleaner, mellower town, not pretty but not ugly; in the bright October sun it almost sparkled. The usual row of stores: Walker's Furniture, Louis's Barber Shop, Evelyn's Beauty Shop, the Savings and Loan, the First State Bank, the I.O.O.F. Lodge, plus branches of national chains—Sears, Ward, Coast-to-Coast—more than in the turn-of-the-century days when, like most small towns, Sauk Centre had been an independent economic entity.

On the corner of Main and Sinclair Lewis Avenue, above the Main Street Drug, was the site of Doc Lewis's office, from which he had issued daily to go home for lunch, so precisely scheduled that the onlookers joked about setting their watches by him. Across the street was the Palmer House Hotel, a red-brick building—not the slatternly pine of Gopher Prairie's hostelry, the Minniemachie House—definitely mellowed, flaunting its period furnishings, a sign at the entrance proudly proclaiming its seventy-fifth year. The Restoration Movement had evidently hit Sauk Centre.

My tour ended with a pilgrimage to the cemetery east of town where Red Lewis is buried in the family plot; I drove straight east on Sinclair Lewis Boulevard to the site, about a mile outside of town. The Minnesota countryside (that Carol—and Lewis—had loved) was lovely, the hills a stippled palette of autumnal oranges, golds, and reds against an enameled blue sky. It was hilly, treeless prairie country, dotted with farms; to my rear in the distance was the town, its treeless streets and brick buildings and wooden houses looking rawer, almost lonely. I remembered Carol's first sighting of Gopher Prairie: "The huddled low wooden houses broke the plains scarcely more than would a hazel thicket. The fields swept up to it, past it. It was unprotected and unprotecting; there was no dignity in it or hope of greatness."[1] Yet that flat little town had produced a Nobel Prize winner, its negative emanations imbuing young Harry Lewis with an anger he transmuted into fierce, gleeful satire.

Lewis's ashes had been flown home to Sauk Centre from Italy, where he died in the care of a pick-up companion, alone and hospitalized, calling the doctors, in his delirium, "Father." At the burial, his older brother, Claude Lewis, poured the ashes from the ornate urn in which they had been shipped into the grave (he wanted to save the urn for a memorial display), but the bitter winter wind gusted some of them away, as though Red Lewis's restless dust was even in death fleeing Sauk Centre. I wandered back and forth among the rows of headstones for half an hour, unable to find the simple marker I had seen depicted in a photograph. Somehow, it didn't seem to matter.

From Minnesota I flew to Omaha, leaving at sunset and watching the inky darkness flood over the earth below, its lakes, gleaming in the last light, scattered about the black land like silver dollars. From Omaha it was a night drive across flat Nebraska prairie land to Grand Island and Willa Cather Country. Red Cloud: the town appeared in her novels as Black Hawk, Sweetwater, Frankfort, Moonstone, Haverford and Hanover, but it was always the same, a magnetizing star. "The Best Years," the last story she wrote before her death in 1947, was a fond remembrance of the house she grew up in, of the townspeople she often criticized and portrayed as a vulgar bourgeois contrast to the heroic pioneers and builders on the prairie.

My car rolled west toward Red Cloud. I was making a roundabout approach in order to go through the rolling country Cather called "The Divide." It was brown-green rolling country, grassy hills and plowed fields in which squatted giant irrigation-pipe contraptions on wheels. Windmills like gaunt gray insects stood lonely in the distance, and empty red barns with doors agape in the wind, cottonwood groves and gnarled oaks shading twisty lanes, new pastel ranch-style farm houses, drowsing villages, half boarded up, and filling stations Edward Hopper might have painted, with signs reading "GAS-EAT."

Red Cloud itself, with its present population of over two thousand, was a smaller town than the one Willa Cather knew. In the 1880s it was booming, and the red Burlington depot, still preserved south of town, received eight trains a day, filled with the foreign immigrants and homesteaders coming in to settle the prairie and make the townspeople's fortunes. Now it is a couple of blocks of busy Main Street and tree-lined little streets and houses with yards spread about on all sides. The Cather home is one of these houses. It sits on the corner of Third and Cedar, a block from downtown, a white frame house only a story and a half in height. It was the best Willa's father, who operated a farm loan and insurance business, could get when the family moved there in 1884. Cather, her biographer Mildred Bennet wrote, always disliked the house's flimsy standardized look—it had been built by a Red Cloud lumberman out of odd boards and had a twin elsewhere in town. The young Willa, a tomboy who defied town opinion, rebelled against the standardized balloon-framehouses of her day; but she always discerned the difference between a house and a home, the external shell and what went on inside.

The house has been restored and is open to visitors, but I found the door locked and waited until one of the hostesses happened by, a woman named Ruth Doudna, who'd come to try to fix up the recorded narration which, she told me, now had the upstairs lecture coming before the downstairs. I said I'd be glad to do the house in reverse order, so we climbed up the stairs and found ourselves in a floor-through attic with unfinished walls, bare brick chimneys in the center, roof shingles for the ceiling. Here Willa and her brothers slept and played; she called it "upstairs," naming it an independent country, which it was—"a story in itself, a secret romance," a refuge existing apart from the grownups' world below. Under the pitch of the roof was Willa's separate little room; it had the same wallpaper that she'd worked at the drugstore to buy, a pattern of roses now brown and peeling. There was a bookcase and the bed where she snuggled under layers of quilts and read, a hot brick at her feet, the snow drifting through the chinks in the shingles. As I stooped over, half in the room, its simple funishings seemed so artless, vulnerable, so I hesitated, then withdrew, as though I'd barged clumsily into Willa Cather's childhood . . .

Red Cloud, and the Cather country around it, had been well mapped and reverently marked for the pilgrim through the efforts of the Willa Cather Pioneer Memorial and Educational Foundation. Every year Cather students assembled here for two weeks of tours and seminars. Homes where prototypes of characters in her novels lived were identified. On Webster Street was the Cather Museum and Foundation Headquarters, located in the old Garber Bank Building with its rather grandiose tower. It was built in the 1880s by Silas Garber, former governor of the state and model for Captain Forrester in *A Lost Lady* (the bank failed, and Garber, like Forrester, lost his fortune).

While I was driving north back to Grand Island, the country left me with one final Cather vision, one not described on any map or guide. The sun was setting, the great, swollen red ball that seems to plummet beneath the rim of the world. Suddenly, I saw a plough on the crest of the hill—not etched against the setting sun, as she had depicted it in that unforgettable image in *My Ántonia*, but nonetheless a distant, moldboard plough, of the kind that broke the plains. I stopped and walked over to it—to discover it was a monument, a plough set in stone, near a historical marker proclaiming the gateway to Catherland. I continued on, the red ball to the west swallowed up by the hills. "The fields below were dark," Cather wrote, "the sky was growing pale, and that forgotten plough had sunk back into its littleness somewhere on the prairies."[3]

I very much doubted that Ed Howe had left any traces in his hometown of Bethany, located in northern Missouri—the town he portrayed in *The Story of A Country Town.* He had, after all, departed it at a young age in 1865. As it turned out, the only mention of Ed Howe was on the county historical marker located along the highway outside of town. As I drove into Bethany, the rain streamed from pewter skies. Bethany (population 2,914) was still a country town. The courthouse, a mausoleumlike limestone building of 1930s WPA architecture, bulked stolidly in the center of the square. The streets were nearly empty, and several of the stores around the square were boarded up.

Driving aimlessly about, I spotted a building with a sign announcing a county historical society museum. I parked and went in. Opening the door, I stumbled into musty darkness like that of a tomb. In the crepuscular light, I made out shelves of dusty artifacts, old pictures on the wall, and other mementoes. I backed out hastily and ran across the street through the pummeling rain to a small house that served as the the town library. The librarian, an ample, cheerful woman, confirmed that no commemoration of Ed Howe's sojourn in Bethany now existed; she added that I was the second person this month who had asked about him; this caused her some puzzlement. But she bustled about fetching me books of local history and set me up at a card table in one corner of the little library.

As the rain descended in sheets outside, I turned the pages of the thick old volumes—standard county histories of the nineteenth century—looking for a trace of the Howe family. There was no mention of his father, the circuit minister, in the section on the clergy. But in the section on the local press, there was brief notice of Rev. Henry Howe purchasing the *Weeekly Union* in 1863, patriotically changing its name to the *Weekly Union of States.* After a year, the historian continued, Henry Howe moved to Council Bluffs, Iowa, leaving the paper in the charge of his sons Ed and James, who ran it until 1865, when they sold it. Those were the only traces left in Bethany of the Howe family—a few cryptic lines in a local history. But for his son's novel, the secret of the Rev. Henry Howe's flight would have remained buried in a musty, forgotten tome.

Staring out through the rain-spattered window, I began idly to wonder if there was a real-life counterpart to the murder-suicide Howe describes in *The Story of a Country Town.* The county history yielded up none that matched Jo Erring's tragic love, and there was no reason that it should, since Howe had transformed the jealousy he felt when he was rejected by a girl into his melodramatic subplot. I did, however, read of two other murders that occurred in the county in 1863, when Ed, only twelve years old, would have been helping his brother run their father's abandoned newspaper. The first erupted out of a long smoldering feud between two neighbors named Christopher Schaeffer and Charles Burger. Schaeffer suspected Burger of shooting his animals, and one day he caught him at it. He promptly ran to fetch his gun, returned and shot Burger dead. This done, he went home and, in the words of the country historian, "placed the muzzle of the loaded gun to his forehead and, touching the trigger with his toe, blew nearly the entire top off his head." The other murder was a Cain and Abel affair. One day, for reasons known only to himself, John Elliott took his knife and cut his brother Hart's throat "from ear to ear." John then pleaded insanity and spent the rest of his life in the insane asylum. He never revealed what it was that had driven him to murder his brother.

Undoubtedly, the *Union of States* reported these crimes. Had young Ed Howe brooded on them—on the frontier boredom and spite, the festering, irrational hatred they revealed? Although he had not portrayed those crimes in his book, they had surely left their mark on his subconscious, like Samuel Clemens's boyhood memory of a man being burned alive in jail had haunted him.

The library was becoming oppressive, a tomb lined with moldering books about dark, inexplicable crimes. I closed the book, carried it back to the librarian, and hurried out to my car. I drove out of Bethany with Ed Howe's memories in hot pursuit. My route soon took me on to a country road, and I inhaled the good smell of fields and wet earth. The skies were clearing as I drove by a country church—the Fairview Baptist Church. The name registered—Fairview was the name of the hamlet where the narrator of Howe's novel first lived, when his father was a country preacher—where Howe himself lived in his boyhood, though the date on the church placed it much later than Ed Howe's time. I stopped and got out. As I walked around my car, I saw a rainbow arching against the blue-gray sky; it seemed to spring from the little graveyard beside the church. The rain, and Ed Howe's gloom, had lifted.

Entering Hannibal, Missouri, the town Mark Twain called St. Petersburg in *Tom Sawyer* and *Huckleberry Finn*, I found myself shunted efficiently by signs off the through highway into the heart of a sort of Mark Twain World—or Tom Sawyer Land. The street on which Samuel Clemens grew up, Hill Street, and the house he grew up in are still there, along with several other period houses. The street slopes straight down to the edge of the great brown Mississippi. The historic area is officially designated Mark Twain Mall and was probably planned as the center of a revival of Hannibal's crumbling, forgotten waterfront; the town had grown away from the river—turned its back on the river whose glory days its famous son had chronicled. Now there are tourist restaurants and fast-food lunch counters and a renovated street of small shops selling handmade crafts. Each of the houses open to visitors harbors a souvenir shop purveying decaled T-shirts, funny hats, pennants, postcards, ashtrays and even some books by Mark Twain.

Lured into the various houses by historical signs, I passed by the restored rooms efficiently shielded by glass, like infant wards in hospitals, and peopled by clothing-store dummies in period dress, posed in tableaux loosely suggested by Mark Twain's life. For a dime in a slot one can hear a recorded lecture—for a dime in a slot one can even hear Mark Twain's own mechanical organ play. It is all a mélange of restoration and tourist-money extractors; and the information conveyed manages to confuse in the worst way the real Sam Clemens and the fictional Tom Sawyer. Still, the people tramping through the houses seemed to love it, judging from their vociferous recollections of this scene or that character from *Tom Sawyer*, which is apparently the novel of every American's childhood.

After a hamburger at a diner where the waitress picks up a phone to relay your order to the cook, I climbed to the top of Holliday's Hill—called Cardiff Hill in *Tom Sawyer*—for a sweeping view of the great river. I could see for miles over hilly green land on the Illinois side; down past the bluffs on the Missouri side was a large island—Jackson's Island in *Huckleberry Finn*, where Huck and Jim hid out. What a great magnet that river seemed, boiling and eddying, sluggishly, inexorably, ceaselessly moving, a great brown viscid highway, on which Hannibal was no longer a stop. Even the river doesn't stop here anymore, I found myself thinking.

Later I drove to Tom Sawyer Cave, two miles south of town, a labyrinthine network of limestone passages, its ceiling smudged with graffiti inscribed by candle-smoke and dating back to the 1840s. The soft-talking, friendly guide gave our party a good running commentary that played down the contrived exhibits such as Injun Joe's treasure—he told us about the real-life Injun Joe, a town character who lived to a good old age, and discoursed knowledgeably on the geology of the caves. Why is it that we Americans often handle the natural sites and local history of them much better than the lives of our writers? Hannibal had become a well-worn stop on the tourists' main line, its mall a mecca for their dollars. Mark Twain would laugh cynically—and count the house. Like Huck, I had the urge to light out for the territory ahead—or, rather, behind, since I was heading back east to Illinois.

The real Spoon River, a nondescript, meandering brown stream, flows through west-central Illinois, between the towns of Petersburg (population 2,632) and Lewiston (population 2,706) where Edgar Lee Masters spent his boyhood and young manhood. Masters is buried in the Oakland Cemetery in Petersburg, "sleeping, sleeping on the hill" like the small-town ghosts who bare their secret souls in his *Spoon River Anthology*. It was to the cemetery I headed first.

I found Masters's grave easily enough; it is near those of his paternal grandparents, at whose farm he spent his happiest times. The body of Ann Rutledge—"Beloved in life of Abraham Lincoln"—also lies there, reinterred from some pioneer potter's field after Masters's poem to her appeared in *Spoon River* and translated her into national legend. Her stone bears lines from his poem, and Masters's own stone is carved with a quotation from "Tomorrow Is My Birthday": "There is no sweeter thing/Nor fate more blessed than to sleep."[4] Perhaps more appropriate would have been the lines written for the character Percival Sharp in *Spoon River*—who is thought to be Masters himself—"I stirred certain vibrations in Spoon River. . ."[5]

On this brilliant autumn day, the Oakland cemetery seemed benign and pastoral. I wandered among rows of sun-dappled monuments, some ornate, others simple, all divulging no secrets beyond the bare dates of birth and death. Only on the grave of a little boy, dating back to the nineteenth century, was there a rare, florid outburst:

> I know his face is hid under the coffin lid
> Closed are his eyes, cold his forehead fair
> Yet my heart whispers that it is not there.

In the bright sunlight that chiseled melancholia with its hysterical denial of death seemed a distant Victorian echo, but later as I was reading Masters's autobiography *Across Spoon River* in the public library, while waiting for a local woman the librarian had called to open the Masters home, I sensed the reality beneath the fustian. Masters writes of the death of his younger brother Alex at age five and of the grief that wracked the family afterward. Then he describes the Petersburg Sunday afternoons when terrible storms loomed up from the west like God's judgment. "Those Sunday afternoons were lugubrious beyond description. There was such ominous silence as the writhing clouds approached and in that silence could be heard an organ in the neighborhood playing 'Depths of Mercy' as a melancholy voice sang those terrible words."[6] In *Spoon River Anthology* Masters mentions his little brother in the poem "Hamlet Micure," referring to "little Paul strangled from diphtheria," and he describes "the little house . . . with its great yard of clover/Running down to the board-fence/Shadowed by the oak tree."[7]

The Masters residence, where the family lived for eight years before moving to Lewiston, turned out to be another of those modest white frame houses built from standard plans in builders' books, so common in the Middle West. Mrs. Lee Gamage, president of the local historical society which tends the house, showed me around. The house was furnished with a few pieces from Masters's time and also the desk he wrote on while living at the Chelsea Hotel in New York and several scrapbooks, with material supplied by Masters's wife, who is still living. In one of the scrapbooks I came across a quotation from the local paper about Masters's burial: "Let us not discuss his books or his philosophy or his individualism," the editor wrote, rejecting him even in death. "Suffice it to say that Edgar Masters has come home." Though he wrote critically of some of the Spoon River people, Masters, like Lewis, could be sentimental about his town, and his attitude was probably more or less expressed in a speech he made to the local boosters club in later years: "No matter where life has taken me, my heart has remained here. . . . I have written books about you with the idea of making you beloved where you are not known."[8] In that he succeeded.

Sherwood Anderson's Clyde, Ohio, is now a place of over four thousand people twenty miles east of Toledo. A 1966 town history still refers to Sherwood Anderson as "the black sheep of the Anderson family." His brother Karl, the successful painter, received much kinder treatment, as did their hardworking mother Emma, who supported the family, dying at forty-five of tuberculosis and overwork. I read this history in the Clyde library, whose friendly librarian would not dream of burning *Winesburg, Ohio*, or any other book. She told me that the book was on the reading list at the high school. I had headed to the library after being directed there by the local newspaper editor, whom I had called at the advice of my motel-keeper (when I asked him about Sherwood Anderson he had first suggested that I look in the phone book). Thus the small-town grapevine led to the library, where there is a small Anderson exhibit in the basement, and the librarian in turn pointed my footsteps toward the lovely old home of Thaddeus Hurd on nearby Buckeye Street.

Thaddeus Hurd is the local historian and, one suspected, keeper of the Anderson flame. An architect, he worked in various cities during his career but came home to spend his retirement in the house that has been in his family since 1904. He acquired his interest in Anderson through paternal influence, for his father, Herman Hurd, was a boyhood chum of Sherwood Anderson. Sherwood courted Herman Hurd's future wife for a time, and the three of them kept in touch the rest of their lives.

Thaddeus Hurd told me that Anderson's two earlier novels had caused hardly a ripple in Clyde; everyone took amazed pride in the fact that "Jobby" Anderson had written a book and laughed at his portrait of his father in *Windy McPherson's Son*. But *Winesburg, Ohio* was another matter. After that book appeared, Mr. Hurd said, Sherwood Anderson became a "nonperson." Hurd, who rereads *Winesburg, Ohio* regularly and speaks feelingly of it as "the Bible," said the town's case against Sherwood Anderson comprised two charges. First, he had written—by the standards of the time, of course—a "dirty book." Beyond that, the author himself was an "immoral man" who had deserted his wife and children. "I can still hear the lady who lived on Buckeye Street," Hurd said. "She was younger than Sherwood but she knew him. She was speaking about him very calmly, then suddenly she got vituperative. 'Any man who leaves a wife and two children is *no good*!' she said. And that was the heart of it."

By then the portraits of Mr. Hurd's grandfather and great-grandfather hanging in the living room had receded into the shadows of late afternoon, and he proposed a "Sherwood Anderson tour" before dark. Clyde seems much smaller than its population of four thousand suggests, and the tour did not take long. We drove, in gathering dusk, to the old fairgrounds, where young Sherwood had hung around the sulky drivers behind the grandstand and got to know the black grooms. It was now a school playing field. Where the old waterworks used to be, there was now a park and a pond that supported a small population of ducks. We drove back through dark, leaf-strewn autumn streets, and the spell of remembered *Winesburg* stories stole over me. I recalled scenes that always seemed to take place in some immemorial cool silent autumn evening, when the streets were dark beneath the over-hanging trees, the frame houses withdrawn into shadowed lawns, a lighted window or two opening upon normal family scenes within that seemed strange and exotic from the night-world outside. One almost expected some distraught Winesburg soul to spring out of the dark and pour forth a disjointed story of secret torment. The vision fled as we stopped across from the old Anderson house. It was a private residence now, fixed up with aluminum siding and a garage, but still another of those small frame houses on a little street in a lonely little town.

We next drove through the business section, which seemed little changed from the old pictures; some of the raspberry-brick blocks were still there, and the town hall, with its original bell. We crossed the main highway that bypasses the town, leading through industrial suburbs to Toledo, and entered the cemetery, where Anderson's mother is buried. There was a historical marker near the entrance, which prompted Hurd to relate how he had urged that Emma Anderson's name be included with those of Clyde's famous sons, including the Civil War general James Birdseye McPherson and the World War II hero Roger Young, subject of the popular patriotic song "The Ballad of Roger Young" and thus the veritable opposite of an unsung Clyde citizen. Hurd said that some people had opposed honoring Mrs. Anderson, feeling that her achievements were not noteworthy; but he, speaking with the older authority of town legend, had reminded them of how she had single-handedly raised the Anderson boys and their sister. And so her name was on the marker. At her grave, Hurd said that Anderson's brother Earl was buried there beside his mother, though there was no stone for him. A wanderer like Sherwood, Earl had died alone in a cheap rooming house in New York. One could imagine the same fate for Sherwood—but for the saving grace of the stories bottled up inside him, which began pouring out that afternoon in Chicago, with the wet snow or rain pelting in through the open window of his room.

We left the cemetery and drove back to the Sherwood Anderson memorial Park, only dedicated in 1976 and still a bare plot of ground near the site of the old town depot. Here had once been the town's thriving center; three hotels for traveling men had stood within a stone's throw—two of them torn down now, Hurd said with regret. He pointed to another empty piece of ground across the road, where, he said, the architect's distaste showing in his voice, a new "mock-Tudor" town hall would soon rise. The old Clyde, inhabited by ghosts of the past, was vanishing.

I stood in the growing darkness, imagining Clyde's heyday—the trains arriving and leaving, important and officious, bearing news and people, clanging and hissing steam. Those were trains that a young man could climb aboard and ride to the cities. "*Winesburg, Ohio* caused a furor that never died down," Hurd said. "People who were upset about it took it to the grave. Only after all those people died could you have a park for Sherwood Anderson in Clyde." A distant train whistle wailed in the night—that plangent, small-town sound—this time heralding the advent of another of those seemingly endless freights that now rumble through Clyde without stopping. My thoughts returned to a small-town boy called George Willard; I seemed to see him coming out of the Willard House—that frame hotel just over there. It is early in the morning, and he is carrying a single bag. He boards the train for the city and sits by the window lost in reverie as the train pulls out. When he remembers to look out the window, "The town of Winesburg had disappeared and his life there had become but a background on which to paint the dreams of his manhood."

A town, a railroad station, a train setting off with a young man, a starting place, a beginning. It recedes behind us and vanishes with all those green and gold summer mornings of boyhood, the air smelling like brown sugar, the cicadas' metronomic droning. A beginning . . . a starting place always there behind us, in memory. And the past decomposes into the bright dust of dreams . . .

Bibliography

Abernethy, Thomas Perkins. *The South in the New Nation 1789–1819.* Baton Rouge, La.: Louisiana State University Press, 1961.

Adams, Henry, *The Education of Henry Adams.* Boston, Houghton Mifflin Co., 1961 © 1918, 1946 Charles F. Adams.

Adams, James Truslow. *The Founding of New England.* Boston and New York: Atlantic–Little Brown, 1921.

———, *Provincial Society*. Chicago: Quadrangle Paperbacks, 1971.

Alcorn, Robert Hayden. *The Biography of a Town 1670–1970.* Hartford, Conn.: 300th Anniversary Committee of the Town of Suffield, 1970.

Allen, Frederick Lewis. *Only Yesterday.* New York: Bantam Books, 1959.

Anderson, Sherwood. *Hello Towns.* Mamaroneck, N.Y.: Paul Appel, 1972.

———. *Home Town.* New York: Alliance Book Corp., 1940.

———. *Memoirs.* New York: Harcourt, 1942.

———. *Poor White.* New York: The Viking Press, 1974.

———. *A Story-Teller's Story*. New York: The Viking Press, 1969.

———. *Winesburg, Ohio.* New York: The Viking Press, 1975.

Atherton, Lewis. *Main Street on the Middle Border*. Chicago: Quadrangle Books, 1966.

Bailey, Anthony. *In the Village.* New York: Alfred A. Knopf, 1971.

Bailyn, Bernard. *The New England Merchants in the Seventeenth Century.* New York: Harper & Row, Torchbooks, 1964.

Baker, Guy S. *History of Halifax, Massachusetts.* Halifax, Mass.: Privately printed, 1976.

Baker, Ronald L., and Marvin Carmony. *Indiana Place Names.* Bloomington, Ind.: Indiana University Press, 1975.

Baldwin, Faith. *New Girl in Town.* New York: Pocket Books, 1977.

Banta, R. E., ed. *Hoosier Caravan.* Bloomington, Ind.: Indiana University Press, 1975.

Barnes, Peter, ed. *The People's Land.* Emmaus, Pa.: Rodale press, 1975.

Baskin, John. *New Burlington.* New York: W. W. Norton, 1976.

Beckwith, H. W. *History of Montgomery County [Indiana].* Chicago: H. H. Hill and N. Iddings Publishers, 1881.

———. *History of Vermillion County* [Illinois]. Chicago: H. H. Hill & Co., 1879.

Bennett, Mildred R. *The World of Willa Cather.* Lincoln, Neb.: University of Nebraska Press, Bison Books, 1961.

Bercovitch, Sacvan. *The Puritan Origins of the American Self.* New Haven, Conn.: Yale University Press, 1975.

Bicknell, A. J., and William T. Comstock. *Victorian Architecture: Two Pattern Books.* Watkins Glen, N.Y.: The American Life Foundation and Study Institute, 1976.

Bicknell, A. J. *Victorian Village Builder.* Watkins Glen, N.Y.: The American Life Foundation and Study Institute, 1976.

Billings, Warren M., ed. *The Old Dominion in the Seventeenth Century.* Chapel Hill, N.C.: University of North Carolina Press, 1975.

Billington, Ray Allen. *The Far Western Frontier 1830–1860.* New York: Harper & Row, Torchbooks, 1962.

———. *The Westward Movement in the United States.* New York: Van Nostrand Reinhold, 1959.

Birbeck, Morris. *Notes on a Journey in America.* London: Ridgway & Sons, 1818.

Blumenthal, Albert. *Small-Town Stuff.* Chicago: University of Chicago Press, 1932.

Bode, Carl, ed. *Midcentury America.* Carbondale and Edwardsville, Ill.: Southern Illinois University Press, 1972.

Boley, Henry. *Lexington in Old Virginia.* Richmond, Va.: Garrett & Massie Publishers, 1974.

Bowers, William L. *The Country Life Movement in America 1900–1920.* Port Washington, N.Y.: Kennikat Press, 1975.

Bradbury, Ray. *Dandelion Wine.* New York: Alfred A. Knopf, 1975.

Bradford, William. *Of Plymouth Plantation.* New York: G. P. Putnam's Sons, Capricorn Boooks, 1962.

Bradford History Committee. *Two Hundred Plus.* Canaan, N.H.: Phoenix Publishing, 1976.

Brooks, Paul. *The View from Lincoln Hill.* Boston and New York: Houghton Mifflin, 1976.

Brooks, Van Wyck. *The Confident Years: 1885–1915.* New York: E. P. Dutton, 1955.

Brosseau, Ray, and Ralph K. Andrist, eds. *Looking Forward.* New York: American Heritage Press, 1970.

Brown, Louise K. *A Revolutionary Town.* Canaan, N.H.: Phoenix Publishing, 1975.

Brownell, Blaine A. *The Urban Ethos in the South 1920–1930.* Baton Rouge, La.: Louisiana State University Press, 1975.

Brownell, Blaine A., and David R. Goldfield, eds. *The City in Southern History.* Port Washington, N.Y.: Kennikat Press, 1977.

Bruner, Edmund, and J. H. Kolb. *Rural Social Trends.* New York: McGraw-Hill, 1933.

Buley, R. Carlyle. *The Old Northwest.* Indianapolis, Ind.: Indiana Historical Society, 1950.

Burby, Raymond J., and Shirley F. Weiss. *New Communities U.S.A.* Lexington, Mass.: Lexington Books, 1976.

Burner, David. *The Politics of Provincialism.* New York: Alfred A. Knopf, 1968.

Burnet, Jacob. *Notes on the Early Settlement of the North-Western Territory.* New York: D. Appleton, 1847.

Bushman, Richard C. *From Puritan to Yankee.* New York: W. W. Norton, 1970.

Butler, Edward W. *Urban Sociology.* New York: Harper & Row, 1976.

Canby, Henry Seidel. *The Age of Confidence.* New York: Farrar & Rinehart, 1934.

Cather, Willa. *Five Stories.* New York: Random House, Vintage Books, 1956.

———. *My Ántonia.* Boston and New York: Houghton Mifflin, 1918.

———. *O Pioneers!* Boston and New York: Houghton Mifflin, 1913.

———. *The Professor's House.* New York: Random House, Vintage Books, 1973.

———. *The Troll Garden.* New York: New American Library, 1961.

Choate, Norman. *Experiments in Town and Country Ministry.* Washington, D.C.: Center for Applied Research in the Apostolate, 1971.

Clark, Norman H. *Everett: A Milltown Biography.* Seattle, Wash.: University of Washington Press, 1970.

Cleland, Robert Glass. *This Reckless Breed of Men.* New York: Alfred A. Knopf, 1950.

Clough, Frank C. *William Allen White of Emporia.* New York: McGraw-Hill, 1941.

The Community. Editors of Time-Life Books. New York: Time-Life Books, 1976.

Conner, Daniel Ellis. *A Confederate in the Colorado Gold Fields.* Donald J. Berthron and Odessa Davenport, eds. Norman, Okla.: University of Oklahoma Press, 1970.

Cook, David M., and Craig G. Swauger. *The Small Town in American Literature.* New York: Harper & Row, 1977.

Coulton, G. G. *Medieval Village, Manor, and Monastery.* New York: Harper, Torchbooks, 1960.

Cowley, Malcolm, ed. *The Portable Faulkner.* New York: The Viking Press, 1977.

Creigh, Dorothy Weyer. *Adams County.* Hastings, Neb.: Adams County–Hastings Centennial Commission, 1972.

———. *Nebraska.* New York: W. W. Norton, 1977.

Crèvcoeur, St. John de. *Sketches of Eighteenth Century America.* New Haven, Conn.: Yale University Press, 1923.

Cushman, Dan. *Montana—The Gold Frontier.* Great Falls, Mont.: Stay Away, Joe Publishers, 1973.

Dana, C. W. *The Garden of the World.* Boston: Wentworth & Co., 1856.

Debo, Angie. *Prairie City.* New York: Alfred A. Knopf, 1944.

Dell, Floyd. *The Briary-Bush.* New York: Alfred A. Knopf, 1921.

———. *Homecoming.* Port Washington, N.Y.: Kennikat, 1978.

———. *Moon-Calf.* New York: Sagamore Press, 1957.

Demos, John. *A Little Commonwealth.* New York: Oxford University Press, 1970.

———, ed. *Remarkable Providences 1600–1760.* New York: George Braziller, 1972.

Dickens, Charles. *American Notes for General Circulation.* London: Chapman and Hall, 1842.

Dillard, J. L. *American Talk.* New York: Random House, 1976.

Dollard, John. *Caste and Class in a Southern Town.* Garden City, N.Y.: Doubleday, Anchor, 1957.

Donaldson, Scott. *The Suburban Myth.* New York: Columbia University Press, 1969.

Douglas, Ben. *History of Wayne County, Ohio.* Indianapolis, Ind.: Robert Douglas, Publisher, 1874.

Dreiser, Theodore. *Sister Carrie: An Authoritative Text, Backgrounds and Sources Criticism:* New York, W. W. Norton, 1970.

Dwight, Timothy. *Travels in New England and New York.* Cambridge, Mass.: The Belknap Press of Harvard University Press, 1969.

Dykstra, Robert. *The Cattle Towns.* New York: Atheneum, 1968.

Eden, Lynn. *Crisis in Watertown.* Ann Arbor, Mich.: University of Michigan Press, 1972.

Eggleston, Edward. *The Hoosier Schoolmaster.* New York: Hart Publishing Co., 1976.

Erwin, Richard T. *A History of Randolph Township.* Hicksville, N.Y.: Exposition Press, 1976.

Esarey, Logan. *The Indiana Home.* Bloomington, Ind.: Indiana University Press, 1976.

Essays on Amherst's History. Amherst, Mass.: The Vista Trust, 1978.

Fairfield, Richard. *Communes U.S.A.* New York: Penguin Books, 1972.

Farr, Finis. *O'Hara.* Boston: Little, Brown, 1973.

Faulk, Odie B. *Tombstone.* New York: Oxford University Press, 1972.

Faulkner, William. *The Hamlet.* New York: Random House, Vintage Books, 1956.

———. *The Town.* New York: Random House, Vintage Books, 1961.

Feldman, Saul D., and Gerald W. Thielbar. *Life Styles.* Boston: Little, Brown, 1972.

Fellman, Michael. *The Unbounded Frame.* Westport, Conn.: Greenwood Press, 1973.

Fischer, Christiane, ed. *Women in the American West 1840–1900.* Hamden, Conn.: The Shoe String Press, Archon Books, 1977.

Ford, "Senator" Ed. *My Home Town.* New York: Howell, Soskin Publishers, 1945.

Ford, Thomas. *A History of Illinois from Its Commencement as a State in 1818 to 1847.* Chicago: S. C. Griggs and Co., 1854.

Frisch, Michael H. *Town into City.* Cambridge, Mass.: Harvard University Press, 1972.

Gale, Zona. *Friendship Village.* New York: Macmillan, 1908.

Garland, Hamlin. *Boy Life on the Prairie.* Lincoln, Neb.: University of Nebraska Press, 1961.

Gass, William H. *In the Heart of the Heart of the Country.* New York: Pocket Books, 1977.

Gates, Paul. *Landlords and Tenants on the Prairie Frontier.* Ithaca, N.Y.: Cornell University Press, 1973.

Gillon, Edmund V. *A New England Town in Early Photographs.* New York: Dover Publications, 1976.

Goist, Park Dixon. *From Main Street to State Street.* Port Washington, N.Y.: Kennikat Press, 1977.

Graff, Polly Anne, and Stewart Graff, eds. *Wolfert's Roost.* Irvington-on-Hudson, N.Y.: The Washington Irving Press, 1971.

Grant, Charles S. *Democracy in the Connecticut Frontier Town of Kent.* New York: W. W. Norton, 1972.

Gray, Richard. *The Literature of Memory.* Baltimore: The Johns Hopkins University Press, 1977.

Greiff, Constance M. *Lost America: From the Atlantic to the Mississippi.* Princeton, N.J.: The Pyne Press, 1974.

———. *Lost America: From the Mississippi to the Pacific.* Princeton, N.J.: The Pyne Press, 1972.

Greven, Philip J. *Four Generations.* Ithaca, N.Y.: Cornell University Press, 1970.

Gronert, Ted. *Sugar Creek Saga.* Crawfordsville, Ind.: Wabash College Press, 1958.

Gross, Robert A. *The Minutemen and Their World.* New York: Hill & Wang, 1976.

Hall, James. *Letters from the West.* Gainesville, Fla.: Scholars' Facsimiles and Reprints, 1967.

Hansen, Harry, ed. *Illinois.* New York: Hastings House, 1974.

Harte, Bret. *The Outcasts of Poker Flat.* New York: New American Library, 1961.

Hatcher, Harlan. *The Western Reserve.* Indianapolis, Ind.: Bobbs-Merrill, 1949.

Havighurst, Walter. *The Heartland.* New York: Harper & Row, 1974.

———. *Wilderness for Sale.* New York: Hastings House, 1956.

Hayden, Dolores. *Seven American Utopias.* Cambridge, Mass.: The M.I.T. Press, 1976.

Heilman, Grant, ed. *Farm Town.* Brattleboro, Vt.: The Stephen Greene Press, 1974.

Hicks, Granville. *Small Town.* New York: Macmillan, 1946.

Hilfer, Anthony Channell. *The Revolt from the Village, 1915–1930.* Chapel Hill, N.C.: University of North Carolina Press, 1969.

Hine, Robert V. *California's Utopian Colonies.* New York: W. W. Norton, 1973.

Historical Statistics of the United States, 1789–1945. U.S. Department of Commerce, Bureau of the Census publication. Washington, D.C.: U.S. Government Printing Office, 1949.

The History of Brown County, Ohio. Chicago: W. H. Beers & Co., 1883.

The History of Darke County, Ohio. Chicago: W. H. Beers & Co., 1880.

The History of Ogle County, Illinois. Chicago: H. F. Kett & Co., 1878.

Hofstadter, Richard. *America at 1750.* New York: Vintage Books, 1973.

Holbrook, Stewart. *The Yankee Exodus.* Seattle: University of Washington Press, 1968.

Hollingshead, A. B. *Elmtown's Youth.* New York: John Wiley & Sons, 1949.

Hollon, W. Eugene. *Frontier Violence.* New York, Oxford University Press, 1974.

Horwitz, Richard P. *Anthropology Toward History.* Middletown, Conn.: Wesleyan University Press, 1978.

Howe, Edgar Watson. *Plain People.* New York: Dodd, Mead, 1929.

———. *Story of a Country Town.* Boston: Houghton Mifflin, 1927.

Howe, Henry. *Historical Collection of Ohio.* Cincinnati: Derby, Bradley & Co., 1847.

Howe, Irving. *Sherwood Anderson.* New York: William Sloane Associates, 1951.

Hussey, E. C. *Victorian Home Building.* Watkins Glen, N.Y.: The American Life Foundation, 1976.

Jackson, John Brinckerhoff. *American Space.* New York: W. W. Norton, 1972.

Jewett, Sarah Orne. *The Country of the Pointed Firs.* Garden City, N.Y.: Doubleday, Anchor, 1956.

Johns-Heine, Patricke, and Hans H. Gerth. "Values in Mass Periodical Fiction, 1921–1940." *The Public Opinion Quarterly,* Vol. 13 (1949) 105–113.

Just, Ward. *A Family Trust.* Boston: Atlantic–Little, Brown, 1978.

Kammen, Michael. *People of Paradox.* New York: Vintage Books, 1973.

Kaplan, Justin. *Mr. Clemens and Mark Twain.* New York: Simon & Schuster, Touchstone Books, 1966.

Kauffman, Henry J. *The American Farmhouse.* New York: Hawthorn Books, 1975.

Kazin, Alfred, *On Native Grounds.* Garden City, N.Y.: Doubleday, Anchor, 1956.

Kerouac, Jack. *The Town and the City.* New York: Harcourt Brace, 1950.

Ketchum, Richard M. *Will Rogers.* New York: American Heritage Publishing Company, 1973.

Klinski, Victor J., ed. *Church and Community.* Washington, D.C.: Center for Applied Research in the Apostolate, 1970.

Koenig, Louis W. *Bryan.* New York: G. P. Putnam's Sons, 1971.

Kramer, Paul, and Frederick L. Holborn, eds. *The City in American Life from Colonial Times to the Present.* New York: G. P. Putnam's Sons, 1970.

Ladd, Everett C. *Ideology in America.* New York: W. W. Norton, 1972.

Lamar, Howard. *The Reader's Encyclopedia of the American West.* New York: Thomas Y. Crowell, 1977.

Langley, Harold D., ed. *To Utah with the Dragoons and Glimpses of Life in Arizona and California 1858–1859.* Salt Lake City: University of Utah Press, 1974.

Lantz, Herman, R. *A Community in Search of Itself.* Carbondale and Edwardsville, Ill.: Southern Illinois University Press, 1972.

Laslett, Peter. *The World We Have Lost.* London: Methuen and Co., 1965.

Lerner, Max. *America as Civilization.* New York: Simon & Schuster, Clarion Books, 1957.

Lesy, Michael. *Wisconsin Death Trip.* New York: Pantheon Books, 1973.

Levering, Julia Henderson. *Historic Indiana.* New York: G. P. Putnam's Sons, 1909.

Lewis, Grace Hegger. *With Love from Gracie.* New York: Harcourt Brace, 1955.

Lewis, Sinclair, *Babbitt.* New York: New American Library, 1961.

———. *Main Street.* New York: New American Library, 1961.

Lingeman, Richard R. *Don't You Know There's a War On?* New York: G. P. Putnam's Sons, 1970.

Lockridge, Kenneth A. *A New England Town.* New York: W. W. Norton, 1970.

Lockwood, George B. *The New Harmony Movement.* New York: Dover Publications, 1971.

Lynd, Robert S., and Helen M. Lynd. *Middletown.* New York: Harcourt Brace & World, 1929.

———. *Middletown in Transition.* New York: Harcourt Brace & World, 1937.

Lynn, Kenneth S. *William Dean Howells.* New York: Harcourt Brace Jovanovich, 1971.

Lytle, Andrew. *A Wake for the Living.* New York: Crown Publishers, 1975.

Mansur, Iva. *A New England Church 1730–1834.* Freeport, Me.: The Bond Wheelwright Co., 1974.

Marshall, Cyril Leek. *The Mayflower Destiny.* Harrisburg, Pa.: Stackpole Books, 1975.

Masters, Edgar Lee. *Across Spoon River.* Farrar, Straus & Giroux, Octagon Books, 1969.

———. *The New Spoon River.* New York: Macmillan, 1968

———. *Spoon River Anthology.* New York: Macmillan, Collier Books, 1962.

Maule, Harry E., and Melville H. Cane, eds. *The Man from Main Street.* New York: Random House, 1953.

Maxwell, William. *Ancestors.* New York: Alfred A. Knopf, 1971.

McCarty, John L. *Maverick Town.* Norman, Okla.: University of Oklahoma Press, 1968.

McCullers, Carson. *The Heart Is a Lonely Hunter.* New York: Bantam Books, 1974.

———. *The Member of the Wedding.* New York: Bantam Books, 1974.

McDermott, John Francis, ed. *Travelers on the Western Frontier.* Urbana, Ill.: University of Illinois Press, 1970.

McMurtry, Larry, *The Last Picture Show.* New York: Dell, 1975.

Mencken, H. L. *Prejudices.* James T. Farrell, ed. New York: Random House, Vintage Books, 1958.

Merk, Frederick. *History of the Western Movement..* New York: Alfred A. Knopf, 1978.

Merriam, H. G., ed. *Way Out West.* Norman, Okla.: University of Oklahoma Press, 1969.

Miller, Perry. *The New England Mind.* Boston: The Beacon Press, 1961.

Mitchell, Edward Valentine. *American Village.* New York: Stackpole Sons, 1938.

Montaigne, François des. *The Plains.* Nancy Alpert Mower and Don Russell, eds. Norman, Okla.: University of Oklahoma Press, 1972.

Morison, Peter A., and Judith P. Wheeler. "Rural Renaissannce in America?" *Population Bulletin*, Vol. 31, No. 3. Washington, D.C.: Population Reference Bureau, 1976.

Morris, Willie. *Yazoo*, New York: Ballantine, 1972.

Morris, Wright. *The Home Place*. Lincoln, Neb.: University of Nebraska Press, Bison Books, 1968.

Mumford, Lewis. *The Human Prospect*. Boston: The Beacon Press, 1955.

———. *The Urban Prospect*. New York: Harcourt, Brace & World, A Harvest Book, 1968.

Myers, John. *The Westerners*. Englewood Cliffs, N.J.: Prentice-Hall, 1969.

Nahm, Milton C. *Las Vegas and Uncle Joe*. Norman, Okla.: University of Oklahoma Press, 1964.

Nathan, George Jean, and H. L. Mencken. *The American Credo*. New York: Farrar, Straus & Giroux, Octagon Books, 1977.

Nicholson, Meredith. *The Valley of Democracy*. New York: Charles Scribner's Sons, 1918.

Nordhoff, Charles. *The Communistic Societies of the United States*. New York: Dover Publications, 1966.

Orwell, George. *In Front of Your Noose, 1945–1950*. Sonia Orwell and Ian Angus, eds., New York: Harcourt Brace Jovanovich, 1968.

Osborn, Frederic J. *Green-Belt Cities*. New York: Schocken Books, 1969.

Parkes, Henry Bamford. *The American Experience*. New York: Random House, Vintage Books, 1959.

Parkman, Ebenezer. *The Diary of Ebenezer Parkman, 1703–1782*. Francis G. Wallett, ed. Worcester, Mass.: American Antiquarian Society, 1974. First Part, 1719–1755.

Parkman, Francis, *The Oregon Trail*. New York: New American Library, 1950.

Parrington, Vernon L. *The Beginnings of Critical Realism in America: 1860–1920*. New York: Harcourt Brace & World, Harbinger Books, 1930.

———. *The Colonial Mind, 1620–1800*. New York: Harcourt Brace & World, Harvest Books, 1927.

———. *The Romantic Revolution, 1800-1860*. New York: Harcourt Brace & World, Harvest Books, 1927.

The Past and Present of Woodford County, Illinois. Chicago: William Le Baron Jr. & Co., 1878.

Peattie, Donald Culross, ed. *Audubon's America*. Boston: Houghton Mifflin Co., 1940.

"The People Left Behind." Publication of the U.S. Dept. of Agriculture, Economic Research Div., Washington, D.C.: U.S. Government Printing Office, 1971.

Peterson, Merrill D., ed., *The Portable Thomas Jefferson*. New York: The Viking Press, 1975.

Philbrick, Francis S. *The Rise of the West, 1754-1830.* New York: Harper & Row, Torchbooks, 1966.

Philips, David R., ed. *The West.* Chicago: Heenry Regnery, A & W Visual Library, 1975.

Powell, Lyman P. *Historic Towns of the Western States.* New York: G. P. Putnam's Sons, 1901.

Power, Richard Lyle. *Planting Corn Belt Culture.* Indianapolis, Ind.: Indiana Historical Society, 1953.

Quinn, Bernard. *The Changing Context of Town and Country Ministry.* Washington, D.C.: Center for Applied Research in the Apostolate, 1970.

Redfield, Robert. *The Little Community. Peasant Society and Culture.* Chicago: University of Chicago Press, 1956.

Reps, John W. *Cities on Stone.* Fort Worth, Texas: Amon Carter Museum of Western Art, 1976.

———. *The Making of Urban America.* Princeton, N.J.: Princeton University Press, 1965.

Rexroth, Kenneth. *Communalism.* New York: The Seabury Press, 1974.

Richter, Conrad. *The Trees.* New York: Alfred A. Knopf, 1940.

———. *The Fields.* New York: Alfred A. Knopf, 1946.

———. *The Town.* New York: Alfred A. Knopf, 1967.

———. *Early Americana.* New York: Alfred A. Knopf, 1964.

———. *The Grandfathers.* New York: Alfred A. Knopf, 1964.

———. *The Rawhide Knot and Other Stories.* New York: Alfred A. Knopf, 1978.

Rideout, Walter B., ed. *Sherwood Anderson.* Englewood Cliffs, N.J.: Prentice-Hall, 1974.

Rifkind, Carole. *Main Street.* New York: Harper & Row, 1977.

Rohrbough, Malcolm J. *The Land Office Business.* New York: Oxford University Press, 1971.

Rölvaag, O. E. *Giants in the Earth.* New York: Harper & Row, 1955.

Rosenberg, Bernard, and David Manning White, eds. *Mass Culture.* New York: Macmillan, The Free Press of Glencoe, 1964.

Rosskam, Edwin. *Roosevelt, New Jersey.* New York: Grossman Publishers, 1972.

Roth, David M., and Freeman Meyer. *From Revolution to Constitution.* Chester, Conn.: The Pequot Press, 1975.

Rural Development—1971. Publication of U.S. Senate, Committee on Agriculture and Forestry. Washington, D.C.: U.S. Government Printing Office, 1972.

Russell, Howard S. *A Long Deep Furrow.* Hanover, N.H.: University Press of New England, 1976.

Sanford, Mollie Dorsey. *Mollie.* Lincoln, Neb.: University of Nebraska Press, 1976.

Schell, Orville. *The Town That Fought to Save Itself*. New York: Pantheon Books, 1976.

Schlesinger, Arthur Meier. *The Rise of the City*. Chicago: Quadrangle Books, 1971.

Schmitt, Martin F., and Dee Brown. *The Settler's West*. New York: Ballantine Books, 1974.

Schmitt, Peter J. *Kalamazoo*. Kalamazoo, Mich.: Kalamazoo City Historical Commission, 1976.

Schorer, Mark. *Pieces of Life*. New York: Farrar, Straus & Giroux, 1977.

———. *Sinclair Lewis*. New York: McGraw-Hill, 1961.

Scully, Vincent. *American Architecture and Urbanism*. New York: Praeger Publishers, 1973.

Sears, Stephen W., and the editors of *American Heritage. Hometown U.S.A.* New York: American Heritage Publishing Company, 1975.

Sewall, Samuel. *The Diary of Samuel Sewall, 1674–1729*. M. Halsey Thomas, ed. New York: Farrar, Straus & Giroux, 1973.

Shinn, Charles Howard. *Mining Camps*. Rodman W. Paul, ed. New York: Harper & Row, Torchbooks, 1965.

Shirer, William L. *20th Century Journey*. New York: Simon & Schuster, 1976.

Shover, John L. *First Majority—Last Minority*. Dekalb, Ill.: Northern Illinois University Press, 1976.

Silverman, Kenneth, ed. *Selected Letters of Cotton Mather*. Baton Rouge, La.: Louisiana State Universtiy Press, 1971.

Slotkin, Richard. *Regeneration Through Violence*. Middletown, Conn.: Wesleyan University Press, 1973.

Small Community Needs. U.S. Dept. of Housing and Urban Development (Contract H-1074). Washington, D.C.: U.S. Government Printing Office, 1971.

Smith, Henry Nash. *Virgin Land*. Cambridge, Mass.: Harvard University Press, 1970.

Smith, Page. *As a City Upon a Hill*. New York: Alfred A. Knopf, 1966.

———. *Daughters of the Promised Land*. Boston and New York: Little, Brown, 1970.

Sobin, Dennis P. *The Future of the American Suburbs*. Port Washington, N.Y.: Kennikat Press, 1971.

Stadtfeld, Curtis. *From the Land and Back*. New York: Charles Scribner's Sons, 1972.

Stegner, Wallace. *Mormon Country*. New York: Hawthorn Books, 1942.

Stein, Maurice R. *The Eclipse of Community*. Princeton, N.J.: Princeton University Press, 1960.

Sternlieb, George, annd James W. Hughes, eds. *Post-Industrial America*. New Brunswick, N.J.: Center for Urban Policy Research, 1975.

Sternsher, Bernard. *Hitting Home*. Chicago: Quadrangle Books, 1970.

Stewart, Elinore Pruitt. *Letters of a Woman Homesteader.* Lincoln, Neb.: University of Nebraska Press, Bison Books, 1961.

Stewart, George R. *American Place Names.* New York: Oxford University Press, 1970.

Stong, Phil. *State Fair.* New York: The Literary Guild, 1932.

Suckow, RRuth. *The Folks.* New York: The Literary Guild, 1934.

Tarkington, Booth. *The Gentleman from Indiana.* New York: Doubleday and McClure, 1899.

———. *The Magnificent Ambersons.* New York: Avon Books, 1960.

Taylor, Samuel W. *The Kingdom or Nothing.* New York: Macmillan, 1976.

———. *Nightfall at Nauvoo.* New York: Avon Books, 1973

Thomas, Benjamin P. *Lincoln's New Salem.* Springfield, Ill.: The Abraham Lincoln Association, 1934.

Tocqueville, Alexis de. *Democracy in America.* New York: Alfred A. Knopf, 1945.

Turner, Frederick Jackson. *The Frontier in American History.* New York: Henry Holt & Co., 1920.

Twain, Mark. *The Autobiography of Mark Twain.* Charles Neider, ed. New York: Harper & Row, 1959.

———. *Roughing It.* New York: New American Library, 1962.

———. *Short Stories of Mark Twain.* New York: Airmont Publishing Co., 1968.

Twelve Southerners, *I'll Take My Stand.* Baton Rouge, La.: Louisiana State University Press, 1930.

Van Dusen, Albert E. *Puritans Against the Wilderness.* Chester, Conn.: The Pequot Press, 1975.

Varenne, Hervé. *Americans Together.* New York: Columbia Teachers College Press, 1977.

Vaughan, Alden T., ed. *The Puritan Tradition in America 1620–1730.* Columbia, S.C.: University of South Carolina Press, 1972.

Vestal, Stanley. *Queen of Cowtowns.* Lincoln, Neb.: University of Nebraska Press, Bison Books, 1972.

Vidich, Arthur I., and Joseph Bensman. *Small Town in Mass Society.* Princeton, N.J.: Princeton University Press, 1968.

Walker, Charles M. *History of Athens County, Ohio.* Cincinnati: Robert Clarke & Co., 1869.

Wall, Joseph Frazier. *Iowa.* New York: W. W. Norton, 1978.

Wallace, Anthony F. C. *Rockdale.* New York: Alfred A. Knopf, 1978.

Warner, W. Lloyd, ed. *Yankee City.* New Haven, Conn. Yale University Press, 1963.

Watkins, T. H., and Charles Watson, Jr. *The Land No One Knows.* San Francisco: Sierra Club Books, 1975.

Webb, Walter Prescott. *The Great Plains.* New York: Grossett & Dunlap, 1973.

Welter, Rush. *The Mind of America 1820-1860*. New York: Columbia University Press, 1975.

Wertenbaker, Thomas J. *The First Americans*. Chicago: Quadrangle Books, 1971.

Wescott, Glenway. *Good-bye Wisconsin*. New York: Harper & Bros., 1928.

West, James, pseud. (Carl Withers). *Plainville, U.S.A.* New York: Columbia University Press, 1945.

Wheeler, Thomas C., ed. *A Vanishing America*. New York: Holt, Rinehart & Winston, 1964.

White, Morton, and Lucia White. *The Intellectual Versus the City*. New York: Oxford University Press, 1977.

White, William Allen. *The Autobiography of William Allen White*. New York: Macmillan, 1946.

———. *Forty Years on Main Street*. New York: Farrar & Rinehart, 1937.

Wilder, Thornton. *Our Town*. John Gassner, ed. In *A Treasury of the Theater*. New York: Simon & Schuster, 1950.

Williams, Raymond. *The Country and the City*. New York: Oxford University Press, 1973.

Wilson, Edmund. *Letters on Literature and Politics, 1912-1972*. Elena Wilson, ed. New York: Farrar, Straus & Giroux, 1977.

Wilson, Helen E. *Gold Fever*. La Mesa, Cal.: Privately published, 1974.

Wilson, Richard Guy, and Sidney K. Robinson. *The Prairie School in Iowa*. Ames, Iowa: Iowa State University Press, 1977.

Wilson, William E. *The Angel and the Serpent*. Bloomington, Ind.: Indiana University Press, 1964.

Winslow, Ola Elizabeth. *Meetinghouse Hill, 1630-1783*. New York: W. W. Norton, 1972.

Withers, Carl. See West, James.

Wolcott, Reed. *Rose Hill*. New York: G. P. Putnam's Sons, 1976.

Wolfe, Thomas. *Look Homeward, Angel*. New York: Charles Scribner's and Sons, 1929.

Wolle, Muriel Sibell. *Stampede to Timberline*. Chicago: The Swallow Press, 1974.

Woodress, James. *Willa Cather*. Lincoln, Neb.: University of Nebraska Press, Bison Books, 1975.

Wrenn, Tony P. and Elizabeth D. Mulloy. *America's Forgotten Architecture*. New York: Pantheon Books, 1967.

Wright, Louis B. *Culture on the Moving Frontier*. Bloomington, Ind.: Indiana University Press, 1955.

———. *Life on the American Frontier*. New York: G. P. Putnam's Sons, 1968.

Zucker, Paul. *Town and Square*. Cambridge, Mass.: The M.I.T. Press, 1970.

Zuckerman, Michael, *Peaceable Kingdoms*. New York: Alfred A. Knopf, 1970.

Notes

Chapter 1

1. Quoted in John W. Reps, *The Making of Urban America* (Princeton, N.J.: Princeton University Press, 1965), p. 160.
2. Quoted in Raymond Williams, *The Country and the City*, (New York: Oxford University Press, 1973), p. 11.
3. Peter Laslett, *The World We Have Lost* (London: Methuen and Co., 1965), p. 64.
4. Quoted in Blaine A. Brownell and David R. Goldfield, eds., *The City in Southern History* (Port Washington, N. Y.: Kennikat Press, 1977), p. 27.
5. Ibid.
6. Warren M. Billings, ed., *The Old Dominion in the Seventeenth Century* (Chapel Hill, N. C.: University of North Carolina Press, 1975), p. 20.
7. Ibid.
8. Quoted in Brownell and Goldfield, *City in Southern History*, p. 30.
9. Ibid., p. 29.
10. Ibid., p. 26.
11. Quoted in Reps, p. 93.
12. Quoted in Brownell and Goldfield, *City in Southern History*, p. 23.
13. Quoted in Page Smith, *As a City Upon a Hill* (New York: Alfred A. Knopf, 1966), p. 6.
14. Quoted in Kenneth A. Lockridge, *A New England Town* (New York: W. W. Norton, 1970), pp.4–5.
15. Ibid.
16. Quoted in Ola Elizabeth Winslow, *Meetinghouse Hill, 1630–1783* (New York: W. W. Norton, 1972), p. 36.
17. Ibid., p. 37.
18. Alden T. Vaughan, *The Puritan Tradition in America 1620–1730* (Columbia, S.C.: University of South Carolina Press, 1972), p. 104.
19. Timothy Dwight, *Travels in New England and New York*, vol. 4 (Cambridge, Mass.: The Belknap Press of Harvard Univ. Press, 1969), p. 319.
20. Quoted in Winslow, *Meetinghouse Hill*, p. 29.
21. Alexis de Tocqueville, *Democracy in America* (New York: Alfred A. Knopf, 1945), p. 58.
22. Quoted in Philip J. Greven, *Four Generations* (Ithaca, N. Y.: Cornell University Press, 1970), p. 45.
23. Vaughan, *Puritan Tradition*, p. 193.
24. Quoted in Michael Zimmerman, *Peaceable Kingdoms* (New York: Alfred A. Knopf, 1970), p. 54.
25. Quoted in Lockridge, *New England Town*, p. 5.
26. Vaughan, *Puritan Tradition*, p. 54.
27. Dwight, *Travels*, p. 319.
28. William Bradford, *Of Plymouth Plantation* (New York: Capricorn Books, 1962), p. 164.
29. Quoted in Richard C. Bushman, *From Puritan to Yankee* (New York: W. W. Norton, 1970), p. 57.

30. Quoted in Charles S. Grant, *Democracy in the Connecticut Frontier Town of Kent* (New York: W. W. Norton, 1972), p. 3.
31. Quoted in Richard C. Bushman, *From Puritan to Yankee* (New York: W. W. Norton, 1970), p. 5.
32. Vaughan, *Puritan Tradition,* p. 135.
33. Ibid., p. 104.
34. Bushman, *Puritan to Yankee,* p. 21.
35. John Demos, ed., *Remarkable Providences 1600-1760* (New York: George Braziller, 1972), p. 170.
36. Vaughan, *Puritan Tradition,* p. 167.
37. Quoted in Zuckerman, p. 117.
38. Demos, *Remarkable Providences,* p. 236.
39. Ibid., pp. 238–39.
40. Vaughan, *Puritan Tradition,* p. 146.
41. Quoted in Robert Hayden Alcorn, *The Biography of a Town 1670–1970* (Hartford, Conn.: 300th Anniversary Committee of the Town of Suffield, 1970), p.88.
42. Ibid.
43. Quoted in Charles S. Grant, *Democracy in the Connecticut Frontier Town of Kent* (New York: W. W. Norton, 1972), p. 162.
44. Vaughan, *Puritan Tradition,* p. 192.
45. Quoted in Grant, *Democracy in Kent,* p. 160.
46. Ebenezer Parkman, *The Diary of Ebenezer Parkman, 1703-1782,* first part: 1719–1755, ed. Francis G. Wallett (Worcestor, Mass.: American Antiquarian Society, 1974), p. 1.
47. Ibid., p. 36.
48. Ibid., p. 19.
49. Ibid., p. 36.
50. Ibid., p. 96.
51. Quoted in Grant, *Democracy in Kent,* p. 165.
52. Quoted in Robert A. Gross, *The Minutemen and Their World* (New York: Hill & Wang, 1976), p. 24.
53. Quoted in Winslow, *Meetinghouse Hill,* pp. 30–31.
54. Quoted in Lockridge, *New England Town,* p. 38.
55. George D. Langdon Jr., "The Franchise and Political Democracy in Plymouth Colony," *William and Mary Quarterly,* 20 (1963): 525–26.
56. Lockridge, *New England Town,* p. 50.
57. Vaughan, *Puritan Tradition,* p. 139.
58. Ibid., pp. 135-36.
59. Parkman, *Diary,* p. 5.
60. Quoted in Grant, *Democracy in Kent,* p. 40.
61. Demos, *Remarkable Providences,* p. 140.
62. Vaughan, *Puritan Tradition,* p. 159.
63. Gross, *Minutemen,* p. 89.
64. Zuckerman, *Peaceable Kingdoms,* p. 89.
65. Quoted in Grant, *Democracy in Kent,* p. 92.
66. Bushman, *Puritan to Yankee,* p. 35.
67. Quoted in Alcorn, *Biography of a Town,* p. 92.
68. Quoted in Bushman, *Puritan to Yankee,* p. 18.
69. Bradford, *Of Plymouth Plantation,* p. 214.

CHAPTER 2

1. Quoted in R. Carlyle Buley, *The Old Northwest: Pioneer Period* 1815–1840, Vol. I (Indianapolis: Indiana Historical Society, 1950), pp. 3–4.
2. Quoted in Ola Elizabeth Winslow, *Meetinghouse Hill* (New York: W. W. Norton), p. 17.
3. Jacob, Burnet, *Notes on the Early Settlement of the North-Western Territory* (New York: D. Appleton & Co., 1847), p. 57.
4. Lyman Powell, ed., *Historic Towns of the Western States* (New York: G. P. Putnam's Sons, 1901), p. 33.
5. Quoted, Ibid, p. 8.
6. Quoted, Buley, Vol. I, p. 101.
7. Quoted in Henry Howe, *Historical Collection of Ohio* (Cincinnati: Derby, Bradley & Co., 1847), p. 264.
8. Quoted in Walter Havighurst, *Wilderness for Sale* (New York: Hastings House, 1956), p. 100.
9. Quoted, Ibid, p. 151.
10. Quoted, Ibid.
11. Quoted, Ibid, p. 155.
12. Quoted, Howe, p. 182.
13. Quoted in Harlan Hatcher, *The Western Reserve* (Indianapolis, Ind.: Bobbs-Merrill, 1949), p. 14.
14. Quoted in Havighurst, p. 66.
15. Quoted in Buley, Vol. I, p. 10.
16. Quoted in Howe, p. 296.
17. Quoted in *The History of Darke County, Ohio* (Chicago: H. H. Beers & Co., 1880), p. 248.
18. Quoted in Richard Lyle Power, *Planting Corn Belt Culture* (Indianapolis: Indiana Historical Society, 1953), p. 13.
19. Howe, p. 296.
20. Quoted in Power, p. 13.
21. Quoted in Buley, Vol. I, p. 378.
22. Quoted, Ibid.
23. Quoted, Ibid.
24. Quoted in Power, p. 9.
25. Quoted in Havighurst, p. 167.
26. Quoted in Frederick Jackson Turner, *The Frontier in American History* (New York: Henry Holt & Co., 1920), p. 153.
27. Quoted in Buley, Vol. I, p. 48.
28. Quoted, Ibid.
29. Quoted in Power, p. 3.
30. Quoted in Turner, p. 351.
31. Quoted in Buley, Vol. II, p. 105.
32. Quoted, Ibid.
33. Quoted, Ibid, p. 106.
34. Quoted in Turner, p. 154.
35. Quoted, Ibid, Vol. I, p. 366.
36. Quoted, Ibid, p. 383.
37. Quoted in Havighurst, p. 243.
38. Quoted in Charles M. Walker, *History of Athens County, Ohio* (Cincinnati, Ohio: Robert Clark & Co., 1869), p. 497.
39. Quoted in H. W. Beckwith, *History of Montgomery County, Indiana* (Chicago: H. H. Hill & N. Iddings, 1881), p. 16.
40. Quoted in Walker, p. 496.
41. Howe, p. 316.
42. Ford, p. 95.
43. Francis S. Philbrick, *The Rise of the West 1754–1830* (New York: Harper & Row, 1965), p. 332.
44. Quoted in Walker, p. 10.
45. Quoted in Buley, Vol. I, p. 16.
46. Quoted in Philbrick, p. 311.
47. Quoted in Power, p. 26.
48. Quoted, Ibid, p. 30.
49. Quoted in Philbrick, p. 311.
50. Quoted, Ibid, p. 312.
51. Quoted in Buley, Vol. II, p. 105.
52. Quoted, Ibid.
53. Turner, p. 200.
54. Quoted in Rush Welter, *The Mind of America 1820–1860* (New York: Columbia University Press, 1957), p. 319.
55. Quoted in Philbrick, p. 354.

56. Quoted in Beckwith, pp. 120–1.
57. Quoted in Paul Gates, *Landlords and Tenants on the Prairie Frontier* (Ithaca, N.Y.: Cornell University Press, 1973), p. 50.
58. Quoted in Buley, Vol. I, p. 110.
59. Quoted, Ibid.
60. Quoted, Ibid, p. 112.
61. Quoted, Ibid.
62. Quoted, Ibid.
63. Quoted in Gates, p. 59.
64. Quoted, Ibid.
65. Quoted in Michael Kammen, *People of Paradox* (New York: Vintage Books, 1973), p. 180.
66. Quoted in Turner, p. 153.
67. Quoted in Buley, Vol. I, p. 16

CHAPTER 3

1. Quoted in Harlan Hatcher, *The Western Reserve* (Indianapolis: Bobbs-Merrill, 1949), p. 65.
2. Quoted, Ibid, pp. 65–66.
3. Quoted in Walter Havighurst, *Wilderness for Sale* (New York: Hastings House, 1956), p. 182.
4. Quoted, Ibid, p. 74.
5. Henry Howe, *Historical Collection of Ohio* (Cincinnati: Derby, Bradley & Co., 1847), p. 439.
6. Ibid.
7. Quoted in Hatcher, p. 111.
8. Quoted, Ibid, p. 75.
9. Quoted in R. Carlyle Buley, *The Old Northwest: Pioneer Period 1815–1840*, Vol. II (Indianapolis: Indiana Historical Society, 1950), p. 147.
10. Quoted, Ibid, Vol. I, p. 26.
11. Quoted in Havighurst, p. 106.
12. Quoted in Richard Lyle Power, *Planting Corn Belt Culture* (Indianapolis: Indiana Historical Society, 1953), p. 49.
13. Quoted in Havighurst, pp. 106–107.
14. Quoted, Ibid, pp. 102–4.
15. Quoted, Ibid, p. 179.
16. Quoted in H.W. Beckwith, *History of Montgomery County, Indiana* (Chicago: H.H. Hill & N. Iddings, 1881), p. 585.
17. Charles Dickens, *American Notes* (New York: Penguin Library, 1972), pp. 215–16.
18. *The Past and Present of Woodford County, Illinois* (Chicago: William LeBaron Jr. & Co., 1878), p.53.
19. Quoted in Rush Welter, *The Mind of America 1820–1860* (New York: Columbia University Press, 1975), p. 313.
20. *The History of Madison County, Ohio* (Chicago: W.H. Beers & Co., 1883), p. 627.
21. Quoted in Howe, p. 194.
22. Ibid, p. 197.
23. Quoted in Buley, Vol. I, p. 373.
24. Thomas Ford, *A History of Illinois from Its Commencement as a State in 1818 to 1847* (Chicago: S.C. Griggs & Co., 1854), p. 86.
25. Beckwith, pp. 119–120.
26. Quoted in Howe, p. 386.
27. *The History of Darke County, Ohio* (Chicago: W.H. Beers & Co., 1880), p. 233.
28. Ford, p.115.
29. Ibid, p. 115.
30. Ibid, p. 90.
31. Ibid, pp. 88–9.
32. Quoted in Welter, p. 315.
33. *History of Darke County*, p. 217.
34. Ibid, p. 238.
35. Quoted in Welter, p. 314.

36. Quoted in Buley, Vol. I, p. 322.
37. Howe, p. 274.
38. Quoted in Beckwith, p. 121.
39. Quoted in Buley, Vol. I, p. 322.
40. Quoted in Howe, p. 152.
41. Quoted in Buley, Vol. I, p. 319.
42. Quoted, Ibid, p. 333.
43. Ibid.
44. Quoted in Walker, pp. 396-7.
45. Quoted in Buley, Vol. I, p. 197.
46. Ibid, p. 182.
47. Quoted in Walker, p. 368.
48. Ibid, p. 231.
49. Quoted in Page Smith, *As a City Upon a Hill* (New York: Alfred A. Knopf, 1966), p. 98.
50. Quoted in Buley, Vol. I, p. 495.
51. Quoted, Ibid.
52. Quoted, Ibid, p. 514.
53. Quoted in Hatcher, p. 153.
54. Quoted in Buley, Vol. I, p. 461.
55. Beckwith, p. 85.
56. Buley, Vol. I, p. 550.
57. Ibid, p. 552.
58. Ibid, p. 554.
59. Quoted in Beckwith, p. 433.
60. Ford, p. 15.
61. Quoted in Hatcher, p. 192.
62. Quoted in Beckwith, p. 127.
63. Quoted in Buley, Vol. I, p. 554.
64. Quoted, Ibid, p. 555.
65. Quoted in Edward Valentine Mithchell, *American Village* (New York: Stackpole Sons, 1938), p. 16.
66. Quoted, Ibid, pp. 17-19.
67. Quoted, Ibid, pp. 24-5.
68. *The History of Ogle County, Illinois* (Chicago: H.F. Kett & Co., 1878), p. 517.
69. Beckwith, p. 203.
70. Ted Gronert, *Sugar Creek Saga* (Crawfordsville, Ind.: Wabash College, 1958), p. 100.
71. Jacob Burnet, *Notes on the Early Settlement of the North-Western Territory* (New York: D. Appleton & Co., 1847), p. 53.
72. *The History of Darke County*, p. 214.
73. *The History of Madison County*, p. 533.
74. Harry Hansen, ed., *Illinois, A Descriptive and Historical Guide* (New York: Hastings House, 1974), p. 717.
75. Quoted in Ben Douglass, *History of Wayne County, Ohio* (Indianapolis: Robert Douglass Publisher, 1874), pp. 270-71.
76. Quoted in *The History of Ogle County*, p. 514.
77. Quoted in *The History of Madison County*, p. 592.
78. Quoted in Paul Gates, *Landlords and Tenants on the Prairie Frontier* (Ithaca, N.Y.: Cornell University Press, 1973), p. 156.
79. Ibid, p. 51.
80. *The History of Darke County*, p. 232.
81. Ibid, p. 231.
82. Ibid, p. 234.
83. Ibid, p. 237.
84. Ibid.
85. Ibid, p. 287.
86. Ibid, p. 263.
87. Conrad Richter, *The Town* (New York: Alfred A. Knopf, 1950), pp. 410-11, 271-3.
88. Quoted in Welter, p. 323.

Chapter 4

1. Charles Howard Shinn, *Mining Camps*, ed. Rodman W. Paul (New York: Harper & Row, Torchbooks, 1965), p. 64.

2. Quoted in Shinn, *Mining Camps*, p. 71.
3. John Brinckerhoff Jackson, *American Space* (New York: W.W. Norton, 1972), p. 194.
4. Quoted in Jackson, *American Space*, p. 197.
5. Ray Allen Billington, *The Far Western Frontier 1830-60* (New York: Harper & Row, Torchbooks, 1962), p. 226.
6. Ibid., p. 218.
7. Quoted in Shinn, *Mining Camps*, p. 219.
8. Quoted in Billington, *Far Western Frontier*, p. 232.
9. Shinn, *Mining Camps*, p. 218.
10. Ibid., p. 214.
11. Ibid., p. 215.
12. Ibid., p. 215.
13. Shinn, *Mining Camps*, p. 211.
14. Quoted in Shinn, *Mining Camps*, p. 240.
15. Ibid., p. 139.
16. Shinn, *Mining Camps*, p. 139.
17. Ibid., p. 140.
18. Ibid., p. 138.
19. Ibid, p. 141.
20. Quoted in Shinn, *Mining Camps*, p. 262.
21. Ibid., p. 208.
22. Ibid., p. 209.
23. Shinn, *Mining Camps*, p. 210.
24. Ibid., p. 211.
25. Quoted in Billington, *Far Western Frontier*, p. 249.
26. Ibid., p. 250.
27. Quoted in John Meyers, *The Westerners* (Englewood Cliffs, N.J.: Prentice Hall, 1969), p. 225.
28. Quoted in Ray Allen Billington, *The Westward Movement in the United States* (New York: Van Nostrand Reinhold, 1959), p. 157.
29. Ibid., p. 158.
30. Ibid., p. 158–59.
31. Ibid., p. 160.
32. Ibid., p. 159.
33. Mark Twain, *Roughing It* (New York: New American Library, 1962), p. 255.
34. Quoted in Christiane Fischer, ed., *Women in the American West 1840-1900* (Hamden, Conn.: The Shoe String Press, Archon Books, 1977), p. 185.
35. Billington, *Far Western Frontier*, p. 26.
36. Muriel Sibell Wolle, *Stampede to Timberline* (Chicago: The Swallow Press, 1974), p. 33.
37. Billington, *Far Western Frontier*, p. 266.
38. Quoted in Albert Blumenthal, *Small-Town Stuff* (Chicago: University of Chicago Press, 1932), p. 29.
39. Vincent Scully, *American Architecture and Urbanism* (New York: Praeger Publishers, 1973), p. 80.
40. Quoted in Odie B. Faulk, *Tombstone* (New York: Oxford University Press, 1972), p. 45.
41. Ibid., p. 187.
42. Ibid.
43. Ibid., p. 109.
44. Ibid., p. 157.
45. Ibid., p. 207–8.
46. Quoted in Stanly Vestal, *Queen of Cowtowns* (Lincoln, Neb.: University of Nebraska Press, Bison Books, 1972), p. 130.
47. Walter Prescott Webb, *The Great Plains* (New York: Grossett & Dunlap, 1973), p. 247.
48. Quoted in Jackson, *American Space*, p. 178.
49. Quoted in Webb, *Great Plains*, p. 122.
50. Quoted in Jackson, *American Space*, p. 180–81.
51. Quoted in Vestal, *Queen of Cowtowns*, p. 35.
52. Ibid., p. 35–36.
53. Ibid., p. 35.
54. Ibid., p. 37.

55. Ibid., p. 96.
56. Ibid., p. 245.
57. Ibid., p. 100.
58. Ibid., p. 168.
59. Quoted in Jackson, *American Space*, p. 179.
60. Quoted in W. Eugene Hollon, *Frontier Violence* (New York: Oxford University Press, 1974), p. 210.
61. Quoted in Vestal, *Queen of Cowtowns*, p. 59.
62. Ibid.
63. Ibid., p. 235.
64. Webb, *Great Plains*, p. 239.

Chapter 5

1. Quoted in T. H. Watkins and Charles Watson, Jr., *The Land No One Knows* (San Francisco: Sierra Club Books, 1975), p. 75.
2. Quoted in Walter Prescott Webb, *The Great Plains* (New York: Grossett & Dunlap, 1973), p. 278.
3. Ibid.
4. Quoted in Watkins and Watson, *The Land No One Knows*, p. 51.
5. Ibid.
6. Quoted in Webb, *The Great Plains*, p. 473.
7. Quoted in Paul Gates, *Landlords and Tenants on the Prairie Frontier* (Ithaca, N. Y.: Cornell University Press, 1973), p. 286.
8. Ibid.
9. Quoted in Dorothy Weyer Creigh, *Adams County* (Hastings, Neb.: Adams County-Hastings Centennial Commission, 1972), p. 10.
10. O. E. Rölvaag, *Giants in the Earth* (New York: Harper & Row, 1955), p. 474.
11. Ibid, p. 475.
12. Webb, *The Great Plains*, p. 506.
13. Christiane Fischer, editor, *Women in the American West 1849-1900* (Hamden, Conn., The Shoe String Press, 1977), p. 44.
14. Elinore Pruitt Stewart, *Letters of a Woman Homesteader* (Lincoln, Neb.: University of Nebraska Press, Bison Books, 1961), p. 214.
15. Ibid., p. 215.
16. Rölvaag, *Giants in the Earth*, p. 158–59.
17. Ibid., p. 387.
18. Thomas C. Cochran and William Miller, *The Age of Enterprise* (New York, Harper & Row, 1961), p. 132.
19. Quoted in Creigh, *Adams County*, p. 907.
20. Ibid., p. 909.
21. Ibid., p. 910.
22. Ibid., p. 1013.
23. Webb, *The Great Plains*, p. 235.
24. Quoted in Creigh, *Adams County*, p. 359–60.
25. Ibid., p. 348.
26. Ibid., p. 16.
27. Quoted in Ray Allen Billington, *The Westward Movement in the United States* (New York: Van Nostrand Reinhold, 1959), p. 86.
28. Richard M. Ketchum, *Will Rogers* (New York: American Heritage Publishing Company, 1973), p. 12.
29. Quoted in Billington, *Westward Movement*, p. 178.
30. Ibid., p. 180.
31. Ibid., p. 183.
32. Ibid., p. 184.
33. Ibid.
34. Ibid., p. 183.

Chapter 6

1. Henry Seidel Canby, *The Age of Confidence* (New York: Farrar & Rinehart, 1934), p. 24.
2. Ibid., p. 259.
3. Ibid., p. 260.
4. Edmund Wilson, *Letters on Literature and Politics 1912–1972*, ed. Elena Wilson (New York: Farrar, Strauss & Giroux, 1977), p. 261.
5. Quoted in Page Smith, *As a City Upon a Hill* (New York: Alfred A. Knopf, 1966), p. 216.
6. Patricke Johns-Heineke and Hans H. Gerth, "Values in Mass Periodical Fiction, 1921–1940" (*The Public Opinion Quarterly*, Vol. 13, 1949), pp. 105–113. In Bernard Rosenberg and David Manning White, editors, *Mass Culture* (New York: Macmillan Publishing Co., 1964), p. 231.
7. Rosenberg and White, p. 230.
8. Canby, *Age of Confidence*, p. 3.
9. Booth Tarkington, *The Gentleman from Indiana* (New York: Doubleday and McClure, 1899), p. 4.
10. Quoted in Raymond Brousseau and Ralph K. Andrist, eds., *Looking Forward* (New York: American Heritage Press, 1970), p. 10.
11. Meredith Nicholson, *The Valley of Democracy* (New York: Charles Scribner's Sons, 1918), p. 61.
12. Quoted in Lewis Atherton, *Main Street on the Middle Border* (Chicago: Quadrangle Books, 1966), p. 38.
13. Guy S. Baker, *History of Halifax, Massachusetts* (Halifax, Mass: Privately printed, 1976), p. 119.
14. Sherwood Anderson, *Memoirs* (New York: Harcourt, 1942), p. 40.
15. Willa Cather, *My Ántonia* (Boston and New York: Houghton Mifflin, 1918), p. 218
16. Quoted in Dorothy Weyer Creigh, *Adams County* (Hastings, Neb.: Adams County–Hastings Centennial Commission, 1972), p. 27.
17. Quoted in Norman H. Clark, *Everett: A Milltown Biography* (Seattle, Wash.: University of Washington Press, 1970), p. 103.
18. Alexis de Tocqueville, *Democracy in America* (New York: Alfred A. Knopf, 1945), pp. 210–11.
19. Lewis Mumford, *The Human Prospect* (Boston: The Beacon Press, 1955), p. 172.
20. Ibid., p. 175.
21. Anderson, *Memoirs*, p. 96.
22. Quoted in Atherton, *Main Street*, p. 97.
23. Ibid., p. 92.
24. William Allen White, *The Autobiography of William Allen White* (New York: Macmillan, 1946), pp. 40, 67.
25. Quoted in Sherwood Anderson, *Home Town* (New York: Alliance Book Corp., 1940), p. 94.
26. Page Smith, *Daughters of the Promised Land* (Boston and New York: Little, Brown, 1970), p. 73.
27. Floyd Dell, *Moon-Calf* (New York: Sagamore Press, 1957), p. 299.
28. Anderson, *Memoirs*, p. 104.
29. Atherton, *Main Street*, p. 86.
30. Quoted in Michael Lesy, *Wisconsin Death Trip* (New York: Pantheon Books, 1973), unpaged.
31. Quoted in Clark, *Everett*, p. 108.
32. Clark, *Everett*, p. 109.
33. Atherton, *Main Street*, p. 116.
34. Quoted in Smith, *City Upon a Hill*, p. 166.

35. Ibid., p. 170.
36. Ibid., p. 171.
37. Canby, *Age of Confidence*, p. 65.
38. Quoted in Smith, *City Upon a Hill*, p. 216.
39. Quoted in Anthony Channell Hilfer, *The Revolt from the Village 1915–1930* (Chapel Hill, N.C.: University of North Carolina Press, 1969), p. 148.
40. Smith, *City Upon a Hill*, p. 172.
41. Ibid.
42. Smith, *Daughters of the Prommised Land*, p. 213.
43. Smith, *City Upon a Hill*, p. 172.
44. Robert Hayden Alcorn, *The Biography of a Town 1670–1970* (Hartford, Conn.: 300th Anniversary Committee of the Town of Suffield, 1970), p. 170.
45. Ibid., p. 185.
46. Quoted in Anderson, *Home Town*, p. 94.
47. Atherton, *Main Street*, p. 87.
48. Michael Lesy, *Wisconsin Death Trip* (New York: Pantheon Books, 1973), unpaged.
49. Quoted in Park Dixon Goist, *From Main Street to State Street* (Port Washington, New York: Kennikat Press, 1977), p. 4.
50. Ibid., p. 4.
51. Quoted in Hilfer, *Revolt from the Village*, p. 25.
52. Ibid., p. 90.
53. Quoted in Atherton, *Main Street*, p. 20.
54. Edgar Watson Howe, *Plain People* (New York: Dodd, Mead, 1929), pp. 1–2.
55. Ibid., p. 4.
56. William Maxwell, *Ancestors* (New York: Alfred A. Knopf, 1971), p. 41.
57. Ibid., p. 29.
58. Atherton, *Main Street*, p. 355.
59. Booth Tarkington, *The Magnificent Ambersons* (New York: Avon Books, 1960), pp. 8–9.
60. Quoted in A.J. Bicknell and William T. Comstock, *Victorian Architecture: Two Pattern Books* (Watkins Glen, N.Y.: The American Life Foundation and Study Institute, 1976), unpaged.
61. Tarkington, *Magnificent Ambersons*, p. 14.
62. E.C. Hussey, *Victorian Home Building* (Watkins Glen, N.Y.: The American Life Foundation, 1976), p. iii.
63. Ibid.
64. Ibid., unpaged.
65. Quoted in Peter J. Schmitt, *Kalamazoo* (Kalamazoo, Mich.: Kalamazoo City Historical Commission, 1976), p. 101.
66. Quoted in Bicknell and Comstock, *Victorian Architecture*, introduction.
67. Ibid.
68. Quoted in Schmitt, *Kalamazoo*, p. 163.
69. Ibid., p. 164.
70. Schmitt, *Kalamazoo*, p. 166.
71. Max Lerner, editor, *The Portable Veblen* (New York: The Viking Press, 1948), p. 169.
72. Ibid., p. 185.
73. Ibid., p. 185.
74. Ibid., p. 186.
75. Sinclair Lewis, *Main Street* (New York: New American Library, 1961), p. 33.
76. Cather, *My Ántonia*, p. 219.
77. Canby, *Age of Confidence*, p. 11.
78. Schmitt, *Kalamazoo*, p. 215.
79. Nicholson, *Valley of Democracy*, p. 62.
80. Ibid., p. 63.
81. Ibid., p. 64.
82. Creigh, *Adams County*, p. 27.
83. Hussey, *Victorian Home Building*, p. 21.

84. Ibid., p. 214.
85. Quoted in Schmitt, *Kalamazoo*, p. 157.
86. Robert S. Lynd and Helen Merrell, *Middletown* (New York: Harcourt Brace & World, 1929), p. 173.
87. Quoted in Carole Rifkind, *Main Street* (New York: Harper & Row, 1977), p. 10.
88. Quoted in Alcorn, *Biography of a Town*, pp. 140–41.
89. Quoted in Brousseau and Andrist, *Looking Forward*, p. 10.
90. Lewis, *Main Street*, p. 37.
91. Ibid.
92. Ibid., p. 38.
93. Ibid., p. 41.
94. Henry Boley, *Lexington in Old Virginia* (Richmond, Va.: Garrett and Massie Publishers, 1974), p. 220.
95. Ibid.
96. Quoted in Rifkind, *Main Street*, p. 56.
97. Rifkind, *Main Street*, p. 56.
98. Ibid., p. 153.
99. Quoted in Rifkind, *Main Street*, p. 145.
100. Glenway Wescott, *Good-bye Wisconsin* (New York: Harper & Bros., 1928), p. 16.
101. Quoted in Brousseau and Andrist, *Looking Forward*, p. 158.
102. Ibid., p. 159.
103. Ibid., p. 156.
104. Alcorn, *Biography of a Town*, p. 233.
105. Mark Schorer, *Pieces of Life* (New York: Farrar, Straus & Giroux, 1977), p. 2.
106. Quoted in Rifkind, *Main Street*, p. 187.
107. Sherwood Anderson, *Hello Towns* (Mamaroneck, N.Y.: Paul Appel, 1972), p. 37.
108. Schorer, *Pieces of Life*, p. 99.
109. Quoted in Robert S. and Helen Merrell Lynd, *Middletown*, p. 246.
110. Atherton, *Main Street*, p. 139.
111. Quoted in Robert S. Lynd and Helen Merrell Lynd, *Middletown*, p. 227.
112. Nicholson, *Valley of Democracy*, p. 198.
113. Ibid., p. 241.
114. Atherton, *Main Street*, p. 185.
115. William L. Shirer, *20th Century Journey* (New York: Simon & Schuster, 1976), p. 158.
116. Canby, *Age of Confidence*, p. 134.
117. Smith, *City Upon a Hill*, p. 75.
118. Atherton, *Main Street*, p. 130.
119. Howe, *Plain People*, p. 45.
120. Hamlin Garland, *Boy Life on the Prairie* (Lincoln, Neb.: University of Nebraska Press, 1961), p. 232.
121. Ibid., pp. 234–35.
122. Ibid., p. 235.
123. Ibid., p. 243.
124. Ibid., p. 250.
125. Ibid., p. 251.
126. Atherton, *Main Street*, p. 320.
127. Quoted in Creigh, *Adams County*, p. 75.
128. Atherton, *Main Street*, p. 66.
129. Quoted in Atherton, *Main Street*, p. 66.
130. Smith, *City Upon a Hill*, p. 231.
131. Ibid., pp. 251–52.
132. Ibid., p. 257.
133. Canby, *Age of Confidence*, p. 31.
134. Thornton Wilder, *Our Town*, in *A Treasury of the Theater*, John Gassner, ed. (New York: Simon & Schuster, 1950), p. 931.
135. Ibid., p. 936.
136. Quoted in Ted Gronert, *Sugar Creek Saga* (Crawfordsville, Ind.: Wabash College Press, 1958), p. 301.
137. Wilder, *Our Town*, p. 936.

138. Ibid., p. 943.
139. Jewett, *Country of the Pointed Firs*, p. 57.
140. Ibid., p. 59.
141. Wilder, *Our Town*, p. 948.
142. Sherwood Anderson, *Poor White* (New York: The Viking Press, 1974), p. 44.
143. W. Lloyd Warner and associates, *Democracy in Jonesville* (New York: Harper and Row, 1949), p. 290.

Chapter 7

1. Arthur Meier Schlesinger, *The Rise of the City* (Chicago: Quadrangle Books, 1971), pp. 79–80.
2. Quoted in Paul Kramer and Frederick L. Holborn, eds., *The City in American Life from Colonial Times to the Present* (New York: G.P. Putnam's Sons, 1970), p. 32.
3. Quoted in Louis W. Koenig, *Bryan* (New York: G.P. Putnam's Sons, 1971), p. 197.
4. Quoted in Arthur Meier Schlesinger, p. 61.
5. Quoted in Vernon L. Parrington, *The Beginnings of Critical Realism in America: 1860–1920* (New York: Harcourt Brace & World, Harbinger Books, 1930), p. 295.
6. Ibid., p. 297.
7. Quoted in Anthony Channell Hilfer, *The Revolt from the Village, 1915–1930* (Chapel Hill, N.C.: University of North Carolina Press, 1969), p. 47.
8. Ibid., p. 53.
9. Quoted in Parrington, *Critical Realism*, p. 289.
10. Quoted in Edgar Watson Howe, *The Story of a Country Town* (Boston: Houghton Mifflin, 1927), p. 5.
11. Edgar Watson Howe, *Plain People* (New York: Dodd Mead, 1929), p. 23.
12. Michael Lesy, *Wisconsin Death Trip* (New York: Pantheon Books, 1973), unpaged.
13. Ibid.
14. Ibid.
15. Quoted, Van Wyck Brooks, *The Confident Years 1885–1915* (New York: E.P. Dutton and Co., 1955), p. 79.
16. Stewart Holbrook, *The Yankee Exodus* (Seattle: University of Washington Press, 1968), p. 265.
17. Quoted in Schlesinger, *Rise of the City*, p. 70.
18. Quoted in Kramer and Holborn, *City in American Life*, p. 28.
19. Schlesinger, *Rise of the City*, p. 14.
20. Quoted in Blaine A. Brownell and David R. Goldfield, eds., *The City in Southern History* (Port Washington, N.Y.: Kennikat Press, 1977), p. 106.
21. Ibid., p. 121.
22. Quoted in William L. Bowers, *The Country Life Movement in America 1900–1920* (Port Washington, N.Y.: Kennikat Press, 1975), p. 38.
23. Ibid., p. 49.
24. Quoted in Lesy, *Wisconsin Death Trip*, unpaged.
25. Quoted in Bowers, *Country Life Movement*, p. 9.
26. May Lerner, editor, *The Portable Veblen* (New York: The Viking Press, 1948), p. 407.
27. Ibid., p. 413.
28. Ibid., p. 414.
29. Ibid., p. 418.

30. Quoted in Frank C. Clough, *William Allen White* (New York: McGraw-Hill, 1941), p. 140.
31. Ibid., p. 141.
32. Ibid.
33. Ibid., p. 417.
34. Ibid., p. 416.
35. Meredith Nicholson, *The Valley of Democracy* (New York: Charles Scribner's Sons, 1918), p. 108.
36. Koenig, *Bryan*, p. 152.
37. Quoted in David Burner, *The Politics of Provincialism* (New York: Alfred A. Knopf, 1968), p. 114.
38. Page Smith, *As a City Upon a Hill* (New York: Alfred A. Knopf, 1966), p. 206.
39. Ibid., p. 207.
40. Ibid.
41. Sherwood Anderson, *Memoirs* (New York: Harcourt, 1942), p. 79.
42. Ibid., pp. 79–81.
43. Henry Seidel Canby, *The Age of Confidence* (New York: Farrar & Rinehart, 1934), pp. 96–97.
44. Ibid., p. 232.
45. Quoted in Burner, *Politics of Provincialism*, p. 8.
46. Ibid.
47. Ibid.
48. Quoted in Smith, *City Upon a Hill*, p. 208.
49. Quoted in Burner, *Politics of Provincialism*, p. 99.
50. Quoted in Howe, *Plain People*, p. 248.
51. Ibid.
52. Frederick Lewis Allen, *Only Yesterday* (New York: Bantam Books, 1959), p. 128.
53. Quoted in Smith, *City Upon a Hill*, p. 263.
54. Zona Gale, *Friendship Village* (New York: Macmillan, 1908), p. 93.
55. Booth Tarkington, *The Gentleman from Indiana* (New York: Doubleday and McClure, 1899), p. 205.
56. Quoted in Hilfer, *Revolt from the Village*, p. 18.
57. Willa Cather, *O Pioneers!* (Boston and New York: Houghton Mifflin, 1913), pp. 122-3.
58. Hilfer, *Revolt from the Village*, p. 23.
59. Booth Tarkingtoon, *Gentleman from Indiana*, p. 182.
60. Ibid.
61. Ibid.
62. Ibid, p. 13.
63. Gale, *Friendship Village*, p. 8.
64. Ibid., p. 105.
65. Ibid., p. 48.
66. Quoted, Vernon L. Parrington, *The Beginnings of Critical Realism in America*, p. 249.
67. Van Wyck Brooks, *The Confident Years: 1885–1915* (New York: E.P. Dutton, 1955), pp. 64–65.
68. Nicholson, *Valley of Democracy*, p. 60.
69. Quoted in Hilfer, *Revolt from the Village*, p. 26.
70. Anthony F.C. Wallace, *Rockdale* (New York: Alfred A. Knopf, 1978), p. 4.
71. Ibid., p. 5.
72. Richard P. Horwitz, *Anthropology Toward History* (Middletown, Conn.: Wesleyan University Press, 1978), p. 78.
73. Robert S. Lynd and Helen M. Lynd, *Middletown* (New York: Harcourt, Brace & World, 1929), p. 8.
74. W. Lloyd Warner, *Yankee City* (New Haven, Conn.: Yale University Press, 1963), p. 158.
75. Ibid., p. 171.
76. Ibid., p. 172.
77. Sherwood Anderson, *Poor White* (New York: The Viking Press, 1974), p. 36.

78. Ibid., pp. 44–45.
79. Anderson, *Memoirs*, p. 102.
80. Sherwood Anderson, *A Story Teller's Story* (New York: The Viking Press, 1969), p. 85.
81. Ibid.
82. Ibid., p. 84.
83. Ibid., pp. 127–28.
84. Ibid., p. 85.
85. Ibid., pp. 198–99.
86. Ibid., p. 200.
87. Anderson, *Memoirs*, p. 124.
88. Ibid.
89. Ibid., pp. 127.
90. Ibid.
91. Anderson, *Story Teller's Story*, p. 295.
92. Quoted in Parrington, *Critical Realism*, p. 371.
93. Anderson, *Story Teller's Story*, p. 327.
94. Sherwood Anderson, *Hello Towns* (Mamaroneck, N.Y.: Paul Appel, 1972), p. 123.
95. Ibid., p. 126.
96. Twelve Southerners, *I'll Take My Stand* (Baton Rouge, La.: Louisiana State University Press, 1930), p. xliv.
97. Ibid., pp. xxx–xxxi.
98. Howe, *Country Town*, p. 228.
99. Quoted in Peter J. Schmitt, *Kalamazoo* (Kalamazoo, Mich.: Kalamazoo City Historical Commission, 1976), p. 158.
100. Ibid.
101. Ibid.
102. Ibid.
103. Ibid.
104. Booth Tarkington, *The Magnificent Ambersons*, pp. 193–5.

Chapter 8

1. Richard Ellman, editor, *The Oxford Book of American Verse* (New York: Oxford University Press, 1976?), p. 422.
2. Van Wyck Brooks, *The Confident Years: 1885–1915* (New York: E.P. Dutton, 1955), p. 309.
3. Theodore Dreiser, *Sister Carrie: An Authoritative Text, Backgrounds and Sources Criticism* (New York: W.W. Norton, 1970), p. 397.
4. Ibid., p. 396.
5. Ibid., p. 369.
6. Quoted, Ibid., p. 478.
7. Quoted, Ibid., p. 519.
8. Edgar Lee Masters, *Across Spoon River* (New York: Farrar, Straus & Giroux, Octagon Books, 1969), p. 283.
9. Ibid., p. 284.
10. Ibid.
11. Dreiser, *Sister Carrie*, p. 431.
12. Masters, *Across Spoon River*, p. 134.
13. Ibid., p. 79.
14. Ibid.
15. Quoted, Dreiser, *Sister Carrie*, p. 395.
16. Ibid., p. 1.
17. Masters, *Across Spoon River*, p. 134.
18. Ibid., p. 338.
19. Ibid.
20. Ibid., p. 339.
21. Edgar Lee Masters, *Spoon River Anthology* (New York: Macmillan, Collier Books, 1962), p. 23.
22. Masters, *Across Spoon River*, p. 286.
23. Ibid., p. 411.
24. Ibid.
25. Masters, *Across Spoon River*, p. 411.
26. Masters, *Spoon River Anthology*, p. 89.

27. Ibid., p. 350.
28. Quoted in Brooks, *Confident Years*, p. 416.
29. Dell, *Homecoming*, p. 211.
30. Masters, *Across Spoon River*, p. 337.
31. Ibid.
32. Sherwood Anderson, *Memoirs* (New York: Harcourt, 1942), p. 336.
33. Ibid.
34. Quoted in *Sinclair Lewis*, Mark Schorer (New York: McGraw-Hill, 1961), p. 278.
35. Anderson, *Memoirs*, p. 336.
36. Ibid., p. 338.
37. Floyd Dell, *The Briary-Bush* (New York: Alfred A. Knopf, 1921), p. 34.
38. Ibid.
39. Anderson, *Memoirs*, p. 344.
40. Ibid., p. 348.
41. Ibid.
42. Ibid.
43. Quoted in William Faulkner, "Sherwood Anderson: An Appreciation" (*Atlantic Monthly*, June, 1953)
44. Ibid.
45. Ibid.
46. Ibid., p. 334.
47. Ibid., p. 341.
48. Ibid.
49. Willa Cather, *A Lost Lady* (New York: Alfred A. Knopf, 1958), p. 104.
50. Ibid.
51. Sinclair Lewis, *Main Street* (New York: New American Library, 1961), p. 148.
52. Irving Howe, *Sherwood Anderson* (New York: William Sloane Associates, 1951), p. 88.
53. Quoted in ibid., p. 89.
54. Dell, *Homecoming*, p. 178.
55. Robert Hayden Alcorn, *The Biography of a Town 1670–1970* (Hartford, Conn.: 300th Anniversary Committee of the Town of Suffield, 1970), p. 182.
56. William L. Shirer, *20th Century Journey* (New York: Simon & Schuster, 1976), pp. 274–75.
57. Quoted in Brooks, *Confident Years*, p. 68.
58. Quoted in Ted Gronert, *Sugar Creek Saga* (Crawfordsville, Ind.: Wabash College Press, 1958), p. 405.
59. Lewis, *Main Street*, p. 6.
60. Frederick Lewis Allen, *Only Yesterday* (New York: Bantam Books, 1959), p. 162.
61. Ibid., p. 163.
62 Vernon L. Parrington, *The Beginnings of Critical Realism in America: 1860–1920* (New York: Harcourt, Brace & World, Harvest Books, 1927), p. 386.
63. Lewis, *Main Street*, p. 432.
64. Grace Hegger Lewis, *With Love from Gracie* (New York: Harcourt, Brace, 1955), p. 90.
65. Ibid.
66. At Sinclair Lewis Interpretive Center, Sauk Centre, Minnesota.
67. Mark Schorer, *Sinclair Lewis* (New York: McGraw-Hill, 1961), p. 147.
68. Quoted in ibid., p. 101.
69. Ibid., p. 100.
70. Ibid., p. 102.
71. Lewis, *Main Street*, p. 154.
72. Quoted in G.H. Lewis, *Love from Gracie*, p. 119.
73. Ibid., p. 117.
74. Lewis, *Main Street*, p. 262.
75. Dell, *Homecoming*, p. 345.
76. Anderson, *Winesburg, Ohio*, p. 243.
77. Edgar Lee Masters, interview with Rose C. Field, *New York Times Book Review*, 9 September 1924, p. 2.
78. Howe, *Sherwood Anderson*, p. 61.
79. Ibid., pp. 61–62.
80. Quoted in ibid., p. 75.

Chapter 9

1. Sherwood Anderson, *Home Town* (New York: Alliance Book Corp., 1940), pp. 4–5.
2. Edmund Bruner and J. H. Kolb, *Rural Social Trends* (New York: McGraw-Hill, 1933) p. 107
3. James West pseud. (Carl Withers), *Plainville, U.S.A.* (New York: Columbia University Press, 1945), p. 81.
4. Ibid, p. 128.
5. W. Lloyd Warner, ed., *Yankee City* (New Haven, Conn.: Yale University Press, 1963), p. 37.
6. W. Lloyd Warner, ed., *Democracy in Jonesville* (New York: Harper & Row, 1949), p. 293.
7. Ibid., p. 23.
8. Quoted in Blaine A. Brownell, The Urban Ethos in the South 1920–1930. (Baton Rouge, La.: Louisiana State University Press, 1975), p. 72
9. West (Withers), *Plainville*, p. 128.
10. Albert Blumenthal, *Small-Town Stuff* (Chicago: University of Chicago Press, 1932), p. 170.
11. Ibid.
12. Robert S. Lynd and Helen M. Lynd, *Middletown* (New York: Harcourt Brace & World, 1929), p. 296.
13. Ibid., p. 296.
14. Bruner and Kolb, *Rural Social Trends*, p. 254.
15. W. Loyd Warner, ed., *Democracy in Jonesville*, p. 121
16. Lynd and Lynd, *Middletown*, p. 302.
17. Ibid., p. 284.
18. Ibid., p. 304.
19. Ibid.
20. Page Smith, *As a City Upon a Hill* (New York: Alfred A. Knopf, 1966), pp. 174–75.
21. Quoted in Smith, *City Upon a Hill*, p. 175.
22. Lynd and Lynd, *Middletown*, p. 81.
23. Warner, *Democracy in Jonesville*, p. 26.
24. Quoted in Finis Farr, *O'Hara* (Boston: Little, Brown and CCo., 1973), p. 164.
25. Blumenthal, *Small-Town Stuff*, p. 163.
26. Ibid., p. 163.
27. Lynd and Lynd, *Middletown in transition*, pp. 458–59.
28. Ibid., p. 459.
29. Ibid., p. 459.
30. Blumenthal, *Small-Town Stuff*, p. 172.
31. Ibid.
32. Ibid., p. 160.
33. Ibid., p. 155.
34. Ibid., p. 156.
35. Robert Hayden Alcorn, *The Biography of a Town 1670–1970* (Hartford, Conn.: 300th Anniversary Committee of the Town of Suffield, 1970), p. 209.
36. Warner, *Jonesville*, p. 32.
37. Ibid.
38. Quoted in Bruner and Kolb, *Rural Social Trends*, p. 258.
39. Blumenthal, *Small-Town Stuff*, p. 105.
40. Ibid., p. 74.
41. Ibid.
42. Ibid., p. 59.
43. West, *Plainville*, pp. 138–39.
44. Blumenthal, *Small-Town Stuff*, p. 146.
45. Robert S. Lynd and Helen M. Lynd, *Middletown in Transition* (New York: Harcourt Brace & World, 1937), p. 453.
46. Quoted in Bruner and Kolb, *Rural Social Trends*, pp. 254–55.
47. Granville Hicks, *Small Town* (New York: Macmillan, 1946), p. 95.
48. Ibid., p. 97.

49. Blumenthal, *Small-Town Stuff*, p. 71.
50. Quoted in Lynd and Lynd, *Middletown in Transition*, p. 103.
51. Ibid., p. 105.
52. Ibid., pp. 111–12.
53. Ibid., p. 109.
54. Ibid., p. 112.
55. Ibid., p. 120.
56. Ibid., p. 123.
57. Ibid., p. 123.
58. Hicks, *Small Town*, p. 106.
59. Blumenthal, *Small-Town Stuff*, p. 296.
60. Ibid., p. 298.
61. Ibid., p. 297.
62. Ibid., p. 321.
63. Ibid., p. 323.
64. West, *Plainville*, p. 91.
65. Hicks, *Small Town*, p. 115.
66. Ibid., p. 117.
67. West, *Plainville*, p. 223.
68. Ibid., p. 225.
69. Hicks, p. 210.
70. Ibid., p. 221.
71. Arthur I. Vidich and Joseph Bensman, *Small Town in Mass Society* (Princeton, N.J.: Princeton University Press, 1968), p. 335.
72. Ibid., p. 334.
73. Ibid., p. 299.
74. Robert Redfield, *The Little Community: Peasant Society and Culture* (Chicago: University of Chicago Press, 1956), p. 146.
75. Redfield, *Little Community*, p. 147.
76. Ibid.
77. F. Scott Fitzgerald, *The Great Gatsby* (New York: Bantam Books, 1945), p. 191.

Chapter 10

1. Harold S. Williams, "Smallness and the Small Town," *Small Town*, October 1977, p. 13.
2. Ibid.
3. Quoted, Ibid., p. 14
4. Quoted, Seth S. King, "St. Cloud, Minn.: A Small City Faces Special Problems," (New York *Times*, Nov. 25, 1971, p. 25.)
5. Peter A. Morison and Judith P. Wheeler, "Rural Renaissance in America?" In *Population Bulletin* (Washington, D.C.: Population Reference Bureau, 1976), Vol. 31, no. 3, p. 22.
6. Quoted in ibid., pp. 4-5.
7. Ibid.
8. Peter Barnes, ed., *The People's Land* (Emmaus, Pa.: Rodale Press, 1975), p. 174.
9. Ibid.
10. Ibid., p. 178.
11. Quoted in Barnes, *People's Land*, p. 180.
12. Ibid.
13 Quoted, Roy Reed, "Influx of Retired People to Ozarks a Mixed Blessing;" (New York *Times*, May 19, 1975), p. 18.
14. Ibid.
15. Ibid.
16. Quoted in Ted Sell, "Problems of Aging: The Elderly Rule Small Towns," *Small Town*, December 1974, p. 5.
17. Edmund Bruner and J.H. Kolb, *Rural Social Trends* (New York: McGraw-Hill, 1933), p. 28.
18. Quoted in Ted Sell, Ibid., p. 6.
19. Ibid.
20. Ibid.
21. Quoted in Albert Blumenthal,

Small-Town Stuff (Chicago: University of Chicago Press, 1932), p. 373.

22. Quoted in "Small New England Town Fights for Survival," *Small Town*, August, 1973, p. 7.
23. *Small Town*, March 1972, p. 2.
24. Quoted in Andrew H. Malcolm, "Amusement Park's Plan Stirs a Quiet Illinois Town," *New York Times*, Nov. 15, 1973, p. 47.
25. Ibid.
26. Ibid.
27. Quoted in *Rural Development—1971*, publication of U.S. Senate, Committee on Agriculture and Forestry (Washington, D.C.: Government Printing Office, 1972), p. 188.
28. Ralph E. Thayer, "Toward a Community Awareness of Growth and Development Problems," *Small Town*, January 1976, pp. 10–11.
29. Gladwyn Hill, "Conflicting Court Actions Perplex Towns Seeking to Curb Growth," *New York Times*, July 29, 1974, p. 18.
30. Quoted in Seth S.. King, "St. Cloud, Minn.," *New York Times*, Nov. 21, 1975, p. 25.
31. Ralph E. Thayer, "Toward a Community Awareness of Growth and Development Problems," *Small Town*, January 1976, p. 10.
32. Gene Summers and Jean M. Lang, "Bringing Jobs to People: Does It Pay?" *Small Town*, September 1976, p. 7.
33. Quoted in John Kifner, "Pulp Mill Plan Splits New Hampshire Town," *New York Times*, Jan. 29, 1976, p. 43.
34. Quoted in Summers and Lang, "Bringing Jobs to People," *Small Town*, September 1976, p. 11
35. Quoted in "Local Industry: When Outsiders Take Control," *Small Town*, February 1975, p. 9.
36. Ibid.
37. Willard F. Mueller, "The Merger's Impact on the Community," *AFL-CIO American Federationist*, June 1971.
38. Ibid.
39. Frederick W. Wagner, John R. Dardis, and Richard K. Magee, "The Impact of Closing an Industrial Plant: The Case of Bogalusa, Louisiana," *Small Town*, May 1978, pp. 5–6.
40. Quoted in Grace Lichtenstein, "A Tiny Wyoming Town Battles Huge Minerals Company Over Environment," *New York Times*, June 8, 1975, p. 51.
41. Quoted in John Kifner, "Pulp Mill Plan," *New York Times*, Jan. 29, 1976, p. 43.
42 Quoted in Douglas Kneeland, "U.S. Aid Rejected By Missouri Town," *New York Times*, May 2, 1973, p. 41.
43. E.B. White, "Letter from the East," *The New Yorker*, Feb. 24, 1975, p. 40.
44. Quoted in "Character of Rural Life Changing with Dramatiic Increase in Crime," *New York Times*, December 27, 1977, p. 22.
45. Ibid.
46. Quoted in Park Dixon Goist, *From Main Street to State Street* (Port Washington, N.Y.: Kennikat Press, 1977), p. 4.
47. Ibid., pp. 4–5.
48. Lewis Mumford, *The Urban Prospect* (New York: Harcourt, Brace & World, a Harvest Book, 1968), p. 224.
49. George Orwell, *In Front of Your Nose, 1945–1950*, Sonia Orwell and Ian Angus, eds. (New York: Harcourt Brace Jovanovich, 1968), p. 216.
50. Hervé Varenne, *Americans Together* (New York: Columbia

Teachers College Press, 1977), p. 204.
51. Ibid.
52. Ibid., pp. 205–6.
53. Ibid., pp. 206–7.
54. Ibid., p. 209.
55. Quoted, Page Smith, *As a City Upon a Hill*, pp. 5–6.
56. William Bradford, *Of Plymouth Plantation* (New York: Capricorn Books, 1962), p. 214.

Epilogue

1. Sinclair Lewis, *Main Street* (New York: New American Library, 1961), p. 30.
2. Willa Cather, "The Best Years," *Five Stories.* (New York: Alfred A. Knopf. A Vintage Book, 1956), p. 130.
3. Willa Cather, *My Ántonia* (Boston and New York: Houghton Mifflin, 1918), p. 245.
4. Tombstone, Oakland Cemetery, Petersburg, Illinois.
5. Edgar Lee Masters, *Spoon River Anthology* (New York: Macmillan, Collier Books, 1962), p. 175.
6. Edgar Lee Masters, *Across Spoon River* (New York: Farrar, Straus & Giroux, Octagon Books, 1969), p. 10.
7. Masters, *Spoon River Anthology*, p. 230.
8. Quoted in *American Heritage*, June 7, 1971.

Index